The American People

BRIEF SECOND EDITION

The American People

Creating a Nation and a Society

VOLUME II: FROM 1865

GARY B. NASH
University of California, Los Angeles

JULIE ROY JEFFREY
Goucher College

JOHN R. HOWE
University of Minnesota

PETER J. FREDERICK
Wabash College

ALLEN F. DAVIS
Temple University

ALLAN M. WINKLER
Miami University

HarperCollinsCollegePublishers

Executive Editor: Bruce Borland
Developmental Editor: John Matthews
Project Editor: Robert Ginsberg
Text and Cover Designer: Nancy Sabato
Cover Illustration/Christine Francis
Art Studio: Vantage Art, Inc.
Photo Researcher: Leslie Coopersmith
Electronic Production Manager: Valerie A. Sawyer
Desktop Administrator: LaToya Wigfall
Manufacturing Manager: Helene G. Landers
Electronic Page Makeup: Americomp
Printer and Binder: RR Donnelley & Sons Company
Cover Printer: The Lehigh Press, Inc.

For permission to use copyrighted material, grateful acknowledgment is made to the copyright holders on p. 711, which is hereby made part of this copyright page.

The American People: Creating a Nation and a Society, Volume II: From 1865, Brief Second Edition

Copyright © 1996 by HarperCollins College Publishers

HarperCollins® and 🏰 ® are registered trademarks of HarperCollins Publishers Inc.

ISBN 0-673-99526-7 (single volume)
ISBN 0-673-99527-5 (volume 1)
ISBN 0-673-99528-3 (volume 2)

98 9 8 7 6 5 4

Contents in Brief

Detailed Contents

Maps and Charts

Preface

The Yoruba people of West Africa have an old saying: "However far the stream flows, it never forgets its source." Why, we wonder, do such ancient societies as the Yoruba find history so important, while modern American students question its relevance? This book aims to end such skepticism about the usefulness of history.

As we near the end of the twentieth century, in an ethnically and racially diverse country caught up in an interdependent global society, history is of central importance in preparing us to exercise our rights and responsibilities as free people. History cannot make good citizens, but without history we cannot understand the choices before us and think wisely about them. Lacking a collective memory of the past, we lapse into a kind of amnesia, unaware of the human condition and the long struggles of men and women everywhere to deal with the problems of their day and to create a better society. Unfurnished with historical knowledge, we deprive ourselves of knowing about the huge range of approaches people have taken to political, economic, and social life; to solving problems; and to conquering the obstacles in their way.

History has a deeper, even more fundamental importance: the cultivation of the private person, whose self-knowledge and self-respect provide the foundation for a life of dignity and fulfillment. Historical memory is the key to self-identity; to seeing one's place in the long stream of time, in the story of humankind.

When we study our own history, that of the American people, we see a rich and extraordinarily complex human story. This country, whose written history began with a convergence of Native Americans, Europeans, and Africans, has always been a nation of diverse peoples—a magnificent mosaic of cultures, religions, and skin shades. This book explores how American society assumed its present shape and developed its present forms of government; how as a nation we have conducted our foreign affairs and managed our economy; how as individuals and in groups we have lived, worked, loved, married, raised families, voted, argued, protested, and struggled to fulfill our dreams and the noble ideals of the American experiment.

Several ways of making the past understandable distinguish this book from most textbooks written in the past twenty years. The coverage of public events like presidential elections, diplomatic treaties, and economic legislation is integrated with the private human stories that underlie them. Within a chronological framework we have woven together our history as a nation, as a people, and as a society. When, for example, national political events are discussed, we analyze their impact on social and economic life at the state and local levels. Wars are described not only as they unfolded on the battlefield and in the salons of diplomats but also on the home front, where they are history's greatest motor of social change. The interaction of ordinary Americans with extraordinary events runs as a theme throughout this book.

Above all, we have tried to show the "humanness" of our history as it is revealed in people's everyday lives. The authors have often used the words of ordinary Americans to capture the authentic human voices of those who participated in and responded to epic events such as war, slavery, industrialization, and reform movements.

GOALS AND THEMES OF THE BOOK

Our primary goal is to provide students with a rich, balanced, and thought-provoking treatment of the American past. By this we mean a history that treats the lives and experiences of

Americans of all national origins and cultural backgrounds, at all levels of society, and in all regions of the country. It also means a history that seeks connections among the many factors—political, economic, technological, social, religious, intellectual, and biological—that have molded and remolded American society over four centuries. And finally it means a history that encourages students to think about how we have all inherited a complex past filled with both notable achievements and thorny problems. The only history befitting a democratic nation is one that inspires students to initiate a frank and searching dialogue with their past.

To speak of a dialogue about the past presumes that history is interpretive. Students should understand that historians are continually reinterpreting the past. New interpretations are often based on the discovery of new evidence, but more often new interpretations emerge because historians reevaluate old evidence in the light of new ideas that spring from the times in which they write and from their personal views of the world.

Through this book, we also hope to promote class discussions, which can be organized around six questions that we see as basic to the American historical experience:

1. How have Americans developed a stable, democratic political system flexible enough to address the wholesale changes that have occurred in the past two centuries, and to what degree has this political system been consistent with the principles of our nation's founding?
2. How has this nation been peopled, from the first inhabitants to many groups that arrived in slavery or servitude during the colonial period down to the voluntary immigrants of today? How have these waves of newcomers contributed to the American cultural mosaic, and how have they preserved elements of their ethnic, racial, and religious heritages?
3. How have economic and technological changes affected daily life, work, family or-

ganization, leisure, the division of wealth, and community relations in the United States?
4. What has been the role of our nation in the world?
5. How have the recurring reform movements in our history dealt with economic, political, and social problems in attempting to square the ideals of American life with the reality?
6. How have American beliefs and values changed over more than four hundred years of history, and how have they varied among different groups—women and men; people of different regions, racial and ethnic backgrounds, religions, and classes?

In writing a history that revolves around these themes, we have tried to describe two dynamics that operate in all societies. First, we observe people continually adjusting to new developments, such as industrialization and urbanization, over which they seemingly have little control; yet we realize that people are not paralyzed by history but rather are the fundamental creators of it. They retain the ability, individually and collectively, to shape the world in which they live and thus in considerable degree to control their own lives. Second, we emphasize the connections that always exist among social, political, economic, technological, and cultural events.

STRUCTURE OF THE BOOK

Part Organization

The chapters of this book are grouped into six parts relating to major periods in American history. Each part begins with a brief *introductory essay* that outlines how the six organizing questions described above are developed in the subsequent chapters.

Chapter Structure

Every chapter begins with a *personal story* recalling the experience of an ordinary or lesser-known American. Chapter 1, for example, starts with the tragic account of Opechancanough, a Powhatan tribesman whose entire life of nearly ninety years was consumed by a struggle against the land, hunger, and alien values brought by Spanish and English newcomers. This brief anecdote serves several purposes. First, it introduces the overarching themes and major concepts of the chapter, in this case the meeting in the North American wilderness of three societies—Native American, European, and African—each with different cultural values, life styles, and aspirations, Second, the personal story launches the chapter in a way that facilitates learning—by engaging the student with a human account. Last, the personal story suggests that history was shaped by ordinary as well as extraordinary people. At the end of the personal story a *brief overview* links the biographical sketch to the text by elaborating the major themes of the chapter.

We aim to facilitate the learning process for students in other ways as well. Every chapter ends with pedagogical features to reinforce and expand the presentation. A *conclusion* briefly summarizes the main concepts and developments elaborated in the chapter and serves as a bridge to the following chapter. A list of *recommended reading* provides supplementary sources for further study or research; novels contemporary to the period are often included. Finally, a *time line* reviews the major events and developments covered in the chapter. Each graph, map, and illustration has been chosen to relate clearly to the narrative.

THE BRIEF EDITION

This text is a Brief Edition of the very successful third edition of *The American People*. This shorter volume—approximately half the length of the complete version—will be particularly useful in one-semester courses and those courses that assign wide readings in primary sources, monographs, or articles in addition to the main text.

The foremost goal of the abridgement was to preserve the distinctive character of the complete text. The balance of political, social, economic, and cultural history remains the same, revolving around the same central, organizing themes previously described. The structure and organization of the text—parts, chapters, sections, and subsections—are largely unchanged. Deletions have been made on a careful line-by-line basis. All important topics are in place, as are the interpretive connections among the many factors molding our society. We have eliminated only detail, extra examples, and illustrative material within sections. While it might have been easier to delete more of the "humanness" of history, leaving room for facts and more facts, we have been careful to retain our focus on history as it is revealed through the lives of ordinary Americans, and the interplay of social and political factors.

We have also tried to provide the support materials necessary to make teaching and learning enjoyable and rewarding. The reader will be the judge of our success. The authors and HarperCollins welcome your comments.

ACKNOWLEDGMENTS

Over the years, as successive editions of this text were being developed, many of our colleagues read and criticized the various drafts of the manuscript. For their thoughtful evaluations and constructive suggestions, the authors wish to express their gratitude to the following reviewers:

Richard H. Abbott, Eastern Michigan University
Kenneth G. Alfers, Mountain View College
Gregg Andrews, Southwest Texas State University
Robert Asher, University of Connecticut, Storrs
Harry Baker, University of Arkansas at Little Rock
Michael Batinski, Southern Illinois University
Gary Bell, Sam Houston State University
Virginia Bellows, Tulsa Junior College

Spencer Bennett, Siena Heights College
James Bradford, Texas A&M University
Neal A. Brooks, Essex Community College
Jeffrey P. Brown, New Mexico State University
Sheri Bartlett Browne, Portland State University
David Brundage, University of California at
    Santa Cruz
Colin Calloway, University of Wyoming
D'Ann Campbell, Indiana University
James S. Chase, University of Arkansas
Vincent A. Clark, Johnson County Community
    College
Neil Clough, North Seattle Community College
Matthew Ware Coulter, Collin County
    Community College
David Culbert, Louisiana State University
John H. De Berry, Somerset Community College
Bruce Dierenfield, Canisius College
John Dittmer, DePauw University
Gordon Dodds, Portland State University
Richard Donley, Eastern Washington University
Robert Downtain, Tarrant County Community
    College
Mark Dyreson, Weber State University
Lori Clune Emerzian, California State University,
    Fresno
Rex L. Field, Palo Alto College
John L. Finnegan, Spokane Community College
Bernard Friedman, Indiana University–Purdue
    University at Indianapolis
Bruce Glasrud, California State University,
    Hayward
Richard Griswold del Castillo, San Diego State
    University
Colonel Williams L. Harris, The Citadel Military
    College
Robert Haws, University of Mississippi
Jerrold Hirsch, Northeast Missouri State
    University
Frederick Hoxie, McNickle Center for Study of
    American Indians
John S. Hughes, University of Texas
Donald M. Jacobs, Northeastern University
Delores Janiewski, University of Idaho, Mt.
    Holyoke

David Johnson, Portland State University
Richard Kern, University of Findlay
Monte Lewis, Cisco Junior College
William Link, University of North Carolina,
    Greensboro
Ronald Lora, University of Toledo
George M. Lubick, Northern Arizona
    University
John C. Massman, St. Cloud State University
Vern Mattson, University of Nevada at Las
    Vegas
Michael McCarthy, Community College of
    Denver
John McCormick, Delaware County
    Community College
Sylvia McGrath, Stephen F. Austin University
James E. McMillan, Denison University
Walter Miszczenko, Boise State University
Norma Mitchell, Troy State University
Gerald F. Moran, University of Michigan,
    Dearborn
William Morris, Midland College
Marian Morton, John Carroll University
Roger Nichols, University of Arizona
Paul Palmer, Texas A&I University
Al Parker, Riverside City College
Judith Parsons, Sul Ross State University
Neva Peters, Tarrant County Junior College
James Prickett, Santa Monica College
Noel Pugash, University of New Mexico
Juan Gomez-Quinones, University of California,
    Los Angeles
George Rable, Anderson College
Joseph P. Reidy, Howard University
Leonard Riforgiato, Pennsylvania State
    University
Randy Roberts, Purdue University
Mary Robertson, Armstrong State University
David Robson, John Carroll University
Sylvia Sebesta, San Antonio College
Herbert Shapiro, University of Cincinnati
David R. Shibley, Santa Monica College
Ellen Shockro, Pasadena City College
Sheila Skemp, University of Mississippi
Kathryn Sklar, Stanford University

Howard Smead, University of Maryland
Gary Scott Smith, Grove City College
James Smith, Virginia State University
John Snetsinger, California Polytechnic State University
Tommy Stringer, Navarro College
Joan E. Supplee, Baylor University
Tom Tefft, Citrus College
John A. Trickel, Richland College
Donna Van Raaphorst, Cuyahoga Community College
Morris Vogel, Temple University
Michael Wade, Appalachian State University
Jackie Walker, James Madison University

SUPPLEMENTS

For Instructors

- *Teaching the American People.* Authors Julie Roy Jeffrey and Peter J. Frederick have written this guide on the basis of ideas generated in the frequent "active learning" workshops held by the authors and have tied it closely to the text. In addition to suggestions on how to generate lively class discussion and involve students in active learning, this supplement also offers a file of exam questions and lists of resources, including films, slides, photo collections, records, and audiocassettes.

- *America Through the Eyes of Its People: A Collection of Primary Sources.* Prepared by Carol Brown of Houston Community College, this one-volume collection of primary documents portraying the rich and varied tapestry of American life contains documents concerning women, Native Americans, African-Americans, Hispanics, and others who helped to shape the course of U.S. history. Designed to be duplicated by instructors for student use, the documents have accompanying student exercises.

- *Discovering American History Through Maps and Views.* Created by Gerald Danzer

of the University of Illinois at Chicago—the recipient of the AHA's 1990 James Harvey Robinson Prize for his work in the development of map transparencies—this set of 140 four-color acetates is a unique instructional tool. It contains an introduction on teaching history through maps and a detailed commentary on each transparency. The collection includes cartographic and pictorial maps, views and photos, urban plans, building diagrams, and works of art.

- *Primary Sources in Gender in American History.* Prepared by Ellen Skinner of Pace University, this collection includes both classic and unique documents from diverse perspectives covering the history of women and gender in American history. The book includes critical thinking questions, bibliography, and contextual headnotes and is available shrinkwrapped with *The American People* at a low cost.

- *Primary Sources in African American History.* Prepared by Roy Finkenbine of Hampton University, this compelling collection includes both social and political documents and covers the history of African-Americans in America. The book includes critical thinking questions, bibliography, and contextual headnotes and is available shrinkwrapped with *The American People* at a low cost.

- *American Impressions: A CD-ROM for U.S. History, Volumes I and II.* This unique and ground-breaking CD-ROM for the U.S. History course is organized in a topical and thematic framework which allows in-depth coverage with a media-centered focus. Hundreds of photos, maps, works of art, graphics, and historical film clips are organized into narrated vignettes and interactive activities to create a tool for both professors and students. The first volume includes: "The Encounter Period," "Revolution to Republic," "A Century of Labor and Reform," and "The Struggle for Equality." A Guide for Instructors provides teaching tips and suggestions for using advanced media in the classroom. The CD-ROM is available in both Macintosh and Windows formats.

- *Visual Archives of American History, 2nd ed.* This two-sided video laserdisc explores history from the meeting of three cultures to the present. It is an encyclopedic chronology of U.S. history offering hundreds of photographs and illustrations, a variety of source and reference maps—several of which are animated— plus 50 minutes of video. For ease in planning lectures, a manual listing barcodes for scanning and frame numbers for all the material is available.

- *A Guide to Teaching American History Through Film.* Written by Randy Roberts of Purdue University, this guide provides instructors with a creative and practical tool for stimulating classroom discussion. The sections include "American Films: A Historian's Perspective," a list of films, practical suggestions, and bibliography. The film listing is presented in narrative form, developing connections between each film and the topics being studied.

- *Video Lecture Launchers.* Prepared by Mark Newman, University of Illinois at Chicago, these video lecture launchers (each 2 to 5 minutes in duration) cover key issues in American history from 1877 to the present. The launchers are accompanied by an instructor's manual.

- *"This Is America" Immigration Videos.* Produced by the American Museum of Immigration, these two 20-minute videos tell the story of American immigrants, relating their personal stories and accomplishments. By showing how the richness of our culture is due to the contributions of millions of immigrant Americans, the videos make the point that America's strength lies in the ethnically and culturally diverse backgrounds of its citizens.

- *Visual Archives of American History.* This video laserdisc provides over 500 photos and 29 minutes of film clips of major events in American history. Each photo or film clip may be instantly accessed, making this collection ideal for classroom use.

- *Transparencies.* A set of more than 40 map transparencies drawn from the text.

- *Test Bank.* This test bank, prepared by Charles Cook, Houston Community College, and J. B. Smallwood, North Texas State University, contains more than 3,500 objective, conceptual, and essay questions. All questions are keyed to specific pages in the text.

- *TestMaster Computerized Testing System.* This flexible, easy-to-master computer test bank includes all the test items in the printed test bank. The TestMaster software allows you to edit existing questions and add your own items. Tests can be printed in several different formats and can include figures such as graphs and tables. Available for IBM and Macintosh computers.

- *QuizMaster.* This new program enables you to design TestMaster-generated tests that your students can take on a computer rather than in printed form. QuizMaster is available separately from TestMaster and can be obtained free through your sales representative.

- *Grades.* A grade-keeping and classroom management software program that maintains data for up to 200 students.

For Students

- *Study Guide and Practice Tests.* This two-volume study guide, created by Julie Roy Jeffrey and Peter J. Frederick, includes chapter outlines, significant themes and highlights, a glossary, learning enrichment ideas, sample test questions, exercises for identification and interpretation, and geography exercises based on maps in the text.

- *Learning to Think Critically: Films and Myths About American History.* Randy Roberts and Robert May of Purdue University use well-known films such as *Gone with the Wind* and *Casablanca* to explore some common myths about America and its past. Many widely held assumptions about our country's past come from or are perpetuated by popular films. Which are true? Which are patently not true? And how does a student of history approach documents, sources, and textbooks with a critical and discerning eye? This short handbook subjects some popular beliefs to historical scrutiny in order to help students develop a method of inquiry for approaching the subject of history in general.

- *Mapping America: A Guide to Historical Geography.* This workbook by Ken L. Weatherbie, Del Mar College, contains 35 sequenced exercises corresponding to the map program in the text, each culminating in a series of interpretive questions about the role of geographical factors in American history.

- *Mapping American History: Student Activities.* Written by Gerald Danzer of the University of Illinois at Chicago, this free map workbook for students features exercises designed to teach students to interpret and analyze cartographic materials as historical documents. The instructor is entitled to a free copy of the workbook for each copy of the text purchased from HarperCollins.

- *Concepts in American History.* This slim volume, written by Robert Asher of the University of Connecticut, contains brief essays on 13 key concepts in American history, including such topics as Republicanism, nativism, feminism, and capitalism.

- *SuperShell II Computerized Tutorial.* Prepared by Ken L. Weatherbie, Del Mar College, this interactive program for IBM computers helps students learn major facts and concepts through drill and practice exercises and diagnostic feedback. SuperShell II provides immediate correct answers, the text page number on which the material is discussed, and a running score of the student's performance maintained on the screen throughout the session. This free supplement is available to instructors through their sales representative.

- *TimeLink Computer Atlas of American History.* This atlas, compiled by William Hamblin of Brigham Young University, is an introductory software tutorial and textbook companion. This Macintosh program presents the historical geography of the continental United States from colonial times to the settling of the West and the admission of the last continental state in 1912. The program covers territories in different time periods, provides quizzes, and includes a special Civil War module.

GARY B. NASH
JULIE ROY JEFFREY
JOHN R. HOWE
PETER J. FREDERICK
ALLEN F. DAVIS
ALLAN M. WINKLER

About the Authors

Gary B. Nash received his Ph.D. from Princeton University in 1964. He is currently Director of the National Center for History in the Schools at the University of California, Los Angeles, where he teaches colonial and revolutionary American history. Among the books Nash has written are *Quakers and Politics: Pennsylvania, 1681–1726* (1968); *Red, White, and Black: The Peoples of Early America* (1974, 1982); *The Urban Crucible: Social Change, Political Consciousness, and the Origins of the American Revolution* (1979); and *Forging Freedom: The Black Urban Experience in Philadelphia, 1720–1840* (1988). His scholarship is especially concerned with the role of common people in the making of history. He wrote Part I and served as a general editor of this book.

Julie Roy Jeffrey earned her Ph.D. in history from Rice University in 1972. Since then she has taught at Goucher College. Honored as an outstanding teacher, Jeffrey has been involved in faculty development activities and curriculum evaluation. Jeffrey's major publications include *Education for Children of the Poor* (1978); *Frontier Women: The Trans-Mississippi West, 1840–1880* (1979); and *Converting the West: A Biography of Narcissa Whitman* (1991). She is the author of many articles on the lives and perceptions of nineteenth-century women. She wrote Parts III and IV in collaboration with Peter Frederick and acted as a general editor of this book.

John R. Howe received his Ph.D. from Yale University in 1962. At the University of Minnesota his teaching interests include early American politics and relations between Native Americans and whites. His major publications include *The Changing Political Thought of John Adams* (1966) and *From the Revolution Through the Age of Jackson* (1973). His major research currently involves a manuscript entitled "The Transformation of Public Life in Revolutionary America." Howe wrote Part II of this book.

Peter J. Frederick received his Ph.D. in history from the University of California, Berkeley, in 1966. Innovative student-centered teaching of American history has been the focus of his career at California State University, Hayward, and since 1970 at Wabash College (1992–1994 at Carleton College). Recognized nationally as a distinguished teacher and for his many articles and workshops for faculty on teaching and learning, Frederick has also written several articles on life-writing and a book, *Knights of the Golden Rule: The Intellectual as Christian Social Reformer in the 1890s*. He coordinated and edited all the "Recovering the Past" sections and co-wrote Parts III and IV of this book.

Allen F. Davis earned his Ph.D. from the University of Wisconsin in 1959. A former president of the American Studies Association, he is a professor of history at Temple University and Director of the Center for Public History. He is the author of *Spearheads for Reform: The Social Settlements and the Progressive Movement* (1967) and *American Heroine: The Life and Legend of Jane Addams* (1973). He is coauthor of *Still Philadelphia* (1983), *Philadelphia Stories* (1987), and *One Hundred Years at Hull-House* (1990). He is currently working on a book on masculine culture in America. Davis wrote Part V of this book.

Allan M. Winkler received his Ph.D. from Yale University in 1974. He is presently teaching at Miami University, where he chairs the History Department. His books include *The Politics of Propaganda: The Office of War Information, 1942–1945* (1978); *Modern America: The United States from the Second World War to the Present* (1985); *Home Front U.S.A.: America During World War II* (1986); and *Life Under a Cloud: American Anxiety About the Atom* (1993). His research centers on the connections between public policy and popular mood in modern American history. Winkler wrote Part VI of this book.

chapter 16

The Union
Reconstructed

In April 1864, one year before Lincoln's assassination, Robert Allston died of pneumonia. His wife, Adele, and daughter, Elizabeth, took over the affairs of their many rice plantations. With Yankee troops moving through coastal South Carolina in the late winter of 1864–1865, Elizabeth's sorrow over the loss of her father turned to "terror" as Union soldiers arrived seeking liquor, firearms, and hidden valuables. The Allston women endured an insulting search and then fled. In a later raid, Yankee troops encouraged the Allston slaves to take furniture and other household goods from the Big Houses, some of which the blacks returned when the Yankees were gone. But before they left, the Union soldiers, in their role as liberators, gave the keys to the crop barns to the semifree slaves.

When the war was over, Adele Allston took an oath of allegiance to the United States and secured a written order commanding the blacks to relinquish these keys. She and Elizabeth made plans to return in the early summer of 1865 to resume control of the family plantations, thereby reestablishing white authority. Possession of the keys to the barns, Elizabeth wrote, would be the "test case" of whether former masters or their former slaves would control land and labor.

Not without some fear, Adele and Elizabeth Allston rode up in a carriage to their former home, Nightingale Hall, to confront their ex-slaves. To their surprise, a pleasant reunion took place. A trusted black foreman handed over the keys to the barns. This harmonious scene was repeated elsewhere.

But at Guendalos, a plantation owned by a son absent during most of the war fighting with the Confederate army, the Allston women met a very different situation. As their carriage arrived, a defiant group of armed ex-slaves lined both sides of the road, following the carriage as it passed by. Tension grew when the carriage stopped. A former black driver, Uncle Jacob, was unsure whether to yield the keys to the barns full of rice and corn, put there by black labor. An angry young man shouted out: "Ef yu gie up de key, blood'll flow." Uncle Jacob slowly slipped the keys back into his pocket.

The tension increased as the blacks sang freedom songs and brandished hoes, pitchforks, and guns in an effort to discourage anyone from going to town for help.

The Allstons spent the night safely, if restlessly, in their house. Early the next morning, they were awakened by a knock at the unlocked front door. Adele slowly opened the door, and there stood Uncle Jacob. Without a word, he gave her the keys.

◦◦═══◉═══◦◦

The story of the keys reveals most of the essential human ingredients of the Reconstruction era. Despite defeat and surrender, southern whites were determined to resume control of both land and labor. Rebellion aside, the law, property titles, and federal enforcement were generally on the side of the original owners of the land.

In this encounter between former slaves and the Allston women, the role of the northern federal officials is most revealing. The Union soldiers, literally and symbolically, gave the keys of freedom to the blacks but did not stay around long enough to guarantee that freedom. Understanding the limits of northern help, Uncle Jacob handed the keys to land and liberty back to his former owner. The blacks at Guendalos knew that if they wanted to ensure their freedom, they had to do it themselves.

The goals of the groups at the Allston plantations were in conflict. The theme of this chapter is the story of what happened to people's various dreams as they sought to form new social, economic, and political relationships during Reconstruction.

For much of the twentieth century, Reconstruction was seen as a disgraceful period in which vindictive northern Radical Republicans imposed a harsh rule of evil carpetbaggers, scalawags, and illiterate blacks on the helpless, defeated South. *Gone with the Wind* reflects this view. In 1935, the black scholar W. E. B. Du Bois challenged this interpretation, suggesting instead that an economic struggle over land and the exploitation of black workers was the crucial focus of Reconstruction. Other historians have shown the beginnings of biracial cooperation and political participation in some southern states and the eventual violent repression of the freedmen's dreams of land, schooling, and votes. This chapter reflects this later interpretation, enriched by an awareness of the ambiguity of human motives and the devastation and divisions of class and race in pursuit of conflicting goals.

THE BITTERSWEET AFTERMATH OF WAR

"There are sad changes in store for both races," the daughter of a Georgia planter wrote in her diary early in the summer of 1865, adding, "I wonder the Yankees do not shudder to behold their work." In order to understand the bittersweet nature of Reconstruction, we must look at the state of the nation in the spring of 1865, shortly after the assassination of President Lincoln.

The United States in 1865

The "Union" was in a state of constitutional crisis in April 1865. The status of the 11 states of the former Confederate States of America was unclear. Lincoln's official position had been that the southern states had never left the Union, which was "constitutionally indestructible." As a result of their rebellion, they were only "out of their proper relation" with the United States. The president, therefore, as commander in chief, had the authority to decide on the basis for setting relations right and proper again.

Lincoln's congressional opponents argued that by declaring war on the Union, the Confederate states had broken their constitutional ties and reverted to a kind of prestatehood status like territories or "conquered provinces." Congress, therefore, which decided on the admission of new states, should resolve the constitutional issues and assert its authority over the reconstruction process. This conflict between Congress and the president reflected the fact that the president had taken on broad powers necessary for rapid mobilization of resources and domestic security during the war. As soon as the war was over, Congress sought to reassert its authority, as it would do after every subsequent war.

In April 1865, the Republican Party ruled victorious and virtually alone. Although less than a dozen years old, the Republicans had won the war, preserved the Union, and enacted a program for economic growth. The Democratic Party, by contrast, was in shambles. Nevertheless, it had been politically important in 1864 for the Republicans to show that the war was a bipartisan effort. A Jacksonian Democrat and Unionist from Tennessee, the tactless Andrew Johnson, had therefore been nominated as Lincoln's vice president. In April 1865, he headed the government.

The United States in the spring of 1865 was a picture of stark economic contrasts. Northern cities hummed with productive activity while southern cities lay in ruins. Roadways and railroad tracks laced the North, while in the South railroads and roads had been devastated. Southern financial institutions were bankrupt, while northern banks flourished. Northern farms,

under increasing mechanization, were more productive than ever before. Southern farms and plantations, especially those that had lain in the path of Sherman's march, were like a "howling waste."

Despite pockets of relative wealth, the South was largely devastated as soldiers demobilized and returned home in April 1865. Yet, as a later southern writer, Wilbur Cash, explained, "If this war had smashed the Southern world, it had left the essential Southern mind and will . . . entirely unshaken." Many southerners wanted nothing less than to resist Reconstruction and restore their old world.

The dominant social reality in the spring of 1865, however, was that nearly four million former slaves were on their own, facing the challenges of freedom. After an initial reaction of joy and celebration, the freedmen quickly became aware of their continuing dependence on former owners.

Hopes Among Freedmen

Throughout the South in the summer of 1865, there were optimistic expectations in the old slave quarters. As Union soldiers marched through Richmond, prisoners in slave-trade jails chanted: "Slavery chain done broke at last! Gonna praise God till I die!" The slavery chain, however, was not broken all at once but link by link. After Union soldiers swept through an area, Confederate troops would follow, or master and overseer would return, and the slaves learned not to rejoice too quickly or openly. "Every time a bunch of No'thern sojers would come through," recalled one slave, "they would tell us we was free and we'd begin celebratin'. Before we would get through somebody else would tell us to go back to work, and we would go." So former slaves became cautious about what freedom meant.

Gradually, the freedmen began to test their new freedom. The first thing they did was to leave the plantation, if only for a few hours or days. Some former slaves cut their ties entirely, leaving cruel and kindly masters alike.

Many freedmen left the plantation in search of members of their families. For some, freedom meant getting married legally. Legal marriage was important morally, but it also served such practical purposes as establishing the legitimacy of children and gaining access to land titles and other economic opportunities. Marriage also meant special burdens for black women who took on the now familiar double role as housekeeper and breadwinner. For many newly married blacks, however, the initial goal was to create a traditional family life, resulting in the widespread withdrawal of women from plantation field labor.

Another way in which freedmen demonstrated their new status was by choosing surnames; names associated with the concept of independence, such as Washington, were common. Emancipation changed black manners around whites as well. Masks were dropped, and old expressions of humility—tipping a hat, stepping aside, feigning happiness, addressing whites with titles of deference—were discarded. For the blacks, these were necessary symbolic expressions of selfhood; they proved that things were now different. To whites, these behaviors were seen as acts of "insolence," "insubordination," and "puttin' on airs."

However important were choosing names, dropping masks, moving around, getting married, and testing new rights, the primary goal for most freedmen was the acquisition of their own land. During the war, some Union generals had placed liberated slaves in charge of confiscated and abandoned lands. In the Sea Islands off the coast of South Carolina and Georgia, blacks had been working 40-acre plots of land and harvesting their own crops for several years. Some blacks held title to these lands. Northern philanthropists had organized others to grow cotton for the Treasury Department to prove the superiority of free labor over slavery.

Many freedmen expected a new economic order as fair payment for their years of involuntary work on the land. As one freedman put it, "Gib us our own land and we take care ourselves; but widout land, de ole massas can hire us or starve us, as dey please." However cautiously expressed, the freedmen had every expectation, fed by the intensity of their dreams, that "forty acres and a mule" would be provided.

The White South's Fearful Response

White southerners had mixed goals at the war's end. Yeoman farmers and poor whites stood side by side with rich planters in bread lines as together they looked forward to the restoration of their land and livelihood. Suffering from "extreme want and destitution," as a Georgia resident put it, white southerners responded with feelings of outrage, loss, and injustice. "I tell you it is mighty hard," said one man, "for my pa paid his own money for our niggers; and that's not all they've robbed us of. They have taken our horses and cattle and sheep *and everything*."

A more dominant emotion, however, was fear. The entire structure of southern society was shaken, and the semblance of racial peace and order that slavery had provided was shattered. Many white southerners could hardly imagine a society without blacks in bondage. Having lost control of all that was familiar and revered, whites feared everything from losing their cheap labor supply to having to sit next to blacks on trains.

The mildest of their fears was the inconvenience of doing various jobs and chores they had rarely done before, like housework. The worst fears of southern whites were rape and revenge. The presence of black soldiers touched off fears of violence. Although demobilization occurred rapidly after Appomattox, a few black militia units remained in uniform, parading with guns in southern cities. Acts of violence by black soldiers against whites, however, were rare.

Believing that their world was turned upside

Both white southerners and their former slaves suffered in the immediate aftermath of the Civil War, as illustrated by this engraving from Frank Leslie's Illustrated Newspaper.

down, the former planter aristocracy set out to restore the old plantation order and appropriate racial relationships. The key to reestablishing white dominance were the "black codes" that state legislatures passed in the first year after the end of the war. Many of the codes granted freedmen the right to marry, sue and be sued, testify in court, and hold property. But these rights were qualified. Complicated passages in the codes explained under exactly what circumstances blacks could testify against whites or own property (mostly they could not) or exercise other rights of free persons. Some rights were denied, including racial intermarriage and the right to bear arms, possess alcoholic beverages, sit on trains except in baggage compartments, be on city streets at night, or congregate in large groups.

Many of the alleged rights guaranteed by the black codes—testimony in court, for example—were passed to induce the federal government to withdraw its remaining troops from the South. This was a crucial issue, for in many places marauding groups of whites were assaulting and terrorizing virtually defenseless freedmen, who clearly needed protection and the right to testify in court against whites.

Because white planters needed the freedmen's labor, the crucial provisions of the black codes were intended to regulate the freedmen's economic status. "Vagrancy" laws provided that any blacks not "lawfully employed," which usually meant by a white employer, could be arrested, jailed, fined, or hired out to a man who would assume responsibility for their debts and future behavior. The codes regulated the work contracts by which black laborers worked in the fields for white landowners, including severe penalties for leaving before the yearly contract was fulfilled and rules for proper behavior, attitude, and manners. In this way, southern leaders sought to reestablish their dominance.

NATIONAL RECONSTRUCTION

The question facing the national government in 1865 was whether it would use its power to support the black codes and the reimposition of racial intimidation in the South or to uphold the newly sought rights of the freedmen. Would the federal government side with the democratic reform impulse in American history, which stressed human rights and liberty, or with the forces emphasizing property, order, and self-interest? Although the primary drama of Reconstruction took place in the conflict between white landowners and black freedmen over land and labor in the South, the struggle over Reconstruction policy among politicians in Washington played a significant role in the local drama, as well as the next century of American history.

The Presidential Plan

After initially calling for punishment of the defeated Confederates for "treason," President

Johnson soon adopted a more lenient policy. On May 29, 1865, he issued two proclamations setting forth his reconstruction program. Like Lincoln, he maintained that the southern states had never left the Union. His first proclamation continued Lincoln's policies by offering "amnesty and pardon, with restoration of all rights of property" to all former Confederates who would take an oath of allegiance to the Constitution and the Union of the United States. However, he made exceptions: ex–Confederate government leaders and rich rebels whose taxable property was valued at over $20,000. Any southerners not covered by the amnesty proclamation could, however, apply for special individual pardons, which Johnson granted to nearly all applicants. By the fall of 1865, only a handful remained unpardoned.

Johnson's second proclamation laid out the steps by which southern states could reestablish state governments. First, the president would appoint a provisional governor, who would call a state convention representing "that portion of the people of said State who are loyal to the United States." This included those who took the oath of allegiance or were otherwise pardoned. The convention should ratify the Thirteenth Amendment, which abolished slavery, void secession, repudiate all Confederate debts, and then elect new state officials and members of Congress.

Under this lenient plan, each of the southern states successfully completed reconstruction and sent newly elected members to the Congress that convened in December 1865. Southern voters defiantly elected dozens of former officers and legislators of the Confederacy, including a few not yet pardoned. Some state conventions hedged on ratifying the Thirteenth Amendment, and some asserted their right to compensation for the loss of slave property. No state provided for black suffrage, and most did nothing to guarantee civil rights, schooling, or economic protection for the freedmen. Less than eight months after Appomattox, Reconstruction seemed to be over.

Congressional Reconstruction

As they looked at the situation late in 1865, northern leaders painfully saw that almost none of their postwar goals were being fulfilled. The South was taking advantage of the president's program to restore the power of the prewar planter aristocracy. The freedmen were receiving neither equal citizenship nor economic independence. And the Republicans were not likely to maintain their political power and stay in office. Would the Democratic Party and the South gain by postwar politics what they had been unable to achieve by civil war?

Congressional Republicans, led by Congressman Thaddeus Stevens of Pennsylvania and Senator Charles Sumner of Massachusetts, decided to assert their own policies for reconstructing the nation. Although branded as "radicals," only for a brief period in 1866 and 1867 did "radical" rule prevail. Rejecting Johnson's notion that the South had already been reconstructed, Congress asserted its constitutional authority to decide on its own membership and refused seats to the newly elected senators and representatives from the old Confederate states. Congress then established the Joint Committee on Reconstruction to investigate conditions in the South. Its report documented disorder and resistance and the appalling treatment and conditions of the freedmen. Even before the report was made final in 1866, Congress passed a civil rights bill to protect the fragile rights of the blacks and extended for two more years the Freedmen's Bureau, an agency providing emergency assistance at the end of the war. President Johnson vetoed both bills, arguing that they were unconstitutional and calling his congressional opponents "traitors."

Johnson's growing anger forced moderates into the radical camp, and Congress passed both bills over his veto. Both, however, were watered down by weakening the power of enforcement.

A white mob burned this freedmen's school during the Memphis riot of May 1866.

had died in the riot. The local Union army commander took his time intervening to restore order, arguing that his troops had "a large amount of public property to guard [and] hated Negroes too." A congressional inquiry found that in Memphis, blacks had "no protection from the law whatever."

A month later, Congress proposed to the states the ratification of the Fourteenth Amendment, the single most significant act of the Reconstruction era. The first section of the amendment sought to provide permanent constitutional protection of the civil rights of freedmen by defining them as citizens. States were prohibited from depriving "any person of life, liberty, or property, without due process of law," and all persons were guaranteed "the equal protection of the laws." In section 2, Congress paved the way for black male suffrage in the South by declaring that states not enfranchising black males would have their "basis of representation reduced" proportionally. Other sections of the amendment denied leaders of the Confederacy the right to hold national or state political office (except by act of Congress), repudiated the Confederate debt, and denied claims of compensation by former slave owners for their lost property.

President Johnson urged the southern states not to ratify the Fourteenth Amendment, and ten states immediately rejected it. Johnson then went on the campaign trail in the midterm election of 1866 to ask voters to throw out the radical Republicans. Vicious name calling and other low forms of electioneering marked this first political campaign since the war's end. The result of the election was an overwhelming victory for the Republicans and a repudiation of Andrew Johnson and his policies.

Therefore, early in 1867, Reconstruction Acts were passed dividing the southern states into five military districts to maintain order and protect the rights of property and persons and defining a new process for readmitting a state.

Southern civil courts, therefore, regularly disallowed black testimony against whites, acquitted whites charged with violence against blacks, sentenced blacks to compulsory labor, and generally made discriminatory sentences for the same crimes. In this judicial climate, racial violence erupted with discouraging frequency.

In Memphis, for example, a race riot occurred in May 1866 that typified race relations during the Reconstruction period. A street brawl erupted between the police and some recently discharged but armed black soldiers. After some fighting and an exchange of gunfire, the soldiers went back to their fort. That night, white mobs, led by prominent local officials, invaded the black section of the city. With the encouragement of the Memphis police, the mobs engaged in over 40 hours of terror, killing, beating, robbing, and raping virtually helpless residents and burning houses, schools, and churches. When it was over, 48 persons, all but two of them black,

Qualified voters, which included blacks and excluded unreconstructed rebels, would elect delegates to state constitutional conventions, which then would write new constitutions guaranteeing black suffrage. After the new voters of the states had ratified the constitutions, elections would be held to choose governors and state legislatures. When a state ratified the Fourteenth Amendment, its representatives to Congress would be accepted, thus completing readmission to the Union.

The President Impeached

At the same time as it passed the Reconstruction Acts, Congress also approved bills to restrict the powers of the president and to establish the dominance of the legislative branch over the executive. The Tenure of Office Act, designed to protect the outspoken secretary of war, Edwin Stanton, from removal by Johnson, limited the president's appointment powers. Other measures restricted his power as commander in chief. Johnson behaved exactly as congressional Republicans had anticipated, vetoing the Reconstruction Acts, issuing orders to limit military commanders in the South, and removing cabinet and other government officials sympathetic to Congress's program. The House Judiciary Committee investigated, charging the president with "usurpations of power," but moderate House Republicans defeated impeachment resolutions to remove Johnson from office.

In August 1867, Johnson finally dismissed Stanton and asked for Senate consent. When the Senate refused, the president ordered Stanton to surrender his office, which he refused, barricading himself inside. This time the House rushed impeachment resolutions to a vote, charging the president with "high crimes and misdemeanors" as detailed in 11 offenses while in office, mostly focusing on alleged violations of the Tenure of Office Act. The three-month trial in the Senate early in 1868 featured impassioned oratory, but in the end, seven moderate Republicans joined

Democrats against conviction, and the effort to find the president guilty as charged fell short of the two-thirds majority required by a single vote.

As the moderate or regular Republicans gained strength in 1868 through their support of the presidential election winner, Ulysses S. Grant, radicalism lost much of its power within Republican ranks. Not for another 100 years would a president again face removal from office through impeachment.

Congressional Moderation

The impeachment crisis revealed that most Republicans were more interested in protecting themselves than the freedmen and in punishing Johnson rather than the South. It is revealing to look not only at what Congress did during Reconstruction but also at what it did not do.

With the exception of Jefferson Davis, Congress did not imprison Confederate leaders, and only one person, the commander of the infamous Andersonville prison camp, was put to death. Congress did not insist on a long-term probationary period before southern states could be readmitted to the Union. It did not reorganize southern local governments. It did not mandate a national program of education for the four million ex-slaves. It did not confiscate and redistribute land to the freedmen, nor did it prevent President Johnson from taking land away from freedmen who had gained possessory titles during the war. It did not, except indirectly, provide economic help to black citizens.

What Congress did do, and that only reluctantly, was grant citizenship and suffrage to the freedmen. Black suffrage gained support after the election of 1868, when General Grant, a military hero regarded as invincible, barely won the popular vote in several states. Congressional Republicans, who had twice rejected a suffrage amendment, took another look at the idea as a way of adding grateful black votes to party rolls. After a bitterly contested fight, repeated in several state ratification contests, the Fifteenth

Amendment, forbidding all states to deny the vote to anyone "on account of race, color, or previous condition of servitude," became part of the Constitution in 1870. A black preacher from Pittsburgh observed that "the Republican party had done the Negro good, but they were doing themselves good at the same time."

For political reasons, therefore, Congress gave blacks the vote but not the land, the opposite priority of what the freedmen wanted. Almost alone, Thaddeus Stevens argued that "forty acres . . . and a hut would be more valuable . . . than the . . . right to vote." But Congress never seriously considered his plan to confiscate the land of the "chief rebels" and to give a small portion of it, divided into 40-acre plots, to the freedmen.

Although most Americans, in the North as well as the South, opposed confiscation and black independent landownership, Congress passed an alternative measure. Proposed by George Julian of Indiana, the Southern Homestead Act of 1866 made public lands available to blacks and loyal whites in five southern states. But the land was of poor quality and inaccessible, and claimants had only until January 1, 1867, to claim their land. But that was nearly impossible for most blacks because they were under contract with white employers until that date. Only about 4,000 black families even applied for the Homestead Act lands, and fewer than 20 percent of them saw their claims completed. The record of white claimants was not much better. Congressional moderation, therefore, left the freedmen economically weak as they faced the challenges of freedom.

Women and the Reconstruction Amendments

One casualty of the Fourteenth and Fifteenth amendments was the goodwill of the women who had been petitioning and campaigning for suffrage for two decades. They had hoped that grateful male legislators would recognize their support for the Union effort during the war and the suspension of their own demands in the interests of the more immediate concerns of preserving the Union, nursing the wounded, and emancipating the slaves. They were therefore shocked to see the wording of the Fourteenth Amendment, which for the first time inserted the word *male* in the Constitution in referring to a citizen's right to vote. Stanton and Anthony campaigned actively against the Fourteenth Amendment, and when the Fifteenth Amendment was proposed, they wondered why the word *sex* could not have been added to the "conditions" no longer a basis for denial of the vote.

Disappointment over the suffrage issue was one of several reasons that led to a split in the women's movement and the formation of two competing organizations in 1869. While some women's rights activists felt that the struggle for black rights should have its day and should not be hindered by linkage to women's demands for the vote, others pointed out that some blacks were also women. Anthony and Stanton, determined to continue their fight for a national amendment for woman suffrage and a long list of other rights, founded the National Woman Suffrage Association (NWSA). The rival American Woman Suffrage Association (AWSA) concentrated its hopes on securing the vote on a state-by-state basis. In the end, both blacks and women would have a long path of struggle ahead of them.

LIFE AFTER SLAVERY

Clinton Fisk, a well-meaning white who helped to found a black college in Tennessee, told freedmen in 1866 that they could be "as free and as happy" working again for their "old master . . . as any where else in the world." For many blacks such pronouncements sounded familiar, reminding them of white preachers' exhortations during slavery to work hard and obey their masters. Ironically, though, Fisk was an agent of the Freedmen's Bureau, the crucial agency intended to ease the transition from slavery to freedom for the four million ex-slaves.

The Freedmen's Bureau

Never in American history has one small agency—underfinanced, understaffed, and undersupported—been given a harder task than was the Bureau of Freedmen, Refugees and Abandoned Lands. Its purposes and mixed successes illustrate the tortuous course of Reconstruction.

The activities of the Freedmen's Bureau included issuing emergency rations of food and providing clothing and shelter to the homeless, hungry victims of the war; establishing medical care and hospital facilities; providing funds for transportation for the thousands of freedmen and white refugees dislocated by the war; helping blacks search for and put their families back together; and arranging for legal marriage ceremonies. The bureau also served as a friend in local civil courts to ensure that the freedmen got fair trials. Although not initially empowered to do so, the agency was responsible for the education of the ex-slaves. To bureau schools came many idealistic teachers from various northern Freedmen's Aid societies.

In addition, the largest task of the Freedmen's Bureau was to serve as an employment agency, tending to the economic well-being of the blacks. This included settling them on abandoned lands and getting them started with tools, seed, and draft animals, as well as arranging work contracts with white landowners. In the area of work contracts, the Freedmen's Bureau served more to "reenslave" the freedmen as impoverished fieldworkers than to set them on their way as independent farmers.

Although some agents were idealistic young New Englanders eager to help slaves adjust to freedom, others were Union army officers more concerned with social order than social transformation. On a typical day, these overworked and underpaid agents would visit courts and schools in their district, supervise the signing of work contracts, and handle numerous complaints, most involving contract violations between whites and blacks or property and domestic disputes among blacks. They were helpful in finding work for the freedmen, but more often than not the agents found themselves defending white landowners by telling the blacks to obey orders, to trust their employers, and to sign and live by disadvantageous contracts.

Despite mounting pressures to support white landowners, personal frustrations, and even threats on their lives, the agents accomplished a great deal. In little more than two years, the Freedmen's Bureau issued 20 million rations (nearly one-third to poor whites), reunited families and resettled some 30,000 displaced war refugees, treated some 450,000 cases of illness and injury, built 40 hospitals and hundreds of schools, provided books, tools, and furnishings—and even some land—to the freedmen, and occasionally protected their economic and civil rights. The historian W. E. B. Du Bois wrote an epitaph for the bureau that might stand for the whole of Reconstruction: "In a time of perfect calm, amid willing neighbors and streaming wealth," he wrote, it "would have been a herculean task" for the bureau to fulfill its many purposes. But in the midst of hunger, sorrow, spite, suspicion, hate, and cruelty, "the work of any instrument of social regeneration was . . . foredoomed to failure."

Economic Freedom by Degrees

The economic failures of the Freedmen's Bureau forced the freedmen into a new economic dependency on their former masters, and both were affected by the changing character of southern agriculture in the postwar years. First, land ownership was concentrated into fewer and even larger holdings than before the Civil War. From South Carolina to Louisiana, the wealthiest tenth of the population owned about 60 percent of the real estate in the 1870s. Second, these large planters increasingly concentrated on one crop, usually cotton, and were tied into the international market. This resulted in a steady drop in food production in the postwar period. Third, reliance on one-crop farming meant that a new credit system emerged whereby most farmers, black and white, depended on local merchants for renting seed, farm implements and animals, provisions, housing, and land. These changes affected race relations and class tensions among whites.

This new system, however, took a few years to develop after emancipation. At first, most freedmen signed contracts with white landowners and worked in gangs in the fields as farm laborers very much as during slavery. But what the freedmen wanted, a Georgia planter correctly observed, was "to get away from all overseers, to hire or purchase land, and work for themselves."

Many blacks therefore broke contracts, ran away, engaged in work slowdowns or strikes, burned barns, and otherwise expressed their displeasure with the contract labor system. Blacks' insistence on autonomy and land of their own was the major impetus for the change from the contract system to tenancy and sharecropping. As a South Carolina freedman put it, "If I can't own de land, I'll hire or lease land, but I won't contract." The sharecroppers were given seed, fertilizer, farm implements, and all necessary food and clothing to take care of their families. In return, the landlord (or a local merchant) told them what to grow and how much and took a share—usually half—of the harvest. The half retained by the cropper, however, was usually needed to pay for goods bought on credit (at huge interest rates) at the landlord's store. Thus the sharecroppers were semiautonomous but remained tied to the landlord's will for economic survival.

Sharecroppers and tenant farmers, though more autonomous than contract laborers, remained dependent on the landlord for their survival.

Under the tenant system, farmers had only slightly more independence. In advance of the harvest, a tenant farmer promised to sell his crop to a local merchant in return for renting land, tools, and other necessities. He was also obligated to purchase goods on credit (at higher prices than whites paid) against the harvest from the merchant's store. At "settling up" time, the income from the sale of the crop was matched with debts accumulated at the store. But tenants usually remained in debt at the end of each year and were then compelled to pledge the next year's crop. Thus a system of debt peonage replaced slavery. Only a very few blacks became independent landowners—about 2 to 5 percent by 1880, but closer to 20 percent in some states by 1900.

These changes in southern agriculture affected yeoman and poor white farmers as well as the freedmen, especially as cotton production doubled between the Civil War and 1880. Like the freedmen, whites, too, were forced to concentrate on growing staples, to pledge their crops against high-interest credit from local merchants, and to face perpetual indebtedness.

Larger planters' reliance on cotton meant fewer food crops, which led to greater dependence on local merchants for provisions and a poorer diet. Poor whites thus faced diminishing fortunes throughout the South. Some became farmhands, earning $6 a month (with board) from other farmers. Other fled to low-paying jobs in urban cotton mills.

In part because their lives were so hard, poor whites persisted in their belief in white superiority. As a federal officer reported in 1866, "The poorer classes of white people ... have a most intense hatred of the Negro, and swear he shall never be reckoned as part of the population." Many poor whites, therefore, joined the Ku Klux Klan and other southern white terror groups that emerged between 1866 and 1868. But however hard life was for poor whites, blacks were far more often sentenced to chain gangs for the slightest crimes and were bound to a life of debt, degradation, and dependency. The

high hopes with which the freedmen had greeted emancipation turned slowly to resignation and disillusionment. Felix Haywood, a former Texas slave, recalled:

> We thought we was goin' to be richer than white folks, 'cause we was stronger and knowed how to work, and the whites ... didn't have us to work for them anymore. But it didn't turn out that way. We soon found out that freedom could make folks proud but it didn't make 'em rich.

Black Self-Help Institutions

It was clear to many black leaders that since white institutions could not fulfill the promises of emancipation, black freedmen would have to do it themselves. Fortunately, the tradition of black community self-help survived in the organized churches and schools of the antebellum free Negro communities and in the "invisible" cultural institutions of the slave quarters. Religion, as usual, was vital. Emancipation brought an explosion in the growth of membership in black churches. The Negro Baptist church grew from 150,000 members in 1850 to 500,000 in 1870. The various branches of the African Methodist Episcopal church increased fourfold in the decade after the Civil War, from 100,000 to over 400,000 members.

Black ministers continued their tradition of community leadership and revivalist preaching. An English visitor to the South in 1867 and 1868, after observing a preacher in Savannah arouse nearly 1,000 people to "sway, and cry, and groan," noted the intensity of black "devoutness."

The freedmen's desire for education was as strong as for religion. A school official in Virginia echoed the observation of many when he said that the freedmen were "down right crazy to learn." This enthusiasm was dampened by the demands of fieldwork and scarce resources for black schools. The first teachers of the black children in the South were unmarried northern women, the legendary "Yankee schoolmarms," sent by groups such as the American Missionary

Along with equal civil rights and land of their own, what the freedmen most wanted was education. Despite white opposition and limited facilities for black schools, one of the most positive outcomes of the Reconstruction era was education in freedmen's schools.

Association. But blacks increasingly preferred their own teachers, who could better understand former slaves. To ensure the training of black preachers and teachers, northern philanthropists founded Howard, Atlanta, Fisk, Morehouse, and other black universities in the South between 1865 and 1867.

Black schools, like churches, became community centers. They published newspapers, provided training in trades and farming, and promoted political participation and land ownership. These efforts made black schools objects of local white hostility. In 1869, in Tennessee alone, 37 black schools were burned to the ground.

White opposition to black education and land ownership stimulated the rise of black nationalism and separatism. In the late 1860s, Benjamin "Pap" Singleton, a former Tennessee slave who had escaped to Canada, organized a land company in 1869 and promoted relocation of

blacks to separatist communities in Kansas, where they would be able to manage their own affairs apart from white interference. When these schemes failed, Singleton and other nationalists urged emigration to Canada and Liberia. Other black leaders, notably Frederick Douglass, continued to assert that suffrage would eventually lead to full citizenship rights within the United States.

RECONSTRUCTION IN THE STATES

Douglass's confidence in the power of the ballot seemed warranted in the enthusiastic early months under the Reconstruction Acts of 1867. With President Johnson neutralized, national Republican leaders were finally in a position to accomplish their political goals. Local Republicans, taking advantage of the inability or refusal of many southern whites to vote, overwhelmingly elected their delegates to state constitutional conventions in the fall of 1867. With guarded optimism and a sense of the "sacred importance" of their work, black and white Republicans turned to the task of creating new state governments.

Republican Rule

Despite popular belief, the southern state governments under Republican rule were not dominated by illiterate black majorities intent on "Africanizing" the South by passing compulsory racial intermarriage laws, as many whites feared. Nor were these governments unusually corrupt or financially extravagant. Nor did they use massive numbers of federal troops to enforce their will. Rather, they tried to do their work in a climate of economic distress and increasingly violent harassment.

A diverse combination of political groups made up the new governments elected under congressional Reconstruction. Labeled the "black and tan" governments by their opponents to suggest domination by former slaves and mulattoes, they were actually predominantly white, with the one exception of the lower house of the South Carolina legislature. The new leadership included an old Whiggish elite class of bankers, industrialists, and others interested far more in economic growth than in radical social reforms; northern Republican capitalists seeking investment opportunities; retired Union veterans; and missionaries and teachers. Such people were unfairly labeled "carpetbaggers."

Moderate blacks also participated in the Republican state governments. A large percentage of black officeholders were mulattoes, many of them well-educated preachers, teachers, and soldiers from the North. Others, such as John Lynch of Mississippi, were self-educated trades-

men or representatives of the small landed class of southern blacks. This class composition meant that black leaders often supported land policies that largely ignored the economic needs of the black masses.

These black politicians were more interested in pursuing political influence and education than land redistribution or state aid to black peasants. They sought no revenge or reversal of power, only, as an 1865 petition said, "that the same laws which govern white men shall govern black men [and that] we be dealt with as others are—in equity and justice."

The primary accomplishment of Republican rule in the South was in eliminating the undemocratic features of earlier state constitutions. All states provided universal men's suffrage and loosened requirements for holding office. The basis of state representation was made fairer by apportioning more legislative seats to the interior regions of southern states. Social and penal laws were also modernized.

Republican governments undertook the task of financially and physically reconstructing the South, overhauling tax systems, and approving generous railroad and other capital investment bonds. Most important, the Republican governments provided for a state-supported system of public schools, absent before in most of the South. As in the North, these schools were largely segregated, but for the first time, rich and poor, black and white alike had access to education. As a result, black school attendance increased from 5 to over 40 percent and white from 20 to over 60 percent by the 1880s. All of this cost money, and the Republicans did indeed greatly increase tax rates and state debts. All in all, the Republican governments "dragged the South, screaming and crying, into the modern world."

Despite its effectiveness in modernizing southern state governments, the Republican coalition did not last very long. In fact, as the map indicates, Republican rule lasted for different periods of time in different states. In some

The Return to the Union During Reconstruction

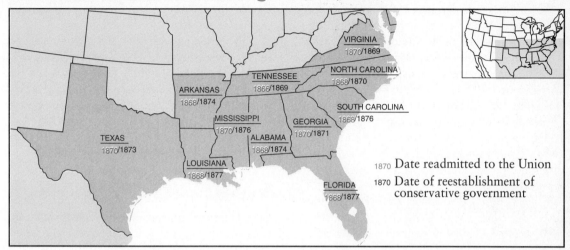

VIRGINIA
1870/1869

NORTH CAROLINA
1868/1870

TENNESSEE
1866/1869

ARKANSAS
1868/1874

SOUTH CAROLINA
1868/1876

MISSISSIPPI
1870/1876

GEORGIA
1870/1871

TEXAS
1870/1873

ALABAMA
1868/1874

LOUISIANA
1868/1877

FLORIDA
1868/1877

1870 Date readmitted to the Union
1870 Date of reestablishment of conservative government

states, Virginia, for example, the Republicans ruled hardly at all. In South Carolina, the unwillingness of black leaders to use their power to help black laborers contributed to their loss of political control to the Democrats. Class tensions and divisions among blacks in Louisiana helped to weaken that Republican regime as well. Republican rule lasted the longest in the black-belt states of the Deep South, where the black population was equal to or greater than the white.

Violence and "Redemption"

Democrats used racial violence, intimidation, and coercion to restore their power. The Ku Klux Klan was only one of several secret organizations that used force and violence against black and white Republicans. The cases of North Carolina and Mississippi are representative in showing how conservative Democrats were able to regain control.

After losing a close election in North Carolina in 1868, conservatives waged a concen-

trated campaign of terror in several counties in the piedmont area. If the Democrats could win these counties in 1870, they would most likely win statewide. In the year prior to the election, several prominent Republicans were killed, including a white state senator, whose throat was cut, and a leading black Union League organizer, who was hanged in the courthouse square with a sign pinned to his breast: "Bewar, ye guilty, both white and black." Scores of citizens were flogged, tortured, fired from their jobs, or forced to flee in the middle of the night from burning homes and barns. The courts consistently refused to prosecute anyone for these crimes. Local papers, in fact, charged that "disgusting negroes and white Radicals" had committed the crimes. The conservative campaign worked. In the election of 1870, some 12,000 fewer Republicans voted in the two crucial counties than had voted two years earlier, and the Democrats swept back into power.

In the state election in Mississippi in 1875, Democrats used similar tactics. In what was called the Mississippi Plan, local Democratic clubs organized themselves into armed militias, marching defiantly through black areas, breaking up Republican meetings, and provoking riots to justify the killing of hundreds of blacks. Armed men were posted during voter registration to intimidate Republicans. At the election itself, anyone still bold enough to attempt to vote was either helped by gun-toting whites to cast a Democratic ballot or driven away from the polls with cannon and clubs. Counties that had earlier given Republican candidates majorities in the thousands managed in 1875 a total of less than a dozen votes!

Democrats called their victory "redemption." As conservative Democratic administrations resumed control of each state government, Reconstruction came to an end. Redemption resulted from a combination of the persistence of white southern resistance, including violence and other coercive measures, and a loss of will to persist in the North.

Congress and President Grant did not totally ignore the violence in the South. Three Force Acts, passed in 1870 and 1871, gave the president strong powers to use federal supervisors to make sure that citizens were not prevented from voting by force or fraud. The third act, known as the Ku Klux Klan Act, declared illegal secret organizations that used disguise and coercion to deprive others of equal protection of the laws. Congress created a joint committee to investigate Klan violence, which reported in 1872 in 13 huge volumes of horrifying testimony. Grant issued proclamations condemning lawlessness and sent some additional troops to South Carolina. However, as reform Republicans realized that black voters supported Grant, they lost interest in defending those voters. Regular Republicans were also not very supportive, since many felt that they could do without black voters. In 1875, Grant's advisers told him that Republicans might lose important Ohio elections if he continued to protect blacks. Thus he decided that year to reject appeals by Mississippi blacks that troops be stationed in their state to

guarantee free elections. Grant declared instead that he and the nation "had tired of these annual autumnal outbreaks."

The federal government did little to stop the reign of terror against black and white Republicans throughout the South. The Force Acts were wholly inadequate and were themselves weakly enforced. Although the Ku Klux Klan's power was officially ended, the attitudes (and tactics) of Klansmen would continue long into the next century.

Reconstruction, Northern Style

The American people, like their leaders, were tired of battles over the freedmen and were shifting their attention to other matters. Frustrated with the difficulties of trying to transform an unwilling South and seemingly ungrateful blacks, the easiest course was to give blacks their citizenship and the vote and move on to something else. After the interruptions of civil war and its aftermath, most Americans were primarily interested in starting families, finding work, and making money. This meant firing furnaces in the new steel plant in Wheeling, West Virginia, pounding in railroad ties for the Central Pacific in the Nevada desert, struggling to teach in a one-room schoolhouse in Vermont for $23 a month, or battling heat, locusts, and railroad rates on a family homestead in Kansas.

At both the individual and national levels, Reconstruction, northern style, meant the continuation of the enormous economic revolution of the nineteenth century. Although failing to effect a smooth transition from slavery to freedom for ex-slaves, Republican northerners were able to accelerate and solidify their program of economic growth and industrial and territorial expansion.

The years between 1865 and 1875 featured not only the rise (and fall) of Republican governments in the South but also the spectacular rise of working-class activity and organization. Stimulated by the Civil War to improve working conditions in northern factories, such groups as trade unions, labor reform associations, and labor parties flourished, culminating in the founding of the National Labor Union in 1866. Before the depression of 1873, an estimated 300,000 to 500,000 American workers had enrolled in some 1,500 trade unions, the largest such increase in the nineteenth century. This growth would inevitably affect class tensions. In 1876, hundreds of freedmen in the rice region along the Combahee River in South Carolina went on strike to protest a 40-cent-per-day wage cut, clashing with local sheriffs and white Democratic rifle clubs. A year later, also over wage cuts, thousands of railroad workers in Pittsburgh, St. Louis, Omaha, and other northern cities went out in a nationwide wave of strikes, clashing with local police and the National Guard.

As economic relations changed, so did the Republican Party. It changed from the party of moral reform to one of material interest. In the continuing struggle in American politics between "virtue and commerce," self-interest was again winning. No longer willing to support an agency like the Freedmen's Bureau, Republican politicians had no difficulty backing huge grants of money and land to the railroads. As blacks were told to go to work and help themselves, the Union Pacific was being given subsidies of between $16,000 and $48,000 for each mile of track laid across western plains and mountains.

By 1869, the year financier Jay Gould almost succeeded in cornering the gold market, the nation was increasingly defined by materialistic "go-getters" and by sordid grasping for wealth and power. Ulysses Grant himself was an honest man, but his judgment of others was flawed. His administration featured a series of scandals that touched several cabinet officers and relatives and even two vice presidents. Under Grant's appointments, outright graft flourished in a half dozen departments. Most scandals involved large sums of public money. The Whiskey Ring affair, for example, cost the public millions of dollars in lost tax revenues siphoned off to government of-

ficials. Gould's gold scam received the unwitting aid of Grant's Treasury Department and the knowing help of his brother-in-law.

Nor was Congress pure in these various schemes. Crédit Mobilier figured in the largest of several scandals in which construction companies for transcontinental railroads (in this case a dummy company) received generous bonds and work contracts in exchange for giving congressmen gifts of money, stocks, and railroad lands. Henry Adams spoke for many Americans when he said that Grant's administration "outraged every rule of decency."

The election of 1872 marked the decline of public interest in moral issues. A "liberal" faction of the Republican Party, unable to dislodge Grant and disgusted with his administration, formed a third party with a reform platform and nominated Horace Greeley, editor of the New York *Tribune,* for president. Democrats, lacking notable presidential candidates, also nominated Greeley, even though he had spent much of his earlier career assailing Democrats as "rascals." Despite his wretched record, Grant easily won a second term.

The End of Reconstruction

Soon after Grant's second inauguration, a financial panic, caused by overconstruction of railroads and the collapse of some crucial eastern banks, created a terrible depression that lasted throughout the mid-1870s. In times of hardship, economic issues dominated politics, further pulling attention away from the plight of the freedmen. As Democrats took control of the House of Representatives in 1874 and looked toward winning the White House in 1876, politicians talked about such issues as new scandals in the Grant administration, unemployment, various proposals for public works expenditures for relief, the availability of silver and greenback dollars, and high tariffs.

No one, it seemed, talked much about the rights and conditions of southern freedmen. In 1875, a guilt-ridden Congress passed Senator

Charles Sumner's civil rights bill, intended to put teeth into the Fourteenth Amendment. But the act was not enforced and was declared unconstitutional by the Supreme Court eight years later. Congressional Reconstruction, long dormant, had ended. The election of 1876 sealed the conclusion.

As their nominee for president in 1876, the Republicans turned to a former governor of Ohio, Rutherford B. Hayes, partly because of his reputation for honesty, partly because he had been an officer in the Union army (a necessity for post–Civil War candidates), and partly because, as Henry Adams put it, he was "obnoxious to no one." The Democrats chose Governor Samuel J. Tilden of New York, who achieved national recognition as a civil service reformer in breaking up the corrupt Tweed Ring.

Tilden won a majority of the popular vote and appeared to have enough electoral votes for victory. Of 20 disputed electoral votes, all but one came from states in the Deep South, where Democrats had applied various versions of the Mississippi Plan to intimidate voters. To resolve the disputed votes, Congress created a special electoral commission, which awarded Hayes all 20 votes, enough to win, 185 to 184.

Outraged Democrats threatened to stop the Senate from officially counting the electoral votes, thus preventing Hayes's inauguration. The country was in a state of crisis, and some Americans wondered if civil war might break out again.

As the inauguration date approached and newspapers echoed outgoing President Grant's call for "peace at any price," the forces of mutual self-interest concluded the "compromise of 1877." The Democrats agreed to suspend resistance to the counting of the electoral votes, and on March 2, Rutherford B. Hayes was declared president. In exchange for the presidency, Hayes ordered the last remaining troops out of the South (South Carolina, Louisiana, and Florida being the last states under military Reconstruction), appointed a former Confederate general to his cabinet, supported federal aid to bolster economic and railroad development in the South, and announced his intentions to let southerners handle race relations themselves. Hayes let it be known that he would not enforce the Fourteenth and Fifteenth amendments, thus initiating a pattern of executive inaction not broken until the middle of the twentieth century. The immediate crisis was averted, officially ending the era of Reconstruction, but the unfulfilled hopes of freedmen continued to smolder beneath the surface of everyday life.

CONCLUSION

A MIXED LEGACY

In the 12 years between Appomattox and Hayes's inauguration, the diverse dreams of victorious northern Republicans, defeated white southerners, and hopeful black freedmen conflicted. There was little chance that all could be realized, yet each group could point to a modest fulfillment of its goals. The compromise of 1877 cemented the reunion of South and North, thus providing new opportunities for economic development in both regions. The Republican Party achieved its economic goals and preserved its political hold on the White House, though not Congress, with two exceptions, until 1932. The ex–Confederate states were brought back into the Union, and southerners retained their firm control of southern lands and black labor, though not without struggle and some changes. To the extent that the peace of 1877 was preserved "at any price," that price was paid by the freedmen.

In 1880, Frederick Douglass summarized Reconstruction for the freedmen, saying that it was a wonder to him "not that freedmen have made so little progress, but, rather, that they have made so much; not that they have been standing still, but that they have been able to stand at all." Indeed, despite their liabilities, the freedmen had made admirable gains in education and in economic and family survival. Although sharecropping and tenancy were harsh systems, black laborers organized themselves to achieve a measure of autonomy and opportunity in their lives that could never be diminished. Moreover, the three great Reconstruction amendments to the Constitution, despite flagrant violation over the next 100 years, held out the promise that the rights of equal citizenship and political participation would yet be fulfilled.

Recommended Reading

The best overviews of the Reconstruction era are John Hope Franklin, *Reconstruction After the Civil War* (1961); Kenneth Stampp, *The Era of Reconstruction, 1865–1877* (1965); and the brilliant work by Eric Foner, *Reconstruction: America's Unfinished Revolution, 1863–1877* (1988).

The fullest, most moving account of the black experience in the transition from slavery to freedom is Leon Litwack's massive and sensitive work, *Been in the Storm So Long: The Aftermath of Slavery* (1980). The southern white response to emancipation is described in Dan T. Carter, *When the War Was Over: The Failure of Self-Reconstruction in the South, 1865–1867* (1985).

The economy of the South and the freedmen's experience with land and labor are described in Roger Ransom and Richard Sutch, *One Kind of Freedom: The Economic Consequences of Emancipation* (1977); and Eric Foner, *Nothing but Freedom: Emancipation and Its Legacy* (1983). An excellent work showing the white experience with tenancy in the changing economy of the South is Stephen Hahn, *The Roots of Southern Populism* (1983). The Freedmen's Bureau is the subject of Donald Nieman, *To Set the Law in Motion: The Freedmen's Bureau and the Legal Rights of Blacks, 1865–1868* (1979). Continuing racial prejudice in the South and North is the subject of C. Vann Woodward, *The Strange Career of Jim Crow*, 3d rev. ed. (1974). See also W. E. B. Du Bois's *Black Reconstruction* (1935) and *The Souls of Black Folk* (1903).

Northern politics during Reconstruction have been widely discussed. See David Donald, *The Politics of Reconstruction* (1965); and Michael Les Benedict, *A Compromise of Principle: Congressional Republicans and Reconstruction, 1863–1869* (1974). Southern politics is best seen in Michael Perman, *The Road to Redemption: Southern Politics, 1869–1879* (1984). Grant's presidency and the abandonment of the freedmen by northern Republicans can be traced in William McFeely, *Grant: A Biography* (1981); and William Gillette, *Retreat from Reconstruction, 1869–1879* (1979). The campaign of violence that ended the Republican governments in the South is told with gripping horror in George C. Rable, *But There Was No Peace: The Role of Violence in the Politics of Reconstruction* (1984).

Five novels written at different times and representing different interpretations of the story of Reconstruction are Albion Tourgée, *A Fool's Errand* (1879); Thomas Dixon, *The Clansman* (1905); W. E. B. Du Bois, *The Quest of the Silver Fleece* (1911); Howard Fast, *Freedom Road* (1944); and Ernest Gaines, *The Autobiography of Miss Jane Pittman* (1971).

Time Line

1865	Civil War ends Lincoln assassinated; Andrew Johnson becomes president Johnson proposes general amnesty and reconstruction plan Racial confusion, widespread hunger, and demobilization Thirteenth Amendment ratified Freedmen's Bureau established	**1870**	Fifteenth Amendment ratified
		1870s–1880s	Black followers of Pap Singleton migrate to Kansas
		1870–1871	Force Acts North Carolina and Georgia reestablish Democratic control
1865–1866	Black codes Repossession of land by whites and freedmen's contracts	**1872**	General Amnesty Act Grant reelected president
		1873	Crédit Mobilier scandal Panic causes depression
1866	Freedmen's Bureau renewed and Civil Rights Act passed over Johnson's veto Southern Homestead Act Ku Klux Klan formed Tennessee readmitted to Union	**1874**	Alabama and Arkansas reestablish Democratic control
		1875	Civil Rights Act Mississippi reestablishes Democratic control
1867	Reconstruction Acts passed over Johnson's veto Impeachment controversy Freedmen's Bureau ends	**1876**	Hayes-Tilden election
		1876–1877	South Carolina, Louisiana, and Florida reestablish Democratic control
1868	Fourteenth Amendment ratified Johnson acquitted Ulysses S. Grant elected president	**1877**	Compromise of 1877; Rutherford B. Hayes assumes presidency and ends Reconstruction
1868–1870	Ten states readmitted under congressional plan	**1880s**	Tenancy and sharecropping prevail in the South Disfranchisement and segregation of southern blacks begins
1869	Georgia and Virginia reestablish Democratic Party control		

part 4

An Industrializing People

1865-1900

In the last quarter of the nineteenth century Americans turned their energies toward transforming their society from one based on agriculture to one based on heavy industry. This era of technological change, industrial growth, and national expansion deeply affected rural Americans and Native Americans as well as urban labor. By 1900, the United States had emerged as one of the world's great industrial powers and had entered the international arena as a new aspiring contender.

Chapters 17, 18, and 19 form a unit. Chapter 17, "Rural America in the Industrial Age," examines the ways in which American farmers modernized and vastly expanded production after the Civil War. Even though agriculture provided the basis for urban industrial development, many farmers did not win the rewards they had anticipated. While the postwar period was difficult for some farmers, it was disastrous for Native Americans. By 1900, the power of the Plains Indians had been broken and the reservation system firmly set in place.

Chapter 18, "The Rise of Smokestack America," focuses on the character of industrial progress and urban expansion. The labor conflicts of the period indicate the difficulty of these years for most working-class Americans.

In Chapter 19, "Politics and Reform," we see how the national politics of the Gilded Age largely ignored the needs of farmers, workers, and other ordinary Americans and how the 1890s became a turning point in American attitudes and political party alignments.

Chapter 20, "Becoming a World Power," demonstrates the international consequences of the country's successful industrialization, its emerging sense of national identity, and its growing role as a world power.

chapter 17

Rural America in the Industrial Age

In 1873, Milton Leeper, his wife, Hattie, and their baby, Anna, climbed into a wagon piled high with their possessions and set out to homestead in Boone County, Nebraska. From their claim, Hattie wrote to her sister in Iowa, "When we get a fine house and 100 acres under cultivation, I wouldn't trade with any one." But Milton had broken in only 13 acres when disaster struck. Hordes of grasshoppers appeared, and the Leepers fled their claim and took refuge in the nearby town of Fremont.

There they stayed for two years. Milton worked first at a store, then hired out to other farmers. Hattie sewed, kept a boarder, and cared for chickens and a milk cow. The family lived on the brink of poverty but never gave up hope. In 1876, the Leepers triumphantly returned to their claim with the modest sum of $27 to help them start over.

The grasshoppers were gone, there was enough rain, and preaching was only half a mile away. The Leepers, like others, began to prosper. Two more daughters were born and cared for in the comfortable sod house, "homely" on the outside but plastered and cozy within. As Hattie explained, the homesteaders lived "just as civilized as they would in Chicago."

Their luck did not last. Hattie, pregnant again, fell ill and died in childbirth along with her infant son. Heartbroken, Milton buried his wife and child and left the claim. The last frontier had momentarily defeated him, although he would try farming in at least four other locations before his death in 1905.

The story of the Leepers illustrates some of the problems confronting rural Americans in the last quarter of the nineteenth century. As a mature industrial economy transformed agriculture and shifted the balance of economic power permanently away from America's farmlands to the country's cities and factories, many farmers found it impossible to realize the traditional dream of rural independence and prosperity. Even bountiful harvests no longer guaranteed success. "We were told . . . to go to work and raise a big crop; that was all we needed," said one farmer. "We went to work and plowed and planted; the rains fell, the sun shone, nature smiled, and we raised the big crop they told us to; and what came of it? Eight cent corn, ten cent oats, two cent beef and no price at all for butter and eggs—that's what came of it." Native Americans also discovered that changes in rural life threatened their values and dreams. As the Sioux leader Red Cloud told railroad surveyors in Wyoming, "We do not want you here. You are scaring away the buffalo."

This chapter explores the agricultural transformation of the late nineteenth century and highlights the ways in which rural Americans—red, white, and black—joined the industrial world and responded to new conditions. The rise of large-scale agriculture in the West, the exploitation of its natural resources, and the development of the Great Plains form a backdrop for the discussion of the impact of white settlement on western tribes and their reactions to white incursions. In an analysis of the South, the efforts of whites to create a "New South" form a contrast to the underlying realities of race, cotton, and economic peonage. The chapter also highlights the protests of blacks and farmers against their places in American life.

MODERNIZING AGRICULTURE

Between 1865 and 1900, the nation's farms more than doubled in number as Americans pushed west of the Mississippi and broke virgin land. In both newly settled and older areas, farmers raised specialized crops with the aid of modern machinery and relied on the expanding railroad system to send them to market. The character of agriculture became increasingly capitalistic. Farmers, as one New Englander pointed out, "must understand farming as a business; if they do not it will go hard with them."

Rural Myth and Reality

The number of Americans still farming the land testified to the continuing vitality of the rural tradition. In the late eighteenth century, Benjamin Franklin praised the country's "industrious frugal farmers," while Thomas Jefferson viewed them as the "deposit for substantial and genuine virtue" and fundamental to the health of the republic.

The notion that the farmer and the farm life symbolized the essence of America persisted as the United States industrialized. The popularity of inexpensive Currier and Ives prints, depicting idyllic rural scenes with sturdy, happy people, suggests how the idealized view of country life captivated Americans.

The prints obscured the often harsh reality of American agriculture. Farmers were no longer the backbone of the work force. In 1860, they represented almost 60 percent of the labor force; by 1900, less than 37 percent of employed Americans were farmers. At the same time, farmers' contribution to the nation's wealth declined from a third to a quarter.

Farmers were increasingly affected by the industrial and urban world. Reliable, cheap transportation allowed them to specialize. Farmers on the Great Plains now grew most of the country's wheat, while those in the Midwest replaced that

This Currier and Ives print expresses an idealized view of rural life, which helps explain the great popularity of these illustrations.

crop with corn used to feed hogs and cattle. Eastern farmers turned to vegetable, fruit, and dairy farming. Cotton continued to dominate the economy of the South, although farmers also raised tobacco, wheat, and rice. In the Far West, grain, fruits, and vegetables predominated.

As farmers specialized in cash crops for national and international markets, their success depended increasingly on outside forces, such as banks, loan companies, middlemen, railroads, and exporters. After 1870, exports of wheat, flour, and animal products rose, with wheat becoming the country's chief cash crop. Thus the cultivation of wheat in Russia and Argentina meant fewer foreign buyers for American grain, and the opening of the Canadian high plains in the 1890s added another competitor.

Farming had become a modern business. "Watch and study the markets and the ways of marketmen . . . learn the art of 'selling well,'" one rural editor advised his readers in 1887. "The work of farming is only half done when the crop is out of the ground."

Like other businesses of the post–Civil War era, farming also increasingly depended on machinery. Harvesters, binders, and other new machines, pulled by work animals, made farm work easier and more efficient. Moreover, they allowed farmers to cultivate far more land than they had been able to do with hand tools, so that by 1900 more than twice as much land was in cultivation as in 1860. But machinery was expensive, and many American farmers had to borrow to buy it. In the decade of the 1880s, mortgage indebtedness grew 2½ times faster than agricultural wealth.

New Farmers, New Farms

As farmers became more like other nineteenth-century businessmen, some became large-scale entrepreneurs. Small family farms still typified American agriculture, but vast mechanized operations devoted to the cultivation of one crop appeared, especially west of the Mississippi River. These farms had huge barns for storage of machinery and a handful of other farm buildings but few gardens, trees, or outbuildings. No churches or villages interrupted the monotony of the landscape.

The bonanza farms, huge wheat farms established in the late 1870s on the northern plains, symbolized the trend to large-scale agriculture. The North Dakota farm that Oliver Dalrymple operated for two Northern Pacific Railroad directors used 200 pairs of harrows and 125 seeders for planting and required 155 binders and 26 steam threshers for harvesting. At peak times, the farm's work force numbered 600 men. The result was a harvest of 600,000 bushels of wheat in 1882.

Overproduction and Falling Prices

Farmers did not initially realize that the new technology might cause problems. As productivity rose, however, the yields for some crops like wheat became so large that the domestic market could not absorb them. The prices farm products commanded steadily declined. In 1867, corn sold for 78 cents a bushel. By 1873, it had fallen to 31 cents and by 1889 to 23 cents. Wheat and cotton prices also spiraled downward.

Because the federal government gradually withdrew paper money from circulation after the Civil War and did not coin much silver, the supply of money rose more slowly than productivity. As a result, prices fell by more than half between the end of the Civil War and 1900. In a deflationary period, farmers received less for their crops but also paid less for their purchases. But deflation increased the real value of debts. In 1888, it took 174 bushels of wheat to pay the interest on a $2,000 mortgage at 8 percent. By 1895, it took 320 bushels.

Farming on the Western Plains, 1880s–1890s

Between 1870 and 1900, the acreage devoted to farming tripled west of the Mississippi as settlers flocked to the Great Plains (North and South Dakota, Kansas, Nebraska, Oklahoma, and Texas). In the mid–nineteenth century, emigrants had deemed the Plains unsuitable for farming and had headed for the Far West. Views of the farming potential of the Plains changed after the Civil War, however. Railroads eager for business as they laid down new lines, town boosters eager for inhabitants, and land speculators eager to sell their holdings all undertook major promotional efforts to lure settlers to the Plains.

Late-nineteenth-century industrial innovations also helped settlers overcome the natural obstacles that made farming on the plains so problematic at midcentury. Because there was so little timber for fencing or housing on the plains, early emigrants had chosen to settle elsewhere. But in the 1870s, Joseph Glidden developed barbed wire as a cheap alternative to timber fencing. Barbed wire fencing could be used to enclose fields on the plains. Other helpful innovations included twine binders, which speeded up grain harvesting, reducing the threat of losing crops to the unpredictable weather, and mail-order steel windmills for pumping water from deep underground wells.

In the first boom period of settlement, lasting from 1879 to the early 1890s, tens of thousands of eager families like the Leepers moved onto the Great Plains and began farming. Some made claims under the Homestead Act, which granted 160 acres to any family head or adult who lived on the claim for five years or who paid $1.25 an acre after six months of residence. Because homestead land was frequently less desirable than land held by railroads and speculators, however, most settlers bought land outright rather than taking up claims. The costs of getting started were thus more substantial than the Homestead Act would suggest. In 1880, some 20 percent of the Plains farmers were tenants who lacked the capital to buy land, and this percentage rose over time.

Many of the new settlers were immigrants, most of whom arrived from Germany, the

Agriculture in the 1880s

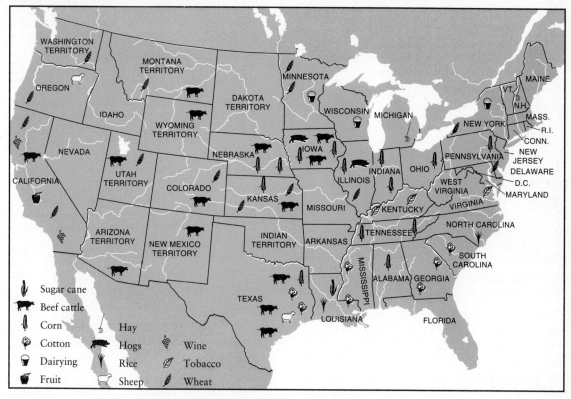

This map reveals the patterns of regional agricultural specialization in the 1880s.

British Isles, and Canada. Many Scandinavians, Czechs, and Poles also moved to the new frontier.

Life on the Plains frontier often proved difficult. The costs of machinery, the vagaries of crops and markets, the pests and natural disasters, the shortage of cash all contributed to the uncertainties of frontier life. Survival was often precarious, and the chances of failure were great. In addition, many settlers found the vast treeless plains depressing. One New England visitor explained, "It has been terrible on settlers, on the women especially, for there is no society and they get doleful and feel almost like committing suicide for want of society." O. E. Rölvaag's novel *Giants in the Earth* (1927) depicts the wife of a Norwegian immigrant farmer driven to madness and death.

But life on the Plains was not always so discouraging as Rölvaag suggested. Willa Cather, who spent her childhood in Nebraska, showed both the harshness and the lure of prairie life in her novels, while letters and diaries also provide a more positive view of farming life. In 1880, six years after Elam Bartholomew had settled in northern Kansas, his journal reveals that 1,081 people stopped at his home. His wife served 783 meals to visitors. Trips to church, parties, sings, and neighborhood get-togethers brightened family life.

Plains settlers had to devise new forms of shelter, using materials readily at hand. The Rawding family posed with their most prized possessions in front of their Nebraska sod house in 1886.

The Plains frontier required many adjustments, however. Scarce water and violent temperature changes demanded resourcefulness and new modes to behavior. Without firewood, farmers learned to burn corncobs and twisted wheat for warmth. The inventive settlers also discovered how to build houses of sod "bricks." Although from a distance such houses often looked like mounds of earth, they were comfortable, cozy, and practical.

The first wave of expansion into the Great Plains halted abruptly by the early 1890s. Falling agricultural prices cut profits. Then, the unusually plentiful rainfall of the 1880s, which had lured farmers to settle semiarid regions, disappeared. A devastating drought followed. The destitute survived on boiled weeds, a few potatoes, and a little bread and butter. Many farmers could not pay their debts and lost their farms to creditors. Some stayed on as tenants. By 1900, two-thirds of homesteaded farms had failed.

Whether individual farmers remained on the Great Plains or whether they retreated to more promising climates, collectively these new agricultural efforts had a significant long-term impact on the region's environment. When farmers removed sod to build their sod houses and broke the prairies with their ploughs in order to plant their crops, they were removing the earth's protective covering. The heavy winds so common on the prairies could lift exposed topsoil and carry it miles away. The deep plowing, which was essential for dry farming techniques introduced after the drought of the 1880s, worsened this situation. The dust bowl of the 1930s was the eventual outcome of these agricultural interventions.

The Early Cattle Frontier, 1860–1890

In the mid-1870s, a clash between two Plains settlers, John Duncan, a cattleman, and Peter Schmidt, a farmer, symbolized the meeting of the farming and cattle frontiers. Some of Duncan's cattle wandered onto Schmidt's property and destroyed his garden. Schmidt ran the cattle off but was outraged at the damage. For years, such incidents had been rare, but as settlement increased in the 1880s and 1890s, they became more common.

The commercial cattle frontier had its roots in Union military strategy. During the war, the North had cut Texas off from its Confederate markets. At the end of the war, five million longhorns were roaming the Texas range. The postwar burst of railroad construction provided a way of turning cattle into dollars. If ranchers drove the cattle north from Texas to railroad connections for shipment to slaughtering and packing houses in cities like Chicago and Kansas City, their value would soar. Thus started the first cattle drives, celebrated in stories, movies, and television. In the late 1860s, cowboys herded thousands of longhorns north to towns like Abilene, Wichita, and Dodge City.

Ranchers on the Great Plains bought some of the cattle. In the late 1870s and early 1880s, huge ranches appeared in eastern Colorado, Wyoming, and Montana and in western Kansas, Nebraska, and the Dakotas. Because the cattle could roam at will over the public domain, they cost owners little as they fattened up.

By the mid-1880s, the first phase of the cattle frontier was ending as farmers moved onto the Plains, bought up public lands once used for grazing, and fenced them in. But the struggle between cattle ranchers and farmers was only one factor in the cattle frontier's collapse. Eager for fat profits, ranchers overstocked their herds. Hungry cattle ate everything in sight, then grew weak as grass became scarce. As one Texan realized, "Grass is what counts. It's what saves us all—as far as we get saved. . . . Grass is what holds the earth together." When cattlemen overstocked the range, their herds devoured the perennial grasses. In their place tough, less nutritious annual grasses sprang up, and sometimes

even these grasses disappeared. Lands once able to support large herds of cattle eventually were transformed into deserts of sagebrush, weeds, and dust.

A winter of memorable blizzards in 1886 killed 90 percent of the cattle. Frantic owners dumped their remaining cattle on the market, getting $8 or even less per animal, compared with the $60 to $70 they had gotten previously. In the aftermath, the ranchers who remained stock raisers adopted new techniques. Experimenting with new breeds, they began to replace their longhorns, to fence in their herds, and to feed them grain during the winter months. Ranching, like farming, was becoming more of a modern business.

Cornucopia on the Pacific

Ranching and farming had a somewhat different history in California. When gold was discovered there in 1849, Americans had rushed west to find it. But as one father told his eager son, "Plant your lands; these be your best gold fields." Little of California's land, however, was actually homesteaded or developed as small family farms. When California entered the Union, Mexican ranchers held vast tracts of land, which never became part of the public domain. Neither Mexican-Americans nor small farmers profited from the 20 years of confusion over the legitimacy of Mexican land titles. Speculators did, however, acquiring much of the Mexican-Americans' land. Consequently, small farmers needed substantial sums to buy land.

California farms were typically larger than farms in the rest of the country. In 1870, the average California farm was 482 acres, whereas the national average farm was only 153 acres. By 1900, two-thirds of the state's agricultural land was occupied by farms of 1,000 acres or more. Small farmers and ranchers did exist, of course, but they found it difficult to compete with large, mechanized operators using cheap migrant laborers, usually Mexican or Chinese.

The value of much of California's agricultural land, especially the southern half of the Central Valley, depended on water. Dams and canals were built to irrigate the parched earth. By 1890, over a quarter of California's farms benefited from irrigation.

Although grain was initially California's most valuable crop, it faced stiff competition from farmers on the Plains and in other parts of the world. Some argued that

> land capable of raising Adriatic figs, Zante currants, French prunes, Malaga raisins, Batavia oranges, Sicily lemons, citrons, limes, dates and olives, and our own incomparable peaches, apricots, nectarines, pears, quinces, plums, pomegranates, apples, English and native walnuts, chestnuts, pecans and almonds, in a climate surpassing that of Italy, is too valuable for the cultivation of simple cereals.

As railroad managers in the 1880s realized the potential profit California's produce represented, they lowered rates and introduced refrigerated railroad cars. Fruit and vegetable production rose. In June 1888, fresh apricots and cherries successfully survived the trip from California to New York. Two years later, 9,000 carloads of navel oranges headed east. Before long California fruit was available in London.

Exploiting Natural Resources

The perspective that led Americans to treat farming as a business was also evident in the ways in which they dealt with the country's abundant natural resources. Gold had been the precious metal originally drawing prospectors to California, but the discovery of other precious materials—silver, iron, copper, coal, lead, zinc, tin—lured thousands west to Colorado, Montana, Idaho, and Nevada as well as to states like Minnesota. The popular conception of the miner as a hardy forty-niner searching for loose placer deposits of gold captures the early days of mining. But by the late nineteenth century, mining relied on machinery, railroads, engineers, and a large work force. It was a big business with high costs and an underlying philosophy that encouraged rapid and thorough exploitation of the earth's resources.

The decimation of the nation's forests went hand in hand with large-scale mining and the railroads that provided the links to markets. Both railroads and mining depended on wood—railroads for wooden ties, mines for shaft timber and ore reduction. The California State Board of Agriculture estimated in the late 1860s that one-third of the state's forests had already disappeared.

The idea that the public lands belonging to the federal government ought to be rapidly developed supported such exploitation of the nation's natural resources. In 1878, Congress passed the Timber and Stone Act, which initially applied to Nevada, Oregon, Washington, and California. This legislation allowed the sale of 160-acre parcels of the public domain that were "unfit for cultivation" and "valuable chiefly for timber." Timber companies were quick to see the possibilities in the new law. They hired men willing to register for claims and then to turn them over to timber interests. By the end of the century, more than 3.5 million acres of the public domain had been acquired under the legislation, and most of it was in corporate hands.

The rapacious exploitation of resources made some Americans uneasy. Many believed that forests played a part in causing rainfall and that their destruction would have an adverse impact on the climate. Others, like the early environmentalist John Muir, lamented the destruction of the country's great natural beauty. In 1868 Muir came upon the Great Valley of California, "all one sheet of plant gold, hazy and vanishing in the distance . . . one smooth, continuous bed of honey-bloom." He soon realized, however, that a "wild, restless agriculture" and "flocks of hoofed locusts, sweeping over the ground like a fire" would destroy this vision of loveliness. Muir became a conservation champion. He played a part in the creation of Yosemite National Park in 1890 and participated in a successful effort to allow President Benjamin Harrison to classify certain parts of the public domain as forest reserves (the Forest Reserve Act of 1891). In 1892, Muir established the Sierra Club. Conservation ideas were more popular in the East, however, than in the West, where the seeming abundance of natural resources and the profit motive diminished support.

THE SECOND GREAT REMOVAL

As farmers settled the western frontier and became entangled in a national economy, they clashed with the Indian tribes who lived on the land. Black Elk, an Ogalala Sioux, recalled an ominous dream:

> A long time ago my father told me what his father told him, that there was once a Lakota [Sioux] holy man, called Drinks Water, who dreamed what was to be; and this was long before the coming of the Wasichus [white men]. He dreamed . . . that a strange race had woven a spider's web all around the Lakotas. And he said: "When this happens, you shall live in square gray houses, in a barren land, and beside those square gray houses you shall starve."

During Black Elk's lifetime, the nightmarish prophecy came true.

Background to Hostilities

As Chapter 13 explained, the lives of most Plains Indians centered on hunting the buffalo. Increased emigration to California and Oregon in the 1840s and 1850s interrupted tribal pursuits and animal migration patterns. During the Civil War, tribes that President Andrew Jackson had earlier resettled in Oklahoma divided in their

Black Elk, pictured here on the left, was a perceptive observer of the deleterious changes experienced by Indians during the latter part of the nineteenth century.

support of the Union and the Confederacy. After the war, however, all "were treated as traitors." The federal government nullified earlier pledges and treaties, leaving Indians defenseless against further incursions on their lands. As settlers pushed into Kansas, the tribes living in Kansas were shunted into Oklahoma.

The White Perspective

At the end of the Civil War, a state of war existed between Indians and whites on the Plains. The shameful massacre of friendly Cheyenne at Sand Creek, Colorado, by the Colorado Volunteers in

1864 sparked widespread hostilities. A congressional commission authorized to make peace on the Plains concluded that "an industrious, thrifty, and enlightened population" of whites would occupy most of the West. All Native Americans should relocate in either the western half of present-day South Dakota, or Oklahoma. There they would learn the ways of white society and "civilized" life.

At two major conferences in 1867 and 1868, Native American chiefs listened to these proposals with mixed feelings. As a Kiowa chief explained, "I don't want to settle. I love to roam over the prairies." None of the agreements extracted were binding since the chiefs had no authority to speak for their tribes. The U.S. Senate dragged its feet in approving the treaties. Supplies promised to Indians who settled in the reserved areas failed to materialize, and wildlife proved too sparse to support them. These Indians soon drifted back to their former hunting grounds.

As General William T. Sherman, Commander of the Army in the West, warned, however, "All who cling to their old hunting ground are hostile and will remain so till killed off." In 1867, he entrusted General Philip Sheridan with the duty of dealing with the tribes. Sheridan introduced a new tactic of winter campaigning. He proposed to seek out the Indians who divided into small groups during the winter and to exterminate them.

The completion of the transcontinental railroad in 1869 added another pressure for "solving" the Indian question. Transcontinental railroads wanted rights-of-way through tribal lands and needed white settlers to make their operations profitable. They carried not only thousands of hopeful settlers to the West but miners and hunters as well.

In his 1872 annual report, the commissioner for Indian affairs, Francis Amasa Walker, proposed a solution for the Indian problem: reservations, where the Indians would be subjected to "a rigid reformatory discipline."

Though Walker considered himself a "friend of humanity" and wished to save the Indians from destruction, he also thought they must "yield or perish."

The Tribal View

Native Americans did not yield passively to such attacks on their ancient way of life and to the violation of treaties. As Black Elk related, his father and many others soon decided that fighting was the only way "to keep our country." But "wherever we went, the soldiers came to kill us, and it was all our country."

Broken promises fed Indian resistance. In 1875, the federal government allowed gold prospectors to stream into the Black Hills, part of the Sioux reservation and one of their sacred places. The Sioux, led by chiefs Sitting Bull, Crazy Horse, and Rain-in-the-Face, took to the warpath. Despite their victory over General George Custer at the Battle of Little Big Horn in 1876, the well-supplied and well-armed U.S. Army finally overwhelmed them. Crazy Horse was murdered. Elsewhere, General Sherman defeated Native American tribes in Texas, while in the Pacific Northwest, Nez Percé chief Joseph surrendered in 1877.

The wholesale destruction of the buffalo contributed to white victory. The animals were central to Indian life, culture, and religion. As one Pawnee chief explained, "Am afraid when we have no meat to offer, Great Spirit . . . will be angry & punish us." Although Plains Indians could be wasteful of buffalo in areas where the animals were abundant, white miners and hunters ultimately destroyed the herds.

The slaughter, which had claimed 13 million animals by 1883, was in retrospect disgraceful. The Indians considered white men demented. "They just killed and killed because they like to do that," said one, whereas when "we hunted the bison . . . [we] killed only what we needed."

The Dawes Act, 1887

Changing federal policy also undermined Native American culture and life. In 1871, Congress ended the practice, in effect since the 1790s, of treating the tribes as sovereign nations. The government urged tribes to establish court systems in place of tribal justice and extended federal jurisdiction to the reservations. Tribes were also warned not to gather for religious ceremonies.

The Dawes Severalty Act of 1887 set the course of federal Indian policy for the rest of the century. Believing that tribal bonds kept Indians in savagery, reformers intended to destroy them. Rather than allotting reservation lands to tribal groups, the act allowed the president to distribute these lands to individuals. Those who accepted allotments would become citizens and presumably forget their tribal identity. Although Indian agents explained that Native Americans opposed the Dawes Act, Congress did not hesitate to legislate on their behalf.

Another motive was also at work. Even if each Indian family head claimed a typical share of 160 acres, millions of "surplus" acres would remain for sale to white settlers. Within 20 years of the Dawes Act, Native Americans had lost 60 percent of their lands.

The Ghost Dance: An Indian Renewal Ritual

By the 1890s, the grim reality of their plight made many Native Americans responsive to the message of Paiute prophet Wovoka, who predicted that natural disasters would eliminate the white race. Dancing Indians would not only avoid this destruction but also gain new strength thanks to the return to life of their ancestors. Believers expressed their faith and hope through the new rituals of ghost dancing and meditation.

Although Wovoka's prophecies discouraged hostile actions against whites, American settlers were uneasy. Indian agents tried to prevent the ghost dances and filed hysterical reports. One agent determined that the Sioux medicine man, Sitting Bull, was a leading troublemaker and attempted to arrest him. In the confusion, Indian police killed Sitting Bull.

Bands of Sioux fled the reservation with the army in swift pursuit. In late December 1890, the army caught up with the Sioux at Wounded Knee Creek and massacred over 200 men, women, and children. An eyewitness described the desolate scene a few days later. "Among the fragments of burned tents . . . we saw the frozen bodies lying close together or piled one upon another."

Thus arose the lament of Black Elk, who saw his people diminished, starving, despairing:

> Once we were happy in our own country and we were seldom hungry, for then the two-leggeds and the four-leggeds lived together like relatives, and there was plenty for them and for us. But then the Wasichus came, and they have made little islands for us and other islands for the four-leggeds, and always these islands are becoming smaller, for around them surges the gnawing flood of the Wasichus; and it is dirty with lies and greed.

THE NEW SOUTH

As the Indians faced an uncertain future, some inhabitants of the South hoped to lift their region out of poverty. Of all the nation's agricultural regions, the South was the poorest. In 1880, southerners' yearly earnings were only half the national average. Some southern publicists during the late nineteenth century, however, dreamed of making the agricultural South the rival of the industrial North.

Postwar Southerners Face the Future

The publicists of the movement for a "New South" argued that southern backwardness did not stem from the Civil War, as so many southerners believed, but from long-standing conditions in southern life, especially a rural economy

Indian Lands and Communities in the United States

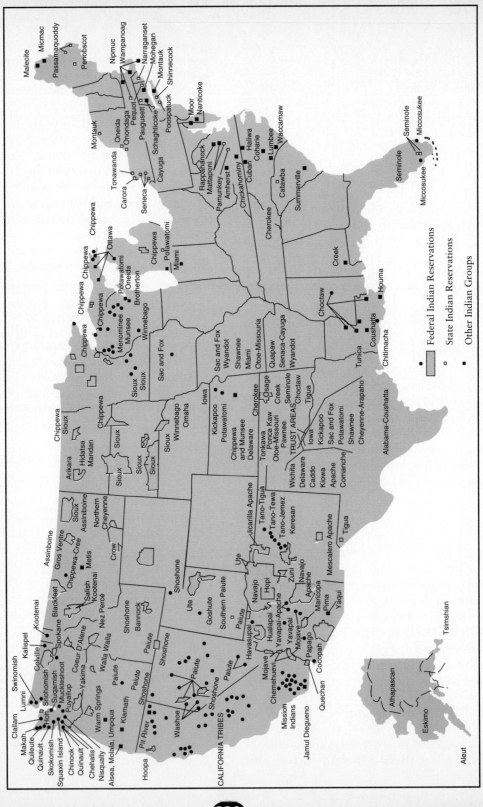

Micmac Malecite Passamaquoddy Penobscot Nipmuc Wampanoag Narraganset Mohegan Montauk Shinnecock Montauk Oneida Onondaga Pequot Paugusett Schaghticoke Poospatuck Moor Nanticoke

Seminole Seminole Miccosukee Miccosukee Seminole

Tonawanda Carora Seneca Cayuga Rappahannock Mattaponi Pamunkey Amherst Chickahominy Cuban Haliwa Coharie Catawba Lumbee Waccamaw Summerville Cherokee Creek Houma

Chippewa Chippewa Chippewa Ottawa Chippewa Potawatomi Chippewa Potawatomi Miami Potawatomi Oneida Brotherton Menominee Munsee Winnebago Chippewa Sac and Fox Sioux Sioux Iowa Winnebago Omaha Sac and Fox Wyandot Shawnee Miami Otoe-Missouria Quapaw Seneca-Cayuga Wyandot Choctaw Coushatta Chitimacha Tunica

Chippewa Sioux Chippewa Arikara Hidatsa Mandan Sioux Sioux Sioux Sioux Sioux Sioux Kickapoo Potawatomi Chippewa and Munsee Delaware Tonkawa Ponca Kaw Otoe-Missouri Pawnee TRUST AREAS Iowa Kickapoo Sac and Fox Potawatomi Shawnee Alabama-Coushatta Creek Osage Seminole Choctaw Tigua Cheyenne-Arapaho

Sioux Assiniboine Sioux Northern Cheyenne Assiniboine Gros Ventre Chippewa-Cree Metis Crow Wichita Delaware Caddo Kiowa Apache Comanche Kickapoo Shawnee

Kootenai Kalispel Colville Swinomish Lummi Clallam Makah Quileute Skokomish Suquamish Muckleshoot Squaxin Island Chinook Quinault Chehalis Nisqually Alsea, Molala, Umpqua Spokane Blackfeet Salish Kootenai Coeur D'Alene Nez Percé Yakima Walla Walla Puyallup Warm Springs Klamath Pit River Hoopa CALIFORNIA TRIBES Washoe Shoshone Shoshone Paiute Paiute Paiute Shoshone Bannock Shoshone Paiute Paiute Ute Goshute Southern Paiute Ute Shoshone Jicarilla Apache Tano-Tigua Tano-Tewa Tano-Jemez Keresan Tigua Mescalero Apache Navajo Hopi Zuni Navajo Apache Mission Indians Jamul Diegueno Chemehuevi Mojave Hualapai Yavapai-Apache Yavapai Mojave Havasupai Maricopa Pima Papago Cocopah Quechan Yaqui

Tsimshian Athapascan Eskimo Aleut

Federal Indian Reservations ●
State Indian Reservations □
Other Indian Groups ■

based on cotton. Power and wealth came not from cotton, they asserted, but from factories, machines, and cities.

In hundreds of speeches, editorials, pamphlets, articles, and books, spokesmen for the New South tried to persuade fellow southerners to abandon prewar ideals that glorified leisure and gentility and adopt the ethic of hard work. To attract essential capital, New South advocates held out inviting opportunities. Several southern state governments offered tax exemptions and cheap convict labor. Texas and Florida awarded the railroads land grants, and cities like Atlanta and Louisville mounted huge industrial exhibitions as incentives to industrial progress. Middle-class southerners increasingly accepted new entrepreneurial values.

During the late nineteenth century, northern money flowed into the southern cotton industry and railroad system. Northern capital helped southern cities to embark on an extended period of expansion. By 1900, some 15 percent of all southerners lived in cities, compared with 7 percent in 1860. (The national averages for these years were 40 percent and 20 percent, respectively.)

The city of Birmingham, Alabama, symbolized the New South. In 1870, the site of the future city was a peaceful cornfield. The next year, two northern real estate speculators arrived on the scene, attracted by the area's rich iron deposits. Despite a siege of cholera and the depression of the 1870s, Birmingham rapidly became the center of the southern iron and steel industry. By 1890, a total of 38,414 people lived in the city. Other southern cities like Richmond and Augusta, Georgia, flourished as well by developing a variety of industries.

The Other Side of Progress

Despite the optimism of New South leaders about matching or even surpassing the North's economic performance, the South made slow progress. Older values persisted, impeding full acceptance of a new economic order. And the southern school system lagged far behind that of the North.

Although new industries and signs of progress abounded, the South did not better its position relative to the North. Whereas in 1860 the South had 17 percent of the country's manufacturing concerns, by 1904 it had only 15 percent. During the same period, the value of its manufactures grew from 10.3 percent of the total value of manufactures in the United States to only 10.5 percent.

Moreover, the South failed to reap many benefits from industrialization. As in the antebellum period, the South remained an economic vassal of the North. Southern businessmen grew in number, but with the exception of the American Tobacco Company, no great southern corporations arose. Instead, southerners worked for northern companies and corporations, which absorbed southern businesses or dominated them financially. By 1900, for example, five corporations directed three-quarters of the railroad mileage in the South (excluding Texas), and northern bankers controlled all five. Northerners also took over the southern steel industry.

As this happened, profits and the power to make decisions flowed north. In many cases, northern directors determined that southern mills and factories could handle only the early stages of processing, while northern factories finished the goods. Thus southern cotton mills sent yarn and coarse cloth north for completion. Southern manufacturers who did finish their products, hoping to improve their chances in the marketplace, found that railroad rate discrimination robbed their goods of any competitive edge.

Individual workers in the new industries received meager rewards. The thousands of women and children in factories were silent testimony to the fact that their husbands and fathers could not earn sufficient wages to keep them at home. As usual, women and children earned lower wages than men. Justifying these policies,

382 PART 4 • AN INDUSTRIALIZING PEOPLE

one Augusta factory president claimed that the employment of children was "a matter of charity with us; some of them would starve if they were not given employment." In general, all workers earned lower wages and worked longer hours in the South than elsewhere. Per capita income was the same in 1900 as it had been in 1860—and only half the national average. Black workers, who made up 6 percent of the southern manufacturing force in 1890, usually had the worst jobs and the lowest wages.

Cotton Still King

Although New South advocates envisioned an industrial society, they always recognized the need for agricultural change. The overdependence on "King Cotton" hobbled southern agriculture by making farmers the victims of far-away market forces and an oppressive credit system. Subdivide old cotton plantations into small diversified farms, Henry Grady, editor of the Atlanta *Constitution,* urged. Truck farming could produce "simply wonderful profits."

A new agricultural South with new class and economic arrangements did emerge, but it was not the one Grady and others envisioned. Despite the breakup of some plantations following the Civil War, large landowners proved resourceful in holding on to their property and in dealing with postwar conditions, as Chapter 16 showed. As landowners adopted new agricultural arrangements, former slaves sank into debt peonage.

White farmers on small and medium-size holdings fared only slightly better than black tenants and sharecroppers. Immediately after the war, high cotton prices tempted them to raise as much cotton as they could. Then prices began a disastrous decline, from 11 cents a pound in 1875 to less than 5 cents in 1894. Yeoman farmers became entangled in debt. Each year, farmers found themselves buying supplies on credit so that they could plant the next year's crop and support their families until harvest time. Each year, thousands of indebted farmers fell further behind. Many lost their land and became tenant

farmers. By 1900, over half the South's white farmers and three-quarters of its black farmers were tenants. Although tenancy was increasing all over rural America, nowhere did it rise more rapidly than in the Deep South.

These patterns had baneful results for individual southerners and for the South as a whole. Caught in a cycle of debt and poverty, few farmers could think of improving agricultural techniques or diversifying crops. In their desperate attempt to pay off debts, they concentrated on cotton, despite falling prices. "Cotton brings money, and money pays debt" was the small farmer's slogan. Landowners also pressured tenants to raise a market crop. Far from diversifying, as Grady had hoped, farmers increasingly limited the number of crops they raised. By 1880, the South was not growing enough food to feed its people adequately. Poor nutrition contributed to chronic bad health and sickness.

The Nadir of Black Life

Grady and other New South advocates painted a picture of a strong, prosperous, and industrialized South, a region that could deal with the troublesome race issue without the interference of any "outside power." Realizing that black labor would be crucial to the transformation he sought, Grady advocated racial cooperation. But since he assumed that blacks were racially inferior, he supported an informal system of segregation.

By the time of Grady's death in 1889, a much harsher perspective on southern race relations was emerging. In 1891, at a national assembly of women's clubs in Washington, D.C., a black woman, Frances Ellen Watkins Harper, anticipated efforts to strip the vote from blacks and appealed to the white women at the meeting not to abandon black suffrage. "Instead of taking the ballot from his hands, teach him how to use it, and add his quota to the progress, strength, and durability of the nation."

The positive approach urged by Harper had no chance of adoption in the late-nineteenth-century political climate. The decision by congressional leaders in 1890 to shelve a proposed civil rights act and the defeat of the Blair bill providing federal assistance for educational institutions made black Americans vulnerable. The traditional sponsor of the rights of freedmen, the Republican Party, left blacks to fend for themselves as a minority in the white South. The courts also abandoned blacks. In 1878, the Supreme Court declared unconstitutional a Louisiana statute banning discrimination in transportation. In 1882, the Court voided the Ku Klux Klan Act of 1871, deciding that the civil rights protections of the Fourteenth Amendment applied to states rather than to individuals. In 1883, the provisions of the Civil Rights Act of 1875, which assured blacks of equal rights in public places, were declared unconstitutional.

Northern leaders did not oppose these actions. In fact, northerners increasingly promulgated negative stereotypes, picturing blacks as either ignorant, lazy, childlike fools or as lying, stealing, raping degenerates. *Atlanta Monthly* in 1890 anticipated a strong current in magazine literature when it expressed doubts that this "lowly variety of man" could ever be brought up to the intellectual and moral standards of whites. Encouraged by northern public opinion, and with the blessing of Congress and the Supreme Court, southern citizens and legislatures sought to make blacks permanently second-class members of southern society.

In the political sphere, white southerners amended state constitutions to disfranchise black voters. By various legal devices—the poll tax, literacy tests, "good character" and "understanding" clauses administered by white voter registrars, and all-white primary elections—blacks lost the right to vote. The most ingenious method was the "grandfather clause," which specified that only citizens whose grandfathers were registered to vote on January 1, 1867, could cast their ballots. This virtually excluded blacks. Although the Supreme Court outlawed such blatantly discriminatory laws as grandfather clauses, a series of other constitutional changes, beginning in Mississippi in 1890 and

spreading to all 11 former Confederate states by 1910, effectively excluded the black vote.

In a second tactic in the 1890s, state and local laws legalized informal segregation in public facilities. Beginning with railroads and schools, "Jim Crow" laws, upheld by the Supreme Court in 1896 in *Plessy* v. *Ferguson*, were extended to libraries, hotels, restaurants, hospitals, asylums, prisons, theaters, parks and playgrounds, cemeteries, toilets, morgues, sidewalks, drinking fountains, and most places where blacks and whites might mingle.

Political and social discrimination made it ever more possible to keep blacks permanently confined to agricultural and unskilled labor and dependent on whites for their material welfare. In 1900, nearly 84 percent of black workers nationwide engaged in some form of agricultural labor as farmhands, overseers, sharecroppers, or tenant or independent farmers or in service jobs, primarily domestic service and laundry work. These had been the primary slave occupations. At the end of the Civil War, at least half of all skilled craftsmen in the South had been black. But by the 1890s, the percentage had decreased to less than 10 percent, as whites systematically excluded blacks from the trades. Such factory work as blacks had been doing was also reduced, largely in order to drive a wedge between poor blacks and whites to prevent unionization. The exclusion of blacks from industry prevented them from acquiring the skills and habits that would enable them to rise into the middle class.

Blacks did not accept their declining position passively. In the mid-1880s, they enthusiastically joined the mass worker organization, the Knights of Labor (discussed in Chapter 18), first in cities such as Richmond and Atlanta, then in rural areas. But as blacks joined, whites withdrew. The flight of whites weakened the organization in the South, and a backlash of white violence finally smashed it.

Against this backdrop, lynchings and other violence against blacks increased. On February 21, 1891, the New York *Times* reported that in Texarkana, Arkansas, a mob apprehended a 32-

year-old black man, Ed Coy, charged with the rape of a white woman, tied him to a stake, and burned him alive. As Coy proclaimed his innocence, his alleged victim herself somewhat hesitatingly put the torch to his oil-soaked body. The *Times* report concluded that only by the "terrible death such as fire . . . can inflict" could other blacks "be deterred from the commission of like crimes." Ed Coy was one of more than 1,400 black men lynched or burned alive during the 1890s. About a third were charged with sex crimes. The rest were accused of a variety of "crimes" related to not knowing their place: marrying or insulting a white woman, testifying in court against whites, having "a bad reputation."

Diverging Black Responses

White discrimination and exploitation nourished new black protest tactics and ideologies. For years, Frederick Douglass had been proclaiming that blacks should remain loyal Americans and count on the promises of the Republican Party. But on his deathbed in 1895, his last words were allegedly, "Agitate! Agitate! Agitate!"

Among black expressions of protest, one was a woman's. In Memphis, Tennessee, editor Ida B. Wells launched a campaign against lynching in 1892. So hostile was the white community's response that Wells carried a gun to protect herself. When white citizens finally destroyed the press and threatened her partner, Wells left Memphis to pursue her activism elsewhere.

Other voices called for black separatism within white America. T. Thomas Fortune wrote in the black New York *Freeman* in 1887 that "there will one day be an African Empire." Three years later, he organized the Afro-American League (a precursor of the NAACP), insisting that blacks must join together to fight the rising tide of discrimination. The league encouraged independent voting, opposed segregation and lynching, and urged the establishment of black institutions like banks to support black businesses.

While some promoted black nationalism, most blacks worked patiently within white society for equality and social justice. In 1887, J. C. Price formed the Citizens Equal Rights Association, which opposed segregation and called for state laws to guarantee equal rights.

Efforts to escape oppression in the South, like "Pap" Singleton's movement to found black towns in Tennessee and Kansas, continued. Blacks founded 25 towns in Oklahoma Territory, as in other states and even Mexico. But these attempts, like earlier ones, were short-lived, crippled by limited funds and the hostility of white neighbors. Singleton eventually recommended migration to Canada or Liberia as a final solution, and later black nationalist leaders also looked increasingly to Africa. But as Douglass had long argued, no matter how important African roots might be, blacks had been in the Americas for generations and would have to win justice and equal rights here.

Most black Americans responded to the slow, moderate self-help program of Booker T. Washington, the best-known black leader in America. Born a slave, Washington had risen through hard work to become the founder (in 1881) and principal of Tuskegee Institute in Alabama, which became the nation's largest and best-known industrial training school. At Tuskegee, young blacks received a highly disciplined education in scientific agricultural techniques and vocational skilled trades. Washington believed that economic self-help and the familiar Puritan virtues of hard work, frugality, cleanliness, and moderation were the way to success. He spent much of his time traveling through the North to secure philanthropic gifts to support Tuskegee. In time, he became a favorite of the American entrepreneurial elite.

Although Washington worked actively behind the scenes for black civil rights, in 1895 in Atlanta he publicly urged that blacks postpone for the time being their pursuit of the vote, civil rights, and social equality with whites and concentrate on gaining an education, vocational training, and economic improvement, especially in agriculture and the trades. Whites throughout the country enthusiastically acclaimed Washington's address, but many blacks called his "Atlanta Compromise" a serious setback in the struggle for black rights. They also believed that if blacks were to improve their lives, they would have to organize.

FARM PROTEST

During the post–Civil War period, many farmers, both black and white, began to realize that only by organizing could they hope to ameliorate the conditions of rural life. Not all were dissatisfied with their lot, however. Farmers in the Midwest and near city markets successfully adjusted to new economic conditions and had little reason for discontent. Farmers in the South and West, by contrast, faced new problems and difficulties that led to the first mass organization of farmers in American history.

The Grange in the 1860s and 1870s

The earliest effort to organize white farmers came in 1867 when Oliver Kelley founded the Order of the Patrons of Husbandry. At first the organization emphasized the improvement of rural social and cultural life, but more aggressive goals soon evolved. Dudley Adams, speaking to an Iowa group in 1870, emphasized the powerlessness of "the immense helpless mob" of farmers, victims of "human vampires." Salvation, Adams maintained, lay in organization.

More and more farmers, especially those in the Midwest and the South, agreed with Adams. The depression of the 1870s (discussed in Chapter 18) sharpened discontent. By 1875, an estimated 800,000 had joined Kelley's organization, now known as the National Grange. The "Farmers' Declaration of Independence," read before local granges on July 4, 1873, called upon farmers to rouse themselves and cast off "the tyranny of monopoly."

Some Granger "reforms" attempted to bypass money-hungry middlemen by establishing buying and selling cooperatives. Although many cooperatives failed, they indicated that farmers realized they could not respond to new conditions on an individual basis but needed to act collectively. Operators of grain elevators drew fire for cheating midwestern farmers. But Grangers saw the railroads, America's first big business, as the greatest offenders. As Chapter 18 will show, cutthroat competition among railroad companies generally brought lower rates. But even though rates dropped nationwide, the railroads often set high rates in rural areas and awarded discriminatory rebates to large shippers.

Other groups also wished to see controls imposed on the railroads. Railroad policies that favored large Chicago grain terminals and long-distance shippers over local concerns victimized many western businessmen. Between 1869 and 1874, both businessmen and farmers in Illinois, Iowa, Wisconsin, and Minnesota lobbied for state railroad laws. The resulting Granger Laws established maximum rates railroads and grain elevators could charge. Other states also sought to control railroads by establishing state regulatory commissions.

Railroad companies and grain elevators quickly challenged the new laws. In 1877, the Supreme Court upheld the legislation in *Munn* v. *Illinois.* Even so, state commissions failed to control long-haul rates, and railroads often raised long-haul charges.

Although the Granger Laws failed to control the railroads, they established an important principle: State legislatures had the power to regulate businesses of a public nature like the railroads. But the failure of the Granger Laws and the Supreme Court's reversal of *Munn* v. *Illinois* in its 1886 *Wabash* v. *Illinois* decision led to greater pressure on Congress to continue the struggle against big business.

The Interstate Commerce Act, 1887

In 1887, Congress responded to farmers, railroad managers who wished to regulate the fierce competition that threatened to bankrupt their companies, and shippers who objected to transportation rates by passing the Interstate Commerce Act. That legislation required that railroad rates be "reasonable and just," that rate schedules be made public, and that practices such as rebates be discontinued. The act also set up the first federal regulatory agency, the Interstate Commerce Commission (ICC), but limited its authority to control over commerce conducted between states.

Like state railroad commissions, the ICC found it difficult to define a reasonable rate. Moreover, thousands of cases overwhelmed the tiny staff in the early months of operation. In the long run, the lack of enforcement power was most serious.

The Farmers' Alliances in the 1880s and 1890s

The Grange declined in the late 1870s as the depression receded. But neither farm organizations nor farm protest died. Depression struck again in the late 1880s and worsened in the 1890s. Official statistics told the familiar story of falling prices for cereal crops grown on the plains and prairies. A bushel of wheat that had sold for $1 in 1870 was worth 60 cents in the 1890s. And while prices declined, the load of debt climbed.

A Kansas farmer's letter reveals some of the human consequences of such trends:

> At the age of 52 years, after a long life of toil, economy and self-denial, I find myself and family virtually paupers. With hundreds of cattle, hundreds of hogs, scores of good horses, and a farm that rewarded the toil of our hands with 16,000 bushels of golden corn, we are poorer by many dollars than we were years ago. What once seemed a neat little fortune and a house of refuge for our declining years . . . has been rendered valueless.

Under these pressures, farmers turned again to organization, education, and cooperation. Farmers' alliances sprang up, grew, and coalesced, and by the late 1880s two organizations dominated: the Northwestern Farmers' Alliance, which was active in Kansas, Nebraska, Iowa, Minnesota, and the Dakotas; and the Southern Farmers' Alliance, which originated in Texas and proceeded to absorb farmers' groups in Arkansas and Louisiana. The Southern Farmers' Alliance, one of the most important reform organizations of the 1880s, sent lecturers throughout the South and onto the western plains. The Alliance's newspaper, the *National Economist,* maintained that "agriculture, as a class, can only be rendered prosperous by radical changes in the laws governing money, transportation, and land." Alliance lecturers proposed various programs that would help realize their slogan: "Equal rights to all, special privileges to none."

On the one hand, the Alliances experimented with buying and selling cooperatives in order to free farmers from the clutches of supply merchants, banks, and other credit agencies. Although these efforts often failed in the long run, they taught the value of cooperation to achieve common goals. On the other hand, the Alliances supported legislative efforts to regulate powerful monopolies and corporations, which they believed gouged the farmer. Many Alliance members also felt that increasing the money supply was critical to improving the position of farmers and supported a national banking system empowered to issue paper money. Finally, the Alliances called for better public schools, state agricultural colleges, and an improvement in the status of women.

By 1890, rural discontent was spreading. In Kansas, hundreds of farmers packed their families into wagons to set off for Alliance meetings or to parade in long lines through the streets of nearby towns and villages. Similar scenes occurred through the West and the South. Never had there been such a wave of organizational activity in rural America. In 1890, more than a million farmers counted themselves as Alliance members.

The Alliance network also included black farmers. In 1888, black and white organizers established the Colored Farmers' Alliance, headed by a white Baptist minister, R. M. Humphrey. The Colored Farmers' Alliance recognized that black and white farmers faced common economic problems, but few initially confronted the fact that many southern cotton farmers depended on black labor and had a different perspective from that of blacks.

The Ocala Platform, 1890

In December 1890, the National Alliance gathered in Ocala, Florida, to develop an official platform. Most delegates felt that the federal government had failed to address the farmers' problems. "Congress must come nearer the people or the people will come nearer the Congress," warned the Alliance's president. The platform called for the direct election of U.S. senators. Alliance members also supported lowering the tariff, emphasizing the need to reduce prices for "the poor of our land." Their money plank proposed a new banking system controlled by the federal government and an increased amount of money in circulation, which, they believed, would lead to inflation, higher prices, and a reduction in debt.

Other platform measures were aimed at freeing farmers from the twin evils of the credit merchant and depressed prices at harvest time. Other demands included a graduated income tax and support for the regulation of transportation and communication networks. If regulation failed, the government was called upon to take over both networks and run them for the public benefit.

These planks, with the demand for aggressive governmental action, departed radically from conventional political norms. Many Americans feared that the organization could upset political arrangements. The New York *Sun* newspaper reported that the Alliance had caused a "panic" in the two major parties. Although the Alliance was not formally in politics, it supported sympathetic candidates in the state and local elections of 1890. A surprising number of these candidates won. Alliance victories in the West harmed the Republican Party enough to cause President Harrison to refer to "our election disaster."

Before long, many Alliance members were pressing for an independent political party, as legislators who had courted Alliance votes conveniently forgot their pledges. One Texas farmer reported that the chairman of the state Democratic executive committee "calls us all skunks" and observed that "anything that has the scent of the plowhandle smells like a polecat" to the Democrats. Among the first to realize the necessity of forming an independent third party was Georgia's Tom Watson. He also recognized that electoral success in the South would depend on unity between white and black farmers.

The People's Party, 1892

In February 1892, the People's, or Populist, Party was established, with almost 100 black delegates in attendance. The party nominated James B. Weaver, Union army veteran from Iowa, as its presidential candidate, and James G. Field, a former Confederate soldier, for vice president.

The platform preamble captured the urgent spirit of the agrarian protest movement in the 1890s:

> We meet in the midst of a nation brought to the verge of moral, political and material ruin. Corruption dominates the ballot box, the legislatures, the Congress.... The fruits of the toil of millions are boldly stolen to build up colossal fortunes ... we breed two great classes—paupers and millionaires.

The charge was clear: "The controlling influences dominating the old political parties have allowed the existing dreadful conditions to develop without serious effort to restrain or prevent them."

The Omaha platform demands, drawn from

the Ocala platform of 1890, were greatly expanded. They included more means of direct democracy, like the secret ballot, and several planks intended to enlist the support of urban labor. The People's Party also endorsed a graduated income tax; the free and unlimited coinage of silver, at a ratio of 16 to 1; and government ownership of railroads, telephone, and telegraph.

The Populist Party attempted to widen the nature of the American political debate by promoting a new vision of the government's role with respect to farmers' problems. But the tasks of weaning the South away from the Democratic Party, encouraging southern whites to work with blacks, and persuading voters of both parties to abandon familiar political ties were monumental.

Despite these obstacles, the new party pressed forward. Unlike the candidates of the major parties in 1892, Weaver campaigned actively. In the South, he faced hostile Democrats who disapproved of attempts to form a biracial political coalition. The results of the campaign were mixed. Although Weaver won over a million popular votes (the first third-party candidate to do so), he carried only four states (Kansas, Colorado, Idaho, and Nevada) and parts of two others for a total of 22 electoral votes. The attempt to break the stranglehold of the Democratic Party on the South had failed, as had its effort to attract urban workers and farmers in the Great Lakes region.

Although the People's Party did not succeed in recruiting a cross-section of American voters in 1892, it gained substantial support. Miners and mine owners in states like Montana and Colorado and in territories like New Mexico favored the demand for coinage of silver. Most Populists, however, were rural Americans in the South and West who stood outside the mainstream of American life. They often lived far from towns, villages, and railroads. Frustrated by the workings of their political, social, and economic world, they responded to a party offering to act as their advocate. They succeeded in electing governors in Kansas and North Dakota, and the party swept the state offices in Colorado. In the South, their losses stemmed from violent opposition and fraud on the part of the Democrats.

Farmers who were better integrated into their world tended to believe that they could work through existing political parties. In 1892, when thousands of farmers and others were politically and economically discontented, they voted for Grover Cleveland and the Democrats, not the Populists.

CONCLUSION

CHANGING RURAL AMERICA

The late nineteenth century brought turbulence to rural America. The "Indian problem," which had plagued Americans for 200 years, was tragically solved for a while, but not without resistance and bloodshed. Few whites found these events troubling. Most were caught up in the challenge of responding to a fast-changing world. White farmers, ranchers, and miners moved into western lands. Southerners struggled to catch up with the North. Blacks protested as they saw their hopes for equal rights thwarted. Some farmers met with success, but others, like Milton Leeper, whose experience was a far cry from the idyllic Currier and Ives depictions of life in the country, found only hardship. Many were caught in a cycle of poverty and debt. Some fled to the cities, where they joined the industrial work force described in the next chapter. Many farmers turned to collective action and politics.

Their actions demonstrate that they did not merely react to events but attempted to shape them.

Recommended Reading

Gilbert C. Fite provides a detailed study of the last agricultural frontier in *The Farmer's Frontier, 1865–1900* (1966). Annette Kolodny deals with women's perceptions of the West in *The Land Before Her: Fantasy and Experience of the American Frontiers, 1630–1860* (1984). Fred C. Luebke has edited a collection of essays dealing with immigrants on the Plains frontier, *Ethnicity on the Great Plains* (1980). Earl Pomeroy covers the Far West in *The Pacific Slope: A History of California, Oregon, Washington, Idaho, Utah, and Nevada* (1965). See also David Montejano, *Anglos and Mexicans in the Making of Texas, 1831–1986* (1987).

R. W. Paul writes of the mining frontier in *Mining Frontiers of the Far West, 1848–1880* (1963). Robert R. Dykstra explores urban development and social tensions on the cattle frontier in *The Cattle Towns: A Social History of the Kansas Cattle Trading Centers* (1970).

On relations between whites and Native Americans, see William T. Hagan, *American Indians* (1979 ed.); and Wilcomb E. Washburn, *The Indian in America* (1975). John G. Neihardt's *Black Elk Speaks* (1932) is the account of a holy man of the Ogalala Sioux.

For views of the New South, see C. Vann Woodward, *The Origins of the New South, 1877–1913* (1951); and Gavin Wright, *Old South, New South: Revolutions in the Southern Economy Since the Civil War* (1986). Also helpful are Robert C. McMath and Orville V. Burton, eds., *Toward a New South: Studies in Post–Civil War Southern Communities* (1982); and Lawrence H. Larsen, *The Rise of the Urban South* (1985). On race relations, see H. N. Rabinowitz, *Race Relations in the Urban South* (1978); and Jacqueline Jones, *Labor of Love, Labor of Sorrow: Black Women, Work, and the Family from Slavery to the Present* (1985).

Lawrence Goodwyn provides a provocative study of Populism in *The Populist Moment: A Short History of the Agrarian Revolt in America* (1978). Other studies include Bruce Palmer, *"Men over Money": The Southern Populist Critique of American Capitalism* (1980); and Peter H. Argersinger, *Populism and Politics: William Alfred Peffer and the People's Party* (1974).

Good novels include Willa Cather, *My Antonia* (1918); and O. E. Rölvaag, *Giants in the Earth* (1927).

Time Line

1860s	Cattle drives from Texas begin	1884	Southern Farmers' Alliance founded
1865–1867	Sioux wars on the Great Plains	1886	Severe winter ends cattle boom *Wabash* v. *Illinois*
1867	National Grange founded	1887	Dawes Severalty Act Interstate Commerce Act Farm prices plummet
1869	Transcontinental railroad completed		
1869–1874	Granger Laws	1888	Colored Farmers' Alliance founded
1873	Financial panic triggers economic depression	1890	Afro-American League founded Sioux Ghost Dance movement Massacre at Wounded Knee Ocala platform
1874	Barbed wire patented		
1875	Black Hills gold rush incites Sioux War	1890s	Black disfranchisement in the South Jim Crow laws passed in the South Declining farm prices
1876	Custer's last stand at Little Big Horn		
1877	*Munn* v. *Illinois* Bonanza farms in the Great Plains	1892	Populist Party formed
		1895	Booker T. Washington's "Atlanta Compromise" address
1880s	"New South"		
1881	Tuskegee Institute founded	1896	*Plessy* v. *Ferguson*
1883–1885	Depression		

chapter 18

The Rise of Smokestack America

By 1883, Thomas O'Donnell, an Irish immigrant, had lived in the United States for over a decade. He was 30 years old, married, with two young children. His third child had died in 1882, and O'Donnell was still in debt for the funeral. Money was scarce, for O'Donnell was a textile worker in Fall River, Massachusetts, and not well educated. "I went to work when I was young," he explained, "and have been working ever since." However, O'Donnell worked only sporadically at the mill. New machines needed "a good deal of small help," and the mill owners preferred to hire man-and-boy teams. Since O'Donnell's children were only 1 and 3, he often saw others preferred for day work. Once, when he was passed over, he recalled, "I said to the boss . . . what am I to do; I have got two little boys at home . . . how am I to get something for them to eat; I can't get a turn when I come here. . . . I says, 'Have I got to starve; ain't I to have any work?' "

O'Donnell was describing his family's marginal existence to a Senate committee that was gathering testimony in Boston in 1883 on the relations between labor and capital. As the senators heard the tale, they asked him why he did not go west. "It would not cost you over $1,500," said one senator. The gap between senator and worker could not have been more dramatic. O'Donnell replied, "Well, I never saw over a $20 bill . . . if some one would give me $1,500 I will go."

From the vantage point of the senator, who had no comprehension of the realities of O'Donnell's life, the fruits of industrial progress were clear. As the United States became a world industrial leader in the years after the Civil War, its factories poured forth an abundance of ever-cheaper goods ranging from steel rails and farm reapers to mass-produced parlor sets. Manufacturing replaced agriculture as the leading source of economic growth between 1860 and 1900. A rural nation of farmers was becoming a nation of industrial workers and city dwellers.

As O'Donnell's testimony illustrates, industrial growth did not benefit everyone. Estimates suggest that perhaps half of the American population was too poor to take advantage of the new goods of the age.

This chapter examines the new order that resulted from the maturing of the American industrial economy between 1865 and 1900. The chapter's central theme grows out of O'Donnell's story: As the United States built up its railroads, cities, and factories, its production and profit orientation resulted in the maldistribution of wealth and power. The social problems that accompanied the country's industrial development would capture the attention of reformers and politicians for decades to come.

THE TEXTURE OF INDUSTRIAL PROGRESS

When Americans went to war in 1861, agriculture was the country's leading source of economic growth. Forty years later, manufacturing had taken its place. As American manufacturing progressed, new regions grew in industrial importance. From New England to the Midwest lay the country's industrial heartland. New England was still a center of light industry, and the Midwest continued to process natural resources. Now, however, the production of iron, steel, and transportation equipment joined the older manufacturing operations there. In the Far West, manufacturers concentrated on processing the region's natural resources, but heavy industry made strides as well. In the South, the textile industry put down roots by the 1890s, although the South as a whole was far less industrialized than either the North or the Midwest.

The Rise of Heavy Industry from 1880 to 1900

Although many factors contributed to the dramatic rise in industrial productivity, the changing nature of the industrial sector itself explains many of the gains. Heavy industry, which produced goods like steel, iron, petroleum, and machinery, grew rapidly and fueled further economic growth. Farmers, who bought machinery for their farms; manufacturers, who installed new equipment; and railroads, which bought steel rails—all contributed to rising productivity figures.

Technological innovations that revolutionized production lay behind the rise of heavy industries such as steel. The introduction of the Bessemer converter and the open-hearth steelmaking method in the 1870s transformed the production process. Both techniques converted iron ore into steel while reducing the need for so many skilled workers.

Dramatic changes in the steel industry resulted. Steel companies developed new forms of vertical organization that provided them with access to raw materials and markets and brought all stages of steel manufacturing, from smelting to rolling, into one mill. Production soared and prices fell.

The production of a cheaper, stronger, more durable material than iron created new goods, new demands, and new markets. Millions of tons of steel went into the making of rails and locomotives, cable suspension bridges, ships, and humbler items such as wire and nails.

New sources of power facilitated the conversion of American industry to mass production. Early manufacturers depended on water power, but with the opening of new anthracite coal deposits, the cost of coal dropped, and American industry rapidly shifted to steam. By 1900, steam engines accounted for 80 percent of the nation's industrial energy supply.

The emergence of a national transportation and communications network was central to economic growth. In 1860, most railroads were located in the East and the Midwest. From 1862 on, the federal and state governments vigorously promoted railroad construction with land grants from the public domain. The first transcontinental railroad, completed in 1869, led to a burst of railroad construction. Four additional transcontinental lines and miles of feeder and branch roads were laid down in the 1870s and 1880s. As railroads crisscrossed the country, Western Union lines arose alongside them. Mass production and distribution depended on fast, efficient, and regular transportation. The completion of the national system both encouraged and supported the adoption of mass production and mass marketing.

Financing Postwar Growth

Such changes demanded huge amounts of capital and the willingness to accept financial risks. The creation of the railroad system alone cost over $1 billion by 1859. Completion of the network required another $10 billion, and foreigners contributed a third of the sum. Americans also eagerly supported new ventures and began to devote an increasing percentage of the national income to investment rather than consumption.

Although savings and commercial banks continued to invest their depositors' capital, investment banking houses like Morgan & Co. played a new and significant role in matching resources with economic enterprises. Investment bankers marketed investment opportunities in corporate bonds (which offered set interest rates and eventually the repayment of principal) and stocks (which paid dividends only if the company made a profit). The market for industrial securities expanded rapidly in the 1880s and 1890s.

Railroads: Pioneers of Big Business

As the nature of the American economy changed, big businesses became the characteristic form of economic organization. The railroads were the pioneers of big business and a great modernizing force in America. After the Civil War, railroad companies expanded rapidly. In 1865, the typical railroad was only 100 miles long. Twenty years later, it was 1,000.

Railroads faced constant high costs of maintaining equipment and lines. In addition, they carried a heavy load of debt, incurred to pay for construction and expansion. Yet railroad freight charges dropped steadily during the last quarter of the century. When two or more lines competed for the same traffic, railroads often offered lower rates than their rivals or secret rebates (cheaper fares in exchange for all of a company's business). Rate wars helped customers, but they could plunge a railroad into bankruptcy. Instability plagued the railroad industry even as it expanded.

In the 1870s, railroad leaders sought stability by eliminating ruinous competition. They established "pools," informal agreements that set uniform rates or divided up the traffic. Yet pools never completely succeeded. Too often, individual companies disregarded their agreements, especially when the business cycle took a downturn. Railroad leaders often tried to offset falling prices by slashing their workers' wages. As a result, railroads faced powerful worker unrest (described later in this chapter).

The size of railroads, the huge costs of construction, maintenance, and repair, and the complexity of operations required unprecedented amounts of capital and new management techniques. In 1854, the directors of the Erie Railroad hired engineer and inventor Daniel McCallum to devise a system to make railroad managers and their employees more accountable. McCallum's system, emphasizing division of responsibilities and a regular flow of information, attracted widespread interest, and railroads became pioneers in rationalized administrative practices and management techniques and models for other businesses in decision making, scheduling, and engineering. Because other big businesses faced similar economic conditions, they also emulated the behavior of the railroads—their competitiveness, their attempts to underprice one another, their eventual interest in merger, and their tendency to cut workers' wages.

Growth in Other Industries

By the last quarter of the century, the textile, metal, and machinery industries equaled the railroads in size. Business expansion was accomplished in one of two ways (or a combination of both). Some owners, like steel magnate Andrew Carnegie, integrated their businesses vertically, by adding operations either before or after the production process. Even though he had introduced the most up-to-date innovations in his steel mills, Carnegie realized he needed his own sources of pig iron, coal, and coke in order to avoid dependence on suppliers. He also acquired steamships and railroads to transport his finished products. Companies that integrated vertically frequently achieved economies of scale through more efficient management techniques.

Other companies copied the railroads and integrated horizontally by combining similar businesses. They sought to gain a monopoly of the market in order to eliminate competition and to stabilize prices. John D. Rockefeller used this strategy to gain control of the oil market.

As giant businesses competed intensely, often cutting wages and prices, they absorbed or eliminated smaller and weaker producers. As a result, business ownership became increasingly concentrated. In 1870, some 808 American iron and steel firms competed in the marketplace. By 1900, the number had dwindled to fewer than 70.

Like the railroads, many big businesses chose to incorporate. Incorporation offered many benefits. Through the sale of stock, businesses could raise funds for large-scale operations. The principle of limited liability protected investors, while the corporation's legal identity ensured its survival after the death of original and subsequent shareholders. Longevity suggested a measure of stability that heightened the attractiveness of a corporation as an investment.

The Erratic Economic Cycle

The transformation of the economy was neither smooth nor steady. Two depressions, one from 1873 to 1879 and the other from 1893 to 1897, surpassed the severity of economic downturns before the Civil War. They were accompanied by widespread unemployment, a phenomenon new to American life.

During expansionary years, manufacturers flooded markets with goods. When the market was finally saturated, sales and profits declined, and the economy spiraled downward. Owners slowed production and laid off workers, who in turn bought less food. As farm prices plummeted, farmers had to cut back on purchases. Business and trade stagnated, and the railroads were finally affected. Eventually, the cycle bottomed out, but in the meantime, millions of workers lost their jobs, thousands of businesses went bankrupt, and many Americans suffered deprivation and hardship.

Pollution

Another negative by-product of the industrial age was widespread pollution. Industrial processes everywhere had an adverse impact on the environment. In the iron and steel city of Birmingham, Alabama, for example, the coke ovens poured smoke, soot, and ashes into the air. Coal tar, a by-product of the coking process, was dumped, and it made the soil so acid that nothing would grow in it.

There was little awareness, however, of the extent or seriousness of environmental damage caused by pollution. Few were concerned that when industrial, human, and animal wastes were disposed of in rivers, they killed off fish and other forms of marine life and the plants that were part of that ecosystem. By the late nineteenth century, pollution of eastern and midwestern rivers as well as lakes had become pronounced. Although Presidents Grover Cleveland and Benjamin Harrison both set aside forest reserves, and there was growing interest in creating national parks, these sorts of actions were limited in scope and did not begin to touch the problems created by the rise of heavy industry and the rapid urban expansion that it stimulated.

URBAN EXPANSION IN THE INDUSTRIAL AGE

The new industrial age engendered rapid urban expansion. Before the Civil War, manufacturers had relied on water power and chosen rural sites for their factories. Now as they shifted to steam power, most favored urban locations that offered them workers, specialized services, local markets, and railroad links to materials and to distant markets.

Cities of all sizes grew. The population of New York and Philadelphia doubled and tripled. Smaller cities in the industrial Midwest, the South, and the Far West also shared in the dramatic growth. In 1870, some 25 percent of Americans lived in cities; by 1900, fully 40 percent of them did.

A Growing Population

What accounted for the dramatic increase in urban population? Certainly not a high birthrate.

The general pattern of declining family size that had emerged before the Civil War continued. By 1900, the average woman bore only 3.6 children, in contrast to 5.2 in 1860. Urban families, moreover, tended to have fewer children than their rural counterparts, and urban infants and children had a higher death rate.

American Urban Dwellers

The swelling population of late-nineteenth-century cities came both from the nation's small towns and farms and from abroad. For rural Americans, the "push" came from the modernization of agricultural life. As farm machines replaced human hands, farm workers increasingly sought work in cities.

By 1890, manufacturing workers were earning hundreds of dollars more a year than farm laborers. Part of the difference between rural and urban wages was eaten up by the higher cost of living in the city, but not all of it. City life also offered excitement and variety to young men and women who had grown up on farms and in small towns.

Novelist Theodore Dreiser captured both the fascination and the dangers of city life. Writing in a style termed literary realism, he examined social problems and cast his characters in carefully depicted local settings. Dreiser's novel *Sister Carrie* (1900) follows a typical country girl as she comes to Chicago. Carrie fantasizes a life of luxury, beyond her means as a mere factory employee. Her desire for comfort and pleasure leads her to affairs with prosperous men. Many readers were shocked that Dreiser never punished Carrie for her "sins."

Southern blacks, often single and young, also migrated to the cities. In the West and the North, blacks made up a tiny part of the population. In southern cities they were more numerous. About 44 percent of Atlanta's residents in the late nineteenth century were black, 38 percent of Nashville's. No matter where they were,

These women and children, photographed as they landed at the Battery in New York City, were part of the new immigration from eastern Europe and Russia.

however, the city offered them few rewards, little glamor, and many dangers.

The New Immigration

In 1870, a "brokenhearted" Annie Sproul stole away from her parents' home in Londonderry, Ireland, to seek a new future in Philadelphia. Probably the disgrace of a love affair prompted Annie's desperate flight, but the young woman was one of many who left their homelands in the nineteenth century. In the 40 years before the Civil War, five million immigrants poured into the United States; from 1860 to 1900, that volume almost tripled. Three-quarters of the newcomers stayed in the Northeast, and many of the rest settled in cities across the nation, where they soon outnumbered native-born whites.

As the flow of immigration increased, the national origin of immigrants shifted. Until 1880, three-quarters of the immigrants, often called the "old immigrants," hailed from the British Isles, Germany, and Scandinavia. Irish and Germans were the largest groups. Then the pattern slowly changed, as the ethnic and religious heterogeneity of the American people was transformed. By 1890, old immigrants composed only 60 percent of the total number of newcomers, while the "new immigrants" from

southern and eastern Europe (Italy, Poland, Russia, Austria-Hungary, Greece, Turkey, and Syria) made up most of the rest. Italian Catholics and eastern European Jews were the most numerous, followed by Slavs.

Efforts to modernize European economies stimulated immigration. New agricultural techniques led European landlords to consolidate their land, evicting longtime tenants. Many younger European farmers emigrated to the United States. Similarly, artisans and craftsmen whose skills were obsolete headed for the United States and other destinations. Government policies pushed others to leave. In eastern Europe, especially in Russia, official persecution of minorities and expansion of the draft for the czar's army led millions of Jewish families and others to emigrate.

Opportunity in the "golden land" of America also attracted thousands. Friends and relatives in America encouraged others to follow. Their letters described favorable living and working conditions and contained promises to help newcomers find work. The phenomenon of immigrants' being recruited through the reports and efforts of their predecessors is known as "chain migration."

Like rural and small-town Americans, Europeans came primarily to work. When times were good and American industry needed large numbers of unskilled laborers, migration was heavy. When times were bad, numbers fell off. Perhaps as many as a third eventually returned to their native lands.

Adding to the stream of foreigners coming to the United States were Mexicans and Chinese laborers. In Mexico, modernization, overpopulation, and new land policies uprooted many inhabitants. Gonzalo Plancarte, a cattle raiser, lost his livelihood in the 1890s when the owner of the hacienda determined to turn his land over to producing goods for export and ended the family's grazing privileges. Eventually Gonzalo headed for the American border. Perhaps 280,000 Mexicans crossed into the United States between 1899 and

Immigration to the United States, 1870-1920

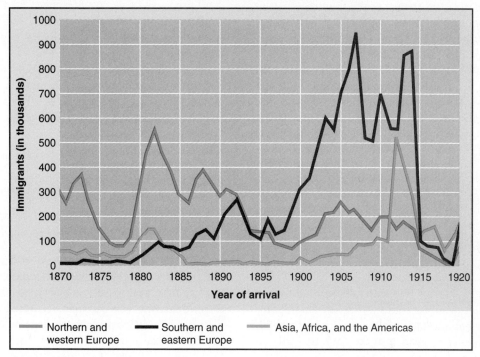

Legend:
- Northern and western Europe
- Southern and eastern Europe
- Asia, Africa, and the Americas

(Y-axis: Immigrants (in thousands); X-axis: Year of arrival, 1870–1920)

1914, many of them finding work on the railroads and in western mines.

Overpopulation, depressed conditions, unemployment, and crop failures brought Asians, most of them from southern China, to the "Land of the Golden Mountains." Although only 264,000 Chinese came to the United States between 1860 and 1900, they constituted a significant minority on the West Coast. Most were unskilled male contract laborers who promised to work for a number of years and then return to their homelands.

The Industrial City, 1880-1900

The late-nineteenth-century industrial city had new physical and social arrangements. By the last quarter of the century, the jumbled arrangements of the antebellum city, whose size and configuration had been limited by the necessity of walking to work, disappeared. Where once substantial houses, businesses, and small artisan dwellings had stood side by side, central business districts emerged. Few people lived downtown, although many worked or shopped there. Surrounding the business center were areas of light manufacturing and wholesale activity with housing for workers. Beyond these working-class neighborhoods stretched middle-class residential areas. Then came the suburbs, with "pure air, peacefulness, quietude, and natural scenery." Scattered throughout the city were pockets of industrial activity surrounded by crowded working-class housing.

This new pattern, with the poorest city residents clustered near the center, is familiar today. However, it reversed the early-nineteenth-century urban form, where much of the most desirable housing was in the heart of the city. New living arrangements were also more segregated by race and class than those in the preindustrial walking city. Homogeneous social and economic neighborhoods emerged, and it became more unusual than before for a poor, working-class family to live near a middle- or upper-class family. Better transportation increasingly allowed middle- and upper-class residents to live away from their work and from grimy industrial districts.

Neighborhoods and Neighborhood Life

Working-class neighborhoods clustered near the center of most industrial cities. Here lived newcomers from the American countryside and crowds of foreigners as well.

Ethnic groups frequently chose to gather in particular neighborhoods, often located near industries requiring their labor. In Detroit in 1880, for example, 37 percent of the city's native-born families lived in one area, while 40 percent of the Irish inhabited the "Irish West Side." Over half the Germans and almost three-quarters of the Poles settled on the city's east side. Although such neighborhoods often had an ethnic flavor, with small specialty shops and foreign-language signs, they were not ethnic ghettos. Immigrants and native-born Americans often lived in the same neighborhoods, on the same streets, and even in the same houses.

Working-class neighborhoods were often what would be called slums today. They were crowded and unsanitary and had inadequate public services. Outdoor privies, often shared by several families, were the rule. Water came from outdoor hydrants, and women had to carry it inside for cooking, washing, and cleaning. Piles of garbage and waste stank in the summer and froze in the winter. In such an environment, death rates were high. Only at the turn of the century did the public health movement, particularly the efforts to treat water supplies with germ-killing chemicals, begin to ameliorate these conditions.

Not every working-class family lived in abject circumstances. Skilled workers might rent comfortable quarters, and a few even owned their own homes. But the unskilled and semiskilled workers were not so fortunate. A Massachusetts survey described the family of an unskilled ironworker crammed into a tenement of four rooms,

> in an overcrowded block, to which belong only two privies for about fifty people. When this place was visited the vault had overflowed in the yard and ... created a stench that was really frightful. . . . The house inside, was badly furnished and dirty, and a disgrace to Worcester.

A wide range of institutions and associations ameliorated the drabness of urban life. Frequently they were based on ethnic ties. Irish associational life, for example, centered on the Roman Catholic parish church, Irish nationalist organizations, and ward politics. Irish saloons were convivial places where men socialized, drank, and talked politics. Jews gathered in their synagogues, Hebrew schools, and Hebrew- and Yiddish-speaking literary groups. Germans had family saloons and educational and singing societies. While such activities may have slowed assimilation into American society and discouraged intergroup contact, they provided companionship, social life, and a bridge between life in the "old country" and life in America. Working-class men and women were far from mere victims of their environment. They found the energy, squeezed out the time, and even saved the money to support networks of social ties and associations.

Black Americans faced the most wretched living conditions of any group in the city. Northern blacks often lived in segregated neighborhoods. In southern cities, they gathered in back alleys and small streets. Many could afford only rented rooms. However, a rich associational life tempered the suffering. Black denominations like the African Methodist Episcopal Church enjoyed phenomenal growth.

Some urban blacks in the late nineteenth century rose into the middle class and, in spite of the heavy odds against them, created the nucleus of professional and artistic life. Henry Ossawa Tanner gained international recognition as a painter by 1900, black educators such as George Washington Williams wrote some of the first African-American histories, and novelists such as Charles W. Chesnutt and William Wells Brown produced noteworthy novels and short stories.

Beyond working-class neighborhoods and pockets of black housing lay streets of middle-class houses, many of which boasted up-to-date gas lighting and bathrooms. Outside, the neighborhoods were cleaner and more attractive than in the inner city. Residents could pay for garbage collection, gaslights, and other improvements.

Streetcar Suburbs

On the fringes of the city were houses for the upper middle class and the rich, who either made their money in business, commerce, and the professions or inherited family fortunes.

Public transportation sped them downtown to their offices and then home again. Robert Work, a modestly successful cap and hat merchant, moved his family to a $5,500 house in West Philadelphia in 1865 and commuted more than four miles to work. The 1880 census revealed his family's comfortable life style. The household included two servants to do the domestic work. The Works enjoyed running hot and cold water, indoor bathrooms, central heating, and other modern conveniences of the age.

The Social Geography of the Cities

In industrial cities of this era, people were sorted by class, occupation, and race. The physical distances between upper- and middle-class neighborhoods and working-class neighborhoods meant that city dwellers often had little firsthand knowledge of people who were different from themselves. Ignorance led to distorted views and social disapproval. Middle-class newspapers unsympathetically described laboring men as "loafing in the sunshine" and criticized the "crowds of idlers, who, day and night,

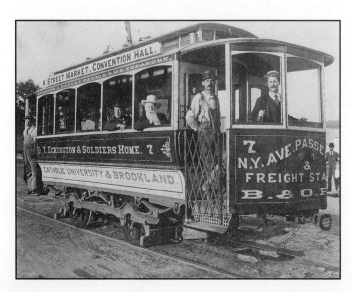

For the middle class, commuting to work from the suburbs became part of the daily routine.

infect Main Street." Yet those "crowds of idlers" were often men who could not find work.

THE LIFE OF THE MIDDLE CLASS

Newspaper comments suggest the economic polarization and social conflict that late-nineteenth-century industrialization spawned. Middle-class Americans found they had much to value in the new age: job and education opportunities, material comforts, and leisure time. By 1900, fully 36 percent of urban families owned their homes.

The expansion of American industry had raised the living standard for increasing numbers of Americans, who were better able to purchase consumer products manufactured, packaged, and promoted in an explosion of technological inventions and shrewd marketing techniques. Among the still familiar products and brands invented or mass-produced for the first time in the 1890s were Del Monte canned fruits and vegetables, Van Camp's pork and beans, Wesson oil, Lipton tea, and Wrigley's Juicy Fruit chewing gum.

More time for recreation like bicycling or watching professional baseball and greater access to consumer goods signaled the power of industrialism to transform the lives of middle-class Americans. Shopping for home furnishings, clothes, and other items became an integral part of many middle-class women's lives. A plentiful supply of immigrant servant girls relieved urban middle-class wives of many housekeeping chores, and smaller families lessened the burdens of motherhood. The new department stores that began to appear in the 1870s profited from women's leisure time and encouraged their desire for material possessions.

New Freedoms for Middle-Class Women

Middle-class women were also gaining new freedoms. Several states granted women more prop-

erty rights in marriage. Women, moreover, finally cast off confining crinolines and bustles in favor of a shirtwaist blouse and ankle-length skirt. This "new woman" was celebrated as *Life* magazine's attractively active, slightly rebellious "Gibson girl."

Using their new freedom, women joined literary societies, charity groups, and reform clubs like the Women's Christian Temperance Union. The General Federation of Women's Clubs, founded in 1890, boasted one million members by 1920. The depression of 1893 stimulated many women to become socially active, investigating slum and factory conditions.

Job opportunities for these educated middle-class women were generally limited to the social services and teaching. Women teachers, frequently hired because they accepted lower pay than men, often faced classes of 40 to 50 children in poorly equipped rooms. By the 1890s, the willingness of middle-class women to work for low pay opened up new forms of employment in office work, nursing, and clerking in department stores.

After the Civil War, educational opportunities for women expanded. New women's colleges such as Smith, Mount Holyoke, Vassar, Bryn Mawr, and Goucher offered programs similar to those at competitive men's colleges, while state schools in the Midwest and the West dropped prohibitions against women. The number of women attending college rose. In 1890, some 13 percent of all college graduates were women; by 1900, this had increased to nearly 20 percent.

Many medical schools refused to accept women students. As a Harvard doctor explained in 1875, a woman's monthly period "unfits her from taking those responsibilities which are to control questions often of life and death." Despite the obstacles, 2,500 women managed to become physicians and surgeons by 1880 (making up 2.8 percent of the total). Women were less successful at breaking into the legal world.

One reason for the greater independence of

American women was that they were having fewer babies. Decreasing family size and an increase in the divorce rate (one out of 12 marriages in 1905) fueled men's fears that the new woman threatened the family, traditional sex roles, and social order. Theodore Roosevelt called this "race suicide" and argued that the falling white birthrate endangered national self-interest.

Arguments against the new woman intensified as many men reaffirmed Victorian stereotypes of "woman's sphere." One male orator in 1896 attacked the new woman's public role because "a woman's brain involves emotions rather than intellect."

Male Mobility and the Success Ethic

As the postwar economy expanded and the structure of American business changed, middle-class men's lives were affected. New job opportunities appeared. Where once the census taker had noted only the occupation of "clerk," now he listed "accountant," "salesman," and "shipping clerk." As the lower ranks of the white-collar world became more specialized, the number of middle-class jobs increased.

To prepare for these new careers, Americans required more education. The number of public high schools in the United States increased from 160 in 1870 to 6,000 in 1900. By 1900, a majority of states and territories had compulsory school attendance laws.

Higher education also expanded in this period. The number of students in colleges and universities nearly doubled, from 53,000 in 1870 to 101,000 in 1900.

Greater specialization and professionalism in education, medicine, law, and business affected male careers. By the 1890s, with government licensing and the rise of professional schools, no longer were tradesmen likely to read up on medicine and become doctors. In this period, organizations like the American Medical Association and the American Bar Association were regulating and professionalizing membership. The number of law schools doubled in the last quarter of the century, and 86 new medical schools were founded in the same period. Dental schools increased from 9 to 56 between 1875 and 1900.

This age of increasing professionalism also gave rise to some new professions. The disciplines of history, economics, sociology, psychology, and political science all date from the last 20 years of the nineteenth century.

The social ethic of the age stressed the availability of economic rewards. Many argued that unlike Europe, where family background and social class determined social rank, in America few barriers held back those of good character and diligent work habits. Anyone doubting this opportunity needed only to be reminded of the rise of two giants of industry, John D. Rockefeller and Andrew Carnegie, who had risen spectacularly through their own efforts.

The best-known popularizer of the rags-to-riches myth was Horatio Alger, Jr. Millions of boys read his 119 novels, with titles like *Luck and Pluck, Strive and Succeed,* and *Bound to Rise.* In a typical Alger novel, the story opens with the hero leading the low life of a shoeshine boy in the streets and wasting what little money he has on tobacco, liquor, gambling, and the theater. A chance opportunity occurs, like diving into the icy waters of the harbor to save the life of the daughter of a local banker, and changes the Alger hero's life. He gives up his slovenly ways to work hard, save his money, and study. Eventually he rises to a prominent position at the bank.

Unlimited and equal opportunity for upward advancement in America has never been as easy as the "bootstraps" ethic maintains. In fact, the typical big businessman was a white, Anglo-Saxon Protestant from a middle- or upper-class family whose father was most likely in business, banking, or commerce.

INDUSTRIAL WORK AND THE LABORING CLASS

David Lawlor, an Irish immigrant who came to the United States as a child in 1872, read Horatio Alger in his free time. Like Alger's heroes, he went to night school and rose in the business world, eventually becoming an advertising executive. But Lawlor's success was exceptional. As industrialization transformed the nature of work and the composition of the work force, traditional opportunities for mobility and even for a secure livelihood seemed to slip away from the grasp of many working-class Americans.

The Impact of Ethnic Diversity

Immigrants made up a sizable portion of the urban working class in the late nineteenth century. They made up 20 percent of the labor force and over 40 percent of laborers in the manufacturing and extractive industries. In cities, where they tended to settle, they accounted for more than half the working-class population.

The fact that more than half of the urban industrial class was foreign and unskilled and often had only a limited command of English influenced industrial work, urban life, labor protest, and local politics. Eager for the unskilled positions rapidly being created as mechanization and mass production took hold, immigrants often had little in common with native-born workers or even with one another. American working-class society became a mosaic of nationalities, cultures, religions, and interests.

The ethnic diversity of the industrial work force helps explain its occupational patterns. At the top of the working-class hierarchy, native-born Protestant whites held a disproportionate share of well-paying skilled jobs. Beneath them, skilled northern European immigrants filled most of the positions in the middle ranks of the occupational structure. Germans, who had training as tailors, bakers, brewers, and shoe-

makers, moved into similar jobs in this country, while Jews became the backbone of the garment industry.

But most of the "new immigrants" from southern and central Europe had no urban industrial experience. They labored in the unskilled, dirty jobs such as relining blast furnaces in steel mills, carrying raw materials or finished products from place to place, or digging ditches. Hiring was often on a daily basis, often arranged through middlemen like the Italian *Padrone*.

At the bottom, blacks occupied the most marginal positions as janitors, servants, porters, and laborers. Racial discrimination generally excluded them from industrial jobs, even though their occupational background differed little from that of rural white immigrants.

The Changing Nature of Work

The rise of big business changed the size and shape of the work force and the nature of work itself. More and more Americans were wage earners rather than independent artisans. The number of manufacturing workers doubled between 1880 and 1900, with the fastest expansion in the unskilled and semiskilled ranks.

But the need for skilled workers remained. New positions, as in steam fitting and structural iron-work, appeared as industries expanded and changed. Increasingly, older skills became obsolete. And all skilled workers faced the possibility that technical advances would eliminate their favored status or that employers would eat away at their jobs by having unskilled helpers take over parts of them.

Work Settings and Experiences

While increasing numbers of American manufacturing workers now labored in factories, some Americans still toiled in small shops and sweatshops tucked away in basements, lofts, or immigrant apartments. Even in these smaller settings, the pressure to produce was almost as relentless as in the factory, for volume, not hours, determined pay. When contractors cut wages, workers had to speed up to earn the same pay.

The organization of work divided workers from one another. In large factories, workers were separated into small work groups and mingled only rarely with the rest of the work force. The clustering of ethnic groups in certain types of work also undermined working-class solidarity. But all workers had one thing in common: a very long working day—usually ten hours a day, six days a week.

Work was usually unhealthy, dangerous, and comfortless. Few owners paid attention to regulations on toilets, drinking facilities, or washing areas. Nor did they concern themselves with the health or safety of their employees. Women bent over sewing machines developed digestive illnesses and curved spines. New drilling machinery introduced in western mines filled the shafts with tiny stone particles that caused lung disease. Accident rates in the United States far exceeded those of Europe's industrial nations. Each year, 35,000 American workers died from industrial mishaps. Iron and steel mills were the main killers, although the railroads alone accounted for 6,000 fatalities a year during the 1890s. The law placed the burden of avoiding accidents on workers.

Industrial jobs were also increasingly specialized and monotonous. Even skilled workers did not produce a complete product, and the range of their skills was narrowing. Cabinetmakers found themselves not crafting cabinets but putting together and finishing pieces made by others. In such circumstances, many skilled workers complained that they were being reduced to drudges and wage slaves.

The Worker's Share in Industrial Progress

The huge fortunes accumulated by industrialists like Andrew Carnegie and John D. Rockefeller during the late nineteenth century dramatized the pattern of wealth concentration that had begun in the early period of industrialization. In 1890, the top one percent of American families possessed over a quarter of the wealth, while the share held by the top 10 percent was about 73 percent. Economic growth still benefited people who influenced its path, and they claimed the lion's share of the rewards.

But what of the workers who tended the machines that lay at the base of industrial wealth? Industry still needed skilled workers and paid them well. Average real wages rose over 50 percent between 1860 and 1900. Skilled manufacturing workers, about a tenth of the nonagricultural working class in the late nineteenth century, saw their wages rise by about 74 percent. But wages for the unskilled increased by only 31 percent. The differential was substantial and widened as the century drew to a close.

A U.S. Bureau of Labor study of working-class families in 1889 revealed great disparities of income: A young girl in a silk mill made $130 a year; a laborer earned $384 a year; a carpenter took home $686. The carpenter's family lived comfortably and breakfasted on meat or eggs, hotcakes, butter, cake, and coffee. The silk worker and the laborer, by contrast, ate bread and butter as the main portion of two of their three daily meals.

For workers without steady employment, rising real wages were meaningless. When times were slow or conditions depressed, as they were between 1873 and 1879 and 1893 and 1897, employers, especially in small firms, laid off both skilled and unskilled workers and reduced wages. Even in a good year like 1890, one out of every five men outside of agriculture had been unemployed at least a month. Since unemployment insurance did not exist, workers had no cushion against losing their jobs.

Although nineteenth-century ideology pictured men as breadwinners, many working-class married men could not earn enough to support their families alone. A working-class family's

Women in the Labor Force, 1870–1900

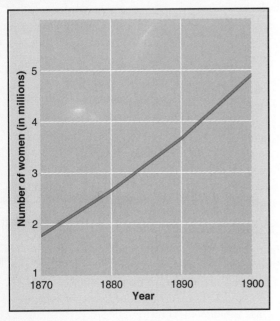

standard of living thus often depended on its number of workers. Married women did not usually take outside employment, although they contributed to family income by taking in sewing, laundry, and boarders. In 1890, only 3.3 percent of married women were to be found in the paid labor force.

The Family Economy

If married women did not work for pay outside their homes, their children did. In 1880, one-fifth of the nation's children between the ages of 10 and 14 held jobs.

Child labor was closely linked to a father's income, which in turn depended on skill, ethnic background, and occupation. Immigrant families more frequently sent their young children out to work (and also had more children) than native-born families. Sending children to work was a means of coping with the immediate

threat of poverty, of financing the education of one of the children, or even of ensuring that children stay near their family.

Women at Work

Many more young people over 14 were working for wages than children. Half of all Philadelphia's students had quit school by that age. Daughters as well as sons were expected to take positions, although young women from immigrant families were more likely to work than young American women. As *Arthur's Home Magazine* for women pointed out, a girl's earnings would help "to relieve her hard-working father of the burden of her support, to supply home with comforts and refinements, to educate a younger brother." By 1900, nearly 20 percent of American women were in the labor force.

Employed women earned far less than men. An experienced female factory worker might be paid between $5 and $6 a week, while an unskilled male laborer could make about $8. About a quarter of working women secured factory jobs. Italian and Jewish women (whose cultural backgrounds virtually forbade domestic work) clustered in the garment industry, while Poles and Slavs went into textiles, food processing, and meatpacking. In some industries, like textiles, women composed an important segment of the work force. But about 40 percent of them, especially those from Irish, Scandinavian, or black families, took jobs as maids, cooks, laundresses, and nurses.

Domestic service meant low wages, unpleasant working conditions, and little free time, usually one evening a week and part of Sunday. A servant received room and board plus $2 to $5 a week. The fact that so many women took domestic work despite the job's disadvantages speaks clearly of their limited opportunities.

The dismal situation facing working women drove some, like Rose Haggerty, into prostitution. Burdened with a widowed and sickly mother and four young brothers and sisters,

Rose was only 14 when she started work at a New York paper bag factory. She earned $10 a month, but $6 went for rent. Her fortunes improved when a friend helped her buy a sewing machine. Rose then sewed shirts at home, often working as long as 14 hours a day, to support her family. Suddenly, the piecework rate for shirts was slashed in half. In desperation, Rose contemplated suicide. But when a sailor offered her money for spending the night with him, she realized she had an alternative. Prostitution meant food, rent, and heat for her family. "Let God Almighty judge who's to blame the most," the 20-year-old Rose reflected, "I that was driven, or them that drove me to the pass I'm in." Prostitution appears to have increased in the late nineteenth century, although there is no way of knowing the actual numbers of women involved.

The unpaid domestic labor of married working-class women was critical to family survival. With husbands away for 10 to 11 hours a day, women bore the burden and loneliness of caring for children and doing the domestic chores, which were time-consuming and arduous without a refrigerator, washing machine, or other labor-saving appliances.

As managers of family resources, married women had important responsibilities. Domestic economies were vital to survival. "In summer and winter alike," one woman explained, "I must try to buy the food that will sustain us the greatest number of meals at the lowest price." Women also supplemented family income by taking in work. Jewish and Italian women frequently did piecework and sewing at home. In the Northeast and the Midwest, between 10 and 40 percent of all working-class families kept boarders.

Black women's working lives reflected the obstacles blacks faced in late-nineteenth-century cities. Although few married white women worked outside the home, black women did so both before and after marriage. In southern cities in 1880, about three-quarters of single black women and one-third of married women worked outside the home. This contrasted to rates for white women of 24 and 7 percent, respectively. Since industrial employers would not hire black women, most of them had to work as domestics or laundresses. The high percentage of married black women in the labor force reflected the marginal wages their husbands earned.

CAPITAL VERSUS LABOR

Class conflict characterized late-nineteenth-century industrial life. While owners reaped most of the profits, bad pay, poor working conditions, and long hours were turning workers into wage slaves. Fashioning their arguments from their republican legacy, workers claimed that the degradation of the country's citizen laborers threatened to undermine the republic itself.

On-the-Job Protests

Workers and employers engaged in a struggle over who would control the workplace. Skilled workers, like iron puddlers and glassblowers, had indispensable knowledge about the production process and practical experience and were in a key position to direct on-the-job actions. Sometimes their goal was to retain control over critical work decisions or to humanize work. Cigar makers clung to their custom of having one worker read to others as they performed their tedious chores. Often workers sought to control the pace of production. Workers also resisted owners' attempts to grasp large profits through unlimited production. Too many goods meant an inhuman pace of work and might result in overproduction, massive layoffs, and a reduction in the prices paid for piecework.

A newspaper account of a glassblowers' strike in 1884 illustrates the clash between capital and labor. With an eye toward bigger profits, the boss tried to increase production. "He knew if the limit was taken off, the men could work ten or twelve hours every day in the week; that in their thirst for the mighty dollar they would kill themselves with labor." But his employees resisted his proposal. Their goal was not riches but a decent pace of work and a respectable wage. Thus "they thundered out no. . . . Threats and curses would not move them."

To protect themselves and preserve the dignity of their labor, workers devised ways of combating employer attempts to speed up the production process. In three industrial firms in the late nineteenth century, one-quarter of the workers stayed home at least one day a week. Some of these lost days were due to layoffs, but not all. The efforts of employers to impose stiff fines on absent workers suggested their frustration at uncooperative workers.

To a surprising extent, workers made the final protest by quitting their jobs altogether. A Massachusetts labor study in 1878 found that although two-thirds of them had been in the same occupation for more than ten years, only 15 percent of the workers surveyed were in the same job. A similar rate of turnover occurred in the industrial work force in the early twentieth century. Workers unmistakably and clearly voted with their feet.

Strike Activity After 1876

The most direct and strenuous attempts to change conditions in the workplace came in the form of thousands of strikes punctuating the late nineteenth century. In 1877, railroad workers staged the first and most violent nationwide industrial strike of the nineteenth century. The immediate cause of the disturbance was the railroad owners' decision to reduce wages. But the rapid spread of the strike from Baltimore to Pittsburgh and then to cities as distant as San Francisco, Chicago, and Omaha, as well as the violence of the strikers, who destroyed railroad property and kept trains idle, indicated more fundamental discontent. An erratic economy, high unemployment rates, and the lack of job se-

curity all contributed to the conflagration. Over 100 people died before federal troops ended the strike. The frenzied response of the propertied class, which saw the strike as the beginning of revolution and favored the intervention of the military, forecast the pattern of later conflicts. Time and time again, middle- and upper-class Americans would turn to the power of the state to crush labor activism.

A wave of confrontations followed the strike of 1877. Between 1881 and 1905, a total of 36,757 strikes erupted, involving over six million workers—three times the strike activity in France. These numbers indicate that far more than the "poorest part" of the workers were involved. Strikes, sabotage, and violence were most often linked to demands for higher wages and shorter hours.

In the period of early industrialization, discontented laborers rioted in their neighborhoods rather than at their workplaces. Between 1845 and the Civil War, however, strikes at the workplace began to replace neighborhood riots. Although workers often called for higher wages, they had only a murky sense that the strike could be a weapon to force employers to improve working conditions.

As an increasing percentage of the work force entered factories, collective actions at the workplace spread. Local and national unions played a more important role in organizing protest, conducting 60 percent of the strikes between 1881 and 1905. By 1891, more than one-tenth of the strikes called by unionized workers were sympathy strikes. Finally, wages became less of an issue among the most highly unionized workers. Workers sought more humane conditions. By the early 1890s, over one-fifth of strikes involved the rules governing the workplace.

Labor Organizing, 1865–1900

The Civil War experience colored labor organizing in the postwar years. As one working-class song pointed out, workers had borne the brunt of that struggle. "You gave your son to the war /

The rich man loaned his gold / And the rich man's son is happy to-day, / And yours is under the mold." Now workers who had fought to save the Union argued that wartime sacrifices justified efforts to gain justice and equality in the workplace.

Labor leaders quickly realized the need for national as well as local organizations to protect the laboring class against "despotic employers." In 1866, several craft unions and reform groups formed the National Labor Union (NLU). Claiming 300,000 members by the early 1870s, the organization supported a range of causes including temperance, women's rights, and the establishment of cooperatives to bring the "wealth of the land" into "the hands of those who produce it," thus ending "wage slavery." They called for an eight-hour day to allow workers the time to cultivate the qualities necessary for republican citizenship. Many of the NLU's specific goals survived, although the organization did not.

The Knights of Labor and the AFL

As the depression of 1873 wound down, a new mass organization, the Noble Order of the Knights of Labor, rose to national importance. Founded as a secret society in 1869, the order became public and national when Terence V. Powderly, an Irish-American, was elected Grand Master Workman in 1879. The Knights of Labor sought "to secure to the workers the full enjoyment of the wealth they create." Since the industrial system denied workers their fair share as producers, the Knights of Labor proposed a cooperative system of production alongside the existing system. Cooperative efforts would give workers the economic independence necessary for citizenship, while an eight-hour day would provide them with the leisure for moral, intellectual, and political pursuits.

The Knights of Labor opened its ranks to all American "producers," defined as all contributing members of society—skilled and unskilled, black and white, men and women. Only the idle and the corrupt (bankers, speculators, lawyers, saloon keepers, and gamblers) were to be excluded.

The organization grew in spurts, attracting miners between 1874 and 1879 and skilled urban tradesmen between 1879 and 1885. Although Powderly frowned on using the strike as a labor weapon, the organization gained members following grass-roots strike activity. In 1886, the Haymarket Riot in Chicago contributed to such a growth in labor militancy that in that single year the membership of the Knights of Labor ballooned from 100,000 to 700,000.

The "riot" at Haymarket was, in fact, a peaceful protest meeting connected with a lockout at the McCormick Reaper Works. When the Chicago police arrived to disperse the crowd, a bomb exploded, killing seven policemen. Although no one knows who planted the bomb, eight anarchists were tried and convicted. Three were executed, one commited suicide, and the others served prison terms.

Labor agitation and turbulence spilled over into politics. In 1884 and 1885, the Knights of Labor lobbied to secure a national contract labor law and state anticonvict labor laws. The organization also pressed successfully for the creation of a federal Department of Labor. Between 1885 and 1888, the Knights of Labor sponsored candidates in 200 towns and cities in 34 states and 4 territories and achieved many electoral victories. Despite local successes, no national labor party emerged.

The Knights of Labor could not sustain their momentum as the voice for the American laboring people. Consumer and producer cooperatives fizzled; the policy of accepting both black and white workers led to strife and discord in the South. The two major parties proved adept at coopting labor politicians. Powderly also bore responsibility for the organization's decline. He was never able to unify or direct his diverse following or control the militant elements that opposed him. Local, unauthorized strike actions were often ill-considered and violent and hurt his cause. By 1890, the membership had dropped to 100,000, although the Knights continued to play a role well into the 1890s.

In the 1890s, the American Federation of Labor (AFL), founded in 1886, replaced the Knights of Labor as the nation's dominant union. The history of the Knights pointed up the problems of a national union that admitted all who worked for wages but officially rejected strike action in favor of the ballot box and arbitration. The leader of the AFL, Samuel Gompers, had a different notion of effective worker organization. Gompers's experience as head of the Cigarmakers' Union in the 1870s and as a founder of the Federation of Organized Trades and Labor Unions in 1881 convinced him that skilled workers should put their specific occupational interests before the interests of workers as a whole. By so doing, they could control the supply of skilled labor and keep wages up.

Gompers organized the AFL as a federation of skilled trades—cigar makers, iron molders, iron workers, carpenters, and others—each one autonomous yet linked through an executive council to work together for prolabor national legislation and mutual support during boycott and strike actions. Gompers was a practical man. He believed in the value of the strike, and he knew from bitter experience the importance of dues high enough to sustain a strike fund through a long, tough fight.

Under Gompers's leadership, the AFL grew from 140,000 in 1886 to nearly one million by 1900. Although his notion of a labor organization was elitist, he succeeded in steering his union through a series of crises, fending off challenges from socialists on his left and corporate opposition to strikes from his right. But there was no room in his organization for the unskilled or for blacks. Nor did the AFL welcome women.

Hostile male attitudes constituted a major barrier against organizing women. Change was slow in coming. When the International Ladies Garment Workers Union (ILGWU) was estab-

lished in 1900, women were the backbone of the organization, but men dominated the leadership.

Working-Class Setbacks

Despite the growth of working-class organizations, workers lost many of their battles with management. Some of the more spectacular clashes reveal why working-class activism often ended in defeat and why so many workers lived precariously on the edge of poverty.

In 1892, silver miners in Coeur d'Alene, Idaho, went on strike when their employers installed machine drills in the mines, reduced skilled workers to shovelmen, and announced a wage cut. The owners, supported by state militiamen and the federal government, successfully broke the strike by using scabs, but not without armed fighting. Several hundred union men were arrested, herded into huge bull pens, and eventually tried and found guilty of a wide variety of charges. Out of the defeat emerged the Western Federation of Miners (WFM), whose chief political goal was an eight-hour law for miners. The pattern of struggle in Coeur d'Alene was followed in many subsequent strikes. In spite of the intimidation tactics of mine owners, the WFM won as many strikes as it lost.

The Homestead and Pullman Strikes of 1892 and 1894

The most serious setback to labor occurred in 1892 at the Homestead steel mills near Pittsburgh, Pennsylvania. Andrew Carnegie had recently purchased the Homestead plant and put Henry Clay Frick in charge. Together they wanted to eliminate the Amalgamated Association of Iron, Steel, and Tin Workers. When the union refused to accept wage decreases, Frick resorted to a lockout. He fenced in the entire plant and hired 300 armed Pinkerton agents to guard it. As they arrived on July 6, they engaged armed steelworkers in a daylong gun battle. Several men on both sides were killed, and the Pinkertons retreated.

Pinkerton detectives are pictured in a Harper's Weekly *engraving of 1892 as they leave the scene of the Homestead steel strike.*

Frick telegraphed Pennsylvania's governor, who sent 8,000 troops to crush both the strike and the union. Two and a half weeks later, Alexander Berkman, a New York anarchist sympathetic to the plight of the oppressed Homestead workers, attempted to assassinate Frick.

Observing these events, Eugene Victor Debs of Terre Haute, Indiana, for many years an ardent organizer of railroad workers, wrote, "If the year 1892 taught the workingmen any lesson worthy of heed, it was that the capitalist class, like a devilfish, had grasped them with its tentacles and was dragging them down to fathomless depths of degradation."

Despite a new depression in 1893, Debs succeeded in combining several of the separate railroad brotherhoods into a united American Railway Union (ARU). Within a year, over 150,000 railroadmen joined the ARU, and Debs won a strike against the Great Northern Railroad.

Debs faced his toughest crisis at the Pullman Palace Car Company in Chicago. Pullman was a model company town where management controlled all aspects of workers' lives. "We are born in a Pullman house, fed from the Pullman shop, taught in the Pullman school, catechized in the Pullman church, and when we die we shall be buried in the Pullman cemetery and go to the Pullman hell," said one worker wryly.

Late in 1893, as the depression worsened, Pullman cut wages by one-third and laid off many workers but made no reductions in rents or prices in the town stores. Those still at work suffered speedups, intimidations, and further wage cuts. Desperate and "without hope," the Pullman workers joined the ARU in the spring of 1894 and went out on strike.

In late June, Debs led the ARU into a sympathy strike in support of the striking Pullman workers. His instructions were to boycott trains handling Pullman cars throughout the West. As the boycott spread, the General Managers Association, which ran the 24 railroads centered in Chicago, came to the Pullman's support, hiring some 2,500 strikebreakers and obtaining state, federal, and judicial support in stopping the strike.

On July 4, President Grover Cleveland ordered federal troops in to crush the strikers. Violence escalated rapidly, and scores of workers were killed.

Debs appealed for wider labor support. When Samuel Gompers refused his support, the strike collapsed. Debs and several other leaders were arrested and found guilty of contempt of a court injunction to end the strike. While in prison, the disillusioned Debs, a lifelong Democrat, became a confirmed socialist. His arrest and the defeat of the Pullman strike provided a deathblow to the American Railway Union. In 1895, the Supreme Court upheld the legality of using an injunction to stop a strike and provided management with a powerful weapon to use against unions in subsequent years.

Many people claimed to accept the idea of worker organizations, but they would not concede that unions should participate in making economic or work decisions. Most employers violently resisted union demands as infringements of their rights to make production decisions, to hire and fire, to lock workers out, to hire scabs, or to reduce wages in times of depression. The sharp competition of the late nineteenth century, combined with a pattern of falling prices, stiffened employers' resistance to workers' demands. State and local governments and the courts frequently supported them in their battles to curb worker activism.

The severe depressions of the 1870s and 1890s also undermined working-class activism. Many unions collapsed during hard times. Of the 30 national unions in 1873, fewer than one-third managed to survive the depression. A far more serious problem was the reluctance of most workers to organize even in favorable times. In 1870, less than one-tenth of the industrial work force belonged to unions. Thirty years later, despite the expansion of the work force, only 8.4 percent (mostly skilled workers) were union members.

Why were workers so slow to join unions? Certainly, diverse work settings and ethnic differences made it difficult for workers to recognize common bonds. Moreover, many native-born Americans still clung to the tradition of individualism. Others continued to nourish dreams of escaping from the working class and entering the ranks of the middle class.

The comments of an Irish woman highlight another important point. "There should be a law . . . to give a job to every decent man that's out of work," she declared, "and another law to keep all them I-talians from comin' in and takin' the bread out of the mouths of honest people." The ethnic and religious diversity of the work force made it difficult to forge a common front.

The perspective of immigrant workers contributed to their indifference to unions and to tension with native-born Americans. Many foreigners planned to return to their homeland and had limited interest in changing conditions in the United States. Moreover, since their goal was to work, they took jobs as scabs. Much of the violence that accompanied working-class actions erupted when owners brought in strikebreakers. Some Americans blamed immigrants for both low wages and failed worker actions. Divisions among workers were often as bitter as those between strikers and employers. When workers divided, employers benefited.

In the 1870s and 1880s, white workers in the West began to blame the Chinese for economic hardships. A meeting of San Francisco workers in 1877 in favor of the eight-hour day exploded into a rampage against the Chinese. In the following years, angry mobs killed Chinese workers in Tacoma, Seattle, Denver, and Rock Springs, Wyoming. "The Chinese must go! They are stealing our jobs!" became a rallying cry for American workers.

Hostility was also expressed at the national level with the Chinese Exclusion Act of 1882. The law, which had the support of the Knights of Labor in the West, prohibited the immigration of both skilled and unskilled Chinese workers for a ten-year period. It was extended in 1892 and made permanent in 1902.

At the same time, many immigrants, especially those who were skilled, did support unions and cooperate with native-born Americans. Irish-Americans played important roles in the Knights of Labor and the AFL. British and Germans also helped build up the unions. Often ethnic bonds served labor causes by tying members to one another and to the community.

The importance of workers' organizations lay not so much in their successful struggles and protests as in the implicit criticism they offered of American society. Using the language of republicanism, many workers lashed out at an economic order that robbed them of their dignity and humanity. As producers of wealth, they protested that so little of it was theirs. As members of the working class, they rejected the middle-class belief in individualism and social mobility.

The Balance Sheet

Except for skilled workers, most laboring people found it impossible to earn much of a share in the material bounty industrialization created. Yet our perception of the harshness of working-class life partly grows out of our own standards of what is acceptable today. Immigrant workers had their own perspectives. The family tenement, one Polish immigrant remarked, "seemed quite advanced when compared with our home" in Poland. American poverty was preferable to Russian pogroms. A ten-hour job in the steel mill might be an improvement over dawn-to-dusk farmwork that brought no wages.

Studies of several cities show that nineteenth-century workers achieved some occupational mobility. One worker in five in Los Angeles and Atlanta during the 1890s, for example, managed to climb into the middle class. Most immigrant workers were stuck in ill-paid, insecure jobs, but their children ended up doing better. Native-born whites, Jews, and Germans rose more swiftly and fell less often than Irish, Italians, or Poles. Cultural attitudes, family size, education, and group leadership all contributed to different ethnic mobility patterns. Jews, for example, valued education and sacrificed to keep

children in school. With an education, they moved upward. The Slavs, however, who valued a steady income over mobility and education, sent their children to work at an early age, believing that these jobs not only helped the family but also provided a head start in securing reliable, stable employment. The southern Italian proverb "Do not make your child better than you are" suggests the value Italians placed on family rather than individual success. Differing attitudes and values led to different aspirations and career patterns.

Two groups enjoyed little mobility. African-Americans were largely excluded from the industrial occupational structure and restricted to unskilled jobs. A study in Los Angeles suggests that Hispanic residents made minimal gains. Their experiences elsewhere may have been much the same.

Although occupational mobility was limited for immigrants, other rewards often compensated for the lack of success at the workplace. Home ownership loomed important for groups like the Irish, while political success or mobility in institutions like the Catholic church provided satisfactions. Likewise, participation in social clubs and fraternal orders compensated in part for lack of advancement at work. Ethnic associations, parades, and holidays provided a sense of identity and security that offset the limitations of the job world.

CONCLUSION

THE COMPLEXITY OF INDUSTRIAL CAPITALISM

The rapid growth of the late nineteenth century made the United States one of the world's industrial giants. Many factors contributed to the "wonderful accomplishments" of the age. They ranged from sympathetic government policies to

the rise of big business and the emergence of a cheap industrial work force. But it was also a turbulent period. Many Americans benefited only marginally from the new wealth. Some of them protested by joining unions, by walking out on strike, or by initiating on-the-job actions. Most lived their lives more quietly and never had the opportunity that Thomas O'Donnell did of telling their story to others. But middle-class Americans began to wonder about the O'Donnells of the country. It is to their concerns, worries, and aspirations that we now turn.

Recommended Reading

The late-nineteenth-century industrial world has been the subject of lively historical investigation. A helpful overview of economic change is provided by Stuart Bruchey, *Growth of the Modern American Economy* (1975); and Robert L. Heilbroner, *The Economic Transformation of America* (1977). Samuel P. Hays gives a useful analysis in *The Response to Industrialism, 1885–1914* (1957).

On big business, see Glenn Porter, *The Rise of Big Business, 1860–1910* (1973); and Olivier Zunz, *Making America Corporate, 1870–1929* (1990). Advertising and its effects are discussed in James D. Norris, *Advertising and the Transformation of American Society, 1865–1920* (1990). Edward C. Kirkland illuminates the business mind in *Dream and Thought in the Business Community, 1860–1900* (1964).

Zane Miller's *Urbanization of America* (1973) provides a good introduction to city growth in the late nineteenth century. Gunther Barth examines urban culture in *The Rise of Modern City Culture in Nineteenth-Century America* (1980). James Borchert explores the black experience in *Alley Life in Washington: Family, Community, Religion, and Folklife in the City, 1850–1970* (1980).

For the immigrant experience, consult Thomas J. Archdeacon, *Becoming American: An Ethnic History* (1983). Alan M. Kraut brings together varied material on immigrants in *The Huddled Masses: The Immigrant in American Society, 1880–1921* (1982).

Studies of the working class include Herbert G. Gutman, *Work, Culture, and Society in Industrializing America* (1976); David M. Gordon, Richard Edwards, and Michael Reich, *Segmented Work, Divided Workers: The Historical Transformation of Labor in the United States* (1982); David T. Rodgers, *The Work Ethic in Industrial America* (1978); David Montgomery, *The Fall of the House of Labor: The Workplace, The State, and American Labor Activism, 1865–1925* (1987); and Theodore Hershberg, ed., *Philadelphia: Work, Space, Family, and Group Experience in the Nineteenth Century* (1981).

Labor conflicts are the focus of Nell Irvin Painter's *Standing at Armageddon in The United States, 1877–1919* (1987). Leon Fink explores the Knights of Labor in several communities in *Workingmen's Democracy: The Knights of Labor and American Politics* (1983). The issue of safety for miners is treated by James Whiteside in *Regulating Danger: The Struggle for Mine Safety in the Rocky Mountain Coal Industry* (1990).

Women and work are the subject of Alice Kessler-Harris, *Out to Work: A History of Wage-Earning Women in the United States* (1982); and Julie Matthaei, *An Economic History of Women in America: Women's Work, the Sexual Division of Labor, and the Development of Capitalism* (1982).

Stephen Thernstrom explores the realities of mobility and assimilation in *Poverty and Progress: Social Mobility in a Nineteenth Century City* (1964) and *The Other Bostonians: Poverty and Progress in the American Metropolis, 1880–1970* (1973). Similar works include Clyde and Sally Griffen, *Natives and Newcomers: The Ordering of Opportunity in Mid-Nineteenth-Century Poughkeepsie* (1978).

Novels depicting the period include Theodore Dreiser, *Sister Carrie* (1900); Stephen Crane, *Maggie: A Girl of the Streets* (1893); Abraham Cahan, *The Rise of David Levinsky* (1917); and Thomas Bell, *Out of This Furnace* (1976 ed.).

Time Line

1843–1884	"Old immigration"	**1879**	Thomas Edison invents incandescent light
1844	Telegraph invented	**1882**	Chinese Exclusion Act
1850s	Steam power widely used in manufacturing	**1885–1914**	"New immigration"
1859	Value of U.S. industrial production exceeds value of agricultural production	**1886**	American Federation of Labor founded Haymarket Riot in Chicago
1866	National Labor Union founded	**1887**	Interstate Commerce Act
1869	Transcontinental railroad completed Knights of Labor organized	**1890**	Sherman Anti-Trust Act
1870	Standard Oil of Ohio formed	**1892**	Standard Oil of New Jersey formed Coeur d'Alene strike Homestead steelworkers strike
1870s–1880s	Consolidation of continental railroad network	**1893**	Chicago World's Fair
1873	Bethlehem Steel begins using Bessemer process	**1893–1897**	Depression
1873–1879	Depression	**1894**	Pullman railroad workers strike
1876	Alexander G. Bell invents telephone	**1900**	International Ladies Garment Workers Union founded Corporations responsible for two-thirds of U.S. manufacturing
1877	Railroad workers hold first nationwide industrial strike		

chapter 19

Politics and Reform

At the start of his best-seller *Looking Backward* (1888), Edward Bellamy likened the American society of his day to a huge stagecoach. Dragging the coach along sandy roads and over steep hills were "the masses of humanity," straining "under the pitiless lashing of hunger." At the top sat the favored few, riding well in breezy comfort. The fortunate few, however, were constantly fearful that they might lose their seats from a sudden jolt, fall to the ground, and have to pull the coach themselves.

Bellamy's famous coach allegory introduced a utopian novel in which the class divisions and pitiless competition of the nineteenth century were replaced by a classless, caring, cooperative new world. Economic anxieties and hardships were supplanted by satisfying labor and leisure.

The novel opens in 1887. The hero, Julian West, a wealthy Bostonian, falls asleep worrying about the effect local labor struggles might have on his upcoming wedding. When he wakes up, it is the year 2000. Utopia had been achieved peacefully through the development of one gigantic trust, owned and operated by the national government. All citizens between 21 and 45 work in an industrial army with equalized pay and work difficulty. In a special division of the industrial army, women worked shorter hours in "lighter occupations." The purpose of equality of the sexes and more leisure, the novel made clear, was to enable women to cultivate their "beauty and grace" and, by extension, to feminize culture and politics.

Bellamy's book was immensely popular. Educated middle-class Americans were attracted by his vision of a society in which humans were both morally good and materially well off. Although the collectivist features of Bellamy's utopia were socialistic, he and his admirers called his system "nationalism." This appealed to a new generation of Americans who had put aside Civil War antagonisms to embrace the greatness of a growing, if now economically divided, nation. In the early 1890s, with Americans buying nearly 10,000 copies of *Looking Backward* every week, over 160 Nationalist clubs were formed to crusade for the adoption of Bellamy's ideas.

The inequalities of wealth described in Bellamy's coach scene reflected a political life in which many participated but only a few benefited. The wealthiest 10 percent, who rode high on the social coach, dominated national politics, while untutored bosses (mostly Irish) held sway in governing cities. Except for token expressions of support, national political leaders ignored the cries of factory workers, immigrants, farmers, blacks, Native Americans, and other victims of the vast transformation of American industrial, urban, and agrarian life in the late nineteenth century. But as the century drew to a close, middle-class Americans like Bellamy, as well as labor and agrarian leaders, proposed various reforms.

In this chapter, we will examine American politics at the national and local level from the end of Reconstruction to the 1890s and look at the growing social and political involvement of educated middle-class reformers. We will conclude with an account of the pivotal importance of the 1890s, which shook many comfortable citizens out of their apathy.

POLITICS IN THE GILDED AGE

In a satirical book in 1873, Mark Twain, with Charles Dudley Warner, used the expression "Gilded Age" to describe the political corruption of Ulysses S. Grant's presidency. The phrase, with its suggestion of shallow glitter, has come to characterize social and political life in the last quarter of the nineteenth century. Ironically, although Gilded Age politics was tainted by corruption and tinted by more color than substance, the period was one of high party vitality: Voter participation in national elections between 1876 and 1896 hovered at an all-time high of 73 to 82 percent of all registered voters.

Behind the pomp, parades, free beer, and lengthy speeches of Gilded Age politics occurred two gradual changes that would greatly affect twentieth-century politics. The first was the development of a professional bureaucracy, which served as a counterfoil to the perceived dangers of majority rule represented by high voter participation. Second, after a period of close elections and party stalemate based on Civil War divisions between Democrats and Republicans, new issues and concerns fostered a party realignment in the 1890s.

Politics, Parties, Patronage, and Presidents

American government in the 1870s and 1880s clearly supported the interests of riders at the top of the coach. Nineteenth-century Americans believed in laissez-faire, a doctrine that argued that all would benefit from an economic life free of government interference. As Republican leader Roscoe Conkling explained, the primary role of government was "to clear the way of impediments and dangers, and leave every class and every individual free and safe in the exertions and pursuits of life." Government regulation of business was in disfavor, but government cooperation with business through policies such as protective tariffs and currency legislation beneficial to financial and commercial interests was another matter.

The Gilded Age, Henry Adams observed, was the most "thoroughly ordinary" period in American politics since Columbus. "One might search the whole list of Congress, Judiciary, and

Politicians in the evenly contested electoral campaigns of the Gilded Age avoided real issues in favor of parades, pomp, patronage, and patriotism. Republican campaigns, invoking Lincoln, reminded voters to "vote as you shot" in the Civil War.

Executive during the twenty-five years 1870–95 and find little but damaged reputation." Adams was especially sensitive to this decline in the quality of democratic politics. His autobiography, *The Education of Henry Adams* (1907), contrasted the low political tone of his own age with the exalted political morality of the days of his grandfather John Quincy Adams and great-grandfather John Adams.

As a result of the weak Johnson and Grant presidencies, Congress emerged in the 1870s as the dominant branch of government. With power in the committee system, the moral quality of congressional leadership was typified by men such as the popular James G. Blaine, who was involved in a bribery scandal in which he was paid for supporting favors to railroads, and Roscoe Conkling, who spent most of his career in patronage conflicts with fellow Republican Party leaders. Though he served in Congress for over two decades, Conkling never drafted a bill. His career was unharmed, for legislation was not Congress's primary purpose.

In 1879, a student of legislative politics, Woodrow Wilson, expressed his disgust with the degradation of Gilded Age politics in eight words: "No leaders, no principles; no principles, no parties." Little differentiated the two major parties. They diverged not over principles but patronage, not over issues but over awarding thousands of government jobs to the winning candidate and his party. An English observer concluded that the most cohesive force in American politics was "the desire for office and for office as a means of gain." The two parties, like two bottles of liquor, bore different labels, yet "each was empty."

Republican votes still came from northeastern Yankee industrial interests and from New England migrants across the Upper Midwest. The main support for Democrats still came primarily from southern whites, northern workers, and Irish Catholic and other urban immigrants. For a few years, Civil War and Reconstruction issues generated clear, ideological party differences. But after 1876, on national issues at least, party labels did indeed mark "empty" bottles.

One reason for avoiding issues in favor of bland platforms and careful campaigning was that the two parties were evenly matched. In three of the five presidential elections between 1876 and 1892, one percent of the vote separated the two major candidates. Although all the presidents in the era except Grover Cleveland were Republicans, the Democrats controlled the House of Representatives in eight of the ten sessions of Congress between 1875 and 1895. As a result, political interest shifted away from Washington to states and cities.

Gilded Age presidents were an undistinguished group. None of them—Rutherford B. Hayes (1877–1881), James Garfield (1881), Chester A. Arthur (1881–1885), Grover Cleveland (1885–1889 and 1893–1897), and Benjamin Harrison (1889–1893)—served two consecutive terms. None was strongly identified with any particular issue. Although Cleveland was the only Democrat in the group, he differed little from the Republicans.

Most Americans expected their presidents to take care of party business by rewarding the faithful with government positions. The scale of patronage was enormous. Garfield complained of having to dispense thousands of jobs as he took office in 1881. He is remembered primarily for being shot early in his administration by a disappointed office seeker. His successor, Chester Arthur, was so closely identified with Conkling's patronage operation that when the shooting of the president was announced, a friend said with shocked disbelief, "My God! Chet Arthur in the White House!"

National Issues

Arthur surprised his doubters by proving himself a capable and dignified president, responsive to the growing demands for civil service reform. Four issues were important at the national level in the Gilded Age: the tariff, currency, civil service, and government regulation of railroads (see Chapter 17). In confronting these issues, legislators tried to serve both their own self-interest and the national interest of an efficient, productive economy. Two additional issues, Indian "reform" and black rights, were submerged in these interests (see Chapter 17).

The tariff was one issue where party, as well as regional attitudes toward the use of government power, made some difference. Republicans believed in using the national government to support business interests and stood for a high protective tariff. Democrats stressed that a low tariff exemplified the "economic axiom . . . that the government is best which governs least." In practice, politicians accommodated local interests in tariff adjustments. Democratic senator Daniel Vorhees of Indiana explained, "I am a protectionist for every interest which I am sent here by my constituents to protect."

Tariff revisions were bewilderingly complex in their acceding to these many special interests. As one senator knowingly said, "The contest over a revision of the tariff brings to light a selfish strife which is not far from disgusting." Most tariffs included a mixture of higher and lower rates that defied understanding.

The question of money was even more complicated. During the Civil War, the federal government had circulated paper money (greenbacks) that could not be exchanged for gold or silver. In the late 1860s and 1870s, proponents of a hard-money policy supported either withdrawing all paper money from circulation or making it convertible to specie. They opposed increasing the volume of money because they thought it would lead to higher prices. Greenbackers, who advocated soft money (currency not exchangeable for gold or silver) urged increasing the supply of paper money. An inadequate money supply, they believed, led to falling prices and an increase in interest rates, which harmed farmers, industrial workers, and all people in debt.

Hard-money interests had more power and influence, and in 1875 Congress put the nation firmly on the gold standard. But as large supplies of silver were discovered and mined in the West, pressure was resumed for increasing the money supply by coining silver. In 1878, the Bland-Allison Act required the Treasury to buy between $2 million and $4 million of silver each month and to coin it as silver dollars. Despite the increase in money supply, the period was not inflationary, but prices fell, disappointing the supporters of soft money. Their response was to push for more silver, which continued the controversy into the 1890s.

The issue of civil service reform was, Henry Adams observed, "a subject almost as dangerous in political conversation in Washington as slavery itself in the old days before the war." The worst feature of the spoils system was that parties financed themselves by assessing holders of patronage jobs, often as much as one percent of their annual salaries. The assassination of Garfield, however, created enough public support to force Congress to take action. The Pendleton Act of 1883 established a system of merit examinations covering about one-tenth of federal offices. Gradually, more bureaucrats fell under its coverage, but parties became no more honest. As campaign contributions from government employees dried up, parties turned to other financial sources, such as corporate contributions.

The Lure of Local Politics

The fact that the major parties did not disagree substantially on issues like money and civil service does not mean that nineteenth-century Americans found politics dull or uninteresting. In fact, far more eligible voters turned out in the late nineteenth century than at any time since. The 78.5 percent average turnout to vote for president in the 1880s contrasts sharply with the less than 55 percent of eligible Americans who voted for president in the 1980s.

Americans were drawn to the polls in part by the fun and games of party parades, buttons, and banners but also by the lure of local issues. For example, Iowa corn farmers turned out to vote for state representatives who favored curbing the power of the railroads to set high grain-shipping rates. But emotional issues of race, religion, nationality, and life style often overrode economic self-interest. While Irish Catholics in New York sought political support for their parochial schools, third-generation middle-class American Protestants from Illinois or Connecticut voted for laws that would compel attendance at public schools.

The influx of the new immigrants, especially in the mushrooming cities, facilitated the rise of urban bosses, whose power to control city government rested on an ability to deliver the votes of poor, uneducated immigrants. In return for votes, bosses like "Big Tim" Sullivan of New York and "Hinky Dink" Kenna of Chicago operated informal welfare systems. They handed out jobs and money for rent, fuel, and bail.

Party leaders also won votes by making political participation exciting. Nineteenth-century campaigns were punctuated by parades, rallies, and oratory. Campaign buttons, handkerchiefs, songs, and other paraphernalia generated color and excitement in political races where substantive issues were not at stake. In the election of 1884, for example, Democrats campaigned against Blaine's record of dishonesty, while Republicans focused on Cleveland's illegitimate child. Cleveland won, in part because a Republican clergyman unwisely called the Democrats the party of "rum, Romanism, and rebellion" on election eve in New York, which delivered the state, and the election, to Cleveland.

Voters may have been cool toward the tariff and civil service, but they expressed strong interest in temperance, anti-Catholicism, compulsory school attendance and Sunday laws, aid to parochial schools, racial issues, restriction of immigration, and "bloody shirt" reminders of the Civil War.

Party membership reflected voter interest in cultural, religious, and ethnic questions. Since the Republican Party had proved its willingness in the past to mobilize the power of the state to reshape society, people who wished to regulate moral and economic life were attracted to it. Catholics and various immigrant groups found the Democratic Party more to their liking because it opposed government efforts to regulate morals. Said one Chicago Democrat, "A Republican is a man who wants you t' go t' church every Sunday. A Democrat says if a man wants t' have a glass of beer on Sunday he can have it."

These differences caused spirited local contests, particularly over prohibition. Many Americans considered drinking a serious social problem. Annual consumption of brewery beer had risen from 2.7 gallons per capita in 1850 to 17.9 in 1880. Rather than trying to persuade individuals to give up drink, as the temperance movement had done earlier in the century, many now sought to make drinking a crime.

In the 1870s in San Jose, California, temperance reformers put on the ballot a local option referendum to ban the sale of liquor in San Jose. Women erected a temperance tent where they held conspicuous daily meetings. On election eve, a large crowd appeared at the temperance tent, but a larger one turned up at a proliquor rally. In the morning, women roamed the streets, urging men to adopt the referendum. Children were marched around to the polls and saloons, singing, "Father, dear father, come home with me now." By afternoon the mood grew ugly, and the women were harassed and threatened by drunken men. The prohibition proposal lost by a vote of 1,430 to 918.

Similarly emotional conflicts occurred in the 1880s at the state level over other issues, especially education. In Iowa, Illinois, and Wisconsin, Republicans sponsored laws mandating that children attend schools that provided instruction in English. The intent of these laws was to undermine parochial schools, which taught in the language of immigrants. In Wisconsin, a law for compulsory school attendance was so strongly anti-Catholic that it backfired. Many voters, disillusioned with Republican moralism, shifted to the Democratic Party.

MIDDLE-CLASS REFORM

Middle-class Americans moved by moral issues such as education and temperance were also concerned by the corruption of urban life and saw the value of the sophisticated and moral thinking they could bring to national life.

Frances Willard and the Women's Christian Temperance Union (WCTU) is an example. As president of the WCTU from 1879 until her death in 1898, Willard headed the largest women's organization in the country. Most members, like Willard, believed drunkenness caused poverty and family violence. But after 1886, the WCTU reversed its position, seeing drunkenness as a result of poverty, unemployment, and bad labor conditions. Willard joined the Knights of Labor in 1887 and by the 1890s had influenced the WCTU to extend its programs in a "do-everything" policy to alleviate the problems of workers, particularly women and children.

The Gospel of Wealth

Frances Willard called herself a Christian socialist because she believed in applying the ethical principles of Jesus to economic life with the aim of reducing inequalities of wealth. But for most Americans in the Gilded Age, Christianity supported the competitive individualistic ethic that justified the lofty place of those at the top. This ethic was endorsed by prominent ministers and others. Episcopal bishop William Lawrence wrote that it was "God's will that some men should attain great wealth."

Industrialist Andrew Carnegie in an article, "The Gospel of Wealth" (1889), celebrated the benefits of better goods and lower prices that resulted from competition. The concentration of wealth in the hands of a few leading industrialists, he concluded, was "not only beneficial but essential to the future of the race." Those most fit would bring order and efficiency out of the chaos of rapid industrialization. Carnegie also insisted that the rich were obligated to spend some of their wealth to benefit their "poorer brethren." He practiced what he preached, establishing over 2,500 libraries and providing substantial funding for education.

Carnegie's ideas about wealth were drawn from an ideology known as social Darwinism, based on the work of Charles Darwin, whose famous *Origin of Species* was published in 1859. Herbert Spencer, an English social philosopher, adopted Darwin's notions of natural selection and the "survival of the fittest" and applied them to human society. Progress, he said, resulted from relentless competition in which the weak failed and were eliminated while the strong climbed to the top. He believed that "the whole effort of nature is to get rid of such as are unfit, to clear the world of them, and make room for better."

Spencer's American followers, like Carnegie and William Graham Sumner, a professor of political economy at Yale, familiarized the American public with the basic ideas of social Darwinism. They emphasized that poverty was the inevitable consequence of the struggle for existence and that attempts to end it were pointless, if not immoral. Sumner, who opposed the monopolistic aims of industrial giants such as John D. Rockefeller, nevertheless scoffed at those who would take power or money away from millionaires. That, he said, would be "like killing off our generals in war."

Social Darwinists also believed in the superiority of the Anglo-Saxon race, which they maintained had reached the highest stage of evolution. Their theories were used to justify race supremacy and imperialism as well as the monopolistic efforts of American businessmen. Railroad magnate James J. Hill said that the absorption of smaller railroads by larger ones was the industrial analogy of the victory in nature of the fit over the unfit. John D. Rockefeller, Jr., told a YMCA class in Cleveland that "the growth of a large business is merely a survival of the fittest." Like the growth of a beautiful rose, "the early buds which grow up around it" must be sacrificed. This was, he said, "merely the working out of a law of nature and a law of God."

Others questioned this rosy outlook. Brooks Adams, brother of Henry, wrote that social philosophers like Spencer and Sumner were "hired by the comfortable classes to prove that everything was all right."

Reform Darwinism and Pragmatism

A number of intellectual reformers directly challenged the gloomy social Darwinian notion that nothing could be done to alleviate poverty and injustice.

Henry George observed that wherever the

highest degree of "material progress" had been realized, "we find the deepest poverty." George's book *Progress and Poverty* (1879) was an early statement of the contradictions of American life. With Bellamy's *Looking Backward,* it was the most influential book of the age, selling two million copies by 1905. George admitted that economic growth had produced wonders but pointed out the social costs and the loss of Christian values. His remedy was to break up landholding monopolists who profited from the increasing value of their land and rents they collected from those who actually did the work. He proposed a "single tax" on the unearned increases in land value received by landlords.

Henry George's optimistic faith in the capacity of humans to effect change appealed to many middle-class intellectuals. Some went beyond George to develop social scientific models that justified reform energy rather than inaction. A sociologist, Lester Frank Ward, and an economist, Richard T. Ely, both found examples of cooperation in nature and demonstrated that competition and laissez-faire had proved both wasteful and inhumane. These reform Darwinists urged instead an economic order marked by caring cooperation and social regulation.

Two pragmatists, John Dewey and William James, established a philosophical foundation for reform. James, a professor at Harvard, argued that while environment was important, so also was human will. People could influence the course of human events. He made it clear that the expression of human sympathies and the aversion to both economic and international war was moral conduct with the most ethical consequences.

James and young social scientists like Ward and Ely rejected the social determinism of Spencer and provided intellectual justification for the struggle against the inequalities of wealth found in many sectors of their society.

Settlements, Revivalism, and the Social Gospel

Jane Addams understood the gap between progress and poverty. She saw it in the misery of the working-class people in Chicago. Addams founded Hull House in Chicago in 1889 "to aid in the solution of the social and industrial problems which are engendered by the modern conditions of life in a great city." Vida Scudder, too, "felt the agitating and painful vibrations" of the depression. This young professor of literature at Wellesley College resolved to do something to alleviate the suffering of the poor. She and six other Smith College graduates formed an organization of college women in 1889 to work in settlement houses.

Other middle-class activists who worried about social conditions were mostly profession-

The young Jane Addams was one of the college-educated women who chose to remain unmarried and pursue a career as an "urban housekeeper" and social reformer, serving immigrant families in the Chicago neighborhood near her Hull House.

als—lawyers, ministers, teachers, journalists, and academic social scientists. The message they began to preach in the 1890s was highly idealistic, ethical, and Christian. They preferred a society marked by cooperation rather than competition, where, as they liked to say, people were guided by the "golden rule rather than the rule of gold." As middle-class intellectuals, they tended to stress an educational approach to problems, but they also ran for public office, crusaded for legislation, mediated labor disputes, and lived in poor neighborhoods.

The settlement house movement typified the blend of idealism and practicality characteristic of middle-class reformers in the 1890s. Addams opened Hull House, and Scudder started Denison House in Boston. A short time later, on New York's Lower East Side, Lillian Wald opened her "house on Henry Street." The primary purpose of the settlement houses was to help immigrant families, especially women, adapt to the realities of urban living in America. This meant launching day nurseries, kindergartens, boarding rooms for working women, and classes in sewing, cooking, nutrition, health care, and English. The settlements also frequently organized sports clubs and coffeehouses for young people as a way of keeping them out of the saloons.

A second purpose of the settlement house movement was to provide college-educated women with meaningful work at a time when they faced professional barriers and to allow them to preserve the strong feelings of sisterhood they had experienced in college. A third goal was to gather data exposing social misery in order to spur legislative action, such as developing city building codes for tenements, abolishing child labor, and improving safety in factories. Hull House, Addams said, was intended in part "to investigate and improve the conditions in the industrial districts of Chicago."

By contrast, another Chicagoan, Dwight Moody, led a wave of urban revivals in the 1870s, which appealed to lower-class rural folk who were either drawn to the city by expectant opportunities or pushed there by economic ruin. Supported by businessmen, who felt that religion would make workers and immigrants more docile, revivalists battled sin through individual conversion rather than by the settlement workers' focus on reform. The revivals helped nearly to double Protestant church membership in the last two decades of the century.

In the 1890s, many Protestant ministers immersed themselves in the Social Gospel movement, which tied salvation to social betterment. Like the settlement house workers, these religious leaders sought to make Christianity relevant to industrial and urban problems. A young Baptist minister in the notorious Hell's Kitchen area of New York City, Walter Rauschenbusch, unleashed scathing attacks on the selfishness of capitalism and church ignorance of socioeconomic issues. His progressive ideas for social justice and a welfare state were later published in two landmark Social Gospel books, *Christianity and the Social Crisis* (1907) and *Christianizing the Social Order* (1912).

Perhaps the most influential book promoting social Christianity was a best-selling novel, *In His Steps,* published in 1897 by Charles Sheldon. *In His Steps* portrayed the dramatic transformations in business relations, tenement life, and urban politics made possible by the work of a few community leaders who resolved to base all their actions on a single question: "What would Jesus do?" Although streaked with naive sentimentality characteristic of much of the Social Gospel, Sheldon's novel prepared thousands of influential middle-class Americans for progressive civic leadership after the turn of the century.

Reforming the City

No late-nineteenth-century institution needed reforming as much as urban government. The president of Cornell University described American city governments as "the worst in Christendom—the most expensive, the most inefficient, and the most corrupt."

Rapid urban growth overburdened city leaders. Population increase and industrial expansion created new demands for service. As city governments struggled to respond to new needs, they raised taxes and incurred vast debts. This combination of rapid growth, indebtedness, and poor services, coupled with the influx of new immigrants, prepared fertile ground for graft and "bossism."

The rise of the boss was directly connected to the growth of the city. As immigrant voters appeared, traditional native-born ruling groups left city government for business, where more money and status beckoned. Into the resulting power vacuum stepped the boss. In an age of urban expansion, bosses dispensed patronage jobs in return for votes and contributions to the party machine. They awarded street railway, gas line, and other utility franchises and construction contracts to local businesses in return for kickbacks and other favors. They also passed on tips to friendly real estate men about the location of projected city improvements. Worse yet, the bosses received favors from the owners of saloons, brothels, and gambling clubs in return for their help with police protection, bail, and influence with the courts. These institutions, however unsavory we might think them today, were vital to the urban economy and played an important role in easing the immigrants' way into American life. For many young women, the brothel was a means of economic survival. For men, the saloon was the center of social life, as well as a place for cheap meals and information about work and aid to their families.

"Bossism" deeply offended middle-class urban reformers, who opposed not only graft and vice but also the perversion of democracy by the exploitation of ignorant immigrants. Urban reformers, whose programs were similar in most cities, not only worked for the "Americanization" of immigrants in public schools (and opposed parochial schooling) but also formed clubs or voters' leagues to discuss the failings of municipal government. Political considerations pervaded every reform issue. Many Anglo-Saxon men favored prohibition partly to remove ethnic saloon owners from politics and supported woman suffrage in part to gain a middle-class political advantage against the predominantly male immigrant community. They proposed to replace the bosses with expert city managers. They hoped to make government less costly and thereby lower taxes. One effect of their emphasis on cost efficiency was to cut services to the poor. Another was to disfranchise working-class and ethnic groups, whose political participation depended on the old ward boss system.

Not all urban reformers were elitist, managerial types. Samuel Jones, for example, both opposed the boss system and had a passionate commitment to democratic political participation by the urban immigrant masses. An immigrant himself, Jones was a self-made man in the rags-to-riches mold, working his way up to the ownership of several oil fields and a factory in Toledo, Ohio. In 1894, Jones resolved "to apply the Golden Rule as a rule of conduct" in his factory. He instituted an eight-hour day for his employees, a $2 minimum wage per day (50 to 75 cents higher than the Toledo average for ten hours), a cooperative insurance program, and an annual 5 percent Christmas dividend. He hired ex-criminals and outcasts that no one else would employ and plastered the Golden Rule all over his factory walls.

Beginning in 1897, Jones was elected to an unprecedented four terms as mayor of Toledo. As a pacifist, he did not believe in violence or coercion of any kind. Therefore, he took away policemen's side arms and heavy clubs. When he sat as judge in police court, he regularly dismissed most cases of petty theft and drunkenness brought before him, charging that the accused were victims of an unjust social order and that only the poor went to jail for such crimes. He refused to advocate closing the saloons or brothels, and when prostitutes were brought before him, he usually dismissed them after fining every man in the room 10 cents—and himself a dollar—for permitting prostitution to exist. The crime rate in Toledo, a notoriously sinful city, decreased during his tenure, and Jones was adored by the plain people. When he died in 1904, nearly 55,000 persons, "tears streaming down their faces," filed past his coffin.

The Struggle for Woman Suffrage

Women served, in Jane Addams's phrase, as "urban housekeepers" in the settlement house and good government movements, which reflected the tension many women felt between their public and private lives, between their obligations to self, family, and society.

Some middle-class women, Addams and Scudder, for example, avoided marriage altogether, preferring the supportive relationships found in the female settlement house community. In fact, the generation of women that came of age in the 1890s married less—and later—than any other in American history.

One way women reconciled the conflicting pressures between their private and public lives, as well as deflected male criticism, was to see their work as maternal. Addams called Hull House "the great mother breast of our common humanity." Frances Willard told Susan B. Anthony in 1898 that "government is only housekeeping on the broadest scale," a job men had botched, thus requiring women's saving participation. But how could they be municipal housekeepers if they could not yet even vote?

In the years after the Seneca Falls Convention in 1848, women's civil and political rights advanced very slowly. Although in several western states they received the right to vote in municipal and schoolboard elections, only the territory of Wyoming, in 1869, had granted full political equality before 1890. Colorado, Utah, and Idaho enfranchised women in the 1890s, but no other states granted suffrage until 1910.

In the 1890s, leading suffragists reappraised the situation. The two wings of the women's rights movement, split since 1869, combined in 1890 as the National American Woman Suffrage Association (NAWSA). Although Elizabeth Cady Stanton and Susan B. Anthony continued to head the association, they were both in their seventies, and effective leadership soon passed to younger leaders, who concentrated on the single issue of the vote rather than dividing their energies among the many causes Stanton and Anthony had espoused. Women of widely divergent political and philosophical views were able to come together on this one issue.

Changing leadership meant a shift from principled to expedient arguments for the suffrage. Since 1848, suffragists had made their argument primarily from principle, citing, as Stanton argued at a congressional hearing in 1892, "our republican idea, individual citizenship." Finding that appeals to principle did not work, the younger generation shifted to three expedient arguments. The first was that women needed to vote to pass self-protection laws that would guard them against rapists, state age-of-consent laws, and unsafe industrial work. The second argument, Addams's notion of urban housekeeping, pointed out that political enfranchisement would further women's role in cleaning up morals, tenements, saloons, factories, and corrupt politics. The third expedient argument was that educated, native-born American women should be given the vote to counteract the undesirable influence of ignorant, illiterate, and immoral male immigrants. In a speech in Iowa in 1894, Carrie Chapman Catt, who would succeed Anthony as president of NAWSA in 1900, argued that the "Government is menaced with great danger . . . in the votes possessed by the males in the slums of the cities," a danger that could be averted only by cutting off that vote and giving it instead to women. In the new century, under the leadership of capable organizers like Catt, suffrage would finally be secured.

THE PIVOTAL 1890s

For years, many Americans have mistakenly called the last decade of the nineteenth century the "gay nineties." The 1890s were, indeed, a decade of sports and leisure, the electrification of the city, and the enormous wealth of the few. But for many more Americans it was also a decade of dark tenement misery, grinding work or desperate unemployment, and poverty.

The 1890s, far from gay, were years of contrasts and crises. The obvious contrast, as Bellamy had anticipated, was between the rich and the poor. The pivotal nature of the decade hinged on this feeling of polarizing unrest and upheaval as the nation underwent the traumas of change. America was transforming itself from a rural to an urban society and experiencing the pressures of rapid industrialization and accompanying changes in the workplace and on farms. Moreover, the new immigration from Europe and the northward, westward, and cityward internal migrations of blacks and farmers added to the "great danger" against which Carrie Catt warned. The depression of 1893 worsened the gaps between rich and poor and accelerated the demands for reform. Government bureaucratic structures began to adapt to the needs of governing a complex specialized society, and Congress slowly shifted away from laissez-faire in order to confront national problems.

Republican Legislation in the Early 1890s

Benjamin Harrison's election to the presidency in 1888 was accompanied by Republican control of both houses of Congress. Though by no means reformers, the Republicans moved forward in the first six months of 1890 with legislation in five areas: pensions for Civil War veterans and their dependents, trusts, the tariff, the money question, and rights for blacks. The De-

pendent Pensions Act, providing generous support of $160 million a year for Union veterans and their dependents, sailed through Congress.

The Sherman Anti-Trust Act declared illegal "every contract, combination . . . or conspiracy in restraint of trade or commerce." Although the bill was vague and not really intended to break up large corporations, the Sherman Act was an initial attempt to restrain large business combinations. But in 1895 the Supreme Court ruled that the law applied only to commerce, not manufacturing.

A bill for higher tariffs, introduced in 1890 by Ohio Republican William McKinley, passed after nearly 500 amendments were added.

The Sherman Silver Purchase Act, a compromise measure that momentarily satisfied almost everyone, ordered the Treasury to buy 4.5 million ounces of silver monthly and to issue treasury notes for it. Silverites were pleased by the proposed increase in the money supply. Opponents felt they had averted the worst, free coinage of silver. The gold standard remained secure.

Republicans were also prepared to confront violations of the voting rights of southern blacks in 1890. President Harrison told the editor of the New York *Tribune,* "I feel very strong upon the question of a free ballot." An elections bill, proposed by Massachusetts senator Henry Cabot Lodge, would protect voter registration and ensure fair elections by setting up mechanisms for investigating charges of bribery and fraud. A storm of disapproval from Democrats greeted the measure. Senate Democrats delayed action with a filibuster.

Meanwhile, Republicans worried that they could not pass both the elections bill and the McKinley Tariff, which was languishing in the Senate. Pennsylvania senator Matt Quay, who had skillfully directed Harrison's election in 1888, proposed that if the Democrats ceased their delaying tactics so that the tariff could come to a vote, the Republicans would agree to put off consideration of the elections bill. The ploy worked, marking the end of major party efforts to protect black voting rights in the South until the 1960s.

The legislative efforts of the summer of 1890, impressive by nineteenth-century standards, fell far short of solving the nation's problems. Trusts grew more rapidly after the Sherman Act than before. Union veterans were pleased by their pensions, but southerners were incensed that Confederate veterans were not covered. Farm prices continued to decline, and gold and silver advocates were only momentarily silenced. Black rights were put off to another time. Polarizing inequalities of wealth remained. Voters abandoned the GOP in droves in the 1890 congressional elections, dropping the number of Republicans in the House from 168 to 88.

Two years later, Cleveland won a presidential rematch with Harrison. His inaugural address underlined the lesson he drew from Republican legislative activism in 1890. "The lessons of paternalism ought to be unlearned," he said, "and the better lesson taught that while the people should ... support their government, its functions do not include the support of the people."

The Depression of 1893

Cleveland's philosophy of government soon faced a difficult test. No sooner had he taken office than began one of the worst depressions ever to grip the American economy, lasting from 1893 to 1897. The depression started in Europe and spread to the United States as overseas buyers cut back on their purchases of American products. Shrinking markets abroad soon crippled American manufacturing. As gold left the country to pay for securities dumped by foreign investors, the nation's supply of money declined.

The collapse in 1893 was also caused by serious overextensions of the economy at home,

especially in railroad construction. Farmers, troubled by falling prices, planted more and more crops, hoping somehow that the market would pick up. As the realization of overextension spread, confidence faltered, then gave way to financial panic. When the stock market crashed early in 1893, investors frantically sold their shares, companies plunged into bankruptcy, and disaster spread. People rushed to exchange paper notes for gold, reducing gold reserves and confidence in the economy even further. Banks called in their loans, which by the end of the year led to 16,000 business bankruptcies and 500 bank failures. Factories closed, and within a year, an estimated three million Americans, 20 percent of the work force, were unemployed. Suddenly people began to look fearfully at the tramps wandering from city to city looking for work. "There are thousands of homeless and starving men in the streets," one young man reported from Chicago, indicating that he had seen "more misery in this last week than I ever saw in my life before."

As in Bellamy's coach image, the misery of the many was not shared by the few, which only increased discontent. While unemployed men foraged in garbage dumps for food, the wealthy gave lavish parties sometimes costing $100,000. At one such affair, diners ate their meal while seated on horses; at another, many guests proudly proclaimed that they had spent over $10,000 on their dresses. While Lithuanian immigrants walked or rode streetcars to Buffalo steel factories to work, wealthy men skimmed across lakes and oceans in huge pleasure yachts. J. P. Morgan owned three, one with a crew of 85 sailors.

Nowhere were these inequalities more apparent than in Chicago during the World's Columbian Exposition, which opened on May 1, 1893, five days before plummeting prices on the stock market began the depression. Built at a cost of $31 million, the Chicago World's Fair celebrated the marvelous mechanical accomplishments of American enterprise. The elegant

The depression of 1893 accentuated contrasts between rich and poor. While well-to-do children enjoyed the giant Ferris wheel and other midway attractions at the Chicago World's Columbian Exposition, slum children played in filthy streets nearby.

design of its buildings and lagoons stimulated a "City Beautiful" movement that made many cities more attractive and enjoyable for their residents. But as well-to-do fairgoers sipped pink champagne, men, women, and children in the immigrant wards of Chicago less than a mile away drank contaminated water, crowded into packed tenements, and looked in vain for jobs.

Despite the magnitude of despair during the depression, national politicians and leaders were reluctant to respond. Only mass demonstrations forced city authorities to provide soup kitchens and places for the homeless to sleep. When an army of unemployed led by Jacob Coxey marched into Washington in the spring of 1894 to press for some form of public work relief, its leaders were arrested for stepping on the grass of the Capitol. Cleveland's reputation for callous disregard for citizens suffering from the depres-

sion worsened later that summer when he sent federal troops to Chicago to crush the Pullman strike.

The president focused his efforts on tariff reform and repeal of the Silver Purchase Act, which he blamed for the depression. Although repeal was ultimately a necessary measure to establish business confidence, in the short run it worsened the financial crisis.

The Crucial Election of 1896

The campaign of 1896, waged during the continuing depression, was one of the most critical in American history. Known as the "battle of the standards," the election was fought in part over the ratio of gold and silver as the standard national currency. Although Cleveland was in disgrace for ignoring depression woes, few leaders in either major party thought the federal government was responsible for alleviating the suffering of the people. But unskilled workers wondered where relief might be found.

As the election of 1896 approached, Populist leaders focused on the issues of silver and whether to fuse with one of the major parties by agreeing on a joint ticket. But fusion required abandoning much of the Populist platform, thus weakening the party's distinctive character. Under the influence of silver mine owners, many Populists became convinced that the hope of the party lay in a single-issue commitment to the free and unlimited coinage of silver at the ratio of 16 to 1. James Weaver expected both parties to nominate gold candidates, which would send disappointed silverites to the Populist standard.

The Republicans, holding their convention first, nominated Senator William McKinley of Ohio on the first ballot. They also cited the familiar argument that prosperity depended on the gold standard and protection and blamed the depression on Cleveland's attempt to lower the tariff.

William Jennings Bryan, surprise nominee at the 1896 Democratic convention, was a vigorous proponent of the "cause of humanity." His surprise nomination threw the country into a frenzy of fear and the Populist Party into a fatal decision over "fusion."

The excitement of the Democratic convention in July contrasted with the staid, smoothly organized Republican one, a pattern to be repeated throughout most of the twentieth century. The surprise nominee of the Democratic convention was an ardent young silverite, William Jennings Bryan, a 36-year-old congressman from Nebraska. Few saw him as presidential material, but as a member of the Resolutions Committee, Bryan arranged to give the closing argument for a silver plank himself. His dramatic speech swept the convention for silver and ensured his own nomination. At the conclusion of what was to become one of the most famous political speeches in American history, Bryan attacked the "goldbugs" and promised, "You shall not press down upon the brow of labor this crown of thorns, you shall not crucify mankind upon a cross of gold."

Populist strategy lay in shambles with the nomination of a Democratic silver candidate. The Democratic vice-presidential candidate, Arthur Sewall, was an East Coast banker and a hard-money man. The Populist convention ultimately nominated Bryan (who thus became the simultaneous nominee of two party conventions), but instead of Sewall chose Populist Tom Watson of Georgia as his running mate. The existence of two silverite slates damaged Bryan's electoral hopes.

During the campaign, McKinley stayed at his home in Canton, Ohio. Republican strategy featured an unprecedented effort to reach voters through a highly sophisticated mass-media campaign, heavily financed by such major corporations as Standard Oil and the railroads. Party leaders hired thousands of speakers to support McKinley and distributed over 200 million pamphlets to a voting population of 15 million. The literature, distributed in 14 languages, was designed to appeal to particular national, ethnic, regional, and occupational groups. To all these people, McKinley was advertised as "the advance agent of prosperity."

In sharp contrast to the Republican stay-at-home policy, Bryan took his case to the people. Three million people in 27 states heard him speak as he traveled over 18,000 miles, giving as many as 30 speeches a day. Bryan's message was simple. Prosperity would return with free coinage of silver. Government policies should attend to the needs of the producing classes rather than the vested interests that believed in the gold standard. "That policy is best for this country," Bryan proclaimed, "which brings prosperity first to those who toil." But his rhetoric favored rural toilers. Few urban workers were inspired by this rhetoric, nor were most immigrants impressed by Bryan's prairie moralizing.

To influential easterners, the brash young

Nebraskan represented a threat to social harmony. Theodore Roosevelt wrote that "this silver craze surpasses belief. Bryan's election would be a great calamity." One newspaper editor said of Bryan that he was just like Nebraska's Platte River: "six inches deep and six miles wide at the mouth." Others branded him a "madman" and an "anarchist."

With such intense interest in the election, it was predictable that voters would turn out in record numbers. When the voting was over, McKinley had won 271 electoral votes to Bryan's 176. Millionaire Mark Hanna jubilantly wired McKinley: "God's in his heaven, all's right with the world." Bryan had been defeated by the largest popular majority since Grant trounced Greeley in 1872.

Although Bryan won over six million votes, more than any previous Democratic winner, he failed to carry the Midwest and the industrial masses. McKinley's promise of a "full dinner pail" was more convincing than the untested formula for free silver. Chance also played a part in Bryan's defeat. Bad wheat harvests in India, Australia, and Argentina drove up grain prices in the world market. Many of the complaints of American farmers evaporated amid rising farm prices.

The New Shape of American Politics

The landslide Republican victory marked the end of the political stalemate that had characterized American politics since the end of the Civil War. Republicans lost their identification with the politics of piety and strengthened their image as the party of prosperity and national greatness, which gave them a party dominance that lasted until the 1930s. The Democrats, who would remain under Bryan's leadership until 1912, took on the mantle of populist moralism but were largely reduced to a sectional party, reflecting narrow southern views on money, race, and national power. The 1896 election demonstrated that the Northeast and the Great Lakes states had acquired so many immigrants that they now controlled the entire nation's political destiny. Populists, demoralized by fusion with a losing campaign, fell apart and disappeared. Asked a despondent Populist, Ignatius Donnelly, "Will the sun of triumph never rise? I fear not." His pessimism was premature, for within the next 20 years most Populist issues were taken over and adopted by politicians of the major parties.

Another result of the election of 1896 was a change in the pattern of political participation. Because the Republicans were so dominant, voters had less and less motivation to cast a ballot. Many black voters in the South, moreover, were disfranchised, and middle-class good government reformers succeeded in reducing the high voter turnout achieved by urban party bosses. Thus the tremendous rate of political participation that had characterized the nineteenth century since the Jackson era gradually declined. In the twentieth century, the low political involvement among poorer Americans was unique among western industrial countries.

McKinley had promised that Republican rule meant prosperity, and as soon as he took office, the economy recovered. Discoveries of gold in the Yukon and the Alaskan Klondike increased the money supply, thus thwarting silver mania until the early 1930s. Industrial production returned to full capacity.

McKinley's election marked not only the return of an era of economic health but also the emergence of the executive as the preeminent focus of the American political system. Just as McKinley's campaign set the pattern for the extravagant efforts to win office that have dominated modern times, his conduct as president foreshadowed the nature of the twentieth-century presidency. McKinley rejected traditional views of the president as the passive executor of laws, instead playing an active role in dealing with Congress and the press. His frequent trips away from Washington testified to his respect for public opinion. Some historians regard McKin- ley as the first modern president in his emphasis on the role of the chief executive in contributing to industrial growth and national power.

CONCLUSION

LOOKING FORWARD

McKinley's triumph in 1896 indicated that in a decade marked by depression, Populist revolt, and cries for action to close the inequalities of wealth, the established order remained intact and politics remained as unresponsive as ever. But in the areas of personal action and the philo- sophical bases for social change, intellectual middle-class reformers like Edward Bellamy, Henry George, William James, Jane Addams, "Golden Rule" Jones, and many others were showing the way to progressive reforms in the new century.

As the year 1900 approached, Henry Adams, still the pessimist, saw an ominous future, predict- ing the explosive and ultimately destructive energy of unrestrained industrial development. But oth- ers, more optimistic, saw America as an exemplary nation, demonstrating to the world the moral superiority of its economic system, democratic institutions, and middle-class Protestant values. Surely the new century, most thought, would see not only the continued perfection of these values and institutions but also the spread of American influence throughout the world.

Recommended Reading

The politics of the Gilded Age is treated usefully in the context of other developments of late-nineteenth-cen- tury life in H. Wayne Morgan, *From Hayes to McKin- ley: National Party Politics, 1877–1896* (1969); and Morton Keller, *Affairs of State: Public Life in Late Nineteenth Century America* (1977). An analysis of politics in the 1890s (and a good example of the "new political history") is R. Hal Williams, *Years of Deci- sion: American Politics in the 1890s* (1978). The new social and political history is well represented by Paul Kleppner, *The Third Electoral System, 1853–1892: Parties, Voters, and Political Cultures* (1979).

The lives of middle-class men and women are un- derstood best by a variety of different approaches. See relevant chapters in Mary Ryan's excellent survey, *Womanhood in America* (1983 ed.). See also Ruth Bordin, *Frances Willard: A Biography* (1986). Social

Darwinism and the success ethic are covered in Richard Hofstadter, *Social Darwinism in American Thought* (1955 ed.); and John Cawelti, *Apostles of the Self-Made Man: Changing Concepts of Success in America* (1965).

Novels that capture the flavor of middle-class life in the late nineteenth century include Mark Twain and Charles Dudley Warner, *The Gilded Age* (1873); Edward Bellamy, *Looking Backward* (1888); William Dean Howells, *The Rise of Silas Lapham* (1885) and *A Hazard of New Fortunes* (1889). Theodore Dreiser, *Sister Carrie* (1900); and Frank Norris, *The Octopus* (1901), depict a middle-class view of both middle- and lower-class life.

On late-nineteenth-century reform see John Sproat, *"The Best Men": Liberal Reformers in the Gilded Age* (1968); and Ralph Luker, *The Social*

Gospel in Black and White: American Racial Reform, 1885–1912 (1991). A study of middle-class urban reformers and the bossism they opposed is John Allswang, *Bosses, Machines, and Urban Voters* (1977). See also William Riordon's delightful recovery of the words of a typical boss, *Plunkitt of Tammany Hall* (1963, originally published in 1905). Biographical or autobiographical accounts of urban reformers include Peter Frederick, *Knights of the Golden Rule: The Intellectual as Christian Social Reformer in the 1890s*

(1976); Jane Addams, *Twenty Years at Hull House* (1910); and Vida Scudder, *On Journey* (1937).

The profound impact of the depression of 1893 is seen in Charles Hoffman, *The Depression of the Nineties: An Economic History* (1970). Populism and the election of 1896 are covered in a straightforward account by Paul Glad, *McKinley, Bryan and the People* (1964). A more recent examination of Populism is Gene Clanton, *Populism: The Humane Preference in America, 1890–1900* (1991).

Time Line

1873	Congress demonetizes silver		Sherman Anti-Trust Act
1875	Specie Resumption Act		Sherman Silver Purchase Act
1877	Rutherford B. Hayes becomes president		McKinley Tariff
			Elections bill defeated
1878	Bland-Allison Act	1890s	Wyoming, Colorado, Utah, and Idaho grant woman suffrage
1879	Henry George, *Progress and Poverty*	1892	Cleveland elected president for the second time; Populist Party wins over a million votes
1880	James A. Garfield elected president		
1881	Garfield assassinated; Chester A. Arthur succeeds to presidency		Homestead steel strike
1883	Pendleton Civil Service Act	1893	World's Columbian Exposition, Chicago
1884	Grover Cleveland elected president W. D. Howells, *The Rise of Silas Lapham*	1893–1897	Financial panic and depression
1887	College Settlement House Association founded	1894	Pullman strike Coxey's march on Washington
1888	Edward Bellamy, *Looking Backward* Benjamin Harrison elected president	1895	*United States* v. *E. C. Knight*
		1896	Charles Sheldon, *In His Steps* (serialized version) Populist Party fuses with Democrats William McKinley elected president
1889	Jane Addams establishes Hull House Andrew Carnegie promulgates "The Gospel of Wealth"	1897	"Golden Rule" Jones elected mayor of Toledo, Ohio Economic recovery begins
1890	General Federation of Women's Clubs founded		

chapter 20

....

Becoming a World Power

In January 1899, the United States Senate was locked in a dramatic debate over whether to ratify the Treaty of Paris concluding the recent war with Spain over Cuban independence. At the same time, American soldiers uneasily faced Filipino rebels across a neutral zone around the outskirts of Manila, capital of the Philippines. Until recent weeks, the Americans and Filipinos had been allies, together defeating the Spanish to liberate the Philippines. The American fleet under Admiral George Dewey had destroyed the Spanish naval squadron in Manila Bay on May 1, 1898. Three weeks later, an American ship brought from exile the native Filipino insurrectionary leader, Emilio Aguinaldo, to lead rebel forces on land while U.S. gunboats patrolled the seas.

At first, the Filipinos looked on the Americans as liberators, helping them win their independence, but when an armistice ended the war in August, American troops denied Filipino soldiers an opportunity to liberate their own capital city and shunted them off to the suburbs. The armistice agreement recognized American rights to "the harbor, city, and bay of Manila," while the proposed Treaty of Paris gave the United States the entire Philippine Island archipelago.

Consequently, tension mounted in Manila. Barroom skirmishes and knifings pervaded the city at night; American soldiers searched houses without warrants and looted stores. Their behavior was not unlike that of the English soldiers in Boston in the 1770s.

On the night of February 4, 1899, Privates William Grayson and David Miller of Company B, 1st Nebraska Volunteers, were on patrol in Santa Mesa, a Manila suburb surrounded on three sides by insurgent trenches. The Americans had orders to shoot any Filipino soldiers found in the neutral area. As the two Americans cautiously worked their way to a bridge over the San Juan River, they encountered four Filipinos and shot three of them. A full-scale battle followed.

The outbreak of hostilities ended the Senate debates. On February 6, the Senate ratified the Treaty of Paris, thus formally annexing the Philippines and sparking a war between the United States and Filipino nationalists.

In a guerrilla war similar to those fought later in the twentieth century in Asia and Central America, Filipino nationalists held out until July 1902, three years longer than the Spanish-American War that caused it and involving far more troops, casualties, and monetary and moral costs.

How did all this happen? What brought Private Grayson halfway around the world to the Philippines? For the first time in history, regular American soldiers found themselves fighting outside North America. The "champion of oppressed nations," as Aguinaldo said, had turned into an oppressor nation itself, imposing the American way of life and American institutions on faraway peoples against their will.

The war in the Philippines marked a critical transformation of America's role in the world. Within a few years at the turn of the century, the United States acquired an empire, however small by European standards, and established itself as a world power. In this chapter, we will review the historical dilemmas of America's role in the world; we will examine the motivations for the intensified expansionism of the 1890s; and we will look at how the fundamental patterns of modern American foreign policy were established for Latin America, Asia, and Europe in the early twentieth century. We will see that the tension between idealism and self-interest that has permeated America's domestic history has guided its foreign policy as well.

STEPS TOWARD EMPIRE

The circumstances that brought Privates Grayson and Miller from Nebraska to the Philippines originated deep in American history. Just as the Puritan John Winthrop sought to set up a "city on a hill" in the New World, a model community of righteous living for others in the world to behold, such idealism became a permanent goal of American policy toward the outside world.

America as a Model Society

Nineteenth-century Americans continued to believe in the nation's special mission. The Monroe Doctrine in 1823 pointed out moral differences between the monarchical, arbitrary governments of Europe and the free republican institutions of the New World. The American Revolutionary model seemed irresistible. In a world that was evil, Americans believed that they stood as a transforming force for good. Many others agreed. The problem was how a nation committed to isolationism was to do the transforming. One way was to encourage other nations to observe and imitate the good example set by the United States. But often other nations preferred their own society or were attracted to competing models of modernization, as has frequently happened in the twentieth century. This implied a more aggressive foreign policy.

Americans have rarely simply focused on perfecting the good example at home, waiting for others to copy it. This requires patience and passivity, two traits not prevalent in Americans. Rather, throughout history, the American people have actively and sometimes forcefully imposed their ideas and institutions on others. The international crusades of the United States, well intentioned if not always well received, have usually been motivated by a mixture of idealism and self-interest.

Early Expansionism

A consistent expression of continental expansionism marked the first century of American independence. Jefferson's purchase of the Louisiana Territory in 1803 and the grasping for Florida and Canada by War Hawks in 1812 signaled an intense American interest in territorial growth. The Cherokee, Seminole, Lakota, Apache, Cheyenne, and other Native American nations found the United States to be far from isolationist. Until midcentury, the United States pursued its "Manifest Destiny"—its conviction that Americans had a mission to spread their civilization across the continent from ocean to ocean (see Chapter 13). But in the 1850s, Americans began to look beyond their own continent. This trend was marked most significantly by Commodore Perry's visit to Japan, the expansion of the China trade, and various expeditions into the Caribbean in search of more cotton lands and a canal connecting the two oceans.

Lincoln's secretary of state, William Seward, believed that the United States was destined to exert commercial domination "on the Pacific ocean, and its islands and continents." His goal was that from markets, raw materials, and trade would come the "regeneration of . . . the East." Toward this end, Seward purchased Alaska from Russia in 1867 for $7.2 million. He also acquired a coaling station in the Midway Islands in the mid-Pacific and paved the way for American commercial expansion in Korea, Japan, and China. Seward dreamed of "possession" of the entire North and Central American continent and ultimately "control of the world."

Expansion After Seward

In 1870, foreshadowing the Philippine debates 30 years later, supporters of President Grant tried without success to force the Senate to annex Santo Domingo (Hispaniola). Senatorial opponents responded that expansionism violated the American principle of self-determination and government by the consent of the governed. They pointed out, moreover, that the native peoples of the Caribbean were brown-skinned, culturally inferior, non-English-speaking, and therefore unassimilable. Finally, they suggested that expansionism might involve foreign entanglements, necessitating a large and expensive navy, growth in the size of government, and higher taxes. The Senate rejected the treaty to annex Santo Domingo.

In 1881, Secretary of State James G. Blaine sought to convene a conference of American nations to promote hemispheric peace and trade. Although motivated mostly by his presidential ambitions, his effort nevertheless led to the first Pan-American Conference eight years later. The Latin Americans may have wondered what Blaine intended, for in 1881 he intervened in three separate border disputes in Central and South America, in each case at the cost of goodwill and trust.

Ten years later, relations with Chile were harmed when several American sailors on shore leave were involved in a barroom brawl in Valparaiso. Two Americans were killed and several others injured. American pride was also injured, and President Benjamin Harrison sent an ultimatum calling for a "prompt and full reparation." After threats of war, Chile complied.

Similar incidents occurred as American expansionists pursued Seward's goals in the Pacific. In the mid-1870s, American sugar-growing interests in the Hawaiian Islands were strong enough to place whites in positions of influence over the native monarchy. In 1875, they obtained a reciprocity treaty admitting Hawaiian sugar duty-free to the United States. When the treaty was renewed and approved in 1887, the United States also gained exclusive rights to build a naval base at Pearl Harbor on the island of Oahu.

In 1891, the strongly nationalist Queen Liliuokalani assumed the throne in Hawaii and promptly abolished the constitution, seeking to establish control over whites in the name of "Hawaii for the Hawaiians." In 1893, with the help of U.S. gunboats and marines, the whites staged a palace coup (a revolution later called

Princess Liliuokalani of Hawaii, in a portrait from the late 1870s or early 1880s. She assumed the Hawaiian throne in 1891 and was deposed in a palace coup two years later.

one "of sugar, by sugar, for sugar") and waited patiently for annexation by the United States, which came during the war in 1898.

U.S. naval forces in the Pacific had skirmishes with Canadian sealing and fishing vessels in the 1880s, and with German naval forces in 1889 in the Samoan Islands. More serious was a conflict with England. In 1895 a long-standing boundary dispute between Venezuela and British Guiana flared up anew after gold was discovered in both lands. The British threatened to intervene against the Venezuelans. President Cleveland, in need of a popular political issue to deflect attention from the depression, discovered the political value of a tough foreign policy by defending a weak sister American republic against the British bully. A strong note citing the Monroe Doctrine was sent to the British, and the possibility of war loomed until both Britain and Venezuela agreed to allow an impartial American commission settle the boundary.

These increasing conflicts in the Caribbean and the Pacific signaled the rise of American presence beyond the borders of the United States. Yet as of 1895, the nation had neither the means nor a consistent policy for enlarging its role in the world. The diplomatic service was small, inexperienced, and unprofessional, and it exhibited insensitive behavior toward native cultures. The U.S. Army, numbering about 28,000 men in the mid-1890s, ranked thirteenth in the world, behind that of Bulgaria. The navy ranked no higher than tenth in size.

EXPANSIONISM IN THE 1890s

In 1893, historian Frederick Jackson Turner wrote that for three centuries, "the dominant fact in American life has been expansion." Turner believed that the frontier played an important role in the development of democracy and liberty in America. He observed that the "extension of American influence to outlying islands and adjoining countries" indicated that expansionism would continue. Turner's observations struck a responsive chord in a country that had always been restless, mobile, and optimistic. With the western American frontier closed, Americans would surely look for new frontiers, for mobility and markets as well as for morality and missionary activity. The motivations for the expansionist impulse of the late 1890s resembled those that had prompted people to settle the New World in the first place: greed, glory, and God. We will examine expansionism as a reflection of profits, patriotism, piety (or moral mission), and politics.

Profits: Searching for Overseas Markets

Senator Albert Beveridge of Indiana bragged in 1898 that "American factories are making more

United States Territorial Expansion to 1900

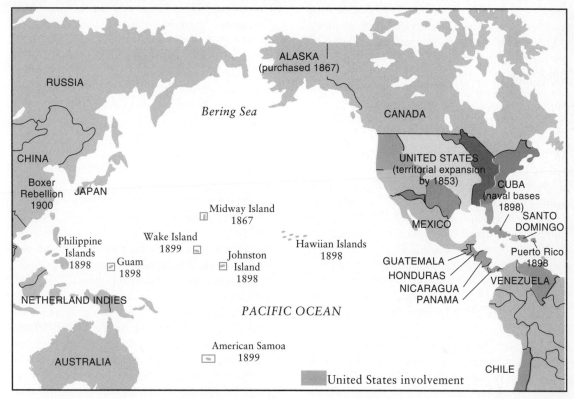

than the American people can use; American soil is producing more than they can consume. Fate has written our policy for us; the trade of the world must and shall be ours." Beveridge believed in the dream of a commercial empire in the islands and adjoining countries of the Caribbean Sea and the Pacific Ocean. American businessmen saw huge profits beckoning in the heavily populated areas of Latin America and Asia, and they began to shape diplomatic and military strategy. As Senator Orville Platt of Connecticut said in 1893, "A policy of isolation did well enough when we were an embryo nation, but today things are different."

Not all businessmen in the 1890s approved of risky new ventures in Asia and Latin America. Some thought it more important in 1897 to se-

cure recovery from the depression than little islands in Asia.

But the decrease in domestic consumption during the depression also encouraged businessmen to expand into new markets to sell surplus goods. They were led by the newly formed National Association of Manufacturers, which emphasized in 1896 "that the trade centres of Central and South America are natural markets for American products."

Despite the depression of the 1890s, products spewed from American factories at a staggering rate. The United States moved from fourth in the world in manufacturing in 1870 to first in 1900. The United States led the world not only in railroad construction (206,631 miles of tracks in 1900, four times more than in 1870) but also in agricultural machinery and mass-produced technological products such as sewing machines, electrical implements, telephones, cash registers, elevators, and cameras. Manufactured goods grew nearly fivefold between 1895 and 1914.

Correspondingly, the total value of American exports tripled, jumping from $434 million in 1866 to nearly $1.5 billion in 1900. By 1914, exports had risen to $2.5 billion, a 67 percent increase over 1900. The increased trade continued to go mainly to Europe. Nevertheless, interest in Asian markets grew, especially as agricultural production continued to increase and prices remained low. Farmers dreamed of selling their surplus wheat to China. James J. Hill of the Great Northern Railroad promoted their hopes by printing wheat cookbooks in various Asian languages and distributed them in the Far East, hoping to fill his westward-bound boxcars and merchant ships with wheat and other grains.

American direct investments abroad also increased, growing from about $634 million to $2.6 billion between 1897 and 1914. At the turn of the century came the formation and growth of America's biggest multinational corporations—the United Fruit Company, Alcoa Aluminum, Amalgamated Copper, Du Pont, American Tobacco, and others, which supported an aggressive foreign policy and the expansion of America's role in the world.

Patriotism: Asserting National Power

American interest in investments, markets, and raw materials abroad reflected a determination not to be left out of the international competition among European powers and Japan for commercial spheres of influence and colonies in Asia, Africa, and Latin America. In 1898, a State Department memorandum stated that "we can no longer afford to disregard international rivalries now that we ourselves have become a com-petitor in the world-wide struggle for trade." The national state, then, had a role in supporting commercial interests.

More Americans, however, saw national glory and greatness as legitimate motivations for expansionism. In the late 1890s, a group of young men centered on Assistant Secretary of the Navy Theodore Roosevelt and Senator Henry Cabot Lodge of Massachusetts emerged as highly influential in shifting from "continentalism" to what Lodge called the "large policy."

The writings of Alfred Thayer Mahan, a naval strategist and author of several books on the importance of sea power to national greatness, greatly influenced the new foreign policy elite. Mahan argued that in a world of Darwinian struggle for survival, national power depended on naval supremacy, control of sea lanes, and vigorous development of domestic resources and foreign markets. He advocated colonies in both the Caribbean and the Pacific, linked by a canal built and controlled by the United States. Strong nations, Mahan wrote, had a special responsibility to dominate weak ones. In a world of constant "strife," where "everywhere nation is arrayed against nation," it was imperative that Americans begin "to look outward." National pride and glory would surely follow.

Piety: The Missionary Impulse

As Mahan's statements suggest, a strong sense of duty and the missionary ideal of doing good for others also motivated expansionism. A statesman once boasted that "with God's help, we will lift Shanghai up and up, ever up, until it is just like Kansas City." Secretary of State Richard Olney agreed, saying in 1898 that "the mission of this country is . . . to forego no fitting opportunity to further the progress of civilization." Motivated by America's sense of itself as a model nation, such statements sometimes rationalized the exploitation and oppression of weaker peoples.

As a missionary put it in 1885, "The Christian nations are subduing the world in order to make mankind free." Josiah Strong, a Congregational minister, was one of the most ardent advocates of American missionary expansionism. Although his book *Our Country* (1885) focused on internal threats to American social order, in a long chapter titled "The Future of the Anglo-Saxon Race," Strong argued that in the struggle for survival among nations, the United States had emerged as the center of Anglo-Saxonism and was "divinely commissioned" to spread the blessings of political liberty, Protestant Christianity, and civilized values over the earth. "This powerful race," he wrote, "will move down upon Mexico, down upon Central and South America, out upon the islands of the sea, over upon Africa and beyond."

Missionaries carried similar Western values to non-Christian lands around the world. China was a favorite target. The number of American Protestant missionaries in China increased from 436 in 1874 to 5,462 in 1914. The estimated number of Christian converts in China jumped from 5,000 in 1870 to nearly 100,000 in 1900. Many Chinese reformist intellectuals who absorbed Western ideas in Christian mission colleges went on to lead the Revolution of 1912 that ended the Manchu dynasty. Economic relations between China and the United States increased at approximately the same rate as missionary activity. The number of American firms in China grew from 50 to 550 between 1870 and 1930, while trade increased 1,500 percent.

Politics: Manipulating Public Opinion

During the expansionist 1890s, public opinion over international issues loomed large in presidential politics for the first time in American history. This process was helped by the growth of a highly competitive popular press, the penny daily newspaper, which brought international issues before a mass readership. When several newspapers in New York City, notably William

Randolph Hearst's *Journal* and Joseph Pulitzer's *World,* competed to see which could stir up more public support for the Cuban rebels in their struggle for independence from Spain, politicians ignored the public outcry at their peril. Daily reports of Spanish atrocities in 1896 and 1897 kept public moral outrage constantly before President McKinley as he considered his course of action.

Politics, then, joined profits, patriotism, and piety in motivating the expansionism of the 1890s. These four impulses interacted to influence the Spanish-American War, the annexation of the Philippine Islands, and the foreign policy of President Theodore Roosevelt.

CUBA AND THE PHILIPPINES

Lying 90 miles off the southern tip of Florida, Cuba had been the object of intense American interest for a half century. Although successful in thwarting American adventurism in Cuba in the 1850s, Spain was unable to halt the continuing struggle of the Cuban people for relief from exploitive labor on the sugar plantations, even after slavery itself ended, and for a measure of autonomy. The most recent uprising, which lasted from 1868 to 1878, had raised tensions between Spain and the United States; it also whetted the Cuban appetite not just for reforms but for complete independence.

The Road to War

When the Cuban revolt flared up anew in 1895, the Madrid government sent General "Butcher" Weyler with 50,000 troops to quell the disturbance. When Weyler began herding rural Cuban citizens into "reconcentration" camps, Americans were outraged. An outpouring of sympathy swept the nation, especially as reports came back of the horrible suffering in the camps.

The Cuban struggle appealed to a country convinced of its role as protector of the weak and defender of the right of self-determination. One editorial deplored Spanish "injustice, oppression, extortion, and demoralization" while describing the Cubans as heroic freedom fighters "largely inspired by our glorious example of beneficent free institutions and successful self-government." But neither President Cleveland nor President McKinley wanted a war over Cuba.

Self-interested motives also played a role. American companies had invested extensively in Cuban sugar plantations. By 1897, trade with Cuba reached $27 million per year. Appeals for reform had much to do with ensuring a stable environment for further investments, as well as for the protection of sugar fields against the ravages of civil war.

A new government in Madrid recalled Weyler, but conditions in Cuba worsened. Although McKinley skillfully resisted the pressure for war, the fundamental causes of the war—Spanish intransigence in the face of persistent Cuban rebellion and American sugar interests and sympathies for the underdog—were seemingly unstoppable.

Events early in 1898 sparked the outbreak of hostilities. Rioting in Havana intensified both Spanish repression and American outrage. As pressures for war increased, a letter from the Spanish minister to the United States, Depuy de Lôme, calling McKinley a "weak" hypocritical politician, was intercepted by spies and made public. Hearst's New York *Journal* called de Lôme's letter "the worst insult to the United States in its history."

A second event was the sinking of the U.S. battleship *Maine,* sent to Havana harbor to protect American citizens. Early in the evening on February 15, a tremendous explosion blew up the *Maine,* killing 262 men. American advocates of war, who assumed Spanish responsibility, called immediately for intervention. Newspaper publishers broadcast slogans like "Remember the *Maine*! To hell with *Spain*!"

Assistant Secretary of the Navy Theodore Roosevelt, who had been preparing for war for some time, said that he would "give anything if President McKinley would order the fleet to Havana tomorrow." Although an official board of inquiry concluded that an external submarine mine caused the disaster, probably a faulty boiler or some other internal problem set off the explosion, a possibility even Roosevelt later conceded.

After the sinking of the *Maine,* Roosevelt took advantage of Secretary of the Navy John D. Long's absence from the office one day to send a cable to Commodore George Dewey, commander of the United States' Pacific fleet at Hong Kong. Roosevelt ordered Dewey to fill his ships with coal and, "in the event" of a declaration of war with Spain, to sail to the Philippines and make sure "the Spanish squadron does not leave the Asiatic coast."

Roosevelt's act was not impetuous, as Long thought, but consistent with naval policies he had been urging upon his more cautious superior for more than a year. Influenced by Mahan, Roosevelt wanted to enlarge the navy, whose growth had been restricted for years. He also believed that the United States should construct an interoceanic canal, acquire the Danish West Indies (the Virgin Islands), annex Hawaii outright, and oust Spain from Cuba. As Roosevelt told McKinley late in 1897, he was putting the navy in "the best possible shape" for "when war began."

The public outcry over the *Maine* drowned out McKinley's efforts to calm the populace and avoid war. Nor was he successful in wringing concessions from Spain. On April 11, 1898, therefore, the president sent an ambiguous message to Congress that seemed to call for war. Two weeks later, Congress authorized the use of troops against Spain and passed a resolution recognizing Cuban independence, actions amounting to a declaration of war. In a significant additional resolution, the Teller Amendment, Congress stated that the United States had no intentions of annexing Cuba, guaranteeing the Cubans the right to determine their own destiny.

An imaginative reconstruction of the celebrated charge of "Teddy's Rough Riders" up Kettle Hill, which so greatly helped Roosevelt's political career.

"A Splendid Little War"

As soon as war was declared, Theodore Roosevelt resigned his post in the Navy Department and prepared to lead a cavalry unit in the war. Black regiments as well as white headed to Tampa, Florida, to be shipped to Cuba. Blacks were especially sympathetic to the Cuban people's struggle. As one soldier wrote in his journal, "Oh, God! at last we have taken up the sword to enforce the divine rights of a people who have been unjustly treated." As the four-month war neared its end in August, John Hay wrote Roosevelt that "it has been a splendid little war; begun with the highest motives, carried on with magnificent intelligence and spirit."

It was a "splendid" war. It was short and relatively easy. Naval battles were won almost without return fire. At both major naval engagements, Manila Bay and Santiago Bay, only two Americans died, one of them from heat prostration while stoking coal. The islands of Guam and Puerto Rico were taken virtually without a shot. Only 385 men died from Spanish bullets, but over 5,000 succumbed to tropical diseases.

The Spanish-American War was splendid in other ways, as letters from American soldiers suggest. One young man wrote that his comrades were all "in good spirits" because oranges

and coconuts were so plentiful and "every trooper has his canteen full of lemonade all the time." Another, however, wrote that "words are inadequate to express the feeling of pain and sickness when one has the fever. For about a week every bone in my body ached and I did not care much whether I lived or not."

Roosevelt's brush with death at Las Guásimas and his celebrated charge up Kettle Hill near Santiago, his flank protected by black troops, made three-inch headlines and advanced not only his political career but also the cause of expansion and national glory.

The Philippines Debates and War

Roosevelt's ordering Dewey to Manila initiated a chain of events that led to the annexation of the Philippines. The most crucial battle of the Spanish-American War occurred on May 1, 1898, when Dewey destroyed the Spanish fleet in Manila Bay. McKinley then began the process of shaping American public opinion to accept the "political, commercial [and] humanitarian" reasons for annexing all 7,000 Philippine islands, Guam, and Puerto Rico. The Treaty of Paris gave the United States all of them in exchange for a $20 million payment to Spain.

The treaty was sent to the Senate for ratification during the winter of 1898–1899. As we have seen, the Senate debate was ended when fighting broke out between American soldiers and Aguinaldo's insurgents near Manila. The Filipino-American War triggered national debates over what to do with the Philippines. After several months of quietly seeking advice and listening to public opinion, McKinley finally recommended annexation. Fellow Republicans confirmed McKinley's arguments for annexation, adding even more racist ones. Filipinos were described as childlike, savage, stunted in size, dirty, and backward. Roosevelt called Aguinaldo "a renegade Pawnee" and said that the Filipinos had no right "to administer the country which they happen to be occupying." The attitudes favoring annexation, therefore, asserted Filipino inferiority and incapacity for self-rule while also reflecting America's proud sense of itself in 1900 as a nation of civilized order and progress.

Other Americans were not so positive about such "progress." A small but vocal group, the Anti-Imperialist League, vigorously opposed war and annexation. They included a cross-section of American dignitaries: ex-Presidents Harrison and Cleveland, Samuel Gompers and Andrew Carnegie, William James, Jane Addams, Mark Twain, and many others.

The major anti-imperialist arguments pointed out how imperialism in general and annexation in particular were unconstitutional and contradicted American ideals regarding the right of self-determination. Moreover, social reforms needed at home demanded American energies and money before foreign expansionism.

Not all anti-imperialist arguments were so noble. One position alleged that since the Filipinos were nonwhite, Catholic, and inferior in size and intelligence, they were unassimilable. Annexation would lead to miscegenation and contamination of Anglo-Saxon blood. Senator Ben Tillman of South Carolina opposed "incorporating any more colored men into the body politic." Some saw the Philippines as a burden that would require American troops to fight distant Asian wars.

The last argument became fact when Private Grayson's encounter started the Filipino-American War. Before it was over in 1902, some 126,500 American troops served in the Philippines, 4,234 died there, and 2,800 more were wounded. The cost was $400 million. Filipino casualties were much worse. In addition to the 18,000 killed in combat, an estimated 200,000 Filipinos died of famine and disease as American soldiers burned villages and destroyed crops and livestock in order to disrupt the economy and deny rebel fighters their food supply. General Jacob H. Smith ordered his troops to "kill and burn and the more you kill and burn, the better you will please me."

As U.S. treatment of the Filipinos during the war became more and more like Spanish mistreatment of the Cubans, the hypocrisy of American behavior became even more evident, especially to black American soldiers who identified with the dark-skinned insurgents. "I feel sorry for these people," a sergeant in the 24th Infantry wrote. "You have no idea the way these people are treated by the Americans here."

The war starkly exposed the hypocrisies of shouldering the white man's burden. Upon reading a report that 8,000 Filipinos had been killed in the first year of the war, Carnegie wrote a letter, dripping with sarcasm, congratulating McKinley for "civilizing the Filipinos. . . . About 8,000 of them have been completely civilized and sent to Heaven. I hope you like it." Another writer penned a devastating one-liner: "Dewey took Manila with the loss of one man—and all our institutions."

The anti-imperialists failed either to prevent annexation or to interfere with the war effort. They were seen as an older, conservative, elite group of Americans, out of tune with the period of exuberant national pride, prosperity, and promise.

Expansionism Triumphant

By 1900, the United States had acquired several island territories, thereby joining the other great world powers. But questions arose over what to do with the new territories. What was their status? Were they colonies? Would they be granted statehood? Did the native peoples of Hawaii, Puerto Rico, Guam, and the Philippines have the same rights as American citizens on the mainland? The answers to these difficult questions emerged in a series of Supreme Court cases, congressional acts, and presidential decisions.

Although slightly different governing systems were worked out for each new territory, the solution in each was to define its status somewhere between subject colony and candidate for statehood. Territorial status came closest. The native people were usually allowed to elect their own legislature for internal lawmaking but had governors and other judicial and administrative officials appointed by the American president. The question of constitutional rights was resolved by deciding that Hawaiians and Puerto Ricans, for example, would be treated differently from Texans and Oregonians. In the "insular cases" of 1901, the Supreme Court ruled that these people would achieve citizenship and constitutional rights only when Congress said they were ready. To the question "Does the Constitution follow the flag?" the answer, as Secretary of State Elihu Root put it, was, "Ye-es, as near as I can make out the Constitution follows the flag—but doesn't quite catch up with it."

McKinley's resounding defeat of Bryan in 1900 clearly revealed the optimistic, nationalistic spirit of the American people, who strongly favored annexation of the Philippines. In the closing weeks of the campaign, Bryan and the Democrats shied away from criticizing the war as imperialist, but Bryan fared no better on other issues. The McKinley forces rightly claimed that under four years of Republican rule, more money, jobs, thriving factories, and manufactured goods had been created. Moreover, McKinley pointed to the tremendous growth in American prestige abroad. Spain had been kicked out of Cuba, and the American flag flew in many places around the globe.

Within one year, the active expansionist, Theodore Roosevelt, went from assistant secretary of the navy to colonel of the Rough Riders to governor of New York. Some Republican politicos sought to slow him down by nominating him for vice president at the Republican convention in 1900. But six months into McKinley's second term, the president was shot and killed by an anarchist, the third presidential assassination in less than 40 years. "Now look," exclaimed party boss Mark Hanna, who had opposed putting Roosevelt on the ticket, "that

damned cowboy is President of the United States!"

ROOSEVELT'S ENERGETIC DIPLOMACY

As president from 1901 to 1909, and as the most dominating American personality for the 15 years between 1897 and 1912, Roosevelt made much fuss and noise about the activist role he thought the United States should play in the world. His energetic foreign policy in Latin America, Asia, and Europe paved the way for the vital role of the United States as a world power.

Foreign Policy as Darwinian Struggle

Roosevelt's personal principles and presidential policies went together. He was an advocate of both individual physical fitness and collective national strength. His ideal was "a nation of men, not weaklings." To be militarily prepared and to fight well were the tests of racial superiority and national greatness. Powerful nations, like individuals, Roosevelt believed, had a duty to cultivate qualities of vigor, strength, courage, and moral commitment to civilized values. In practical terms this meant developing natural resources, building large navies, and being ever prepared to fight. "I never take a step in foreign policy," he wrote, "unless I am assured that I shall be able eventually to carry out my will by force."

Although known for his advice to "speak softly and carry a big stick," Roosevelt often not only wielded a large stick but spoke loudly as well. Despite his bluster, Roosevelt was usually restrained in the exercise of force. He won the Nobel Peace Prize in 1906 for helping to end the Russo-Japanese War. The purpose of the big stick and the loud talk was to preserve order and peace in the world. "To be prepared for war," he

The "big stick" became a memorable image in American diplomacy as Teddy Roosevelt sought to make the United States a policeman not only of the Caribbean basin but also of the whole world.

said, "is the most effectual means to promote peace."

Roosevelt divided the world into civilized and uncivilized nations, the former usually defined as Anglo-Saxon and English-speaking. The civilized nations had a responsibility to "police" the uncivilized, not only maintaining order but also spreading superior values and institutions. Roosevelt regarded this "international police power" as the "white man's burden," a phrase originated by English imperialist author Rudyard Kipling.

Roosevelt also believed in the balance of power. Strong, advanced nations like the United States had a duty to use their power to preserve order and peace. The 1900 census had recently revealed that the United States, with 75 million people, was much more populous than Great Britain, France, or Germany. Since all of these

nations had many colonies in Asia and Africa it seemed time for Americans to exercise a greater role in world affairs, and to assert its primacy in the Western Hemisphere.

Roosevelt developed a highly personal style of diplomacy. Rather than relying on the Department of State, he preferred face-to-face contact and personal exchange of letters with foreign ambassadors, ministers, and heads of state. A British emissary observed that Roosevelt had a "powerful personality" and a commanding knowledge of the world. As a result, ministries from London to Tokyo respected both the president and the power of the United States.

"In a crisis the duty of a leader is to lead," Roosevelt said. When he wanted Panama, Roosevelt bragged later, "I took the Canal Zone," and while Congress debated his actions, the building of the canal across Panama began. Roosevelt's energetic executive activism in foreign policy set a pattern followed by nearly every twentieth-century American president.

Taking the Panama Canal

In justifying the intervention of 2,600 American troops in Honduras and Nicaragua in 1906, Philander Knox, secretary of state from 1909 to 1913, said, "We are in the eyes of the world, and because of the Monroe Doctrine, held responsible for the order of Central America, and its proximity to the Canal makes the preservation of peace in that neighborhood particularly necessary." The Panama Canal was not yet finished when Knox spoke, but it had already become a vital cornerstone of United States policy in the region.

Panama was a province of Colombia and could not negotiate with the United States. In 1903, the Colombian senate rejected a treaty negotiated by Secretary of State John Hay, but mostly on nationalistic, not financial, grounds. Roosevelt, angered by this rebuff, called the Colombians "Dagoes" and "foolish and homicidal corruptionists," who tried to "hold us up" like highway robbers.

Aware of Roosevelt's fury, encouraged by hints of American support, and eager for the economic benefits the building of a canal would bring, Panamanian nationalists in 1903 staged a revolution led by several rich families and a Frenchman, Philippe Bunau-Varilla of the New Panama Canal Company. The bloodless revolution occurred on November 3; the next day, Panama declared its independence. On November 6, the United States officially recognized the new government in Panama. Although Roosevelt did not formally encourage the revolution, it would not have occurred without American money and the presence of American troops, who prevented Colombian troops from landing to suppress the rebellion.

On November 18, Hay and Bunau-Varilla signed a treaty establishing the American right to build and operate a canal through Panama and to exercise "titular sovereignty" over the 10-mile-wide Canal Zone. The Panamanian government protested the treaty, to no avail, and a later government called it "the treaty that no Panamanian signed."

Policeman of the Caribbean

As late as 1901, the Monroe Doctrine was still regarded, according to Roosevelt, as the "equivalent to an open door in South America." To the United States, this meant that although no nation had a right "to get territorial possessions," all nations had equal commercial rights in the Western Hemisphere south of the Rio Grande. But as American investments poured into Central America and Caribbean islands, that policy changed to one of the primary right of the United States to dominant influence in the lands of the Caribbean basin. Order was indispensable for profitable economic activity.

After the Spanish were expelled from Cuba, the United States supervised the island under Military Governor General Leonard Wood until 1902, when the Cubans elected their own congress and president. The United States honored Cuban independence, as it had promised to do in the Teller Amendment. But through the Platt Amendment, which Cubans reluctantly attached to their constitution in 1901, the United States obtained many economic rights in Cuba, a naval base at Guantanamo Bay, and the right of intervention if Cuban sovereignty were ever threatened. Newspapers in Havana assailed this violation of their newfound independence.

American policy intended to make Cuba a model of how a newly independent nation could achieve orderly self-government with only minimal guidance. When in 1906 an internal political crisis threatened the infant nation, however, Roosevelt sent warships and troops, at Cuba's request "to restore order and peace and public confidence." As he left office in 1909, Roosevelt proudly proclaimed that "we have done our best to put Cuba on the road to stable and orderly government." The road was paved with sugar. United States trade with Cuba increased from $27 million in the decade before 1898 to an average of $43 million per year during the following decade. Along with economic development, American political and even military involvement in Cuban affairs continued throughout the century. The Platt Amendment provided the excuse for United States intervention at nearly every Cuban election, because the losing side would call on the United States to overturn the results—a pattern that hampered the independent development of the Cuban political system.

The pattern repeated itself throughout the Caribbean region. United States warships discouraged European intervention in the Dominican Republic in 1904. Two years later, the United States intervened in Guatemala and Nicaragua, where American bankers controlled nearly 50 percent of all trade.

Roosevelt's policy of intervention as "an international police power," he said in his annual message in 1904, was necessary to have "stable, orderly and prosperous neighbors." This doctrine, known as the Roosevelt Corollary to the Monroe Doctrine, justified American intervention in Caribbean countries to protect property, loans, and investments and to maintain order. This meant supporting the brutal regimes of wealthy elites who owned most of the land, suppressed the poor and efforts for reform, and acted as surrogates of American policy.

After 1904, the Roosevelt Corollary was invoked in several Caribbean countries. Intervention usually required the landing of U.S. Marines to counter the threat posed by political instability and bankruptcy to American economic interests: railroads, mines, and the production of sugar, bananas, and coffee. Roosevelt's successors, William Howard Taft and Woodrow Wilson, pursued the same interventionist policy. Later presidents, including Lyndon Johnson, Ronald Reagan, George Bush, and Bill Clinton, would do likewise.

Opening the Door to China

Another area that attracted American commercial interest was China. Throughout the nineteenth century, American relations with China were restricted to a small but profitable trade. While Britain, France, Germany, and Russia had advantageous trade treaties with China as well as spheres of influence, Americans tended to disdain European imperialism, though they, too, wanted to participate in the trade. American attitudes toward the Chinese people reflected this confusion of motives. Some Americans held an idealized view of China as the center of Eastern wisdom and saw a "special relationship" between the two nations. But the dominant American attitude viewed the Chinese as heathen, exotic, backward, and immoral.

The annexation of Hawaii, Samoa, and the Philippines in 1898–1899 convinced Secretary of State Hay that the United States should announce its own policy for China. The result was the Open Door notes of 1899–1900, which declared the principle of equal access to commercial rights in China by all nations and called on all countries to respect the "territorial and administrative integrity" of China. This second principle opened the way for a larger American role in Asia, offering China protection from foreign invasions and preserving a balance of power in the Far East.

An early test of this new role came during the Boxer Rebellion in 1900. The Boxers were a society of young traditionalist Chinese in revolt against both the Manchu dynasty and the growing Western presence and influence in China. During the summer of 1900, fanatical Boxers killed some 242 missionaries and other foreign-

United States Involvement in Central America and the Caribbean, 1898-1939

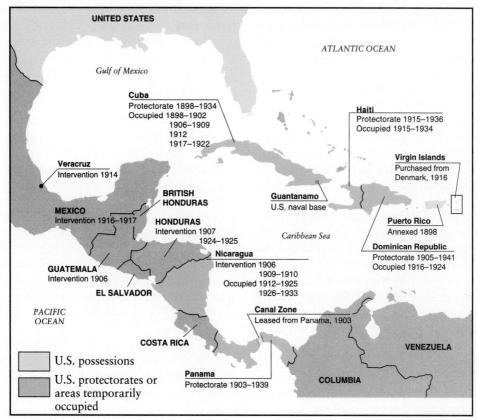

UNITED STATES

ATLANTIC OCEAN

Gulf of Mexico

Cuba
Protectorate 1898–1934
Occupied 1898–1902
1906–1909
1912
1917–1922

Haiti
Protectorate 1915–1936
Occupied 1915–1934

Virgin Islands
Purchased from
Denmark, 1916

Veracruz
Intervention 1914

**BRITISH
HONDURAS**

Guantanamo
U.S. naval base

MEXICO
Intervention 1916–1917

HONDURAS
Intervention 1907
1924–1925

Caribbean Sea

Puerto Rico
Annexed 1898

Nicaragua
Intervention 1906
1909–1910
Occupied 1912–1925
1926–1933

Dominican Republic
Protectorate 1905–1941
Occupied 1916–1924

GUATEMALA
Intervention 1906

EL SALVADOR

*PACIFIC
OCEAN*

Canal Zone
Leased from Panama, 1903

| | U.S. possessions |
| | U.S. protectorates or areas temporarily occupied |

COSTA RICA

Panama
Protectorate 1903–1939

COLUMBIA

VENEZUELA

ers and besieged the foreign legation quarter of Peking. Eventually, an international military force of 19,000 troops, including some 3,000 Americans sent from the Philippines, marched on Peking to end the siege.

Although the American relationship with China was plagued by the exclusionist immigration policy, the idea that the United States had a unique guardian relationship with China persisted into the twentieth century. Since Japan had ambitions in China, this created a rivalry between Japan and the United States, testing the American commitment to preserve the Open

Door in China, the territorial integrity of China, and the balance of power in Asia.

Japan and the Balance of Power

Because of population pressures on the limited land mass of Japan, as well as war and the quest for economic opportunities, Japanese immigration to the United States dramatically increased around the turn of the century. Coming first as unmarried males working on western railroads and in Pacific Coast canneries, mines, and logging camps, immigrants from Japan increased from 25,000 in the 1890s to 125,000 between 1901 and 1908. Like the earlier Chinese immigrants, they were met with nativist hostility and discrimination. At Roosevelt's instigation, the Japanese agreed to limit the migration of unskilled workers to the United States in a gentleman's agreement signed in 1907.

Roosevelt also relied on the use of diplomacy and negotiation in his effort to balance Asian powers against one another. The Boxer Rebellion of 1900 left Russia, which had 50,000 troops in Manchuria, the strongest nation in eastern Asia. Roosevelt's admiration for the Japanese as a "fighting" people and a valuable factor in "the civilization of the future" contrasted with his low respect for the Russians, whom he described as "corrupt," "treacherous," and "incompetent." As Japan moved into Korea and Russia into Manchuria, Roosevelt hoped that each would check the growing power of the other.

Because of increasing Russian strength, Roosevelt welcomed news in 1904 that Japan had launched a successful surprise attack on Port Arthur in Manchuria, beginning the Russo-Japanese War. He was equally pleased when the Japanese expressed interest in ending the war. His goal was to achieve peace and leave a balanced situation. "It is best," he wrote, that Russia be left "face to face with Japan so that each may have a moderative action on the other." The negotiations and resulting treaty were carried out in the summer of 1905 near Portsmouth, New Hampshire. No single act better symbolizes the new posture of American power and presence in the world than the signing of a peace treaty ending a war in Manchuria between Russia and Japan halfway around the globe in New Hampshire!

The Treaty of Portsmouth left Japan dominant in Manchuria, but in return, in the Root-Takahira Agreement of 1908, Japan promised to honor U.S. control in the Philippines and to make no further encroachments into China.

These agreements over territorial divisions barely covered up the tensions in Japanese-American relations. Some Japanese were angry that they had not received in the Portsmouth Treaty the indemnities they had wanted from Russia, and they blamed Roosevelt. American insensitivity to the immigration issue also left bad feelings. In Manchuria, U.S. Consul General Willard Straight aggressively pushed an anti-Japanese program of financing capital investment projects in banking and railroads. The United States was in Japan's way, and rumors of war circulated in the world press.

It was clearly time for Roosevelt's version of the "big stick." In 1907, he told Secretary of State Root that he was "more concerned over the Japanese situation than almost any other. Thank Heaven we have the navy in good shape." From 1900 to 1905, outlays to the navy rose from $56 to $117 million. Such a naval spending binge was without precedent in peacetime. In 1907, Roosevelt sent his new, modernized "Great White Fleet" on a goodwill tour around the world. The first stop was the Japanese port of Yokohama. For the time being, the balance of power in Asia was preserved.

Preventing War in Europe

Although the United States was actively involved in Latin America and Asia, toward Europe the traditional policies of neutrality and nonentanglement continued. Still, there was an American role to be played even there, and Roosevelt was eager to play it.

Roosevelt believed that the most serious threats to world peace and civilized order lay in relationships among Germany, Great Britain, and France. He established two fundamental policies toward Europe that with only minor variations would define the U.S. role throughout the century. The first was to make friendship with Great Britain the cornerstone of U.S. policy. The second was to prevent the outbreak of a general war in Europe among strong nations.

Toward this end, Roosevelt depended on his personal negotiating skills and began the practice of summit diplomacy.

Throughout most of the nineteenth century, England was America's chief enemy and commercial rival. But the Venezuelan crisis and a number of other events at the turn of the century shocked the United States and England into an awareness of their mutual interests. Roosevelt supported British imperialism because he favored the dominance of "the English-speaking race" and believed that England was "fighting the battle of civilization." Furthermore, both nations worried about growing German power in Europe, Africa, and East Asia. As German naval power increased, England had to bring its fleet closer to home. Friendly allies were needed to police parts of the world formerly patrolled by the British navy. England therefore concluded a mutual-protection treaty with Japan in 1902 and willingly let the Americans police Central America and the Caribbean Sea. As Roosevelt left the presidency in 1909, one of his final acts was to proclaim the special American friendship with Great Britain.

German Kaiser Wilhelm II often underestimated the solidity of Anglo-American friendship and thought that Roosevelt was really pro-German, an error the American president skillfully used. The Moroccan crisis in 1905 and 1906 is illustrative. European powers competed for colonies and spheres of influence in Africa as well in Asia. Germany resented French dominance along the North African coast in Morocco. The kaiser precipitated a crisis in the summer of 1905 by delivering a bellicose speech in Casablanca, Morocco, intended to split the British and French entente and to force an opening of commercial doors in Morocco. As war threatened, Roosevelt intervened, arranging a conference of European powers in Algeciras, Spain, to avert conflict. The treaty signed in 1906 prevented war and settled the issues of commerce and police administration in Morocco favorably for the French.

In 1911 retired president Roosevelt wrote that there would be nothing worse than that "Germany should ever overthrow England and establish the supremacy in Europe she aims at." German interest "to try her hand in America," he thought, would surely follow. To avert such horrors, Roosevelt's policy for Europe included cementing friendship with England and, while maintaining official neutrality, using diplomacy to prevent hostilities among European powers. The relationship between Great Britain and Germany continued to deteriorate, however, leading to the outbreak of World War I in 1914.

CONCLUSION

THE RESPONSIBILITIES OF POWER

Since the earliest settlements in Massachusetts Bay, Americans had struggled with the dilemma of how to do good in a world that did wrong. Roosevelt said in 1910 that because of "strength and geographical situation," the United States had itself become "more and more, the balance of power of the whole world." This ominous responsibility was also an opportunity to extend American economic, political, and moral influence around the globe.

As president in the first decade of the twentieth century, Roosevelt established aggressive American policies toward the rest of the world. Americans dominated and policed Central

America and the Caribbean Sea, annexed the Philippines, and worked to preserve the balance of power in Asia. In Europe, the United States sought to remain neutral, cement Anglo-American friendship, and prevent "civilized" nations from going to war.

Throughout the period, the fundamental ambivalence of America's sense of itself as a model "city on a hill," an example to others, remained. But Americans learned that it was difficult for the United States to be both responsible and good, both powerful and loved. The American people thus learned to experience both the satisfactions and the burdens, the profits and the costs, of the missionary role.

Recommended Reading

The best overviews of the emergence of America as a world power in the late nineteenth century, each emphasizing different motives for expansion, are Walter La Feber, *The New Empire: An Interpretation of American Expansion, 1860–1898* (1963); Robert Beisner, *From the Old Diplomacy to the New, 1865–1900* (1975); and Charles Campbell, *The Transformation of American Foreign Relations, 1865–1900* (1976).

On the immediate causes of expansionism in the 1890s and the war with Spain, see David Healy, *U.S. Expansion: Imperialist Urge in the 1890s* (1970). Particular aspects of American expansion are discussed in William Widenor, *Henry Cabot Lodge and the Search for an American Foreign Policy* (1980); and Emily Rosenberg, *Spreading the American Dream: American Economic and Cultural Expansion, 1890–1945* (1982). McKinley's leadership is covered in Lewis Gould, *The Presidency of William McKinley* (1980); and John Dobson, *Reticent Expansionism: The Foreign Policy of William McKinley* (1988).

On the Spanish-American War, see David Trask, *The War with Spain in 1898* (1981); and a fascinating account of the war experiences of black soldiers,

Willard Gatewood, Jr., *"Smoked Yankees" and the Struggle for Empire: Letters from Negro Soldiers, 1898–1902* (1971). The brutal suppression of the Philippine rebels is described in Stanley Karnow, *In Our Image: America's Empire in the Philippines* (1989); and Richard Welch, *Response to Imperialism: The United States and the Philippine-American War, 1899–1902* (1979). Some anti-imperialists are treated in Robert Beisner, *Twelve Against Empire: The Anti-Imperialists, 1898–1900* (1975). Relations with Asian countries are discussed in Ronald Takaki, *Strangers from a Different Shore: A History of Asian Americans* (1989).

The standard work on Roosevelt's foreign policy is Howard Beale, *Theodore Roosevelt and the Rise of America to World Power* (1956). Newer interpretations can be found in Raymond Esthus, *Theodore Roosevelt and the International Rivalries* (1970); and Frederick Marks II, *Velvet on Iron: The Diplomacy of Theodore Roosevelt* (1979). Walter La Feber has documented how thoroughly American interests have dominated Central America in *The Panama Canal* (1978) and *Inevitable Revolutions: The United States in Central America* (1983).

Time Line

1823	Monroe Doctrine
1857	Trade opens with Japan
1867	Alaska purchased from Russia
1870	Failure to annex Santo Domingo (Hispaniola)
1875	Sugar reciprocity treaty with Hawaii
1877	United States acquires naval base at Pearl Harbor
1878	United States acquires naval station in Samoa
1882	Chinese Exclusion Act
1889	First Pan-American Conference
1890	Alfred Mahan publishes *Influence of Sea Power upon History*
1893	Hawaiian coup by American sugar growers
1895	Cuban revolt against Spanish Venezuelan boundary dispute
1896	Weyler's reconcentration policy in Cuba McKinley-Bryan presidential campaign
1897	Theodore Roosevelt's speech at Naval War College

1898	January	De Lôme letter
	February	Sinking of the battleship *Maine*
	April	Spanish-American War; Teller Amendment
	May	Dewey takes Manila Bay
	July	Annexation of Hawaiian Islands
	August	Americans liberate Manila; war ends
	December	Treaty of Paris; annexation of the Philippines

1899	Senate ratifies Treaty of Paris Filipino-American War begins American Samoa acquired
1899–1900	Open Door notes
1900	Boxer Rebellion in China William Mckinley reelected president
1901	Supreme Court insular cases McKinley assassinated; Theodore Roosevelt becomes president
1902	Filipino-American War ends U.S. military occupation of Cuba ends Platt Amendment Venezuela debt crisis
1903	Panamanian revolt and independence Hay–Bunau-Varilla Treaty
1904	Theodore Roosevelt elected president Roosevelt Corollary
1904–1905	Russo-Japanese War ended by treaty signed at Portsmouth, N.H.
1904–1906	United States intervenes in Nicaragua, Guatemala, Cuba
1905–1906	Moroccan crisis
1906	Roosevelt receives Nobel Peace Prize
1907	Gentleman's agreement with Japan
1908	Root-Takahira Agreement
1909	U.S. Navy ("Great White Fleet") sails around the world
1911	U.S. intervenes in Nicaragua
1914	Opening of the Panama Canal World War I begins
1916	Partial home rule granted to the Philippines

part 5

A Modernizing People

1900-1945

The first half of the twentieth century was filled with tumultuous changes: two world wars, the worst economic depression the modern world has endured, and spectacular advances in technology. By 1945, the automobile, the airplane, plastics, radio, television, and the atomic bomb had transformed the country, and most Americans lived in urban areas.

Chapter 21, "The Progressives Confront Industrial Capitalism," discusses progressivism, the first modern American reform movement. It examines the nation's struggle to maintain democratic order in an urban and industrial age and to adapt its institutions to the arrival of millions of immigrants.

Chapter 22, "The Great War," describes U.S. involvement in World War I, a crusade to "make the world safe for democracy," in Woodrow Wilson's words. The wartime situation gave new opportunities to blacks and other minorities and began the process of government–business cooperation that would increase bureaucracy and change the very nature of the American system of free enterprise.

Chapter 23, "Affluence and Anxiety," covers the period between World War I and the stock market crash of 1929—a time of prosperity for some, and of fear and intolerance for others.

Chapter 24, "The Great Depression and the New Deal," focuses on the Depression decade, a time of unprecedented economic collapse, and the New Deal, a major American reform movement that promoted the power of the federal government to stimulate the economy and to pass a variety of social programs.

In Chapter 25, "World War II," we discover that war, rather than the New Deal, ended the Depression. World War II stimulated the economy and at the same time released American crusading zeal in an all-out effort to defeat Germany and Japan. During the war, Americans tended to see the world divided between good and evil; yet the United States emerged as the most prosperous and most powerful nation on earth. The euphoria would not last long as peace devolved into the Cold War and competition with the Soviet Union for world domination.

chapter 21

The Progressives Confront Industrial Capitalism

Frances Kellor received her law degree in 1897 from Cornell University but decided that she was more interested in solving the nation's social problems than in practicing law. She moved to Chicago, studied sociology, and trained herself as a social reformer. Kellor believed passionately that poverty and inequality could be eliminated in America.

Like many progressives, Kellor believed that environment was more important than heredity in determining ability, prosperity, and happiness. Better schools and better housing, she thought, would produce better citizens. Even criminals, she argued, were simply victims of environment. Kellor demonstrated that poor health and deprived childhoods explained the only differences between criminals and college students.

Kellor was an efficient professional. Like the majority of the professional women of her generation, she never married but devoted her life to social research and social reform. She lived for a time at Hull House in Chicago and at the College Settlement in New York, centers not only of social research and reform but also of lively community.

While staying at the College Settlement, Kellor researched and wrote a muckraking study of employment agencies, published in 1904 as *Out of Work*. She revealed how employment agencies exploited immigrants, blacks, and other recent arrivals in the city. Kellor's book, like the writing of most progressives, spilled over with moral outrage. But Kellor went beyond moralism to suggest corrective legislation at the state and national levels.

Convinced of the need for a national movement to push for reform legislation, Kellor helped to found the National Committee for Immigrants in America, which tried to promote a national policy "to make all these people Americans," and a federal bureau to organize the campaign. Eventually she helped establish the Division of Immigrant Education within the Department of Education. A political movement led by

Theodore Roosevelt excited her most. More than almost any other single person, Kellor had been responsible for alerting Roosevelt to the problems the immigrants faced in American cities. When Roosevelt formed the new Progressive Party in 1912, she was one of the many social workers and social researchers who joined him. She campaigned for Roosevelt and directed the Progressive Service Organization, to educate voters in all areas of social justice and welfare after the election. After Roosevelt's defeat and the collapse of the Progressive Party in 1914, Kellor continued to work for Americanization. She spent the rest of her life promoting justice, order, and efficiency and trying to find ways for resolving industrial and international disputes.

Frances Kellor's life illustrates two important aspects of progressivism, the first nationwide reform movement of the modern era: first, a commitment to promote social justice, to assure equal opportunity, and to preserve democracy; and second, a search for order and efficiency in a world complicated by rapid industrialization, immigration, and spectacular urban growth. Progressivism reached a climax in the years from 1900 to 1914. The reform impulse seems to run in cycles in American history, and the progressive movement was one of those times in American history (others were the 1830s, the 1930s, and the 1960s) when a majority of Americans agreed that changes were needed in American society. This chapter traces the important aspects of progressivism, a broad and diverse movement that influenced almost all areas of American life. It examines the social justice movement, life among workers, the reform movements in the cities and states, and finally, progressivism at the national level during the administrations of Theodore Roosevelt and Woodrow Wilson, the first thoroughly modern presidents.

THE SOCIAL JUSTICE MOVEMENT

The "progressive movement" was actually a number of movements focusing on the problems created by a rapidly expanding urban and industrial world. Progressivism had roots in the 1890s, when many reformers were shocked by the devastation caused by the depression of 1893, and they were influenced by reading Henry George's *Progress and Poverty* (1879) and Edward Bellamy's *Looking Backward* (1888), as well as literature of the Social Gospel movement.

The Progressive World View

Intellectually, the progressives were influenced by the Darwinian revolution. They believed that the world was in flux, and they rebelled against the fixed and the formal in every field. One of the philosophers of the movement, John Dewey, wrote that ideas could become instruments for change. William James, in his philosophy of pragmatism, denied that there were universal truths; ideas should be judged by their usefulness. Most of the progressives were environmentalists who were convinced that environment was much more important than heredity in forming character. Thus if one could build better schools and houses, one could make better people and a more perfect society. But they also believed that some groups could be molded and changed more easily than others. Thus progressivism did not usually mean progress for blacks.

Progressivism sought to bring order and efficiency to a world that had been transformed by rapid growth and new technology. The progressive leaders were almost always middle-class, and they quite consciously tried to teach their middle-class values to the immigrants and the working class. They were part of a statistics-minded, realistic generation. They conducted surveys, gathered facts, wrote reports about every conceivable problem, and usually had faith that their reports would lead to change. Their urge to document came out in haunting photographs of young workers taken by Lewis Hine, in the stark and beautiful city paintings by John Sloan. They pondered such questions as: What is the proper relation of government to society? To big business? How much responsibility does society have to care for the poor and needy?

The Muckrakers

One group of writers who exposed corruption and other evils in American society were labeled "muckrakers" by Theodore Roosevelt. Not all muckrakers were reformers—some merely wanted to profit from the scandals—but the reformers learned from their techniques of exposé. Editors of magazines such as *American, McClure's,* and *Cosmopolitan* eagerly published the articles of investigative reporters who wanted to tell the public what was wrong in American society.

Lincoln Steffens, a young California jour-

nalist, wrote articles for *McClure's* exposing the connections between respectable urban businessmen and corrupt politicians. When published in 1904 as *The Shame of the Cities,* Steffens's account became a battle cry for people determined to clean up the graft in city government. Ida Tarbell, a teacher turned journalist, revealed John D. Rockefeller's ruthless ways and his unfair business practices in her *History of the Standard Oil Company* (1904).

After Steffens and Tarbell achieved popular success, many others followed. Realistic fiction also portrayed social problems. For example, Frank Norris in *The Octopus* (1901) dramatized the railroads' stranglehold on the farmers.

Working Women and Children

Nothing disturbed the social justice progressives more than the sight of children, sometimes as young as 8 or 10, working long hours in dangerous and depressing factories. Young people had worked in factories since the beginning of the industrial revolution, but that did not make the practice any less repugnant to the reformers. "Children are put into industry very much as we put in raw material," Jane Addams objected, "and the product we look for is not better men and women, but better manufactured goods."

Florence Kelley was one of the most important leaders in the crusade against child labor. Raised in an upper-class Philadelphia family, she studied law when she could find no attorney in Chicago to argue a child labor case against some of the prominent corporations. She passed the bar exam and argued the cases herself.

Although Kelley and the other child labor reformers won a few cases, they quickly recognized the need for state laws if they were going to have any real influence. Reformers, marshaling their evidence about the tragic effects on growing children of long working hours in dark and damp factories, pressured the Illinois state legislature into passing an anti–child labor law.

Nothing tugged at the heartstrings of the reformers more than the sight of little children, sullen and stunted, working long hours in factory, farm, and mine. These children, coal miners in Pennsylvania, were carefully posed by Lewis Hine while he worked for the National Child Labor Committee in 1911.

A few years later, however, the state supreme court declared the law unconstitutional.

Judicial opposition was one factor leading reformers to the national level in the first decade of the twentieth century. Florence Kelley again led the charge. In 1899, she had become secretary of the National Consumers League, an organization that enlisted consumers in a campaign to lobby elected officials and corporations to ensure that products were produced under safe and sanitary conditions. It was not Kelley, however, but Edgar Gardner Murphy, an Alabama clergyman, who suggested the formation of the National Child Labor Committee. Like many other Social Gospel ministers, Murphy believed that the church should reform society as well as save souls. He was appalled by the number of young children working in southern textile mills, where they were exposed to great danger and condemned to "compulsory ignorance" (because they dropped out of school).

The National Child Labor Committee led a campaign for child labor legislation. While two-thirds of the states passed some form of child

labor law between 1905 and 1907, many had loopholes that exempted a large number of children, including newsboys and youngsters who worked in the theater. Despite reformers' efforts, compulsory school attendance laws did more to reduce the number of children who worked than federal and state laws, which proved difficult to pass and even more difficult to enforce.

The crusade against child labor was a typical social justice reform effort. Its orgins lay in the moral indignation of middle-class reformers. But reform went beyond moral outrage as reformers gathered statistics, took photographs documenting the abuse of children, and used their evidence to push for legislation first on the local level, then in the states, and eventually in Washington.

Like other progressive reform efforts, the battle against child labor was only partly successful. Too many businessmen, both small and large, were profiting from employing children at low wages. And some parents, who often desperately needed the money their children earned in the factories, opposed the reformers and even broke the law to allow their children to work.

In Denver and Chicago, reformers organized juvenile courts where judges had the authority to put delinquent youths on probation, take them from their families and make them wards of the state, or assign them to an institution. The juvenile court often helped prevent young delinquents from adopting a life of crime. Yet the juvenile offender was frequently deprived of all rights of due process, a fact that the Supreme Court finally recognized in 1967, when it ruled that children were entitled to procedural rights when accused of a crime.

Closely connected with the anti–child labor movement was the effort to limit the hours of women's work. It seemed inconsistent to protect a girl until she was 16 and then give her the "right to work from 8 A.M. to 10 P.M., thirteen hours a day, seventy-eight hours a week for $6." Florence Kelley and the National Consumers League led the campaign. In 1908, the Supreme

Lewis Hine, Carolina Cotton Mill, *1908.*

Court, in *Muller* v. *Oregon*, upheld the Oregon ten-hour law largely because reformer Josephine Goldmark had detailed the danger and disease that factory women faced. Most states fell into line with the Supreme Court decision and passed protective legislation for women, though many companies found ways to circumvent the laws. Even ten hours work a day seemed too long to some women. One factory worker stated. "I have four children and have to work hard at home. Make me awful tired. I would like nine hours. I get up at 5:30. When I wash, I have to stay up till one or two o'clock."

By contending that "women are fundamentally weaker than men," the reformers won some protection for women workers. But their arguments that women were weaker than men would eventually be used to reinforce gender segregation of the work force for the next half century.

In addition to working for protective legislation for working women, the social justice pro-

gressives also campaigned for woman suffrage. Addams argued that urban women not only could vote intelligently but also needed the vote to protect, clothe, and feed their families. Women in an urban age, she suggested, needed to be municipal housekeepers. The progressive insistence that all women needed the vote helped to push woman suffrage toward the victory that would come during World War I.

Much more controversial than either votes for women or protective legislation was the movement for birth control. The Comstock Law of 1873 made it illegal to promote or even write about contraceptive devices, but Margaret Sanger, a nurse who had watched poor women suffer from too many births and even die from dangerous illegal abortions, spoke out. Sanger obtained the latest medical and scientific European studies of birth control methods and in 1914 explained in her magazine, *The Woman Rebel,* and in a pamphlet, *Family Limitation,* that women could separate sex from procreation. She was promptly indicted for violation of the postal code and fled to Europe to avoid arrest. Birth control remained controversial and in most states illegal for many years. Yet Sanger helped to bring the topic of sexuality and contraception out into the open. When she returned to the United States in 1921, she founded the American Birth Control League, which became the Planned Parenthood Federation in 1942.

Home and School

The reformers believed that better housing and education could transform the lives of the poor and create a better world. Books such as Jacob Riis's *How the Other Half Lives* (1890) horrified them. With vivid language and haunting photographs, Riis had documented the overcrowded tenements, the damp, dark alleys, and the sickness and despair that affected people who lived in New York's slums. He labored to replace New York's worst slums with parks and playgrounds. In the first decade of the twentieth century, the progressives called attention to the effect of urban overcrowding and tried to pass tenement house laws in several cities, but the laws were often evaded or modified. In 1910, they organized the National Housing Association, and some of them looked ahead to federal laws and even to government-subsidized housing.

The housing reformers combined moral zeal with practical tactics. One reformer's guide, *How to Furnish and Keep House in a Tenement Flat,* recommended "wood-stained and uncluttered furniture surfaces, iron beds with mattresses, and unupholstered chairs. . . . Walls must be painted not papered . . . screens provide privacy in the bedrooms; a few good pictures should grace the walls." But often immigrant family ideals and values differed from those of the middle-class reformers. Despite the reformers' efforts to separate life's functions into separate rooms, most immigrants still crowded into the kitchen and hung religious objects rather than "good pictures" on the walls.

While some middle-class women reformers were concerned about immigrants' housekeeping, others began to realize that the domestic tasks expected of women of all classes kept many of them from taking their full place in society. Charlotte Perkins Gilman, author of *Women and Economics* (1898), dismantled the traditional view of "woman's sphere" and sketched an alternative. Suggesting that entrepreneurs ought to build apartment houses designed to allow women to combine motherhood with careers, she advocated shared kitchen facilities and a common dining room, a laundry run by efficient workers, and a roof-garden day nursery with a professional teacher.

Next to better housing, the progressives stressed better schools as a way to produce better citizens. Public school systems were often rigid and corrupt. Far from producing citizens who would help to transform society, the schools seemed to reinforce the conservative habits that blocked change. A reporter who traveled around the country in 1892 discovered mindless teachers who drilled pupils through repetitive rote learning.

Progressive education, like many other aspects of progressivism, revolted against the rigid and the formal in favor of flexibility and change. John Dewey was the key philosopher of progressive education. Having grown up in Vermont, he tried throughout his life to create a sense of the small rural community in the city. In his laboratory school at the University of Chicago, he experimented with new educational methods. He replaced the school desks, which were bolted down and always faced the front, with seats that could be moved into circles and arranged in small groups. The movable seat, in fact, became one of the symbols of the progressive education movement.

Dewey insisted that the schools be child-centered, not subject-oriented. Teachers should teach children rather than teach history or mathematics. History and math should be related to the students' experience. Students should learn by doing. They should not just learn about democracy; the school itself should operate like a democracy.

Crusades Against Saloons, Brothels, and Movie Houses

Given their faith in the reforming potential of healthy and educated citizens, it was logical that most social justice progressives opposed the sale of alcohol. They saw eliminating drinking as part of the process of reforming the city and conserving human resources.

Americans did drink great quantities of beer, wine, and hard liquor, and the amount they consumed rose rapidly after 1900, peaking between 1911 and 1915. The modern antiliquor movement was spearheaded in the 1880s and 1890s by the Women's Christian Temperance Union and after 1900 by the Anti-Saloon League and a coalition of religious leaders and social reformers. During the progressive era, temperance forces had considerable success in influencing legislation. Seven states passed temperance laws between 1906 and 1912.

The reformers tended to focus on the saloon and its social life. Drug traffic, prostitution, and political corruption all seemed linked to the saloon. Although they never quite understood the role alcohol played in the social life of many ethnic groups, Jane Addams and other settlement workers appreciated the saloon's importance as a neighborhood social center. Addams started a coffeehouse at Hull House in an attempt to lure the neighbors away from the evils of the saloon.

The progressives joined forces with other prohibition groups, and their combined efforts led to victory on December 22, 1917, when Congress sent to the states for ratification a constitutional amendment prohibiting the sale, manufacturing, or importing of intoxicating liquor within the United States. The spirit of sacrifice for the war effort facilitated its rapid ratification.

In addition to the saloon, the progressives saw the urban dance hall and the movie theater as threats to the morals and well-being of young people, especially young women. The motion picture, invented in 1889, developed as an important form of entertainment during the first decade of the twentieth century. But not until World War I, when D. W. Griffith produced long feature films, did the movies begin to attract a middle-class audience. The most popular of these early films was Griffith's *The Birth of a Nation* (1915), a blatantly racist and distorted epic of black debauchery during Reconstruction. Many early films had plots that depicted premarital sex, adultery, and violence, and, unlike later films, many attacked authority and had tragic endings. *The Candidate* (1907) showed an upper-class reform candidate who gets dirt thrown at him for his efforts to clean up the town. The film *Down with Women* (1907) showed well-dressed men denouncing woman suffrage and the incompe-

tence of the weaker sex, but throughout the film only strong women are depicted. In the end, when the hero is arrested, a woman lawyer defends him.

Although reformers disapproved of the dark theaters, often located near saloons, for young immigrant women, who made up the bulk of the audience at most urban movie theaters, the films provided rare exciting moments in their lives. One daughter of strict Italian parents remarked, "The one place I was allowed to go by myself was the movies. I went to the movies for fun. My parents wouldn't let me go anywhere else, even when I was twenty-four."

Saloons, dance halls, and movie theaters all seemed dangerous to progressives interested in improving life in the city because all appeared to be somehow connected with the worst evil of all, prostitution. Campaigns against prostitution had been waged since the early nineteenth century, but they were nothing compared with the progressives' crusade to wipe out what they called "the social evil." All major cities and many smaller ones appointed vice commissions and made elaborate studies of prostitution.

The progressive antivice crusade attracted many kinds of people, for often contradictory reasons. Racists and immigration restrictionists maintained that inferior people—blacks and recent immigrants, especially those from southern and eastern Europe—became prostitutes and pimps. Others had a variety of motives. Most progressives, however, stressed the environmental and especially the economic causes of vice. "Do you suppose I am going back to earn five or six dollars a week in a factory," one prostitute asked an investigator, "when I can earn that amount any night and often much more?"

Despite all their reports and all the publicity, the progressives failed to end prostitution and did virtually nothing to address its roots in poverty. They wiped out a few red-light districts, closed a number of brothels, and managed to push a bill through Congress (the Mann Act of 1910) that prohibited the interstate transport of women for immoral purposes. Perhaps more important, in several states they got the age of consent for women raised, and in 20 states they made the Wassermann test for syphilis mandatory for both men and women before a marriage license could be issued.

THE WORKER IN THE PROGRESSIVE ERA

Progressive reformers sympathized with industrial workers who struggled to earn a living for themselves and their families. The progressives sought protective legislation—particularly for women and children—unemployment insurance, and workers' compensation. But often they had little understanding of what it was really like to sell one's strength by the hour. For example, they supported labor's right to organize at a time when labor had few friends, yet they often opposed the strike as a weapon against management.

Adjusting to Industrial Labor

John Mekras arrived in New York from Greece in 1912 and traveled immediately to Manchester, New Hampshire, where he found a job in the giant Amoskeag textile mill. He did not speak a word of English. He later remembered,

> the man who hands out the jobs sent me to the spinning room. There I don't know anything about the spinning. I'm a farmer ... I don't know what the boss is talking about.

Mekras didn't last long at the mill. He was one of the many industrial workers who had difficulty adjusting to factory work in the early twentieth century.

Many workers, whether they were from Greece, from eastern Europe, from rural Vermont, or from Michigan, confronted a bewildering world based on order and routine. Unlike farm or craft work, factory life was dominated by the clock, the bell tower, and the boss. The workers continued to resist the routine and pace of factory work, and they subtly sabotaged the employers' efforts to control the workplace as they had done in an earlier period (see Chapters 11 and 18). They stayed at home on holidays, took unauthorized breaks, and set their own informal productivity schedules. Often they were fired or quit. In the woolen industry, the annual turnover of workers between 1907 and 1910 was more than 100 percent. In New York needle-worker shops in 1912 and 1913, the turnover rate was over 250 percent. Overall in American industry, one-third of the workers stayed at their jobs less than a year.

This industrial work force, still composed largely of immigrants, had a fluid character. Many migrants, especially those from southern and eastern Europe, expected to stay only for a short time and then return to their homeland. Many men came alone—70 percent in some years. They saved money by living in a boardinghouse. In 1910, two-thirds of the workers in Pittsburgh made less than $12 a week, but by lodging in boardinghouses and paying $2.50 a month for a bed, they could save perhaps one-third of their pay. "Here in America one must work for three horses," one immigrant wrote home. "The work is very heavy, but I don't mind it," another wrote.

About 40 percent of those who immigrated to America in the first decade of the twentieth century returned home, according to one estimate. In years of economic downturn, such as 1908, more Italians and Austro-Hungarians left the United States than entered it. For many immigrants, the American dream never materialized.

The nature of work continued to change in the early twentieth century as industrialists extended late-nineteenth-century efforts to make their factories and their work forces more efficient, productive, and profitable. In some industries, the introduction of new machines revolutionized work and eliminated highly paid

Immigration to the United States, 1900-1920

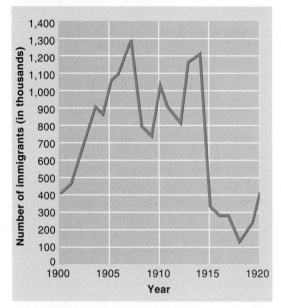

Source: U.S. Bureau of the Census

skilled jobs. Glassblowing machines invented about 1900, for example, replaced thousands of glassblowers or reduced them from craftsmen to workers. Power-driven machines, better-organized operations, and, finally, the moving assembly line, perfected by Henry Ford, transformed the nature of work and turned many laborers into unskilled tenders of machines.

While some skilled weavers and glassblowers were transformed into unskilled operators, the introduction of the machines themselves created the need for new skilled workers. In the auto industry, for example, the new elite workers were the mechanics and tool and die men who kept the assembly line running. Although these new skilled artisans survived, the trend toward mechanization was unstoppable, and even the most skilled workers were eventually removed from making decisions about the production process.

More than machines changed the nature of industrial work. The principles of scientific management, which set out new rules for organizing work, were just as important. The key figure was Frederick Taylor, an engineer at Midvale Steel Company in Philadelphia. Taylor was obsessed with efficiency. He emphasized centralized planning, systematic analysis, and detailed instructions. Most of all, he studied all kinds of workers and timed the various components of their jobs with a stopwatch.

As Taylor himself explained, scientific management meant "the deliberate gathering in on ... management's side of all of the great mass of traditional knowledge, which in the past has been in the heads of the workmen, and in the physical skill and knack of the workman which he has acquired through years of experience." Taylor's approach was designed to reduce the need for skilled workers, to limit workers' scope for self-direction, and to control closely their productivity. Not surprisingly, many workers resented the drive for efficiency and control. "We don't want to work as fast as we are able to," one machinist remarked. "We want to work as fast as we think it comfortable for us to work."

Union Organizing

The progressive reformers had little understanding of the revolution going on in the factory. Samuel Gompers, head of the American Federation of Labor, however, was quick to recognize that Taylorism would reduce workers to "mere machines." Under his guidance the AFL prospered during the progressive era. Between 1897 and 1904, union membership grew from 447,000 to over two million, with three out of every four union members claimed by the AFL. By 1914, the AFL alone had over two million members. Gompers's "pure and simple unionism" was most successful among coal miners, railroad workers, and the building trades. As we saw in Chapter 18, Gompers ignored the growing army of unskilled and immigrant workers and concentrated on raising the wages and improving the working conditions of the skilled craftsmen who were members of unions affiliated with the AFL.

For a time, Gompers's strategy seemed to work. Several industries negotiated with the AFL as a way of avoiding disruptive strikes. But cooperation was short-lived. Labor unions were defeated in a number of disastrous strikes, and the National Association of Manufacturers launched an aggressive counterattack. The NAM and other employer associations provided strikebreakers, used industrial spies, and blacklisted union members to prevent them from obtaining other jobs.

The Supreme Court came down squarely on management's side, ruling in the *Danbury Hatters* case in 1908 that trade unions were subject to the Sherman Anti-Trust Act. Thus union members themselves could be held personally liable for money lost by a business during a strike. Courts at all levels sided overwhelmingly with employers. They often declared strikes illegal and were quick to issue restraining orders, making it impossible for workers to interfere with the operation of a business.

Working women and their problems aroused more sympathy among progressive reformers than the plight of working men. The number of women working outside the home increased steadily during the progressive era, from over 5 million in 1900 to nearly 8.5 million in 1920. But few belonged to unions, and the policy of Gompers and the other labor leaders was generally to oppose organizing women workers.

Many upper-class women reformers tried to help these working women in a variety of ways. Tension and misunderstanding often cropped up between the reformers and the working women, but one organization in which there was genuine cooperation was the Women's Trade Union League. Founded in 1903, the league was organized by Mary Kenney and William English Walling, a socialist and reformer. The league established branches in most large eastern and midwestern cities and served for more than a decade as an important force in helping to organize women into unions.

Garment Workers and the Triangle Fire

Thousands of young women, most of them Jewish and Italian, were employed in the garment industry in New York City. Most were between 16 and 25; some lived with their families, and others lived alone or with a roommate. They worked a 56-hour, six-day week and made about $6 for their efforts. Like other industries, garment manufacturing had changed in the first decade of the twentieth century. Once conducted in thousands of dark and dingy tenement rooms, now all the operations were centralized in large loft buildings in lower Manhattan. These buildings were an improvement over the sweating labor of the tenements, but many were overcrowded, and they had few fire escapes or safety features. In addition, the owners applied scientific management techniques in order to increase their profits, making life miserable for the workers. Most of the women had to rent their sewing machines and even had to pay for the electricity they used. They were penalized for mistakes or for talking too loudly. They were usually supervised by a male contractor, who badgered and sometimes even harassed them.

In 1909, some of the women went out on strike to protest the working conditions. The International Ladies' Garment Workers Union (ILGWU) and the Women's Trade Union League supported them. But strikers were beaten and sometimes arrested by unsympathetic policemen and by strikebreakers on the picket lines. At a mass meeting held at Cooper Union in New York on November 22, 1909, Clara Lemlich, a young shirtwaist worker who had been injured on the picket line and was angered by the long speeches and lack of action, rose and in an emotional speech in Yiddish demanded a general strike. The entire audience pledged its agreement. The next day, all over the city, the shirt-waist workers went out on strike. "The uprising of the twenty thousand," as the strike was called, startled the nation.

The shirtwaist workers won, and in part the success of the strike made the garment union one of the most powerful in the AFL. But the victory was limited. Over 300 companies accepted the union's terms, but others refused to go along. The young women went back to work amid still oppressive and unsafe conditions. That became dramatically obvious on Saturday, March 25, 1911, when a fire broke out on the eighth floor of the ten-story loft building housing the Tri-angle Shirtwaist Company near Washington Square in New York. Within minutes, the top three floors of the factory were a raging inferno. Many exit doors were locked. The elevators broke down. There were no fire escapes. Forty-six women jumped to their deaths, some of them in groups of three and four holding hands. Over 100 died in the flames.

Shocked by the Triangle fire, the state legis-lature appointed a commission to investigate working conditions in the state. The result was state legislation limiting the work of women to 54 hours a week, prohibiting labor by children under 14, and improving safety regulations in factories. One supporter of the bills in Albany was a young state senator named Franklin De-lano Roosevelt.

Another investigative commission, the fed-eral Industrial Relations Commission, which was created in 1912 to study the causes of indus-trial unrest and violence, conducted a detailed study of a violent labor-management conflict in Colorado, known as the Ludlow Massacre. A strike broke out in the fall of 1913 in the vast mineral-rich area of southern Colorado, much of it controlled by the Colorado Fuel and Iron In-dustry, a company largely owned by the Rocke-feller family. It was a paternalistic empire where workers lived in company towns and sometimes in tent colonies. They were paid in company scrip and forced to shop at the company store.

When the workers, supported by the United Mine Workers, went on strike demanding an eight-hour day, better safety precautions, and the removal of armed guards, the company refused to negotiate. The strike turned violent, and in the spring of 1914, strikebreakers and national guardsmen fired on the workers. Eleven children and two women were killed in an attack on a tent city near Ludlow, Colorado.

The Industrial Relations Commission stated in its report that violent class conflict could be avoided only by limiting the use of armed guards and detectives, by restricting monopoly, by pro-tecting the right of the workers to organize, and, most dramatically, by redistributing wealth through taxation. The commission's report, not surprisingly, fell on deaf ears. Most progressives, like most Americans, denied the commission's conclusion that class conflict was inevitable.

Radical Labor

In 1905, a group of about 200 radicals met in Chicago to form a new union as an alternative to the AFL. The Industrial Workers of the World, or IWW, would welcome all workers: the un-skilled, and even the unemployed, as well as women, blacks, Asians, and all other ethnic groups. Attending the organizational meeting were Daniel De Leon of the Socialist Labor Party, Eugene Debs, one of the outstanding radi-cal leaders in the country, and Mary Harris Jones, widely known as "Mother" Jones. Jones had been a dressmaker, a Populist, and a mem-ber of the Knights of Labor. During the 1890s, she had marched with miners' wives on the picket line in western Pennsylvania. She was im-prisoned and denounced, but by 1905 she was already a legend.

Presiding at the Chicago meeting was "Big Bill" Haywood. He had been a cowboy, a miner, and a prospector. Somewhere along the way he had lost an eye and mangled a hand, but he had a booming voice and a passionate commitment to "the emancipation of the working class from the slave bondage of capitalism." Denouncing Gompers and the AFL, he talked of class conflict. "The purpose of the IWW," he proclaimed, "is to bring the workers of this country into the possession of the full value of the product of their toil."

The IWW remained a small organization, troubled by internal squabbles and disagreements. It succeeded in organizing textile workers in the Northeast as well as itinerant lumbermen and migratory workers in the Northwest. But in other places, especially in times of high unemployment, the Wobblies, as they were called, helped the unskilled workers vent their anger against their employers.

Many American workers still did not feel, as European workers did, that they were engaged in a perpetual class struggle with their capitalist employers. The AFL, not the IWW, became the dominant American labor movement. But for a few, the IWW represented a dream of what might have been. For others, its presence, though small and largely ineffective, meant that perhaps someday a European-style working-class movement might develop in America.

REFORM IN THE CITIES AND STATES

The reform movements of the progressive era usually started at the local level, then moved to the state and finally to the nation's capital. Progressivism in the cities and states had roots in the depression and discontent of the 1890s. The movement's leaders were often the professional and business classes. They intended to bring order out of chaos and to modernize the city and the state during a time of swift growth.

Municipal Reformers

American cities grew rapidly in the last part of the nineteenth and the first part of the twentieth centuries. New York, which had a population of

1.2 million in 1880, grew to 3.4 million by 1900 and 5.6 million in 1920. Chicago expanded even more dramatically, from 500,000 in 1880 to 1.7 million in 1900 and 2.7 million in 1920. Los Angeles was a town of 11,000 in 1880 but multiplied ten times by 1900, and then increased another five times, to more than a half million, by 1920.

The spectacular and continuing growth of the cities caused problems and created a need for housing, transportation, and municipal services. But it was the kind of people who were moving into the cities that worried many observers. Americans from the small towns and farms continued to throng to the urban centers, but immigration produced the greatest surge in population. Fully 40 percent of New York's population and 36 percent of Chicago's was foreign-born in 1910; if one included the children of the immigrants, the percentage approached 80 percent in some cities. The new immigrants from eastern and western Europe, according to Francis Walker, the president of MIT, were "beaten men from beaten races, representing the worst failures in the struggle for existence." They seemed to threaten the American way of life and the very tenets of democracy.

Fear of the city and its new inhabitants motivated progressive municipal reform efforts. Urban problems seemed to have reached a crisis stage.

The twentieth-century reformers, mostly middle-class citizens like those in the nineteenth, wanted to regulate and control the sprawling metropolis, restore democracy, reduce corruption, and limit the power of the political bosses and their immigrant allies. When these reformers talked of restoring power to the people, they usually meant ensuring control for people like themselves. The chief aim of municipal reform was to make the city more organized and efficient for the business and professional classes who were to control its workings.

Municipal reform movements varied from city to city. In Boston, the reformers tried to

Chapter 21 • The Progressives Confront Industrial Capitalism **467**

Cities grew so rapidly that they often ceased to work. This 1909 photograph shows Dearborn Street looking south from Randolph in Chicago. Horse-drawn vehicles, streetcars, pedestrians, and even a few early autos clogged the intersection and created the urban inefficiency that angered municipal reformers.

strengthen the power of the mayor, break the hold of the city council, and eliminate council corruption. They succeeded in removing all party designations from city election ballots, and they extended the term of the mayor from two to four years. But to their chagrin, in the election of 1910, John Fitzgerald, grandfather of John F. Kennedy and foe of reform, defeated their candidate. In other cities, the reformers used different tactics, but they almost always conducted elaborate studies and campaigned to reduce corruption.

The most dramatic innovation was the replacement of both mayor and council with a nonpartisan commission of administrators. This innovation began quite accidentally when a hurricane devastated Galveston, Texas, in Septem-ber 1900. The existing government was helpless to deal with the crisis, so the state legislature appointed five commissioners to run the city during the emergency. The idea spread and proved most popular in small to medium-size cities in the Midwest and the Pacific Northwest. By World War I, more than 400 cities had adopted the commission form. Dayton, Ohio, went one step further: After a disastrous flood in 1913, the city hired a city manager to run the city and to report to the elected council. Government by experts was the perfect symbol of what most municipal reformers had in mind.

The commission and the expert manager did not replace the mayor in most large cities. One of the most flamboyant and successful of the progressive mayors was Tom Johnson, elected mayor of Cleveland in 1901. During his two terms in city hall, he managed to reduce transit fares and to build parks and municipal bath houses throughout the city. Johnson also broke the connection between the police and prostitution in the city by promising the madams and the brothel owners that he would not bother them if they would be orderly and not steal from their customers or pay off the police. His most controversial move, however, was to advocate city ownership of the street railroads and utilities (sometimes called municipal socialism). Johnson was defeated in 1909 in part because he alienated many powerful business interests, but one of his lieutenants, Newton D. Baker, was elected mayor in 1911 and carried on many of his programs. Cleveland was one of many cities that began to regulate municipal utilities or to take them over from the private owners.

The City Beautiful

In Cleveland, both Tom Johnson and Newton Baker promoted the arts, music, and adult education. They also supervised the construction of a civic center, a library, and a museum. Most other American cities during the progressive era set out to bring culture and beauty to their centers. They were influenced at least in part by the great, classical White City constructed for the Chicago World's Fair of 1893 and by the grand European boulevards such as the Champs-Elysées in Paris. The architects of the "city beautiful movement" tried to make the city more attractive and meaningful for the middle and upper classes. The museums and the libraries were closed on Sundays, the only day the working class could possibly visit them.

The social justice progressives, especially those connected with the social settlements, were more concerned with neighborhood parks and playgrounds than with the ceremonial boulevards and grand buildings. Hull House established the first public playground in Chicago.

Most progressives had an ambivalent atti-

tude toward the city. They feared it, and they loved it. One of Tom Johnson's young assistants, Frederic C. Howe, wrote a book called *The City: The Hope of Democracy* (1905). Hope or threat, the progressives realized that the United States had become an urban nation and that the problems of the city had to be faced.

Reform in the States

The progressive movements in the states had many roots and took many forms. In some states, especially in the West, progressive attempts to regulate railroads and utilities were simply an extension of populism. In other states, the reform drive bubbled up from reform efforts in the cities. Most states passed initiative and referendum laws, allowing citizens to originate legislation and to overturn laws passed by the legislature, and recall laws, which gave the people a way to remove elected officials. Many states passed social justice measures as well. Maryland enacted the first workers' compensation law in 1902, paying employees for days missed because of job-related injuries. Illinois approved a law aiding mothers with dependent children. Several states passed anti–child labor bills, and Oregon's ten-hour law restricting women's labor became a model for other states.

The states with the most successful reform movements elected strong and aggressive governors: Charles Evans Hughes in New York, Hoke Smith in Georgia, Hiram Johnson in California, Woodrow Wilson in New Jersey, and Robert La Follette in Wisconsin. After Wilson, La Follette was the most famous and in many ways the model progressive governor.

The depression of 1893 hit Wisconsin hard. More than a third of the state's citizens were out of work; farmers lost their farms, and many small businesses went bankrupt. At the same time, the rich seemed to be getting richer. As grass-roots discontent spread, several newspapers joined the battle and denounced special privilege and corruption. Everyone could agree on the need for tax reform, railroad regulation, and more participation of the people in government.

La Follette, a lawyer who had had little interest in reform, took advantage of the general mood of discontent to win the governorship in 1901. A shrewd politician, he used professors from the University of Wisconsin, in the capital, to prepare reports and do statistical studies. Then he worked with the legislature to pass a state primary law and an act regulating the railroads. "Go back to the first principles of democracy; go back to the people" was his battle cry. He became a national figure and was elected to the Senate in 1906.

Although the progressive movement had mixed results, it did improve government and make it more responsible to the people in states like Wisconsin. The spirit of reform that swept the country was real, and progressive movements on the local level did eventually have an impact on Washington, especially during the administrations of Theodore Roosevelt and Woodrow Wilson.

THEODORE ROOSEVELT AND THE SQUARE DEAL

President William McKinley was shot in Buffalo, New York, on September 6, 1901, by Leon Czolgosz, an anarchist. He died eight days later, making Theodore Roosevelt, at 42, the youngest man ever to become president. The nation mourned its fallen leader, while in many cities anarchists and other radicals were rounded up for questioning.

No one knew what to expect from Roosevelt, but under his leadership, progressivism reshaped the national political agenda. While early progressive reformers had attacked problems at the state or local level, the emergence of a national industrial economy had spawned conditions that demanded national solutions.

Progressives at the national level turned their attention to the workings of the economic system. They examined the railroads and other large corporations, threats to the natural environment, and the quality of the products of American industry. As they fashioned legislation to remedy the flaws in the economic system, they vastly expanded the power of the national government.

A Strong and Controversial President

Roosevelt came to the presidency with considerable experience. He had served a term in the New York state assembly, spent four years as a United States civil service commissioner, and served two years as the police commissioner of New York City. His exploits in the Spanish-American War brought him to the public's attention, but he had also been an effective assistant secretary of the navy and a reform governor of New York. While police commissioner and governor, he had been influenced by housing reformer Jacob Riis and other progressives. He came from an upper-class family, had written a number of books, and was one of the most intellectual presidents since Thomas Jefferson. But none of these things assured that he would be a progressive in office.

Roosevelt loved being president. He called the office a "bully pulpit," and he enjoyed talking to the people and the press. The American people quickly adopted him as their favorite. They called him "Teddy" and named a stuffed bear after him.

Roosevelt became the strongest president since Lincoln. He revitalized the executive branch, reorganized the army command structure, and modernized the consular service. He established the Bureau of Corporations, appointed independent commissions staffed with experts, and enlisted talented and well-trained men to work for the government. "TR," as he became known, also called a White House conference on the care of dependent children. He angered many social justice progressives by not going far enough. But he was the first president to listen to the pleas of the progressives and to learn from them.

Dealing with the Trusts

One of Roosevelt's first actions as president was to attempt to control the large industrial corporations. He took office in the middle of an unprecedented wave of business consolidation. Between 1897 and 1904, some 4,227 companies combined to form 257 large corporations. The Sherman Anti-Trust Act of 1890 had been virtually useless in controlling the trusts, but a new outcry from muckrakers and progressives called for regulation. Roosevelt opposed neither bigness nor the right of businessmen to make money. But he thought some businessmen arrogant, greedy, and irresponsible. "We draw the line against misconduct, not against wealth," he said.

To the shock of much of the business community, he directed his attorney general to file suit to dissolve the Northern Securities Company, a giant railroad monopoly put together by James J. Hill and financier J. P. Morgan. The government won its case and proceeded to prosecute some of the largest corporations, including Standard Oil of New Jersey and the American Tobacco Company. Although Roosevelt's antitrust policy did not end the power of the giant corporations or even alter their methods of doing business, it did breathe some life into the Sherman Anti-Trust Act, and it increased the role of the federal government as regulator. It also caused large firms such as U.S. Steel to diversify in order to avoid antitrust suits.

Roosevelt sought to strengthen the power of the Interstate Commerce Commission (ICC) to regulate rate and rebate abuses by the railroads through two proposed bills. Although opponents in Congress weakened the bills, the legislative effort resulted in the Elkins Act of 1903, which attempted to end the railroads' practice of granting rebates to shippers, and the Hepburn

Act of 1906, which authorized the ICC to examine the account books of corporations and determine a maximum shipping rate. Despite their intent, however, these laws failed to end abuses or satisfy the farmers and small businessmen who had always been the railroads' chief critics.

Roosevelt firmly believed in corporate capitalism. He detested socialism and felt much more comfortable around business executives than labor leaders. Yet he saw his role as mediator and regulator. His view of the power of the presidency was illustrated in 1902 during the anthracite coal strike. Led by John Mitchell of the United Mine Workers, the coal miners went on strike to protest low wages, long hours, and unsafe working conditions. In 1901, a total of 513 coal miners had been killed. The mine owners refused to talk to the miners. They hired strikebreakers and used private security forces to threaten and intimidate the workers.

In the fall of 1902, schools began closing for lack of coal, and it looked like many citizens would suffer through the winter. Coal, which usually sold for $5 a ton, rose to $14. Roosevelt called the owners and representatives of the union to the White House. He appointed a commission that included representatives of the union as well as the community. Within weeks, the miners went back to work with a 10 percent raise.

Meat Inspection and Pure Food and Drugs

Roosevelt's first major legislative reform began almost accidentally in 1904 when Upton Sinclair, a 26-year-old muckraking journalist, started research on the Chicago stockyards. Sinclair boarded at the University of Chicago Settlement while he did research, conducted interviews, and wrote the story that would be published in 1906 as *The Jungle*.

Sinclair's novel told of the Rudkus family, who emigrated from Lithuania to Chicago filled with ambition and hope. But the American dream failed for them. Sinclair documented exploitation in his fictional account, but his description of contaminated meat drew more attention.

Selling 25,000 copies in its first six weeks, *The Jungle* disturbed many people, including Roosevelt, who ordered a study of the meatpacking industry. The resulting Meat Inspection Act of 1906 was a compromise. It enforced some federal inspection and mandated sanitary conditions in all companies selling meat in interstate commerce, but it did not require the dating of all meat. But the bill was a beginning. It illustrates how muckrakers, social justice progressives, and public outcry eventually led to reform legislation. It also shows how Roosevelt used the public mood and manipulated the political process to get a bill through Congress.

Taking advantage of the publicity that circulated around *The Jungle,* a group of reformers, writers, and government officials pushed for legislation to regulate the sale of food and drugs. Many packaged and canned foods contained dangerous chemicals and impurities. One popular remedy, Hosteter's Stomach Bitters, was revealed on analysis to contain 44 percent alcohol. Coca-Cola, a popular soft drink, contained a small amount of cocaine, and many medicines were laced with opium. Many people, including women and children, became alcoholics or drug addicts in their quest to feel better. The Pure Food and Drug Act, which passed Congress on the same day in 1906 as the Meat Inspection Act, was not a perfect bill, but it prevented some of the worst abuses, including eliminating the cocaine from Coca-Cola.

Conservation Versus Preservation

Although Roosevelt was pleased with the new legislation regulating the food and drug industries, he considered his conservation program his most important domestic achievement. For more than a century, American natural resources appeared to be inexhaustible, but by 1900 it had become obvious to many that forests had been destroyed, rivers polluted and filled with silt, land eroded, and other resources exploited for private gain. In 1902, with Roosevelt's enthusiastic support, Congress passed the Newlands Acts, named after Francis Newlands, an ardent conservationist from Nevada. Officially known as the National Reclamation Act, it set aside the proceeds from the sale of public land in sixteen western states to pay for the construction of irrigation projects in those states. Although it tended to help big farmers more than small producers, the Newlands Act federalized irrigation for the first time.

In 1908, Roosevelt convened a White House Conservation Conference, which resulted in the appointment of a National Conservation Commission charged with making an inventory of the natural resources of the entire country. To chair the commission Roosevelt appointed Gifford Pinchot, forestry expert and ardent conservationist, who advocated selective logging, fire control, and limited grazing on public lands.

Pinchot's policies pleased many in the timber and cattle industries but angered some as too restrictive. Preservationist John Muir, who believed passionately in preserving the land in a wilderness state, denounced the Pinchot approach. Muir helped to organize the Sierra Club in 1892 and also led the successful campaign to create Yosemite National Park in California.

An outdoorsman since his youth, Roosevelt used his executive authority to more than triple the land set aside for national forests, bringing the total to over 150 million acres. Use of such areas increased as many middle-class Americans took up hiking, camping, and other outdoor activities, while children joined the Boy Scouts (founded 1910) and the Camp Fire Girls (1912).

The conflicting philosophies of Pinchot and Muir were dramatically demonstrated by the controversy over Hetch-Hetchy, a remote valley deep within Yosemite National Park. Muir and his followers wanted to keep it an unspoiled wilderness, but the mayor of San Francisco wanted a dam and reservoir to supply his growing city with water. The Hetch-Hetchy affair was fought out in newspapers, magazines, and the halls of Congress, but in the end, the conservationists won out over the preservationists. Roosevelt and Congress sided with Pinchot, the dam was built, and the valley was turned into a lake. But the debate over how to use the nation's land and water would continue throughout the twentieth century.

Progressivism for Whites Only

Like most of his generation, Roosevelt thought in stereotyped racial terms. Although he appointed several qualified blacks to minor federal posts, notably Dr. William D. Crum to head the Charleston, South Carolina, customs house in 1905, at other times he seemed insensitive to the needs and feelings of black Americans. This was especially true in his handling of the Brownsville, Texas, riot of 1906. Members of a black army unit stationed there, angered by discrimination against them, rioted one hot August night. Exactly what happened no one was sure, but one white man was killed and several wounded. Waiting until after the midterm elections of 1906, Roosevelt ordered all 167 members of three companies dishonorably discharged. It was an unjust punishment for an unproved crime, and 66 years later the secretary of the army granted honorable discharges to the men, most of them by that time dead.

During the progressive era, even the most advanced progressives seldom included blacks in their reform schemes. Hull House, like most social settlements, was segregated, although Jane Addams spoke out repeatedly against lynching and supported the founding of the National Association for the Advancement of Colored People in 1909.

The most important black leader who argued for equality and opportunity for his people

was W. E. B. Du Bois. As revealed in Chapter 18, Du Bois differed dramatically with Booker T. Washington on strategies to improve the position of blacks in American life. While Washington advocated vocational education, Du Bois argued for the best education possible for the most talented tenth of the black population. While Washington preached compromise and accommodation to the dominant white society, Du Bois increasingly urged militant action to assure equality. Du Bois called a meeting of young and militant blacks in 1905. They met in Canada, not far from Niagara Falls, and issued an angry statement. "We want to *pull down* nothing but we don't propose to be pulled down," the platform announced. "We believe in *taking what we can get* but we don't believe in being satisfied with it and in permitting anybody for a moment to imagine we're satisfied." The Niagara movement, as it came to be called, combined with the NAACP in 1910, and Du Bois became editor of its journal, *The Crisis*. The NAACP was a typical progressive organization, seeking to work within the American system to promote reform. But to Roosevelt and many others who called themselves progressives, the NAACP seemed dangerously radical.

William Howard Taft

After eight years as president, Roosevelt decided to step down. He handpicked as his successor William Howard Taft, who had been a distinguished lawyer, federal judge, and Roosevelt's secretary of war. After defeating William Jennings Bryan for the presidency in 1908, Taft quickly ran into difficulties. In some ways, he seemed more progressive than Roosevelt. His administration instituted more suits against monopolies in one term than Roosevelt had in his nearly two full terms. He supported the eight-hour workday and legislation to make mining safer and urged the passage of the Mann-Elkins Act in 1910, which strengthened the ICC

Tuskegee Institute followed Booker T. Washington's philosophy of black advancement through accommodation to the white status quo. Here students study American history, but most of their time was spent in vocational training.

by giving it more power to set railroad rates and extending its jurisdiction over telephone and telegraph companies. Taft and Congress also authorized the first tax on corporate profits. He also encouraged the process that eventually led to the passage of the federal income tax, which was authorized under the Sixteenth Amendment, ratified in 1913. That probably did more to transform the relationship of the government to the people than all other progressive measures combined.

Taft's biggest problem was his style. He was a huge man, weighing over 300 pounds. An uninspired speaker, he also lacked Roosevelt's political skills. Many progressives were annoyed when he signed the Payne-Aldrich Tariff, which midwesterners thought left rates on cotton and

wool cloth and other items too high and played into the hands of the eastern industrial interests. Even Roosevelt was infuriated when his successor reversed many of his conservation policies. Roosevelt broke with Taft, letting it be known that he was willing to run again for president. This set up one of the most exciting and significant elections in American history.

The Election of 1912

Woodrow Wilson won the Democratic nomination for president in 1912. Born two years before Roosevelt, Wilson was the son and grandson of Presbyterian ministers. Well educated, with a Ph.D. from the Johns Hopkins University in Baltimore, Wilson published a book, *Congressional Government* (1885), that established his reputation as a shrewd analyst of American politics. He taught history briefly at Bryn Mawr College near Philadelphia and at Wesleyan in Connecticut before moving to Princeton. Less flamboyant than Roosevelt, he was an excellent public speaker with the power to convince people with his words.

In 1902, Wilson was elected president of Princeton University. Later, as governor of New Jersey, he showed courage as he quickly alienated some of the conservatives who had helped to elect him. Building a coalition of reformers, he worked with them to pass a direct primary law and a workers' compensation law. He also created a commission to regulate transportation and public utility companies. By 1912, Wilson not only was an expert on government and politics but had also acquired the reputation of a progressive.

Roosevelt, who lost the Republican nomination to Taft, startled the nation by walking out of the convention and forming a new political party, the Progressive Party. The new party would not have been formed without Roosevelt, but the party was always more than Roosevelt. It appealed to progressives from all over the country who had become frustrated with the conservative leadership in both major parties.

Many social workers and social justice progressives supported the Progressive Party because of its platform, which contained provisions they had been advocating for years. The Progressives supported an eight-hour day, a six-day week, the abolition of child labor under age 16, and a federal system of accident, old age, and unemployment insurance. Unlike the Democrats, the Progressives also endorsed woman suffrage. Most supporters of the Progressives in 1912 did not realistically think they could win, but they were convinced that they could organize a new political movement that would replace the Republican Party, just as the Republicans had replaced the Whigs after 1856.

The enthusiasm for Roosevelt and the Progressive Party was misleading, for behind the unified facade lurked many disagreements. Roosevelt had become more progressive on many issues since leaving the presidency. He even attacked the financiers "to whom the acquisition of untold millions is the supreme goal of life, and who are too often utterly indifferent as to how these millions are obtained." But he was not as committed to social reform as some of the delegates. Perhaps the most divisive issue was the controversy over seating black delegates from several southern states. A number of social justice progressives fought hard to include a plank in the platform supporting equality for blacks and for seating the black delegation. Roosevelt, however, did not agree with them, and in the end, he prevailed.

The political campaign in 1912 became a contest primarily between Roosevelt and Wilson, with Taft, the Republican candidate and incumbent, ignored by most reporters who covered the campaign. Roosevelt spoke of the "New Nationalism." In a modern industrial society, he argued, large corporations were "inevitable and necessary." What was needed was not the breakup of the trusts but a strong president and increased power in the hands of the federal government to regulate business and industry and to ensure the rights of labor, women and children, and other groups.

Wilson talked of the "New Freedom." He emphasized the need for the Jeffersonian tradition of limited government with open competition. He spoke of the "curse of bigness" and argued against too much federal power: "If America is not to have free enterprise, then she can have freedom of no sort whatever." "What I fear is a government of experts," Wilson declared, implying that Roosevelt's New Nationalism would lead to regulated monopoly and even collectivism.

The level of debate during the campaign was impressive, making this one of the few elections in American history when important ideas were actually discussed. It also marked a watershed for political thought for liberals who rejected Jefferson's distrust of a strong central government. It is easy to exaggerate the differences between Roosevelt and Wilson. Both of them urged reform within the American system. Both defended corporate capitalism, and both opposed socialism and radical labor organizations such as the IWW. Both wanted to promote more democracy and to strengthen conservative labor unions. Both were very different in style and substance from the fourth candidate, Eugene Debs, who ran on the Socialist Party ticket in 1912.

Debs, in 1912, was the most important socialist leader in the country. Although socialism was always a minority movement in the United States, it had its greatest success in the first decade of the twentieth century. Thirty-three cities including Milwaukee, Wisconsin; Reading, Pennsylvania; Butte, Montana; Jackson, Michigan; and Berkeley, California, chose socialist mayors. Socialists Victor Berger from Wisconsin and Meyer London from New York were elected to Congress. The most important socialist periodical, *Appeal to Reason,* published in Girard, Kansas, increased its circulation from about 30,000 in 1900 to nearly 300,000 in 1906. Socialism appealed to some reformers, frustrated with the slow progress of reform, and to recent immigrants, who brought with them a European sense of class differences.

A tremendously appealing figure and a great orator, Debs had run for president in 1900, 1904, and 1908, but in 1912 he reached much wider audiences in more parts of the country. His message called for "wresting control of government and industry from the capitalists and making the working class the ruling class of the nation and the world." Debs polled almost 900,000 votes in 1912 (6 percent of the popular vote), the best showing ever for a socialist in the United States. Wilson received 6.3 million votes, Roosevelt a little more than 4 million, and Taft 3.5 million. Wilson garnered 435 electoral votes, Roosevelt 88, and Taft only 8.

WOODROW WILSON AND THE NEW FREEDOM

Wilson was elected largely because Roosevelt and the Progressive Party split the Republican vote. But once elected, Wilson became a vigorous and aggressive chief executive. Like Roosevelt, Wilson became more progressive during his presidency.

Tariff and Banking Reform

Wilson was not as charismatic as Roosevelt, but he was an outstanding orator who dominated through the force of his intellect. His ability to push his legislative program through Congress during his first two years in office was matched only by Franklin Roosevelt during the first months of the New Deal and by Lyndon Johnson in 1965.

Within a month of his inauguration, Wilson went before a joint session of Congress to outline his legislative program. By appearing in person before Congress, he broke a precedent established by Thomas Jefferson. First on his agenda was tariff reform. The Underwood Tariff, passed in 1913, was not a free-trade bill, but it did reduce the schedule for the first time in many years.

Attached to the Underwood bill was a provision for a small and slightly graduated income tax, which had been made possible by the passage of the Sixteenth Amendment. The income tax was enacted to replace the money lost from lowering the tariff. Wilson seemed to have no interest in using it to redistribute wealth in America.

The next item on Wilson's agenda was reform of the banking system. A financial panic in 1907 had revealed the need for a central bank, but few people could agree on the exact nature of the reforms. A congressional committee, led by Arsène Pujo of Louisiana, had revealed a massive consolidation of banks and trust companies and a system of interlocking directorates and informal arrangements that concentrated resources and power in the hands of a few firms such as the J. P. Morgan Company. But talk of banking reform alarmed conservative Democrats and the business community.

The bill that passed Congress established the Federal Reserve System, providing for 12 Federal Reserve Banks and a Federal Reserve Board appointed by the president. The bill also created a flexible currency, based on federal reserve notes, that could be expanded or contracted as the situation required. The Federal Reserve System, while not perfect, appealed to the progressives' desire for order and efficiency.

Despite these reform measures, Wilson was not very progressive in some of his actions during his first two years in office. He failed to support proposed long-term rural credit financed by the federal government, a woman suffrage amendment, and an anti–child labor bill. He also ordered the segregation of blacks in several federal departments. When southern Democrats, suddenly in control in many departments, began dismissing black federal officeholders, especially those "who boss white girls," Wilson did nothing.

Moving Closer to a New Nationalism

How to control the great corporations in America was a question Wilson and Roosevelt debated extensively during the campaign. Wilson's solution was the Clayton Act, submitted to Congress in 1914. The bill prohibited a number of unfair trading practices, outlawed the interlocking directorate, and made it illegal for corporations to purchase stock in other corporations if this tended to reduce competition. Labor leaders protested that the bill had no provision exempting labor organizations from prosecution under the Sherman Anti-Trust Act. When a section was added exempting both labor and agricultural organizations, Samuel Gompers hailed it as labor's Magna Carta. It was hardly that, because the courts interpreted the provision so that labor unions remained subject to court injunctions during strikes despite the Clayton Act.

More important than the Clayton Act, which both supporters and opponents realized was too vague to be enforced, was the creation of the Federal Trade Commission (FTC), modeled after the ICC, with enough power to move directly against corporations accused of restricting competition. The Federal Trade Commission, however, did not end monopoly, and the courts in the next two decades did not increase the government's power to regulate business.

Neither Roosevelt nor Wilson satisfied the demands of the advanced progressives. Most of the efforts of the two progressive presidents were spent trying to regulate economic power rather than to promote social justice. Their most important legacy, however, was that they reasserted presidential authority, modernized the executive branch, and began the creation of the federal bureaucracy, which has had a major impact on the lives of Americans in the twentieth century.

Both Roosevelt and Wilson used the presidency as a "bully pulpit" to make pronouncements, create news, and influence policy. For example, both presidents called White House conferences and appointed committees and commissions. Roosevelt strengthened the Interstate Commerce Commission and Wilson created the Federal Trade Commission, both of which were the forerunners of many other federal regulatory bodies. And by breaking precedent and actually delivering his annual message in person before a joint session of Congress, Wilson symbolized the new power of the presidency.

The new bureaus, committees, and commissions brought to Washington a new kind of expert, trained in the universities, at the state and local level, and in the voluntary organizations. The expert, the commission, the statistical survey, and the increased power of the executive branch were all legacies of the progressive era.

CONCLUSION

THE LIMITS OF PROGRESSIVISM

The progressive era was a time when many Americans set out to promote reform because they saw poverty, despair, and disorder in a country transformed by immigration, urbanism, and industrialism. The progressives, largely middle-class whites, sought to help the poor, the immigrants, and the working class, but they rarely worried about blacks. They talked of the need for more democracy, but they often succeeded in promoting bureaucracy and a government run by experts. They believed there was a need to regulate business, promote efficiency, and spread social justice, but their regulatory laws tended to aid business and to strengthen corporate capitalism. By contrast, most of the industrialized nations of western Europe passed legislation during this period providing for old-age pensions and health and unemployment insurance.

Progressivism had its roots in the 1890s and reached a climax in the early twentieth century. Women played important roles in organizing reform and eventually began to fill positions in the new agencies in the state capitals and in Washington. Neither Theodore Roosevelt nor Woodrow Wilson was an advanced progressive, but during both their administrations, progressivism achieved some success. Progressivism would be altered by World War I, but it survived, with its strengths and weaknesses, to affect American society through most of the twentieth century.

Recommended Reading

A good starting point for exploring the progressive movement is Arthur S. Link and Richard L. McCormick, *Progressivism* (1983). Intellectual background is provided in David Noble, *The Progressive Mind, 1890–1917* (1970). Paul Boyer, *Urban Masses and Moral Order in America, 1820–1920* (1978), finds a continuity of the reform impulse across a century and rates fear of immigrants and a desire for social control as the most important ingredients of progressivism. Robert M. Crunden, *Ministers of Reform* (1982), stresses the religious motivation and includes art, architecture, literature, and music in his analysis. More recent studies include Robert B. Westbrook,

John Dewey and American Democracy (1991); and Susan Curtis, *Consuming Faith: The Social Gospel and Modern American Culture* (1991).

Allen F. Davis, *Spearheads for Reform* (1967), emphasizes the social justice movement. Ruth Rosen, *The Lost Sisterhood* (1982); and Mark T. Connelly, *The Response to Prostitution in the Progressive Era* (1980), tell the fascinating story of the crusade against prostitution. Louis Filler, *The Muckrakers* (1976), is the best place to begin a study of the journalists who helped to create a social movement. Dewey W. Grantham, *Southern Progressivism* (1983), details the impact of the movement in a region often thought to have missed much of the reform impulse. The struggle for women's rights can be followed in Aileen S. Kraditor, *The Ideas of the Woman Suffrage Movement, 1890–1920* (1965). August Meier, *Negro Thought in America, 1880–1915* (1963), is still the best introduction to black movements during the progressive period. David Montgomery, *The Fall of the House of Labor* (1988), tells the story of workers and the labor movement during the period.

John Morton Blum, *The Progressive Presidents* (1980), and John Milton Cooper, Jr., *The Warrior and the Priest* (1983), give interesting interpretations of Roosevelt and Wilson. Nick Salvatore, *Eugene V. Debs* (1982), is the best biography of America's most influential radical.

Relevant novels include Theodore Dreiser, *Sister Carrie* (1900), a classic of social realism; Upton Sinclair, *The Jungle* (1906), a muckraking novel about the meatpacking industry; and Charlotte Perkins Gilman, *Herland* (1915), the story of a female utopia.

Time Line

1901	McKinley assassinated; Theodore Roosevelt becomes president Robert La Follette elected governor of Wisconsin Tom Johnson elected mayor of Cleveland U.S. Steel formed
1902	Anthracite coal strike
1903	Women's Trade Union League founded
1904	Roosevelt elected president Lincoln Steffens publishes *The Shame of the Cities*
1905	Frederic C. Howe writes *The City: The Hope of Democracy* Industrial Workers of the World formed
1906	Upton Sinclair publishes *The Jungle* Meat Inspection Act Pure Food and Drug Act
1907	Financial panic
1908	*Muller v. Oregon* *Danbury Hatters* case William Howard Taft elected president

1909	Herbert Croly publishes *The Promise of American Life* NAACP founded
1910	Ballinger-Pinchot controversy Mann-Elkins Act
1911	Frederick Taylor publishes *The Principles of Scientific Management* Triangle Shirtwaist Company fire
1912	Progressive Party founded by Theodore Roosevelt Woodrow Wilson elected president Children's Bureau established Industrial Relations Commission founded
1913	Sixteenth Amendment (income tax) ratified Underwood Tariff Federal Reserve System established Seventeenth Amendment (direct election of senators) passed
1914	Clayton Act AFL has over two million members Ludlow Massacre in Colorado

chapter 22

The Great War

On April 7, 1917, the day after the United States officially declared war on Germany, Edmund P. Arpin, Jr., a young man of 22 from Grand Rapids, Wisconsin, decided to enlist in the army. It was not patriotism that led him to join the army but his craving for adventure and excitement. After training at Fort Sheridan, Illinois, Arpin finally arrived with his unit in Liverpool on December 23, 1917, aboard the *Leviathan,* a German luxury liner that the United States had interned when war was declared and pressed into service as a troop transport. In England, he discovered that American troops were not greeted as saviors. Hostility against the Americans simmered partly because of the previous unit's drunken brawls. Drinking also seems to have been a preoccupation of the soldiers in Arpin's outfit, but Arpin spent most of the endless waiting time learning to play contract bridge.

Arpin saw some of the horror of war when he went to the front with a French regiment as an observer, but his own unit did not engage in combat until October 1918, when the war was almost over. He took part in the bloody Meuse-Argonne offensive, which helped end the war. Wounded in the leg in an assault on an unnamed hill and awarded a Distinguished Service Cross for his bravery, Arpin later learned that the order to attack had been recalled but word had not reached him in time. When the armistice came, Arpin was recovering in a field hospital.

Edward Arpin was in the army for two years. He was one of 4,791,172 Americans who served in the army, navy, or marines. He was one of the two million who went overseas, and one of the 230,074 who were wounded. Some of his friends were among the 48,909 who were killed. When he was mustered out of the army in March 1919, he felt lost and confused, but in time, he settled down. He became a successful businessman, married, and raised a family. A member of the American Legion, he periodically went to conventions and reminisced with men from his division about their escapades in France.

Just as the Great War changed the life of Edmund P. Arpin, Jr., so too did it alter the lives of most Americans. Trends begun during the progressive era accelerated. The power and influence of the federal government increased. Not only did the war promote woman suffrage, prohibition, and public housing, but it also helped to create an administrative bureaucracy that blurred the lines between public and private, between government and business—a trend that would continue throughout the twentieth century.

Woodrow Wilson talked of a "war to end all wars" and a war "to make the world safe for democracy." His optimism, moralism, and missionary zeal helped to transform the war into a great crusade, which most Americans enthusiastically joined.

In this chapter, we travel the twisted path that led the United States into the war and share the wartime experiences of American men and women overseas and at home. The chapter concludes with a look at the idealistic efforts to promote peace at the end of the war.

THE EARLY WAR YEARS

Few Americans expected the Great War that erupted in Europe in the summer of 1914 to affect their lives. When a Serbian student terrorist assassinated Archduke Franz Ferdinand of Austria-Hungary in Sarajevo, the capital of the province of Bosnia, a place most Americans had never heard of, it precipitated a series of events leading to the most destructive war the world had ever known.

The Causes of War

Despite Theodore Roosevelt's successful peacekeeping attempts in the first decade of the century (see Chapter 20), relationships among the European powers had not improved. Intense rivalries for empire turned minor incidents in Africa, Asia, or the Balkans into events that threatened world peace. As European nations armed, they drew up a complex series of treaties. Austria-Hungary and Germany (the Central Powers) became military allies, while Britain, France, and Russia (the Allied Powers) agreed to assist one another in case of attack.

The incident in Sarajevo destroyed the precarious balance of power. The leaders of Austria-Hungary determined to punish Serbia for the assassination. Russia mobilized to aid Serbia. Germany, supporting Austria-Hungary, declared war on Russia and France. England hesitated, but when Germany invaded Belgium in order to attack France, England declared war, and the slaughter began. Europeans "have reverted to the condition of savage tribes roaming the forests and falling upon each other in a fury of blood and carnage," the New York *Times* announced.

The American sense that the nation would never succumb to the barbarism of war, combined with the fact that the Atlantic Ocean separated Europe from the United States, contributed to a great sense of relief after the first shock of the war began to wear off. Woodrow Wilson's official proclamation of neutrality on August 4, 1914, reinforced the belief that the United States had no major stake in the outcome of the war and would stay uninvolved. The president was preoccupied with his own personal tragedy. His wife, Ellen Axson Wilson, died of Bright's disease the day after his proclamation. Two weeks later, still engulfed by his own grief, he urged all Americans to "be neutral in fact as well as in name, . . . impartial in thought as well as in action."

American Reactions

Many social reformers despaired when they heard the news from Europe. Even during its first months, the war seemed to deflect energy

Europe During the Great War

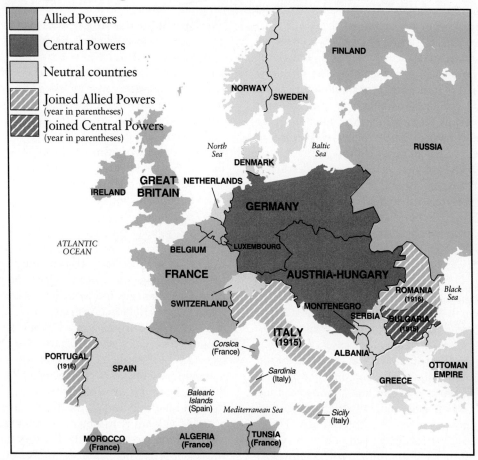

The Great War had an impact on all of Europe, even on the few countries that managed to remain neutral. Russia left the war in 1917, the same year that the United States joined the fight.

away from reform. Jane Addams of Hull House helped to organize the Woman's Peace Party.

While many people worked to promote an international plan to end the war through mediation, others could hardly wait to take part in the great adventure. Hundreds of young American men, most of them students or recent college graduates, volunteered to join ambulance units, to take part in the war effort without actually fighting. Among the most famous of them were Ernest Hemingway, John Dos Passos, and E. E.

Cummings, who later turned their wartime adventures into literary masterpieces. Others volunteered for service with the French Foreign Legion or joined the Lafayette Escadrille, a unit of pilots made up of well-to-do American volunteers attached to the French army. Many of these young men were inspired by an older generation who pictured war as a romantic and manly adventure. One college president talked of the chastening and purifying effect of armed conflict, while Theodore Roosevelt projected an image of war that was something like a football game, where red-blooded American men could test their idealism and manhood.

Alan Seeger, a writer and poet who believed in the noble purpose of the war, joined the French Foreign Legion. "You have no idea how beautiful it is to see the troops undulating along the road . . . with the captains and lieutenants on horse back at the head of the companies," he wrote his mother. When Seeger was killed in 1916, he became an instant hero.

Many Americans visualized war as a romantic struggle for honor and glory because the only conflict they remembered was the "splendid little war" of 1898. But this would be a cruel modern war in which men died by the thousands, cut down by a more efficient technology of killing.

The New Military Technology

The German Schlieffen plan called for a rapid strike through Belgium to attack Paris and the French army from the rear. However, the French stopped the German advance at the Battle of the Marne in September 1914, and the fighting soon bogged down in a costly and bloody routine. Soldiers on both sides dug miles of trenches and strung out barbed wire to protect them. Thousands died in battles that gained only a few yards or nothing at all. Rapid-firing rifles, improved explosives, incendiary shells, smokeless bullets, and tracer bullets all added to the destruction. Most devastating of all, however, was the improved artillery, sometimes mounted on trucks and directed by spotters using wireless radios, that could fire over the horizon and hit targets many miles behind the lines.

The technology of defense, especially the machine gun, neutralized the frontal assault, the most popular military tactic since the American Civil War. As one writer explained: "Three men and a machine gun can stop a battalion of heroes." But the generals on both sides continued to order their men to charge to their almost certain deaths.

The war was both a traditional and a revolutionary struggle. It was the last war in which cavalry was used and the first that employed new military technologies. By 1918, airplanes, initially used only for observation, were creating terror below with their bombs. Tanks made their first tentative appearance in 1916, but it was not until the last days of the war that this new offensive weapon began to neutralize the machine gun. Poison gas, first used in 1914, added a new element of fear to a war of already unspeakable horror. But then military technicians on both sides developed the gas mask, allowing the defense to counter the new offensive weapons.

Difficulties of Neutrality

Despite Wilson's efforts to promote neutrality, ties of language and culture tipped the balance for most Americans in favor of the Allied cause. About eight million Austrian- and German-Americans lived in the United States, and some supported the cause of the Central Powers. They viewed Kaiser Wilhelm II's Germany as a progressive parliamentary democracy. The anti-British sentiment of some Irish-Americans led them to take sides not so much for Germany as against England. A few Swedish-Americans distrusted Russia so vehemently that they had difficulty supporting the Allies. A number of American scholars, physicians, and intellectuals fondly remembered studying in Germany. To them, Germany meant great universities and cathedrals, music and culture. It also represented social planning, health insurance, unemployment compensation, and many programs for which the progressives had been fighting.

Other reasons made real neutrality nearly impossible. American trade with the Allies was much more important than with the Central Powers. Wilson's advisers, especially Robert Lansing and Edward House, openly supported the French and the British, as did most newspaper owners and editors. Gradually for Wilson, and probably for most Americans, the perception that England and France were fighting to preserve civilization from the forces of Prussian evil replaced the idea that all Europeans were barbaric and decadent. But the American people were not yet willing to go to war to save civilization. Let France and England do that.

Woodrow Wilson also sympathized with the Allies for practical and idealistic reasons. He believed that by keeping the United States out of the war, he might control the peace. The war, he hoped, would show the futility of imperialism and would usher in a world of free trade in products and ideas.

Remaining neutral while maintaining trade with the belligerents became increasingly difficult. Remaining neutral while speaking out about the peace eventually became impossible. The need to trade and the desire to control the peace finally led the United States into the Great War.

World Trade and Neutrality Rights

The United States was part of an international economic community in 1914 in a way that it had not been a hundred years earlier during the Napoleonic Wars. The outbreak of war in the summer of 1914 caused an immediate economic panic in the United States. On July 31, 1914, the Wilson administration closed the stock exchange to prevent the unloading of European securities and panic selling. It also adopted a policy discouraging loans by American banks to belligerent nations. Most difficult was the matter of neutral trade. Wilson insisted on the rights of Americans to trade with both the Allies and the Central Powers, but Great Britain instituted an illegal naval blockade, mined the North Sea, and began seizing American ships, even those carrying food and raw materials to Italy, the Netherlands, and other neutral nations.

Wilson eventually accepted British control of the seas. His conviction that the destinies of the United States and Great Britain were inter-

twined outweighed his idealistic belief in free trade. Consequently, American trade with the Allies rose while with the Central Powers it declined. At the same time, the United States government eased restrictions on private loans to belligerents, and the British and French quickly obtained loans.

Germany retaliated against British control of the seas with submarine warfare. The new weapon, the U-boat (*Unterseeboot*), created unprecedented problems. Nineteenth-century international law obligated a belligerent warship to warn a passenger or merchant ship before attacking, but the chief advantage of the submarine was surprise. Rising to the surface to issue a warning would have meant being blown out of the water by an armed merchant ship.

On February 4, 1915, Germany announced a submarine blockade of the British Isles. Until Britain gave up its campaign to starve the German population, the Germans would sink even neutral ships. Wilson warned Germany that it would be held to "strict accountability" for illegal destruction of American ships or lives.

On May 7, 1915, a German U-boat torpedoed the British luxury liner *Lusitania* off the Irish coast. The liner, which was not armed but was carrying war supplies, sank in 18 minutes. Nearly 1,200 people, including many women and children, drowned. Among the dead were 128 Americans. Suddenly Americans confronted the horror of total war fought with modern weapons, a war that killed civilians, including women and children, just as easily as it killed soldiers.

Although some Americans called for a declaration of war, Wilson and most Americans had no idea of going to war in the spring of 1915, but the president refused to take William Jennings Bryan's advice and prevent further loss of American lives by simply prohibiting all Americans from traveling on belligerent ships. Instead, he sent a series of protest notes demanding reparation for the loss of American lives and a pledge from Germany that it would cease attacking ocean liners without warning. Bryan resigned as secretary of state over the tone of the notes and charged that the United States was not being truly neutral. The president replaced him with Robert Lansing, who was much more eager than Bryan to oppose Germany, even at the risk of war.

The tense situation eased late in 1915. After a German U-boat sank the British steamer *Arabic*, claiming two American lives, the German ambassador promised that Germany would not attack ocean liners without warning (the *Arabic* pledge). But the *Lusitania* crisis caused an outpouring of books and articles urging the nation to prepare for war. Preparedness groups called for a bigger army and navy and a system of universal military training.

Wilson sympathized with the preparedness groups, and despite great opposition, especially from southern and western congressmen, he signed the Army Reorganization Bill in June 1916. This law increased the regular army to just over 200,000 and integrated the National Guard into the defense structure. Few Americans, however, expected those young men to go to war. One of the most popular songs of 1916 was "I Didn't Raise My Boy to Be a Soldier." Even before American soldiers arrived in France, however, Wilson used the army and the marines in Mexico and Central America.

Intervening in Mexico and Central America

Woodrow Wilson came to office in 1913 planning to promote liberal and humanitarian ends, not only in domestic policies but also in foreign affairs. Wilson had a vision of a world purged of imperialism, a world of free trade, but a world where American ideas and American products would find their way. With his secretary of state, William Jennings Bryan, Wilson denounced the "big stick" and "dollar diplomacy" of the Roosevelt and Taft years. Yet in the end, his adminis-

tration used force more systematically than those of his predecessors.

The diplomacy of idealism did not last long. After a disastrous civil war in the Dominican Republic, the United States offered in 1915 to take over the country's finances and police force. But when the Dominican leaders rejected a treaty making their country virtually a protectorate of the United States, Wilson ordered in the marines. They took control of the government in May 1916. Although Americans built roads, schools, and hospitals, people resented their presence. In neighboring Haiti, the situation was different, but the results were similar. The marines landed at Port-au-Prince in the summer of 1915 to prop up a pro-American regime. In Nicaragua, the Wilson administration kept in place the marines sent by Taft in 1912 to preserve the pro-American regime of Adolfo Díaz and acquired the right, through treaty, to intervene at any time to preserve order and protect American property. Except for a brief period in the mid-1920s, the marines remained until 1933.

Wilson's policy of intervention ran into greatest difficulty in Mexico, a country whose rulers had long welcomed American investors. By 1910, Americans controlled 75 percent of the mines, 70 percent of the rubber, and 60 percent of the oil. In 1911, however, Francisco Madero, a reformer, came to power. Two years later, he was deposed and murdered by order of Victoriano Huerta, the head of the army. This was the situation when Wilson became president.

To the shock of many diplomats and businessmen, Wilson refused to recognize the Huerta government. Instead, he set out to remove what he called a "government of butchers" and "to exert every influence [the U.S.] can to secure Mexico a better government under which all contracts and business concessions will be safer than they have ever been." When the United States landed troops at Veracruz, angry Mexican mobs destroyed American property wherever they could find it. Wilson's action outraged many Europeans and Latin Americans as well as Americans.

Wilson's military intervention succeeded in forcing Huerta out of power, but a civil war had erupted between forces led by Venustiano Carranza and those led by General Francisco "Pancho" Villa. With arms from the United States, Carranza, who was considered less radical than Villa, was victorious. When an angry Villa led what was left of his army in a raid on Columbus, New Mexico, in March 1916, Wilson sent an expedition under Brigadier General John Pershing to track down Villa and his men. Pershing's army charged 300 miles into Mexico but was unable to catch the retreating rebel. Tensions rose as Wilson refused to withdraw the American troops. In January 1917, just as war with Mexico seemed inevitable, Wilson agreed to recall the troops and to recognize the Carranza government. If it had not been for the growing crisis in Europe, it is likely that war would have resulted.

The tragedy was that Wilson, who idealistically wanted the best for the people of Mexico and Central America and who thought he knew exactly what they needed, managed to intervene too often and too blatantly to protect the strategic and economic interests of the United States. In the process, his policy alienated onetime friends of the United States.

THE UNITED STATES ENTERS THE WAR

A significant minority of Americans opposed going to war in 1917, but once involved, the government and the American people made the war into a patriotic crusade.

The Election of 1916

As 1915 turned to 1916, Wilson had to think of reelection as well as of preparedness, submarine warfare, and the Mexican campaign. At first glance, the president's chances of reelection seemed poor. He had won in 1912 only because Theodore Roosevelt and the Progressive Party had split the Republican vote.

Wilson was aware that he had to win over progressive voters who had favored Roosevelt in 1912. In January 1916, he appointed Louis D. Brandeis to the Supreme Court. The first Jew ever to sit on the High Court, Brandeis had always championed reform causes. In August, Wilson put heavy pressure on Congress and obtained passage of the Workmen's Compensation Bill, which gave some protection to federal employees, and the Keatings-Owen Child Labor Bill, which prohibited the shipment in interstate commerce of goods produced by children under 14 and in some cases under 16. The Keatings-Owen bill, later declared unconstitutional, was a far-reaching proposal that for the first time used federal control over interstate commerce to dictate the conditions under which businessmen could manufacture products.

To attract farm and labor support, Wilson supported the Federal Farm Loan Act, which created 12 Federal Farm Loan Banks to extend long-term credit to farmers, and the Adamson Act, which established an eight-hour day for all interstate railway workers. Within a few months, Wilson reversed the New Freedom doctrines he had earlier supported and brought the force of the federal government into play on the side of reform. The flurry of legislation early in 1916 provided one climax to the progressive movement. The strategy seemed to work, for progressives of all kinds enthusiastically endorsed the president.

The Republicans nominated Charles Evans Hughes, a former governor of New York and future Supreme Court justice. Their platform called for neutrality and preparedness. As the campaign progressed, the peace issue became more and more important, and the cry "He kept us out of war" echoed through every Democratic rally.

The election was extremely close. In fact, Wilson went to bed on election night thinking he had lost the presidency. He won by carrying the West as well as the South.

Deciding for War

In January 1917, Wilson went before the Senate and outlined a plan for a negotiated settlement before either side had achieved victory. It would be a peace among equals, "a peace without victory," a peace without indemnities and annexations.

The German government refused to accept a peace without victory and on January 31, 1917, announced that it would sink on sight any ship, belligerent or neutral, sailing toward England or France. In retaliation, the United States broke diplomatic relations with Germany. As goods began to pile up in warehouses and American ships stayed idly in port, however, pressure mounted to arm American merchant ships. An intercepted telegram from the German foreign secretary, Arthur Zimmermann, to the German minister in Mexico increased anti-German feeling. If war broke out, the German minister was to offer Mexico the territory it had lost in Texas, New Mexico, and Arizona in 1848. In return, Mexico would join Germany in a war against the United States. When this telegram was released to the press on March 1, 1917, many Americans demanded war against Germany. Wilson still hesitated.

As the country waited on the brink of war, news of revolution in Russia reached Washington. In the long run, that event would prove as important as the war itself. The March 1917 revolution in Russia was a spontaneous uprising of the workers, housewives, and soldiers against the oppressive government of Czar Nicholas II and its inept conduct of the war. At first, Wilson and other Americans were enthusiastic about the new republic led by Alexander Kerensky. The overthrow of the feudal aristocracy seemed in the spirit of the American Revolution. But within months, the revolution took a more extreme turn. Vladimir Ilyich Ulyanov, known as Lenin, returned from exile in Switzerland and led the radical Bolsheviks to victory over the Kerensky regime in November 1917.

Lenin, a brilliant lawyer and revolutionary tactician, was a follower of Karl Marx (1818–1883), a German intellectual and radical philosopher. Believing that capitalism and imperialism went hand in hand, Lenin argued that the only way to end imperialism was to end capitalism. The new Soviet Union, not the United States, was the model for the rest of the world to follow; communism, Lenin predicted, would eventually dominate the globe. The Russian Revolution posed a threat to Wilson's vision of the world and to his plan to bring the United States into the war "to make the world safe for democracy."

More disturbing than the first news of revolution in Russia, however, was the situation in the North Atlantic, where German U-boats sank five American ships between March 12 and March 21, 1917. Wilson no longer hesitated. On April 2, he urged Congress to declare war. The war resolution swept the Senate 82 to 6 and the House of Representatives 373 to 50.

A Patriotic Crusade

Not all Americans applauded the declaration of war. Some pacifists and socialists opposed the war. But whether they supported the war or not, for most Americans in the spring of 1917, the war seemed remote. A few days after the war was declared, one senator, hearing a report on supplies that would be needed by an American army in France, exclaimed, "Good Lord! You're not going to send soldiers over there, are you?"

To convince senators and citizens alike that the war was real and that American participation was just, Wilson appointed a Committee on Public Information, headed by George Creel, a muckraking journalist from Denver. The Creel Committee launched a gigantic propaganda campaign to win support for the war.

The patriotic crusade soon became stri-

The Great War, which seemed to some to be an idealistic crusade, was incredibly costly in lives and property.

dently anti-German and anti-immigrant. Most school districts banned the teaching of German, "a language that disseminates the ideals of autocracy, brutality and hatred." Anything German became suspect. Occasionally, the patriotic fever led to violence. The most notorious incident happened in East St. Louis, which had a large German population. A mob seized Robert Prager, a young German-American, in April 1918, stripped off his clothes, dressed him in an American flag, marched him through the streets, and lynched him. The eventual trial led to the acquittal of the ringleaders on the grounds that the lynching was a "patriotic murder."

The Wilson administration, of course, did not condone domestic violence and murder, but heated patriotism led to irrational hatreds and fears of subversion. Suspect were not only German-Americans but also radicals, pacifists, and others. In New York, the black editors of *The Messenger* were given 2½-year jail sentences for the paper's article "Pro-Germanism Among Negroes." The Los Angeles police ignored complaints that Mexicans were being harassed because after learning of the Zimmer-

mann telegram, they believed that all Mexicans were pro-German. In his home state of Wisconsin, Senator Robert La Follette, who had voted against the war resolution, was burned in effigy.

On June 15, 1917, Congress, at Wilson's behest, passed the Espionage Act, which provided imprisonment of up to 20 years or a fine of up to $10,000, or both, for persons who aided the enemy or who "willfully cause . . . insubordination, disloyalty, mutiny or refusal of duty in the military . . . forces of the United States. . . ." The act also authorized the postmaster general to prohibit from the mails any matter he thought advocated treason or forcible resistance to United States laws. Using the act, Postmaster General Albert S. Burleson banned the magazines *American Socialist* and *The Masses* from the mails.

Congress later added the Trading with the Enemy Act and a Sedition Act. The latter prohibited disloyal, profane, scurrilous, or abusive remarks about the form of government, flag, or uniforms of the United States. Eugene Debs was sentenced to ten years in prison for opposing the war. In 1919, the Supreme Court upheld the conviction, even though Debs had not explicitly urged the violation of the draft laws. Not all Americans agreed with the decision, for while still in prison, Debs polled close to one million votes in the presidential election of 1920. Ultimately, the government prosecuted 2,168 persons under the Espionage and Sedition acts and convicted about half of them. But these figures do not include the thousands informally persecuted and deprived of their liberties and their right of free speech. The attorney general of the United States, speaking of opponents of government policies, said, "May God have mercy on them for they need expect none from an outraged people and an avenging government."

The Civil Liberties Bureau, an outgrowth of the American Union Against Militarism, protested the blatant abridgment of freedom of speech during the war, but the protests fell on deaf ears at the Justice Department and in the White House. Rights and freedoms have been reduced or suspended during all wars, but the massive disregard for basic rights was greater during World War I than during the Civil War. Wilson was so convinced his cause was just that he ignored the rights of those who opposed him.

Raising an Army

How should a democracy recruit an army in time of war? The debate over a volunteer army versus the draft had been going on for several years before the United States entered the war. Wilson and his secretary of war, Newton Baker, both initially opposed the draft. In the end, however, both concluded that it was the most efficient way to organize military manpower. Ironically, it was Theodore Roosevelt who tipped Wilson in favor of the draft. Even though his health was failing and he was blind in one eye, the old Rough Rider was determined to recruit a volunteer division and lead it personally against the Germans. The thought of his old enemy Theodore Roosevelt blustering about Europe so frightened Wilson that he supported the Selective Service Act in part, at least, to prevent such volunteer outfits as Roosevelt planned. On June 5, 1917, some 9.5 million men between the ages of 21 and 31 registered, with little protest. In August 1918, Congress extended the act to men 18 to 45. In all, over 24 million men registered and over 2.8 million were inducted, making up over 75 percent of soldiers who served in the war.

The draft worked well, but not perfectly. Because local draft boards had so much control, favoritism and political influence allowed some to stay at home. Draft protests erupted in a few places, the largest in Oklahoma, where a group of tenant farmers planned a march on Washington to take over the government and end the "rich man's war." The Green Corn Rebellion, as it came to be called, died before it got started. A local posse arrested about 900 rebels and took them off to jail.

Some men escaped the draft. Some were deferred because of war-related jobs, while others resisted by claiming exemption for reasons of conscience. However, thousands of conscientious objectors were inducted. Some accepted noncombat positions; others went to prison for refusing to serve.

THE MILITARY EXPERIENCE

Family albums in millions of American homes contain photographs of young men in uniform, some of them stiff and formal, some of them candid shots of soldiers on leave in Paris or Washington or Chicago. These photographs testify to the importance of the war to a generation of Americans. For some, the war was a tragic event as they saw the horrors of the battlefield firsthand. For others, it was a liberating experience and the most exciting period in their lives.

The American Doughboy

The typical soldier, according to the Medical Department, stood 5 feet 7½ inches tall, weighed 141½ pounds, and was about 22 years old. He probably watched a movie called *Fit to Fight,* which warned him about the dangers of venereal disease. The majority of the American soldiers had not attended high school. The median amount of education for native whites was 6.9 years and for immigrants 4.7 years but was only 2.6 years for southern blacks. As many as 31 percent of the recruits were declared illiterate. Fully 29 percent of the recruits were rejected as physically unfit for service, which shocked the health experts.

Most World War I soldiers were ill-educated and unsophisticated young men. The military experience changed their lives and often their attitudes. Women also contributed to the war effort as telephone operators and clerk-typists in the navy and the marines. Some went overseas as army and navy nurses. Others volunteered for a tour of duty with the Red Cross, the Salvation Army, or the YMCA. Yet the military experience in World War I was predominantly male. Even going to training camp was a new and often frightening experience. A leave in Paris or London, or even in New York or New Orleans, was an adventure to remember for a lifetime. Even those who never got overseas or who never saw a battle experienced subtle changes. Many soldiers saw their first movie in the army or had their first contact with trucks and cars, safety razors, or cigarettes. The war experience also caused many men to abandon the pocket watch for the more convenient wristwatch, which had been considered effeminate before the war.

The Black Soldier

Blacks had served in all American wars, but black soldiers had most often performed menial work and belonged to segregated units. Black leaders hoped it would be different this time. Shortly after the United States entered the war, W. E. B. Du Bois, the black leader and editor of *The Crisis,* predicted that the war experience would cause the "walls of prejudice" to crumble. But the walls did not crumble, and the black soldier never received equal or fair treatment during the war.

White draft boards were more generous in exempting whites than blacks. Jim Crow laws also posed problems for black soldiers. In August 1917, violence erupted in Houston, Texas, involving soldiers from the regular army's all-black 24th Infantry Division. Harassed by the Jim Crow laws, which had been tightened for their benefit, a group of soldiers went on a rampage, killing 17 white civilians. Over 100 soldiers were court-martialed; 13 were condemned to death. Those convicted were hanged three days later before any appeals could be filed. Sec-

retary of War Baker made it clear that the army had no intention of upsetting the status quo. The basic government policy was of complete segregation and careful distribution of black units throughout the country.

Some blacks were trained as junior officers and were assigned to the all-black 92nd Division, where the high-ranking officers were white. But most of the black soldiers, including about 80 percent of those sent to France as stevedores and common laborers, worked under the supervision of white noncommissioned officers. Other black soldiers acted as servants, drivers, and porters for the white officers. It was a demeaning and ironic policy for a government that advertised itself as standing for justice, honor, and democracy.

Over There

The conflict that Wilson called the war "to make the world safe for democracy" had become a contest of stalemate and slaughter. Hundreds of thousands had died on both sides, but victory remained elusive. To this ghastly war Americans made important contributions. In fact, without their help, the Allies might have lost. But the American contribution was most significant only in the war's final months. When the United States entered the conflict in the spring of 1917, the fighting had dragged on for nearly three years. After a few rapid advances and retreats, the war in western Europe had settled down to a tactical and bloody stalemate. By the spring of 1917, the British and French armies were down to their last reserves. Italy's army had nearly collapsed. In the east, the Russians were engaged in a bitter internal struggle, and in November, the Bolshevik Revolution would cause them to sue for a separate peace.

A few token American regiments arrived in France in the summer of 1917 under the command of General John J. "Black Jack" Pershing, who had fought in the Spanish-American War

Assigned to segregated units, black soldiers were also excluded from white recreation facilities. Here black women in Newark, New Jersey, aided by white social workers, entertain black servicemen.

and led the Mexican expedition in 1916. The first Americans saw action near Verdun in October 1917. By March 1918, over 300,000 American soldiers had reached France, and by the time the war ended in November 1918, more than two million.

The United States forces were kept separate from the French and British divisions, with the exception of four regiments of black soldiers who were assigned to the French army. Despite the American warning to the French not to "spoil the Negroes" by allowing them to mix with the French civilian population, these soldiers fought so well that the French later awarded three of the regiments the Croix de Guerre, their highest unit citation.

In the spring of 1918, with Russia out of the war, the Germans launched an all-out, desperate offensive to win the war before full American military and industrial power became a factor in the contest. By late May, the Germans had

pushed to within 50 miles of Paris. American troops were thrown into the line and helped stem the German advance. Americans also took part in the Allied offensive led by General Ferdinand Foch of France in the summer of 1918. In September, over one-half million American troops fought near St. Mihiel in the first battle where large numbers of Americans were pressed into action. The Americans suffered over 7,000 casualties, but they captured more than 16,000 German soldiers.

In the fall of 1918, the combined British, French, and American armies drove the Germans back. Faced with low morale among the German soldiers and finally the mutiny of the German fleet and the surrender of Austria, Kaiser Wilhem II abdicated on November 8, and the Armistice was signed on November 11. More than a million American soldiers took part in the final Allied offensive near the Meuse River and the Argonne forest. It was in this battle that

Edmund Arpin was wounded. Many of the men were inexperienced, and some, who had been rushed through training as "90-day wonders," had never handled a rifle before arriving in France. There were many disastrous mistakes and bungled situations.

The all-black 92nd Division, which had been deliberately dispersed around the United States and had never trained as a unit, was ordered at the last minute to a particularly difficult position on the Meuse-Argonne line. They had no maps and no wire-cutting equipment. Battalion commanders lost contact with their men, and on several occasions the men broke and ran in the face of enemy fire. The division was withdrawn in disgrace, and for years politicians and military leaders used this incident to point out that black soldiers would never make good fighting men, ignoring the difficulties under which the 92nd fought and the valor shown by black troops assigned to the French army.

The war produced a few American heroes. Joseph Oklahombie, a Choctaw, overran several German machine gun nests and captured more than 100 German soldiers. Sergeant Alvin York, a former conscientious objector from Tennessee, single-handedly killed or captured 160 Germans using only his rifle and pistol. The press made him a celebrity, but his heroics were not typical. Artillery, machine guns, and, near the end, tanks, trucks, and airplanes won the war.

With few exceptions, the Americans fought hard and well. While the French and British criticized American inexperience and disarray, they admired their exuberance, their "pep," and their ability to move large numbers of men and equipment efficiently. Sometimes it seemed that Americans simply overwhelmed the enemy with their numbers.

The United States entered the war late but still lost more than 48,000 service personnel and had many more wounded. Disease claimed 15 of every 1,000 American soldiers each year (compared with 65 per 1,000 in the Civil War). But the British lost 900,000 men, the French 1.4 million, and the Russians 1.7 million. The United States contributed huge amounts of men and supplies in the last months of the war, and that finally tipped the balance. But it had entered late and sacrificed little compared to France and England. That would influence the peace settlement.

The end of the Great War brought relief and joy to many, but the fall of 1918 also witnessed the outbreak of an unusually lethal flu epidemic. The conditions of life in the war zones and the movement of large numbers of troops and civilian refugees apparently contributed to the emergence of an extremely virulent form of influenza that spread around the world and claimed over 20 million lives. In a two-year period, the virus struck in three waves, becoming more lethal with each advance and killing young men, women, and children as well as the old and weak. In the United States, over half a million died in what may be considered an indirect legacy of the war.

DOMESTIC IMPACT OF THE WAR

For at least 30 years before the United States entered the Great War, a debate raged over the proper role of the federal government in regulating industry and protecting people who could not protect themselves. Even within the Wilson administration, advisers disagreed on the proper role of the federal government. The war and the problems it raised increased the power of the federal government in a variety of ways. The wartime experience did not end the debate, but the United States emerged from the war a more modern nation, with more power residing in Washington.

Financing the War

The war, by one calculation, cost the United States over $33 billion. Interest and veterans' benefits bring the total to nearly $112 billion. Early on, when an economist suggested that the war might cost the United States $10 billion, everyone laughed. Yet many in the Wilson administration knew the war was going to be expensive, and they set out to raise the money by borrowing and by increasing taxes.

Secretary of the Treasury William McAdoo shouldered the task of financing the war. A war must be "a kind of crusade," he remarked. His campaign to sell liberty bonds to ordinary American citizens at a very low interest rate called forth patriotic sentiment. "Lick a Stamp and Lick the Kaiser," one poster urged. Celebrities such as film stars Mary Pickford and Douglas Fairbanks promoted the bonds, and McAdoo employed the Boy Scouts to sell them. "Every Scout to Save a Soldier" was the slogan. The public responded enthusiastically, but they discovered after the war that their bonds had dropped to about 80 percent of face value.

McAdoo's other plan to finance the war involved raising taxes. The War Revenue Act of 1917 boosted the tax rate sharply, levied a tax on excess profits, and increased estate taxes. Another bill the next year raised the tax on the largest incomes to 77 percent. The wealthy protested, but a number of progressives were just as unhappy with the bill, for they wanted to confiscate all income over $100,000 a year. Despite taxes and liberty bonds, however, World War I, like the Civil War, was financed in large part by inflation. Food prices, for example, nearly doubled between 1917 and 1919.

Increasing Federal Power

At first, Wilson tried to work through a variety of state agencies to mobilize the nation's resources. The need for more central control and authority soon led Wilson to create a series of federal agencies to deal with the war emergency. The first crisis was food. Poor grain crops for two years and an increasing demand for American food in Europe caused shortages. To solve the problem, Wilson appointed Herbert Hoover, a young engineer who had won great prestige as

head of the Commission for Relief of Belgium, to direct the Food Administration. Hoover set out to meet the crisis not so much through government regulation as through an appeal to the patriotism of farmers and consumers alike. He instituted a series of "wheatless" and "meatless" days and urged housewives to cooperate. In Philadelphia, a large sign announced, "FOOD WILL WIN THE WAR; DON'T WASTE IT."

The War Industries Board, led by Bernard Baruch, a shrewd Wall Street broker, used the power of the government to control scarce materials and, on occasion, to set prices and priorities. The government itself went into the shipbuilding business. The largest shipyard, at Hog Island, near Philadelphia, employed as many as 35,000 workers, but the yard did not launch its first ship until the late summer of 1918—too late to affect the outcome of the war.

The government also got into the business of running the railroads. When a severe winter and a lack of coordination brought the rail system near collapse in December 1917, Wilson put all the nation's railroads under the control of the United Railway Administration. The government spent more than $500 million to improve the rails and equipment, and in 1918 the railroads did run more efficiently than they had under private control. Some businessmen resented government rules and regulations, but most came to agree with Baruch that a close working relationship with government could improve the quality of their products, promote efficiency, and increase profits.

War Workers

The Wilson administration sought to protect and extend the rights of organized labor during the war, while at the same time mobilizing the workers necessary to keep the factories running. The National War Labor Board insisted on adequate wages and reduced hours, and it tried to prevent the exploitation of women and children working under government contracts. On one

Women proved during the war that they could do "men's work." These shipyard workers even dressed like men, but the war did not change the American ideal that a woman's place was in the home.

occasion, when a munitions plant refused to accept the War Labor Board's decision, the government simply took over the factory. When workers threatened to strike, the board often ruled that they either work or be drafted into the army.

The Wilson administration favored the conservative labor movement of Samuel Gompers and the AFL, while the Justice Department put the radical Industrial Workers of the World "out of business." Beginning in September 1917, federal agents conducted massive raids on IWW offices and arrested most of the leaders.

Samuel Gompers took advantage of the crisis to strengthen the AFL's position to speak for labor. He made it clear that he opposed the IWW as well as socialists and communists. Convincing Wilson that it was important to protect the rights of organized labor during wartime, he announced that "no other policy is compatible with the spirit and methods of democracy." As the AFL won a voice in homefront policy, its membership increased from 2.7 million in 1916 to over 4 million in 1917. Organized labor's wartime gains, however, would prove only temporary.

The war opened up industrial employment opportunities for black men. With four million men in the armed forces and the flow of immigrants interrupted by the war, American manufacturers for the first time hired blacks in large numbers. Northern labor agents and the railroads actively recruited southern blacks, but the news of jobs in northern cities spread by word of mouth as well. By 1920, more than 300,000 blacks had joined the "great migration" north. As blacks moved north, thousands of Mexicans crossed into the United States as immigration officials relaxed the regulations because of the need for labor in the farms and factories of the Southwest.

The war also created new employment opportunities for women. One poster announced, "Stenographers, Washington Needs You." Women responded to these appeals out of patriotism, as well as out of a need to increase their earnings and to make up for inflation, which diminished real wages. Women went into every kind of industry. They labored in brickyards and in heavy industry, became conductors on the railroad, and turned out shells in munition plants. They even organized the Woman's Land Army to mobilize female labor for the farms. They demonstrated that women could do any kind of job, whatever the physical or intellectual demands. One black woman who gave up her position as a live-in servant to work in a paper-box factory declared:

> I'll never work in nobody's kitchen but my own any more. No indeed, that's the one thing that makes me stick to this job, but when you're working in anybody's kitchen, well you out of luck. You almost have to eat on the run; you never get any time off.

As black women moved out of domestic service, they took jobs in textile mills or even in the stockyards. Racial discrimination, however, even in the North, prevented them from moving very far up the occupational ladder.

The war accelerated trends already under way in women's employment. It increased the need for telephone operators, sales personnel, secretaries, and other white-collar workers, and in these occupations women soon became a majority. Telephone operator, for example, became an almost exclusively female job. There were 15,000 operators in 1900 but 80,000 in 1910, and by 1917 women represented 99 percent of all operators as the telephone network spanned the nation. In the end, the war provided limited opportunities for some women, but after the soldiers returned home, the gains made by women almost disappeared. There were 8 million women in the work force in 1910 and only 8.5 million in 1920.

The Climax of Progressivism

Many progressives, especially the social justice progressives, opposed the United States' entry into the war until a few months before the nation declared war. But after April 1917, many began to see the "social possibilities of war." They deplored the death and destruction, the abridgment of freedom of speech, and the patriotic spirit that accompanied the war. But they praised the social planning stimulated by the conflict. They approved the Wilson administration's support of collective bargaining, the eight-hour day, and protection for women and children in industry. They welcomed the experiments with government-owned housing projects, woman suffrage, and prohibition. Many endorsed the government takeover of the railroads and control of business during the war.

One of the best examples of the progressives' influence on wartime activities was the Commission on Training Camp Activities, set up early in the war to solve the problem of mobilizing, entertaining, and protecting American servicemen at home and abroad. Chairman of the commission was Raymond Fosdick, a former settlement worker. The commission organized community singing, baseball, post exchanges, theaters, and even university extension lectures for the servicemen.

The Commission on Training Camp Activi-

ties also incorporated the progressive crusades against alcohol and prostitution. The Military Draft Act prohibited the sale of liquor to men in uniform and gave the president power to establish zones around military bases where prostitution and alcohol would be prohibited. Some military commanders protested, and at least one city official argued that prostitutes were "God-provided means for the prevention of the violation of innocent girls, by men who are exercising their 'God-given passions.'" Yet the commission, with the full cooperation of the Wilson administration, set out to wipe out sin, or at least to put it out of the reach of servicemen. When the boys go to France, the secretary of war remarked, "I want them to have invisible armour to take with them. I want them to have armour made up of a set of social habits replacing those of their homes and communities."

France tested the "invisible armour." It proved impossible to keep the soldiers away from sex and liquor. Both the British and the French armies had tried to solve the problem of venereal disease by licensing and inspecting prostitutes. Georges Clemenceau, the French premier, found the American attitude toward prostitution difficult to comprehend. On one occasion, he offered to provide the Americans with licensed prostitutes. General Pershing considered the letter containing the offer "too hot to handle." So he gave it to Fosdick, who showed it to Baker, who remarked, "For God's sake, Raymond, don't show this to the President or he'll stop the war." The Americans never accepted Clemenceau's offer, and he continued to be baffled by the American progressive mentality.

Suffrage for Women

In the fall of 1918, while American soldiers were mobilizing for the final offensive in France and hundreds of thousands of women were working in factories and serving as Red Cross and Salvation Army volunteers near the army bases, Woodrow Wilson spoke before the Senate to ask its support of woman suffrage, which he maintained was "vital to the winning of the war." Wilson had earlier opposed the vote for women, and many people still argued that the vote would make women less feminine, more worldly, and less able to perform their primary tasks as wives and mothers.

Carrie Chapman Catt, an efficient administrator and tireless organizer from Iowa, devised the strategy that finally secured the vote for women. In 1915, Catt became president of the National American Woman Suffrage Association (NAWSA), the organization founded in 1890 and based in part on the society organized by Elizabeth Cady Stanton and Susan B. Anthony in 1869. Catt coordinated the state-campaigns with the work in Washington, directing a growing army of dedicated workers. The Washington headquarters sent precise information to the states on ways to pressure congressmen in local districts. In Washington, they maintained a file on each congressman and senator.

The careful planning began to produce results, but a group of more militant reformers, impatient with the slow progress, broke off from NAWSA to form the National Woman's Party (NWP) in 1916. This group was led by Alice Paul, a Quaker from New Jersey, who had participated in some of the suffrage battles in England. Paul and her group picketed the White House, chained themselves to the fence, and blocked the streets. They carried banners that asked, "MR. PRESIDENT, HOW LONG MUST WOMEN WAIT FOR LIBERTY?" In the summer of 1917, the government arrested more than 200 women and charged them with "obstructing the sidewalk." It was just the kind of publicity the militant group sought, and it made the most of it. Wilson, fearing even more embarrassment, began to cooperate with the more moderate reformers.

The careful organizing of the NAWSA and the more militant tactics of the NWP both contributed to the final success of the woman suffrage crusade. Early in 1919, the House of Representatives passed the suffrage amendment 304 to 90, and the Senate approved by a vote of 56

to 25. Fourteen months later, the required 36 states had ratified the amendment, and women at last had the vote.

PLANNING FOR PEACE

On January 8, 1918, in part to counteract the Bolshevik charge that the war was merely a struggle among imperialist powers, Woodrow Wilson announced his plan to organize the peace. Called the Fourteen Points, it argued for "open covenants of peace openly arrived at," freedom of the seas, equality of trade, the self-determination of all peoples. But his most important point, the fourteenth, called for an international organization, a "league of nations," to preserve peace.

The Paris Peace Conference

Late in 1918, Wilson announced that he would head the American delegation in Paris. Wilson's entourage included Secretary of State Lansing, Edward House, and a number of other advisers. Conspicuously missing, however, was Henry Cabot Lodge or any other Republican senator. This would prove a serious blunder, for the Republican-controlled Senate would have to approve any treaty negotiated in Paris. In Paris, Wilson faced the reality of European power politics and ambitions and the personalities of David Lloyd George of Great Britain, Vittorio Orlando of Italy, and Georges Clemenceau of France.

Though Wilson was more naive and more idealistic than his European counterparts, he was a clever negotiator who won many concessions at the peace table, sometimes by threatening to go home if his counterparts would not compromise. The European leaders were determined to punish Germany and enlarge their empires. Wilson, however, believed that he could create a new kind of international relations based on his Fourteen Points. He achieved limited acceptance of the idea of self-determination, his dream that each national group could have its own country and that the people should decide in what country they wanted to live.

The peacemakers carved the new countries of Austria, Hungary, and Yugoslavia out of what had been the Austro-Hungarian Empire. In addition, they created Poland, Czechoslovakia, Finland, Estonia, Latvia, and Lithuania, in part to help contain the threat of bolshevism in eastern Europe. France was to occupy the industrial Saar region of Germany for 15 years, with a plebiscite at the end of that time to determine whether the people wanted to become a part of Germany or France. Italy gained the port city of Trieste.

Wilson won some points at the peace negotiations, but he also had to make major concessions. He was forced to agree that Germany should pay reparations (later set at $56 billion), lose much of its oil- and coal-rich territory, and admit to its war guilt. He accepted a mandate system, to be supervised by the League of Nations, that allowed France and Britain to take over portions of the Middle East and allowed Japan to occupy Germany's colonies in the Pacific. He acquiesced when the Allies turned Germany's African colonies into "mandate possessions" because they did not want to allow the self-determination of blacks in areas they had colonized. Wilson also did not win approval for freedom of the seas or the abolition of trade barriers, but he did gain endorsement for the League of Nations, the organization he hoped would prevent all future wars.

Women for Peace

While the statesmen met at Versailles to sign the peace treaty hammered out in Paris and to divide up Europe, a group of prominent women from all over the world, including many from the Central Powers, met in Zurich, Switzerland. The American delegation was led by Jane Addams and included Florence Kelley of the National Consumers League; Alice Hamilton, a professor at Harvard Medical School; and Jeannette Rankin, a congresswoman from Montana (one

of the few states where women could vote). They met amid the devastation of war to promote a peace that would last. At their conference they formed the Women's International League for Peace and Freedom. Electing Addams president of the new organization, they denounced the harsh peace terms, which called for disarmament of only one side and exacted great economic penalties against the Central Powers. Prophetically, they predicted that the peace treaty would result in the spread of hatred and anarchy and "create all over Europe discords and animosities which can only lead to future wars."

Hate and intolerance were indeed legacies of the war. Also hanging over the peace conference was the Bolshevik success in Russia. The threat of revolution seemed so great that Wilson and the Allies sent American and Japanese troops into Russia in 1919 to attempt to defeat the Bolsheviks and create a moderate republic. But by 1920, the troops had failed in their mission and withdrew.

Wilson's Failed Dream

Probably most Americans supported the concept of the League of Nations in the summer of 1919. Yet in the end, the Senate refused to accept American membership in the League. The League of Nations treaty, one commentator has suggested, was killed by its friends and not by its enemies.

First there was Lodge, who had earlier endorsed the idea of some kind of international peacekeeping organization but who objected to Article 10, claiming that it would force Americans to participate in the wars of foreigners. Then there was Wilson, whose only hope of passage of the treaty in the Senate was a compromise to bring moderate senators to his side. But Wilson refused to compromise or to modify Article 10 to allow Congress the opportunity to decide whether or not the United States would support the League in time of crisis. While stumping the country to win popular support for the League treaty, Wilson collapsed in Pueblo, Colorado. He was rushed back to Washington, where a few days later he suffered a massive stroke. For the next year and a half, the president was incapable of running the government. Protected by his second wife and his closest advisers, Wilson became irritable and depressed and unable to lead a fight for the League. For a year and a half the country limped along without a president.

After many votes and much maneuvering, the Senate finally killed the League treaty in March 1920. Had the United States joined the League of Nations, it probably would have made little difference in the international events of the 1920s and 1930s. Nor would American participation have prevented World War II. The United States did not resign from the world of diplomacy or trade, nor did the United States with that single act become isolated from the rest of the world. But the rejection of the League treaty was symbolic of the refusal of many Americans to admit that the world and America's place in it had changed dramatically since 1914.

CONCLUSION

THE DIVIDED LEGACY OF THE GREAT WAR

For Edmund Arpin and many of his friends, the war was a great adventure. For others who served, the war's results were more tragic. Many died. Some came home injured, disabled by poison gas, or unable to cope with the complex world that had opened up to them.

The war created job opportunities for blacks and women, and farmers suddenly discovered a demand for their products. The passage of the woman's suffrage amendment and the use of federal power to promote justice and order pleased reformers. Once the war ended, however, much federal legislation was dismantled or reduced in effectiveness, and votes for women had little initial impact on social legislation.

The Great War marked the coming of age of the United States as a world power, but the country seemed reluctant to accept the new responsibility. The war stimulated patriotism and pride in the country, but it also increased intolerance. The shared experience of the Great War years, including contact among soldiers from various regions of the country, expanded employment opportunities for blacks and women, and with the growth of advertising, also contributed to the development of a more uniform mass culture. With this mixed legacy from the war, the country entered the new era of the 1920s.

RECOMMENDED READING

On Woodrow Wilson's foreign policy, see Arthur S. Link, *Woodrow Wilson: Revolution, War, and Peace* (1979). Ellis W. Hawley, *The Great War and the Search for Modern Order* (1979), emphasizes the long-term impact of the war.

The best general account of the American military involvement in the Great War is Edward M. Coffman, *The War to End All Wars* (1968). Arthur D. Barbeau and Florette Henri, *The Unknown Soldiers: Black American Troops in World War I* (1974), describes the experience of blacks in the military. David M. Kennedy, *Over Here* (1980), is the most comprehensive survey of the impact of the war on American society.

More specialized studies include Carol S. Gruber, *Mars and Minerva* (1975), on the impact of the war on higher education; and Nancy F. Cott, *The Grounding of Modern Feminism* (1987), on the relationship between suffrage and feminism. Frederick C. Luebke, *Bonds of Loyalty* (1974), details the experience of German-Americans. On the impact of the Russian Revolution on American policy and attitudes, see John L. Gaddis, *Russia, the Soviet Union, and the United States* (1978). For the Mexican intervention,

see P. Edward Haley, *Revolution and Intervention* (1970).

Paul Fussell, *The Great War and Modern Memory* (1975), focuses primarily on the British experience but is indispensable for understanding the importance of the war for the generation that lived through it.

Many novels focus on the war. Erich Maria Remarque highlights the horror of war from the European point of view in *All Quiet on the Western Front* (1929). John Dos Passos shows war as a bitter experience in *Three Soldiers* (1921), and Ernest Hemingway portrays its futility in *Farewell to Arms* (1929).

Time Line

1914	Archduke Ferdinand assassinated; World War I begins American troops invade Mexico and occupy Veracruz
1915	Germany announces submarine blockade of Great Britain *Lusitania* sunk *Arabic* pledge
1916	Expedition into Mexico Wilson reelected Workmen's Compensation Bill Keatings-Owen Child Labor Bill Federal Farm Loan Act National Woman's Party founded
1917	Germany resumes unrestricted submarine warfare United States breaks relations with Germany Zimmermann telegram Russian Revolution
1917	United States declares war on Germany Espionage Act Committee on Public Information established Trading with the Enemy Act Selective Service Act War Industries Board formed
1918	Sedition Act Flu epidemic sweeps nation Wilson's Fourteen Points American troops intervene in Russian Revolution
1919	Paris peace conference Eighteenth Amendment prohibits alcoholic beverages Senate rejects Treaty of Versailles
1920	Nineteenth Amendment grants woman suffrage

chapter 23

······························

Affluence and Anxiety

John and Lizzie Parker were black sharecroppers in central Alabama. They had two daughters, one age 6, the other already married. The whole family worked hard in the cotton fields, but they had little to show for their labor. One day in 1917, Lizzie straightened her shoulders and declared, "I'm through. I've picked my last sack of cotton. I've cleared my last field."

Like many southern blacks, the Parkers sought opportunity and a better life in the North. During World War I there was a shortage of workers, and some companies sent special trains into the South to recruit blacks. John Parker signed up with a mining company in West Virginia. The company offered free transportation for his family. "You will be allowed to get your food at the company store and there are houses awaiting for you," the agent promised.

They soon discovered that life in the company town in West Virginia was little better than the life they left in Alabama. John ran away and drifted to Detroit, where he got a job with the American Car and Foundry Company. It was 1918, and the pay was good. After a few weeks, he rented an apartment and sent for his family. For the first time, Lizzie had a gas stove and an indoor toilet, and Sally, who was now 7, started school. It seemed as if their dream had come true.

Detroit was not quite the dream, however. Many whites did not welcome blacks in their neighborhoods. Sally was beaten up by a gang of white youths at school. The Ku Klux Klan also made life uncomfortable for the blacks who had moved north to seek jobs and opportunity.

Suddenly the war ended, and almost immediately John lost his job. The Parkers were forced to leave their apartment for housing in a section just outside the city near Eight Mile Road. This black ghetto had dirt streets and the shack had no indoor plumbing and no electricity, only a pump in the yard and an outhouse.

The recession winter of 1921–1922 was particularly difficult. John could find only part-time employment, while Lizzie worked as a domestic servant for white families. The shack they called home was freezing cold, and it was cramped because their married daughter and her husband had joined them in Detroit.

Lizzie did not give up her dream, however. With strength, determination, and a sense of humor, she kept the family together. By the end of the decade, Sally had graduated from high school, and the Parkers finally had electricity and indoor plumbing in the house, though the streets were still unpaved. The Parkers had improved their lot, but they still lived outside Detroit—and, in many ways, outside America.

Like most Americans in the 1920s, the Parkers pursued the American dream of success. For them, a comfortable house and a steady job, a new bathroom, and an education for their younger daughter constituted that dream. The 1920s has often been referred to as the "jazz age," a time when the American people supposedly had one long party complete with flappers, speakeasies, illegal bathtub gin, and the Charleston. This frivolous interpretation has some basis in fact, but most Americans did not share in the party, for they were too busy struggling to make a living in a tumultuous time of social, economic, and technological change.

In this chapter, we will explore some of the conflicting trends of an exciting decade. First, we will examine the currents of intolerance that influenced almost all the events and social movements of the time. We will also look at some developments in technology, especially the automobile, which changed life for almost everyone during the 1920s and created the illusion of prosperity for all. We will then focus on groups—women, blacks, industrial workers, and farmers—who had their hopes raised but not always fulfilled during the decade. We will conclude by looking at the way business, politics, and foreign policy were intertwined during the age of Harding, Coolidge, and Hoover.

POSTWAR PROBLEMS

The years immediately following the end of World War I were marked by domestic dissension. The enthusiasm for social progress and the sense of common purpose that had energized Americans during the war evaporated. During 1919 Americans experienced strikes, violence, and a wave of fear that Bolsheviks, blacks, foreigners, and others were destroying the American way.

Red Scare

Americans have often feared radicals and other groups that seemed to be conspiring to overthrow the American way. In the 1840s, the 1890s, and at other times in the past, Catholics, Mormons, Populists, immigrants, and holders of many political views have all been attacked as dangerous and "un-American." But before 1917, anarchists seemed to pose the worst threat. After the Russian Revolution, *Bolshevik* became the most dangerous radical, while *communist* was transformed from a member of a utopian community to a dreaded, menacing subversive. In the spring of 1919, with the Russian announcement of a policy of worldwide revolution and with Communist uprisings in Hungary and Bavaria, many Americans feared that the Communists planned to take over the United States. There were a few American Communists, but they never really threatened the United States or the American way of life.

However, some idealists, like John Reed, found developments in Russia inspiring. Reed, the Harvard-educated son of a wealthy businessman, converted to socialism. In Europe shortly after the war began, he witnessed the bloody Bolshevik takeover in 1917. His eyewitness account, *Ten Days That Shook the World,* optimistically predicted a worldwide revolution. However, when he saw how little hope there was for that revolution in postwar America, he returned to the Soviet Union. By the time he died from typhus in 1920, the authoritarian nature of the new Russian regime had disillusioned him.

Working-Class Protest

Relatively few Americans, even among those who had been socialists, and fewer still among the workers, joined the Communist Party. Perhaps in all there were 25,000 to 40,000, and those were split into two groups, the American Communist Party and the Communist Labor Party. The threat to the American system of government was very slight. But in 1919, the Communists seemed to be a threat, particularly as a series of devastating strikes erupted across the country. Workers in the United States had suffered from wartime inflation, which had almost doubled prices between 1914 and 1919, while most wages remained the same. During 1919, more than four million workers took part in 4,000 strikes. Few wanted to overthrow the government; they demanded higher wages, shorter hours, and in some cases more control over the workplace.

On January 21, 1919, some 35,000 shipyard workers went on strike in Seattle, Washington. Within a few days, a general strike paralyzed the city; transportation and business stopped. The mayor of Seattle called for federal troops. Within five days, using strong-arm tactics, the mayor put down the strike and was hailed across the country as a "red-blooded patriot."

Yet the strikes continued, spreading in September to U.S. Steel and Bethlehem Steel. Blaming the strikes on the Bolsheviks, the owners imported strikebreakers, provoked riots, broke up union meetings, and finally used police and soldiers to end the strike. While the steel strike was still in progress, the police in Boston went on strike. The Boston newspapers blamed the strike on Communist influence. Calvin Coolidge, then governor of Massachusetts, quickly broke the strike and fired the policemen.

Several bomb incidents in 1919 also convinced some that revolution was around the corner, even though most American workers wanted only shorter hours, better working conditions, and a chance to realize the American dream.

The strikes and bombs, combined with the general postwar mood of distrust and suspicion, persuaded many people of a real and immediate threat to the nation. No one was more convinced than Attorney General A. Mitchell Palmer. From a Quaker family in a small Pennsylvania town, the attorney general had graduated from Swarthmore College and had been admitted to the Pennsylvania bar in 1893 at the age of 21. After serving three terms as a congressman, he helped swing the Pennsylvania delegation to Wilson at the 1912 convention. Wilson offered him the post of secretary of war, but Palmer's pacifism led him to refuse. He did support the United States' entry into the war, however, and served as alien property custodian, a job created by the Trading with the Enemy Act. This position apparently convinced him of the danger of radical subversive activities in America. The bombing of his home intensified his fears, and in the summer of 1919, he determined to find and destroy the Red network. He organized a special antiradical division within the Justice Department and put a young man named J. Edgar Hoover in charge of coordinating information on domestic radical activities.

Obsessed with the "Red menace," Palmer instituted a series of raids, beginning in November 1919. Simultaneously, in several cities, his men rounded up 250 members of the Union of

Russian Workers, many of whom were beaten and roughed up in the process. In December, 249 aliens, including the famous anarchist Emma Goldman, were deported, although very few were Communists and even fewer had any desire to overthrow the government of the United States. Palmer's men arrested 500 people in Detroit and 800 in Boston.

The Palmer raids, which probably constituted the most massive violation of civil liberties in America history to this date, found few dangerous radicals but did fan the flames of fear and intolerance in the country. In Indiana, a jury quickly acquitted a man who had killed an alien for yelling, "To hell with the United States."

Palmer became a national hero for ferreting out Communists, but Assistant Secretary of State Louis Post insisted that the arrested aliens be given legal rights, and in the end only about 600 were deported, out of the more than 5,000 arrested. The worst of the "Red Scare" was over by the end of 1920, but the fear of radicals and the emotional patriotism colored the rest of the decade.

The Red Scare promoted many patriotic organizations, such as the American Legion, the American Defense Society, the Sentinels of the Republic, the United States Flag Association, and the Daughters of the American Revolution. Such groups were often united by an obsessive fear of Communists and radicals.

Some organizations targeted women social reformers. One group attacked the "Hot-House, Hull House Variety of Parlor Bolshevists." Even the Needlework Guild and the Sunshine Society were accused of being influenced by Communists. The connections were made only through the use of half-truths, innuendo, and outright lies. To protest their charges did little good, for the accusers knew the truth and would not be deflected from their purpose of exterminating dangerous radicals.

The Sacco-Vanzetti Case

One result of the Red Scare was the conviction of two Italian anarchists, Nicola Sacco and Bar-

tolomeo Vanzetti. Arrested in 1920 for allegedly murdering a guard during a robbery of a shoe factory in South Braintree, Massachusetts, the two were convicted and sentenced to die in the summer of 1921 on what many liberals considered circumstantial and flimsy evidence. Indeed, it seemed to many that the two Italians, who spoke in broken English and were admitted anarchists, were punished because of their radicalism and their foreign appearance. Many intellectuals in Europe and America rallied to their defense, but all appeals failed, and the two were executed in the electric chair on August 23, 1927.

Ku Klux Klan

While the superpatriotic societies exploited the fear that radicals and Bolsheviks were subverting the American way of life from within, the Ku Klux Klan went further. The Klan was organized in Georgia by William J. Simmons, a lay preacher, salesman, and member of many fraternal organizations. He adopted the name and white-sheet uniform of the old antiblack Reconstruction organization that was glorified in 1915 in the immensely popular but racist feature film *Birth of a Nation*. Simmons appointed himself head ("Imperial Wizard") of the new Klan.

Unlike the original organization, which took almost anyone who was white, the new Klan was thoroughly Protestant and explicitly antiforeign, anti-Semitic, and anti-Catholic. It opposed the teaching of evolution; glorified old-time religion; supported immigration restriction; denounced short skirts, petting, and "demon rum"; and upheld patriotism and the purity of women. The Klan grew rapidly after the war because of aggressive recruiting but also because of the fear and confusion of the period.

The Klan flourished in small towns and rural areas in the South, where it set out to keep the returning black soldiers in their "proper place," but it soon spread throughout the country, and at least half the members came from urban areas. At the peak of its power, the Klan

The Klan, with its elaborate rituals and its white uniforms, exploited the fear of blacks, Jews, liberals, and Catholics while preaching "traditional" American values.

had several million members. The Klan's power declined after 1924, but widespread fear of Catholicism and everything perceived as un-American remained.

A PROSPERING ECONOMY

Although the decade after World War I was a time of considerable intolerance and anxiety, it was also a time of industrial expansion and widespread prosperity. Fueled by new technology, more efficient planning and management, and innovative advertising, industrial production almost doubled during the decade, and the gross national product rose by an astonishing 40 percent. A construction boom created new suburbs around American cities, while a new generation of skyscrapers transformed the cities themselves. However, the benefits of this prosperity fell unevenly on the many social groups comprising American society.

The Rising Standard of Living

Signs of the new prosperity appeared in many forms. Millions of sturdy homes and apartments were built and equipped with the latest conveniences. The number of telephones installed nearly doubled between 1915 and 1930. Plastics, rayon, and cellophane altered the habits of millions of Americans, while new products, such as cigarette lighters, reinforced concrete, dry ice, and Pyrex glass, created new demands unheard of a decade before.

In sharp contrast to the nineteenth century, Americans had more leisure time, a shorter work week, and often vacation with pay. The American diet also improved during the decade. Health improved and life expectancy increased.

Educational opportunities also expanded. In 1900, only one in ten young people of high school age remained in school. By 1930, that number had increased to six in ten, and much of the improvement came in the 1920s. In 1900, only one college-age person in 33 attended an institution of higher learning; by 1930, the ratio was one in seven, and over a million people were enrolled in the nation's colleges.

The Evolution of the Modern Corporation

The structure and practice of American business were transformed in the 1920s. After a crisis created by the economic downturn of 1920–1922, business boomed until the crash of 1929. Mergers increased during the decade, creating such giants as General Electric, General Motors, Sears Roebuck, Du Pont, and U.S. Rubber. By 1930, the 200 largest corporations controlled almost half the corporate wealth in the country. Large businesses also diversified during the decade. GE and Westinghouse began to produce household appliances and radios; Du Pont moved into plastics, paints, dyes, and film.

But perhaps the most important business trend of the decade was the emergence of a new kind of manager. No longer did family entrepreneurs make decisions relating to prices, wages, or output. Alfred P. Sloan, Jr., an engineer who reorganized General Motors, was a prototype of the new kind of manager. He divided the company into components, freeing the top managers to concentrate on planning new products, controlling inventory, and integrating the whole operation. Marketing and advertising became as important as production, and many businesses began to spend more money on research. The new manager often had a large staff but owned no part of the company. He was usually an expert at cost accounting and analyzing data. Increasingly, he was a graduate of one of the new business colleges.

The new managers introduced pensions, recreation facilities, cafeterias, and, in some cases, paid vacations and profit-sharing plans. The managers were not being altruistic, however; "welfare capitalism" was designed to reduce worker discontent and to discourage labor unions. Planning was the key to the new corporate structure, and planning often meant a continuation of the business-government cooperation that had developed during World War I. All the planning and the new managerial authority failed to prevent the economic collapse of 1929, but the modern corporation survived the Depression to exert a growing influence on American life in the 1930s and after.

Electrification

The 1920s also marked the climax of the "second industrial revolution." During the late nineteenth century, American industry had primarily manufactured goods intended for other producers. In the first quarter of the twentieth century, as industries like coal, textiles, and steel stabilized or declined, new manufacturing concerns that produced rubber, synthetic fabrics, chemicals, and petroleum arose. They focused on goods for consumers, such as silk stockings, washing machines, and cars.

Powering the second industrial revolution was electricity. Between 1900 and 1920, the replacement of steam power by electricity worked as profound a change as had the substitution of steam power for water power after the Civil War. In 1902, electricity supplied a mere 2 percent of all industrial power; by 1929, this figure rose to fully 80 percent. Less than one of every ten American homes was supplied with electricity in 1907, but more than two-thirds were by 1929. Powered by electricity, American industries reached new heights of productivity. By 1929, the work force was turning out twice as many goods as a similarly sized work force had ten years before.

Electricity brought dozens of gadgets and labor-saving devices into the home; washing machines, electric irons, vacuum cleaners, electric toasters, and sewing machines lightened housework. The "Great White Ways" of the cities symbolized progress, but they also made the darkness of slums and hamlets seem even more forbidding.

Automobile Culture

Automobile manufacturing, like electrification, underwent spectacular growth in the 1920s. The automobile was one major factor in the postwar economic boom. It stimulated and transformed the petroleum, steel, and rubber industries. The auto forced the construction and improvement of streets and highways and caused the spending of millions of dollars on labor and concrete.

The auto changed American life in myriad ways. It led to the decline of the small crossroads store as well as many small churches because the rural family could now drive to the larger city or town. The tractor changed methods of farming. Trucks replaced the horse and wagon and altered the marketing of farm products. Buses began to eliminate the one-room school, because it was now possible to transport students to larger schools. The automobile allowed young people for the first time to escape the chaperoning of parents. It was hardly the "house of prostitution on wheels" that one judge called it, but it did change courting habits in all parts of the country.

Gradually, as the decade progressed, the automobile became not just transportation but a sign of status. Advertising helped create the impression that it was the symbol of the good life, of sex, freedom, and speed. The auto in turn transformed advertising and design. It even altered the way products were purchased. By 1926, three-fourths of the cars sold were bought on some kind of deferred-payment plan. Installment credit, first tried by a group of businessmen in Toledo, Ohio, in 1915 to sell more autos, was soon used to promote sewing machines, refrigerators, and other consumer products. "Buy now, pay later" became the American way.

The United States had a love affair with the auto from the beginning. The number of registered motor vehicles rose from 8,000 in 1900 to nearly 27 million in 1929. Automobile culture was a mass movement.

The auto industry, like most American businesses, went through a period of consolidation in the 1920s. In 1908, more than 250 companies were manufacturing automobiles in the United States. By 1929, only 44 remained.

A pioneer of the auto industry, Henry Ford is often credited with inventing the assembly line. In actuality it was the work of a team of engineers. But the Ford Motor Company was the first organization to perfect the moving assembly line and mass-production technology. Introduced in 1913, the new method reduced the time it took to produce a car from 14 hours to an hour and a half.

In 1914, Ford startled the country by announcing that he was increasing the minimum pay of the Ford assembly-line worker to $5 a day (almost twice the national average pay for factory workers). Ford did not do so for humanitarian reasons. He wanted a dependable work force and understood that skilled workers were less likely to quit if they received good pay.

Henry Ford was not easy to work for. One newspaper account in 1928 called him "an industrial fascist—the Mussolini of Detroit." He ruthlessly pressured his dealers and used them to bail him out of difficult financial situations. Instead of borrowing money from a bank, he forced dealers to buy extra cars, trucks, and tractors. He used spies on the assembly lines and fired workers and executives at the least provocation. But he did produce a car that transformed America.

The Model T, which cost $600 in 1912, was reduced gradually in price until it sold for only $290 in 1924. The "Tin Lizzie," as it was affectionately called, was light and easily repaired. Replacement parts were standardized and widely available. The Model T did not change from year to year, and it did not deviate from its one color, black. The Model A, introduced in 1927, was never as popular or as successful as the Model T.

The Exploding Metropolis

The automobile enabled American cities to expand into the countryside. In the late nineteenth century, railroads and streetcars had created suburbs near the major cities, but the great expansion of suburban population occurred in the 1920s. Shaker Heights, a Cleveland suburb, was in some ways a typical development. Built on the site of a former Shaker community, the new suburb was planned and developed by two businessmen. They controlled the size and style of the homes and restricted buyers. No blacks were allowed. Curving roads led off the main auto boulevards, while landscaping and natural areas contributed to a parklike atmosphere. The suburb increased in population from 1,700 in 1919 to over 15,000 in 1929, and the price of lots multiplied by 10 during the decade. Other suburbs grew in an equally spectacular manner. The biggest land boom of all occurred in Florida, where the city of Miami mushroomed from 30,000 in 1920 to 75,000 in 1925.

The automobile transformed every city, but the most spectacular growth of all took place in two cities that the car virtually created. Detroit grew from 300,000 in 1900 to 1,837,000 in 1930, while Los Angeles expanded from 114,000 in 1900 to 778,000 in 1930. With sprawling subdivisions connected by a growing network of roads, Los Angeles was the city of the future.

While cities expanded horizontally during the 1920s, sprawling into the countryside, city centers grew vertically. A building boom that peaked near the end of the decade created new skylines for most urban centers. Even cities such as Tulsa, Dallas, Kansas City, Memphis, and Syracuse built skyscrapers.

A Communications Revolution

Changing communications altered the way many Americans lived as well as the way they conducted business. The telephone, first demonstrated in 1876, was found in 13 million homes by the end of the 1920. Commercial radio broadcasting, begun by WWJ in Detroit in the summer of 1920, was an immediate success. Five hundred stations took to the airwaves in 1922 alone. By the end of the decade, people in all sections of the country were humming the same popular songs. Actors and announcers became celebrities. The music, voice, and sound of the radio marked the end of silence and, to a certain extent, the end of privacy. Even more dramatic was the phenomenon of the movies. Forty million viewers a week went to the movies in 1922, and by 1929, that had increased to over 100 million. Charlie Chaplin, Rudolph Valentino, Lillian Gish, and Greta Garbo were more famous and more important to millions of Americans than most government officials were.

Not only movie stars became celebrities in the 1920s. Sports figures such as Babe Ruth, Bobby Jones, Jack Dempsey, and Red Grange were just as famous. The great spectator sports of the decade owed much to the increase of leisure time and to the automobile, the radio, and the mass-circulation newspaper. Thousands drove automobiles to college towns to watch football heroes perform. Millions listened for scores or read about the results the next day. One writer in 1924 called this era "the age of play." He might better have called it "the age of the spectator." The popularity of sports, like the movies and radio, was in part the product of technology.

The year 1927 seemed to mark the beginning of the new age of mechanization and progress. That was the year Henry Ford produced his 15-millionth car and introduced the Model A. During that year, radio-telephone service was established between San Francisco and Manila. The first radio network was organized (CBS), and the first talking movie was released (*The Jazz Singer*). In 1927, the Holland Tunnel, the first underwater vehicular roadway, connected New York and New Jersey. It was also the year that Charles Lindbergh flew from New York to Paris in his single-engine plane in 33½ hours. Lindbergh was not the first to fly the Atlantic, but he was the first to fly it alone, an accomplishment that won him $25,000 in prize money and captured the world's imagination. He was young and handsome, and his feat seemed to represent not only the triumph of an individual but also the triumph of the machine. When Americans cheered Lindbergh, they were reaffirming their belief in the American dream and their faith in individual initiative as well as in technology.

HOPES RAISED, PROMISES DEFERRED

The 1920s was a time when all kinds of hopes seemed realizable. "Don't envy successful salesmen—be one!" one advertisement screamed.

Buy a car. Build a house. Start a career. Invest in land. Invest in stocks. Make a fortune.

Not all Americans, of course, were intent on making a stock market killing or expected to win a huge fortune. Some merely wished to retain traditional values in a society that seemed to question them. Others wanted a steady job or perhaps a new appliance. Many discovered, however, that no matter how modest their hopes might be, they lay tantalizingly out of reach.

Clash of Values

During the 1920s, radio, movies, advertising, and mass-circulation magazines promoted a national, secular culture. But this new culture, which emphasized consumption, pleasure, upward mobility, even sex, clashed with traditional values of hard work, thrift, church, family, and home. Still, many Americans feared that new cultural values, scientific breakthroughs, and new ideas like bolshevism, relativism, Freudianism, and biblical criticism threatened their familiar way of life. A trial over the teaching of evolutionary ideas in high school in the little town of Dayton, Tennessee, symbolized the clash of the old versus the new.

The scientific community and most educated people had long accepted the basic concepts of evolution, if not all the details of Charles Darwin's theories. But many Christians, especially those from Protestant evangelical churches, accepted the Bible as the literal truth and opposed Darwin's ideas. Several states, including Tennessee, passed laws forbidding the teaching of evolution.

John Scopes, a young biology teacher, volunteered to test the law by teaching evolutionary theory to his class, and the state of Tennessee brought him to trial. The American Civil Liberties Union hired Clarence Darrow, perhaps the country's most famous defense lawyer, to defend Scopes; the World Christian Fundamentalist Association engaged William Jennings Bryan, former presidential candidate and secretary of state, to assist the prosecution. Bryan was old and

tired (he died only a few days after the trial), but he was still an eloquent and deeply religious man. In cross-examination, Darrow reduced Bryan's statements to intellectual rubble and revealed also that Bryan was at a loss to explain much of the Bible. He could not explain how Eve was created from Adam's rib or where Cain got his wife. Nevertheless, the jury declared Scopes guilty, for he had clearly broken the law. He was fined $100, though the case was later dismissed by a higher state court. But the press from all over the country covered the trial and upheld science and academic freedom.

Immigration and Migration

Just as the Scopes trial demonstrated a degree of resistance to change, a similar attitude was apparent in many Americans' views on immigration. Anyone perceived as "un-American" seemed to threaten the old ways. A movement to restrict immigration had existed for decades. An act passed in 1882 prohibited the entry of criminals, paupers, and the insane, and special agreements between 1880 and 1908 restricted both Chinese and Japanese immigration. But it was the fear and intolerance of the war years and the period right after the war that resulted in major restrictive legislation.

The first strongly restrictive immigration law passed in 1917 over President Wilson's veto. It required a literacy test for the first time (an immigrant had to read a passage in one of a number of languages). The bill also prohibited the immigration of certain political radicals. The literacy test did not stop the more than one million immigrants who poured into the country in 1920 and 1921, however.

In 1921 Congress limited European immigration in any one year to 3 percent of the number of each nationality present in the country in 1910. Congress changed the quota in 1924 to 2 percent of those in the country in 1890, in order to limit immigration from southern and eastern Europe and ban all immigration from Asia. The

John Steuart Curry was one of the 1920s regionalist painters who found inspiration in the American heartland. In Baptism in Kansas, he depicts a religious ritual that underscores the conflict between rural and
urban values.

National Origins Act of 1927 set an overall limit
of 150,000 European immigrants a year, with
more than 60 percent coming from Great Britain
and Germany but less than 4 percent from Italy.
Restrictive immigration laws, sponsored by Republicans, helped to attract American Jews, Italians, and Poles to the Democratic Party.

The immigration acts of 1921, 1924, and
1927, in sharply limiting European immigration
and virtually banning Asian immigrants, cut off
the streams of cheap labor that had provided
muscle for an industrializing country since the
early nineteenth century. At the same time, by
exempting immigrants from the Western Hemisphere, the new laws opened the country to
Mexican laborers who were eager to escape

poverty in their own land and to work in the
fields and farms of California and the Southwest.

Mexican immigrants soon became the country's largest first-generation immigrant group.
Nearly half a million arrived in the 1920s, in
contrast to only 31,000 in the first decade of the
century. Some worked on farms; others migrated
to industrial cities such as Detroit, St. Louis, and
Kansas City. Northern companies recruited
them and paid their transportation. During the
1920s, El Paso, Texas, became more than half
Mexican, San Antonio a little less than half. Like
black Americans, the Mexicans found opportunity by migrating, but they did not escape prejudice or hardship.

Just as foreign immigrants were attracted to jobs in the United States, from 1915 to 1920 blacks migrated north in great numbers seeking a better life. One young black man wrote to the Chicago *Defender* from Texas that he would prefer to go to Chicago or Philadelphia, but "I don't care where so long as I go where a man is a man." Most black migrants were young and unskilled. They found work in the huge meatpacking plants of Chicago, East St. Louis, Omaha, and Kansas City and in the shipyards and steel mills. The black population of Chicago increased from 44,000 in 1910 to 234,000 by 1930. Cleveland's black population grew eightfold between 1910 and 1930.

Blacks unquestionably improved their lives by moving north. But most were like the Parkers, their dreams only partly fulfilled. Most crowded into segregated housing and faced prejudice and hate. "Black men stay South," the Chicago *Tribune* advised and offered to pay the transportation for any who would return. The presence of more blacks in the industrial cities of the North led to the development of black ghettos and increased the racial tension that occasionally flared into violence.

One of the worst race riots took place in Chicago in 1919. The riot began at a beach on a hot July day. A black youth drowned in a white swimming area. Blacks claimed he had been hit by stones, but the police refused to arrest any of the white men. A group of blacks attacked the police, and the riot was on. It lasted four days. Several dozen people were killed and hundreds were wounded.

Race riots broke out in other places as well in the early 1920s. The wave of violence and racism angered and disillusioned W. E. B. Du Bois, who had urged blacks to close ranks and support the American cause during the war. In an angry editorial for *The Crisis,* he called upon blacks

to fight a sterner, longer more unbending battle against the forces of hell in our own land. *We return. We return from fighting. We return fight-*

ing. Make way for Democracy; we saved it in France, and by the Great Jehovah, we will save it in the United States of America, or know the reason why.

Marcus Garvey: Black Messiah

Du Bois was not the only militant black leader in the postwar years. A flamboyant Jamaican fed a growing sense of black pride during that time. Marcus Garvey arrived in New York at the age of 29. Largely self-taught, he was an admirer of Booker T. Washington. Although he never abandoned Washington's philosophy of self-help, he thoroughly transformed it. Washington focused on economic betterment through self-help; Garvey saw self-help as a means of political empowerment by which African peoples would reclaim their homelands from European powers.

In Jamaica, Garvey had founded the Universal Negro Improvement Association. By 1919, he had established 30 branches in the United States and the Caribbean. He also set up the newspaper *The Negro World,* the Black Cross Nurses, and a chain of grocery stores, millinery shops, and restaurants. His biggest project was the Black Star Line, a steamship company, to be owned and operated by blacks. Advocating the return of blacks to Africa, he declared himself the "provisional president of Africa," a title he adopted from Eamon De Valera, the first "provisional president of Ireland." He glorified the African past and preached that God and Jesus were black.

Garvey won converts, mostly among lower-middle-class blacks, through the force of his oratory and the power of his personality, but especially through his message of black pride. Thousands of his followers invested their money in the Black Star Line. The line soon collapsed, however, in part because white entrepreneurs sold Garvey inferior ships and equipment. Garvey was arrested for using the mails to defraud shareholders and was sentenced to five years in prison. President Coolidge commuted the sentence. Ordered deported as an undesirable alien,

Marcus Garvey (second from right), shown dressed in his favorite uniform, became a hero for many black Americans.

Garvey left America in 1927. Despite Garvey's failures, he convinced thousands of American blacks that they could join together and accomplish something and that they should feel pride in their heritage and their future.

The Harlem Renaissance and the Lost Generation

A group of black writers, artists, and intellectuals who settled in Harlem after the war sought a way to be both black and American. Alain Locke, the first black Rhodes scholar and a dapper professor of philosophy at Howard University, was in one sense the father of the renaissance. His collection of essays and art, *The New*

Negro (1925), announced the movement to the outside world and outlined black contributions to American culture and civilization. Langston Hughes, a poet and novelist born in Missouri, went to high school in Cleveland, lived in Mexico, and traveled in Europe and Africa before settling in Harlem. He wrote bitter but laughing poems, using black vernacular to describe the pathos and the pride of American blacks. In *Weary Blues*, he adapted the rhythm and beat of black jazz and the blues to his poetry. Jazz was an important force in Harlem in the 1920s, and many prosperous whites came from downtown to listen to Louis Armstrong, Fletcher Henderson, Duke Ellington, and other black musicians.

The Harlem writers struggled with how to be both black and intellectual. They worried that they depended on white patrons, who introduced them to writers and artists in Greenwich Village and made contacts for them at New York publishing houses. Many of the white patrons pressured the black writers to conform to the white elite idea of black authenticity. Jean Toomer wrote haunting poems trying to explore the difficulty of black identity, and in a novel, *Cane* (1923), he sketched maladjusted, almost grotesque characters who expressed some of the alienation that many writers felt in the 1920s.

Many black writers felt alienated from American society. They tried living in Paris or in Greenwich Village, but most felt drawn to Harlem, which in the 1920s was rapidly becoming the center of black population in New York City. Much of the work of the Harlem writers was read by very small numbers, but another generation of young black intellectuals in the 1960s still struggling with the dilemma of how to be both black and American would rediscover it.

One did not need to be black to be disillusioned with society. Many white intellectuals, writers, and artists also felt alienated from what they perceived as the materialism, conformity, and provincial prejudice that dominated American life. Many writers of this postwar "Lost

Generation," including F. Scott Fitzgerald, Ernest Hemingway, E. E. Cummings, and T. S. Eliot, moved to Europe, where they wrote novels, plays, and poems about America.

For many writers, the disillusionment began with the war itself. Hemingway eagerly volunteered to go to Europe as an ambulance driver. But when he was wounded on the Italian front, he reevaluated the purpose of the war and the meaning of all the slaughter. His novel *The Sun Also Rises* (1926) is the story of the purposeless European wanderings of a group of Americans. But it is also the story of Jake Barnes, made impotent by a war injury. His "unreasonable wound" is a symbol of the futility of life in the postwar period.

F. Scott Fitzgerald epitomized some of the despair of his generation, which had "grown up to find all Gods dead, all wars fought, all faiths in man shaken." His best novel, *The Great Gatsby* (1925), was a critique of the American success myth. The book describes the elaborate parties given by a mysterious businessman, who, it turns out, has made his money illegally as a bootlegger. Gatsby hopes to win back a beautiful woman who has forsaken him for another man. But wealth won't buy happiness, and Gatsby's life ends tragically, as so many lives seemed to end in the novels written during the decade.

Sherwood Anderson's novel *Winesburg, Ohio* (1919) and Sinclair Lewis's *Main Street* (1920) and *Babbitt* (1922) criticized the narrowness of midwestern small-town middle-class culture. H. L. Mencken, who edited the *American Mercury* in Baltimore, denounced what he called "the booboisie."

Ironically, while intellectuals despaired over American society and complained that art could not survive in a business-dominated civilization, literature flourished. The novels of Hemingway, Fitzgerald, Lewis, William Faulkner, and Gertrude Stein, the plays of Eugene O'Neill and Maxwell Anderson, the poetry of T. S. Eliot, Hart Crane, E. E. Cummings, and Marianne Moore, and the work of many black writers

marked the 1920s as one of the most creative decades in American literature.

Women Struggle for Equality

In the eventful postwar decade, women not only won the right to vote, as seen in Chapter 22; they also adopted changes in their ways of living and working. Any mention of the role of women in the 1920s brings to mind the image of the flapper—a young woman with a short skirt, bobbed hair, and a boyish figure doing the Charleston, smoking, drinking, and being very casual about sex. F. Scott Fitzgerald's heroines in novels like *This Side of Paradise* (1920) and *The Great Gatsby* (1925) provided the role models for young people to imitate, and movie stars such as Clara Bow and Gloria Swanson, aggressively seductive on the screen, supplied even more dramatic examples of flirtatious and provocative behavior.

Without question, women acquired more sexual freedom and more control over their reproductive lives in the 1920s. Contraceptives, especially the diaphragm, became more readily available during the decade, and Margaret Sanger, who had been indicted for sending birth control information through the mail in 1914, organized the first American birth control conference in 1921. Family size declined during the decade (from 3.6 children in 1900 to 2.5 in 1930), and young people were apparently more inclined to marry for love than for security.

Despite more freedom for women, however, the double standard persisted. "When lovely woman stoops to folly, she can always find someone to stoop with her," one male writer announced, "but not always someone to lift her up again to the level where she belongs."

Women's lives were shaped by other innovations of the 1920s. Electricity, running water, washing machines, vacuum cleaners, and other labor-saving devices made housework easier for the middle class but did not reduce time spent doing housework. Standards of cleanliness rose, and women were urged to make their houses more spotless than any nineteenth-century housekeeper would have felt necessary. At the same time, magazines and newspapers bombarded women with advertising urging them to buy products to make themselves better housekeepers.

More women worked outside the home. The greatest expansion of jobs for women was in white-collar occupations that were being feminized—secretary, bookkeeper, clerk, telephone operator. In 1930, fully 96 percent of stenographers were women. Although more married women had jobs (an increase of 25 percent during the decade), most of them held low-paying jobs, and most single women assumed that marriage would terminate their employment.

For some working women—secretaries and teachers, for example—marriage often led to dismissal. According to one businessman, married women are "very unstable in their work; their first claim is to home and children." Considering these attitudes, it is not surprising that the disparity between male and female wages widened during the decade. By 1930, women earned only 57 percent of what men were paid. Although the proportion of women lawyers and bankers increased slightly during the decade, the rate of growth declined, and the number of women doctors and scientists dropped. In the 1920s, women acquired some sexual freedom and a limited amount of opportunity outside the home, but the promise of the prewar feminist movement and the hopes that accompanied the suffrage amendment remained unfulfilled.

Winning the vote for women did not assure equality. In most states, a woman's service belonged to her husband. Women could vote, but often they could not serve on juries. In some states, women could not hold office, own a business, or sign a contract without their husbands' permission. Women were usually held responsible for an illegitimate birth, and divorce laws almost always favored men.

Alice Paul, who had led the militant National Women's Party in 1916, chained herself to the White House fence once again to promote an equal rights amendment to the Constitution. The amendment received support in Wisconsin and several other states, but many women opposed it on the grounds that such an amendment would cancel the special legislation to protect women in industry that had taken so long to enact in the two decades before.

Rural America in the 1920s

Most farmers did not share in the prosperity of the 1920s. Responding to worldwide demands and rising prices for wheat, cotton, and other products, many farmers invested in more land, tractors, and farm equipment during the war. The prices tumbled. In the postwar depression, many farmers could not pay their debts. Because the value of land fell, they often lost both mortgage and land and still owed the bank money.

The changing nature of farming was part of the problem. The use of chemical fertilizers and new hybrid seeds increased the yield per acre. The use of tractors and trucks made farming more efficient and released for cash crops land formerly used to raise feed for horses and mules. Production increased at the very time that worldwide demand for American farm products declined.

Large commercial operations, using mechanized equipment, produced most of the cash crops. Many small farmers found themselves unable to compete with agribusiness. Some of them, along with many farm laborers, solved the problem of declining rural profitability by leaving the farms. In 1900, fully 40 percent of the labor force worked on farms; by 1930, only 21 percent earned their living from the land.

Few farmers could afford the products of the new technology. While many middle-class urban families were buying new cars, radios, and bathrooms, only one farm family in ten had electricity in the 1920s. The lot of the farm wife had not changed for centuries. She ran a domestic factory, did all the household chores, and helped on the farm as well.

As they had done in the nineteenth century, farmers tried to act collectively. They sought to influence legislation in the state capital and in Washington. Most of their effort went into the McNary-Haugen Farm Relief Bill, which would have provided for government support for key agricultural products. The bill was introduced a number of times between 1924 and 1928 without success, but farm organizations in all parts of the country learned how to work together to influence Congress. That would have important ramifications for the future.

The Workers' Share of Prosperity

Hundreds of thousands of workers improved their standard of living in the 1920s, yet inequality grew. Real wages increased 21 percent between 1923 and 1929, but corporate dividends went up by nearly two-thirds in the same period. The workers did not profit from the increased production they helped to create, and that boded ill for the future. The richest 5 percent of the population increased their share of the wealth from a quarter to a third, and the wealthiest one percent controlled a whopping 19 percent of all income. Even among workers there was great disparity. Those employed on the auto assembly lines or in the new factories producing radios saw their wages go up, and many saw their hours decline. Yet the majority of American working-class families did not earn enough to move them much beyond the subsistence level.

While some workers prospered in the 1920s, organized labor fell on hard times. Labor union membership fell from about 5 million in 1921 to less than 3.5 million in 1929. A number of large employers lured workers away from unions with promises that seemed to equal union benefits: profit-sharing plans, pensions, and their own company unions.

The more aggressive unions like the United Mine Workers, led by the flamboyant John L. Lewis, also encountered difficulties. The union's attempt to organize the mines in West Virginia had led to violent clashes between union members and imported guards. President Harding called out troops in 1921 to put down an "army organized by the strikers." The next year, Lewis called the greatest coal strike in history, and further violence erupted, especially in Williamson County, Illinois. Internal strife also weakened the union, and Lewis had to accept wage reductions in the negotiations of 1927.

Organized labor, like so many other groups, struggled desperately during the decade to take advantage of the prosperity. It won some victories, and it made some progress. But American affluence was beyond the reach of many groups during the decade. Eventually the inequality would lead to disaster.

THE BUSINESS OF POLITICS

Business, especially big business, prospered in the 1920s, and the image of businessmen, enhanced by their important role in World War I, rose further. The government reduced regulation, lowered taxes, and cooperated to aid business expansion at home and abroad. Business and politics, always intertwined, were especially allied during the decade. Republican presidents Harding, Coolidge, and Hoover favored an activist federal government whose main interest was big business. Wealthy financiers such as Andrew Mellon and Charles Dawes played important roles in formulating both domestic and foreign policy. Even more significant, a new kind of businessman was elected president in 1928. Herbert Hoover, international engineer and efficiency expert, was the very symbol of the modern techniques and practices that many people confidently expected to transform the United States and the world.

Harding and Coolidge

The Republicans, almost assured of victory in 1920 because of bitter reaction against Woodrow Wilson, nominated Warren G. Harding, a former newspaper editor from Ohio. To balance the ticket, the Republicans chose as their vice-presidential candidate Calvin Coolidge of Massachusetts, who had gained attention by his firm stand during the Boston police strike. The Democrats, after 44 roll calls, finally nominated Governor James Cox of Ohio and picked Franklin D. Roosevelt, a young politician from New York, as his running mate. Harding won in a record landslide, but less than 50 percent of the eligible voters went to the polls.

In contrast to the reform-minded Presidents Roosevelt and Wilson, Harding reflected the conservatism of the 1920s. He was a jovial man who brought many Ohio friends to Washington and placed them in positions of power. At a little house a few blocks from the White House on K Street, Harry Daugherty, Harding's attorney general and longtime associate, held forth with a group of friends. Amid bootleg liquor and the atmosphere of a brothel, they did a brisk business in selling favors, taking bribes, and organizing illegal schemes. Harding was not personally corrupt, and the nation's leading businessmen approved of his policies of higher tariffs and lower taxes. Nor did he spend all his time drinking with his cronies. He called a conference on disarmament and another to deal with the problems of unemployment, and he pardoned Eugene Debs, who had been in prison since the war. When he died suddenly in August 1923, the American people genuinely mourned him.

Only after Harding's vice president, Calvin Coolidge, succeeded to the presidency did the full extent of the corruption and scandals of the Harding administration come to light. A Senate committee discovered that the secretary of the interior, Albert Fall, had illegally leased government-owned oil reserves in the Teapot Dome section of Wyoming to private business interests in return for over $300,000 in bribes. Illegal activities were also discovered in the Veterans Administration and elsewhere in government. Harding's attorney general resigned in disgrace, the secretary of the navy barely avoided prison, two of Harding's advisers committed suicide, and the secretary of the interior was sentenced to jail.

Coolidge was dour and taciturn, but honest. No hint of scandal infected his administration or his personal life. He ran for election in 1924 with the financier Charles Dawes as his running mate. There was little question that he would win. The Democrats were so equally divided between northern urban Catholics and southern rural Protestants that it took 103 ballots before they nominated John Davis, an affable corporate lawyer with little national following. A group of dissidents, mostly representing the farmers and the laborers dissatisfied with both nominees, formed a new Progressive Party and nominated Robert La Follette of Wisconsin for president. They drafted a platform calling for government ownership of railroads and ratification of the child labor amendment. La Follette received nearly 5 million votes, only 3.5 million short of

Warren G. Harding (left) and Calvin Coolidge were immensely popular in the 1920s, but later historians criticized them and rated them among the worst of American presidents.

Davis's total. But Coolidge and prosperity won easily.

Symbolizing the pro-business attitude of the Harding and Coolidge administrations was the wealthy Andrew Mellon, appointed secretary of the treasury by Harding and retained in that post by the next two presidents. Mellon set out to lower individual and corporate taxes. In 1922, Congress, with Mellon's endorsement, repealed the wartime excess profits tax, and increased tax exemptions for families. In 1928, Congress reduced taxes further, removed most excise taxes, and lowered the corporate tax rate. The 200 largest corporations increased their assets during the decade from $43 billion to $81 billion. Coolidge observed, "The chief business of the American people is business."

Herbert Hoover

One bright light in the lackluster Harding and Coolidge administrations was Herbert Hoover, who served as secretary of commerce under both presidents. Hoover had made a fortune as an international mining engineer before 1914 and then earned the reputation of a great humanitarian for his work managing the Belgian Relief Committee and directing the Food Administration.

While secretary of commerce, Hoover used the force of the federal government to regulate, stimulate, and promote, but he believed first of all in American free enterprise and local volunteer action to solve problems. In 1921, he convinced Harding of the need to do something about unemployment during the postwar recession. The president's conference on unemployment, convened in September 1921, marked the first time the national government had admitted any responsibility to the unemployed. The result of the conference (the first of many on a variety of topics that Hoover was to organize) was a flood of publicity, pamphlets, and advice from experts. Most of all, the conference urged state and local governments and businesses to cooper-

ate on a volunteer basis to solve the problem. The primary responsibility of the federal government, Hoover believed, was to educate and promote. With all his activity and his organizing, Hoover got the reputation during the Harding and Coolidge years as an efficient and progressive administrator, and he became one of the most popular figures in government service.

Foreign Policy in the 1920s

The decade of the 1920s is often remembered as a time of isolation, when the United States rejected the League of Nations treaty and turned its back on the rest of the world. In fact, the United States remained involved—indeed, increased its involvement—in international affairs during the decade. Although the United States never joined the League of Nations or the World Court, it cooperated with many League agencies and conferences and took the lead in trying to reduce naval armaments and to solve the problems of international finance caused in part by the war.

Indeed, business, trade, and finance marked the decade as one of international expansion. With American corporate investments overseas growing sevenfold during the decade, the United States was transformed from a debtor to a creditor nation. The United States also continued its involvement in the affairs of South and Central American countries. Yet the United States took up its role of international power reluctantly and with a number of contradictory and disastrous results.

"We seek no part in directing the destiny of the world," Harding announced in his inaugural address, but even Harding discovered that international problems would not disappear. One that required immediate attention was the naval arms race.

At the Washington Conference on Naval Disarmament, which convened in November 1921, Secretary of State Charles Evans Hughes startled the delegates by proposing a ten-year "holiday" on the construction of warships and by offering to sink or scrap 845,000 tons of American ships, including 30 battleships. He urged Britain and Japan to do the same.

The conference participants ultimately agreed to fix the tonnage of capital ships at a ratio of the United States and Great Britain, 5; Japan, 3; and France and Italy, 1.67. Japan agreed only reluctantly, but when the United States promised not to fortify its Pacific island possessions, the Japanese yielded. The conference was hailed as the first time in history that the major nations of the world had agreed to disarm. And it was the United States that took the lead by offering to be the first to scrap its battleships.

American foreign policy in the 1920s tried to reduce the risk of international conflict, resist revolution, and make the world safe for trade and investment. American diplomats argued for an open door to trade in China, but in Latin America the United States had always assumed a special and distinct role. Throughout the decade, American investment in agriculture, minerals, petroleum, and manufacturing increased in the countries to the south.

The United States also continued the process of intervention begun earlier. By the end of the decade, the United States controlled the financial affairs of ten Latin American nations. The marines were withdrawn from the Dominican Republic in 1924, but that country remained a virtual protectorate of the United States until 1941. The government ordered the marines from Nicaragua in 1925 but sent them back the next year when a liberal insurrection, led by the charismatic Augusto Sandino, threatened the conservative government. One American coffee planter decided in 1931 that the American intervention had been a disaster. "Today we are hated and despised," he announced. "This feeling has been created by employing American marines to hunt down and kill Nicaraguans in their own country." In 1934, Sandino was murdered by General Anastasio Somoza, a ruthless leader supported by the United States. For more than 40 years, Somoza and his two sons ruled Nicaragua as a private fiefdom, a legacy not yet resolved in that strife-torn country.

Mexico frightened American businessmen in the mid-1920s by beginning to nationalize foreign holdings in oil and mineral rights. Coolidge appointed Dwight W. Morrow of the J. P. Morgan Company as ambassador, and his conciliatory attitude led to agreements protecting American investments. Throughout the decade, the goal of U.S. policy toward Central and South America, whether in the form of negotiations or intervention, was to maintain a special sphere of influence.

The United States' policy toward Europe during this period was not always consistent or carefully thought out. At the end of the war, European countries owed the United States over $10 billion, with Great Britain and France responsible for about three-fourths of that amount. Nearly the only way European nations could repay the United States was by exporting products, but in a series of tariff acts, especially the Fordney-McCumber Tariff of 1922 and the Hawley-Smoot Tariff of 1930 Congress erected a protective barrier to trade. American policy of high tariffs (a counterproductive policy for a creditor nation) caused retaliation and restrictions on American trade, which American corporations were trying to increase.

The inability of the European countries to export products to the United States and to repay their loans was intertwined with the reparation agreement made with Germany. Germany's economy was in disarray after the war, with inflation raging and its industrial plant throttled by the peace treaty. By 1921, Germany was defaulting on its payments. The United States, which believed a healthy Germany important to the stability of Europe and of world trade, instituted a plan engineered by Charles Dawes whereby the German debt would be renegotiated and spread over a longer period. In the meantime, American bankers and the American government loaned Germany hundreds of millions of dollars. In the end, the United States loaned money to Germany so it could make payments to Britain and France so that those countries could continue their payments to the United States.

The United States had replaced Great Britain as the dominant force in international finance, but the nation in the 1920s was a reluctant and inconsistent world leader. Although the United States was hesitant to get involved in multinational agreements, in 1928 it signed the idealistic Kellogg-Briand pact, which outlawed war. Eventually 62 nations signed, but the only power behind the treaty was moral force rather than economic or military sanctions.

The Survival of Progressivism

The decade of the 1920s was a time of reaction against reform, but progressivism did not simply die. It survived in many forms through the period that Jane Addams called a time of "political and social sag." For example, child labor reformers worked through the Women's Trade Union League, the Consumers League, and other organizations to promote a child labor amendment to the Constitution after the 1919 law was declared unconstitutional in 1922.

The greatest success of the social justice movement was the 1921 Sheppard-Towner Maternity Act, one of the first pieces of federal social welfare legislation, the product of long progressive agitation. A study conducted by the Children's Bureau discovered that more than 3,000 mothers died in childbirth in 1918 and that more than 250,000 infants also died. The United States ranked eighteenth out of 20 countries in maternal mortality and eleventh in infant deaths. Josephine Baker, the pioneer physician and founder of the American Child Health Association, was not being ironic when she remarked, "It's six times safer to be a soldier in the trenches in France than to be born a baby in the United States."

The maternity bill called for a million dollars a year to assist the states in providing medical aid, consultation centers, and visiting nurses to teach expectant mothers how to care for themselves and their babies. The bill was controversial from the beginning. The American Medical Association and others attacked this bill as leading to socialism. Some opponents argued that it was put forward by extreme feminists or "inspired by foreign experiments in Communism."

Despite the opposition, the bill passed Congress and was signed by President Harding in 1921. The appropriation for the bill was only for six years, and the opposition, again raising the specter of a feminist-socialist-communist plot, succeeded in repealing the law in 1929.

Temperance Triumphant

Another survival of progressivism was the the temperance movement. Prohibition, like child labor reform and maternity benefits, was an important effort to conserve human resources. By 1918, over three-fourths of the people in the country lived in dry states or counties, but it was the war that allowed the anti-saloon advocates to associate prohibition with patriotism. "We have German enemies across the water," one prohibitionist announced. "We have German enemies in this country too. And the worst of all our German enemies, the most treacherous, the most menacing are Pabst, Schlitz, Blatz and Miller." In 1919, Congress passed the Volstead Act banning the brewing and selling of beverages containing more than one-half of one percent alcohol. The thirty-sixth state ratified the Eighteenth Amendment in June 1919, but the country had, for all practical purposes, been dry since 1917.

The prohibition experiment probably did reduce the total consumption of alcohol in the country, but most people who wanted to drink during the "noble experiment" found a way. Speakeasies replaced saloons, and people consumed bathtub gin, home brew, and many strange and dangerous concoctions. Bartenders invented the cocktail to disguise the poor quality of liquor, and women, at least middle- and upper-class women, began to drink in public for the first time. Prohibition also created great bootlegging rings, which were tied to organized crime in many cities. Al Capone of Chicago was the most famous underworld figure whose power and wealth were based on the sale of illegal alcohol. Many supporters of prohibition slowly came to favor its repeal, some because it reduced the power of the states, others because it stimulated too much illegal activity and because it did not seem to be worth the social and political costs.

The Election of 1928

The decade of the 1920s ended as it had begun, with a Republican administration. On August 2, 1927, President Coolidge announced simply, "I do not choose to run for President in 1928." Hoover immediately became the logical Republican candidate and easily won the nomination. In a year when the country was buoyant with optimism and when prosperity seemed as if it would go on forever, few doubted that Hoover would be elected.

The Democrats nominated Alfred Smith, a Catholic Irish-American from New York. With his New York accent, his opposition to prohibition, and his flamboyant style, he contrasted sharply with the more sedate Hoover. Racial and religious prejudice played a role in this campaign, as it had in others. But looked at more closely, the two candidates differed little. Both were self-made men, both were "progressives."

Hoover won in a landslide, 444 electoral votes to 76 for Smith, who carried only Massachusetts and Rhode Island outside the Deep South. But the 1928 campaign revitalized the Democratic Party. Smith polled nearly twice as many votes as the Democratic candidate in 1924, and for the first time the Democrats carried the nation's 12 largest cities.

Stock Market Crash

Hoover, as it turned out, had only six months to apply his progressive and efficient methods to running the country because in the fall of 1929, the prosperity that seemed endless suddenly came to a halt. In 1928 and 1929, rampant speculation made the stock market boom. Money could be made everywhere—in real estate and business ventures, but especially in the stock market.

Only a small percentage of the American people had previously invested in the stock market, but a large number got into the game in the late 1920s because it seemed a safe and sure way to make money. The economy was booming. The New York *Times* index of 25 industrial stocks, which had reached 100 in 1924, rose to 245 by the end of 1927.

Then the orgy started. During 1928, the market rose to 331. Many investors and speculators began to buy on margin (borrowing in order to invest). Businessmen and others began to invest money in the market that would ordinarily have gone into houses, cars, and other goods. Yet even at the peak of the boom, probably only about 1.5 million Americans owned stock.

In early September 1929, the New York *Times* index peaked at 452 and then began to drift downward. On October 23, the market lost 31 points. The next day ("Black Thursday"), it first seemed that everyone was trying to sell, but at the end of the day the panic appeared over. It was not. By mid-November, the market had plummeted to 224, about half what it had been two months before. This represented a loss on paper of over $26 billion. The market continued to go down. Tens of thousands of investors lost everything. There was panic and despair, but the legendary stories of executives jumping out of windows were grossly exaggerated.

CONCLUSION

A New Era of Prosperity and Problems

The stock market crash ended the decade of prosperity and revealed the weakness of the economy. The fruits of economic expansion had been unevenly distributed. Not enough people could afford to buy the autos, refrigerators, and other products pouring from American factories. Prosperity had been built on a shaky foundation. When that foundation crumbled in 1929, the nation slid into a major depression.

More than most decades, the 1920s was a time of paradox and contradictions. It was a time of prosperity, yet a great many people, including farmers, blacks, and other ordinary Americans, did not prosper. It was a time of reaction against reform, yet progressivism survived. It was a time when intellectuals felt disillusioned with America, yet it was one of the most creative and innovative periods for American writers, who described its foibles and intolerance.

Recommended Reading

Lively reading about the 1920s is Frederick Lewis Allen, *Only Yesterday* (1931). Much better balanced, however, is William E. Leuchtenburg, *The Perils of Prosperity* (1958). Two very different views of foreign policy during the decade can be found in L. Ethan Ellis, *Republican Foreign Policy, 1921–33* (1968), and William Appleman Williams, *The Tragedy of American Diplomacy* (1959).

Robert K. Murray, *Red Scare* (1955), describes the hate and intolerance that erupted after the war. See also Kenneth Jackson, *The Ku Klux Klan and the City, 1915–1930* (1967). On Hispanic migration to the Southwest, see Sarah Deutsch, *No Separate Refuge* (1987). Nancy F. Cott, *The Grounding of Modern Feminism* (1987), tracks the role of women during the decade. The experiences of ordinary Americans are treated in Margaret Marsh, *Suburban Lives* (1990); and Lizabeth Cohen, *Making a New Deal: Industrial Workers in Chicago, 1919–1939* (1990).

Nathan Huggins, *Harlem Renaissance* (1971), and Frederick Hoffman, *The Twenties* (1955), are indispensable for the study of the literary trends during this innovative decade. Robert T. Sklar, *Movie-Made America* (1976), is excellent on Hollywood and the film industry. Roland Marchand, *Advertising the American Dream* (1985), is the best place to begin a study of the impact of advertising. On the Scopes trial and religious fundamentalism, see George M. Marsden, *Fundamentalism and American Culture* (1980).

Andrew Sinclair, *The Available Man* (1965); Donald R. McCoy, *Calvin Coolidge* (1967); Oscar Handlin, *Al Smith and His America* (1958); and Joan Hoff Wilson, *Herbert Hoover: The Forgotten Progressive* (1975), chart the lives and activities of some of the political leaders. John Kenneth Galbraith, *The Great Crash, 1929* (1954), explains how the 1920s came to a tragic end.

Time Line

1900–1930	Electricity powers the "second industrial revolution"	**1924**	Coolidge elected president Peak of Ku Klux Klan activity Immigration Quota Law
1917	Race riot in East St. Louis, Illinois	**1925**	Scopes trial in Dayton, Tennessee F. Scott Fitzgerald, *The Great Gatsby* Alain Locke, *The New Negro* Claude McKay, *Home to Harlem* 5 million enameled bathroom fixtures produced
1918	World War I ends		
1919	Treaty of Versailles Strikes in Seattle, Boston, and elsewhere Red Scare and Palmer raids Race riots in Chicago and other cities Marcus Garvey's Universal Negro Improvement Association spreads		
		1926	Ernest Hemingway, *The Sun Also Rises*
		1927	National Origins Act McNary-Haugen Farm Relief bill Sacco and Vanzetti executed Lindbergh flies solo, New York to Paris First talking movie, *The Jazz Singer* Henry Ford produces 15-millionth car
1920	Warren Harding elected president Women vote in national elections First commercial radio broadcast Sacco and Vanzetti arrested Sinclair Lewis, *Main Street*		
1921	Immigration Quota Law Disarmament Conference First birth control conference Sheppard-Towner Maternity Act	**1928**	Herbert Hoover elected president Kellogg-Briand Treaty Stock market soars
1921–1922	Postwar depression	**1929**	27 million registered cars in country 10 million households own radios 100 million people attend movies Stock market crash
1922	Fordney-McCumber Tariff Sinclair Lewis, *Babbitt*		
1923	Harding dies; Coolidge becomes president Teapot Dome scandal		

chapter 24

The Great Depression and the New Deal

Diana Morgan grew up in a small North Carolina town, the daughter of a prosperous cotton merchant. She lived the life of a "southern belle," oblivious to the country's social and political problems. But the Depression changed that. She came home from college for Christmas vacation during her junior year to discover that her world had fallen apart. Her father's business had failed, her family didn't have a cook or a cleaning woman anymore, and their house was being sold for back taxes. She was confused and embarrassed. Sometimes it was the little things that were the hardest to bear. Friends would come from out of town, and there would be no ice because her family did not own an electric refrigerator and they could not afford to buy ice. "There were those frantic arrangements of running out to the drug store to get Coca-Cola with crushed ice, and there'd be this embarrassing delay, and I can remember how hot my face was." Like many Americans, Diana Morgan and her family blamed themselves for what happened to them during the Depression.

Diana Morgan had never intended to work outside the home. But she found a position with the Civil Works Administration, a New Deal agency, where at first she had to ask humiliating questions of the people applying for assistance to make sure they were destitute. "Do you own a car?" "Does anyone in the family work?" One day, a woman who had formerly cooked for her family came in to apply for help. Each was embarrassed to see the other in changed circumstances.

She had to defend the New Deal programs to many of her friends, who accused her of being sentimental and told her that the poor, especially poor blacks, did not know any better than to live in squalor. "If you give them coal, they'd put it in the bathtub," was a charge she often heard. But she knew "they didn't have bathtubs to put coal in. So how did anybody know that's what they'd do with coal if they had it?"

Diana Morgan's experience working for a New Deal agency influenced her life and her attitudes; it made her more of a social activist. Her Depression experience gave her a greater appreciation for the struggles of the country's poor and unlucky.

The Great Depression changed the lives of all Americans and separated that generation from the one that followed. An exaggerated need for security, the fear of failure, a nagging sense of guilt, and a real sense that it might happen all over again divided the Depression generation from everyone born after 1940.

The Depression dominated the decade of the 1930s despite imaginative efforts and massive spending by Franklin Roosevelt's New Deal. The New Deal was not a radical movement; but it did establish a minimum welfare state, as the government accepted limited responsibility to manage the economy, subsidize farmers, and promote social insurance and minimum wage laws. Greater government involvement in the social welfare of the country had important consequences for the American people and nation.

This chapter explores the causes and consequences of the Great Depression. We will look at the efforts of Herbert Hoover and Franklin Roosevelt to combat the Depression. We will also examine the great strides in technology during the 1930s, when innovative developments in radio, movies, and the automobile affected the lives of most Americans.

THE GREAT DEPRESSION

There had been recessions and depressions in American history, notably in the 1830s, 1870s, and 1890s, but nothing compared to the devastating economic collapse of the 1930s. The Great Depression was all the more shocking because it came after a decade of unprecedented prosperity when most experts assumed that the United States was immune to a downturn in the business cycle. The Great Depression had an impact on all areas of American life; perhaps most important, it destroyed American confidence in the future.

The Depression Begins

Few people anticipated the stock market crash in the fall of 1929. But even after the collapse of the stock market, few expected the entire economy to go into a tailspin. By 1932, at least one of every four American breadwinners was out of work, and industrial production had almost ground to a halt.

Why did the nation sink deeper and deeper into depression? The answer is complex, but the prosperity of the 1920s, it appears in retrospect, was superficial. Farmers and coal and textile workers had suffered all through the 1920s from low prices, and the farmers were the first group in the 1930s to plunge into depression. But other aspects of the economy also lurched out of balance. Two percent of the population received about 28 percent of the national income, while the lower 60 percent only got 24 percent. Businesses increased profits while holding down wages and the prices of raw materials. The result was that American workers, like American farmers, did not have the money to buy the goods they helped to produce.

Well-to-do Americans were speculating a significant portion of their money in the stock market. Their illusion of permanent prosperity helped fire the boom of the 1920s, just as their pessimism and lack of confidence helped exaggerate the depression in 1931 and 1932.

Other factors were also involved. The stock

market crash revealed serious structural weaknesses in the financial and banking systems (7,000 banks had failed during the 1920s). The Federal Reserve Board, fearing inflation, tightened credit—exactly the opposite of the action it should have taken to fight a slowdown in purchasing. Economic relations with Europe contributed to deepening depression. High American tariffs during the 1920s had reduced trade. When American investment in Europe declined in 1928 and 1929, European economies declined. As the European financial situation worsened, the American economy spiraled downward.

Hoover and the Depression

Initial business and government reactions to the stock market crash were optimistic. "All the evidence indicates that the worst effects of the crash upon unemployment will have been passed during the next sixty days," Herbert Hoover reported. His upbeat first statements were calculated to prevent further panic.

The Agricultural Marketing Act of 1929 set up a $500-million revolving fund to help farmers organize cooperative marketing associations and to establish minimum prices. But as agricultural prices plummeted and banks foreclosed on farm mortgages, the available funds proved inadequate. The Farm Board was helpless to aid the farmer who could not meet mortgage payments because the price of grain had fallen so rapidly. Nor could it help the Arkansas woman who stood weeping in the window as her possessions, including the cows, which all had names, were sold one by one.

Hoover acted aggressively to stem the economic collapse. More than any president before him, he used the power of the federal government and the office of the president to deal with an economic crisis. Nobody called it a depression for the first year at least, for the economic problems seemed very much like earlier cyclic recessions. Hoover called conferences of businessmen and labor leaders. He met with mayors and governors and encouraged them to speed up public works projects. He created agencies and boards, such as the National Credit Corporation and the Emergency Committee for Employment, to obtain voluntary action to solve the problem. Hoover even supported a tax cut, which Congress enacted in December 1929, but it did little to stimulate spending. Hoover also went on the radio in his effort to convince the American people that the fundamental structure of the economy was sound.

The Collapsing Economy

Voluntary action and psychological campaigns could not stop the Depression. The stock market, after appearing to bottom out in the winter of 1930–1931, continued its decline, responding in part to the European economic collapse that threatened international finance and trade.

But more than a collapsing market afflicted the economy. Over 1,300 additional banks failed in 1930. Despite Hoover's pleas, many factories cut back on production, and some simply closed. U.S. Steel announced a 10 percent wage cut in 1931. As the auto industry laid off workers, the unemployment rate rose to over 40 percent in Detroit. More than 4 million Americans were out of work in 1930, and at least 12 million by 1932. Foreclosures and evictions created thousands of personal tragedies. While the middle class watched in horror as their life savings disappeared, the rich began to hoard gold and to fear revolution.

There was never any real danger of revolution. Some farmers organized to dump their milk to protest low prices, and when a neighbor's farm was sold, they gathered to hold a penny auction, bidding only a few cents for equipment and returning it to their dispossessed neighbor. But everywhere people despaired as the Depression deepened in 1931 and 1932. For unemployed blacks and for many tenant farmers, the Depression had little immediate effect because

Unemployment Rate, 1929–1940

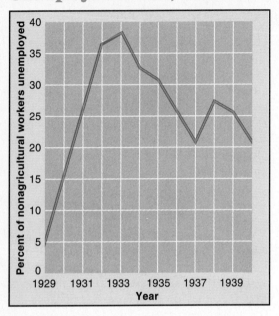

Source: U.S. Bureau of the Census

their lives were already so depressed. Most Americans (the 98 percent who did not own stock) hardly noticed the stock market crash; for them, the Depression meant the loss of a job or a bank foreclosure. For Diana Morgan, it was learning that her father's business and the family home had been lost; for some farmers, it was burning corn rather than coal because the price of corn had fallen so low that it was not worth marketing.

For some in the cities, the Depression meant not having enough money to feed the children. "Have you ever heard a hungry child cry?" asked Lillian Wald of the Henry Street Settlement. "Have you seen the uncontrollable trembling of parents who have gone half starved for weeks so that the children may have food?" In Chicago, children fought with men and women over the garbage dumped by the city trucks.

Many Depression victims blamed themselves. A businessman who lost his job and had to stand in a relief line remembered years later how he would bend his head low so nobody would recognize him.

The Depression probably disrupted women's lives less than men's. There were many exceptions, of course, but when men lost their jobs, their identity and sense of purpose as the family breadwinner were shattered. For women, however, even when money was short, there was still cooking, cleaning, and mending. Many women, in addition, took in laundry, found room for a boarder, and made the clothes they formerly would have bought. Many families were forced to move in with relatives. The marriage rate, the divorce rate, and the birthrate all dropped during the decade.

Hoover reacted to growing despair by urging more voluntary action. "We are going through a period," he announced in February 1931, "when character and courage are on trial, and where the very faith that is within us is under test." He insisted on maintaining the gold standard and a balanced budget, but so did almost everyone else. Hoover increasingly blamed the Depression on international economic problems, and he was not entirely mistaken. The whole world was gripped by depression, but as it deepened, Americans began to blame Hoover for some of the disaster. The president became isolated and bitter. The shanties that grew near all the large cities were called "Hoovervilles," and the privies, "Hoover villas."

Hoover did try innovative schemes. More public works projects were built during his administration than in the previous 30 years. He attempted to rescue banks and businesses that were near failure. When private effort failed, he turned reluctantly to Congress, which passed a bill early in 1932 authorizing the Reconstruction Finance Corporation. The RFC was capitalized at $500 million, but a short time later that was increased to $3 billion. It was authorized to make loans to banks, insurance companies, farm mortgage companies, and railroads. Its effectiveness was limited, however, because it funded

The worst result of the Depression was hopelessness and despair. Those emotions are captured in this painting of an unemployment office by Isaac Soyer.

only those financial institutions capable of putting up collateral, so that small, weak banks, for example, could not qualify for support. Similarly, public works projects had to include potential earnings for repayment. The RFC did help shore up a number of shaky financial institutions and remained the major government finance agency until World War II. But it became much more effective under Roosevelt because it provided loans directly to industry.

Hoover also asked Congress to make home mortgages more readily available. The Federal Home Loan Bank Act of 1932 became the basis for the Federal Housing Administration of the New Deal years. He also pushed the passage of the Glass-Steagall Banking Act of 1932, which expanded credit in order to make more loans available to businesses and individuals. Hoover

firmly believed in loans, but not direct subsidies, and he thought it was the responsibility of state and local governments, as well as of private charity, to provide direct relief to the unemployed and the needy.

The Bonus Army

Many World War I veterans lost their jobs during the Depression, and beginning in 1930, they lobbied for the payment of their veterans' bonuses, not due until 1945. In May 1932, about 17,000 veterans marched on Washington. Some took up residence in a shantytown, called Bonus City, in the Anacostia flats outside the city.

The House passed a bonus bill, but in mid-June, the Senate defeated it. Most of the veterans, disappointed but resigned, accepted a free railroad ticket home. Several thousand remained, however, along with some wives and children, in the unsanitary shacks during the steaming summer heat. Among them were a small group of committed Communists and other radicals. Hoover finally called out the U.S. Army to disperse them. General Douglas MacArthur, the army chief of staff, ordered the army to disperse the veterans. He described the Bonus marchers as a "mob . . . animated by the essence of revolution." With tanks, guns, and tear gas, the army routed the veterans. Two Bonus marchers were killed, and several others were injured. "What a pitiful spectacle is that of the great American Government, mightiest in the world, chasing unarmed men, women and children with Army tanks," commented a Washington newspaper. The army was not attacking revolutionaries in the streets of Washington but was routing bewildered, confused, unemployed men who had seen their American dream collapse.

The Bonus army fiasco, bread lines, and Hoovervilles became the symbols of Hoover's presidency. He deserved better because he tried to use the power of the federal government to solve growing and increasingly complex economic problems. But in the end, his personality and background limited him. Willing to use the federal government to support business, he could not accept federal aid for the unemployed. He feared an unbalanced budget and a large federal bureaucracy. Ironically, his policies led in the next years to a massive increase in federal power and in the federal bureaucracy.

ROOSEVELT AND THE FIRST NEW DEAL

The Republicans nominated Herbert Hoover for a second term, but in the summer of 1932, the Depression and Hoover's unpopularity opened the way for the Democrats. After a shrewd campaign, Franklin D. Roosevelt, governor of New York, emerged from the pack and won the nomination. Roosevelt, distantly related to Theodore

Roosevelt, had served as an assistant secretary of the navy during World War I and had been the Democratic vice-presidential candidate in 1920. Crippled by infantile paralysis not long after, he had recovered enough to serve as governor of New York for two terms, though he was not especially well known by the general public in 1932.

Governor Roosevelt had become the first governor to support state aid for the unemployed. But it was difficult to tell during the presidential campaign exactly what he stood for. The truth was that Roosevelt did not have a master plan to save the country. Yet he won overwhelmingly, carrying more than 57 percent of the popular vote.

In his inaugural address, Roosevelt announced confidently, "The only thing we have to fear is fear itself." This, of course, was not true, for the country faced the worst crisis since the Civil War, but Roosevelt's confidence and his ability to communicate with ordinary Americans were obvious early in his presidency. He instituted a series of radio "fireside chats" to explain to the American people what he was doing to solve the nation's problems. When he said "my friends," millions believed that he meant it, and they wrote letters to him in unprecedented numbers to explain their needs.

Roosevelt surrounded himself with intelligent and innovative advisers. His cabinet was made up of a mixture of people from different backgrounds who often did not agree with one another. Harold Ickes, the secretary of the interior, was a Republican lawyer from Chicago. Another Republican, Henry Wallace of Iowa, a plant geneticist and agricultural statistician, became the secretary of agriculture. Frances Perkins, the first woman ever appointed to a cabinet post, became the secretary of labor. A disciple of Jane Addams and Florence Kelley, she had been a settlement resident, secretary of the New York Consumers League, and an adviser to Al Smith.

In addition to the formal cabinet, Roosevelt created an informal "Brain Trust," which included Adolph Berle, Jr., Rexford Tugwell, and

Harry Hopkins. Eleanor Roosevelt, the president's wife, traveled widely, giving speeches and listening to the concerns of women, minorities, and ordinary Americans. Attacked by critics who thought she had too much power, she courageously took stands on issues of social justice and civil rights. She helped push the president toward social reform.

Roosevelt proved to be an adept politician. He took ideas, plans, and suggestions from conflicting sources and combined them. He had "a flypaper mind," one of his advisers decided. Roosevelt was an optimist and opportunist by nature. And he believed in action.

His first New Deal, lasting from 1933 to early 1935, focused mainly on recovery from the Depression and relief for the poor and unemployed. Congress passed legislation to aid business, the farmers, and labor and authorized public works projects and massive spending to put Americans back to work. No single ideological position united all the programs, for Roosevelt was a pragmatist who was willing to try a variety of programs. More than Hoover, he believed in economic planning and in government spending to help the poor.

Roosevelt's caution and conservatism shaped the first New Deal. He did not promote socialism or suggest nationalizing the banks. He was even careful in authorizing public works projects to stimulate the economy. The New Deal was based on the assumption that it was possible to create a just society by superimposing a welfare state on the capitalistic system, leaving the profit motive undisturbed. During the first New Deal, Roosevelt believed he would achieve his goals through cooperation with the business community. Later he would move more toward reform, but at first his primary concern was simply relief and recovery.

One Hundred Days

Because Roosevelt took office in the middle of a major crisis, a cooperative Congress was willing to pass almost any legislation that he put before it. Not since Woodrow Wilson's first term did a president orchestrate Congress so effectively. In three months, a bewildering number of bills were rushed through. Many would have far-reaching implications for the relationship of government to society. Unlike Hoover, Roosevelt was willing to use direct government action to solve the problems of depression and unemployment. As it turned out, none of the bills passed during the first 100 days cured the Depression, but taken together, the legislation constituted one of the most innovative periods in American political history.

The most immediate problem Roosevelt faced was the condition of the banks. Many had closed. Using a forgotten provision of a World War I law, Roosevelt declared a four-day bank holiday. Three days later, an emergency session of Congress approved his action and within hours passed the Emergency Banking Relief Act. The bill gave the president broad powers over financial transactions, prohibited the hoarding of gold, and allowed for the reopening of sound banks, sometimes with loans from the Reconstruction Finance Corporation. Within the next few years, Congress passed additional legislation that gave the federal government more regulatory power over the stock market and over the process by which corporations issued stock. It also passed the Banking Act of 1933, which strengthened the Federal Reserve System, established the Federal Deposit Insurance Corporation, and insured individual deposits up to $5,000.

The Democratic platform in 1932 called for reduced government spending and an end to prohibition. Roosevelt moved quickly on both. The Economy Act, which passed Congress easily, reduced government salaries and cut veterans' pensions. However, other bills passed the same week called for increased spending. The Beer-Wine Revenue Act legalized 3.2 beer and light wines and levied a tax on both. The Twenty-first Amendment, ratified on December 5, 1933, repealed the Eighteenth Amendment and ended the prohibition experiment.

Congress granted Roosevelt great power to devalue the dollar and to manipulate inflation. Bankers and businessmen feared inflation, but farmers and debtors favored an inflationary policy as a way to raise prices and put more money in their pockets. "I have always favored sound money," Roosevelt announced, "and I do now, but it is 'too darned sound' when it takes so much of farm products to buy a dollar." He rejected the more extreme inflationary plans supported by many congressmen from the agricultural states, but he did take the country off the gold standard. No longer would paper currency be redeemable in gold. After experimenting with pushing the price of gold up by buying it in the open market, Roosevelt and his advisers fixed the price at $35 an ounce in January 1934 (against the old price of $20.63). This inflated the dollar by about 40 percent, but some still cried for more inflation.

Relief Measures

Roosevelt believed in economy in government and in a balanced budget, but he also wanted to help the unemployed and the homeless. One survey estimated in 1933 that 1.5 million Americans were homeless. One man with a wife and six children from Latrobe, Pennsylvania, who was being evicted wrote, "I have 10 days to get another house, no job, no means of paying rent, can you advise me as to which would be the most humane way to dispose of myself and family, as this is about the only thing that I see left to do."

Roosevelt's answer was the Federal Emergency Relief Administration (FERA), which Congress authorized with an appropriation of $500 million in direct grants to cities and states. A few months later, Roosevelt created a Civil Works Administration (CWA) to put more than four million people to work on various state, municipal, and federal projects. Hopkins, who ran both agencies, believed it was much better to pay people to work than to give them charity. An accountant working on a road project said, "I'd rather stay out here in that ditch the rest of my life than take one cent of direct relief."

The CWA was not always effective, but in just over a year, the agency built or restored a half million miles of roads and constructed 40,000 schools and 1,000 airports. Roosevelt, however, feared that the program was costing too much and might create a permanent class of relief recipients. In the spring of 1934, he ordered the CWA closed down.

The Public Works Administration (PWA), directed by Harold Ickes, in some respects overlapped the work of the CWA, but it lasted longer. Between 1933 and 1939, the PWA built hospitals, courthouses, school buildings, low-cost housing, and other projects. One purpose of the PWA was economic pump priming—the stimulation of the economy and consumer spending through the investment of government funds. Afraid that there might be scandals in the agency, Ickes spent money slowly and carefully. PWA projects, however, did little to stimulate the economy.

Agricultural Adjustment Act

In 1933, most farmers were desperate as mounting surpluses and falling prices drastically cut their incomes. Congress passed a number of bills in 1933 and 1934 to deal with the agricultural crisis, but the New Deal's principal solution to the farm problem was the Agricultural Adjustment Act (AAA), which sought to control the overproduction of basic commodities so that farmers might regain the purchasing power they had enjoyed before World War I. To guarantee these "parity prices" (the average prices in the years 1909–1914), the production of major agricultural staples—wheat, cotton, corn, hogs, rice, tobacco, and milk—would be controlled by paying the farmers to reduce their acreage under cultivation. The AAA levied a tax at the processing stage to pay for the program.

The act aroused great disagreement among

farm leaders and economists, but the controversy was nothing compared with the outcry from the public over the initial action of the AAA in the summer of 1933. To prevent a glut on the cotton and pork markets, the agency ordered 10 million acres of cotton plowed up and 6 million little pigs slaughtered. It seemed unnatural, even immoral, to kill pigs and plow up cotton when millions of people were underfed and in need of clothes.

The Agricultural Adjustment Act did raise the prices of some agricultural products. But it helped the larger farmers more than the small operators, and it was often disastrous for the tenant farmers and sharecroppers, whom crop reduction made expendable. Many tenant farmers were simply cast out on the road with a few possessions and nowhere to go. The long-range significance of the AAA, which was later declared unconstitutional, was the establishment of the idea that the government should subsidize farmers for limiting production.

Industrial Recovery

The flurry of legislation during the first days of the Roosevelt administration contained something for almost every group. The National Industrial Recovery Act (NIRA) was designed to help business, raise prices, control production, and put people back to work. The act established the National Recovery Administration (NRA) with the power to set fair competition codes in all industries. To run the NRA, Roosevelt appointed Hugh Johnson, who had helped organize the World War I draft and served on the War Industries Board. Johnson used his wartime experiences and the enthusiasm of the bond drives to rally the country around the NRA. There were parades and rallies, even a postage stamp; and industries that cooperated could display a blue eagle, the symbol of the NRA. "We Do Our Part," the posters and banners proclaimed, but the results were somewhat less than the promise.

Section 7a of the NIRA established the National Labor Board to see that workers' rights were respected. But the board, usually dominated by businessmen, often interpreted the labor provisions of the contracts loosely. In addition, small businessmen complained that the NIRA was unfair to their interests. Any attempt to set prices led to controversy.

When the Supreme Court declared the NIRA unconstitutional in 1935, few people complained. The labor provisions of the act were picked up later by the National Labor Relations Act, sponsored by New York's Democratic senator Robert Wagner.

Civilian Conservation Corps

One of the most popular and successful of the New Deal programs, the Civilian Conservation Corps (CCC), combined work relief with the preservation of natural resources. It put young unemployed men between the ages of 18 and 25 to work on reforestation, road and park construction, flood control, and other projects. The men lived in the more than 1,500 work camps and earned $30 a month, $25 of which had to be sent home to their families. Some complained that the CCC camps, run by the U.S. Army, were too military. Others protested that the CCC did nothing for unemployed young women, so a few special camps were organized for them; however only 8,000 women took part in a program that by 1941 had included 2.5 million men. Overall, the CCC was one of the most successful and least controversial of all the New Deal programs.

Tennessee Valley Authority

Roosevelt, like his Republican namesake, believed in conservation. He promoted flood control projects and added millions of acres to the country's national forests, wildlife refuges, and fish and game sanctuaries. But the most important New Deal conservation project was the Tennessee Valley Authority (TVA).

For many people, the Depression meant homeless despair. Here an Oklahoma family who have lost their farm walk with all their possessions along the highway.

Congress authorized the TVA as an independent public corporation with the power to sell electricity and fertilizer and to promote flood control and land reclamation. The TVA built nine major dams and many minor ones between 1933 and 1944, affecting parts of Virginia, North Carolina, Georgia, Alabama, Mississippi, Tennessee, and Kentucky. It promoted everything from flood control to library bookmobiles. For residents of the valley, it meant cheaper electricity, radios, electric irons, washing machines, and other appliances for the first time. The largest federal construction project ever launched, it also created jobs for many thousands who helped build the dams. But government officials and businessmen who feared that the experiment would lead to socialism always curbed the regional planning possibilities of the TVA.

Critics of the New Deal

The furious legislative activity during the first 100 days of the New Deal helped alleviate the pessimism and despair hanging over the country. Stock market prices rose slightly, and industrial production was up 11 percent at the end of 1933. Still, the country remained locked in depression, and nearly 12 million Americans were without jobs. Yet Roosevelt captured the imagination of ordinary Americans everywhere. Hundreds of thousands of letters poured into the White House, so many that eventually 50 people had to be hired to answer them. "If ever there was a saint, he is one," declared a Wisconsin woman.

But conservatives were not so sure that Roosevelt was a savior; in fact, many businessmen began to fear that the president was leading the country toward socialism.

The conservative revolt against Roosevelt surfaced in the summer of 1934 as the congressional elections approached. A group of disgruntled politicians and businessmen formed the Liberty League, which supported conservative or at least anti–New Deal candidates for Congress, but it had little influence. In the election of 1934, the Democrats increased their majority from 310 to 319 in the House and from 60 to 69 in the Senate (only the second time in the twentieth century that the party in power had increased its control of Congress).

While some thought the New Deal too radical, others maintained that the government had not done enough to help the poor. One source of criticism was the Communist Party, which increased its membership from 7,500 in 1930 to 75,000 in 1938. While a majority who joined the party came from the working class, communism had a special appeal to writers, intellectuals, and some college students during a decade when the American dream had turned into a nightmare.

A larger number of Americans, however, were influenced by other movements promising easy solutions to poverty and unemployment. In Minnesota, Governor Floyd Olson, elected on a Farm-Labor ticket, accused capitalism of causing the Depression and startled some listeners when he thundered, "I hope the present system of government goes right to hell." In California, old-age pension schemes were promoted by Upton Sinclair and Dr. Francis E. Townsend.

More threatening to Roosevelt were the protest movements led by Father Charles E. Coughlin and Senator Huey P. Long. Father Coughlin, a Roman Catholic priest from a Detroit suburb, attracted an audience of 30 to 45 million to his national radio show. At first, he supported Roosevelt's policies, but later he savagely attacked the New Deal as excessively pro-business. Mixing religious commentary with visions of a society operating without bankers and big businessmen, he roused his audience with blatantly anti-Semitic appeals. Most often the "evil" bankers he described were Jewish—the Rothschilds, Warburgs, and Kuhn-Loebs. Anti-Semitism reached a peak in the 1930s, so Jews, rather than Catholics, bore the brunt of nativist fury. Groups like the Silver Shirts and the German-American Bund lashed out against Jews. To members of these groups and others like them, Father Coughlin's attacks made sense.

Huey Long, like Coughlin, had a charisma that won support from the millions still trying to survive in a country where the continuing depression made day-to-day existence a struggle. Elected governor of Louisiana in 1928, he promoted a "Share the Wealth" program. He taxed the oil refineries and built hospitals, schools, and thousands of miles of new highways. By 1934, he was the virtual dictator of his state, personally controlling the police and the courts. Long talked about a guaranteed income for all American families and promised pensions for the elderly and college educations for the young. He would pay for these programs by taxing the rich and liquidating the great fortunes. Had not an assassin's bullet cut Long down in September 1935, he might have mounted a third-party challenge to Roosevelt.

THE SECOND NEW DEAL

Responding in part to the discontent of the lower middle class but also to the threat of various utopian schemes, Roosevelt moved his programs in 1935 toward the goals of social reform and social justice. At the same time, he departed from attempts to cooperate with the business community.

Work Relief and Social Security

The Works Progress Administration (WPA), authorized by Congress in April 1935, was the first massive attempt to deal with unemployment. The WPA employed about three million people a year on a variety of socially useful projects, such as bridges, airports, libraries, roads, and golf courses. A minor but important part of the WPA funding supported writers, artists, actors, and musicians.

Only one member of a family could qualify for a WPA job, and first choice always went to the man. A woman could qualify only if she headed the household. But eventually more than 13 percent of the people who worked for the WPA were women, although their most common employment was in the sewing room, where old clothes were made over. "For unskilled men we have the shovel. For unskilled women we have only the needle," one official remarked.

The WPA inevitably aroused some criticism, but it did useful work; the program built nearly 6,000 schools, more than 2,500 hospitals, and 13,000 playgrounds. More important, it gave millions of unemployed Americans a chance to support their families. The National Youth Administration (NYA) supplemented the work of the WPA and assisted young men and women between the ages of 16 and 25, many of them students.

By far the most enduring reform came with the passage of the Social Security Act of 1935. By the 1930s, the United States remained the only major industrial country without such a program. The number of people over 65 in the country increased from 5.7 million in 1925 to 7.8 million in 1935, and that group demanded action.

The Social Security Act of 1935 was a compromise. It provided old-age and survivor insurance to be paid for by a tax of one percent on both employers and employees. The benefits initially ranged from $10 to $85 a month. The act also established a cooperative federal-state system of unemployment compensation. Other provisions authorized federal grants to the states to assist in caring for the crippled and the blind. Finally, the Social Security Act provided some aid to dependent children. This provision would eventually expand to become the largest federal welfare program.

Although the National Association of Manufacturers denounced social security, it was actually a conservative and incomplete system. In no other country was social insurance paid for in part by a regressive tax on the workers' wages. The law also excluded many people, including those who needed it most, such as farm laborers and domestic servants. It discriminated against married women wage earners, and it failed to protect against sickness. Yet for all its weaknesses, it was one of the most important New Deal measures. A landmark in American social legislation, it marked the beginning of the welfare state that would expand significantly after World War II.

Aiding the Farmers

The flurry of legislation in 1935 and early 1936, often called the "second New Deal," also included an effort to help American farmers. Over 1.7 million farm families had incomes of under $500 annually in 1935, and 42 percent of all those who lived on farms were tenants. The Resettlement Administration (RA) set out to relocate tenant farmers on land purchased by the government. Lack of funds and fears that the Roosevelt administration was trying to establish Soviet-style collective farms limited the effectiveness of the RA program.

Much more important in improving the lives of farm families was the Rural Electrification Administration (REA), which was authorized in 1935 to loan money to cooperatives to generate and distribute electricity in isolated rural areas not served by private utilities. When the REA's lines were finally attached, they dramatically changed the lives of millions of farm families.

In the hill country west of Austin, Texas, for example, no electricity existed until the end of the 1930s. There were no bathrooms because bathrooms required running water, and running water depended on an electric pump. Women

A farmer and his sons race to find shelter from a dust storm in Cimarron County, Oklahoma, in 1936. A combination of factors, including overplanting that destroyed the natural sod of the Great Plains, resulted in the devastating dust storms of the 1930s. Without sod to protect the soil from the wind, thousands of acres of the Great Plains just blew away.

and children hauled water constantly—for infrequent baths, for continuous canning (because without a refrigerator, fruits and vegetables had to be put up almost immediately or they spoiled), and for washday. Washday, always Monday, meant scrubbing clothes by hand with harsh soap on a washboard; it meant boiling clothes in a large copper vat over a wood stove and stirring them with a wooden fork.

It was memory of the difficult life in the hill country that inspired a young congressman from Texas, Lyndon Johnson, to work to bring rural electrification to the area. In November 1939, the lights finally came on in the hill country, plugging the area into the twentieth century.

The Dust Bowl: An Ecological Disaster

Some farmers profited from the agricultural legislation of the 1930s, but most of those who tried to farm on the Great Plains fell victim to years of drought and dust storms. Record heat waves and below-average rainfall in the 1930s turned an area from the Oklahoma panhandle to western Kansas into a giant dust bowl. A single storm on May 11, 1934, removed 300 million tons of topsoil and turned day into night. Between 1932 and 1939 there was an average of fifty dust storms a year. Cities kept their street lights on for twenty-four hours a day. Dust covered everything from food to bedspreads and piled up in dunes in city streets and barnyards. Thousands died of "dust pneumonia." One woman remembered what it was like at night: "A trip for water to rinse the grit from our lips, and then back to bed with washcloths over our noses, we try to lie still, because every turn stirs the dust on the blankets."

A 1936 survey of twenty counties in the heart of the dust bowl concluded that 97.6 percent of the land suffered from erosion and more than 50 percent was seriously damaged. By the end of the decade 10,000 farm homes were abandoned to the elements, 9 million acres of farmland was reduced to a wasteland, and three and a half million people had abandoned their farms and joined a massive migration to find a better life. More than 350,000 left Oklahoma during the decade and moved to California, a place that seemed to many like the promised land. But the name Okie came to mean any farm migrant. The plight of these wayfarers was immortalized by John Steinbeck in his novel about the Joad family, *The Grapes of Wrath* (1939).

The dust bowl was a natural disaster, but it was aided and exaggerated by human actions and inactions. The semiarid plains west of the 98th meridian were not suitable for intensive agriculture. Overgrazing, too much plowing, and indiscriminate planting over a period of sixty years exposed the thin soil to the elements. When the winds came in the 1930s, much of the land simply blew away.

The Roosevelt administration did try to deal with the problem. The Taylor Grazing Act of 1934 restricted the use of the public range in an attempt to prevent overgrazing, and it also closed 80 million acres of grassland to further settlement. The Civilian Conservation Corps and other New Deal agencies planted trees, and the Soil Conservation Service promoted drought-resistant crops and contour plowing, but it was too little and too late. Even worse, according to some authorities, government measures applied after the disaster of 1930 encouraged farmers to return to raising wheat and other inappropriate crops, leading to more dust bowl crises in the 1950s and 1970s.

Controlling Corporate Power and Taxing the Wealthy

In the summer of 1935, Roosevelt also moved to control the large corporations, and increase taxes paid by the well-to-do. The Public Utility Holding Company Act, passed in 1935, gave various government commissions the authority to regulate and control the power companies, 12 of which controlled over half of the country's power. The act gave each company five years to demonstrate that its services were efficient. This was one of the most radical attempts to control corporate power in American history.

In 1935, Roosevelt criticized the "unjust concentration of wealth and economic power" and persuaded Congress to increase estate and gift taxes and raise the income tax rates at the top.

The New Deal for Labor

Like many progressive reformers, Roosevelt was more interested in improving the lot of working people by passing social legislation than by strengthening the bargaining position of organized labor. Yet he saw labor as an important balance to the power of industry, and he listened to his advisers, especially to Frances Perkins and to Senator Robert Wagner of New York, who

Distribution of Income, 1935–1936

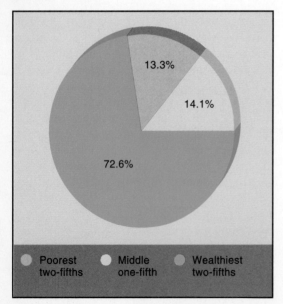

Poorest two-fifths   Middle one-fifth   Wealthiest two-fifths

Source: U.S. Bureau of the Census

persistently brought up the needs of organized labor.

After strikes in San Francisco, Minneapolis, and Toledo, Roosevelt supported the Wagner Act, officially called the National Labor Relations Act, which outlawed blacklisting and a number of other practices and reasserted labor's right to organize and to bargain collectively. The act also established a Labor Relations Board with the power to certify a properly elected bargaining unit. The act did not require workers to join unions, but it made the federal government a regulator, or at least a neutral force, in management-labor relations. That alone made the National Labor Relations Act one of the most important New Deal reform measures.

The Roosevelt administration's friendly attitude toward organized labor helped to increase union membership from under 3 million in 1933 to 4.5 million by 1935. Many groups, however, were left out, including farm laborers, unskilled workers, and women. Only about 3 percent of working women belonged to unions, and women earned only about 60 percent of wages paid to men for equivalent work.

Still, many people resented the fact that women were employed at all. The Brotherhood of Railway and Steamship Clerks ruled that no married woman whose husband could support her was eligible for a job. One writer had a perfect solution for the unemployment problem: "Simply fire the women, who shouldn't be working anyway, and hire the men." The American Federation of Labor had little interest in organizing unskilled workers, but a new group of committed and militant labor leaders emerged in the 1930s to take up that task. John L. Lewis, the eloquent head of the United Mine Workers, was the most aggressive. He was joined by David Dubinsky of the International Ladies' Garment Workers and Sidney Hillman, president of the Amalgamated Clothing Workers. Both were socialists who believed in economic planning, but both had worked closely with social justice progressives. These new progressive

labor leaders formed the Committee of Industrial Organization (CIO) within the AFL and set out to organize workers in the steel, auto, and rubber industries. Rather than separating workers by skill or craft as the AFL preferred, they organized everyone into an industrywide union much as the Knights of Labor had done in the 1880s. They also used new and aggressive tactics. When a foreman tried to increase production or enforce discipline, the union leaders would simply pull the switch and declare a spontaneous strike. This "brass knuckle unionism" worked especially well in the auto and rubber industries.

In 1936, the workers at three rubber plants in Akron, Ohio, went on strike without permission from the leaders. Instead of picketing outside the factory, they occupied the buildings and took them over. The "sit-down strike" became a new protest technique. After sit-down strikes against General Motors plants in Atlanta, Georgia, and Flint, Michigan, General Motors finally accepted the United Auto Workers as their employees' bargaining unit.

The General Motors strike was the most important event in a critical period of labor upheaval. A group of workers using disorderly but largely nonviolent tactics (as would the civil rights advocates in the mid-1960s) demanded their rights under the law. They helped to make labor's voice heard in the decision-making process in major industries where labor had long been denied any role. They also helped to raise the status of organized labor in the eyes of many Americans.

"Labor does not seek industrial strife," Lewis announced. "It wants peace, but a peace with justice." As the sit-down tactic spread, violence often accompanied justice. Chrysler capitulated. But the Ford Motor Company used hired gunmen to discourage the strikers. A bloody struggle ensued before Ford agreed to accept the UAW as the bargaining agent. Even U.S. Steel came to terms with the Steel Workers Organizing Committee, but other steel companies refused to go along. In Chicago on Memorial Day in 1937, a confrontation between the police and peaceful pickets at the Republic Steel plant resulted in ten deaths. In the "Memorial Day Massacre," as it came to be called, the police fired without provocation into a crowd of workers and their families, who had gathered near the plant in a holiday mood. All ten of the dead were shot in the back.

Despite the violence and management's use of undercover agents within unions, the CIO gained many members. William Green and the leadership of the AFL were horrified at the aggressive tactics of the new labor leaders. They expelled the CIO leaders from the AFL only to see them form a separate Congress of Industrial Organization (the initials stayed the same). By the end of the decade, the CIO had infused the labor movement with a new spirit. Accepting unskilled workers, blacks, and others who had never belonged to a union before, they won increased pay, better working conditions, and the right to bargain collectively in most of the basic American industries. Jim Cole, a black butcher at one of the meatpacking plants in Chicago, tried to join the Amalgamated Butchers and Meat Cutters, an AFL union, but they turned him away because he was black. He later joined the CIO.

America's Minorities in the 1930s

A half million blacks joined unions through the CIO during the 1930s, and many blacks were aided by various New Deal agencies. Yet the familiar pattern of discrimination, low-paying jobs, and intimidation through violence persisted. Lynchings in the South actually increased in the New Deal years, rising from 8 in 1932 to 28 in 1933 and 20 in 1935.

The migration of blacks to northern cities, which had accelerated during World War I, continued during the 1930s. The collapse of cotton prices forced black farmers and farm laborers to flee north for survival. But since most were poorly educated, they were eligible for only the most menial jobs.

Black leaders attacked the Roosevelt administration for supporting or allowing segregation in government-sponsored facilities. The TVA model town of Norris, Tennessee, was off limits for blacks, and AAA policies actually drove blacks off the land in the South. The CCC segregated black and white workers, and the PWA financed segregated housing projects. Blacks ought to realize, a writer in the NAACP journal *The Crisis* warned in 1935, "that the powers-that-be in the Roosevelt administration have nothing for them."

Roosevelt, fearing that he might antagonize southern congressmen whose backing he needed, refused to support the two major civil rights bills of the era, an antilynching bill and a bill to abolish the poll tax. Yet Harold Ickes and Harry Hopkins worked to ensure that blacks were given opportunities in the CCC, the WPA, and other agencies. By 1941, black federal employees totaled 150,000, more than three times the number during the Hoover administration.

Partly responsible for the presence of more black employees was the "black cabinet," a group of more than 50 young blacks who had appointments in almost every government department and New Deal agency. The group met on Friday evenings at the home of Mary McLeod Bethune, promoter of black education and member of the advisory committee of the National Youth Administration. Bethune had a large impact on New Deal policy and on the black cabinet. She spoke out forcefully, she picketed and protested, and she intervened shrewdly to obtain civil rights and more jobs for black Americans.

W. E. B. Du Bois, in the meantime, had become disillusioned with the reform of race relations through integration with white society. He resigned from the NAACP in 1934 and eventually joined the Communist Party and moved to Ghana, where he died in 1963.

Eleanor Roosevelt, who was educated in

part by Mary McLeod Bethune, was committed to civil rights for blacks. In 1939, when the Daughters of the American Revolution refused to allow Marian Anderson, a black concert ɡer, to use their stage, Mrs. Roosevelt publicly protested and resigned her membership in the DAR. She also arranged for Anderson to sing from the steps of the Lincoln Memorial, where 75,000 people gathered to listen and to support civil rights for all black citizens.

Many Mexicans who had been actively recruited for American farms and businesses in the 1920s lost their jobs in the Depression decade. Hundreds of thousands drifted from the urban barrios to small towns and farms in the Southwest looking for work.

A few found work with the CCC or the WPA, but to be employed, an applicant had to qualify for state relief, and that eliminated most migrants. The primary solution was not to provide aid for Mexicans but to ship them back to Mexico. A trainload of repatriates left Los Angeles every month during 1933, and officials deported thousands from other cities. One estimate placed the number sent back in 1932 at 200,000, including some American citizens.

During the Depression, Native Americans also experienced hunger, disease, and despair, and their plight was compounded by years of exploitation. Since the Dawes Act of 1887 (described in Chapter 17), government policy had sought to make the Indian into a property-owning farmer and to limit tribal rights. Native Americans lost over 60 percent of the 138 million acres granted them in 1887. The government declared some of the land surplus and encouraged individuals to settle on 160 acres and adopt the "habits of civilized life." Few Native Americans profited from this system, but many whites did. Just as other progressives sought the quick assimilation of immigrants, the progressive era Indian commissioners sped up the allotment process to increase Indian detribalization. But many Native Americans who remained on the reservations were not even citizens. Finally,

in 1924, Congress granted citizenship to all Indians born in the United States. The original Americans became United States citizens, but that did not end their suffering.

Franklin Roosevelt brought a new spirit to Indian policy by appointing John Collier as commissioner of Indian affairs. Collier, who had organized the American Indian Defense Association in 1923 was primarily responsible for the passage of the Indian Reorganization Act of 1934, which sought to restore the political independence of the tribes and to end the allotment policy of the Dawes Act.

The bill also sought to promote "the study of Indian civilization" and to "preserve and develop the special cultural contributions and achievements of such civilization, including Indian arts, crafts, skills and traditions." Not all Indians agreed with the new policies. Some chose to become members of the dominant culture, and the Navajos voted to reject the Reorganization Act. Still, the Indian Reorganization Act and a more concerned attitude during the New Deal led to a reversal of land policy, a revival of interest in tribal identity, and a recognition of the importance of Indian culture, language, and ritual.

Women and the New Deal

Like some minorities, women made certain gains during the 1930s, but obstacles remained. While employment in general for women was not easy during a period of high unemployment for men, more women occupied high government positions in the Roosevelt administration than in any previous administration. The most visible was Frances Perkins, whose appointment as secretary of labor made her the first woman member of the cabinet. Katharine Lenroot, director of the Children's Bureau, and Mary Anderson, head of the Women's Bureau, selected many other women to serve in their agencies. With the support of Eleanor Roosevelt, Molly Dewson, a social worker who became head of the Women's

Division of the Democratic Committee and then an adviser to the president, worked to achieve a number of firsts: two women appointed ambassadors, a judge on the U.S. Court of Appeals, the director of the mint, and many women in government agencies.

Despite the number of women working for the government, feminism declined in the 1930s, and the image of woman's proper role continued to be housewife and mother.

THE LAST YEARS OF THE NEW DEAL

The New Deal was not a consistent or well-organized effort to end the Depression and restructure society. Roosevelt was a politician and a pragmatist, unconcerned about ideological or programmatic consistency. The first New Deal in 1933 and 1934 concentrated on relief and recovery, while the legislation passed in 1935 and 1936 was more involved with social reform. In many ways, the election of 1936 marked the high point of Roosevelt's power and influence. After 1937, in part because of the growing threat of war, but also because of increasing opposition in Congress, the pace of social legislation slowed. Yet several measures passed in 1937 and 1938 had such far-reaching significance that some historians refer to a third New Deal. Among the new measures were bills that provided for a minimum wage and for housing reform.

The Election of 1936

The Republicans in 1936 nominated a moderate, Governor Alfred Landon of Kansas. Roosevelt, helped by signs that the economy was recovering and supported by a coalition of the Democratic South, organized labor, farmers, and urban voters, won easily. A majority of black Americans for the first time deserted the party of Lincoln, not because of Roosevelt's interest in civil rights for blacks but because New Deal re-

lief programs assisted many poor blacks. Roosevelt won by over 10 million votes, carrying every state except Maine and Vermont. "To some generations much is given," Roosevelt announced in his acceptance speech; "of other generations much is expected. This generation has a rendezvous with destiny." Now he had a mandate to continue his New Deal social and economic reforms.

The Battle of the Supreme Court

The president's first action in 1937 was to announce a plan to reform the Supreme Court and the judicial system. The Court had invalidated a number of New Deal bills, including the NIRA and the first version of AAA. Increasingly angry at the "nine old men" who seemed to be destroying New Deal initatives and defying Congress's will, Roosevelt determined to create a more sympathetic Court. He hoped to gain power to appoint an extra justice for each justice over 70 years of age, of whom there were six. His plan also called for modernizing the court system at all levels, but that plan got lost in the public outcry over the Court-packing scheme.

Roosevelt's plan to nullify the influence of the older and more reactionary justices foundered. Many congressmen from his own party refused to support him. After months of controversy, Roosevelt withdrew the legislation and admitted defeat.

Ironically, though he lost the battle of the Supreme Court, Roosevelt won the war. By the spring of 1937, the Court began to reverse its position and in a 5–4 decision upheld the National Labor Relations Act. When Justice Willis Van Devanter retired, Roosevelt was able to make his first Supreme Court appointment, thus assuring at least a shaky liberal majority on the Court. But Roosevelt triumphed at great cost. His attempt to reorganize the Court was the most unpopular action he took as president, and even some of his supporters were dismayed by

sion, the government must spend massive amounts of money on goods and services in order to increase demand and revive production. The economy responded slowly to increased government spending but never fully recovered until wartime expenditures, beginning in 1940, eliminated unemployment and ended the Depression.

The Third New Deal

Despite increasing hostility, Congress passed a number of important bills in 1937 and 1938 that completed the New Deal reform legislation. In 1937, the Farm Security Administration (FSA) was created to aid tenant farmers, sharecroppers, and farm owners who had lost their farms. More than a million men, women, and children were drifting aimlessly and hopelessly looking for work. The drought that had created a "dust bowl" in the Southwest worsened their plight. The FSA, which provided loans to grain collectives, also set up camps for migratory workers.

Congress passed a new Agricultural Adjustment Act in 1938 that tried to solve the continuing problem of farm surpluses. The new act replaced the processing tax, which the Supreme Court had declared unconstitutional, with direct payments from the federal treasury to farmers; added a soil conservation program; and provided for the marketing of surplus crops. Like its predecessor, the new act tried to stabi-

struction of low-cost housing. By 1939, however, only 117,000 units had been built, and many of them soon became problems rather than solutions.

In the long run, New Deal housing legislation had a greater impact on middle-class housing policies and patterns. During the first 100 days of the New Deal, at Roosevelt's urging, Congress passed a bill creating the Home Owners Loan Corporation (HOLC), which over the next two years made more than $3 billion in low-interest loans and helped over a million people save their homes from foreclosure. The HOLC also introduced the first long-term fixed-rate mortgages and established a uniform system of real estate appraisal that tended to undervalue urban property, especially in neighborhoods that were old, crowded, and ethnically mixed. This was the beginning of the practice later called "redlining" that made it nearly impossible for certain prospective homeowners to obtain a mortgage in many urban areas.

The Federal Housing Administration (FHA), created in 1934 by the National Housing Act, expanded and extended many of these HOLC policies. New Deal housing policies helped to make the suburban home with the long FHA mortgage part of the American way of life, but the policies also contributed to the decline of many urban neighborhoods.

Just as important as housing legislation was the Fair Labor Standards Act, which Congress passed in June 1938. It applied to industries engaged in interstate commerce and called for a minimum wage of 25 cents an hour, to rise in two years to 40 cents an hour, and a maximum workweek of 44 hours, to be reduced to 40 hours. Congress exempted many groups, including farm laborers and domestic servants. Nevertheless, when it went into effect, 750,000 workers immediately received raises, and by 1940, some 12 million had had pay increases. The law also prohibited child labor in interstate commerce, making it the first permanent federal law to prohibit youngsters under 16 from working. And without emphasizing the matter, the law made no distinction between men and women.

The New Deal had many weaknesses, but it did dramatically increase government support for the needy. In 1913, local, state and federal governments spent $21 million on public assistance. By 1932, that had risen to $218 million; by 1939, it was $4.9 billion.

THE OTHER SIDE OF THE 1930s

The Great Depression and the New Deal so dominate the history of the 1930s that it is easy to conclude that nothing else happened, that there were only bread lines and relief agencies. But there is another side of the decade. A communications revolution changed the lives of middle-class Americans. The sale of radios and attendance at movies increased during the 1930s, and literature flourished. And automobiles facilitated travel.

Taking to the Road

"People give up everything in the world but their car," a banker in Muncie, Indiana, remarked during the Depression. Although automobile production dropped off after 1929 and did not recover until the end of the 1930s, the number of motor vehicles registered had swelled to over 32 million by 1940. People who could not afford new cars drove used ones. The fact that even many poor Americans owned cars shocked visitors from Europe, where automobiles were still only for the rich. Tourist courts sprang up across the country to accommodate travelers. In their predecessors of the motel there were no doormen, no bellhops, no register to sign. At the tourist court, all the owner wanted was the automobile license number.

The Electric Home

Just as travel became more convenient for families that owned automobiles, life at home also benefited from new technological developments. The sale of electrical appliances increased throughout the decade, with refrigerators leading the way. In 1930, the number of refrigerators produced exceeded the number of iceboxes for the first time.

Replacing an icebox with an electrical refrigerator, as many middle-class families did in the 1930s, altered more than the appearance of the kitchen. It also changed habits and life styles, especially for women. An icebox was part of a culture that included icemen, ice wagons (or ice trucks), picks, tongs, and a pan that had to be emptied continually. The refrigerator required no attention beyond occasional defrosting of the freezer compartment. Like the streamlined automobile, the sleek refrigerator became a symbol of progress and modern civilization in the 1930s. At the end of the decade, in 1939, the World's Fair in New York glorified the theme of a streamlined future, carefully planned and based on new technology.

The electric washing machine and electric iron revolutionized washday. Packaged and canned goods became more widely available during the decade, making food preparation easier.

Popular Pastimes

During the Depression, many people found themselves with time on their hands and sought out ways of spending it. The 1920s was a time of spectator sports, of football and baseball heroes, of huge crowds that turned out to see boxing matches. These sports continued during the Depression decade, although attendance suffered. Softball and miniature golf also became popular.

Many popular games of the period had elaborate rules and directions. Contract bridge swept the country during the decade, and Monopoly was the most popular game of all. Produced by Parker Brothers, Monopoly was a fantasy of real estate speculation in which chance, luck, and the roll of the dice determined the winner.

The 1930s was also a time of fads and instant celebrities, created by radio, newsreels, and businessmen ready to turn almost anything to commercial advantage. The leading box office attraction between 1935 and 1938 was Shirley Temple, an adorable child star. She inspired dolls, dishes, books, and clothes. The media also focused on five identical girl babies born to a couple in northern Ontario in 1934. The Dionne quintuplets appeared on dozens of magazine covers and endorsed every imaginable product. Both Shirley Temple and the Dionne quintuplet craze were products of the new technology, especially radio and the movies.

Radio's Finest Hour

The number of radio sets purchased increased steadily during the 1930s. In 1929, slightly more than 10 million households owned radios; by 1939, fully 27.5 million households had radio sets. Families gathered around the radio at night to listen to and laugh at Jack Benny or Edgar Bergen and Charlie McCarthy or to try to solve a murder mystery with Mr. and Mrs. North. "The Lone Ranger," another popular program, had 20 million listeners by 1939. During the day there were soap operas.

The magic of radio allowed many people to feel connected to distant places and to believe they knew the radio performers personally. Radio was also responsible for one of the biggest hoaxes of all time. On October 31, 1938, Orson Welles broadcast "The War of the Worlds" so realistically that thousands of listeners really believed that anyone i demonstr

The

The 19 Between 60 and the movies every week. Talking films had replaced the silent variety in the late 1920s, and attendance soared. Though it fell off slightly in the early 1930s, by 1934 movie viewing was climbing again. For many families, even in the depth of the Depression, movie money was as important as food money.

The movies were a place to take a date, to go with friends, or to go as a family. Movies could be talked about for days. Young women tried to speak like Greta Garbo or to hold a cigarette like Joan Crawford. Jean Harlow and Mae West so popularized blonde hair that sales of peroxide shot up. Young men tried to emulate Clark Gable or Cary Grant, and one young man admitted that it was "directly through the movies that I learned to kiss a girl on her ears, neck, and cheeks, as well as on the mouth." The animated cartoons of Walt Disney, one of the true geniuses of the movie industry, were so popular that Mickey Mouse was more famous and familiar than most human celebrities.

Literary Reflections of the 1930s

Though much of the literature of the 1930s reflected the decade's troubled currents, reading continued to be a popular and cheap entertainment. John Steinbeck, whose later novel *The Grapes of Wrath* (1939) followed the fortunes of the Joad family, described the plight of Mexican migrant workers in *Tortilla Flat* (1935). John Dos Passos's trilogy *U.S.A.* (1930–1936) conveyed a deep pessimism about American capitalism. William Faulkner's fictional Yoknapatawpha County, brought to life in *The Sound and the Fury, As I Lay Dying, Sanctuary,* and *Light*

THE AMBIVALENCE OF THE GREAT DEPRESSION

The New Deal, despite its great variety of legislation, did not end the Depression, nor did it solve the problem of unemployment. For many Americans looking back on the decade of the 1930s, the most vivid memory was the shame and guilt of being unemployed, the despair and fear that came from losing a business or being evicted from a home or an apartment.

New Deal legislation did not solve the country's problems, but it did strengthen the federal government, especially the executive branch. Federal agencies like the Federal Deposit Insurance Corporation and programs like social security influenced the daily lives of most Americans,

and rural electrification, the WPA, and the CCC changed the lives of millions. The New Deal also established the principle of federal responsibility for the health of the economy, initiated the concept of the welfare state, and dramatically increased government spending to help the poor.

The New Deal promoted social justice and social reform, but it provided little for people at the bottom of American society. The New Deal did not prevent business consolidation, and, in the end, it probably strengthened corporate capitalism. Roosevelt, with his colorful personality and his dramatic response to the nation's crisis, dominated his times in a way few presidents have done.

Recommended Reading

Robert S. McElvaine, *The Great Depression* (1984), is the best single volume on the subject. Donald Worster, *Dust Bowl* (1979), describes the impact of the Depression and the drought in the Southwest. Robert S. McElvaine, ed., *Down and Out in the Great Depression* (1983), uses letters written to Eleanor and Franklin Roosevelt to describe the reaction of ordinary Americans.

On the New Deal, see Paul K. Conkin, *The New Deal* (1967); Anthony J. Badger, *The New Deal: The Depression Years* (1989); and Steve Fraser and Gary Gertstle, eds., *The Rise and Fall of the New Deal Order* (1989). James MacGregor Burns, *Roosevelt: The Lion and the Fox* (1956), is still the best one-volume biography.

Specialized studies of the Depression and the New Deal abound. Harvard Sitkoff, *A New Deal for Blacks* (1978), discusses the limited attention given to blacks during the decade. On Collier and the Indian New Deal, see Kenneth R. Philip, *John Collier's Crusade for Indian Reform* (1977). Mark Reisler, *By the Sweat of Their Brow* (1976), describes the plight of Mexican-Americans. Susan Ware, *Beyond Suffrage* (1981), depicts the lot of women during the New Deal era. Irving Bernstein, *Turbulent Years* (1969), discusses the American worker and organized labor. Alan Brinkley, *Voices of Protest* (1982), tells the story of Father Coughlin and Huey Long. The other side of the 1930s can be followed in Warren Sussman, ed., *Culture and Commitment* (1973).

John Steinbeck shows Okies trying to escape the dust bowl in his novel *The Grapes of Wrath* (1939). James Farrell describes growing up in Depression Chicago in *Studs Lonigan* (1932–1935). Richard Wright details the trials of a young black man in *Native Son* (1940).

Time Line

1929	Stock market crashes Agricultural Marketing Act
1930	Depression worsens
1932	Reconstruction Finance Corporation established Glass-Steagall Banking Act Bonus march on Washington Franklin D. Roosevelt elected president
1933	Emergency Banking Relief Act Federal Emergency Relief Act Twenty-first Amendment repeals Eighteenth, ending prohibition Agricultural Adjustment Act National Industrial Recovery Act Civilian Conservation Corps Tennessee Valley Authority established Public Works Administration established
1934	Unemployment peaks Federal Housing Administration established Indian Reorganization Act
1935	Second New Deal begins Works Progress Administration established Social Security Act Rural Electrification Act National Labor Relations Act Public Utility Holding Company Act Committee for Industrial Organization (CIO) formed
1936	United Auto Workers hold sit-down strikes against General Motors Roosevelt reelected president Economy begins rebound
1937	Attempt to expand the Supreme Court Economic collapse Farm Security Administration established National Housing Act
1938	Fair Labor Standards Act Agricultural Adjustment Act

chapter 25

World War II

N. Scott Momaday, a Kiowa Indian born at Lawton, Oklahoma, in 1934, grew up on Navajo, Apache, and Pueblo reservations. He was only 11 when World War II ended, yet the war changed his life. Shortly after the United States entered the war, Momaday's parents moved to New Mexico, where his father got a job with an oil company and his mother worked in the civilian personnel office at an Army Air Force base. Like many couples, they had struggled through the hard times of the Depression. The war meant jobs.

Momaday's best friend was Billy Don Johnson, "a reddish, robust boy of great good humor and intense loyalty." Together they played war, digging trenches and dragging themselves through imaginary mine fields. Like most Americans, they believed that World War II was a good war fought against evil empires. The United States was always right, the enemy always wrong. It was an attitude that would influence Momaday and his generation for the rest of their lives.

Momaday's only difficulty was that his Native American face was often mistaken for that of an Asian. Almost every day on the school playground, someone would yell, "Hi ya, Jap," and a fight was on.

Near the end of the war, his family moved again, as so many families did, so that his father might get a better job. This time they lived right next door to an air force base, and Scott fell in love with the B-17 "Flying Fortress" bomber.

Looking back on his early years, Momaday reflected on the importance of the war in his growing up. "I see now that one experiences easily the ordinary things of life," he decided, "the things which cast familiar shadows upon the sheer, transparent panels of time, and he perceives his experience in the only way he can, according to his age." Though Momaday's youth was affected by the fact that he was male, was an Indian, and lived in the Southwest, the most important influence was that he was an American growing up during the war. Ironically, his parents, made U.S. citizens by an act of Congress in 1924 like all Native Americans living in Arizona and New Mexico, were denied the right to vote by state law.

Still, Momaday thought of himself not so much as an Indian as an American, and that too was a product of his generation. But as he grew to maturity, he became a successful writer and spokesman for his people. In 1969, he won the Pulitzer Prize for his novel *House Made of Dawn*. He also recorded his experiences and memories in a book called *The Names* (1976).

Despite the fact that no American cities were bombed and the country was never invaded, World War II influenced almost every aspect of American life. The war ended the Depression and unemployment. It also ended the last remnants of American isolationism. The United States emerged from the war in 1945 as the most powerful and most prosperous nation in the world.

This chapter traces the events during the 1930s that finally led to American participation in the most devastating war the world had seen. It recounts the diplomatic and military struggles of the war and the search for a secure peace. It also seeks to explain the impact of the war on ordinary Americans on their attitudes, and on their way of life. The war brought prosperity to some as it brought death to others.

THE TWISTING ROAD TO WAR

Looking back on the events between 1933 and 1941 that eventually led to American involvement in World War II, it is easy to be critical of decisions made or actions not taken. Leaders who must make decisions, however, never have the advantage of retrospective vision; they have to deal with situations as they find them, and they never have all the facts.

Foreign Policy in the 1930s

In March 1933, Roosevelt faced not only overwhelming domestic difficulties but also international crisis. The worldwide depression had caused near financial disaster in Europe. Germany had defaulted on its reparations installments, and most European countries were unable to keep up the payments on their debts to the United States.

Roosevelt had no master plan in foreign policy, just as he had none in the domestic sphere. At first, it seemed that the president would cooperate in some kind of international economic agreement on tariffs and currency. But during the June 1933 international economic conference in London, he undercut the American delegation by refusing to go along with any international agreement. Solving the American domestic economic crisis seemed more important to Roosevelt in 1933 than international economic cooperation. His actions signaled a decision to go it alone in foreign policy in the 1930s.

Roosevelt did, however, alter some of the foreign policy decisions of previous administrations. For example, he recognized the Soviet government, hoping to gain a market for surplus American grain. Although the expected trade bonanza never materialized, the Soviet Union agreed to pay the old debts and to extend rights to American citizens living in the Soviet Union. Diplomatic recognition opened communications between the two emerging world powers.

Led by Secretary of State Cordell Hull, Roosevelt's administration extended the Good Neighbor policy Hoover had initiated and completed the removal of American military forces from Haiti and Nicaragua in 1934. In a series of pan-American conferences, Roosevelt joined in pledging that no country in the hemisphere would intervene in the "internal or external affairs" of any other.

The first test of that pledge came in Cuba, where a revolution threatened American investments of more than a billion dollars. But the United States did not send troops. Instead Roosevelt dispatched special envoys to work out a conciliatory agreement with the revolutionary government. A short time later, when a coup led by Fulgencio Batista overthrew the revolutionary government, the United States not only recognized the Batista government but also offered a large loan and agreed to abrogate the Platt Amendment (which made Cuba a virtual protectorate of the United States) in return for the rights to a naval base.

Using presidential powers granted by the Trade Agreements Act of 1934, the Roosevelt administration negotiated a series of agreements that improved trade. By 1935, half of American cotton exports and a large proportion of other products were going to Latin America. So the Good Neighbor policy was also good business for the United States.

Another test for Latin American policy came in 1938 when Mexico nationalized the property of a number of American oil companies. Instead of intervening, as many businessmen urged, the State Department patiently worked out an agreement that included some compensation for the companies.

Neutrality in Europe

Around the time that Roosevelt was elected president, Adolf Hitler came to power in Germany. Born in Austria in 1889, Hitler had served as a corporal in the German army during World War I. Like many other Germans, he was angered by the Treaty of Versailles. But he blamed Germany's defeat on the Communists and the Jews.

Hitler, the leader of the National Socialist Party of the German Workers (*Nazi* is short for *National*), became chancellor of Germany on January 30, 1933, and within months the Reichstag (parliament) suspended the constitution, making Hitler *Führer* (leader) and dictator. His Fascist regime concentrated political and economic power in a centralized state. He intended to conquer Europe and to make the German Third Reich (empire) the center of a new civilization.

In 1934, Hitler announced a program of German rearmament, violating the Versailles Treaty of 1919. Meanwhile, in Italy, a Fascist dictator, Benito Mussolini, was building a powerful military force and threatening to invade the East African country of Ethiopia. These ominous rumblings in Europe frightened Americans, who never again wanted to get involved in a European conflict.

On many college campuses, students demonstrated against war. On April 13, 1934, a day of protest around the country, students at Smith College placed white crosses on the campus as a memorial to the people killed in the Great War and those who would die in the next one. The next year, even more students went on strike for a day. Students joined organizations like Veterans of Future Wars and Future Gold Star Mothers and protested the presence of the Reserve Office Training Corps on their campuses. They were determined never again to support a foreign war. But in Europe, Asia, and Africa, there were already rumblings of another great international conflict.

Ethiopia and Spain

In May 1935, Italy invaded Ethiopia and made quick work of the small and poorly equipped Ethiopian army. The Ethiopian war, remote as it seemed, frightened Congress, which passed a Neutrality Act authorizing the president to prohibit all arms shipments to nations at war and to advise all United States citizens not to travel on belligerents' ships except at their own risk. Remembering the process that led the United States into World War I, Congress was determined that it would not happen again. Roosevelt used the authority of the Neutrality Act of 1935 to impose an arms embargo. The embargo had little impact on Italy, but it was disastrous for the poor African nation. Italy quickly defeated Ethiopia, and by 1936, Mussolini had joined forces with Germany to form the Rome-Berlin Axis.

"We shun political commitments which might entangle us in foreign war," Roosevelt announced in 1936. "We are not isolationist except in so far as we seek to isolate ourselves completely from war." But isolation became more difficult when a civil war broke out in Spain in 1936. General Francisco Franco, supported by the Catholic church and large landowners, revolted against the republican government. Germany and Italy aided Franco, sending planes and other weapons, while the Soviet Union came to the support of the Spanish republican Loyalists. Most American Catholics and many anticommunists sided with Franco. But many American radicals, even those opposed to all war a few months before, found the Loyalist cause worth fighting and dying for. Over 3,000 Americans joined the Abraham Lincoln Brigade, and hundreds were killed fighting fascism in Spain.

The U.S. government tried to stay neutral and to ship arms and equipment to neither side. In 1937, Congress passed another Neutrality Act, this time making it illegal for American citizens to travel on belligerents' ships. The act extended the embargo on arms and made even nonmilitary items available to belligerents only on a cash-and-carry basis.

In a variety of ways, the United States tried to avoid repeating the mistakes that had led it into World War I. Unfortunately, World War II, which moved closer each day, would be a different kind of war, and the lessons of the first war would be of little use.

War in Europe

Roosevelt had no carefully planned strategy to deal with the rising tide of war in Europe in the late 1930s. He was by no means an isolationist, but he wanted to keep the United States out of the European conflagration.

Hitler, however, was on the move. In 1936 Hitler's troops marched into the Rhineland, an area demilitarized by the peace terms following World War I. In March 1938 he annexed Aus-

tria. Six months later he demanded the cession of Sudetenland, an adjacent part of Czechoslovakia. In a meeting at Munich on September 29, 1938, Britain and France agreed that Hitler could take Sudetenland, and Hitler, in turn, agreed to make no further territorial demands. The Munich Accords have since been held up as a lesson on the price of appeasing a dictator. Within six months, Hitler's armies had overrun the rest of Czechoslovakia.

Little protest came from the United States. Most Americans sympathized with the victims of Hitler's aggression, and eventually some were horrified at rumors of the murder of hundreds of thousands of Jews. August 23, 1939, brought news of a Nazi-Soviet pact. Fascism and communism were political philosophies supposedly in deadly opposition, but Nazi Germany and Soviet Russia had now signed a nonaggression pact. A week later, Hitler's army attacked Poland, marking the official beginning of World War II. Britain and France honored their treaties and came to Poland's defense. "This nation will remain a neutral nation," Roosevelt announced, "but I cannot ask that every American remain neutral in thought as well."

Roosevelt asked for a repeal of the embargo section of the Neutrality Act and for the approval of the sale of arms on a cash-and-carry basis to France and Britain. The United States would help the countries struggling against Hitler, but not at the risk of entering the war or even at the threat of disrupting the civilian economy. Yet Roosevelt did take some secret risks. In August 1939, Albert Einstein, a Jewish refugee from Nazi Germany, and other distinguished scientists warned the president that German researchers were at work on an atomic bomb. Fearing the consequences of a powerful new weapon in Hitler's hands, Roosevelt authorized funds for a top-secret project to build an American bomb first. Only a few advisers and key members of Congress knew of the project, which was officially organized in 1941 and would ultimately change the course of human history.

The war in Poland ended quickly. With Germany attacking from the west and the Soviet Union from the east, the Poles were overwhelmed in a month. The fall of Poland in September 1939 brought a lull in the fighting.

Great Britain sent several divisions to aid the French against the expected German attack, but for months nothing happened. Then on April 9, 1940, Germany attacked Norway and Denmark with a furious air and sea assault. A few weeks later, using armed vehicles supported by massive air strikes, the German *Blitzkrieg* swept through Belgium, Luxembourg, and the Netherlands. A week later, the Germans stormed into France. The famed Maginot line, a series of fortifications designed to repulse a German invasion, was useless as German mechanized forces swept around the end of the line and attacked from the rear. The French guns, solidly fixed in concrete and pointing toward Germany, were never fired. France surrendered in June as the British army fled back across the English Channel from Dunkirk.

Roosevelt reacted cautiously to events in Europe. He approved the shipment to Britain of 50 overage American destroyers. In return, the United States received the right to establish naval and air bases on British territory from Newfoundland to Bermuda and British Guiana.

In July 1940, Roosevelt also signed a measure authorizing $4 billion to increase the number of American naval warships. In September, Congress passed the Selective Service Act, which provided for the first peacetime draft in the history of the United States. As the war in Europe reached a crisis in the fall of 1940, the American people were still undecided about the proper response.

The Election of 1940

Part of Roosevelt's reluctance to aid Great Britain more energetically came from his genuine desire to keep the United States out of the war, but it was also related to the presidential campaign waged during the crisis months of the summer and fall of 1940. Roosevelt broke a long tradition by seeking a third term. He marked the increasing support he was drawing from the liberal wing of the Democratic party by selecting liberal farm economist Henry Wallace of Iowa as his running mate. The Republicans chose Wendell Willkie of Indiana, the most persuasive and exciting Republican candidate since Theodore Roosevelt. Yet in an atmosphere of international crisis, most voters chose to stay with Roosevelt. He won, 27 million to 22 million, and carried 38 of 48 states.

Lend-Lease

After the election, Roosevelt invented a scheme for sending aid to Britain without demanding payment, which Britain could not afford. He called the arrangement "lend-lease," and compared it to lending a garden hose to a neighbor whose house was on fire. The Lend-Lease Act, which Congress passed in March 1941, allowed the United States to lend or lease armaments to any country considered essential to American defense. The receiving country had only to agree to return the items after the war. The lend-lease program destroyed the fiction of neutrality.

By that time, German submarines were sinking a half million tons of shipping each month in the Atlantic. In June, Roosevelt proclaimed a national emergency and ordered the closing of German and Italian consulates in the United States. On June 22, Germany suddenly attacked the Soviet Union. It was one of Hitler's biggest blunders of the war, for now his armies had to fight on two fronts. In November 1941, Roosevelt extended lend-lease aid to Russia.

By the autumn of 1941, the United States was virtually at war with Germany in the Atlantic. It was not Germany, however, but Japan that catapulted the United States into World War II.

The Path to Pearl Harbor

Japan, controlled by ambitious military leaders, was the aggressor in the Far East as Hitler's Germany was in Europe. Intent on becoming a major world power yet desperately needing natural resources, especially oil, Japan was willing to risk war with China, the Soviet Union, and even the United States to get those resources. Japan invaded Manchuria in 1931 and launched an all-out assault on China in 1937. The Japanese leaders assumed that at some point the United States would go to war if Japan tried to take the Philippines, but the Japanese attempted to delay that moment as long as possible by diplomatic means. For its part, the United States feared the possibility of a two-front war and was willing to delay the confrontation with Japan until it had dealt with the German threat. Thus between 1938 and 1941, the United States and Japan engaged in a kind of diplomatic shadow boxing.

The United States did exert economic pressure on Japan, demanding that the Japanese withdraw from China. Beginning in July 1939, the United States gradually reduced trade shipments to Japan, but Japan continued on its course of expansion, occupying French Indochina in 1940 and 1941. In July 1941, Roosevelt froze all Japanese assets in the United States, effectively embargoing trade with Japan.

As the crisis developed, Roosevelt had an advantage in the negotiations with Japan, for the United States had broken the Japanese diplomatic code. But Japanese intentions were hard to decipher from the intercepted messages. The American leaders knew Japan was planning an attack, but they did not know when or where. In September 1941, the Japanese decided to strike at the United States sometime after November

unless the United States offered real concessions. The strike came at Pearl Harbor, the main American Pacific naval base, in Hawaii.

On the morning of December 7, 1941, Japanese airplanes launched from aircraft carriers attacked the United States fleet at Pearl Harbor. The surprise attack destroyed or disabled 19 ships (including 5 battleships) and 150 planes and killed 2,335 soldiers and sailors and 68 civilians. On the same day, the Japanese launched attacks on the Philippines, Guam, and the Midway Islands, as well as on the British colonies of Hong Kong and Malaya. The next day, with only one dissenting vote, Congress declared war on Japan. Jeannette Rankin, a member of Congress from Montana who had voted against the war resolution in 1917, voted no again on December 8, 1941. Three days later, Japan's allies, Germany and Italy, declared war on the United States. This time, Congress replied unanimously in declaring war on them.

December 7, 1941, was a day that would "live in infamy," in the words of Franklin Roosevelt. It was also a day that would have far-reaching implications for American foreign policy and for American attitudes toward the world. The surprise attack united the country as nothing else could have. Even isolationists quickly rallied behind the war effort.

After the shock and anger subsided, Americans searched for a villain. A myth persists to this day that the villain was Roosevelt, who, the story goes, knew of the Japanese attack but failed to warn the military commanders so that the American people might unite behind the war effort against Germany. But Roosevelt did not know. There was no specific warning that the attack was coming against Pearl Harbor, and the American ability to read the Japanese coded messages was no help because the fleet kept radio silence. The irony was that the Americans, partly because of racial prejudice against the Japanese, underestimated their ability.

Even more important in the long run than

An exploding American battleship at Pearl Harbor, December 7, 1941. The attack on Pearl Harbor united the country and came to symbolize Japanese treachery and American lack of preparedness. Photographs such as this were published throughout the war to inspire Americans to work harder.

the way the attack on Pearl Harbor united the American people was its effect on a generation of military and political leaders. Pearl Harbor became the symbol of unpreparedness. For a generation that experienced the anger and frustration of the attack on Pearl Harbor by an unscrupulous enemy, the lesson was to be prepared and ready to stop an aggressor before it had a chance to strike at the United States. The smoldering remains of the sinking battleships at Pearl Harbor on the morning of December 7, 1941, and the history lesson learned there would influence American policy not only during World War II but also in Korea, Vietnam, and the international confrontations of the 1980s.

THE HOME FRONT

World War II had an impact on all aspects of society—the economy, the movies and radio, even attitudes toward women and blacks. For many people, the war represented opportunity and the end of the Depression. For others, the excitement of faraway places meant that they could

never return home again. For still others, the war left lasting scars.

Mobilizing for War

Converting American industry to war production was a complex task. Many corporate executives refused to admit that an emergency existed. Shortly after Pearl Harbor, Roosevelt created the War Production Board (WPB) and appointed Donald Nelson, executive vice president of Sears, Roebuck, to mobilize the nation's resources for an all-out war effort. The WPB offered businesses cost-plus contracts, guaranteeing a fixed and generous profit. Often the government also financed new plants and equipment.

The Roosevelt administration leaned over backward to gain the cooperation of businessmen. The president appointed many business executives to key positions, some of whom, like Nelson, served for a dollar a year. He also abandoned antitrust actions in all industries that were remotely war related.

The policy worked. Both industrial production and net corporate profits nearly doubled during the war. Large commercial farmers also profited. The war years accelerated the mechanization of the farm. At the same time, the farm population declined by 17 percent. The consolidation of small farms into large ones and the dramatic increase in the use of fertilizer made farms more productive and farming more profitable for the large operators.

Many government agencies in addition to the War Production Board helped to run the war effort efficiently. The Office of Price Administration (OPA) set prices on thousands of items to control inflation and also rationed scarce products. The National War Labor Board (NWLB) had the authority to set wages and hours and to monitor working conditions and could, under the president's wartime emergency powers, seize industrial plants whose owners refused to cooperate.

Membership in labor unions grew rapidly during the war, from a total of 10.5 million in 1941 to 14.7 million in 1945. This increase was aided by government policy. In return for a "no-strike pledge," the NWLB allowed agreements that required workers to retain their union membership through the life of a contract. Labor leaders, however, were often not content with the raises permitted by the NWLB. In the most famous incident, John L. Lewis broke the no-strike pledge of organized labor by calling a nationwide coal strike in 1943. When Roosevelt ordered the secretary of the interior to take over the mines, Lewis called off the strike. But this bold protest did help raise miners' wages.

In addition to wage and price controls and rationing, the government tried to reduce inflation by selling war bonds and by increasing taxes. The war made the income tax a reality for most Americans for the first time.

Despite some unfairness and much confusion, the American economy responded to the wartime crisis and turned out the equipment and supplies that eventually won the war. American industries built 300,000 airplanes, 88,140 tanks, and 3,000 merchant ships. Although the national debt grew from about $143 billion in 1943 to $260 billion in 1945, the government policy of taxation paid for about 40 percent of the war's cost. In a limited way, the tax policy also tended to redistribute wealth, which the New Deal had failed to do. The top 5 percent income bracket, which controlled 23 percent of the disposable income in 1939, accounted for only 17 percent in 1945.

Patriotic Fervor

In European and Asian cities, the horror and destruction of war were everywhere. But in the United States, the war was remote. The government tried to keep the country united behind the war effort. The Office of War Information, staffed by writers and advertising executives, controlled the news the American public received about the war. It promoted patriotism and presented the American war effort in the best possible light.

The government also sold war bonds, not only to help pay for the war and reduce inflation but also to sell the war to the American people. As had been true during World War I, movie stars and other celebrities appeared at war bond rallies. Schoolchildren purchased war stamps and faithfully pasted them in an album until they had accumulated stamps worth $18.75, enough to buy a $25 bond (redeemable ten years later). In the end, the government sold over $135 billion in war bonds.

Those too old or too young to join the armed forces served in other ways. Thousands became air raid wardens or civilian defense and Red Cross volunteers. They raised victory gardens and took part in scrap drives. Even small children could join the war effort by collecting old rubber, waste paper, and kitchen fats. Some items, including gasoline, sugar, butter, and meat, were rationed, but few people complained. Newspaper and magazine advertising characterized ordinary actions as speeding victory or impeding the war effort. "Hoarders are the same as spies," one ad announced. "Everytime you decide *not* to buy something you help win the war."

Internment of Japanese-Americans

Wartime campaigns not only stimulated patriotism but also promoted hate for the enemy. "You and I don't hate the Nazis because they are Germans. We hate the Germans because they are Nazis," announced a character in one of Helen MacInnes's novels. But before long, most Americans ceased to make distinctions. All Germans seemed evil, although the anti-German hysteria that had swept the country during World War I never developed.

The Japanese were easier to hate than the Germans. The attack on Pearl Harbor created a special animosity toward the Japanese, but the depiction of the Japanese as warlike and subhuman owed something to a long tradition of fear of the so-called yellow peril and a distrust of all Asians. The movies, magazine articles, cartoons, and posters added to the image of the Japanese soldier or pilot with a toothy grin murdering innocent women and children or shooting down helpless Americans.

The racial stereotype of the Japanese played a role in the treatment of Japanese-Americans during the war. Some prejudice was shown against German- and Italian-Americans, but Japanese-Americans were the only group confined in concentration camps in the greatest mass abridgment of civil liberties in American history.

At the time of Pearl Harbor, about 127,000 Japanese-Americans lived in the United States, most on the West Coast. About 80,000 were nisei (Japanese born in the United States and holding American citizenship) and sansei (the sons and daughters of nisei); the rest were issei (aliens born in Japan who were ineligible for U.S. citizenship). Although many retained cultural and linguistic ties to Japan, they posed no more threat to the country than did the much larger groups of Italian-Americans and German-Americans. But their physical characteristics made them stand out as the others did not. After Pearl Harbor, an anti-Japanese panic seized the West Coast.

West Coast politicians and ordinary citizens urged the War Department and the president to evacuate the Japanese. The president capitulated and issued Executive Order 9066 authorizing the evacuation in February 1942.

Eventually, the government built the "relocation centers" in remote, often arid, sections of the West. The camps were primitive and unattractive. "When I first entered our room, I became sick to my stomach," a Japanese-American woman remembered. "There were seven beds in the room and no furniture nor any partitions to separate the males and the females of the family. I just sat on the bed, staring at the bare wall." The government evacuated about 110,000 Japanese. Those who were forced to leave their homes, farms, and businesses lost almost all their property and possessions.

The evacuation of the Japanese-Americans appears in retrospect to have been unjustified. Even in Hawaii, where a much larger Japanese population existed, the government attempted no evacuation, and no sabotage and little disloyalty occurred. The government allowed Japanese-American men to volunteer for military service, and many served bravely in the European theater. The 442nd Infantry Combat Team, made up entirely of nisei, became the most decorated unit in all the military service—another indication of the loyalty and patriotism of the Japanese-Americans. In 1988, Congress belatedly voted limited compensation for the Japanese-Americans relocated during World War II.

Black and Hispanic Americans at War

The United States in 1941, even in much of the North, remained a segregated society. Blacks

Japanese-American children on their way to a "relocation center." For many Japanese-Americans, but especially for the children, the nightmare of the relocation camp experience would stay with them all their lives.

could not live, eat, travel, work, or go to school with the same freedom whites enjoyed. Blacks profited little from the revival of prosperity and the expansion of jobs early in the war. Blacks who joined the military were usually assigned to menial jobs as cooks or laborers and were always assigned to segregated units with whites as the high-ranking officers. The myth that black soldiers had failed to perform well in World War I persisted.

Some black leaders found it especially ironic that as the country prepared to fight Hitler and his racist policies, the United States persisted in its own brand of racism. "A jim crow Army cannot fight for a free world," announced *The Crisis,* the journal of the NAACP. In 1941, A. Philip Randolph, who had organized and led the Brotherhood of Sleeping Car Porters, planned a march on Washington to demand equal rights.

The threat of as many as 100,000 blacks marching in protest in the nation's capital alarmed Roosevelt. At first he sent his assistants, including his wife, Eleanor, who was greatly admired in the black community, to dissuade Randolph from such drastic action. Finally, he talked to Randolph in person on June 18, 1941. Randolph and Roosevelt struck a bargain. Roosevelt refused to desegregate the armed forces, but in return for Randolph's calling off the march, the president issued Executive Order 8802, which stated that it was the policy of the United States that "there shall be no discrimination in the employment of workers in defense industries or government because of race, creed, color or national origin." He also established the Committee on Fair Employment Practices (FEPC) to carry out the order, but it was never effectively enforced.

Blacks continued to experience discrimination in other areas of life as well. Many black soldiers were angered and humiliated throughout the war by being made to sit in the back of buses and being barred from hotels and restaurants. Years later, one former black soldier recalled being refused service in a restaurant in Salina, Kansas, while the same restaurant served German prisoners from a camp nearby. "We continued to stare," he recalled. "This was really happening. . . . The people of Salina would serve these enemy soldiers and turn away black American G.I.'s."

Many black Americans improved their economic conditions during the war by taking jobs in war industries in northern and western cities. But they did not escape racial prejudice. In Detroit, a major race riot broke out in the summer of 1943. Polish-Americans had protested a public housing development that promised to bring blacks into their neighborhood. In one year, more than 50,000 blacks moved into that city, already overcrowded with many others seeking wartime jobs.

The riot broke out on a hot, steamy day at a municipal park where a series of incidents led to fights between black and white young people

Even before the United States entered the war, black families like this one moved north to look for work and a better life. This massive migration would change the racial mix in northern cities.

and then to looting in the black community. Before federal and state troops restored order, 34 had been killed (25 blacks and 9 whites), and rioters had destroyed more than $2-million worth of property. Other riots broke out in Mobile, Los Angeles, New York, and Beaumont, Texas. In all these cities, and in many others where the tension did not lead to open violence, the legacy of bitterness and hate lasted long after the war.

Mexican-Americans, like most minority groups, profited during the war from the increased job opportunities provided by wartime industry. But they, too, faced prejudice and discrimination.

In California and in many parts of the Southwest, Mexicans and Mexican-Americans could not use public swimming pools. Often lumped together with blacks, they were excluded from certain restaurants. Usually they were limited to menial jobs and were constantly harassed by the police, picked up for minor offenses, and jailed on the smallest excuse. In Los Angeles, the anti-Mexican prejudice flared into violence. The increased migration of Mexicans into the city and old hatreds created a volatile situation. Most of the hostility and anger focused on Mex-

ican gang members, or *pachucos,* especially those wearing zoot suits (long, loose coats with padded shoulders, ballooned pants pegged at the ankles, and a wide-brimmed hat).

The zoot-suiters especially angered soldiers and sailors who were stationed or on leave in Los Angeles. After a number of provocative incidents, the violence reached a peak on June 7, 1943, when gangs of servicemen, often in taxicabs, combed the city, attacking all the young zoot-suiters they could find or anyone who looked Mexican. The servicemen, joined by others, beat up the Mexicans, stripped them of their clothes, and then gave them haircuts. The police, both civilian and military, looked the other way, and when they did move in, they arrested the victims rather than their attackers. *Time* magazine called the riots "the ugliest brand of mob action since the coolie race riots of the 1870s."

THE SOCIAL IMPACT OF THE WAR

Modern wars have been incredibly destructive of human lives and property, and they have social results as well. The Civil War ended slavery and ensured the triumph of the industrial North for years to come; it left a legacy of bitterness and transformed the race question from a sectional to a national problem. World War I assured the success of woman suffrage and prohibition, caused a migration of blacks to northern cities, and ushered in a time of intolerance. World War II also had many social results. It altered patterns of work, leisure, education, and family life; caused a massive migration of people; created jobs; and changed life styles. It is difficult to overemphasize the impact of the war on the generation that lived through it.

Wartime Opportunities

The war caused many Americans to move to other parts of the country. More than 15 million civilians moved during the war, flocking to cities, where defense jobs were readily available. They moved west: California alone gained more than two million people during the war. But they also moved out of the South into the northern cities, while a smaller number moved from the North to the South. Late in the war, when a shortage of farm labor developed, some reversed the trend and moved back onto the farms.

The World War II migrants poured into industrial centers; 200,000 came to the Detroit area, nearly a half million to Los Angeles, and about 100,000 to Mobile, Alabama. They put pressure on the schools, housing, and other services. Often they had to live in new Hoovervilles, trailer parks, or temporary housing. Bill Mauldin, the war cartoonist, showed a young couple with a child buying tickets for a movie, with the caption: "Matinee, heck—we want to register for a week."

For the first time in years, many families had money to spend, but they had nothing to spend it on. The last new car rolled off the assembly line in February 1942. There were no washing machines, refrigerators, or radios in the stores, little gasoline and few tires to permit weekend trips.

The war required major adjustments in American family life. With several million men in the service and others far away working at defense jobs, the number of households headed by a woman increased dramatically. The number of marriages also rose sharply. Early in the war, a young man could be deferred if he had a dependent, and a wife qualified as a dependent. Later, many servicemen got married, often to women they barely knew, because they wanted a little excitement and perhaps someone to come home to. The birthrate also began to rise in 1940, reversing a long decline. The illegitimacy rate also went up, and from the outset of the war, the divorce rate began to climb sharply. Yet most of the wartime marriages survived, and many of the women left at home looked ahead to a time after the war when they could settle down to a normal life.

Women Workers for Victory

Another impact of the war was the opening of industrial jobs to women. Thousands of women took jobs in heavy industry that formerly would have been considered unladylike. They built tanks, airplanes, and ships, but they still earned less than men.

By 1943, with many men drafted and male unemployment virtually nonexistent, the government was quick to suggest that it was women's patriotic duty to take their place on the assembly line. A popular song was "Rosie the Riveter," who was "making history working for victory."

At the end of the war, the labor force included 19.5 million women. In 1944, women's weekly wages averaged $31.21, compared with $54.65 for men, reflecting women's more menial tasks and their low seniority as well as outright discrimination. Still, many women enjoyed factory work. "Boy have the men been getting away with murder all these years," exclaimed a Pittsburgh housewife. "Why I worked twice as hard selling in a department store and got half the pay." In addition to lower pay, women workers often had to endure catcalls, whistles, and more overt sexual harassment on the job.

Black women faced the most difficult situation during the war, and often when they applied for work, they were told, "We have not yet installed separate toilet facilities" or "We can't put a Negro in the front office." Not until 1944 did the telephone company in New York City hire a black telephone operator. Married women with young children also found it difficult to find work. They found few day-care facilities and were often informed that they should be home with their children.

Many women war workers quickly left their jobs after the war ended. Some left by choice, but many were laid off, because the law guaranteed to returning male veterans their former jobs. As war industries slowed down, dismissals ran twice as high for women as for men. The war had only temporarily shaken the notion that a woman's place was at home.

Entertaining the People

According to one survey, Americans listened to the radio an average of 4½ hours a day during the war. The major networks increased their news programs from less than 4 percent to nearly 30 percent of broadcasting time. Americans heard Edward R. Murrow broadcasting from London during the German air blitz with the sound of the air raid sirens in the background. They listened to Eric Sevareid cover the battle of Burma and describe the sensation of jumping out of an airplane. They also relied on commentators like H. V. Kaltenborn or Gabriel Heatter to explain what was happening around the world.

The serials, the standard fare of daytime radio, also adopted wartime themes. Dick Tracy tracked down spies, while Stella Dallas took a job in a defense plant.

Music, which took up a large proportion of radio programming, also conveyed a war theme. There was "Goodbye, Mama (I'm Off to Yoko-hama)" and "Praise the Lord and Pass the Am-munition." But more numerous were songs of romance and love, songs about separation and hope for a better time after the war. The dance-able tunes of Glenn Miller and Tommy Dorsey became just as much a part of wartime memories as ration books and far-off battlefields.

For many Americans, the motion picture became the most important leisure activity and a part of their fantasy life during the war. Attendance at the movies averaged about 100 million individuals a week. There might not be gasoline for weekend trips or Sunday drives, but the whole family could go to the movies.

Musical comedies, cowboy movies, and historical romances remained popular during the war, but the conflict intruded even on Hollywood. Newsreels that offered a visual synopsis of the war news, always with an upbeat message and a touch of human interest, preceded most movies. Their theme was that the Americans were winning the war, even if early in the conflict there was little evidence to that effect. Many feature films also had a wartime theme, picturing the war in the Pacific complete with grinning, vicious Japanese villains (usually played by Chinese or Korean character actors). In the beginning of these films, the Japanese were always victorious, but in the end, they always got "what they deserved."

The movies set in Europe differed somewhat from those depicting the Far Eastern war. British and Americans, sometimes spies, sometimes downed airmen, could dress up like Germans and get away with it. They outwitted the Germans at every turn, sabotaging important installations and finally escaping in a captured plane.

The GIs' War

GI, the abbreviation for *government issue*, became the affectionate designation for the ordinary soldier in World War II. The GIs came from every background and ethnic group. Ernie Pyle, one of the war correspondents who chronicled the authentic story of the ordinary GI, wrote of soldiers "just toiling from day to day in a world full of insecurity, discomfort, homesickness, and a dulled sense of danger."

Bill Mauldin, another correspondent, told the story of the ordinary soldier in a series of cartoons featuring two tired and resigned infantrymen, Willie and Joe. In one cartoon Willie says, "Joe, yestiddy ya saved my life an' I swore I'd pay you back. Here's my last pair of dry socks." For the soldier in the front line, the big strategies were irrelevant. The war seemed a constant mixup; much more important were the little comforts and staying alive.

In the midst of battle, the war was no fun, but only one soldier of eight who served ever saw combat, and even for many of those the war was a great adventure (just as World War I had been). World War II catapulted young men and women out of their small towns and urban neighborhoods into exotic places where they met new people and did new things.

The war was important for Mexican-Americans, who were drafted and volunteered in great numbers. A third of a million served in all branches of the military, a larger percentage than for many other ethnic groups.

Many Native Americans also served. In fact, many Indians were recruited for special service in the Marine Signal Corps. One group of Navajos completely befuddled the Japanese with a code based on their native language. "Were it not for the Navajos, the Marines would never have taken Iwo Jima," one Signal Corps officer declared. But the Navajo code talkers and all other Indians who chose to return to the reservations after the war were ineligible for veterans' loans, hospitalization, and other benefits. They lived on federal land, and that, according to the law, canceled all the advantages that other veterans enjoyed after the war.

For black Americans, who served throughout the war in segregated units and faced prejudice wherever they went, the military experience also had much to teach. Fewer blacks were sent overseas, and fewer were in combat outfits, so the percentage of black soldiers

killed and wounded was low. Many illiterate blacks, especially from the South, learned to read and write in the service. Blacks who went overseas began to realize that not everyone viewed them as inferior. One black army officer said, "What the hell do we want to fight the Japs for anyhow? They couldn't possibly treat us any worse than these 'crackers' right here at home."

Because the war lasted longer than World War I, its impact was greater. In all, over 16 million men and women served in some branch of the military service. About 322,000 were killed in the war, and more than 800,000 were wounded. The 12,000 listed as missing just disappeared. The war claimed many more lives than World War I and was the nation's costliest after the Civil War. But because of penicillin, blood plasma, sulfa drugs, and rapid battle-field evacuation, the wounded in World War II were twice as likely to survive as in World War I.

Women in Uniform

Women had served in all wars as nurses and cooks and in other support capacities, and during World War II many continued in these traditional roles. A few nurses landed in France just days after the Normandy invasion. Nurses served with the army and the marines in the Pacific. They dug their own foxholes and treated men under enemy fire. Sixty-six nurses spent the entire war in the Philippines as prisoners of the Japanese. Most nurses, however, served far behind the lines tending the sick and wounded. Army nurses who were given officer rank were forbidden to date enlisted men.

Though nobody objected to women's serving as nurses, not until April 1943 did women physicians win the right to join the Army and Navy Medical Corps. Congress authorized full military participation for women (except for combat) because of the military emergency and the argument that women could free men for combat duty. World War II thus became the first war in which women were given regular military status. About 350,000 women joined up, most in the Women's Army Corps (WACS) and the women's branch of the navy (WAVES), but others served in the coast guard and the marines.

Men were informed about contraceptives and encouraged to use them, but information about birth control was explicitly prohibited for women. Rumors charged many servicewomen with sexual promiscuity. One cause for immediate discharge was pregnancy; yet the pregnancy rate for both married and unmarried women remained low.

Despite difficulties, women played important roles during the war, and when they left the service (unlike the women who had served in other wars), they had the same rights and privileges as the male veterans. And like male soldiers, many of the women who served had their lives changed and their horizons expanded.

A WAR OF DIPLOMATS AND GENERALS

Pearl Harbor catapulted the country into war with Japan, and on December 11, 1941, Hitler declared war on the United States, forcing it to fight the Axis powers in both Europe and Asia.

War Aims

Why was the United States fighting the war? What did it hope to accomplish in a peace settlement once the war was over? Roosevelt and the other American leaders never really decided. In a speech before Congress in January 1941, Roosevelt had mentioned the four freedoms: freedom of speech and expression, freedom of worship, freedom from want, and freedom from fear. For many Americans, this was what they were fighting for. Roosevelt spoke vaguely of the need to extend democracy and to establish a peacekeeping organization, but in direct contrast to Woodrow

Wilson's Fourteen Points, he never spelled out in any detail the political purposes for fighting.

Roosevelt and his advisers, realizing that it would be impossible to mount an all-out war against both Japan and Germany, decided to fight a holding action in the Pacific at first while concentrating efforts against Hitler in Europe, where the immediate danger seemed greater. The United States joined the Soviet Union and Great Britain in a difficult but ultimately effective alliance to defeat Nazi Germany. British prime minister Winston Churchill and Roosevelt got along well, although they often disagreed on strategy and tactics. Roosevelt's relationship with Soviet leader Joseph Stalin was much more strained, but often he agreed with the Russian leader about the way to fight the war. Stalin, a ruthless leader who had maintained his position of power only after eliminating hundreds of thousands of opponents, distrusted both the British and the Americans, but he needed them, just as they depended on him. Without the tremendous sacrifices of the Soviet army and people in 1941 and 1942, Germany would have won the war before the vast American military and industrial might could be mobilized.

1942: Year of Disaster

The first half of 1942 was disastrous for the Allied cause. In the Pacific, the Japanese captured the Dutch East Indies with their vast riches in rubber, oil, and other resources. They swept into Burma, took Wake Island and Guam, and invaded the Aleutian Islands of Alaska. They pushed the American garrison on the Philippines onto the Bataan peninsula and finally onto the tiny island of Corregidor, where U.S. General Jonathan Wainwright surrendered more than 11,000 men to the Japanese. American reporters tried to play down the disasters, concentrating their stories on the few American victories and on tales of American heroism against overwhelming odds.

In Europe, the Germans pushed deep into

World War II: Pacific Theater

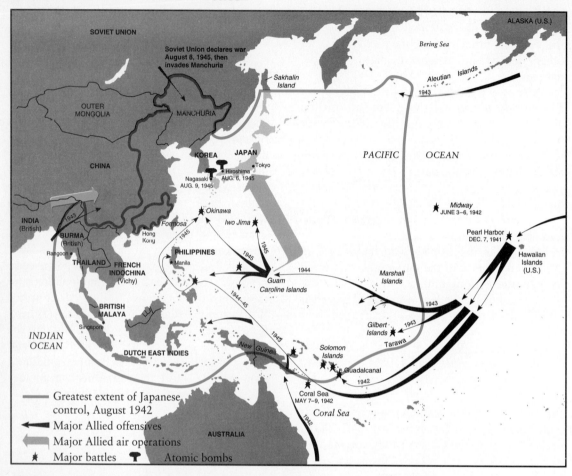

After the surprise attack on Pearl Harbor, the Japanese extended their control in the Pacific from Burma to the Aleutian Islands and almost to Australia. But after American naval and air victories at Coral Sea and Midway in 1942, the Japanese were increasingly on the defensive.

Russia, threatening Moscow. In North Africa, General Erwin Rommel and his mechanized divisions, the Afrika Korps, drove the British forces almost to Cairo in Egypt and threatened the Suez Canal. In contrast to World War I, which had been a war of stalemate, the opening phase of World War II was marked by air strikes and swift advances. In the Atlantic, German submarines sank British and American ships more rapidly than they could be replaced. For a few dark months in 1942, it seemed that the Berlin-Tokyo Axis would win the war before the United States got itself ready to fight.

The Allies could not agree on the proper military strategy in Europe. Stalin demanded a second front, an invasion of Europe in 1942, to relieve the pressure on the Soviet army, which faced 200 German divisions along a 2,000-mile front. Roo-

World War II: European and North African Theaters

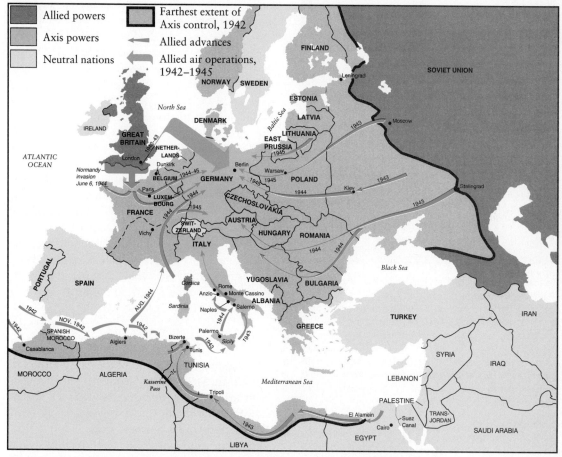

The German war machine swept across Europe and North Africa and almost captured Cairo and Moscow, but after major defeats at Stalingrad and El Alamein in 1943, the Axis powers were in retreat. Many lives were lost on both sides before the Allied victory in 1945.

sevelt agreed to an offensive in 1942. But in the end, the invasion in 1942 came not in France but in North Africa. The decision was probably right from a military point of view, but it taught the Soviets to distrust Britain and the United States. The delay in opening the second front probably contributed indirectly to the Cold War after 1945.

Attacking in North Africa in November 1942, American and British troops tried to link up with a beleaguered British army. The American army, enthusiastic but inexperienced, met little resistance in the beginning, but at Kasserine Pass in Tunisia, the Germans counter attacked and destroyed a large American force, inflicting 5,000 casualties.

To gain a cease-fire in conquered French territory in North Africa, the United States recognized Admiral Jean Darlan as head of its provisional government. Darlan persecuted the Jews, exploited the Arabs, imprisoned his opponents, and

The death camp Buchenwald, established by the Nazis in 1937, was liberated by American troops on April 13, 1945. One of the survivors was Elie Wiesel (shown here third from the right, middle level), whose mother and sister died in Auschwitz and whose father died in Buchenwald. Wiesel emigrated to the United States in 1956 and subsequently published an autobiographical novel, Night, in which he described the horrors of existence in the concentration camp. For his efforts in exposing the evils of the Holocaust, he received the Nobel Prize for Peace in 1986.

collaborated with the Nazis. The Darlan compromise reinforced Soviet distrust of the United States and angered many Americans as well.

Roosevelt also aided General Francisco Franco, the Fascist dictator in Spain, in return for safe passage of American shipping into the Mediterranean. But the United States also supplied arms to the left-wing resistance in France, to the Communist Tito in Yogoslavia, and Ho Chi Minh, the anti-French resistance leader in Indochina. Roosevelt also authorized large-scale lend-lease aid to the Soviet Union. Although liberals criticized his support of dictators, Roosevelt was willing to do almost anything to win the war. Military expediency often dictated his political decisions.

Even on one of the most sensitive issues of the war, the plight of the Jews in occupied Europe, Roosevelt's solution was to win the war as quickly as possible. By November 1942, confirmed information had reached the United States that the Nazis were systematically exterminating Jews. Yet the Roosevelt administration did nothing for more than a year, and even then it did scandalously little to rescue European Jews from the gas chambers. Widespread anti-Semitic feelings in the United States in the 1940s and the fear of massive Jewish immigration help to explain the failure of the Roosevelt administration to act. Roosevelt could not have prevented the Holocaust, but vigorous action on his part could have saved many thousands of lives during the war.

Roosevelt was not always right, nor was he even consistent, but people who assumed he had a master strategy or a fixed ideological position misunderstood the American president.

A Strategy for Ending the War

The commanding general of the Allied armies in the North African campaign emerged as a genuine leader. Born in Texas, Dwight D. Eisenhower spent his boyhood in Abilene, Kansas. His small-town background made it easy for biographers and newspaper reporters to make him into an American hero. Eisenhower was only a lieutenant colonel when World War II erupted. He was quickly promoted to general and achieved a reputation as an expert planner and organizer. Not a brilliant field commander, he had the ability to get diverse people working together, which was crucial where British and American units had to cooperate.

The American army moved slowly across North Africa, linked up with the British, invaded Sicily in July 1943, and finally stormed ashore in Italy in September. The Italian campaign proved long and bitter. The Allies did not reach Rome until June 1944, and they never controlled all of Italy.

United States into the dominant international power.

Americans greeted the end of the war with joy and relief. They looked forward to the peace and prosperity for which they had fought. Yet within two years, the peace would be jeopardized by the Cold War, and the United States would be rearming its former enemies, Japan and Germany, to oppose its former friend, the Soviet Union. The irony of that situation reduced the joy of the hard-won peace and made the American people more suspicious of their government and its foreign policy.

Recommended Reading

On the process by which the United States got involved in World War II, see Robert Dallek, *Franklin D. Roosevelt and American Foreign Policy* (1979); Waldo Heinricks, *Threshold of War* (1988); and Robert A. Divine, *The Reluctant Belligerent* (1979). For United States policy toward Central America, see Walter La Feber, *Inevitable Revolutions: The United States in Central America* (1983).

On the war, see Robert Leckie, *Delivered from Evil* (1987); Martin J. Sherwin, *A World Destroyed* (1975); Warren Kimball, *The Juggler: Franklin Roosevelt as Wartime Statesman* (1991); Herbert Feis, *The Atomic Bomb and the End of World War II* (1966); and Stephen Ambrose, *Eisenhower* (1983). John W. Dower, *War Without Mercy* (1986), and Akira Iriye, *The Origins of the Second World War in Asia and the Pacific* (1988), deal with the war against Japan.

Ross Gregory, *America 1941* (1988), is a fascinating account of the United States on the eve of the war. John Morton Blum, *V Was for Victory* (1976), and Richard Polenberg, *War and Society* (1972), are excellent books about the home front. Ruth Milkman, *Gender at Work* (1987), describes women during the war. Richard M. Dalfuime, *Desegregation of the U.S. Armed Forces* (1975), describes race relations in the military during the war. Roger Daniels, *Concentration Camp U.S.A.* (1971), details the relocation of Japanese-Americans during the war. David S. Wyman, *The Abandonment of the Jews* (1984), tells the story of American policy toward the victims of the Holocaust. Other books about the domestic scene include Nicholas Lemann, *The Promised Land: The Great Black Migration and How It Changed America* (1991); Mauricio Mazon, *The Zoot-Suit Riots* (1984); and Bill Gilbert, *They Also Served: Baseball and the Homefront* (1992).

Irwin Shaw's novel *The Young Lions* (1948) tells what fighting the war was like.

Time Line

1931–1932	Japan seizes Manchuria	1941	Lend-Lease Act
			Proposed black march on Washington
1933	Hitler becomes German chancellor		Germany attacks Russia
	United States recognizes the Soviet Union		Japanese assets in United States frozen
	Roosevelt extends Good Neighbor policy		Japanese attack Pearl Harbor; United States declares war on Japan
1934	Germany begins rearmament		Germany declares war on the United States
1935	Italy invades Ethiopia	1942	Internment of Japanese-Americans
	First Neutrality Act		Second Allied front in Africa launched
1936	Spanish civil war begins	1943	Invasion of Sicily
	Second Neutrality Act		Italian campaign; Italy surrenders
	Roosevelt reelected		United Mine Workers strike
1937	Third Neutrality Act		Race riots in Detroit and other cities
1938	Hitler annexes Austria, occupies Sudetenland	1944	Normandy invasion (Operation Overlord)
	German persecution of Jews intensifies		Congress passes GI Bill
			Roosevelt elected for a fourth term
1939	Nazi-Soviet Pact	1945	Yalta conference
	German invasion of Poland; World War II begins		Roosevelt dies; Harry Truman becomes president
1940	Roosevelt elected for a third term		Germany surrenders
	Selective Service Act		Successful test of atomic bomb
1941	FDR's "Four Freedoms" speech		Hiroshima and Nagasaki bombed; Japan surrenders
	Executive order outlaws discrimination in defense industries		

part 6

A
Resilient
People

1945-1993

The final section of *The American People* traces the recent history of the United States and highlights themes developed earlier in the text. We will explore the sense of mission the Cold War with the Soviet Union inspired, the growing role of the federal government in promoting the well-being of its citizens, and the reaction against that role. Finally, we will examine the continuing struggle to realize national ideals of liberty and equality in racial, gender, and social relations as new waves of immigration from Latin America and Asia increased the diversity of the American people.

Chapters 26 and 27 are paired. Chapter 26, "Chills and Fever During the Cold War," shows how the United States moved from an uneasy friendship with the Soviet Union to disillu-

sionment and hostility. Chapter 27, "Postwar Growth and Social Change," describes the expansion of self-interest in an age of extensive material growth and new patterns of regulation.

Chapters 28 and 29 are paired as well. Chapter 28, "The Rise and Fall of the Liberal State," describes the debate in the 1960s and 1970s over the appropriate role of government with regard to ensuring the welfare of all citizens. Chapter 29, "The Struggle for Social Reform," examines the continuing reform impulse that had its roots in the earliest days of American society.

In Chapter 30, "The Triumph of Conservatism," we explore the 1970s and 1980s in terms of economic and demographic developments, and we examine the 1992 presidential election.

chapter 26
....
Chills and Fever
During the Cold War

Val Lorwin was in Paris in November 1950 when word of the charges against him arrived. A State Department employee, on leave of absence after 16 years of government service, he was in France working on a book. Now he had to return to the United States to defend himself against the accusation that he was a member of the Communist Party and thus a loyalty and security risk.

Lorwin had begun to work for the government in 1935, serving in a number of New Deal agencies, then in the Labor Department and on the War Production Board before he was drafted during World War II. While in the army, he was assigned to the Office of Strategic Services, an early intelligence agency, and he was frequently granted security clearances in the United States and abroad.

Lorwin, however, did have a left-wing past as an active Socialist in the 1930s. He had supported the unionization of southern tenant farmers and the provision of aid to the unemployed. He and his wife, Madge, drafted statements or stuffed envelopes to support their goals. But that activity was wholly open and legal, and Lorwin had from the start been aggressively anticommunist in political affairs.

Suddenly, Lorwin, like others in the period, faced the nightmare of secret charges against which the burden of proof was entirely on him and the chance of clearing his name slim. Despite his spotless record, Lorwin was told that an unnamed accuser had identified him as a Communist. He was entitled to a hearing if he chose, or he could resign.

Lorwin requested a hearing, held late in 1950. Still struck by the absurdity of the situation, he refuted all accusations but made little effort to cite his own positive achievements. At the conclusion, he was informed that the government no longer doubted his loyalty but considered him a security risk, grounds nonetheless for dismissal from his job.

When he appealed the judgment, Lorwin was again denied access to the identity of his accuser. This time, however, he thoroughly prepared his defense. At the hearing, a total of 97 witnesses either spoke under oath on Lorwin's behalf or left sworn written depositions testifying to his good character and meritorious service. In March 1952, Lorwin was finally cleared for both loyalty and security.

Though he thought he had weathered the storm, Lorwin's troubles were not yet over. His name appeared on one of the lists produced by Senator Joseph McCarthy of Wisconsin, the most aggressive anticommunist of the era, and Lorwin was again victimized. The next year, he was indicted for making false statements to the State Department Loyalty-Security Board. The charges this time proved as specious as before. Finally, in May 1954, admitting that its special prosecutor had deliberately lied to the grand jury and had no legitimate case, the Justice Department asked for dismissal of the indictment. Lorwin was cleared at last and went on to a distinguished career as a labor historian.

<hr/>

Lorwin was more fortunate than some victims of the anticommunist crusade. People rallied around him and he survived the witch-hunt of the early 1950s. Not everyone was as lucky.

The Cold War, which unfolded soon after the end of World War II, powerfully affected all aspects of American life. The same sense of mission that had infused America in the Spanish-American War, World War I, and World War II now impelled most Americans to see themselves struggling against communism at home and abroad. This chapter explores that continuing sense of mission and its consequences.

CONFLICTING WORLD VIEWS

The Cold War was rooted in long-standing disagreements between the major powers regarding the shape of the postwar world. The United States, strong and secure, was intent on spreading its vision of freedom and economic opportunity around the world. The Soviet Union, concerned about its own security after a devastating war, demanded politically sympathetic neighbors on its borders. Each nation felt threatened by the interests of the other, and actions by both sides sparked reactions that culminated in the Cold War.

The American Stance

The United States emerged from World War II more powerful than any nation ever before.

Now it sought to use that might to achieve the kind of order that could sustain American aims. American policymakers, following in Woodrow Wilson's footsteps, hoped to spread the values that provided the underpinning of the American dream—liberty, equality, and democracy. They also hoped for a world where economic enterprise could thrive. With the American economy operating at full speed as a result of the war, world markets were needed once the fighting stopped. Government officials wanted to eliminate trade barriers—imposed by the Soviet Union and other nations—to provide outlets for industrial products and for surplus farm commodities like wheat, cotton, and tobacco. As the largest source of goods for world markets, with exports totaling $14 billion in 1947, the United States required open channels for growth to continue.

Soviet Aims

The Soviet Union formulated its own goals after World War II. Historically, Russia had usually had a strongly centralized, sometimes even autocratic, government, and that tradition—as much as communist ideology, with its stress on class struggle and the inevitable triumph of a proletarian state—guided Soviet policy.

During the war, the Soviets had played down the notion of world revolution they knew the other allies found threatening and had mobilized support for more nationalistic goals. As the struggle drew to a close, they talked little of world conquest, emphasizing socialism within the nation itself.

Rebuilding was a necessary priority. Devastated by the war, the Soviet Union concentrated on reconstruction as its first priority. Soviet agriculture and industry were a shambles and had to be revived. But revival demanded internal security. The Soviets feared vulnerability along their western flank. Such anxieties had a historical basis, for in the early nineteenth century, Napoleon had reached the gates of Moscow. Twice in the twentieth century, invasions had come from the west, most recently when Hitler had attacked in 1941. Haunted by fears that the Germans would recover quickly, the Soviets demanded defensible borders and neighboring regimes sympathetic to their aims.

Cold War Leadership

Both the United States and the Soviet Union had strong leadership as the Cold War unfolded. On the American side, first Harry Truman, then Dwight Eisenhower accepted the centralization of authority Franklin Roosevelt had begun, as the executive branch became increasingly powerful in guiding foreign policy. In the Soviet Union, first Joseph Stalin, then Nikita Khrushchev provided equally forceful direction.

Harry S Truman served as president of the United States in the first postwar years. He was an unpretentious man who took a straightforward approach to public affairs. He was, however, ill prepared for the office he assumed in the final months of World War II. His three months as vice president had done little to school him in the complexity of postwar issues.

Yet Truman matured swiftly. Impulsive and aggressive, he made a virtue out of rapid response. At his first press conference, he answered questions so quickly that reporters could not record his answers. A sign on the president's White House desk read "The Buck Stops Here." His rapid-fire decisions had important consequences for the Cold War.

Truman served virtually all of the term to which Roosevelt had been elected, then won another for himself in 1948. In 1952, war hero Dwight D. Eisenhower, who won the presidency for the Republican Party for the first time in 20 years, succeeded him.

Eisenhower stood in stark contrast to his predecessor. His easy manner and warm smile made him widely popular. On occasion, in press conferences or other public gatherings, his comments came out convoluted and imprecise. Yet appearances were deceiving, for beneath his casual approach was real shrewdness.

Eisenhower had not taken the typical route to the presidency. After his World War II success, he served as army chief of staff, president of Columbia University, and then head of the North Atlantic Treaty Organization. Despite his lack of formal political background, he had a genuine ability to get people to compromise and to work together.

Ike's limited experience with everyday politics conditioned his sense of the presidential role. Whereas Truman was accustomed to political infighting and wanted to take charge, Eisenhower saw things differently. "You do not *lead* by hitting people over the head. Any damn fool can do that," he said, "but it's usually called 'assault'— not 'leadership.'" Even so, Ike knew exactly where he wanted to go and worked behind the scenes to get there.

Though the personal styles of Truman and Eisenhower differed, they both subscribed to traditional American attitudes about self-determination and the superiority of American political institutions and values. Both distrusted Soviet ventures during and after the war.

Truman accepted collaboration with the Soviet Union during the struggle as a marriage of necessity, but he became increasingly hostile to Soviet moves as the war drew to an end. Like Truman, Eisenhower believed that communism was a monolithic force struggling for world supremacy and that the Kremlin in Moscow was orchestrating subversive activity around the globe. Like Truman, he viewed the Soviet system as "a tyranny that has brought thousands, millions of people into slave camps and is attempting to make all mankind its chattel." Yet Eisenhower was still a military man with a measure of caution who could practice accommodation when it served his ends.

The leader of the Soviet Union at the war's end was Joseph Stalin. Possessing almost absolute power, he had presided over monstrous purges against his opponents in the 1930s. Now he was determined to rebuild Soviet society, if possible with Western assistance, and to keep eastern Europe within the Soviet sphere of influence.

Stalin's death in March 1953 left a vacuum in Soviet political affairs. His successor, Nikita S. Khrushchev, used his position as party secretary to consolidate his power. Purges of the party bureaucracy took place, and five years after Stalin's death, Khrushchev held the offices of both prime minister and party secretary. Known for rude behavior, Khrushchev once pounded a table at the United Nations with his shoe while the British prime minister was speaking. During Khrushchev's regime, the Cold War continued, but there were now brief periods when relations between the two powers became less hostile.

ORIGINS OF THE COLD WAR

The Cold War developed by degrees. With the Fascist threat defeated, disagreements about the shape of the postwar world brought the Soviet Union and the United States into conflict. Such conflicts caused suspicion and distrust. As confrontation followed confrontation, the two nations behaved, according to Senator J. William Fulbright, "like two big dogs chewing on a bone."

Disillusionment with the USSR

In September 1945, more than half (54 percent) of a U.S. national sample trusted the Soviets to cooperate with the Americans in the postwar years. Two months later, the figure had dropped to 44 percent, and by February 1946, to 35 percent.

As Americans soured on the Soviet Union, they began to equate the Nazi and Soviet systems and to transfer their hatred of Hitler's Germany to the Soviet Communists. Just as they had in the 1930s, authors, journalists, and public officials began to point to similarities between the regimes, some of them quite legitimate. Both states, they contended, maintained total control over communications and could eliminate political opposition whenever they chose. Both states used terror to silence dissidents. Soviet labor camps in Siberia were now compared to German concentration camps. After the American publication in 1949 of George Orwell's frightening novel *1984*, *Life* magazine noted in an editorial that the ominous figure Big Brother was but a "mating" of Hitler and Stalin. Truman spoke for many Americans when he said in 1950 that "there isn't any difference between the totalitarian Russian government and the Hitler government. . . . They are all alike. They are . . . police state governments."

The lingering sense that the nation had not acted quickly enough to resist totalitarian aggression in the 1930s heightened American fears. Had the United States stopped the Germans, Italians, or Japanese, it might have prevented the long, devastating war. The free world had not responded quickly enough before and was determined never to repeat the same mistake.

The Polish Question

The first clash between East and West came, even before the war ended, over Poland. Soviet demands for a government willing to accept Soviet influence clashed with American hopes for a more representative structure patterned after the Western model.

"We must stand up to the Russians," Truman said, "and not be easy with them." Truman's unbending stance in an April 1945 meeting with Soviet foreign minister Vyacheslav Molotov on the question of what kind of government should lead Poland contributed to the deterioration of Soviet-American relations.

Truman and Stalin met face to face for the first time at the Potsdam Conference in July 1945, the last of the meetings held by the Big Three during the war. There, as they considered the Soviet-Polish boundary, the fate of Germany, and the American desire to obtain an unconditional surrender from Japan, the two leaders sized each other up. It was Truman's first exposure to international diplomacy at the highest level, and it left him confident of his abilities. When he learned during the meeting of the first successful atomic bomb test in New Mexico, he became even more determined to insist on his positions.

Economic Pressure on the USSR

One major source of controversy in the last stage of World War II was the question of American aid to its allies. Responding to congressional pressure at home to limit foreign assistance as hostilities ended, Truman acted impulsively. Six days after V-E Day signaled the end of the European war in May 1945, he issued an executive

order cutting off lend-lease supplies to the Allies. Although the policy affected all nations receiving aid, it hurt the Soviet Union most of all.

The United States intended to use economic pressure in other ways as well. The USSR desperately needed financial assistance to rebuild after the war and, in January 1945, had requested a $6 billion loan. Roosevelt hedged, hoping to win concessions in return. In August, the Soviets renewed their application, this time for only $1 billion. The new president dragged his heels, hoping to use the loan as a lever to gain access to new markets in areas traditionally dominated by the Soviet Union. Unwilling to help promote American trade in such areas, Stalin refused the offer of a loan with such conditions and launched his own five-year plan instead.

Declaring the Cold War

As Soviet-American disagreements increased, both sides stepped up their rhetorical attacks. Stalin spoke out first, in 1946, asserting his confidence in the triumph of the Soviet system. Capitalism and communism were on a collision course, he argued, and a series of cataclysmic disturbances would tear the capitalist world apart.

Supreme Court Justice William O. Douglas called Stalin's ominous speech "the declaration of World War III." In response, England's former prime minister, Winston Churchill, declared that "from Stettin in the Baltic to Trieste in the Adriatic, an iron curtain has descended across the Continent."

CONTAINING THE SOVIET UNION

Containment formed the basis of postwar American policy. Both political parties determined to check Soviet expansion. In an increasingly contentious world, the American government formulated rigid policies to maintain the upper hand. The Soviet Union responded in an equally rigid manner.

Containment Defined

George F. Kennan was primarily responsible for defining the new policy. Chargé d'affaires at the American embassy in the Soviet Union, he sent off an 8,000-word telegram to the State Department after Stalin's speech in February 1946. Kennan argued that Soviet-American hostility stemmed from "the Kremlin's neurotic view of world affairs," which in turn came from "the traditional and instinctive Russian sense of insecurity." Soviet fanaticism would not soften, regardless of how accommodating American policy became. Therefore, it had to be opposed at every turn.

Kennan's analysis struck a resonant chord in Washington. It made his diplomatic reputation, led to his assignment to an influential position in the State Department, and encouraged him to publish an extended analysis, under the pseudonym "Mr. X," in *Foreign Affairs*. "The whole Soviet governmental machine, including the mechanism of diplomacy," he wrote, "moves inexorably along the prescribed path, like a persistent toy automobile wound up and headed in a given direction, stopping only when it meets with some unanswerable force." Many Americans agreed with Kennan that Soviet pressure had to "be contained by the adroit and vigilant application of counter-force at a series of constantly shifting geographical and political points."

The concept of containment provided the philosophical justification for the hard-line stance that Americans, both in and out of government, adopted. Containment created the framework for military and economic assistance around the globe.

The Truman Doctrine

The Truman Doctrine represented the first major application of containment policy. The new policy was devised to respond to conditions in the eastern Mediterranean. The Soviet Union was pressuring Turkey for joint control of the Dardanelles, the passage between the Black Sea and the Mediterranean. Meanwhile, a civil war in Greece pitted Communist elements against the ruling English-aided right-wing monarchy. Revolutionary pressures threatened to topple the government.

In February 1947, the British ambassador to the United States informed the State Department that his exhausted country could no longer give Greece and Turkey economic and military aid. Would the United States now move into the void? The State Department was willing, but the conservative Congress had to be persuaded.

Administration leaders knew they needed bipartisan support to accomplish such a major policy shift. Senator Arthur Vandenberg of Michigan, a key Republican, warned that the administration had to begin "scaring hell out of the country" if it was serious about a bold new course of containment.

Truman took Vandenberg's advice to heart. On March 12, 1947, he told Congress, in a statement that came to be known as the Truman Doctrine, "I believe that it must be the policy of the United States to support free peoples who are resisting subjugation by armed minorities or by outside pressures." Unless the United States acted, the free world might not survive. To avert that calamity, he urged Congress to appropriate $400 million for military and economic aid to Turkey and Greece. Not everyone agreed with Truman's overblown description of the situation, but Congress passed his foreign aid bill.

In its assumption that Americans could police the globe, the Truman Doctrine was a major step in the advent of the Cold War. Truman's address, observed financier Bernard Baruch, "was tantamount to a declaration of . . . an ideological or religious war." Journalist Walter Lippmann was more critical. He termed the new containment policy a "strategic monstrosity" that could embroil the United States in disputes around the world. In the two succeeding decades, Lippmann proved correct.

The Marshall Plan, NATO, and NSC-68

The next step involved extensive economic aid for postwar recovery in western Europe. At the war's end, most of Europe was economically and politically unstable, thereby offering opportunities to the Communist movement. Decisive action was needed, for as the new secretary of state, George Marshall, declared, "The patient is sinking while the doctors deliberate." Another motive was eagerness to bolster the European economy to provide markets for American goods.

Marshall revealed the administration's willingness to assist European recovery in June 1947. He asked all troubled European nations to draw up an aid program that the United States could support, a program "directed not against any country or doctrine but against hunger, poverty, desperation, and chaos." The proposed program would assist the ravaged nations, provide the United States with needed markets, and advance the nation's ideological aims. American aid, Marshall pointed out, would permit the "emergence of political and social conditions in which free institutions can exist." The Marshall Plan and the Truman Doctrine, Truman noted, were "two halves of the same walnut."

In the end, American officials agreed to provide $17 billion over a period of four years to 16 cooperating nations. Though some members of Congress feared spreading American resources too thin, in early 1948 Congress committed the nation to funding European economic recovery, and the containment policy moved forward another step.

Closely related to the Marshall Plan was a concerted Western effort to rebuild Germany and to reintegrate it into a reviving Europe. At Yalta, Allied leaders had agreed on zonal occupation of Germany and on reparations Germany would pay the victors. Four zones, occupied by the Soviets, Americans, British, and French, had been established for postwar administration. A year after the end of the war, however, the balance of power in Europe had shifted. With the Soviet Union threatening to dominate eastern Europe, the West moved to fill the vacuum in central Europe. In late 1946, the Americans and British merged their zones for economic purposes and began to assign administrative duties to Germans. By the middle of 1947, the process of rebuilding West German industry was under way.

In mid-1948, the Soviet Union attempted to force the other nations out of Berlin, which, like Germany itself, was divided into zones after the war. Soviet refusal to allow the other Allies land access to West Berlin, located in the Soviet zone of Germany, led to a U.S. and Royal Air Force airlift that flew over two million tons of supplies to the beleaguered Berliners. The fliers named it Operation Vittles, and it broke the Soviet blockade.

The next major link in the containment strategy was the creation of a military alliance in Europe to complement the economic program. After the Soviets tightened their control of Hungary and Czechoslovakia, the United States in 1949 took the lead in establishing NATO, the North Atlantic Treaty Organization. Twelve nations formed the alliance, vowing that an attack against any one member would be considered an attack against all, to be met by appropriate armed force.

The Senate, formerly opposed to such military pacts, approved this time, and the United States established its first military treaty ties with Europe since the American Revolution. Congress also voted military aid for its NATO allies. The Cold War had softened long-standing American reluctance to become closely involved with European affairs.

In 1949, two significant events—the success of the Communists in the Chinese civil war and the Soviet detonation of an atomic device—led the United States to define its aims still more

An American and British airlift in 1948 brought badly needed supplies to West Berliners isolated behind a Soviet blockade of the city. By refusing to allow the Western powers to reach the city, located within the Soviet zone, the Russians hoped to drive them from Berlin, but the airlift broke the blockade.

specifically. The National Security Council, organized in 1947 to provide policy coordination, produced a paper, NSC-68, which shaped American policy for the next 20 years.

NSC-68 built on the Cold War rhetoric of the Truman Doctrine. It assumed that conflict between East and West was unavoidable, and that negotiation was useless, for the Soviets could never be trusted to bargain in good faith.

Having eliminated important options to resolving differences through traditional channels of diplomacy, NSC-68 then called for a massive increase in defense spending from the $13 billion set for 1950 to as much as $50 billion per year. The costs were huge, the document argued, but

necessary for the United States if the free world was to survive.

Containment in the 1950s

Containment, the keystone of American policy throughout the Truman years, was the rationale for the Truman Doctrine, the Marshall Plan, NATO, and NSC-68. In the 1950s, however, under Eisenhower's administration, containment came under attack as too cautious to counter the threat of communism.

For most of Eisenhower's two terms, John Foster Dulles was secretary of state. A devout Presbyterian who hated atheistic communism,

Cold War Europe in 1950

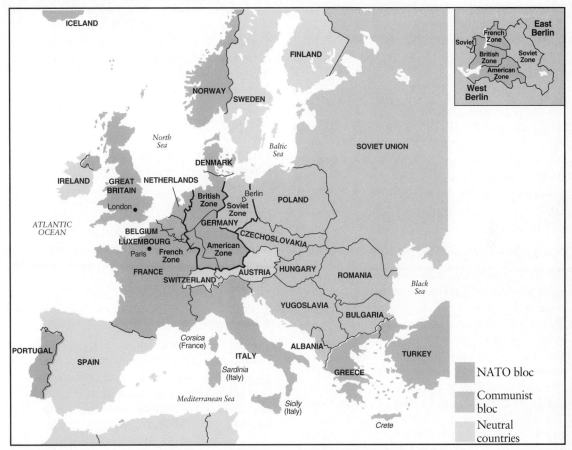

This map shows the rigid demarcation between East and West during the Cold War. Although there were a number of neutral countries in Europe, the other nations found themselves in a standoff, as each side tried to contain the possible advances of the other. The small inset map in the upper right-hand corner shows the division of Berlin that paralleled the division of Germany itself after World War II.

he sought to move beyond containment to a holy crusade to promote democracy and to free the countries under Soviet domination.

Eisenhower, more conciliatory and realistic than Dulles, recognized the impossibility of changing the governments of Russia's satellites. He also understood the need for caution. In mid-1953, as East Germans mounted anti-Soviet demonstrations, the United States kept its dis-

tance. In 1956, when Hungarian "freedom fighters" rose up against Soviet domination, the United States again stood back as Soviet forces smashed the rebels. Because Western action could have precipitated a more general conflict, Eisenhower refused to translate rhetoric into action. Throughout the 1950s, the policy of containment, largely as it had been defined earlier, remained in effect.

AMERICAN POLICY IN ASIA, THE MIDDLE EAST, AND LATIN AMERICA

Although containment resulted from the effort to promote European stability, the United States, in a dramatic departure from its history of non-involvement, extended the policy to meet challenges around the globe. In Asia, the Middle East and Latin America, the United States discovered the tremendous appeal of communism as a social and political system and found that ever greater efforts were required to advance American aims.

The Chinese Revolution

America's commitment to containment became stronger with the Communist victory in the Chinese civil war in 1949. China, an ally during World War II, had struggled against the Japanese, while at the same time it fought a domestic conflict rooted deep in the Chinese past—in widespread poverty, disease, oppression by the landlord class, and national humiliation at the hands of foreign powers. Mao Zedong (Mao Tse-tung),* founder of a branch of the Communist Party, wished to reshape China in a Communist mold. Opposing the Communists were the Nationalists, led by Jiang Jieshi (Chiang Kai-shek). By the early 1940s, Jiang Jieshi's regime was exhausted, hopelessly inefficient, and corrupt. Mao's movement, meanwhile, grew stronger during the Second World War as he opposed the Japanese invaders and won the loyalty of the peasant class.

After the war, Jiang fled in 1949 to the island of Taiwan. There he nursed the improbable belief that his was still the rightful government of all China and that he would one day return.

---

*Chinese names are rendered in their modern *Pinyin* spelling. At first occurrence, the older (usually Wade-Giles) spelling is given in parentheses.

The United States failed to understand the long internal conflict in China or the immense popular support Mao had generated. As the Communist army moved toward victory, the New York *Times* termed the group a "nauseous force," a "compact little oligarchy dominated by Moscow's nominees."

Secretary of State Dean Acheson considered granting diplomatic recognition to the new regime but backed off after the Communists seized American property, harassed American citizens, and openly allied themselves with the Russians.

Tension with China increased during the Korean War and then again in 1954 when Mao's government began shelling Nationalist positions on the offshore islands of Quemoy and Matsu. Eisenhower, now president, was again unwilling to respond forcefully.

The War in Korea

The Korean War marked America's growing intervention in Asian affairs. Concern about China and determination to contain communism led the United States into the struggle, but American objectives were not always clear and were largely unrealized after three years of war.

The conflict in Korea stemmed from tensions lingering after World War II. Korea, long under Japanese control, hoped for independence after Japan's defeat. But the Allies temporarily divided Korea along the 38th parallel when the rapid end to the Pacific struggle allowed Soviet troops to accept Japanese surrender in the north while American forces did the same in the south. The Soviet-American line, initially intended as a matter of military convenience, hardened after 1945, just as a similar division rigidified in Germany, and in time the Soviets set up a government in the north and the Americans a government in the south. Each Korean government hoped to reunify the country on its own terms.

North Korea moved first. On June 25, 1950, North Korean forces invaded South Korea

The Korean War

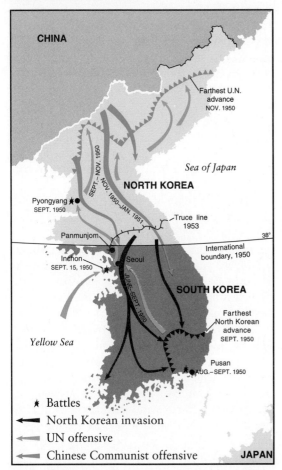

This map shows the ebb and flow of the Korean War. North Korea crossed the 38th parallel first, then the UN offensive drove the North Koreans close to the Chinese border, and finally the Chinese Communists entered the war and drove the UN forces back below the 38th parallel. The armistice signed at Panmunjom in 1953 provided a dividing line very close to the prewar line.

by crossing the 38th parallel. Following Soviet-built tanks, North Korean troops steadily advanced against South Korean soldiers.

The United States was taken by surprise, but Truman responded vigorously. He declared, "If this was allowed to go unchallenged it would

mean a third world war, just as similar incidents had brought on the second world war."

Truman readied American naval and air forces and directed General Douglas MacArthur in Japan to supply South Korea. The United States also went to the United Nations Security Council, which branded North Korea an aggressor and called on members of the organization to assist the south in repelling aggression and restoring peace.

The president first ordered American air and naval forces into battle south of the 38th parallel, then American ground forces as well. Following a daring amphibious invasion that pushed the North Koreans back to the former boundary line, United Nations troops crossed the 38th parallel, hoping to reunify Korea under an American-backed government. Despite Chinese signals that this movement toward their border threatened their security, the United States pressed on. In October, Chinese troops appeared briefly in battle, then disappeared. The next month, the Chinese mounted a full-fledged counterattack, which pushed the UN forces back below the dividing line again.

The resulting stalemate provoked a bitter struggle between Douglas MacArthur and his civilian commander in chief. A brilliant but arrogant general, MacArthur called for retaliatory air strikes against China, but Truman was trying to conduct a limited war.

MacArthur's public statements, issued from the field, finally went too far. In April 1951, he argued that the American approach in Korea was wrong, and that "there is no substitute for victory." Truman had no choice but to relieve him for insubordination.

The Korean War continued into Eisenhower's presidency. During the campaign of 1952, Eisenhower promised to go to Korea, and three weeks after his election, he did so. When truce talks bogged down again in May 1953, the new administration privately threatened the Chinese with the use of atomic weapons and a massive military campaign. This brought about a resumption of the peace talks. Finally, on July 27,

1953, an armistice was signed. The Republican administration had managed to do what the preceding Democratic administration could not. After three long years, the unpopular war had ended.

American involvement carried a heavy price: 54,000 Americans dead and many more wounded. But those figures paled beside the numbers of Korean casualties. As many as two million may have died in North and South Korea, and countless others were maimed.

The war also significantly changed American attitudes and institutions. This was the first war in which United States forces fought in integrated units. President Truman, as commander in chief, had ordered the integration of the armed forces in 1948, over the opposition of many generals, and blacks became part of all military units. Their successful performance led to acceptance of military integration.

The Korean War years also saw military expenditures soar from $13 billion in 1950 to about $47 billion three years later as defense spending followed the guidelines proposed in NSC-68. Whereas the military absorbed less than a third of the federal budget in 1950, a decade later it took one-half. More than a million military men were stationed around the world. At home, an increasingly powerful military establishment became closely tied to corporate and scientific communities and created a military-industrial complex that employed 3.5 million Americans by 1960.

The Korean War had important political effects as well. It led the United States to sign a peace treaty with Japan in September 1951 and to rely on that nation to maintain the balance of power in the Pacific. At the same time, the struggle poisoned relations with the People's Republic of China and ensured a diplomatic standoff that lasted more than 20 years.

Civil War in Vietnam

Indochina had been under French control since the middle of the nineteenth century. During World War II, the Japanese occupied the area but allowed French collaborators to direct internal affairs. An independence movement, led by the Communist organizer and revolutionary Ho Chi Minh, sought to expel the Japanese conquerors. In 1945, the Allied powers faced the decision of how to deal with Ho and his nationalist movement.

Franklin Roosevelt, like Woodrow Wilson, believed in self-determination and wanted to end colonialism. But France was determined to regain its colony, and by the time of his death, Roosevelt had backed down.

Ho Chi Minh meanwhile had established the Democratic Republic of Vietnam in 1945. Although the new government enjoyed widespread support, the United States refused to recognize it. The head of the American Office of Strategic Services mission predicted that if the French sought to regain control, the Vietnamese would fight to the death.

A long, bitter struggle between the French and the forces of Ho Chi Minh did break out and became entangled with the larger Cold War. President Truman was less concerned about ending colonialism than with checking growing Soviet power in Europe and around the world. He needed France to balance Soviet strength in Europe, and that meant cooperating with the French in Vietnam.

Though Ho did not, in fact, have close ties to the Soviet state and was committed to his independent nationalist crusade, Truman and his advisers, who saw communism as a monolithic force, assumed wrongly that Ho took orders from Moscow. Hence in 1950, the United States formally recognized the French puppet government in Vietnam. The United States also provided economic assistance to France. By 1954, the United States was paying over three-quarters of the cost of the war.

After Eisenhower took office, France's position deteriorated. Dulles was eager to assist the French; the chairman of the Joint Chiefs of Staff even contemplated using nuclear weapons. But

Eisenhower refused to intervene directly. The French fortress at Dien Bien Phu finally fell, and an international conference in Geneva divided Vietnam along the 17th parallel, with elections promised in 1956 (but never held) to unify the country and determine its political fate.

As a result of that division, two new states emerged. Ho Chi Minh held power in the north, while in the south Premier Ngo Dinh Diem, a fierce anticommunist, formed a separate government. Intent on taking France's place in Southeast Asia, the United States supported the Diem government and refused to sign the Geneva agreement. In the next few years, American aid increased and military advisers began to assist the South Vietnamese. The United States had taken the first steps toward involvement in a ruinous war halfway around the world that would later escalate out of control.

The Middle East

Cold War attitudes also influenced American responses to events in the Middle East. That part of the world had tremendous strategic importance as the supplier of oil for the industrialized nations. During World War II, the major Allied powers occupied Iran, with the provision that they would leave within six months of the war's end. As of early 1946, both Great Britain and the United States had withdrawn, but the Soviet Union, which bordered on Iran, remained. Stalin claimed that earlier security agreements had not been honored and, further, demanded oil concessions. A threat of vigorous American action, however, forced the Soviets to back down and withdraw.

The Eisenhower administration maintained its interest in Iran. In 1953, the CIA helped the local army overthrow the government of Mohammed Mossadegh, which had nationalized oil wells formerly under British control, and place the shah of Iran securely on the Peacock Throne.

After the coup, British and American companies regained command of the wells, and thereafter the United States government provided military assistance to the shah.

A far more serious situation emerged west of Iran. In 1948, the United Nations attempted to partition Palestine into an Arab state and a Jewish state. Truman officially recognized the new state of Israel 15 minutes after it was proclaimed. But recognition could not end bitter animosities between Arabs, who felt they had been robbed of their territory, and Jews, who felt they had finally regained a homeland after the horrors of the Holocaust. As Americans looked on, Arab forces from Egypt, Trans-Jordan, Syria, Lebanon, and Iraq invaded Israel, but the Israelis won the war and added territory to what they had been given by the UN.

The United States cultivated close ties with Israel but could not afford to lose the friendship of oil-rich Arab states or allow them to fall into the Soviet orbit. In Egypt, Arab nationalist General Gamal Abdel Nasser planned a great dam on the Nile River to produce electricity, while he proclaimed his country neutral in the Cold War. Dulles offered American financial support for the Aswan Dam project, but Nasser also began discussions with the Soviet Union. The secretary of state furiously withdrew the American offer. Left without funds for the dam, Nasser seized and nationalized the British-controlled Suez Canal in July 1956. At the same time, he closed the canal to Israeli ships. All of Europe feared that Nasser would disrupt the flow of oil from the Middle East.

In October and November, Israeli, British, and French military forces invaded Egypt. Eisenhower, who had not been consulted, was irate. Realizing that the attack might push Nasser into the arms of Moscow, the United States sponsored a UN resolution condemning the attacking nations and cut off oil from England and France. These actions persuaded them to withdraw.

In 1958, the United States again intervened

The Middle East in 1949

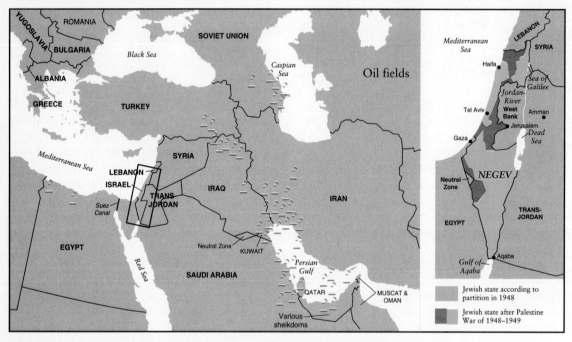

This map shows the extensive oil resources that made the Middle East such an important region, and the shifting boundaries of Israel as a result of the war following its independence in 1948. Notice how its size increased after its victory in the first of a series of Middle Eastern conflicts.

in the Middle East. Eisenhower authorized the landing of 14,000 soldiers in Lebanon to prop up a right-wing government challenged from within.

Restricting Revolt in Latin America

The Cold War also affected relations in Latin America, the United States' traditional sphere of influence. In 1954, Dulles sniffed Communist activity in Guatemala and ordered CIA support for a right-wing coup that overthrew the elected government of reform-minded Colonal Jacobo Arbenz Guzmán. The property of the United Fruit Company that Arbenz had seized was restored, but at the cost of aborting needed reform. The effort in Guatemala also fed strong anti-American feeling throughout Latin America.

In 1959, when Fidel Castro overthrew the dictatorial regime of Fulgencio Batista in Cuba, the shortsightedness of American policy became even clearer. Nationalism and the thrust for social reform were powerful forces in Latin America, as in the rest of the Third World. But when Castro confiscated American property in Cuba, the Eisenhower administration cut off exports and severed diplomatic ties. In response, Cuba turned to Russia for support.

ATOMIC WEAPONS AND THE COLD WAR

Throughout the Cold War period, the atomic bomb was a crucial factor in world affairs. Atomic weapons were destructive enough, but when the United States and the Soviet Union both developed hydrogen bombs, an age of overkill began.

Sharing the Secret of the Bomb

The United States, with British aid, had built the first atomic bomb in secrecy. Soviet spies, however, discovered that the Americans were at work on the bomb. By 1943, a program to create a Soviet atomic bomb was under way.

The question of sharing the atomic secret was pressing in the immediate postwar years. Secretary of War Henry L. Stimson favored cooperating with the Soviet Union. Recognizing the futility of trying to cajole the Soviets while "having this weapon ostentatiously on our hip," he suggested that "their suspicions and their distrust of our purposes and motives will increase." Only mutual accommodation could bring international cooperation.

But the United States never followed Stimson's advice. Truman, increasingly worried about the Soviet presence in eastern Europe, vowed to retain the technological advantage. He resisted a more flexible approach until the creation of a "foolproof method of control" over atomic weapons. Most Americans agreed.

For a time the administration sought a means of international arms control. The United States proposed an international agency to provide atomic energy control. This plan failed as negotiations collapsed.

The United States then moved toward its own internal mechanism of control. The Atomic Energy Act of 1946 established the Atomic Energy Commission to supervise all atomic energy development in the United States. It also opened the way to a nuclear arms race once the USSR developed its own bomb.

Nuclear Proliferation

As the atomic bomb found its way into popular culture, Americans at first showed more excite-

ment than fear. In Los Angeles, the "Atom Bomb Dancers" appeared at the Burbank Burlesque Theater. In 1946, the Buchanan Brothers recorded a song called "Atomic Power."

In September 1949, reporters were called to the White House and told: "We have evidence that within recent weeks an atomic explosion occurred in the U.S.S.R." Over the Labor Day weekend, a U.S. Air Force weather reconnaissance plane on a routine mission had picked up air samples showing higher than normal radioactivity counts. Other samples confirmed this, and scientists soon concluded that the Soviets had conducted a nuclear test.

The American public was shocked. Suddenly the security of being the world's only atomic power vanished. Harold C. Urey, a Nobel Prize–winning scientist, summed up the feelings of many Americans: "There is only one thing worse than one nation having the atomic bomb—that's two nations having it."

In early 1950, Truman authorized the development of a new hydrogen superbomb, potentially far more devastating than the atomic bomb. Edward Teller, a physicist on the Manhattan Project, had contemplated the possibility that fusion might release energy in even greater amounts. Now he had his chance to proceed.

By 1953, both the United States and the Soviet Union had unlocked the secret of the hydrogen bomb. Rumors circulated that the first test of a hydrogen device in the Pacific Ocean in 1952 had created a hole in the ocean floor 175 feet deep and a mile wide. Later, after the 1954 BRAVO test, Lewis Strauss, Atomic Energy Commission chairman, admitted that "an H-bomb can be made . . . large enough to take out a city." Then, in 1957, shortly after the news that the Soviets had successfully tested their first intercontinental ballistic missile (ICBM), Americans learned that the Soviets had fired the first satellite, *Sputnik,* into outer space. The apparent inferiority of American rocketry and the openness of the country to attack caused serious concern.

The discovery of radioactive fallout added another dimension to the nuclear dilemma. Fallout became publicly known after the BRAVO blast showered Japanese fishermen 85 miles away with radioactive dust. They became ill with radiation sickness, and several months later, one of them died. The Japanese, who had been the first to experience the effects of atomic weapons, were outraged and alarmed. Elsewhere people began to realize the terrible impact of the new weapons.

Authors in both the scientific and the popular press focused attention on radioactive fallout. Radiation, physicist Ralph Lapp observed, "cannot be felt and possesses all the terror of the unknown." Nevil Shute's best-selling 1957 novel *On the Beach,* and the film that followed, described a war that released so much radioactive waste that all life in the Northern Hemisphere disappeared, while the Southern Hemisphere waited for the residue to come closer and bring the same deadly end. In 1959, when *Consumer Reports* warned of the contamination of milk with strontium-90 as a result of nuclear fallout, public alarm grew.

The discovery of fallout provoked a bomb shelter craze. More and more companies advertised ready-made shelters to eager consumers. A firm in Miami reported many inquiries about shelters costing between $1,795 and $3,895, depending on capacity, and planned 900 franchises. By the end of 1960, an estimated one million family shelters had been built.

"Massive Retaliation"

As Americans grappled with the consequences of nuclear weapons, government policy came to depend increasingly on an atomic shield. Truman authorized the development of a nuclear arsenal but also stressed conventional forms of defense. After his election in 1952, Eisenhower decided to rely on atomic weapons rather than combat

forces as the key to American defense. Dulles developed the policy of "massive retaliation." The United States was willing and ready to use nuclear weapons against communist aggression "at places of our own choosing." The policy allowed troop cutbacks and promised to be cost-effective by giving "more bang for the buck."

Massive retaliation provided for an all-or-nothing response, leaving no middle course, no alternatives between nuclear war and retreat. Critics called Dulles's foreign policy "brinkmanship" and wondered what would happen if the line were crossed in the new atomic age. Eisenhower himself was horrified when he saw reports indicating what nuclear weapons could do, and with characteristic caution he did his best to ensure that the rhetoric of massive retaliation did not lead to war.

THE COLD WAR AT HOME

The Cold War also affected domestic affairs and led to the creation of an internal loyalty program that produced serious violations of civil liberties. As Americans began to suspect Communist infiltration at home, some determined that they must root out any traces of communism inside the United States.

Truman's Loyalty Program

As the Truman administration mobilized support for its containment program in the immediate postwar years, its rhetoric became increasingly shrill and unrealistic. According to Attorney General J. Howard McGrath, there were "many Communists in America," each bearing "the germ of death for society."

When administration officials perceived an internal threat to security, Truman responded by appointing a Temporary Commission on Employee Loyalty. He also wanted to undercut the

Republican charge that the Democrats were "soft on communism."

On the basis of the report from his temporary commission, Truman established a new Federal Employee Loyalty Program by executive decree in 1947. In the same week he announced his containment policy, Truman ordered the FBI to check its files for evidence of subversive activity and then to bring suspects before a new Civil Service Commission Loyalty Review Board. Initially, the program included safeguards and assumed that a challenged employee was innocent until guilt had been proved. But as the Loyalty Review Board assumed more and more power, it came to overlook individual rights. Employees could now be attacked with little chance to fight back. Although the Truman loyalty program examined several million employees and found grounds for dismissing only several hundred, it still bred fear of subversion.

The Congressional Loyalty Program

While Truman's loyalty probe investigated government employees, Congress embarked on its own program. The Smith Act of 1940 had made it a crime to advocate or teach the forcible overthrow of the U.S. government. In 1949, Eugene Dennis and ten other Communist leaders were found guilty under its terms. In 1951, the Supreme Court upheld the Smith Act, clearing the way for the prosecution of nearly 100 other Communists.

The McCarran Internal Security Act of 1950 further circumscribed Communist activity by declaring that it was illegal to conspire to act in a way that would "substantially contribute" to establishing a totalitarian dictatorship in America. Members of Communist organizations had to register with the attorney general and could not obtain passports or work in areas of national defense. Congress passed the measure over Truman's veto and provided further legal backing for the anticommunist crusade. The American Communist Party, which had never been large, even in the Depression, declined still further. Membership, numbering about 80,000 in 1947, fell to 55,000 in 1950 and 25,000 in 1954.

The investigations of the House Committee on Un-American Activities (HUAC) contributed to that decline. Intent on rooting out subversion, HUAC probed the motion picture industry in 1947. Protesting its scare tactics, some people the committee summoned refused to testify under oath. They were scapegoated for their stand. The so-called Hollywood Ten, a group of writers, were cited for contempt of court and sent to federal prison. At that, Hollywood knuckled under and blacklisted anyone with even a marginally questionable past. No one on these lists could find jobs at the studios anymore.

Congress made a greater splash with the Hiss-Chambers case. Whittaker Chambers, a former Communist who had broken with the party in 1938 and had become a successful editor of *Time,* charged that Alger Hiss had been a Communist in the 1930s. Hiss was a distinguished New Dealer who had served in the Agriculture Department before becoming assistant secretary of state. Now out of the government, he was president of the Carnegie Endowment for International Peace. He denied Chambers's charge, and the matter might have died there had not freshman congressman Richard Nixon taken up the case. Nixon finally extracted from Hiss an admission that he had once known Chambers. Outside the hearing room, Hiss sued Chambers for libel, whereupon Chambers changed his story and charged that Hiss was a Soviet spy.

Hiss was indicted for perjury, for lying under oath about his former relationship with Chambers. The case made front-page news around the nation. Chambers appeared unstable and changed his story several times. Yet Hiss, too, seemed contradictory in his testimony and never adequately explained how some copies of stolen State Department documents had been typed on a typewriter he had once owned. The first trial ended in a hung jury; the second trial, in January 1950, sent Hiss to prison for almost four years.

After Hiss's conviction but before his appeal, Dean Acheson supported his friend. Regardless of what happened, he said, "I do not intend to turn my back on Alger Hiss." Decent though his affirmation was, it caused the secretary of state political trouble. Truman too was broadly attacked for his comments about the case. The dramatic Hiss case helped to discredit the Democrats and to justify the even worse witch-hunt that followed.

The Second Red Scare

The key anticommunist warrior in the 1950s was Joseph R. McCarthy, senator from Wisconsin, who claimed he had in his hand a list of 205 known Communists in the State Department, then reduced the number of names to 57. He prompted mixed reactions. A subcommittee of the Senate Foreign Relations Committee, after investigating, called his charge a "fraud and a hoax." As his support grew, however, Republicans realized his partisan value and egged him on.

McCarthy selected assorted targets. In the elections of 1950, he attacked Millard Tydings, the Democrat from Maryland who had chaired the subcommittee that dismissed McCarthy's first accusations. A doctored photograph, showing Tyding with deposed American Communist party head Earl Browder, helped bring about Tydings's defeat. McCarthy called Dean Acheson the "Red Dean of the State Department" and slandered George C. Marshall as "a man steeped in falsehood."

A demagogue throughout his career, McCarthy liked to play tough for press and televi-

sion coverage. He did not mind appearing disheveled, unshaven, and half sober. He used obscenity and vulgarity freely.

McCarthy's tactics worked because the public was alarmed about the Communist threat. The arrest in 1950 of Julius and Ethel Rosenberg further aroused fears of subversion from within. The Rosenbergs, a seemingly ordinary American couple with two small children, were charged with stealing and transmitting atomic secrets to the Russians. To many Americans, it was inconceivable that the Soviets could have developed the bomb on their own. Only treachery could explain the Soviet explosion of an atomic device.

The next year, the Rosenbergs were found guilty of espionage and sentenced to death. Although some argued, then and today, that the Rosenbergs were victims of hysteria, efforts to prevent their execution failed. In 1953, they were put to death, but anticommunism continued unabated.

When the Republicans won control of the Senate in 1952, McCarthy's power grew. He became chairman of the Government Operations Committee and head of its Permanent Investigations Subcommittee. He now had a stronger base and two dedicated assistants, Roy Cohn and G. David Schine.

As McCarthy's anticommunist witch-hunt continued, Eisenhower became uneasy. He disliked the senator but, recognizing his popularity, was reluctant to challenge him.

With the help of Cohn and Schine, McCarthy pushed on, and finally he pushed too hard. In 1953, the army drafted Schine and then refused to allow the preferential treatment that Cohn insisted his colleague deserved. Angered, McCarthy began to investigate army security and even top-level army leaders themselves. When the army charged that McCarthy was going too far, the Senate investigated the complaint.

The Army-McCarthy hearings began in April 1954 and lasted 36 days. Televised to a fascinated nationwide audience, they demonstrated

Senator Joseph McCarthy's spurious charges inflamed anticommunist sentiment in the 1950s. Here he uses a chart of Communist Party organization in the United States to suggest that the nation was at risk unless subversives were rooted out.

the power of TV to shape people's opinions. Americans saw McCarthy's savage tactics on screen. He came across to viewers as irresponsible and destructive, particularly in contrast to Boston lawyer Joseph Welch, who argued the army's case with quiet eloquence.

The hearings shattered McCarthy's mystical appeal. In broad daylight, before a national television audience, his ruthless methods no longer made sense. The Senate finally summoned the courage to condemn him for his conduct. Conservatives there turned against McCarthy because by attacking Eisenhower and the army, he was no longer limiting his venom to Democrats and liberals. Although McCarthy remained in office, his influence disappeared. Three years later, at the age of 48, he died a broken man.

Yet for a time he had exerted a powerful hold in the United States. Some members of both parties spoke out against him, but most did not.

His crusade thus encouraged, McCarthy pressed on until he went too far.

The Casualties of Fear

The anticommunist crusade promoted a pervasive sense of suspicion in American society. In the late 1940s and early 1950s, dissent no longer seemed safe. Civil servants, government workers, academics, and actors all came under attack and found that the right of due process often evaporated as the Cold War Red Scare gained ground. Seasoned China experts lost their positions in the diplomatic service, and social justice legislation faltered.

This paranoia affected American life in countless ways. In New York, subway workers were fired when they refused to answer questions about their own political actions and beliefs. Navajos in Arizona and New Mexico, facing starvation in the bitter winter of 1947–1948, were denied government relief because of charges that their communal way of life was communistic and therefore un-American. Black actor Paul Robeson, who along with W. E. B. Du Bois criticized American foreign policy, was accused of Communist leanings, found few opportunities to perform, and eventually, like Du Bois, lost his passport. Hispanic laborers faced deportation for membership in unions with left-wing sympathies. In 1949, the Congress of Industrial Organizations (CIO) expelled 11 unions with a total membership of more than one million for alleged domination by Communists. Val Lorwin, introduced at the beginning of the chapter, weathered the storm of malicious accusations and was finally vindicated, but others were less lucky. They were the unfortunate victims as the United States became consumed by the passions of the Cold War.

CONCLUSION

THE COLD WAR IN PERSPECTIVE

The Cold War was the greatest single force affecting American society in the decade and a half after World War II. In the early years after the war, policymakers and commentators justified the American stance as a bold and courageous effort to meet the Communist threat. Later, particularly in the 1960s, as the public started to have doubts about the course of American foreign policy, revisionist historians began to argue that American policy was misguided, insensitive to Soviet needs, and a contributing factor to the worsening frictions.

The Cold War stemmed from a competition for international influence between the two great world powers. After World War II, the American vision of what the postwar world should be like clashed with the goals of Communist powers and with anticolonial movements in Third World countries. The Cold War, with its profound effects at home and abroad, was the unfortunate result.

Recommended Reading

Walter LaFeber, *America, Russia, and the Cold War, 1945–1990* (6th ed., 1991), is the best brief account of the Cold War from beginning to end. Other good sources include John Lewis Gaddis, *Strategies of Containment: A Critical Appraisal of Postwar American National Security Policy* (1982); and Thomas G. Patterson, *On Every Front: The Making of the Cold War* (1979).

For foreign policy in the Eisenhower period, see Robert A. Divine, *Eisenhower and the Cold War* (1981); and H. W. Brands, Jr., *Cold Warriors: Eisenhower's Generation and American Foreign Policy* (1988).

On the Korean War, see Burton I. Kaufman, *The*

Korean War: Challenges in Crisis, Credibility, and Command (1986), for an excellent survey of the foreign policy implications of the war. Joseph C. Goulden, *Korea: The Untold Story of the War* (1982), is a popular account of the struggle. James A. Michener's novel *The Bridges at Toko-Ri* (1953) provides a sense of the frustrations during the war.

On the anticommunist crusade, see Thomas C. Reeves, *The Life and Times of Joe McCarthy: A Biography* (1982), and David M. Oshinsky, *A Conspiracy So Immense: The World of Joe McCarthy* (1983). See also Allen Weinstein, *Perjury: The Hiss-Chambers Case* (1978); and Ronald Radash and Joyce Milton, *The Rosenberg File: A Search for Truth* (1984).

Time Line

1945	Yalta Conference Roosevelt dies; Harry Truman becomes president Potsdam Conference	**1950–1953**	Korean War
1946	American plan for control of atomic energy fails Atomic Energy Act Iran crisis Churchill's "Iron Curtain" speech	**1951**	Japanese-American Treaty *Dennis* v. *United States*
1947	Truman Doctrine Federal Employee Loyalty Program House Un-American Activities Committee (HUAC) investigates the movie industry	**1952**	Dwight D. Eisenhower elected president McCarthy heads Senate Permanent Investigations Subcommittee
1948	Marshall Plan launched Berlin airlift Israel created by UN Hiss-Chambers case Truman elected president	**1953**	Stalin dies; Khrushchev consolidates power East Germans stage anti-Soviet demonstrations Shah of Iran returns to power in CIA-supported coup
1949	Soviet Union tests atomic bomb North Atlantic Treaty Organization (NATO) established George Orwell publishes *1984* Mao Zedong's forces win Chinese civil war; Jiang Jieshi flees to Taiwan	**1954**	Fall of Dien Bien Phu ends French control of Indochina Geneva Conference Guatemalan government overthrown with CIA help Mao's forces shell Quemoy and Matsu Army-McCarthy hearings
1950	Truman authorizes development of the hydrogen bomb Alger Hiss convicted Joseph McCarthy's Wheeling (W. Va.) speech on subversion NSC-68 McCarran Internal Security Act	**1956**	Suez incident Hungarian "freedom fighters" suppressed Eisenhower reelected
		1957	Soviets launch *Sputnik* satellite
		1958	U.S. troops sent to support Lebanese government
		1959	Castro deposes Batista in Cuba

chapter 27

Postwar Growth and Social Change

Ray Kroc, an ambitious salesman, headed toward San Bernardino, California, on a business trip in 1954. For more than a decade he had been selling "multimixers"—stainless steel machines that could make six milkshakes at once—to restaurants and soda shops around the United States. On this trip he was particularly interested in checking out a hamburger stand run by Richard and Maurice McDonald, who had bought eight of his "contraptions" and could therefore make 48 shakes at the same time.

Always eager to increase sales, Kroc wanted to see the McDonald's operation for himself. As he watched the lines of people at the San Bernardino McDonald's, he saw the reason for their success. The McDonald brothers sold only standard hamburgers and french fries, but they had developed a system that was fast, efficient, and clean. It drew on the automobile traffic that moved along Route 66. And it was profitable indeed. Sensing the possibilities, Kroc proposed that the two owners open other establishments as well. When they balked, he negotiated a 99-year contract that allowed him to sell the fast-food idea and the name—and their golden arches design—wherever he could.

On April 15, 1955, Kroc opened his first McDonald's in Des Plaines, a suburb of Chicago. Three months later, he sold his first franchise in Fresno, California. Others soon followed. Kroc persuaded people to put up the capital, and he provided them with specifications guaranteed to ensure future success. For his efforts, he received a percentage of the gross take.

From the start, Kroc insisted on standardization. Every McDonald's looked the same. All menus and prices were exactly the same, and Kroc demanded that the establishments be clean. No pinball games or cigarette machines were permitted.

McDonald's, of course, was an enormous success. When Kroc died in 1984, a total of 45 billion burgers had been sold at 7,500 outlets in 32 countries.

The success of McDonald's provides an example of the development of new trends in the 1950s in the United States. Kroc capitalized on the changes of the automobile age.

He understood that a restaurant, not in the city but along the highways, where it could draw on heavier traffic, had a better chance of success. He understood that the franchise notion provided the key to rapid growth. He sensed, too, the importance of standardization and uniformity.

This chapter describes the structural changes in American society in the decade and a half after World War II. We will examine how economic growth, spurred by technological advances, transformed the patterns of American life at home and at work. Self-interest triumphed over idealism as most Americans obtained material comfort previously unknown. But even as it promoted economic growth, the government was obliged to acknowledge the claims of minorities. In their protests against continuing social and economic injustice, blacks, Indians, and Hispanics highlighted the limits of the postwar American dream.

ECONOMIC BOOM

In spite of anxieties about the Cold War, most Americans were optimistic after 1945. As servicemen returned home and resumed their lives, a baby boom brought unprecedented population growth. The simultaneous economic boom that took the nation by surprise had an even greater impact as new technology and new products flooded the market.

The Peacetime Economy

The wartime prosperity continued in the postwar years. Americans enjoyed one of the most sustained periods of economic expansion the United States had ever known, as it solidified its position as the richest nation in the world.

The statistical evidence of economic success was impressive. The gross national product (GNP) jumped from just over $200 billion in 1940 to about $300 billion in 1950 and by 1960 had climbed above $500 billion. Per capita income rose from $2,100 in 1950 to $2,435 in 1960. Almost 60 percent of all families in the country were now part of the middle class, a dramatic change from the class structure in the nineteenth and early twentieth century.

Personal resources fueled economic growth. During World War II, American consumers had been unable to spend all they earned because production had been concentrated in the manufacture of weapons needed for the war. With accumulated savings of $140 billion at war's end, consumers were ready to purchase whatever they could. Equally important was the 22 percent rise in real purchasing power between 1946 and 1960.

The automobile industry was a key part of the economic boom. Limited to the production of military vehicles during World War II, the auto industry expanded dramatically in the postwar period. Two million cars were made in 1946, four times as many in 1955.

The development of a massive interstate highway system also stimulated auto production and so contributed to prosperity. The Interstate Highway Act of 1956 provided $26 billion, the largest public works expenditure in American history, to build over 40,000 miles of federal highways, linking all parts of the United States.

Though highways added to the problem of pollution and triggered urban flight, the interstate complex was hailed as a key to the country's material development. President Eisenhower wrote: "More than any single action by the government since the end of the war, this one would change the face of America."

House construction contributed to economic growth as well. Much of the stimulus came from the GI Bill of 1944. In addition to giving returning servicemen priority for many jobs and providing educational benefits, it offered low-interest home mortgages, and millions of former soldiers took advantage of the measure to buy into the American dream.

Federal policy also helped sustain the expansion by allowing businesses to buy almost 80 percent of the factories built by the government during the war for much less than they cost. Even more important was the dramatic rise in defense spending as the Cold War escalated. In 1947, when the Department of Defense was established, the defense budget stood at $13 billion. With the onset of the Korean War, it rose to $22 billion in 1951 and to about $47 billion in 1953. Between 1949 and 1960, spending for space research increased from $49 million to $401 million. As federal expenditures reached 20 percent of the GNP by the 1950s, it was clear that a major economic transformation had occurred.

Peaceful, prosperous, and productive, the country had become "the affluent society," in economist John Kenneth Galbraith's phrase. The concentration of income remained the same—the bottom half of the population still earned less than the top tenth—but the ranks of middle-class Americans grew.

The Corporate World

After 1945, the major corporations increased their hold on the American economy. Government policy in World War II had encouraged the growth of big business and produced tremendous industrial concentration. During the war, half of all military contracts were awarded to three dozen giants. In 1940, some 100 companies accounted for 30 percent of all manufacturing output in the United States. Three years later, that figure had risen to 70 percent.

Industrial concentration continued after the war, making oligopoly—domination of a given industry by a few firms—a feature of American capitalism. At the same time, the booming economy encouraged the development of conglomerates—firms that diversified with holdings in a variety of industries. International Telephone and Telegraph, for example, purchased Avis Rent-a-Car, Continental Baking, Sheraton Hotels, Levitt and Sons Home Builders, and Hartford Fire Insurance. That pattern, widely duplicated, protected companies against instability in one particular area. It also led to the further development of finance capitalism to help put the deals together, just as the demands of consolidation in the late nineteenth century had opened the way for bankers like J.P. Morgan (see Chapter 19).

While expanding at home, large corporations also moved increasingly into foreign markets, as they had in the 1890s. But at the same time they began to build plants overseas, where labor costs were cheaper. In the decade after 1957, General Electric built 61 plants abroad, and numerous other firms did the same.

In the post-1945 period, the close business-government ties that had developed during the war grew stronger. Federal dollars fueled research that in turn accounted for new industrial expansion.

Corporate planning, meanwhile, developed rapidly, as firms hired managers, trained in business schools, who could maximize profit.

The Workers' World

As corporations changed, so did the world of work. In the years after World War II, the United

States reversed a 150-year trend and became less a nation of goods producers and more a country of service providers. By 1956, a majority of the American people held white-collar jobs. Salaried rather than paid by the hour, these white-collar workers served as corporate managers, teachers, salespersons, and office workers.

Work in the huge corporations became even more impersonal than before. Money and material well-being were the prizes of corporate life. But white-collar employees paid a price for comfort. Corporations, preaching that teamwork was far more important than individuality, indoctrinated employees and conveyed the appropriate standards of conduct. RCA issued company neckties. IBM had training programs to teach employees the company line. Some large firms set up training programs to show wives how their own behavior could help their husbands' careers. Social critic C. Wright Mills observed, "When white-collar people get jobs, they sell not only their time and energy but their personalities as well."

Blue-collar workers also prospered in the postwar years. Labor union strength peaked as the war ended. The American Federation of Labor and the Congress of Industrial Organizations merged into the AFL-CIO in 1955. The new organization, led by building trade unionist George Meany, represented more than 90 percent of the country's 17.5 million union members. Union activity brought real improvements in income.

With higher, more predictable incomes, workers were more willing to limit strike activity. Labor peace prevailed, but at the expense of the last vestiges of autonomy in the workplace. Workers fell increasingly under the control of middle-level managers and watched anxiously as companies automated at home or expanded abroad, where labor was cheaper.

The union movement stalled in the mid-1950s. The heavy industries providing workers who gravitated to the union movement were no longer growing. As membership began to fall, unions tried to expand their base by reaching out to new groups—less skilled minority workers and white-collar service-oriented employees—but they proved difficult to organize.

The Agricultural World

The agricultural world changed even more than the industrial world in postwar America. New technology revolutionized farming. Improved planting and harvesting machines and better fertilizers and pesticides brought massive gains in productivity.

Increasing profitability led to agricultural consolidation. In the 25 years after 1945, average farm size almost doubled, and farmers left the land in increasing numbers. At the end of World War II, farmers made up one-fourth of the nation's work force (down from one-third in 1935). Over the next 25 years, 25 million people left the rural life behind, until only 5 percent of the population remained on farms in 1970.

Population Shifts and the New Suburbs

In post–World War II America, a growing population marked prosperity's return. During the Great Depression, the birthrate had dropped to an all-time low of 19 births per 1,000 population as hard times obliged people to delay marriage and parenthood. As World War II boosted the economy, the birthrate began to rise again, as millions of Americans began families. The "baby boom" peaked in 1957, with a rate of more than 25 births per 1,000. In that year, 4.3 million babies were born, one every seven seconds.

The rising birthrate was the dominant factor affecting population growth, but the death rate was also declining. Miracle drugs, such as streptomycin and aureomycin, played a large part in curing illnesses. Life expectancy rose: Midway through the 1950s, the average was 70 years for whites and 64 for blacks, compared with 55 for whites and 45 for blacks in 1920.

Birth and Population Rates, 1900–1960

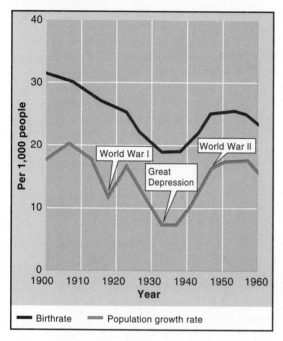

Source: U.S. Bureau of the Census

The baby boom had a powerful impact on family and social patterns and material needs. Many women who had taken jobs during the war now left the work force to raise their children and care for their homes. The demand grew for diaper services and baby foods. When they entered school, the members of the baby boom generation strained the educational system.

As Americans became more populous, they also became more mobile. For many generations, lower-class Americans had been the most likely to move; now geographic mobility spread to the middle class. Each year in the 1950s, over a million farmers left their farms in search of new employment. Other Americans moved to look for better jobs. Bob Moses of Baltimore simply wandered a while after returning home from the war. Traveling in a 1937 Chevrolet with some high school friends, Moses was going

"nowhere in particular, just roaming. We'd see a kink in a river on the map, and head there." After regimented military life, it was good to be free.

The war had produced increasing movement, most of it westward, as people gravitated toward the cities where shipyards, airplane factories, and other industrial plants were located. After the war, that migration pattern persisted, as the West and the Southwest continued to grow. Sun Belt cities like Houston, Albuquerque, Tucson, and Phoenix underwent phenomenal expansion. In the 1950s, Los Angeles pulled ahead of Phildelphia as the third largest city in the United States. By 1963, California had passed New York as the nation's most populous state.

After the war, another form of movement became even more important in the United States. Millions of white Americans fled the inner cities to suburban fringes. As central cities became places where poor nonwhites clustered, new urban and racial problems emerged.

For people of means, cities were places to work and then to leave at 5 o'clock. In Manhattan, south of City Hall, the noontime population of 1.5 million dropped to 2,000 during the night. The area, said writer John Brooks, was "left pretty much to thieves, policemen, and rats" after nightfall.

As the cities declined, the suburbs blossomed. If the decade after World War I had witnessed a rural-to-urban shift, the decades after World War II saw a reverse shift to the regions outside the central cities, usually accessible only by car. By the end of the 1950s, a third of all Americans resided in suburbs.

A key figure in the suburbanization movement was William J. Levitt, a builder eager to gamble and reap the rewards of a growing demand. Levitt recognized the advantages of mass production during World War II, when his firm put up dwellings for war workers. Aware that the GI Bill made mortgage money readily available, he felt that suburban development was a

Step-by-step mass production, with units completed in assembly-line fashion, was the key to William Levitt's approach to housing. But the suburban developments he and others created were marked by street after street of houses that all looked the same.

sure bet. But to cash in, Levitt knew he had to use new construction methods.

Mass production was the key. Working on a careful schedule, Levitt's team brought precut and preassembled materials to each site, put them together, and then moved on to the next location. As on an assembly line, tasks were broken down into individual steps. Groups of workers performed but a single job, moving from one tract to another. By this method, construction costs at Levittown, New York, a new community of 17,000 homes built in the late 1940s, were only $10 per square foot, compared with the $12 to $15 common elsewhere. Levitt provided a model for other developers.

Government-insured mortages, especially for veterans, fueled the housing boom. So did fairly low postwar interest rates. Mortgage interest rates were in the affordable 5 percent range.

Suburbanization changed the landscape of the United States. Huge tracts of land now contained acres of standardized squares, each bearing a house with a two-car garage and a manicured lawn. Woods disappeared, for it was cheaper to cut down all trees than to work around them. Folksinger Malvina Reynolds described the new developments she saw:

Little boxes on the hillside
Little boxes made of ticky tacky

Little boxes on the hillside
Little boxes all the same.
There's a green one and a pink one
And a blue one and a yellow one
And they're all made out of ticky tacky
And they all look just the same.

As suburbs flourished, businesses followed their customers out of the cities. Shopping centers catered to the suburban clientele, offering easy parking and convenient late hours. They also undermined the downtown department stores.

The Environmental Impact

Rapid development of the suburbs often took place without extensive planning and encroached on some of the nation's most attractive rural areas. Before long, virtually every American city was ringed by an ugly highway lined with eating places, shopping malls, and auto dealerships. Billboard advertisements dotted the landscape.

Responding to the increasingly cluttered terrain, architect Peter Blake ruthlessly attacked the practices of the 1950s in his muckraking book *God's Own Junkyard: The Planned Deterioration of America's Landscape*, published in 1964. The largely pictorial account indicted the careless attitudes toward the environment that led to the "uglification" of a once lovely land.

Despite occasional accounts like Blake's, there was little real consciousness of environmental issues in the post–World War II years. Yet the very prosperity that created the dismal highway strips in the late 1940s and 1950s was leading more and more Americans to appreciate natural environments as necessary parts of their rising standard of living. The shorter workweek provided more free time, and many Americans now had the means for longer vacations. They began to explore mountains and rivers and ocean shores, and to consider how to protect them. In 1958, Congress established the National Outdoor Recreation Review Commission, a first step toward consideration of environmental issues that became far more common in the next decade.

Technology Supreme

Rapid technological change occurred in the postwar years. Computers led the way. Wartime advances led to large but workable calculators, followed in the postwar years by machines that contained their own internal instructions and memories. After the development of the transistor by three scientists at Bell Laboratories in 1948, the computer became faster and more reliable, and transformed American society as surely as industrialization had changed it a century before.

Television was even more important commercially. Developed in the 1930s, it became a major influence on American life after World War II. In 1946, there were fewer than 17,000 sets; by 1949, Americans bought some 250,000 a month; and by 1960, three-quarters of all American families owned at least one set. In 1955, the average American family tuned in four to five hours each day.

Young Americans grew up to the strains of "Winky Dink and You," "The Mickey Mouse Club," and "Howdy Doody Time" in the 1950s. Older viewers enjoyed situation comedies like "I Love Lucy" and "Father Knows Best" and live dramas such as "Playhouse 90."

Americans maintained an ardent love affair with new appliances and gadgets. Tiny transistors powered not only computers and radios but also miniature hearing aids that could fit into the frame of a pair of eyeglasses. Stereophonic hi-fi sets, using new transistor components, provided better sound. By the end of the 1950s, most families had at least one automobile, as well as a refrigerator, washing machine, television, and vacuum cleaner.

One ominous technological trend was the advent of automation. Mechanization was not new, but now it became far more widespread, threatening both skilled and unskilled workers. In 1952, the Ford Motor Company began using automatic drilling machines in an engine plant and found that 41 workers could do a job 117 had done before. The implications of falling purchasing power as machines replaced workers were serious for an economy dependent on consumer demand.

The Consumer Culture

The modern American economy depended on consumption. Purchasing new goods and gadgets became easier with the expansion of consumer credit. Installment plans facilitated buying a new car, while credit cards encouraged other expenditures. Consumer credit mushroomed from $8.4 billion in 1946 to nearly $45 billion in 1958.

Advertising, which had faltered when the economy collapsed in the 1930s, began to revive during the war as firms sought to keep the public aware of consumer goods, even those in short supply. With the postwar boom, advertisers again began to hawk their wares.

Motivational research became more sophisticated, uncovering new ways of persuading people to buy. Taking the place of radio, television played an important part in conveying the spirit of consumption to millions of Americans. Shows like "The Price Is Right" stressed consumption in direct ways: Contestants won goods for quoting their correct retail price. Drawing on a talent that was sharpened in the shopping centers and department stores, the show encouraged the acquisition of ever more material goods.

Americans welcomed the postwar affluence. They had weathered the poverty and unemployment of the 1930s, made sacrifices during a long war, and now intended to enjoy their newfound abundance and leisure time. By 1950, most wage laborers worked a 40-hour week, and 60 percent of nonagricultural workers enjoyed paid vacations, whereas few had in 1930. Most Ameri-

cans regarded all this as their due, sometimes neglecting to look beyond the immediate objects of their desire. The decade, journalist William Shannon wrote, was one of "self-satisfaction and gross materialism. . . . The loudest sound in the land has been the oink and grunt of private hoggishness. . . ."

CONSENSUS AND CONFORMITY

As the economy grew, an increasing sense of sameness pervaded American society. This was the great age of conformity, when members of all social groups learned to emulate those around them rather than strike out on their own. Television contributed to growing conformity by providing young and old with a common, visually seductive experience. Escaping the homogenizing tendencies was difficult.

Conformity in School and Religious Life

The willingness to conform to group norms affected colleges and universities, where cautious students sought security. They joined fraternities and sororities and engaged in panty raids and other pranks but took little interest in world affairs.

Americans also returned to their churches in record numbers. Church membership doubled between 1945 and 1970. In part, church attendance reflected a desire to challenge "godless communism" at the height of the Cold War and to find some solace from the threat of annihilation in a nuclear war; in part, it resulted from the power of suggestion that led Americans to do what others did. By the end of the 1950s, fully 95 percent of all Americans identified with some religious denomination.

Dwight Eisenhower reflected the national mood when he observed that "our government makes no sense unless it is founded in a deeply felt religious faith—and I don't care what it is."

In 1954, Congress added the words "under God" to the pledge to the flag and the next year voted to require the phrase "In God We Trust" on all American currency.

Back to the Kitchen

During World War II, as servicemen went overseas, women left their homes to work. After 1945, there was a period of adjustment as the men returned. In the 1950s, traditional gender roles were reaffirmed, even though, paradoxically, more women entered the work force than ever before.

Men viewed themselves as the primary breadwinners and wanted their jobs waiting for them after the war. For women, the situation was more difficult. Many had enjoyed working during the war and were reluctant to retreat to the home, although the government and employers persistently encouraged them to do so.

By the 1950s, the issue was settled. The baby boom increased average family size and made the decision to remain home easier. The flight to the suburbs gave women more to do, and they settled into the routines of redecorating their homes and gardens and transporting children to and from activities and schools.

In 1956, *Life* magazine produced a special issue on women. Profiling Marjorie Sutton, the magazine spoke of the "Busy Wife's Achievements" as "Home Manager, Mother, Hostess, and Useful Civic Worker." Married at 16, Marjorie was now busy with the PTA, Campfire Girls, and charity causes. She cooked and sewed for her family, which included four children, supported her husband by entertaining 1,500 guests a year, and worked out on the trampoline "to keep her size 12 figure." Marjorie Sutton reflected the widespread social emphasis on marriage and home.

Despite the reaffirmation of the old ideology that a woman's place was in the home, the decade of the 1950s was a period of unnoticed but important change. Because the supply of single women workers was diminished by the low birthrate of the Depression years and by increased schooling and early marriage, older married women began entering the labor force in large numbers for the first time. In 1940, only 15 percent of American wives had jobs. By 1950, 21 percent were employed, and ten years later, the figure had risen to 30 percent. Moreover, married women now accounted for more than half of all working women, a dramatic reversal of earlier patterns.

Women stepped into the new jobs created by economic expansion, clustering in office, sales, and service positions, occupations already defined as female. They and their employers considered their work subordinate to their primary role as wives and mothers.

Black women worked as always but often lost the jobs they had won during the war. As the total percentage of women in the Detroit automobile industry dropped from 25 to 7.5, for example, jobs for black women nearly disappeared. Their median income at the end of the 1940s was less than half of white women. But during the 1950s, they succeeded both in moving into white-collar positions and improving their income. By 1960, more than a third of all black women had clerical, sales, service, or professional jobs, and their paychecks were 70 percent of those of white women.

Despite women's mixed experiences, society continued to view women in traditional ways. The belief that women's main role was still at home justified paying them low wages and denying them promotions. This view was reinforced by the portrayal of women in movies, television programs, and popular literature.

Sexuality was a troublesome if compelling topic in the postwar years. In 1948, Alfred C. Kinsey published *Sexual Behavior in the Human Male.* Kinsey was an Indiana University zoologist who had previously studied the gall wasp. When asked to teach a course on marriage problems, he found little published material about human sexual activity and decided to collect his own. He compiled case histories of 5,300 white males, analyzed their personal backgrounds, and recorded patterns of sexual behavior.

Kinsey shocked the country with his statistics on premarital, extramarital, and otherwise illicit sexual activity. Among males who went to college, he concluded, 67 percent had engaged in sexual intercourse before marriage; 84 percent of those who went to high school but not beyond had done the same. Thirty-seven percent of the total male population had experienced some kind of overt homosexual activity. One out of every six farm boys in America had copulated with animals. Kinsey published a companion volume, *Sexual Behavior in the Human Female* (1953), that detailed many of the same sexual patterns. Although critics denounced the books, both sold widely, for they opened the door to a subject that had previously been considered taboo. Interest in sexuality was reflected in the fascination with sex goddesses like actress Marilyn Monroe and with male fantasies of women, visible in *Playboy,* which first appeared in 1953.

Cultural Rebels

Not all Americans fit the stereotypes of the 1950s. Some were alienated from the culture and rebelled against its values. Even as young people struggled to meet the standards and expectations of their peers, they were intrigued by Holden Caulfield, the main figure in J. D. Salinger's popular novel *The Catcher in the Rye* (1951). Holden, a sensitive student at boarding school, felt surrounded by "phonies" who threatened his individuality and independence. Holden's ill-fated effort to preserve his own integrity in the face of pressures to conform struck a resonant chord in many readers.

A group of writers, often called the "beat generation," espoused unconventional values in their stories, poems, and "happenings." Confronting apathy and conformity, they insisted there were alternatives. Stressing spontaneity and spirituality, they claimed that intuition was

more important than reason, Eastern mysticism more valuable than Western faith. The "beats" went out of their way to challenge the norms of respectability. They rejected materialism, engaged in overt sexual activity designed to shock, and helped popularize the use of marijuana.

Their literary work reflected their approach to life. Jack Kerouac typed his best-selling novel *On the Road* (1957), describing free-wheeling trips across country, on a 250-foot roll of paper. Lacking conventional punctuation and paragraph structure, the book was a paean to the free life the beats espoused.

Poet Allen Ginsberg, like Kerouac a Columbia University dropout, became equally well known for his poem "Howl." Written during a wild weekend in 1955 while Ginsberg was under the influence of drugs, the poem was a scathing critique of the modern, mechanized culture and its effects.

The popularity of Salinger, Kerouac, and Ginsberg owed much to a revolution in book publishing and to the democratization of education that accompanied the program of GI educational benefits. More Americans than ever before acquired a taste for literature, and they found huge numbers of inexpensive books available because of the "paperback revolution." The paperback, introduced in 1939, dominated the book market after World War II. By 1965, readers could choose among some 25,000 titles.

The signs of cultural rebellion also appeared in popular music and art. A young Tennessee singer named Elvis Presley made "rock and roll" the new music of the young. American painters, led by Jackson Pollock and his "New York school," discarded the easel, laid gigantic canvases on the floor, and then used trowels, putty knives, and sticks to apply paint, glass shards, sand, and other materials in wild explosions of color. Known as abstract expressionists, these painters regarded the unconscious as the source of their artistic creations. Like much of the literature of rebellion, abstract expressionism reflected the artist's alienation from a world becoming filled with nuclear threats, computerization, and materialism.

DOMESTIC POLICY UNDER TRUMAN AND EISENHOWER

In the prosperous postwar era, pressures from the expanding middle class and from rapid growth influenced public policy. Two dissimilar men exercised presidential leadership in the decade and a half after World War II. Democrat Harry S Truman took the same aggressive stance at home as he adopted in foreign affairs. A conservative Congress, however, blocked him at every turn. His Republican successor, Dwight D. Eisenhower, created a very different imprint. Genial and calm, even when facing an opposition Congress himself, the war hero conveyed to Americans the feeling that everything was all right.

Reconversion

Truman's first priority when the war ended was reconversion—the transition to a peacetime economy. Servicemen returned rapidly. The number on active duty dropped from 12 million in 1945 to 1.6 million in mid-1947, causing competition in the housing and employment markets.

Truman also recognized the need to keep the cap on inflation. When wartime price controls ended, prices rose. A year and a half after the end of the war, the consumer price index was up almost 25 percent.

Finally, Truman had to deal with the problem of labor unrest. Massive layoffs left 2.7 million workers without jobs by March 1946. Wage issues were unresolved as well. After the wartime years of restraint, workers wanted pay increases they regarded as long overdue. Furthermore, many more of them belonged to unions. The percentage of nonagricultural workers who were union members rose from 13 percent in 1935 to 27 percent in 1940 and to 35 percent by 1945. When wage demands were refused, millions of workers walked out. In 1946, some 4.6 million workers marched on picket lines, more than had turned out ever before in the history of the United States. They struck in the automobile, steel, and electrical industries, the railroads, and the soft-coal mines. When Truman argued that the national interest was compromised by strikes in those industries, he alienated many working-class Americans, a major segment of the Democratic coalition that his predecessor, Franklin Roosevelt, had put together in the 1930s.

Postwar Public Policy

Even as he grappled with the immediate problems of postwar reconversion, Truman addressed broader questions. Less than a week after the end of World War II, Truman called on Congress to pass legislation guaranteeing all Americans jobs, decent housing, educational opportunities, and a variety of other rights outlined in a 21-point program. During the next ten weeks, Truman sent blueprints of further proposals to Congress, including health insurance and atomic energy legislation. This liberal program soon ran into fierce political opposition.

The debate surrounding the Employment Act of 1946 hinted at the fate of Truman's proposals. The Employment Act was a deliberate effort to apply the theory of English economist John Maynard Keynes to maintain economic equilibrium and prevent depression. The initial bill committed the government to maintaining full employment by monitoring the economy and taking remedial actions in case of decline. Those actions included tax cuts and spending programs to stimulate the economy and reduce unemployment.

Liberals hailed the measure, but business groups opposed it. Congress cut the proposal to bits. As finally passed, the act created a Council of Economic Advisers to make recommendations to the president, who was to report annually on the state of the economy. But it stopped short of committing the government to using fiscal tools to maintain full employment when economic indicators turned downward. The act was only a modest continuation of New Deal attempts at economic planning.

Truman Against a Conservative Congress

As the midterm elections of 1946 approached, Truman and his supporters knew they were vulnerable. Often seeming like a petty, bungling administrator, Truman became the butt of countless political jokes. Support for Truman dropped from 87 percent of those polled after he assumed the presidency to 32 percent in November 1946. Republicans won majorities in both houses of Congress for the first time since the 1928 elections, and a majority of the governorships as well.

After the 1946 election, Truman faced an unsympathetic 80th Congress. Republicans and conservative Democrats, dominating both houses, sought to reverse the liberal policies of the Roosevelt years. When the new Congress met, it moved to cut federal spending and reduce taxes.

Congress also struck at Democratic labor policies. Republicans wanted to check labor unions, and in 1947, they passed the Taft-Hartley Act, which intended to limit the power of unions by restricting the weapons they could employ. Revising the Wagner Act of 1935, the legislation spelled out unfair labor practices (such as preventing workers from working if they wished) and outlawed the closed shop whereby an employee had to join a union before getting a job. The law allowed states to prohibit the union shop, which forced workers to join the union after they had been hired. The act also gave the president the right to call for an 80-day cooling-off period in strikes affecting national security and required union officials to sign non-Communist oaths in order to use governmental machinery designed to protect their rights. Tru-

man vigorously opposed the bill, but Congress passed it over his veto.

The Fair Deal and Its Critics

In 1948, Truman won the Democratic nomination despite his waning popularity, but the Democratic Party was split by the civil rights issue.

When liberals defeated a moderate platform proposal and pressed for a stronger stand on black civil rights; angry delegates from Mississippi and Alabama stormed out of the convention. They later formed the States' Rights, or "Dixiecrat," party, nominated Governor J. Strom Thurmond of South Carolina as their presidential candidate, and affirmed their support for continued racial segregation.

Meanwhile, Henry A. Wallace, for seven years secretary of agriculture, then vice president during Roosevelt's third term and secretary of commerce after that, was mounting his own challenge. Truman had fired Wallace from his cabinet for supporting a more temperate stand on Soviet relations. Now Wallace became the presidential candidate of the Progressive Party.

In that fragmented state, against the first real third-party challenges since 1912, the Democrats faced the Republicans, who coveted the White House after 16 years out of power. Once again they nominated Thomas E. Dewey, the governor of New York. Egocentric and stiff, Dewey was hardly a charismatic figure. Still, the polls uniformly picked the Republicans to win.

Truman, as the underdog, conducted a vigorous campaign. He appealed to ordinary Americans as an unpretentious man engaged in an uphill fight. Speaking without a prepared text in his choppy, aggressive style, he warmed to crowds, and they warmed to him. "Give 'em hell, Harry," they yelled. "Pour it on." He did.

All the polls predicted a Republican win. But the pollsters were wrong. On election day, despite the bold headline "Dewey Defeats Truman" in the Chicago *Daily Tribune*, the incumbent president scored one of the most unex-

In one of the nation's most extraordinary political upsets, Harry Truman beat Thomas E. Dewey in 1948. Here an exuberant Truman holds a newspaper headline printed while he slept, before the vote turned his way.

pected political upsets in American history, winning 303–189 in the electoral college. Democrats also swept both houses of Congress.

Truman won primarily because he was able to revive the major elements of the Democratic coalition that Franklin Roosevelt had constructed more than a decade before. Despite the rocky days of 1946, Truman managed to hold on to labor, farm, and black votes.

With the election behind him, Truman pursued his liberal program, which became known as the "Fair Deal." Some parts of Truman's Fair Deal worked; others did not. The minimum wage was raised, and social security programs were expanded. A housing program brought modest gains but did not really meet housing needs. A farm program, aimed at providing income support to farmers if prices fell, never made it through Congress. Most of his civil rights program failed to win congressional sup-

port. The American Medical Association undermined the effort to provide national health insurance, and Congress rejected a measure to provide federal aid to education.

Committed to checking the perceived Soviet threat, Truman allowed his domestic program to suffer. As defense expenditures mounted, correspondingly less money was available for projects at home.

The Election of Eisenhower

In 1952, Truman had the support of only 23 percent of the American people, and all indicators pointed to a political shift. The Democrats nominated Adlai Stevenson, Illinois's able, articulate, and moderately liberal governor. The Republicans turned to Dwight D. Eisenhower, the World War II hero Americans knew as Ike.

The Republicans called the Democrats "soft

on communism." They criticized assorted scandals surrounding Truman's cronies and friends. The president himself was blameless, but some of the people near him were not. The Republicans also promised to end the unpopular Korean War.

Eisenhower won a massive victory at the polls. He received 55 percent of the vote and carried 41 states. The new president took office with a Republican Congress as well and had little difficulty gaining a second term four years later.

"Modern Republicanism"

Eisenhower believed firmly in limiting the presidential role. He wanted to reduce the growth of the federal government. Eisenhower sometimes termed his approach "dynamic conservatism" or "modern Republicanism," which, he explained, meant "conservative when it comes to money, liberal when it comes to human beings."

Above all, economic concerns dominated the Eisenhower years. The president and his chief aides wanted desperately to preserve the value of the dollar, pare down levels of funding, cut taxes, and balance the budget after years of deficit spending.

To achieve those aims, the president appointed George Humphrey, a fiscal conservative, as secretary of the treasury. Humphrey's approach to reducing spending did not exclude "using a meat axe." The business-oriented administration was willing to risk unemployment to keep inflation under control.

Eisenhower supported the passage of the Submerged Lands Act in 1953. That measure transferred control of about $40 billion worth of oil lands from the federal government to the states. The New York *Times* called it "one of the greatest and surely the most unjustified giveaway programs in all the history of the United States."

The administration also sought to reduce federal activity in the electric-power field. Eisenhower favored private rather than public development of power. He opposed a TVA proposal for expansion to provide power to the Atomic Energy Commission and instead authorized a private group, the Dixon-Yates syndicate, to build a plant in Arkansas to meet the need. Later, when charges of scandal arose, the administration canceled the agreement, but the basic preference for private development remained.

As a result of the administration's reluctance to stimulate the economy too much, the annual rate of economic growth declined from 4.3 percent between 1947 and 1952 to 2.5 percent between 1953 and 1960. The country suffered three recessions in Eisenhower's eight years. During the slumps, the deficits that Eisenhower so wanted to avoid increased.

Eisenhower's understated approach led to a legislative stalemate, particularly when the Democrats regained control of Congress in 1954. Opponents of the president gibed at Ike's restrained stance. Yet he was often active behind the scenes pursuing his favorite programs. By accepting the fundamental features of the welfare state the Democrats had created, he ensured that it would not be rolled back. For all the jokes at his expense, Eisenhower remained popular with the voters.

THE OTHER AMERICA

In the years after World War II, not all Americans enjoyed the prosperity and privileges of the growing middle class. Poverty existed in inner cities and rural areas. Minorities began to press for equal treatment and equal rights. Black Americans and Jews, in the forefront of the civil rights struggle, were joined by Hispanics and Native Americans, who built their protest movements on the model of black protest but moved more slowly than blacks.

Poverty amid Affluence

Many people in the "affluent society" lived in poverty. Economic growth favored the upper and middle classes. Although the popular "trickle-down" theory argued that economic expansion brought benefits to all classes, little, in fact, reached the citizens at the bottom of the ladder. In 1960, according to the Federal Bureau of Labor Statistics, a yearly subsistence-level income for a family of four was $3,000 and for a family of six, $4,000. The Bureau reported that 40 million people (almost a quarter of the population) lived below those levels and nearly the same number only marginally above the line.

Michael Harrington, Socialist author and critic, exposed those conditions in *The Other America,* a devastating account that shocked the country when it appeared in 1962. The poor were everywhere. Harrington described the "economic underworld" in New York City, where "Puerto Ricans and Negroes, alcoholics, drifters, and disturbed people" sought daily positions as "dishwashers and day workers, the fly-by-night jobs" at employment agencies. He also explained the plight of the rural poor—tenant farmers and migrant workers.

Black Americans and Civil Rights

Blacks became increasingly restive in the post–World War II years, particularly as economic changes affected traditional employment patterns. In the South, as cotton farmers turned to less labor-intensive crops like soybeans and peanuts, they ousted their tenants. Between 1930 and 1960, the southern agricultural population declined from 16 million to 6 million. Millions of blacks moved to southern cities, where they found better jobs, better schooling, and freedom from landlord control. Some achieved middle-class status. Still not entirely free, these southern blacks were now ready to attack Jim Crow.

Millions of blacks also headed for northern cities between 1940 and 1960. And since northern blacks could vote and usually voted for the Democrats, civil rights became an issue that northern Democratic leaders could not avoid.

Blacks had increased their demands for change during World War II. They had won some concessions (see Chapter 26) but not enough to satisfy rising black aspirations. Meanwhile, black servicemen returning from the war vowed to reject second-class citizenship and helped mobilize a grass-roots movement. Adam Clayton Powell, a Harlem preacher (and later congressman), warned that the black man "is ready to throw himself into the struggle to make the dream of America become flesh and blood, bread and butter, freedom and equality. He walks conscious of the fact that he is no longer alone—no longer a minority."

The racial question was dramatized in 1947 when Jackie Robinson broke the color line and began playing major league baseball with the Brooklyn Dodgers. After Robinson's trailblazing effort, other blacks, formerly confined to the old Negro leagues, started to move into the major leagues, then into professional football and basketball.

A somewhat reluctant Truman supported the civil rights movement. A moderate on questions of race who believed in political equality, not social equality, he yielded to the growing strength of the black vote. In 1946, Truman appointed a Committee on Civil Rights to investigate the problem of lynchings and other brutalities against blacks and to make recommendations. The committee's report, released in October 1947, showed that blacks remained second-class citizens in every area of American life. The report set a civil rights agenda for the next two decades.

Though Truman hedged at first, in February 1948 he sent a ten-point civil rights program to

Congress—the first presidential civil rights program since Reconstruction. When the southern wing of the Democratic Party bolted later that year, he moved forward even more aggressively. First he issued an executive order barring discrimination in the federal establishment. Then he ordered equality of treatment in the military services. Manpower needs in the Korean War led to the elimination of the last restrictions, particularly when the army found that integrated units performed well.

Elsewhere the administration pushed reforms. The Justice Department, not previously supportive of NAACP litigation on behalf of equal rights for blacks, entered the battle against segregation and filed briefs challenging the constitutionality of restrictions in housing, education, and interstate transportation. Those helped build the pressure for change that influenced the Supreme Court. Congress, however, did little.

Integrating the Schools

In the 1950s, as the civil rights struggle gained momentum, the judicial system played a crucial role. The NAACP was determined to overturn the doctrine established in *Plessy* v. *Ferguson* in 1896. In that decision, the Supreme Court had declared that segregation of the black and white races was constitutional if the facilities used by each were "separate but equal." The decree had been used for generations to sanction rigid segregation, primarily in the South, even though separate facilities were seldom, if ever, equal.

A direct challenge came in 1951 when Oliver Brown, the father of 8-year-old Linda Brown, sued the school board of Topeka, Kansas, to allow his daughter to attend a school for white children that she passed as she walked to the bus that carried her to a black school farther away. The case reached the Supreme Court, which on May 17, 1954, released its bombshell ruling in *Brown* v. *Board of Education*. For more than a decade, Supreme Court decisions had gradually expanded black civil rights, and

now the Court unanimously decreed that "separate facilities are inherently unequal" and concluded that the "separate but equal" doctrine had no place in public education. A year later, the Court turned to the question of implementation and declared that local school boards, acting with the guidance of lower courts, should move "with all deliberate speed" to desegregate their facilities.

Charged with the ultimate responsibility for executing the law was Dwight Eisenhower, who privately thought the decision was wrong but knew that according to the Constitution it was his duty to see that the law was carried out. Even while urging sympathy for the South in its period of transition, he acted immediately to desegregate the Washington, D.C., schools as a model for the rest of the country. He also ordered desegregation in navy yards and veterans' hospitals.

Even so, the South resisted. In district after district, vicious scenes occurred. The crucial confrontation came in Little Rock, Arkansas, in 1957. A desegregation plan, to begin with the token admission of a few black students to Central High School, was ready to go into effect. Just before the school year began, Governor Orval Faubus declared on television that it would not be possible to maintain order if integration took place. National Guardsmen, posted by the governor to keep the peace and armed with bayonets, turned away nine black students as they tried to enter the school. After three weeks, a federal court ordered the troops to leave. When the black children entered, the white students, spurred on by their elders, belligerently opposed them, chanting such slogans as "Two, four, six, eight, we ain't gonna integrate." In the face of hostile mobs, the black children left the school.

With the lines drawn, attention focused on the moderate man in the White House, who faced a situation in which Little Rock whites were clearly defying the law. As a former military officer, Ike knew that such resistance could not be tolerated. He called out federal troops to protect the rights of black citizens, ordered paratroopers to Little Rock, and placed National Guardsmen under federal command. The black children entered the school and attended classes with the military protecting their rights. Thus desegregation began.

Black Gains on Other Fronts

Meanwhile, blacks themselves began organizing in ways that advanced the civil rights movement. The crucial event occurred in Montgomery, Alabama, in December 1955. Rosa Parks, a 42-year-old black seamstress who was also secretary of the state NAACP, sat down in the front of a bus in a section reserved by custom for whites. Tired from a hard day's work, she refused when ordered to move back. The police were called at the next stop, and Parks was arrested for violating the segregation laws. Although she had not intended to challenge the law or cause a scene, her stance marked a new phase in the civil rights movement.

In Montgomery, black civil rights officials seized the issue. The next evening, resistance began. Fifty black leaders met to discuss the case and decided to organize a massive boycott of the bus system. Martin Luther King, Jr., the 27-year-old minister of the Baptist church where the meeting was held, soon emerged as the preeminent spokesman of the protest.

Fifty thousand blacks walked or formed car pools to avoid the transit system. Their actions cut gross revenue on city buses by 65 percent. Almost a year later, the Supreme Court ruled that bus segregation, like school segregation, violated the Constitution, and the boycott ended. But the mood it fostered continued, and peaceful protest became a way of life for many blacks.

Meanwhile, a concerted effort developed to guarantee black voting rights. The provisions of

Baptist minister Martin Luther King, Jr., emerged as the black spokesman in the Montgomery, Alabama, bus boycott and soon became the most eloquent African-American leader of the entire civil rights movement. Drawing on his religious background, he was able to mobilize blacks and whites alike in the struggle for equal rights.

the Fifteenth Amendment notwithstanding, many states had circumvented the law for decades (see Chapter 16). Some required a poll tax or a literacy test or an examination of constitutional understanding. Blacks often found themselves excluded from the polls.

Largely because of the legislative genius of Senate majority leader Lyndon B. Johnson of Texas, the civil rights bill, the first since Reconstruction, moved toward passage. With his eye on the presidency, Johnson wanted to establish his credentials as a man who could look beyond narrow southern interests. Paring the bill down to the provisions he felt would pass, Johnson pushed the measure through.

The Civil Rights Act of 1957 created a Civil Rights Commission and empowered the Justice Department to go to court in cases where blacks were denied the right to vote. The bill was a compromise measure, yet it was the first successful effort to protect civil rights in 82 years.

Again led by Johnson, Congress passed the Civil Rights Act of 1960, which set stiffer punishments for people who interfered with others' right to vote but again stopped short of authorizing federal registrars to register blacks to vote and so was generally ineffective.

The civil rights movement made important strides during the Eisenhower years, though little of the progress resulted from the president's leadership. Rather, the efforts of blacks themselves and the ruling of the Supreme Court brought significant change. The period of grassroots civil rights activities, now launched, would continue in the 1960s.

Mexican Migrant Laborers

In the years after World War II, Spanish-speaking groups in the United States suffered from many of the same problems as blacks. They came mainly from Puerto Rico, Mexico, and Central America. Often unskilled and illiterate, they gravitated to the cities like other less fortunate Americans.

Chicanos, or Mexican-Americans, the most numerous newcomers, faced peculiar difficulties and widespread discrimination. During World War II, as the country faced a labor shortage at home, American farmers sought Mexican *braceros* (helping hands) to harvest their crops. A program to encourage the seasonal immigration of farm workers continued after the war when the government signed a Migratory Labor Agreement with Mexico. Between 1948 and 1964, some 4.5 million Mexicans were brought to the United States for temporary work. *Braceros* were expected to return to Mexico at the end of their labor contract, but they often stayed, hoping to better their lives in America. Joining them were millions more who entered the country illegally.

Conditions were harsh for the *braceros* even in the best of times. In periods of economic difficulty, they worsened. During the 1953–1954 recession, the government mounted Operation Wetback to deport illegal entrants and *braceros* who had remained in the country illegally. Deportations numbered 1.1 million. But the *bracero* program continued, and in 1956 a record 445,000 *braceros* crossed the border to work on American farms.

The political attacks in the heated days of the Red Scare also brought persecution to Chicanos active in radical causes. Agapito Gómez had lived in the United States for 25 years. He had an American-born wife. Nonetheless, he found himself questioned for past union activities. In the 1930s, he had been part of a Depression relief organization and had joined the CIO. When he refused to divulge the names of people with whom he had worked, immigration officials took away his alien card.

In addition to economic oppression, Chicanos in all walks of life faced discrimination in the schools, uncertain access to public facilities, and occasional exclusion from the governing process, which they did not always understand. Like blacks, they protested such restrictions and sometimes met with success. The post--World War II years saw increasing political awareness on the part of Mexican-Americans and new aggressiveness in fighting for their rights.

Sometimes action resulted from a particular event. Chicanos, for example, established the American GI Forum when a Texas funeral home refused to bury a Mexican-American casualty of World War II. When the group's protest led to a burial in Arlington National Cemetery, it was clear that concerted action could succeed.

Meanwhile, in the waning months of the war, a court case challenging Mexican-American segregation in the schools began. Gonzalo Méndez, an asparagus grower and a U.S. citizen who had lived in Orange County, California, for 25 years, filed suit to permit his children to attend the school reserved for Anglo-Americans, which was far more attractive than the Mexican one to which they had been assigned. A federal district court upheld his claim in the spring of 1945, and two years later, the circuit court affirmed the original ruling. With the favorable decision, other communities filed similar suits and began to press for integration of their schools.

Chicanos also faced police brutality, particularly in the cities with the largest Chicano populations. Los Angeles, with its large number of Chicanos, was the scene of numerous unsavory racial episodes.

Protests continued, yet in the 1950s, Chicano activism was fragmented. Some Mexican-Americans considered their situation hopeless. While new and aggressive challenges appeared, fully effective mobilization had to wait for another day.

Native Americans

American Indians also acted to defend their interests, but with even greater difficulties. Not only did they have to fight the forces of cultural and technological change that were eroding tribal tradition, but they also had to resist the federal government's reversal of New Deal Indian policy.

Just after the end of World War II, Native Americans achieved an important victory when Congress established the Indian Claims Commission. The commission was mandated to review tribal cases pleading that ancestral lands had been illegally taken from them through violation of federal treaties. Hundreds of tribal suits against the government in federal courts were now possible. Many of them would lead to large settlements of cash—a form of reparation for past injustices—and sometimes the return of long-lost lands.

The Eisenhower administration turned away from the New Deal policy of government support for tribal autonomy. In the Indian Reorganization Act of 1934, the government had stepped in to restore lands to tribal ownership and end their loss or sale to outsiders. In 1953, the administration adopted a new approach, known as the "termination" policy. The government proposed settling all outstanding claims and eliminating reservations as legitimate political entities. To encourage their assimilation into mainstream society, the government offered small subsidies to families who would leave the reservations and relocate in the cities.

The new policy victimized the Indians. With their lands no longer federally protected and their members deprived of treaty rights, many tribes became unwitting victims of people who wanted to seize their land. The new policy caused great disruption as the government terminated tribes like the Klamaths in Oregon, the Menominees in Wisconsin, the Alabamas and Coushattas in Texas, and bands of Paiutes in Utah. At the same time, the policy spurred Indian activism. The National Congress of American Indians mobilized opposition to the federal program. In 1958, the Eisenhower administration ended termination without a tribe's consent. The policy continued to have the force of law, but implementation ceased.

CONCLUSION

QUALMS AMID AFFLUENCE

In general, the United States during the decade and a half after World War II was stable and secure. Recessions occurred periodically, but the economy righted itself after short downturns. For the most part, business boomed. Millions of middle-class Americans moved to the suburbs to enjoy what they considered the good life.

Some Americans, however, did not share in the prosperity. Though black Americans and other minority groups were beginning to mobilize, their protests remained peaceful.

Toward the end of the 1950s, after the Soviet Union became the first nation to place a satellite in orbit, a wave of anxiety swept the nation. Some Americans began to criticize the materialism that had apparently caused the nation to fall behind.

Criticisms and anxieties notwithstanding, the standard of living remained high for many of the nation's citizens. Healthy and comfortable, upper- and middle-class Americans assumed that their society would continue to prosper. But the "other Americans" had begun to make their voices heard, and the echoes would reverberate loudly in future years.

Recommended Reading

A number of good books describe domestic developments in the years between 1945 and 1960. David Brody, *Workers in Industrial America* (1980), and James R. Green, *The World of the Worker* (1980), deal perceptively with labor issues. Kenneth T. Jackson, *Crabgrass Frontier: The Suburbanization of the United States* (1985), focuses on the growth of suburbs; William Leuchtenburg, *A Troubled Feast* (1983), is a perceptive assessment of the entire post-1945 period that focuses on the consumer culture that came into prominence after World War II.

Robert J. Donovan, *Conflict and Crisis: The Presidency of Harry S. Truman, 1945–1948* (1977), is a detailed overview of Truman's first term. *Tumultuous Years: The Presidency of Harry S. Truman* (1982), by the same author, carries the story through the second term. Harry S. Truman, *Memoirs,* 2 vols. (1955, 1956), is Truman's own account of his years at the top.

For a general introduction to the Eisenhower period, see Charles C. Alexander, *Holding the Line: The Eisenhower Era, 1952–1961* (1975). Dwight D. Eisenhower, *Mandate for Change, 1953–1956* (1963), is the first volume of Ike's memoirs of his years in office; *Waging Peace* (1965) is the concluding volume.

Stephen E. Ambrose, *Eisenhower: The President* (1984), is an excellent account of the White House years.

On women, William H. Chafe, *The American Woman: Her Changing Social, Economic, and Political Roles, 1920–1970* (1972), is an outstanding survey of women's struggle. Betty Friedan, *The Feminine Mystique* (1963), is a compelling book describing the stereotypical role of women in the 1950s as they focused on being housewives and mothers.

For further details on civil rights, see Harvard Sitkoff, *The Struggle for Black Equality, 1954–1980* (1981), a readable survey of the movement since the early 1950s. David J. Garrow, *Bearing the Cross: Martin Luther King, Jr., and the Southern Christian Leadership Conference* (1986), is a good account of King and his role. Taylor Branch, *Parting the Waters: America in the King Years, 1954–1963* (1988), vividly records the conflicts in the movement. Rodolfo Acuña, *Occupied America: A History of Chicanos,* 3d ed. (1988), gives insight into the Chicanos' struggle in the years after World War II. Alvin M. Josephy, Jr., *Now That the Buffalo's Gone* (1982), details Indian struggles over the past several decades.

Time Line

1944	GI Bill Passed	**1951**	J. D. Salinger's *Catcher in the Rye*
1945	World War II ends Wave of strikes in heavy industries	**1952**	Dwight D. Eisenhower elected president
1946	Truman vetoes bill extending Office of Price Administration Prices rise by 25 percent in 18 months Union strikes in the auto, coal, steel, and electrical industries Employment Act Dr. Spock's *Baby and Child Care*	**1953**	Submerged Lands Act
		1954	*Brown* v. *Board of Education*
		1955	Montgomery bus boycott begins First McDonald's opens in Illinois AFL and CIO merge
		1956	Eisenhower reelected Interstate Highway Act Allen Ginsberg's "Howl"
1947	Taft-Hartley Act Jackie Robinson breaks the color line in major league baseball	**1957**	Little Rock school integration crisis Civil Rights Act Baby boom peaks with 4.3 million births Soviet Union launches *Sputnik*
1948	Executive order bars discrimination in federal government Armed forces begin to desegregate "Dixiecrat" party formed Truman defeats Dewey Kinsey report on human sexuality Transistor developed at Bell Laboratories	**1959**	One-third of all Americans reside in suburbs
		1960	Three-fourths of all families own a TV Civil Rights Act GNP hits $500 billion
1949	Truman launches Fair Deal		
1950	*Asociación Nacional México- Americana* formed		

chapter 28

The Rise and Fall of the Liberal State

Ron Kovic was an all-American boy. Born in 1946, he grew up on Long Island. Life was secure in the comfortable post–World War II years, as Kovic shared the dreams of millions of others his age. "I loved baseball more than anything else in the world," he later recalled, "playing catch-a-fly-you're-up for hours with a beat-up old baseball." When baseball did not occupy him, television did.

Anxious moments occasionally intervened. Kovic, like others, wondered how the Russians had managed to put a satellite into space before the United States. He grew up fearing "the Communist threat." But, like most Americans, Kovic had an unquestioning confidence in the "American way." Caught up in the spirit of the New Frontier, Kovic was stunned when President John F. Kennedy was shot. "I truly felt I had lost a dear friend," he wrote.

After graduating from high school, Kovic enlisted in the marines. The desire to be a hero carried him through basic training and a first tour of duty in the war in Vietnam. Proud of what he was doing, he signed up for a second tour. Only then did the conflict begin to tear him apart.

Kovic was increasingly haunted by his conduct in the war. He accidently shot and killed an American corporal and, as if to atone for his deed, plunged on even more aggressively to serve his country. Yet that effort, too, ended in disaster when men in his unit shot at shadowy figures moving in a village hut, only to learn that they had killed and wounded innocent children.

Later Kovic was hit in the foot and then took a 30-caliber sniper bullet in the spine. The pain in his foot vanished, but so did all sensation below his chest. Suddenly, all he could feel was "the worthlessness of dying right here in this place at this moment for nothing."

Ron Kovic returned from the war paralyzed from the chest down. As he went from hospital to hospital, seeing the muscle tone of his legs disappear, he grew to believe that he had been trapped in a meaningless crusade and then left to dangle on his own. He became one of the many protesters who finally helped bring the war to an end.

Ron Kovic's passage through the 1960s and 1970s reflected that of American society as a whole. Millions of Americans shared his positive views as the period began. And like Ron Kovic, they were then consumed by doubts about the government's role as the United States became more and more involved in Vietnam.

This chapter describes both the climax of twentieth-century liberalism and its subsequent decline. We will examine first the Democratic initiatives, then the Republican responses, as American politics shifted course in the 1960s and 1970s. In pondering the possibilities of reform, we will outline the various efforts to devise an effective political response to structural changes in the post–World War II economy and follow the fate of those efforts as they became intertwined with the nation's ill-conceived anticommunist crusade in Vietnam.

THE HIGH-WATER MARK OF LIBERALISM

American priorities changed as Dwight Eisenhower came to the end of his second term. The Republican administration's acceptance of New Deal and Fair Deal commitments helped to create a consensus on the major role of the federal government in American life. The Democrats who won office in the 1960s wanted to broaden that role. Dismayed at the problems of poverty, unemployment, and racism, they sought to manage the economy more effectively, eradicate poverty, and protect the civil rights of all Americans. Midway through the decade they came close to achieving their goals.

In this section we will examine the personalities and leadership qualities of liberal presidents Kennedy and Johnson and the changing role of government before taking up the domestic programs of the Kennedy and Johnson administrations and supportive role played by the Supreme Court.

Liberal Leadership

The liberal Democratic leaders of the 1960s took an activist view of the presidency. They believed that the president should set national priorities and then work closely with Congress to ensure the passage of legislation. Whereas Eisenhower had been more comfortable working behind the scenes with legislators, first John Kennedy, then Lyndon Johnson, hoped to use the White House as a "bully pulpit" as Theodore Roosevelt had done. Kennedy encountered fierce resistance from the legislative branch; Johnson was far more successful in implementing his program.

John F. Kennedy, who won the presidency in 1960, seemed to symbolize the commitment to energetic leadership. At 43, he was the youngest man ever elected president. Son of a former ambassador to England and grandson of an Irish-American mayor of Boston, he appeared vigorous and articulate, able to make good on his campaign promise to get the country moving again.

Keenly aware of shifting political patterns, he recognized the need to use the techniques of advertising in his bid for the presidency. Above all he realized the power of television in taking his case to the American people.

In the 1960 campaign, Kennedy squared off against Richard Nixon, the Republican nominee, in the first televised presidential debates. Seventy million Americans turned on their sets to watch the two men in the first debate. Kennedy projected a more dynamic image; Nixon looked worn out and ill at ease.

In the election of 1960, John Kennedy squared off against Richard Nixon in the first televised presidential debates. Nearly 80 million people watched Kennedy establish his credibility with a smooth performance in the four debates.

Kennedy also had the capacity to voice his aims in understandable and eloquent language. During the campaign, he pointed to "uncharted areas of science and space, unsolved problems of peace and war, unconquered pockets of ignorance and prejudice, unanswered questions of poverty and surplus" that Americans must confront, for "the New Frontier is here whether we seek it or not." He made the same point even more movingly in his inaugural address: "The torch has been passed to a new generation of Americans—born in this century, tempered by war, disciplined by a hard and bitter peace, proud of our ancient heritage." Many were inspired by his concluding call to action: "And so, my fellow Americans: Ask not what your country can do for you—ask what you can do for your country."

For Kennedy, strong leadership was all-important. He surrounded himself with talented assistants. On his staff were 15 Rhodes scholars

and several famous authors. The secretary of state was Dean Rusk, a former member of the State Department who had then served as president of the Rockefeller Foundation. The secretary of defense was Robert S. McNamara, the highly successful president of the Ford Motor Company, who had proved creative in mobilizing talented assistants—"whiz kids"—and in using computer analysis to turn the company around.

Further contributing to the attractive Kennedy image were his glamorous wife, Jacqueline, and the glittering social occasions the Kennedys hosted. Energy, exuberance, and excitement filled the air. The administration seemed like the Camelot of King Arthur's day, popularized in a Broadway musical in 1960.

Despite his charismatic appeal, Kennedy faced real problems as president. He had won office despite seemingly insuperable odds and had become the first Catholic in the White House, but his victory over Nixon was razor-thin. The electoral margin of 303 to 219 concealed the close popular tally, in which he triumphed by less than 120,000 of 68 million votes. Without an overwhelming popular mandate and without sufficient liberal support in Congress, he found it difficult to make good on his promises.

Facing reelection in 1964, Kennedy wanted not only to win the presidency for a second term but also to increase Democratic strength in Congress. In November 1963, he traveled to Texas, where he hoped to unite the state's Democratic Party for the upcoming election. Dallas, one of the stops on the trip, had a reputation as being less than cordial to the administration. On November 22, as the presidential party entered the city in an open car, the group encountered friendly crowds. Suddenly shots rang out, and Kennedy slumped forward. Desperately wounded, he died a short time later at a Dallas hospital. Lee Harvey Oswald, the assassin, was himself shot and killed a few days later in the jail where he was being held.

Vice President Lyndon B. Johnson succeeded Kennedy as president of the United States.

Though less polished, Johnson was a more effective political leader than Kennedy and brought his own special skills and vision to the presidency. Johnson was a man of energy and force. Always manipulative and often vulgar, he was, Dean Acheson once told him, "not a very likable man." But he was successful in the passion of his life—politics.

Schooled in Congress and influenced by FDR, Johnson was the most able legislative leader of the postwar years. As Senate majority leader, he became famous for his ability to get things done. Like Kennedy, Johnson was determined to wield presidential power aggressively and to use the media to shape public opinion.

Johnson ran the Senate with tight control and established a credible record for himself and his party during the Eisenhower years. He was the Democrat most responsible for keeping liberal goals alive in a conservative time, as he tried to broaden his own appeal in his quest for the presidency. Unsuccessful in 1960, he agreed to take the second spot under JFK. As vice president, he felt uncomfortable with the Kennedy crowd, useless and stifled in his new role.

Despite his ambivalence about Kennedy, Johnson sensed the profound shock that gripped the United States after the assassination and was determined to utilize Kennedy's memory to achieve his own vision of a society in which the comforts of life would be more widely shared and poverty eliminated.

The Changing Role of Government

The liberal agenda reflected the changing role of government. By 1960, government had become a major factor in ordinary people's lives. The New Deal and World War II had brought the unprecedented expansion of government's role. In the 1930s, the White House became an initiator of legislation and worked closely with Congress, while new agencies administered relief and recovery programs (see Chapter 24). The process

continued during World War II, when the number of civilians working for the federal government more than tripled between 1940 and 1945. Though the number declined somewhat at the war's end, the government still employed close to 2.5 million people throughout the 1950s. Federal expenditures, which had stood at $3.1 billion in 1929, rose to $75 billion in 1953 and passed $150 billion in the 1960s. Defense spending rose dramatically during the Cold War years, but at the same time, the government extended old-age pensions and unemployment benefits to its citizens and took increasing responsibility for other social needs.

By 1960, most Americans accepted, even embraced, government's expanded role. The major political debate revolved around the question of how far that expansion should continue and which groups should benefit from it. Demands heard in the late 1940s and the 1950s—for educational assistance, for federal health care, for more extensive welfare benefits—now became part of the political agenda in the 1960s.

The New Frontier

As president from 1961 to 1963, John Kennedy sought to maintain an expanding economic system and to extend social welfare programs. Regarding civil rights, he espoused liberal goals and social justice, although his policies were limited (see Chapter 29 for a full discussion of civil rights). On the economic front, he tried to end the lingering recession by working with the business community, while controlling price inflation at the same time.

Those two goals conflicted when, in the spring of 1962, the large steel companies sought what the administration regarded as excessive price increases. Determined to force the steel companies to back down, Kennedy pressed for a congressional investigation. When the Defense Department threatened to deny contracts to the offending companies, they gave in and reinstituted the earlier price levels. Although Kennedy

The American landing on the moon resulted from Kennedy's commitment to the space program.

won, he paid a price for his victory. Business leaders concluded that this Democratic administration, like all the others, was hostile to business. In late May, six weeks after the steel crisis, the stock market plunged in the greatest drop since the Great Crash of 1929. Kennedy received the blame.

It now seemed doubly pressing to end the recession. Adopting a Keynesian approach to economic growth, in June 1962, Kennedy announced that deficits, properly used, might help the economy. In early 1963, he called for a $13.5 billion cut in corporate taxes over the next three years. While that cut would cause a large deficit, it would also provide capital to stimulate the economy and ultimately increase tax revenues.

Opposition mounted. Conservatives refused to accept the basic premise that deficits would stimulate economic growth. Liberals, economist John Kenneth Galbraith among them, claimed that it would be better to stimulate the economy by spending for social programs rather than by cutting taxes. Why, he wondered, have "a few

more dollars to spend if the air is too dirty to breathe, the water is too polluted to drink, the commuters are losing out in the struggle to get in and out of cities, the streets are filthy, and the schools are so bad that the young, perhaps wisely, stay away?" In Congress, opponents pigeonholed the proposal in committee, and there it remained. Nor did Congress pass legislation that Kennedy proposed for federal aid for education, medical care for the elderly, housing subsidies, and urban renewal. His new minimum-wage measure passed Congress only in pared-down form.

Kennedy was more successful in securing funding for the exploration of space. As first Alan Shepard, then John Glenn, flew in space, Kennedy proposed that the United States commit itself to landing a man on the moon and returning him to earth before the end of the decade. Congress assented and increased funding of the National Aeronautics and Space Administration (NASA).

Kennedy also succeeded in establishing the Peace Corps, which sent men and women overseas to assist developing countries.

If Kennedy's successes were moderate in comparison with his failures, he had begun to set a new liberal agenda that provided a model for the administrations that followed. He had reaffirmed the importance of executive leadership in the effort to extend the boundaries of the welfare state. And he had committed himself to using modern economics to maintain fiscal stability.

The Great Society in Action

Like Kennedy, Lyndon Johnson had an expansive vision of the possibilities of reform. Using his considerable political skills, he succeeded in pushing through Congress the most extensive reform program in American history. "Is a new world coming?" the president asked. "We welcome it, and we will bend it to the hopes of man."

Johnson began to develop the support he

needed the day he took office. In his first public address, delivered to Congress and televised nationwide, he embraced Kennedy's liberal program. He began, in a measured tone, with the words, "All I have, I would have given gladly not to be standing here today." He asked members of Congress to work with him, and he underscored the theme "Let us continue" throughout his speech.

As a first step, Johnson determined to secure the measures Kennedy had been unable to extract from Congress. By the spring of 1964, the outlines of his own expansive vision were taking shape, and he had begun to use the phrase "Great Society" to describe his reform program. Successful even before the election of 1964, his landslide victory over conservative Republican challenger Barry Goldwater of Arizona validated his approach. LBJ received 61 percent of the popular vote and an electoral tally of 486 to 52 and gained Democratic congressional majorities of 68–32 in the Senate and 295–140 in the House.

Johnson provided strong executive leadership in support of his proposals. He appointed task forces that included legislators to study problems and suggest solutions, worked with them to draft bills, and maintained close contact with congressional leaders through a sophisticated liaison staff. Not since the FDR years had there been such a coordinated effort, and it resulted in the strongest legislative program since the New Deal.

Civil rights reform was an integral part of the Great Society program (see Chapter 29), along with welfare state measures. Following Kennedy's lead, Johnson pressed for a tax cut to stimulate the economy. To gain conservative support, he agreed to hold down spending; the tax bill passed. With the tax cut in hand, the president pressed for the poverty program that Kennedy had begun to plan. For the first time in American history, the government developed a program specifically directed at ending poverty. The Economic Opportunity Act of 1964 created

an Office of Economic Opportunity to provide education and training for unskilled young people trapped in the poverty cycle, VISTA (Volunteers in Service to America) to assist the poor at home, and assorted community action programs to give the poor themselves a voice in improving housing, health, and education in their own neighborhoods.

Johnson also won passage of important legislation in health, education, and aid for the poor. Medicare, a medical assistance plan, was tied to the established social security system and limited to the elderly. Medicaid met the needs of the poor below the age of 65 who could not afford private insurance. The Medicare-Medicaid program was the most important extension of federally directed social benefits since the Social Security Act of 1935. Johnson was similarly successful in his effort to provide aid for elementary and secondary schools and rent supplements for the poor.

Congress, meanwhile, reformed the restrictive immigration policy, which for decades had rested on racial and national quotas. The Immigration Act of 1965 replaced the 1924 quota system with a new yearly limit of 170,000 people from the Eastern Hemisphere and 120,000 from the Western Hemisphere. Family members of United States citizens were exempted from the quotas, as were political refugees. In the 1960s, some 350,000 immigrants entered the United States annually; in the 1970s, the number exceeded 400,000 a year. This new immigration brought different groups to America and helped revive a sense of ethnic consciousness.

Meanwhile, the federal government provided new forms of aid, such as legal assistance for the poor, financial grants to colleges and universities, and support for artists and scholars through the new National Endowments for the Arts and Humanities.

At the same time, the Great Society reflected the stirring of the environmental movement. In 1962, naturalist Rachel Carson alerted the public to the dangers of pesticide poisoning and environmental pollution in her book *Silent Spring*. Johnson recognized the need to do something about caustic fumes in the air, lethal sludge in rivers and streams, and the steady disappearance of wildlife. The National Wilderness Preservation System Act of 1964 set aside 9.1 million acres of wilderness, while Lady Bird Johnson, the president's wife, led a beautification campaign to eliminate unsightly billboards and junkyards along the nation's highways, and Congress passed other measures to limit air and water pollution.

A Sympathetic Supreme Court

The Supreme Court also supported and promoted social change in the 1960s. Under the leadership of Chief Justice Earl Warren, the Court followed the lead it had taken in 1954 in *Brown* v. *Board of Education*. Having dealt with the issue of school segregation, the Court moved against Jim Crow practices in other public establishments.

The Court also supported civil liberties. It began to protect the rights of individuals who held radical political views. Similarly, in *Gideon* v. *Wainwright* (1963), the justices decided that poor defendants in serious cases had the right to free legal counsel. In *Escobedo* v. *Illinois* (1964), they ruled that a suspect had to be given access to an attorney during questioning. In *Miranda* v. *Arizona* (1966), they argued that offenders had to be warned that statements extracted by the police could be used against them and that they could remain silent.

Other decisions similarly broke new ground. *Baker* v. *Carr* (1962) opened the way to reapportionment of state legislative bodies, according to the standard, defined a year later by Justice William O. Douglas's words, of "one person, one vote." This crucial ruling helped break the political control of lightly populated rural districts in many state assemblies and similarly made the United States House of Representatives much more responsive to urban and sub-

urban issues. Meanwhile, the Court outraged conservatives by ruling that prayer could not be required in the public schools and that obscenity laws could no longer restrict allegedly pornographic material that might have some "redeeming social value."

The Great Society Under Attack

For a few years, the Great Society worked as Johnson had hoped. The tax cut proved effective. The budget deficit dropped, unemployment fell, and inflation remained under control. Medical programs provided a measure of security for the old and the poor. Education flourished as schools were built, and salaries increased in response to the influx of federal aid.

Yet the gains proved short-lived. No real effort had been made to redistribute income. Nor was enough money allocated to the new social programs. As Michael Harrington concluded, "What was supposed to be a social war turned out to be a skirmish and, in any case, poverty won."

Although the Great Society was criticized by both the left and the right, it accomplished much in widening the web of federal activity. It might have accomplished even more had not a series of internal contradictions and external challenges intruded.

The Great Society suffered from the start from factionalism. Civil rights activists disagreed with white southern Democrats over how strongly the government should push for equal rights; the urban poor who pressed for increased political power fought with political bosses who had been the backbone of the Democratic Party and who wanted to preserve their strength.

At the same time, the Great Society suffered from the consequences of the Vietnam War (see Chapter 26 for the origins of the war and the last section of this chapter for its escalation). LBJ's decision to try to maintain the war and commitments at home without raising taxes fueled an inflation that soon jumped out of control. Congress finally got into the act and responded by slashing Great Society programs. As hard economic choices became increasingly necessary, many decided the country could no longer afford social reform on the scale Johnson had proposed.

THE DECLINE OF LIBERALISM

After eight years of Democratic rule, many Americans questioned the liberal agenda and the ability of the government to solve social problems. The war had polarized the country, and the Democratic Party was under attack. Republicans, capitalizing on the alienation sparked by the Vietnam War, determined to scale down the commitment to social change and pay more attention to white, middle-class Americans. While, like Dwight Eisenhower a decade and a half before, they accepted some social programs as necessary for the well-being of modern America, they were resolved to reduce spending and cut back the federal bureaucracy.

Republican Leadership

Nixon had long dreamed of holding the nation's highest office. In 1968, his chances seemed good as the Vietnam War split the Democratic Party. Americans were tired of the drawn-out, expensive war, and Johnson had announced that he would not seek another term. As Senator Eugene McCarthy promoted his candidacy, Robert F. Kennedy, the charismatic brother of the slain president, launched his own bid for the nomination. It ended in his assassination, which shook the country. Inheriting the role of leading contender was Vice President Hubert H. Humphrey.

The Democratic national convention was a disaster. Militant protesters found themselves pitted against Mayor Richard Daley, longtime boss of Chicago, who vowed to use his police force to keep order. On the climactic evening

when the convention nominated Humphrey, the police ran amok, clubbing not only demonstrators but also reporters, bystanders, and anyone else in the way.

Complicating the general election was the third-party campaign of Governor George C. Wallace of Alabama, who exploited racial tensions for his own ends.

Nixon's nomination by the Republicans was a triumph in a turbulent career. Running for vice president in 1952, Nixon had almost been dropped from the ticket when charges of a slush fund surfaced. Only his maudlin televised appeal to the American public saved him then. After his loss to Kennedy in 1960 and his defeat in a race for governor of California in 1962, his political career appeared over. But after the Goldwater disaster in 1964, Nixon began to campaign for Republican candidates and reestablished a base of support.

In the election, Nixon received 43.4 percent of the popular vote, not quite one percent more than Humphrey, with Wallace capturing the rest, but it was enough to give Nixon a majority in the electoral college. The Democrats won both houses of Congress.

In and out of office, Nixon was a remote man, lacking humor and grace. As one of his speech-writers said, there was "a mean side to his nature" that he strove to conceal. Earlier in his career he was labeled "Tricky Dick." He was most comfortable alone or with a few wealthy friends. Even at work he insulated himself, preferred written contacts to personal ones, and often retreated to a small room in the executive office building to be alone.

Philosophically, Nixon disagreed with the liberal faith in federal planning and wanted to decentralize social policy. But he agreed with his liberal predecessors that the presidency ought to be the engine of the political system. Faced with a Congress dominated by Democrats and their allocations of money for programs which he opposed, he impounded, or refused to spend, funds Congress had authorized. Later commentators would see the Nixon years as the height of the "imperial presidency."

In Nixon's cabinet sat only white, male Republicans. Yet for the most part, Nixon worked around his cabinet, relying on other White House staff appointees. In domestic affairs, Arthur Burns, a former chairman of the Council of Economic Advisers, and Daniel Patrick Moynihan, a Harvard professor of government (and a Democrat), were the most important. In foreign affairs, the major figure was Henry A. Kissinger, another Harvard government professor, even more talented and ambitious, who directed the National Security Council staff and later became secretary of state.

Still another tier of White House officials insulated the president from the outside world and carried out his commands. Advertising executive H. R. Haldeman, a tireless Nixon campaigner, became chief of staff. Lawyer John Ehrlichman started as a legal counselor and rose to become chief domestic adviser. Haldeman and Ehrlichman came to be known as the "Berlin Wall" for the way they guarded the president's privacy. Another lawyer, John Mitchell, known as "El Supremo" by the staff, and as "the Big Enchilada" by Ehrlichman, assumed the post of attorney general and gave the president daily advice.

The Republican Agenda

Although Nixon had come to political maturity in Republican circles, he accepted the basic contours of the welfare state and sought to systematize its programs. Despite reservations at first, he proved willing to use economic tools to maintain stability.

The economy was faltering when Nixon assumed office. Nixon responded to inflation by tightening monetary and fiscal policy. Later he imposed wage and price controls to stop inflation and used monetary and fiscal policies to stimulate the economy. After his reelection in 1972, however, he lifted wage and price controls, and inflation began to rise again.

A number of factors besides the Vietnam War contributed to the spiral of rising prices. Large grain sales to Russia in 1972, coupled with crop disasters, caused inflation in grain prices. In 1973, events in the Middle East caused oil prices to rise dramatically. Although OPEC (the Organization of Petroleum Exporting Countries) had slowly raised oil prices in the early 1970s, the 1973 war between Israel, Egypt, and Syria led Saudi Arabia to impose an embargo on oil shipped to Israel's ally, the United States. Other OPEC nations quadrupled their prices. Dependent on imports for one-third of their energy needs, Americans faced shortages and skyrocketing prices. When the embargo ended in 1974, prices remained high.

The oil crisis affected all aspects of American economic life. Manufacturers, farmers, homeowners—all were touched by high energy prices. A loaf of bread that had cost 28 cents in the early 1970s jumped to 89 cents, and automobiles cost 72 percent more in 1978 than they had in 1973. Accustomed to filling up their cars' tanks for only a few dollars, Americans were shocked at paying 65 cents a gallon. In 1974, inflation reached 11 percent. But as higher energy prices encouraged consumers to cut back on their purchases, the nation also entered a recession. Unemployment climbed to 9 percent, the highest level since the 1930s. Inflation and high unemployment were worrisome bedfellows.

As economic growth and stability eluded him, Nixon also tried to reorganize rapidly expanding welfare programs. At the urging of domestic adviser Daniel Moynihan, Nixon endorsed an expensive but feasible work-incentive program, which would have guaranteed a minimum yearly stipend of $1,600 to a family of four, with food stamps providing about $800 more. Though promising, the program died in the Senate, but it indicated what the administration hoped to do.

As he tried to manage the economy, Nixon also worked to restore "law and order" in the United States. Political protest—and rising crime rates, increased drug use, and more permissive attitudes toward sex—brought a growing backlash on the part of working-class and many middle-class Americans. Nixon decided to use government power to silence disruption in an effort to strengthen his own political constituency. He lashed out at demonstrators—he called the students "bums" at one point. His vice president and hatchet man, Spiro Agnew, called opposition elements, and students in particular, "ideological eunuchs" who made up an "effete corps of impudent snobs."

Another part of Nixon's effort to promote stability involved attacking the media, which he regarded as biased and hostile toward him personally. Agnew spearheaded the attack on the television networks.

Most important, however, was Attorney General John Mitchell's effort to curb domestic protest by seeking enhanced powers for a campaign on crime, sometimes at the expense of individuals' constitutional rights. One part of Mitchell's plan involved reshaping the Supreme Court, which had rendered increasingly liberal decisions on the rights of defendants in the past decade and a half. In his first term, Nixon had the extraordinary opportunity to name four judges to the Court, and he nominated men who shared his views. His first choice was Warren E. Burger as chief justice to replace the liberal Earl Warren, who was retiring. Burger, a moderate, was confirmed quickly. The next two men he nominated showed such racial biases or limitations that the Senate refused to confirm them. Nixon then appointed Harry Blackmun, Lewis F. Powell, Jr., and William Rehnquist, all able and qualified, and all inclined to tilt the Court in a more conservative direction.

Over the next few years, the Court shifted to the right. It narrowed defendants' rights and upheld pornography laws if they reflected community standards. In the controversial 1973 *Roe* v. *Wade* decision, however, the Court legalized abortion, stating that women's rights included the right to control their own bodies. This decision was one that feminists, a group hardly supported by the president, had ardently sought.

Watergate and Its Aftermath

Faced with a solidly Democratic Congress, the Nixon administration found its legislative initiatives blocked. In this situation, Nixon was determined to end the stalemate by winning a second term and sweeping Republican majorities into both houses of Congress in 1972. His efforts to gain a decisive Republican victory at the polls led to excesses that brought his demise.

In his reelection campaign, Nixon relied on aides who were fiercely loyal and prepared to do anything to win. He also drew on the assistance of White House counsel John Dean, former CIA agent E. Howard Hunt, and former FBI agent G. Gordon Liddy.

The Committee to Re-elect the President (CREEP), headed by John Mitchell, who resigned as attorney general, launched a massive fund-raising drive, aimed at collecting as much money as it could before the reporting of contributions became necessary under a new campaign-finance law. That money could be used for any purpose, including payments for the performance of dirty tricks aimed at disrupting the opposition's campaign. Other funds financed an intelligence branch within CREEP that had Liddy at its head and included Hunt.

Early in 1972, Liddy and his lieutenants proposed an elaborate scheme to wiretap the phones of various Democrats and to disrupt their nominating convention. Twice Mitchell refused to go along, arguing that the plan was too risky and expensive. Finally he approved a modified version of the plan to tap the phones of the Democratic National Committee at its headquarters in the Watergate apartment complex in Washington, D.C. Mitchell, formerly the top justice official in the land, had authorized breaking the law.

The wiretapping attempt took place on the evening of June 16 and ended with the arrest of those involved. They carried with them money and documents that could be traced to CREEP and incriminate the reelection campaign. Reelection remained the most pressing priority, so Nixon's aides played the matter down and used federal resources to head off the investigation. When the FBI traced the money carried by the burglars to CREEP, the president authorized the CIA to call off the FBI on the grounds that national security was at stake. Though not involved in the planning of the break-in, the president was now party to the cover-up. In the succeeding months, he authorized payment of hush money to silence Hunt and others. Top members of the administration, including Mitchell, perjured themselves in court to shield the higher officials who were involved.

Nixon won the election of 1972 in a landslide, trouncing his opponent, George McGovern, a liberal senator from South Dakota. He failed, however, to gain the congressional majorities necessary to support his programs.

When the Watergate burglars were brought to trial, they pleaded guilty and were sentenced to jail, but the case refused to die. Two zealous reporters, Bob Woodward and Carl Bernstein of the Washington *Post,* eventually linked Mitchell to Watergate. A Senate investigation then revealed that the White House had been involved in the episode.

In May 1973, the Senate committee began televised public hearings, reminiscent of the earlier McCarthy hearings of the 1950s. As millions of Americans watched, the drama built. John Dean, seeking to save himself, testified that Nixon knew about the cover-up, and other staffers revealed a host of illegal activities undertaken at the White House: Money had been paid to the burglars to silence them; State Department documents had been forged to smear a previous administration; wiretaps had been used to prevent top-level leaks. The most electrifying moment was the disclosure that the the president had in his office a secret taping system that recorded all conversations. Tapes could verify or disprove the growing rumors that Nixon had in

fact been party to the cover-up all along. But Nixon would not release the tapes.

More and more Americans now believed that the president had played a role in the cover-up. *Time* magazine ran an editorial headlined "The President Should Resign," and Congress considered impeachment. In late July 1974, the House Judiciary Committee, made up of 21 Democrats and 17 Republicans, voted to impeach the president on the grounds of obstruction of justice, abuse of power, and refusal to obey a congressional subpoena to turn over his tapes. A full House of Representatives vote still had to occur, and the Senate would have to preside over a trial before removal could take place. But for Nixon the handwriting was on the wall.

After a brief delay, on August 5 Nixon obeyed a Supreme Court ruling and released the tapes. Despite a troubling 18½-minute silence, they contained clear evidence of his complicity in the cover-up. Four days later, on August 9, 1974, Nixon became the first American president ever to resign.

Although the power of government and of the presidency had expanded greatly in the 1960s and 1970s, the Watergate episode seemed disturbing and scandalous evidence that the appropriate balance of power had disappeared. As the scandal wound down, many began to question the centralization of power in the American political system and to cite the "imperial presidency" as the cause of recent abuses. Others simply lost faith in the presidency altogether. Disillusionment over the American involvement in Vietnam and revelations concerning the Watergate affair contributed to the cumulative distrust of politics in Washington and to the steady decrease in political participation.

Gerald Ford: Caretaker President

Gerald Ford succeeded to the presidency in the aftermath of the Watergate affair. He had become vice president in 1973 when Nixon's first vice president, Spiro Agnew, resigned in disgrace for accepting bribes. An unpretentious middle-American Republican who believed in the traditional virtues, Ford faced the difficult task of trying to use his authority to restore national confidence at a time when the misuse of presidential power had caused the crisis.

Ford worked quickly to restore trust in the government. He promised to cooperate both with Congress and with American citizens. The new president then pardoned Richard Nixon barely a month after his resignation. Haldeman, Ehrlichman, Mitchell, Dean, and other Nixon administration officials faced indictment, trial, and imprisonment for their part in the Watergate affair, but their former leader, even before a hearing, was to go free of prosecution for any crimes committed while president. Ford's action raised doubts about his judgment and caused angry demonstrations.

In domestic policy, Ford followed the direction established during the Nixon years. Economic problems proved most pressing in 1974 as inflation, fueled by oil-price increases, rose to 11 percent a year, unemployment stood at 5.3 percent, and gross national product declined. Not since Franklin Roosevelt took office in the depths of the Great Depression had a new president faced economic difficulties so severe.

Ford tried to restore confidence through his WIN campaign, calling on Americans to "Whip Inflation Now" by saving more and by planting their own vegetable gardens to challenge rising prices in the stores. The plan failed and soon disappeared.

At last convinced of the need for strong governmental action, the administration introduced a tight-money policy as a means of curbing inflation. It led to the most severe recession since the Depression, with unemployment peaking at 12 percent in 1975. Congress pushed for an antirecession spending program. Recognizing political reality, Ford endorsed a multibillion-dollar tax cut coupled with higher unemployment benefits. The economy made a modest recovery, although inflation and unemployment remained high, and federal budget deficits soared.

Ford's dilemma was that his belief in limited presidential involvement set him against liberals who still argued that strong executive leadership was necessary to make the welfare state work. When he failed to take the initiative, Congress intervened, and the two branches of government became embroiled in conflict. Ford vetoed numerous bills, including those creating a consumer protection agency and expanding programs in education, housing, and health. In response, Congress overrode a higher percentage of vetoes than at any time since the presidency of Franklin Pierce more than a century before.

The Carter Interlude

In the election of 1976, the nation's bicentennial year, Ford faced Jimmy Carter, former governor of Georgia. Carter, appealing to voters distrustful of political leadership, portrayed himself as an outsider. He stressed that he was not from Washington and that, unlike many of those mired in past scandals, he was not a lawyer.

Carter won a 50 to 48 percent majority of the popular vote and a 297 to 240 tally in the electoral college. He did well with the working class, blacks, and Catholics, and he won most of the South.

Carter was a graduate of the Naval Academy, trained as a manager and an engineer. A modest man by nature, he hoped to take a restrained approach to the presidency and thereby defuse its imperial stamp.

Initially, voters saw him as a reform Democrat committed to his party's liberal goals, but he was hardly the old-line liberal some Democrats had hoped for. Though he called himself a populist, his political philosophy and priorities were never clear, and he seemed to respond to problems in a haphazard way. His status as an outsider, touted during the campaign, led him to ignore traditional political channels when he assumed power. Like Herbert Hoover, he was a technocrat in the White House at a time when liberals wanted a visionary to help them overcome hard times.

In economic affairs, Carter gave liberals some hope at first as he permitted a policy of deficit spending. When inflation rose to about 10 percent a year in 1979, he slowed down the economy and cut the deficit slightly. Contraction of the money supply led to greater unemployment and many small business failures. Budget cuts fell largely on social programs and distanced Carter from reform-minded Democrats who had supported him three years before. Yet even that effort to arrest growing deficits was not enough. When the budget released in early 1980 still showed high spending levels, the financial community reacted strongly. Bond prices fell, and interest rates rose dramatically.

Similarly, Carter disappointed liberals by his failure to construct an effective energy policy in the face of OPEC's rising oil prices. His program, bogged down in Congress for 26 months, eventually committed the nation to move from oil dependence to reliance on coal, possibly even on sun and wind, and established a new synthetic-fuel corporation. Nuclear power seemed less attractive as costs rose and accidents, such as the near disaster at Three Mile Island (see Chapter 29), occurred.

Carter further upset liberals by beginning deregulation—the removal of governmental controls in economic life. Arguing that certain restrictions established over the past century ended competition and increased consumer costs, he supported decontrol of oil and natural gas prices to spur production. He also deregulated the railroad, trucking, and airline industries.

THE CONTINUING COLD WAR AND ITS CONSEQUENCES

As executive and legislative leaders struggled to define the government's role in domestic affairs, the Cold War continued to dominate America's role abroad. Involvement in the quagmire of Vietnam was the unfortunate result. Extrication from the war demanded the same kind of redefinition of role that was occurring on the domestic front.

Kennedy's Confrontations

John Kennedy entered office determined to stand firm in the face of Russian power. During the campaign, he declared: "The enemy is the communist system itself—implacable, insatiable, unceasing in its drive for world domination."

Kennedy's most imaginative approach to the Cold War involved the promotion of "peaceful revolution" in unaligned Third World countries. By providing nonmilitary assistance programs that increased agricultural productivity and built modern transportation and communications systems, Kennedy hoped to promote stable, pro-Western governments throughout Latin America, Africa, and Asia.

While these efforts in developing nations proceeded, Kennedy saw direct challenges from the Soviet Union almost from the beginning of his presidency. The first came at the Bay of Pigs in the spring of 1961. Cuban-American relations had been strained since Fidel Castro's revolutionary army had overthrown the dictatorial Fulgencio Batista, a longtime American ally, in 1959. As Castro expropriated private property of major American corporations, which for decades had dominated the Cuban economy, the U.S. government became increasingly concerned. A radical regime in Cuba, leaning toward the Soviet Union, could provide a model for upheaval elsewhere in Latin America and threaten the venerable Monroe Doctrine.

Just before Kennedy assumed office, the United States broke diplomatic relations with Cuba. The CIA, meanwhile, was covertly training anti-Castro exiles to storm the Cuban coast at the Bay of Pigs. The American planners assumed the invasion would lead to an uprising of the Cuban people against Castro. When Kennedy learned of the plan, he approved it.

The invasion, on April 17, 1961, was an unmitigated disaster. Cuban forces kept troops from coming ashore, and there was no popular uprising to greet the invaders. The United States stood exposed to the world, attempting to overthrow a sovereign government. It had broken agreements not to interfere in the internal affairs of hemispheric neighbors and had intervened clumsily and unsuccessfully.

Although chastened by the debacle at the Bay of Pigs, Kennedy remained determined to deal sternly with the perceived Communist threat. In June 1961, the Russians were pressing for a settlement regarding Berlin that would reflect the reality of the city's division into eastern and western zones since World War II and prevent the flight of East Germans to the West. Fearful that the Soviet effort signaled designs on the Continent as a whole, Kennedy responded aggressively, seeking $3 billion more in defense appropriations, more men for the armed forces, and funds for a civil defense fallout shelter program, as if to warn of the possibility of nuclear war. After the Russians erected a wall in Berlin to seal off their section, the crisis eased.

The next year, a new crisis arose. Fidel Castro, understandably fearful of the American threat to Cuban independence after the Bay of Pigs invasion, secured Russian assistance. According to American aerial photographs in October 1962, the Soviet Union had begun to place offensive missiles on Cuban soil. Cuba insisted that the missiles were defensive and in any event they did not change the strategic balance significantly, for the Soviets could still wreak untold damage on American targets from bases farther away, and American missiles stood on the borders of the Soviet Union in Turkey. But with Russian weapons installed just 90 miles from American shores, appearance was more important than strategic balance. Kennedy was determined to confront the Russians (not the Cubans) and win.

The president went on nationwide TV to tell the American people about the missiles and to demand their removal. He declared that the United States would not shrink from the risk of nuclear war and announced a naval blockade around Cuba to prevent Soviet ships from bringing in additional missiles. He called the move a quarantine, for a blockade was an act of war.

As the Soviet ships steamed toward the blockade and the nations stood "eyeball to eyeball" at the brink, the American and Russian people held their breath. After several days, the tension broke, but only because Khrushchev called the Russian ships back and then sent a long letter to Kennedy pledging to remove the missiles if the United States ended the blockade and promised to stay out of Cuba altogether. The United States agreed, having already announced its intention to remove its own missiles from Turkey. With that the crisis ended.

The Cuban missile crisis was the most terrifying confrontation of the Cold War. But Kennedy emerged from the crisis as a hero who had stood firm. His reputation was enhanced, as was the image of his party in the coming congressional elections. One consequence of the crisis was the establishment of a Soviet-American hot line to avoid similar episodes in the future. Another was Russia's determination to increase its nuclear arsenal so that it would never again be exposed as inferior to the United States.

Escalation in Vietnam

Believing that the power and prestige of the United States had been damaged by the Bay of Pigs and the confrontation over the Berlin Wall, Kennedy was determined to achieve Cold War victories in other parts of the world. Thus he willingly increased American involvement in Southeast Asia. Unsympathetic to Ho Chi Minh's regime in North Vietnam, the United States had steadily increased its support to South Vietnam. By the time Eisenhower left the presidency in 1961, some 675 American military advisers were assisting the South Vietnamese. By the end of 1963, the number had risen to more than 16,000.

Despite American backing, South Vietnamese leader Ngo Dinh Diem was rapidly losing support within his own country. American officials began to realize that Diem would never reform. After receiving assurances that the United States would not object to an internal coup, South Vietnamese military leaders assassinated Diem and seized the government.

Kennedy understood the importance of popular support for the South Vietnamese government if that country were to maintain its independence. But he was reluctant to withdraw and let the Vietnamese solve their own problems. When Kennedy met with a violent death shortly after Diem's assassination, Lyndon Johnson faced a situation in flux in Vietnam.

Johnson shared many of Kennedy's assumptions about the threat of communism. Like Kennedy, Johnson believed in the domino theory, which held that if one country in a region fell, others were bound to follow. In 1965, he sent 20,000 troops to the Dominican Republic to help buttress a military junta. His flimsy claims about the threat of communism and the importance of protecting American tourists created a wedge between his administration and liberals.

That wedge would widen over the question of Vietnam. Kennedy had expanded American forces there; Johnson took the Vietnam War and made it his own. Soon after assuming office, he reached a fundamental decision that guided policy for the next four years. South Vietnam was more unstable than ever after the assassination of Diem. Guerrillas, known as Viet Cong, challenged the regime, aided by Ho Chi Minh and the North Vietnamese. "I am not going to lose Vietnam," Johnson said. "I am not going to be the President who saw Southeast Asia go the way China went."

In the election campaign of 1964, Johnson posed as a man of peace. All the while, however, he was planning to increase American involvement in the war.

In August 1964, Johnson cleverly obtained congressional authorization for the war. North Vietnamese torpedo boats, he announced, had, without provocation, attacked American destroyers in the international waters of the Gulf of Tonkin, 30 miles from North Vietnam. Only later did it become clear that the American ships had violated the territorial waters of North Vietnam by assisting South Vietnamese commando raids in offshore combat zones. With the details of the attack still unclear, Johnson used the episode to obtain from Congress the "Gulf of Tonkin Resolution," giving him authority to "take all necessary measures to repel any armed attack against the forces of the United States and to prevent further aggression."

Military escalation began in earnest in February 1965, and a few months later, the president sent American ground troops into action, marking a crucial turning point in the Americanization of the Vietnam War. Only 25,000 American soldiers were in Vietnam at the start of 1965. By the end of the year, there were 184,000, and the number swelled to 385,000 in 1966, 485,000 in 1967, 543,000 in 1968.

American forces became direct participants in the fight to prop up a dictatorial regime in faraway South Vietnam. Although a more effective government headed by Nguyen Van Thieu and Nguyen Cao Ky was finally established, the level of violence increased. Saturation bombing of North Vietnam continued. Fragmentation bombs, killing and maiming countless civilians, and napalm, which seared off human flesh, were used extensively. Similar destruction wracked South Vietnam. Yet the North Vietnamese and their revolutionary allies in South Vietnam pressed on. Like LBJ, they sought not compromise but victory.

Americans began to protest their involvement in the war. The first antiwar teach-in took place in March 1965 at the University of Michigan. Others soon followed. "Make love, not war," slogans proclaimed as more and more students became involved in political demonstrations at dozens of colleges. "Hey, hey, LBJ. How many kids did you kill today?" opponents of the war chanted. In 1967, some 300,000 people marched in New York City. In Washington, D.C., 100,000 tried to close down the Pentagon.

The Vietnam War

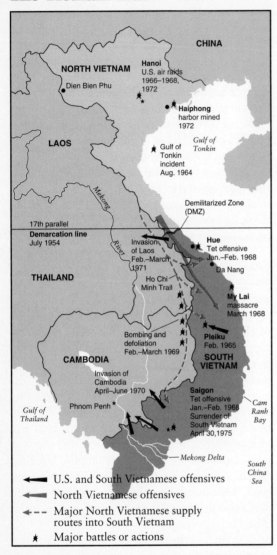

CHINA

NORTH VIETNAM

Hanoi
U.S. air raids
1966–1968,
1972

Dien Bien Phu

Haiphong
harbor mined
1972

LAOS

Gulf of Tonkin

★ Gulf of
Tonkin
incident
Aug. 1964

Mekong River

Demilitarized Zone
(DMZ)

17th parallel
Demarcation line
July 1954

Invasion
of Laos
Feb.–March
1971

Hue
Tet offensive
Jan.–Feb. 1968

THAILAND

Da Nang

Ho Chi
Minh Trail

My Lai
massacre
March 1968

Bombing and
defoliation
Feb.–March 1969

Pleiku
Feb. 1965

CAMBODIA

**SOUTH
VIETNAM**

Invasion of
Cambodia
April–June 1970

*Gulf of
Thailand*

Phnom Penh ★

Saigon
Tet offensive
Jan.–Feb. 1968
Surrender of
South Vietnam
April 30,1975

*Cam
Ranh
Bay*

— *Mekong Delta*

*South
China
Sea*

◀━━ U.S. and South Vietnamese offensives

◀━ North Vietnamese offensives

◀- - - Major North Vietnamese supply
routes into South Vietnam

★ Major battles or actions

*This map shows the major campaigns of the Vietnam War.
The North Vietnamese Tet offensive of early 1968 turned the
tide against U.S. participation in the war and led to peace
talks. The American invasion of Cambodia in 1970 provoked
serious opposition.*

Working-class and middle-class Americans began to sour on the war as well. Watching nightly television reports that featured graphic representations of the death and destruction, they wondered about their nation's purposes and actions.

In early 1968, the North Vietnamese mounted the massive Tet offensive, attacking provincial capitals and district towns in South Vietnam. In Saigon, they struck the American embassy, Tan Son Nhut air base, and the presidential palace. Though beaten back, they won a psychological victory. American audiences came to realize that the war perhaps could not be won.

When Richard Nixon assumed office in 1969, he gave top priority to extricating the deeply divided United States from Vietnam while still finding a way to win the war. He embarked on the policy of Vietnamization, which entailed removing American forces and replacing them with Vietnamese ones. At the same time, Americans launched ferocious air attacks on North Vietnam. "Let's blow the hell out of them," Nixon ordered. Between 1968 and 1972, American troop strength dropped from 543,000 to 39,000. Yet as the transition occurred, the South Vietnamese steadily lost ground to the Viet Cong.

War protests multiplied in 1969 and 1970. In November 1969, as a massive protest demonstration took place in Washington, D.C., stories surfaced about a massacre of civilians in Vietnam the year before. Journalist Seymour M. Hersh had heard rumors about an episode at My Lai and had begun to piece together an account of what had occurred. His efforts provided the American people with horrifying evidence of the war's brutality.

At My Lai, a small village in South Vietnam, American soldiers rounded up the villagers—women, children, and old men—and gunned them down in cold blood. Private Paul Meadlo recalled:

We huddled them up. We made them squat down.... I poured about four clips into the group.... The mothers was hugging their children. . . . Well, we kept right on firing. They was waving their arms and begging. . . . I still dream about it. About the women and children in my sleep. Some days . . . some nights, I can't even sleep.

While the My Lai incident led many to wonder about American conduct of the war, incidents on several college campuses made them question the use of troops at home. Nixon's policy prompted the episodes. Still looking for victory in Vietnam, Nixon announced that American and Vietnamese troops were invading Cambodia to clear out the Communist enclaves there. The United States, he said, would not stand by as "a pitiful helpless giant" when there were actions it could take to stem the Communist advance.

Nixon's invasion of Cambodia brought renewed demonstrations on college campuses, some with tragic results. At Kent State, in Ohio, disgruntled students gathered downtown but were dispersed by local authorities. The next evening, groups of students collected around the ROTC building, began throwing firecrackers and rocks at the structure, and then set it on fire and watched it burn to the ground.

The governor of Ohio ordered the National Guard to the university. In the ensuing confrontation, the soldiers fired at the students. When the firing ceased, four students lay dead, nine wounded. Two of the dead had been demonstrators, who were more than 250 feet away when shot. The other two were innocent bystanders, almost 400 feet from the troops.

Students around the country, as well as other Americans, were outraged by the attack. Many were equally disturbed about a similar attack at Jackson State University in Mississippi. Policemen and highway patrolmen poured automatic weapon fire into a women's dormitory without warning. When the shooting stopped, two people were dead, more wounded. The dead there, however, were black students at a black institution, and white America paid less attention to that attack.

In 1971, the Vietnam War made major

headlines once more when the New York *Times* began publishing a secret Department of Defense account of American involvement in the war. The so-called Pentagon Papers, leaked by Daniel Ellsberg, a defense analyst, gave Americans a firsthand look at the fabrications and faulty assumptions that had guided the steady expansion of the struggle. Even though the study stopped with the Johnson years, the Nixon administration was furious and tried, without success, to halt publication of the series.

Vietnam remained a political football as Nixon ran for reelection in 1972. Negotiations aimed at a settlement were under way, and just days before the election, Henry Kissinger announced, "Peace is at hand." A cease-fire was finally signed in 1973, and American troops were brought home.

After Nixon left office, Gerald Ford called for more aid for the South Vietnamese, but Congress refused, leaving the crumbling government of South Vietnam to fend for itself. As the North Vietnamese consolidated their hold over the entire country, Republicans hailed Kissinger for having freed the United States from the Southeast Asian quagmire. *The New Republic* wryly observed that Kissinger brought peace to Vietnam in the same way Napoleon brought peace to Europe: by losing.

The conflict was finally over, but the costs were immense. In the longest war in its history, the United States lost almost 58,000 men, with far more wounded or maimed. Blacks and Chicanos suffered more than whites since they were disproportionately represented in combat units. The nation spent over $150 billion on the unsuccessful war. Domestic reform had slowed, then stopped. American society had been deeply divided. Only time would heal the wounds.

Détente

If the Republicans' Vietnam policy was a questionable success, accomplishments were impressive in other areas. Nixon, the Red-baiter of the past, was able to deal successfully with the Com-

When Ohio National Guardsmen fired on a crowd of antiwar demonstrators and killed four students, even prowar Americans were shocked. This photograph shows the grief and outrage of others who survived the savage shooting of innocent bystanders.

munist powers, reversing the direction of American policy since World War II. He relied heavily on Kissinger, who understood the tensions within the Communist realm, and exploited them to restore better American relations with both the Soviet Union and China.

Nixon's most dramatic step was opening formal relations with the People's Republic of China. In the two decades since Mao Zedong's victory on the Chinese mainland in 1949, the United States had never recognized the PRC, regarding Jiang Jieshi's rump government on Taiwan as the rightful government of the Chinese people. In 1971, with an eye on the forthcoming political campaign, the administration began softening its rigid stand. Nixon believed that he could open a dialogue with the Chinese Communists without political harm, for he had long been a vocal critic of communism and could hardly be accused of being "soft" on it. He knew

also that the coverage of a dramatic trip could give him a boost in the press.

Nixon went to China in February 1972. He met with Chinese leaders Mao Zedong and Zhou Enlai (Chou En-lai), talked about international problems, exchanged toasts, and saw some of the major sights. Though formal relations were not yet restored, détente between the two countries had begun.

Seeking to play one Communist state against the other, Nixon also visited Russia, where he was likewise warmly welcomed. After several cordial meetings, the president and Soviet premier Leonid Brezhnev agreed to limit missile stockpiles, work together in space, and ease long-standing restrictions on trade. Businessmen applauded the new approach, and most Americans approved of détente.

When Gerald Ford assumed office, he followed the policies begun under Nixon. Kissinger

Nixon shifted the course of Chinese-American relations by his dramatic visit to the People's Republic. He met Chinese officials for the first time, visited the Great Wall and other sites, and then reported back enthusiastically to the American people.

remained secretary of state and continued to play an influential role in foreign affairs. Ford continued the Strategic Arms Limitation Talks (SALT) that provided hope for eventual nuclear disarmament. He also accepted the Helsinki Accords, which defined European security arrangements and underscored basic human rights. He pursued friendly relations with China and elsewhere maintained the spirit of détente, even while rejecting the term.

Human Rights Diplomacy

Jimmy Carter enjoyed a number of notable successes in conducting a more modest foreign policy, though he had had little diplomatic experience when he took office. Deeply religious, he sought to make American policy adhere to the Christian standards that were part of his personal life.

Carter's major achievement involved the Middle East, where Israel and the Arab nations had fought a series of bitter wars. His personal diplomacy helped bring about a peace treaty, signed in March 1979, between Israel and Egypt. After 30 years of hostilities, the two nations were at peace.

At home, Carter fought for Senate acceptance of two treaties turning the Panama Canal over to Panama by the year 2000. Resentment had grown in Panama over the presence of a foreign power. In the agreements, accepted by the margin of a single vote, the United States retained certain rights in the event of crisis but otherwise yielded to Panamanian demands.

In Asia, Carter successfully followed Nixon's initiatives by extending diplomatic recognition to the People's Republic of China. American wheat farmers and businessmen eyed the Chinese market of nearly a billion people with enthusiasm, and American diplomats were eager to keep China and Russia at odds.

With the Soviet Union, Carter was less successful. His commitment to human rights caused him to lend verbal support to Russian dissidents, which antagonized the Soviets. One prickly issue was arms control. Negotiations for a more comprehensive strategic arms limitation treaty than the agreement of 1972 were protracted, but the SALT II agreement was reached in June 1979. The Soviet invasion of Afghanistan in December 1979, however, complicated ratification. The Russians considered internal agitation there a threat to their security and invaded the country. After a year and a half of watching the bloody involvement, Carter responded by calling the Soviet move the most serious blow to world peace since World War II. He postponed presenting SALT II to the Senate and imposed an American boycott of the 1980 Olympic Games in Moscow. Détente was effectively dead.

Carter also stumbled in his effort to defuse a major crisis with Iran. Americans had long supported the shah of Iran. Overlooking the corruption and abuse in his regime, they viewed him as a reliable supplier of oil and defender of stability in the Persian Gulf region. In January 1979, revolutionary groups drove the shah from power. In his place sat the Ayatollah Ruholla Khomeini, an Islamic priest who returned from exile in Paris to lead a new fundamentalist Islamic regime.

When Carter admitted the shah to the United States for medical treatment in October 1979, angry Iranian students seized the American embassy in Tehran and held 53 Americans hostage. The prisoners were blindfolded, bound, and beaten. Some suffered solitary confinement and endured mock executions. In the United States, their ordeal became a national cause. Unwilling to return the shah or to apologize for past American support for his now discredited regime, Carter broke diplomatic relations and froze Iranian assets, but his actions brought no results and his popularity plummeted. The Iranians finally agreed to free the hostages in early 1981, but not until the very day Carter left office did the prisoners end their 444-day ordeal. Congressional hearings in 1987 would subsequently reveal that Reagan administration officials had obtained the release of the hostages by secretly and illegally selling arms to Iran (see the discussion of the Iran-Contra affair in Chapter 30).

CONCLUSION

POLITICAL READJUSTMENT

America's political role, at home and abroad, changed significantly in the decade and a half after Dwight Eisenhower left the presidency. First Democrats, then Republicans accepted the need for large-scale government intervention to meet the social and economic problems that accompanied the modern industrial age. They endorsed a process under way since the New Deal and strengthened the nation's commitment to a capitalist welfare state. They committed the nation to a similar role in maintaining an anticommunist stability in the continuing Cold War.

Most Americans, like Ron Kovic, welcomed the nation's approach. They embraced the message of John Kennedy and the New Frontier and endorsed the programs that resulted. But over time, like Kovic, they began to question the tenets of liberalism as the economy faltered and the country became mired in Vietnam. Slowly, the optimism that had characterized the 1960s evaporated. A more conservative approach to domestic and foreign problems emerged.

Recommended Reading

For a good introduction to the basic foreign and domestic policies of the 1960s, see Jim F. Health, *Decade of Disillusionment: The Kennedy-Johnson Years* (1975). Herbert S. Parmet, *JFK: The Presidency of John F. Kennedy* (1983), is a comprehensive account of Kennedy's White House years.

Doris Kearns, *Lyndon Johnson and the American Dream* (1976), is a readable analysis of the Johnson presidency by a political scientist and former White House fellow. Robert A. Caro, *The Years of Lyndon Johnson: The Path to Power* (1983), describes LBJ's ascent. In *The Promise of Greatness* (1976), Sar A. Levitan and Robert Taggart argue that Great Society goals were realistic and that the programs enacted made a difference. Lyndon Johnson, *The Vantage Point: Perspectives of the Presidency* (1971), is LBJ's own autobiographical overview of his presidential years. An excellent appraisal of the Johnson years is Robert Dallek's *Lone Star Rising: Lyndon Johnson and His Times* (1990). For an excellent analysis of the 1960s, see Allen J. Matusow, *The Unraveling of America: A History of Liberalism in the 1960s* (1984).

On the Nixon presidency, Rowland Evans, Jr., and Robert D. Novak, *Nixon in the White House* (1972), offers the best assessment of public policy and politics in the first term. Richard Nixon, *RN: The Memoirs of Richard Nixon* (1978), is his own account of his life and achievements. Stephen Ambrose, *Nixon: The Education of a Politician, 1913–1962* (1987), is a good survey of Nixon's prepresidential period.

For the Watergate affair, J. Anthony Lukas, *Nightmare: The Underside of the Nixon Years* (1976), provides the background necessary to understand the scandal and places that crisis in the proper perspective.

On Gerald Ford, Richard Reeves, *A Ford, Not a Lincoln* (1975), is a penetrating account of how Ford functioned as president.

A great deal has been written about the Vietnam War. George C. Herring, *America's Longest War: The United States and Vietnam, 1950–1975* (1979), is the best brief account of American policy in that conflict, particularly in the 1960s and thereafter. Al Santoli, *Everything We Had: An Oral History of the Vietnam War by Thirty-three American Soldiers Who Fought It* (1981), is a collection of first-person narratives about the struggle.

Time Line

1960	John F. Kennedy elected president	1969	SALT talks begin
1961	Bay of Pigs invasion fails	1970	U.S. invasion of Cambodia
	Khrushchev and Kennedy meet in Vienna		Kent State and Jackson State shootings
	Berlin Wall constructed	1971	New York *Times* publishes Pentagon Papers
1962	JFK confronts steel companies		
	Cuban missile crisis	1972	Nixon visits China and the Soviet Union
1963	Kennedy assassinated; Lyndon B. Johnson becomes president		Watergate break-in
	Buddhist demonstrations in Vietnam		Nixon reelected
	President Diem assassinated in Vietnam		SALT I treaty on nuclear arms
1964	Gulf of Tonkin Resolution	1973	Vietnam cease-fire agreement
	Economic Opportunity Act initiates War on Poverty		Arab oil embargo
	Johnson reelected		Watergate hearings in Congress
1965	Vietnam conflict escalates		Spiro Agnew resigns as vice president
	Marines sent to Dominican Republic	1974	OPEC price increases
	Teach-ins begin		Inflation hits 11 percent
	Department of Housing and Urban Development established		Unemployment reaches 7.1 percent
	Elementary and Secondary Education Act		Nixon resigns; Gerald R. Ford becomes president
1966	National Traffic and Motor Vehicle Safety Act		Ford pardons Nixon
	Department of Transportation established	1975	South Vietnam falls to the Communists
1967	Antiwar demonstrations		Unemployment reaches 12 percent
1968	Robert F. Kennedy assassinated	1976	Jimmy Carter elected president
	Antiwar demonstrations increase	1977	Carter energy program, human rights policy
	Tet offensive in Vietnam		Panama Canal treaties
	Police and protesters clash at Democratic national convention	1978	Israeli-Egyptian peace accords at Camp David
	Richard Nixon elected president	1979	Russians invade Afghanistan
	My Lai massacre		Iranian revolution overthrows shah
1969	Moratorium against the Vietnam War		SALT II agreement on nuclear arms
		1979–1981	Iranian hostage crisis

chapter 29

....

The Struggle for
Social Reform

Ann Clarke—as she chooses to call herself now—always wanted to go to college. But girls from Italian families rarely did when she was growing up. Her mother, a Sicilian immigrant and widow, asked her brother for advice: "Should Antonina go to college?" "What's the point?" he replied. "She's just going to get married." Responsive to family needs, Ann finished the high school commercial course in three years and became a legal secretary on Wall Street. She was proud of her ability to bring money home to her family.

When World War II began, Ann wanted to join the WACS. "Better you should be a prostitute," her mother said. Ann went off to California instead, where she worked at resorts. When she left California, she vowed to return to that land of freedom and opportunity.

After the war, Ann married Gerard Clarke, a college man with an English background. Her children would grow up accepted with Anglo-Saxon names. Over the next 15 years, Ann devoted herself to her family. By the early 1960s, her three children were all in school, and she enrolled at Pasadena City College. It was not easy. Family still came first. A simple problem was finding time to study. When doing dishes or cleaning house, she memorized lists of dates, historical events, and other material for school.

Her conflict over her studies was intensified by her position as one of the first older women to go back to college. "Sometimes I felt like I wanted to hide in the woodwork," she admitted. Often her teachers were younger than she was. It took four years to complete the two-year program. But she was not yet done. She wanted a bachelor's degree. Back she went, this time to California State College at Los Angeles.

As the years passed and the credits piled up, Ann became an honors student and graduated at the top of her class. Then she returned to school for a teaching credential. Receiving her certificate at age 50, she faced the irony of social change. Once denied opportunities, Italians had been assimilated into American society. Now she was just another Anglo in Los Angeles, caught in a changing immigration wave; the city now sought Hispanics and other minorities to teach in the schools. Jobs in education were scarce, and she was close to "retirement age," so she became a substitute in Mexican-American areas for the next ten years, specializing in bilingual education.

Meanwhile, Ann was troubled by the Vietnam War and by the social adjustments that resulted. Her son grew long hair and a beard and attended protest rallies. Her daughter came home from college in boots and a leather miniskirt designed to shock. Ann accepted her children's changes as relatively superficial, confident in their fundamental values; "they were good kids." She trusted them, even as she worried.

Ann Clarke's experience paralleled that of millions of women in the 1960s and 1970s. Caught up for years in traditional patterns of family life, these women began to recognize their need for something more. Like blacks, Hispanics, Native Americans, and other groups, American women struggled to transform the conditions of their lives and the rights they enjoyed within American society.

This chapter describes the reform impulse that accompanied the effort to define the government's responsibility for economic and social stability described in Chapter 28. Like earlier reform efforts, this modern struggle attempted to fulfill the promise of the American past and to provide liberty and equality in racial, gender, and social relations. Its voices, however, came more from those on the mudsills of society than from middle-class activists.

THE BLACK STRUGGLE FOR EQUALITY

The quest for equality by black Americans sparked all other struggles for civil rights. Stemming from an effort dating back to the Civil War and Reconstruction, the movement had gained momentum in the mid-twentieth century (see Chapter 27 for the gains of the 1950s), but change was slow.

Confrontation

A spectrum of organizations, some old, some new, spearheaded the challenge to segregation in the courts and organized nonviolent direct action that relied on grass-roots support. The National Association for the Advancement of Colored People (NAACP), founded in 1910, remained committed to overturning the legal bases for segregation. Other activist organizations included the Congress of Racial Equality (CORE), established in 1942; the Southern Christian Leadership Conference (SCLC), an organization of southern black clergy, founded in 1957 by Martin Luther King, Jr., and others after their victory at Montgomery; and the Student Non-Violent Coordinating Committee (SNCC, pronounced "snick"), formed in 1960. Recruiting young Americans who had not been involved in the civil rights struggle, SNCC would become far more militant and confrontational than the older, gradualist organizations.

The importance of grass-roots efforts for reform was evident as early as 1960 when black college students sat down at a segregated Woolworth's lunch counter and deliberately violated

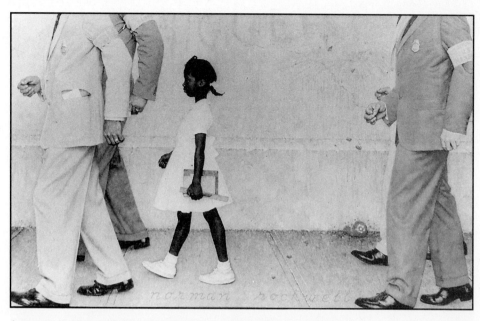

A painting by Norman Rockwell that illustrates the perception by many Americans in the North of the inequity and frustration of the initial efforts at school integration in the South. In many cases, black students were forced to run a gauntlet of white protesters under the protection of federal officials. The strict segregation that had existed in the South for so long was often highly resistant to change.

southern segregation laws by refusing to leave. The sit-ins captured media attention, and soon thousands of blacks were involved in the campaign. The following year, the sit-ins gave rise to freedom rides, aimed at testing southern transportation facilities, recently desegregated by a Supreme Court decision. Organized initially by CORE and aided by SNCC, the program sent groups of blacks and whites together on buses heading south and stopping at terminals along the way. The riders, peaceful themselves, anticipated confrontations that would publicize their cause and generate political support.

In North and South alike, consciousness of the need to combat racial discrimination grew. The civil rights movement became the most powerful moral campaign since the abolitionist crusade before the Civil War. Black and white participants in the movement came from every direction.

Anne Moody, who grew up in a small town in Mississippi, personified the awakening of black consciousness. Through her own efforts, Moody became the first of her family to go to college. Once there, she found her own place in the civil rights movement. At Tougaloo College, near Jackson, Mississippi, she joined the NAACP and also became involved in the activities of SNCC and CORE. Slowly, she noted, "I could feel myself beginning to change. For the first time I began to think something would be done about whites killing, beating, and misusing Negroes. I knew I was going to be a part of whatever happened." She participated in sit-ins where she was thrashed and jailed for her role, but she remained deeply involved.

In violation of southern law, black college students refused to leave a lunch counter, launching a new campaign in the struggle. Here the students wait patiently for service, or forcible eviction, as a way of dramatizing their determination to end segregation.

Many whites also joined the struggle in the South. Mimi Feingold, a white student at Swarthmore College in Pennsylvania, helped picket Woolworth's in Chester, Pennsylvania, and sought to unionize Swarthmore's black dining hall workers. In 1961, after her sophomore year, she headed south to join the freedom rides sponsored by CORE.

In 1962, the civil rights movement accelerated. James Meredith, a black air force veteran and student at Jackson State College, sought to enter the all-white University of Mississippi, only to be rejected on racial grounds. Suing to gain admission, he carried his case to the Supreme Court, where Justice Hugo Black affirmed his claim. But then Governor Ross Barnett, an adamant racist, asserted that Meredith would not be admitted, whatever the Court deci-

sion. With such positions staked out, a major riot began. Tear gas covered the university grounds, and by the end of the riot, two men lay dead and hundreds hurt.

An even more violent confrontation began in April 1963, in Birmingham, Alabama, where local black leaders encouraged Martin Luther King, Jr., to launch another attack on southern segregation. Forty percent black, the city was rigidly segregated along racial and class lines. King later explained, "We believed that while a campaign in Birmingham would surely be the toughest fight of our civil rights careers, it could, if successful, break the back of segregation all over the nation."

Though the demonstrations were nonviolent, the responses were not. City officials declared that protest marches violated city regulations against parading without a license and, over a five-week period, they arrested 2,200 blacks, some of them schoolchildren. Police Commissioner Eugene "Bull" Connor used high-pressure fire hoses, electric cattle prods, and trained police dogs to force the protesters back. As the media recorded the events, Americans watching television and reading newspapers were horrified. The images of violence in Birmingham created mass sympathy for black Americans' civil rights struggle.

Kennedy's Response

John Kennedy claimed to be sickened by the pictures from Birmingham but insisted that he could do nothing, even though he had sought and won black support in 1960. The narrowness of his election victory made him reluctant to press white southerners on civil rights when he needed their votes on other issues. Kennedy failed to sponsor any civil rights legislation. Nor did he fulfill his campaign promise to end housing discrimination by presidential order, despite gifts of numerous bottles of ink. Not until November 1962, after the midterm elections, did he take a modest action—an executive order ending segregation in federally financed housing.

Events finally forced Kennedy to take bolder actions. In the James Meredith confrontation, the president, like his predecessor in the Little Rock crisis, had to send federal troops to restore control and to guarantee Meredith's right to attend. The administration also forced the desegregation of the University of Alabama and helped arrange a compromise providing for desegregation of Birmingham's municipal facilities, implementation of more equitable hiring practices, and formation of a biracial committee. And when white bombings aimed at eliminating black leaders in Birmingham caused thousands of blacks to abandon nonviolence and rampage through the streets, Kennedy readied federal troops to intervene.

The events in Birmingham helped to push Kennedy to honor the commitments he had made during the campaign. In a nationally televised address, he called the quest for equal rights "a moral issue" and asked, ". . . are we to say to the world, and much more importantly, to each other that this is a land of the free except for the Negroes. . . ?" Hours after he spoke, assassins killed Medgar Evers, a black NAACP official, in his own driveway in Jackson, Mississippi.

Kennedy sent Congress a new civil rights bill, which prohibited segregation in public places, banned discrimination wherever federal money was involved, and advanced the process of school integration. Polls showed that 63 percent of the nation supported his stand.

To lobby for passage of that measure, civil rights leaders, pressed from below by black activists, arranged a massive march on Washington in August 1963. More than 200,000 people gathered from across the country and demonstrated enthusiastically. Celebrities were present: Ralph Bunche, James Baldwin, Sammy Davis, Jr., Harry Belafonte, Jackie Robinson, Lena Horne. The folk music artists of the early 1960s were there as well. Joan Baez, Bob Dylan, and Peter, Paul, and Mary sang songs associated with the movement such as "Blowin' in the Wind" and "We Shall Overcome."

But the high point of the day was the address by Martin Luther King, Jr., the nation's preeminent spokesman for civil rights and proponent of nonviolent protest. King proclaimed his faith in the decency of his fellow citizens and in their ability to extend the promises of the Constitution and the Declaration of Independence to every American. With all the power of a southern preacher, he implored his audience to share his faith.

"I have a dream," King declared, "that one day this nation will rise up and live out the true meaning of its creed: 'We hold these truths to be self-evident, that all men are created equal.' I have a dream that one day on the red hills of Georgia, the sons of former slaves and the sons

of former slave-owners will be able to sit together at the table of brotherhood." It was a fer-
vent appeal, and one to which the crowd responded. Each time King used the refrain "I
have a dream," thousands of blacks and whites
roared together.

Despite the power of the rhetoric, and despite large Democratic majorities, strong white
southern resistance to the cause of civil rights remained, and as of November 1963, Kennedy's
bill was still bottled up in committee.

Civil Rights Under Johnson

Lyndon Johnson was more successful than
Kennedy in advancing civil rights. His first legislative priority on assuming office was civil
rights reform, although his earlier record on the
issue was mixed. A southerner from Texas, he
broke with the South when he guided the Civil
Rights Act of 1957 through Congress.

In 1963, Johnson revived Kennedy's civil
rights proposal, which had been sidetracked in
Congress. Seizing the opportunity provided by
Kennedy's assassination, Johnson told Congress,
"No memorial oration or eulogy could more
eloquently honor President Kennedy's memory
than the earliest possible passage of the civil
rights bill." He pushed the bill through Congress, heading off a Senate filibuster by persuading his old colleague, minority leader Everett
Dirksen, to work for cloture—a two-thirds vote
to cut off debate. In June 1964, the Senate for
the first time imposed cloture to advance a civil
rights measure, and passage soon followed. "No
army can withstand the strength of an idea
whose time has come," Dirksen commented.

The Civil Rights Act of 1964 outlawed
racial discrimination in all public accommoda-
tions and authorized the Justice Department to
act with greater authority in school and voting
matters. In addition, an equal-opportunity provision prohibited discriminatory hiring on
grounds of race, gender, religion, or national origin in firms with more than 25 employees. The

legislation was one of the great achievements of
the 1960s.

Johnson realized that the Civil Rights Act of
1964 was only a starting point, since widespread
discrimination still existed in American society.
Despite the voting rights measures of 1957 and
1960, blacks still found it difficult to vote in
large areas of the South. Freedom Summer,
sponsored by SNCC and other civil rights
groups in Mississippi in 1964, focused attention
on the problem by sending black and white students south to work for black rights. Early in the
summer, two whites, Michael Schwerner and
Andrew Goodman, and one black, James
Chaney, were murdered. By the end of the summer, 80 workers had been beaten, 1,000 arrests
had been made, and 37 churches had been
bombed.

Early in 1965, Alabama police clubbed and
tear-gassed demonstrators in an aborted march
from Selma to the state capital at Montgomery.
Events in Selma forced President Johnson first to
send the National Guard to protect another
march to Montgomery, led by Martin Luther
King, Jr., and second to ask Congress for a voting bill that would close the loopholes of the previous two acts.

The Voting Rights Act of 1965, perhaps the
most important law of the decade, singled out
the South for its restrictive practices and authorized the U.S. attorney general to appoint federal
examiners to register voters where local officials
were obstructing the registration of blacks. In
the year after passage of the act, 400,000 blacks
registered to vote in the Deep South; by 1968,
the number reached a million.

BLACK POWER CHALLENGES
LIBERAL REFORM

Despite passage of the Civil Rights Act of 1964
and the Voting Rights Act of 1965, racial discrimination remained in both North and South.
De facto segregated schools, wretched housing,

and inadequate job opportunities were continuing problems. As civil rights moved north, dramatic divisions within the movement emerged.

One episode that contributed to a black sense of betrayal by white liberals occurred at the Democratic national convention of 1964 in Atlantic City. SNCC, active in the Freedom Summer project in Mississippi, had founded the Freedom Democratic Party as an alternative to the all-white delegation that was to represent the state. Before the credentials committee, black activist Fannie Lou Hamer testified that she had been beaten, jailed, and denied the right to vote. Yet the committee's final compromise, pressed by President Johnson, who worried about losing southern support in the coming election, was that the white delegation would still be seated, with two members of the protest organization offered seats at large. That response hardly satisfied those who had risked their lives and families to try to vote in Mississippi. As civil rights leader James Forman observed, "Atlantic City was a powerful lesson, not only for the black people from Mississippi, but for all of SNCC. . . . No longer was there any hope . . . that the federal government would change the situation in the Deep South." SNCC, once a religious, integrated organization, began to change into an all-black cadre that could mobilize poor blacks for militant action. "Liberation" was replacing civil rights as a goal.

Increasingly, angry blacks argued that the nation must no longer withhold the rights pledged in its founding credo. James Baldwin, a prominent black author, wrote that unless change came soon, the worst could be expected: "If we do not now dare everything, the fulfillment of that prophecy, recreated from the Bible in song by a slave, is upon us: God gave Noah the rainbow sign, No more water, the fire next time!"

Even more responsible for focusing aggressive black sentiment was Malcolm X. Born Malcolm Little and raised in ghettos from Detroit to New York, he hustled numbers and prostitutes in the big cities. Later, in prison, he became a convert to the Nation of Islam and a disciple of black leader Elijah Muhammad. He began to preach that the white man was responsible for the black man's condition and that blacks had to help themselves.

Malcolm was impatient with the moderate civil rights movement and its nonviolent sit-ins. Espousing black separatism and black nationalism for most of his public career, he argued for black control of black communities, preached an international perspective embracing African peoples in diaspora, and appealed to blacks to fight racism "by any means necessary."

Malcolm X became the most dynamic spokesman for poor blacks since Marcus Garvey in the 1920s. Though he was assassinated by a black antagonist in 1965, his perspective helped shape the ongoing struggle against racism.

One man influenced by Malcolm's message was Stokely Carmichael. Born in Trinidad, he came to the United States at the age of 11 and grew up with an interest in political affairs and black protest. He participated in pickets and demonstrations and was beaten and jailed. Frustrated with the strategy of civil disobedience, he urged field-workers to carry weapons for self-defense. It was time for blacks to cease depending on whites, he argued, and to make SNCC into a black organization. His election as head of SNCC in 1966 reflected the organization's growing radicalism.

The split in the black movement became clear in June 1966 when Carmichael's followers challenged those of Martin Luther King, Jr., during a march in Mississippi. King still adhered to nonviolence and interracial cooperation. Carmichael, just out of jail, jumped onto a flatbed truck to address the group. "This is the twenty-seventh time I have been arrested—and I ain't going to jail no more!" he shouted. "The only way we gonna stop them white men from whippin' us is to take over. We been saying freedom for six years and we ain't got nothing. What we gonna start saying now is Black

Power!" Carmichael had the audience in his hand as he repeated, "We ... want ... Black ... Power!"

Meanwhile, other blacks proposed more drastic action. The Black Panthers formed a militant organization that vowed to eradicate not only racial discrimination but capitalism as well. H. Rap Brown, who followed Carmichael as head of SNCC, became known for his statement that "violence is as American as cherry pie."

Violence often accompanied the more militant calls for reform. Riots erupted in Rochester, New York City, and several New Jersey cities in 1964. In 1965, in the Watts neighborhood of Los Angeles, a massive uprising lasting five days left 34 dead, more than 1,000 injured, and hundreds of structures burned to the ground. Violence broke out again in other cities in 1966 and 1967. When Martin Luther King, Jr., fell before a white assassin's bullet in April 1968, angry blacks reacted by demonstrating once more in cities around the country.

"SOUTHERN STRATEGY" AND SHOWDOWN ON CIVIL RIGHTS

Richard Nixon, elected president in 1968, was less sympathetic to the cause of civil rights than his predecessors. In 1968, the Republicans had won only 12 percent of the black vote, leading Nixon to conclude that any effort to woo the black electorate would endanger his attempt to obtain white southern support.

From the start, the Nixon administration sought to scale back the federal commitment to civil rights. It moved, at the start of Nixon's first term, to reduce appropriations for fair-housing enforcement. Then the Department of Justice tried to block an extension of the Voting Rights Act of 1965. Although Congress approved the extension, the administration's position on racial issues was clear. When South Carolina senator Strom Thurmond and others tried to suspend federal school desegregation guidelines, the Jus-

tice Department lent support by urging a delay in meeting desegregation deadlines in 33 of Mississippi's school districts. When a unanimous Supreme Court rebuffed the effort, Nixon disagreed publicly with the decision.

Nixon also faced the growing controversy over busing as a means of desegregation, a highly charged issue in the 1970s. Transporting students from one area to another to attend school was nothing new. By 1970, over 18 million students, almost 40 percent of those in the United States, rode buses to school. Yet when busing became tangled with the question of integration, it inflamed passions.

In the South, before the Supreme Court endorsed integration, busing had long been used to maintain segregated schools. Some black students in Selma, Alabama, for example, traveled 50 miles by bus to an entirely black trade school in Montgomery, even though a similar school for whites stood nearby. Now, however, busing had become a means of breaking down racial barriers.

The issue came to a head in North Carolina, in the Charlotte-Mecklenburg school system. A desegregation plan involving voluntary transfer was in effect, but many blacks still attended largely segregated schools. A federal judge ruled that the district was not in compliance with the latest Supreme Court decisions, and in 1971, the Supreme Court ruled that district courts had broad authority to order the desegregation of school systems—by busing, if necessary.

Earlier, Nixon had opposed such busing. Now he proposed a moratorium or even a restriction on busing and went on television to denounce it. Although Congress did not accede to his request, southerners knew where the president stood.

As the busing mandate spread to the North, resistance spilled out of the South. In many of the nation's largest northern cities, schools were as rigidly segregated as in the South, largely because of residential patterns. This segregation was called *de facto* to differentiate it from the *de jure* or legal segregation that had existed in the South. Mississippi senator John C. Stennis, a bitter foe of busing, hoped to stir up the North by making it subject to the same standards as the South. His proposal, adopted in the Senate, required that the government enforce federal desegregation guidelines uniformly throughout the nation or not use them at all. Court decisions subsequently ordered many northern cities to desegregate their schools.

In Boston, the effort to integrate proved rockier than anywhere else in the North. In 1973, 85 percent of the blacks in Boston attended schools that had a black majority. More than half the black students were in schools that were 90 percent black. In June 1974, a federal judge ordered that busing begin. The first phase, involving 17,000 pupils, was to start in the fall of that year.

For many younger students, being bused to different elementary schools went smoothly. Reassigned high school students were less fortunate. A white boycott at South Boston High cut attendance from the anticipated 1,500 to less than 100 on the first day. Buses bringing in black students were stoned, and some children were injured. White working-class South Bostonians felt that they were being asked to carry the burden of middle-class liberals' racial views. Similar resentments and anger triggered racial episodes elsewhere. In many cases, white families either enrolled their children in private schools or fled the city altogether.

Nixon hoped to slow down the civil rights movement, and to a degree he did. His successor, Gerald Ford, never came out squarely against civil rights, but his lukewarm approach demonstrated a weakening of the federal commitment.

The situation was less inflamed at the college level, but the same pattern held. Blacks made significant progress until the Republican administrations in the late 1960s and 1970s slowed the movement for civil rights. Integration at the post-secondary level came easier as federal affirmative-action guidelines brought more blacks into colleges and universities. In 1950, only 83,000 black students were enrolled in institutions of higher education. A decade later, more than one million were working for college degrees. Black enrollment in colleges reached 9.3 percent of the college population in 1976, dropped back to 9.1 percent in 1980, just what it had been in 1973, then rose to 10.2 percent in 1990.

As blacks struggled on the educational and occupational fronts, some whites protested that gains came at their expense and amounted to "reverse discrimination." In 1973 and 1974, for example, Allan Bakke, a white, applied to the medical school at the University of California at Davis. Twice rejected, he sued on the grounds that a racial quota reserving 16 of 100 places for minority-group applicants was a form of reverse discrimination that violated the Civil Rights Act of 1964. In 1978, the Supreme Court ordered Bakke's admission to the medical school but also upheld the consideration of race in admissions policies, even while arguing that quotas could no longer be imposed.

Jimmy Carter, president when the *Bakke* decision was handed down, tried to adopt a more active approach than his Republican predecessors. He brought a number of qualified blacks into his administration. Some, like Andrew Young, his ambassador to the United Nations, were highly visible. But his lack of support for increased social programs for the poor hurt the majority of black citizens and strained their loyalty to the Democratic Party.

By the early 1980s, for the first time since Reconstruction, black voting rights had brought to political office a host of new leaders. Black political candidates won mayoral elections in the 1980s in major cities, including Detroit, Los Angeles, Cleveland, Chicago, and New York. In 1989, Douglas Wilder of Virginia became the first African-American ever to be elected governor of any state. Equally impressive were the presidential campaigns of the Reverend Jesse Jackson in 1984 and 1988. Though he did not win the nomination, his campaign indicated the important African-American presence in politics.

Yet cutting against the grain of those strides forward in electoral politics were backward steps in the struggle for social and economic equality.

After steady progress toward integration in the 1970s and 1980s, residential and school re-segregation began to occur. Racial separation in urban neighborhoods was part of the problem. More important was the erosion of the commitment to civil rights and the economic policies (discussed in Chapter 30) pursued during the Republican administrations of the 1980s and early 1990s. Ronald Reagan opposed busing to achieve racial balance, and his attorney general worked to dismantle affirmative-action programs. Initially reluctant to support extension of the enormously successful Voting Rights Act of 1965, Reagan relented only under severe criticism from Republicans as well as Democrats. He directed the Internal Revenue Service to cease banning tax exemptions for private schools that discriminated against blacks, only to see that move overturned by the Supreme Court in 1983. He also weakened the Civil Rights Commission by appointing members who did not support its main goals.

The courts similarly weakened the commitment to equal rights. As a result of Reagan's judicial appointments, and those of his successor, George Bush, federal courts stopped pushing for school integration. The *Freeman* v. *Pitts* decision in 1992 granted a suburban Atlanta school board relief from a desegregation order on the grounds that it was not possible to counteract massive demographic shifts. This was the second time in two years that the Court granted a local board such relief.

The civil rights movement underscored the democratic values on which the nation was based, but the gap between rhetoric and reality remained. Given a wavering presidential commitment to reform in the 1970s and 1980s, only

pressures from reform groups kept the faltering civil rights movement alive.

THE WOMEN'S MOVEMENT

The black struggle for equality in the 1960s and 1970s was accompanied by a women's movement that grew out of the agitation for civil rights but soon developed a life of its own. That struggle, like the struggles by Hispanics and Native Americans, employed the confrontational approach and the vocabulary of the civil rights movement to create sufficient pressure for change. Using proven strategies, it sometimes proceeded even faster than the black effort.

Attacking the Feminine Mystique

Many white women joined the civil rights movement only to find that they were second-class citizens. Men, black and white, held the policy positions and relegated women to menial chores when not actually involved in demonstrations or voter drives. Many women also felt sexually exploited by male leaders. Stokely Carmichael's comment only underscored their point. "The only position for women in SNCC," he said, "is prone."

Although the civil rights movement helped spark the women's movement, broad social changes provided the preconditions. During the 1950s and 1960s, increasing numbers of married women entered the labor force, and half of all women worked. Yet, in 1963, the average working woman earned only 63 percent of what a man could expect; in 1973, only 57 percent. Just as important, many more young women were attending college. By 1970, women earned 41 percent of all B. A.'s awarded, in comparison to only 25 percent in 1950. These educated young women held high hopes for themselves.

When women tried to rely on Title 7 of the 1964 Civil Rights bill, which prohibited discrim-

Women in the Work Force, 1920-1990

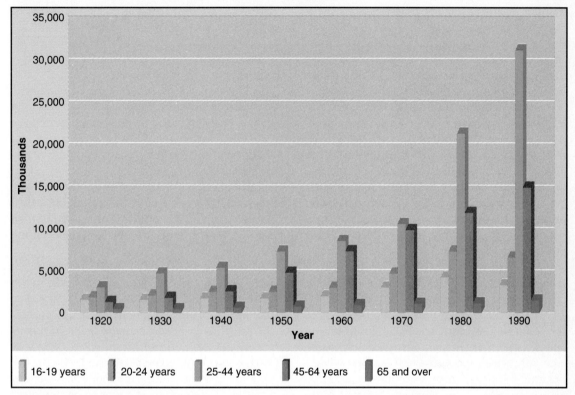

This graph shows the dramatic increase in the number of women in the work force in the 1970s, 1980s, and 1990s. Note particularly the rise in the number of working women 25–44 years old. *Source: U.S. Bureau of the Census.*

ination on the basis of gender as well as race, they discovered that the Equal Employment Opportunities Commission regarded women's complaints of discrimination as far less important than those of blacks.

In 1966, a group of 28 professional women, including Betty Friedan, established the National Organization for Women (NOW) "to take action to bring American women into full participation in the mainstream of American society *now.*" By full participation the founders not only meant fair pay and equal opportunity but a new, more egalitarian form of marriage. NOW also attacked "the false image of women ... in the media." By 1967, some 1,000 women had

joined the organization, and four years later, its membership reached 15,000.

NOW was a political pressure group. To radical feminists, who had come up through the civil rights movement, NOW's agenda failed to confront adequately the problem of gender discrimination. They tried, through the technique of consciousness raising, to help women understand the extent of their oppression and to analyze their experience as a political phenomenon.

Feminism at High Tide

A 1970 survey of first-year college students showed that men interested in such fields as business, medicine, engineering, and law out-numbered women eight to one; by 1975, the ratio had dropped to three to one. The proportion of women beginning law school quadrupled between 1969 and 1973. Women gained access to the military academies and entered senior officer ranks, but were still restricted from combat command ranks. Similarly, many employers systematically excluded women from certain positions, and women usually held "female" jobs in the clerical, sales, and service sectors. But changes were under way. For example, Title 9 of the Education Amendments of 1972 barred gender bias in federally assisted education activities and programs, made the admission of women easier, and changed the nature of intercollegiate athletics. By 1980, fully 30 percent of the participants in intercollegiate athletics were women, compared with 15 percent before Title 9 had become law.

A flurry of publications spread the ideas of the women's movement. In 1972, Gloria Steinem and several other women founded a new magazine, *Ms.,* which succeeded beyond their wildest dreams. By 1973, there were almost 200,000 subscribers. *The New Woman's Survival Catalogue* provided useful advice to women readers. *Our Bodies, Ourselves,* a handbook published by a woman's health collective, encouraged women to understand and control their bodies; it sold 850,000 copies between 1971 and 1976.

These new books and magazines differed radically from older women's magazines like *Good Housekeeping* and *Ladies' Home Journal,* which focused on women's domestic interests. *Ms.,* in dramatic contrast, dealt with abortion, employment, discrimination, and other feminist issues, such as the Equal Rights Amendment.

Women both in and out of NOW worked for congressional passage, then ratification, of the Equal Rights Amendment (ERA) to the Constitution. Passed by Congress in 1972, it stated simply, "Equality of rights under the law shall not be denied or abridged by the United States or by any State on account of sex." Thirty of the re-quired 38 states quickly ratified it, a few others followed, and for a time final approval seemed imminent.

Other feminist groups adopted more radical positions. Some insisted that legal changes were not enough. Traditional gender and family roles would have to be discarded, they maintained. Socialist feminists claimed that it was not enough to strike out at male domination, for capitalist society itself was responsible for women's plight. Only through the process of revolution could women be free.

Moderates and radicals alike attracted opposition. Nixon sided with the traditionalists when in 1971 he vetoed an appropriation for day-care centers with the argument that they undermined the sanctity of the family.

Women themselves resisted feminism for many reasons. Many felt the women's movement was contemptuous of women who stayed at home to perform traditional tasks. In politics, Phyllis Schlafly headed a nationwide campaign to block ratification of the ERA. "It won't do anything to help women," she said, "and it will take away from women the rights they already have, such as the right of a wife to be supported by her husband, the right of a woman to be exempted from military combat, and the right, if you wanted it, to go to a single-sex college." The ERA, she predicted, would lead to the establishment of coed bathrooms, the elimination of alimony, and the legalization of homosexual marriage.

Schlafly and her allies had their way. Within a few years of passage of the ERA, 35 states had agreed to the measure, but then the momentum disappeared. By mid-1982, the ERA was dead.

Even so, the 1980s brought significant gains. In politics, women won mayoral races in the nation's major cities. Far more women were elected to state legislatures and to Congress. In 1981, President Ronald Reagan appointed Sandra Day O'Connor as the first woman Supreme Court justice, and in 1984, Geraldine Ferraro, a Democratic member of Congress, became the

Women marched to mobilize support for ratification of the Equal Rights Amendment, but the campaign failed as opponents aroused public fears and blocked support in a number of key states. A decade after passage, the ERA was dead.

first woman vice-presidential candidate of a major party.

Despite substantial gains, women still faced serious problems. Access to new positions did not change their concentration in lower-paying jobs. In 1985, most women still served as secretaries, cashiers, bookkeepers, registered nurses, and waitresses. In 1985, full-time working women still earned only 63.6 cents for every dollar earned by men. Their concentration in the so-called pink-collar positions—traditional women's jobs—made further improvement difficult. Arguments that women should receive equal pay for equal work now led to demands for equal pay for different jobs of similar value. Comparable-worth cases began to work their way through the courts.

Women were likewise worried about the erosion of their right to abortion. Despite the 1973 Supreme Court decision legalizing abortion, the issue remained very much alive. The number of abortions increased dramatically in the decade after the decision. By some estimates, 10 million lawful abortions were performed in that decade, or one for every three births. In response, "pro-life" forces mobilized. They lobbied to cut off federal funds that allowed the poor to obtain the abortions that the better-off could pay for themselves; they insisted that abortions should be performed in hospitals and not in less expensive clinics; and they worked to reverse the original decision itself.

Though the Supreme Court, which included the first woman in its history, reaffirmed its judgment in 1983, the pro-life movement was not deterred. In 1989, a solidifying conservative majority on the Court ruled in *Webster* v. *Reproductive Health Services* that while women's right to abortion remained intact, state legislatures could impose limitations if they chose. With that judgment, a major legislative debate over the issue began, and numerous states began to mandate restrictions. In response, the courts heard still further cases to determine what should remain legal. In 1992, in *Planned Parenthood* v. *Casey,* the Supreme Court reaffirmed what it termed the "essence" of the right to abortion, while permitting further state restrictions.

Outside of the legal arena, pro-life groups engaged in civil disobedience campaigns and harassment tactics to discourage or prevent women from seeking abortions. They picketed and tried to block access to clinics, and many screamed epithets at women approaching the clinics. A few extremists resorted to violence, including the murder of clinic personnel and arson.

Despite counterattacks against women's right of reproductive choice, the women's movement flourished in the 1970s and 1980s. In the tenth-anniversary issue of *Ms.* magazine, in 1982, founding editor Gloria Steinem noted the differences a decade had made. "Now, we have words like 'sexual harassment' and 'battered women,'" she wrote. "Ten years ago, it was just called 'life.'"

HISPANIC RIGHTS

Hispanics, like women, profited from the example of blacks in the struggle for equality. Long denied equal access to the American dream, they became more vocal and confrontational as their numbers increased in the postwar years. Puerto Ricans in the Northeast, Cubans in Florida, and Chicanos in California and Tejanos in Texas developed a heightened sense of solidarity and group pride as they began to assert their own rights. In 1970, some 9 million people declared they were of Spanish origin; in 1980, the figure was 14.6 million; and in 1990 it was 20.8 million, as increases far outstripped the aggregate

César Chávez organized the United Farm Workers to give migrant Mexican workers representation in their struggle for better wages and working conditions.

American increase. But median household income remained less than three-fourths of that of Anglos, and inferior education and political weakness reinforced social and cultural separation.

César Chávez and the Politics of Confrontation

In the 1960s and 1970s, Mexican-Americans began to use confrontational tactics and pressure politics. In the election of 1960, Mexican-Americans supported Kennedy, helping him win Texas. In 1961, Henry B. González was elected to Congress from San Antonio. Three years later, Elizo ("Kika") de la Garza of Texas won election to the House and Joseph Montoya of New Mexico went to the Senate. Chicanos were gaining a political voice and began to anticipate the day when it could help them improve their lives.

More important than political representation, which came only slowly, was direct action. César Chávez, founder of the United Farm Workers, proved what could be done by organizing one of the most exploited and ignored groups of laboring people in the country, the migrant farm workers of the West. Chávez concentrated on migrant Mexican fieldhands, who worked long hours in the fields for meager pay. By 1965, his organization had recruited 1,700 members.

Chávez first took on the grape growers of California. Calling the grape workers out on strike, the union demanded better pay and working conditions as well as the recognition of the union. When the growers did not concede, Chávez launched a nationwide consumer boycott of their products. Although the Schenley Corporation and several wine companies came to terms, others held out. In 1966, the DiGiorgio Corporation agreed to permit a union election but then rigged the results. When California governor Edmund G. Brown, Sr., launched an investigation that resulted in another election, he became the first major political figure to support the long-powerless Chicano fieldhands. This time, the United Farm Workers won. Similar boycotts of lettuce and other products harvested by exploited labor also ended in success. In 1975, César Chávez's long struggle for farmworkers ended in the successful passage in California of a measure that required growers to bargain collectively with the elected representatives of the workers. Farmworkers had never been covered by the National Labor Relations Board. Now they had achieved the legal basis for representation that could help bring higher wages and improved working conditions. And Chávez had become a national figure.

Meanwhile, Mexican-Americans pressed for reform in other areas as well. In the West and Southwest, Mexican-American studies programs flourished. By 1969, at least 50 were available in California alone. They offered degrees, built library collections, and gave Chicanos access to their own past. The campuses also provided a network linking students together and mobilizing them for political action.

Beginning in 1968, Mexican-American students began to protest conditions in their overcrowded and run-down secondary schools. In March 1968, some 10,000 Chicano students walked out of five high schools in Los Angeles. Their actions inspired other walkouts in Colorado, Texas, and other parts of California and led to demands for Hispanic teachers, counselors, and courses and better facilities.

At the same time, new organizations emerged. A few years before, teenager David Sánchez and four Chicanos in East Los Angeles had formed a group called Young Citizens for Community Action. Gradually the organization evolved from a service club to a defensive patrol. Now known as Young Chicanos for Community Action, the group adopted a paramilitary stance. Its members became identified as the Brown Berets and formed chapters throughout the Midwest and Southwest.

Other Hispanics began to organize politically. In Texas José Angel Gutiérrez formed a cit-

izens' organization, which evolved into the La Raza Unida political party and successfully promoted Mexican-American candidates for political offices. Throughout the 1970s, it gained strength in the West and Southwest.

Hispanics made a particular point of protesting against the Vietnam War. Because the draft drew most heavily from the poorer segments of society, the Hispanic casualty rate was far higher than that of the population at large. In 1969, the Brown Berets organized the National Chicano Moratorium Committee and staged antiwar demonstrations. They argued that this was a racial war, with black and brown Americans being used against their Third World compatriots. Some of the rallies ended in confrontations with the police. News reporter Rubén Salazar, active in exposing questionable police activity, was killed in one such episode in 1970, and his death brought renewed charges of police brutality.

Aware of the growing numbers and growing demands of Hispanics, the Nixon administration sought to defuse their anger and win their support. Cuban-American refugees, strongly opposed to communism, shifted toward the Republican Party, which they assumed was more likely eventually to intervene against Fidel Castro. Meanwhile, Nixon courted Chicanos by dangling political positions, government jobs, and promises of better programs for Mexican-Americans. The effort paid off; Nixon received 31 percent of the Hispanic vote in 1972. Rather than reward his Hispanic followers, however, the president moved to cut back the poverty program, begun under Johnson, that assisted many of them.

Despite occasional gains in the 1970s and 1980s, Hispanics faced continuing problems. Spanish-speaking students often found it difficult to move through the educational system. In 1987, fully 40 percent of all Hispanic high school students did not graduate. Only 31 percent of the Hispanic seniors were enrolled in college-preparatory courses. Hispanic students frequently received little help from guidance counselors. Anel Albarran, a Mexican immigrant who arrived in East Los Angeles when she was 11, applied to UCLA when a special high school teacher encouraged her and made sure that she received help in choosing the necessary courses. By contrast, her regular counselor asked her two months before graduation whether she had considered college: "All he had wanted to do during high school was give me my classes and get me out of the room."

A growing network of Hispanic educators and programs worked to ease the way for future students. "Ten years ago, there was no national Chicano academic community," declared Arturo Madrid, president of the National Chicano Council on Higher Education, in 1982. "Now we have a professional presence in higher education." A colleague estimated that there were 5,000 Chicano faculty members in 1980, compared with 2,000 a decade before, and the numbers continued to grow.

Hispanics slowly extended their political gains as well. In San Antonio, Rudy Ortiz was appointed mayor pro tem in 1978, and Henry Cisneros was elected mayor in 1982. At the same time, Colorado state legislator Federico Peña was elected mayor of Denver. In New Mexico, Governor Toney Anaya called himself the nation's highest elected Hispanic and worked to create a national "Hispanic force." Among Hispanic administrators appointed at the national level of government, Lauro Cavazos, named U.S. secretary of education in 1988, Henry G. Cisneros, appointed secretary of housing and urban development in 1993, and Federico Peña, secretary of transportation, also appointed in 1993, are the most prominent.

NATIVE AMERICAN PROTEST

Like Hispanics, Native Americans continued to suffer second-class status as the 1960s began. But, partly inspired by the confrontational tactics of other groups, they became more aggressive in their efforts to claim their rights and to improve living and working conditions. The years saw not only a renewed aggressiveness but also phenomenal population growth—from 550,000 in 1960 to 1,959,000 in 1990.

Tribal Voices

During the Eisenhower years, the federal government's policy of termination was in effect. That effort to force Indians to assimilate into mainstream American life by relocating them in cities had worked poorly. Thousands of Native Americans traded reservation poverty for urban poverty.

In the 1960s, Indians began to assert themselves. At a conference in Chicago in 1961, several hundred Indians asked the Kennedy administration for the right to help make decisions about programs and budgets for the tribes. A group of college-educated Indians at the conference formed a National Indian Youth Council aimed at reestablishing Indian national pride. Over the next several decades, the council helped change the attitudes of tribal leaders, who were frequently called Uncle Tomahawks and "apples" (red outside, white inside) for their willingness to sacrifice their people's needs to white demands.

Indians successfully promoted their own values and designs. Native American fashions became more common, museums and galleries displayed Indian art, and Indian jewelry found a new market. The larger culture came to appreciate important work by Native Americans. In 1968, N. Scott Momaday won the Pulitzer Prize for his book *House Made of Dawn*. Vine Deloria's *Custer Died for Your Sins* (1969) had even wider readership. Meanwhile popular films like *Little Big Man* (1970) and, several decades later, the Academy Award–winning *Dances with Wolves* (1990) provided sympathetic portrayals of Indian history. Indian studies programs developed in colleges and universities. Organizations like the American Indian Historical Society in San Francisco protested traditional textbook treatment of Indians and demanded more honest portrayals.

Indian Activism

At the same time, Native Americans became more confrontational. Like other groups, they worked through the courts when they could but also challenged authority in more aggressive ways when necessary.

Led by a new generation of leaders, Native Americans tried to protect what was left of their tribal lands. "Everything is tied to our homeland," D'Arcy McNickle, a Flathead anthropologist, told other Indians in 1961.

The new activism was apparent on the Seneca Nation's Allegany reservation in New York State. Although the Senecas' right to the land was established by a treaty made in 1794, the federal government had planned since 1928 to build the Kinzua Dam there as part of a flood control project. In 1956, after hearings to which the Indians were not invited and about which they were not informed, Congress appropriated funds for the project. The dam was eventually built, and although the government belatedly passed a $15 million reparations bill, money did not compensate for the loss of 10,000 acres of land that contained sacred sites, hunting and fishing grounds, and homes.

The Seneca did somewhat better in the 1970s. When New York State tried to condemn a section of Seneca land for a superhighway running through part of the Allegany reservation, the Indians again went to court. In 1981, the state finally agreed to an exchange: state land elsewhere in addition to a cash settlement in return for an easement through the reservation. That decision encouraged tribal efforts in Montana, Wyoming, Utah, New Mexico, and Arizona to resist similar incursions on reservation lands.

Native American leaders then brought a

wave of lawsuits charging violations of treaty rights. In 1967, in the first of many decisions upholding the Indian side, the U.S. Court of Claims ruled that the government had forced the Seminole in Florida to cede their land in 1823 for an unreasonably low price. The court directed the government to pay additional funds 144 years later. In other litigation, Indian tribes fought to protect their water rights and fishing rights.

The activist American Indian Movement (AIM) was founded in 1968 by George Mitchell and Dennis Banks, Chippewa living in Minneapolis. AIM sought to help neglected Indians in the city. It managed to get Office of Economic Opportunity funds channeled to Indian-controlled organizations. It also established patrols to protect drunken Indians from harassment by the police. As its successes became known, chapters formed in other cities.

The new militancy was dramatized in November 1969, when a landing party of 78 Indians seized Alcatraz Island in San Francisco Bay to protest symbolically the inability of the Bureau of Indian Affairs to "deal practically" with questions of Indian welfare. They converted the island, with its defunct federal prison, into a cultural and educational center, but in 1971 federal officials removed them.

Other, similar protests followed. In 1972, militants launched the Broken Treaties Caravan to Washington. For six days, insurgents occupied the Bureau of Indian Affairs. In 1973, AIM took over the South Dakota village of Wounded Knee, where in 1890 the U.S. 7th Calvary had massacred the Sioux. The reservation surrounding the town was mired in poverty. Half the families were on welfare, alcoholism was widespread, and 81 percent of the student population had dropped out of school. The occupation was meant to dramatize these conditions and to draw attention to the 371 treaties AIM leaders claimed the government had broken. Federal officials responded by encircling the area and, when AIM tried to bring in supplies, killed one Indian and wounded another. The confrontation

The American Indian Movement's armed occupation of Wounded Knee, South Dakota, site of a late-nineteenth-century massacre of the Sioux, resulted in bloodshed that dramatized the government's unfair treatment of Native Americans.

ended with a government agreement to reexamine the treaty rights of the Indians, although little of substance was subsequently done.

At the same time, Native Americans devoted increasing attention to providing education and developing business and legal skills. Because roughly half of the Indian population continued to live on reservations, many tribal communities founded their own colleges. In 1971, the Oglala Sioux established Oglala Lakota College on the Pine Ridge Reservation in South Dakota. Nearby Sinte Gleska College on the Rosebud Reservation was the first to offer accredited four-year and graduate programs. The number of Indians in college rose from a few hundred in the early 1960s to tens of thousands by 1980. Between 1980 and 1990, Native American enrollment in higher education institutions increased by over 23 percent.

Some tribal communities developed business skills, although traditional Indian attitudes hardly fostered the capitalist perspective. "Now we're beginning to realize that, if we want to be self-sufficient, we're going to have to become entrepreneurs ourselves," observed Iola Hayden, the Comanche executive director of Oklahomans for Indian Opportunity. The Choctaw in Mississippi were perhaps the most successful, cutting their 1979 unemployment rate of 50 percent in half by the mid-1980s.

Indians themselves studied law and acted as legal advocates for their own people in the court cases they were filing. They have worked for tribes directly and have successfully argued for tribal jurisdiction in conflicts between whites and Indians on the reservations.

Government Response

Indian protest brought results. The outcry against termination in the 1960s led the Kennedy and Johnson administrations to steer a middle course, neither endorsing nor disavowing the policy. Instead they tried to bolster reservation economies and raise standards of living by persuading private industries to locate on reservations and by promoting the leasing of reservation lands to energy and development corporations. In the 1970s, however, the Navajo, Northern Cheyenne, Crow, and other tribes sought to cancel or renegotiate such leases, fearing "termination by corporation."

The Native American cry for self-determination brought Indian involvement in the poverty program of the Great Society in the mid-1960s. Two agencies, the Area Redevelopment Administration (later the Economic Development Administration) and the Office of Economic Opportunity, responded to Indian pressure by making their resources available. Indians could devise programs and budgets and administer programs themselves. They were similarly involved with Great Society housing, health, and education initiatives. Finally, in 1975, Congress passed the Indian Self-Determination and Education Assistance acts. Though both laws were limited, they nonetheless reflected the government's decision to respond to Indian pressure.

SOCIAL AND CULTURAL PROTEST

As blacks, Hispanics, and Native Americans agitated, middle-class American society experienced an upheaval unlike any it had known before. Young people in particular rejected the stable patterns of affluent life their parents had forged in the decade before. Some embraced radical political activity; many more adopted new standards of sexual behavior, music, and dress. In time their actions spawned still other protests as Americans tried to make the political and social world more responsive than before.

The Student Movement

Among young Americans who came of age in the 1960s, many, especially from the large mid-

dle class, moved on to some form of higher education. By the end of the 1960s, college enrollment was more than four times what it had been in the 1940s.

In college, some students joined the struggle for civil rights. Hopeful at first, they gradually became discouraged by the limitations of the government's commitment, despite the rhetoric of Kennedy and the New Frontier.

Out of that disillusionment arose the radical spirit of the New Left. Civil rights activists were among those who in 1960 organized Students for a Democratic Society (SDS). In 1962, SDS issued a manifesto, the Port Huron Statement, written largely by Tom Hayden of the University of Michigan, and calling for the creation of a "New Left." "We are people of this generation, bred in at least modest comfort, housed now in universities, looking uncomfortably at the world we inherit," it began. It went on to deplore the vast social and economic distances separating people from each other and to condemn the isolation and estrangement of modern life. The document called for a better system, "a democracy of individual participation."

The first blow of the growing student rebellion came at the University of California in Berkeley. There civil rights activists became involved in a confrontation that quickly became known as the free speech movement. It began in September 1964 when the university refused to allow students to distribute protest material outside the main campus gate. The students, many of whom had worked in the movement in the South, argued that their tables were off campus and therefore not subject to university restrictions on political activity. When police arrested one of the leaders, students surrounded the police car and kept it from moving all night.

The university regents brought charges against the student leaders, including Mario Savio. When the regents refused to drop the charges, the students occupied the administration building. Then, as in the South, police stormed in and arrested the students in the building. A student strike, with faculty aid, mobilized wider support for the right to free speech.

The free speech movement at Berkeley was basically a plea for traditional liberal reform. Students sought only the reaffirmation of a long-standing right, the right to express themselves as they chose, and they aimed their attacks at the university, not at society as a whole. The attack broadened as the ferment at Berkeley spread to other campuses in the spring of 1965. Students sought a greater voice in university affairs, argued for curricular reform, and demanded admission of more minority students. Their success in gaining their demands changed the shape of American higher education.

The mounting protest against the escalation of the Vietnam War fueled and refocused the youth movement. Confrontation became the new tactic of radical students, and protest became a way of life. Between January 1 and June 15, 1968, hundreds of thousands of students staged 221 major demonstrations at more than 100 educational institutions.

The next year, in October 1969, the Weathermen, a militant fringe group of SDS, sought to show that the revolution had arrived with a frontal attack on Chicago, scene of the violent Democratic convention of 1968. The Weathermen, taking their name from a line in a Bob Dylan song—"You don't need a weatherman to know which way the wind blows"—came from all over the country. Dressed in hard hats, jackboots, work gloves, and other padding, they rampaged through the streets with clubs and pipes, chains and rocks. They ran into the police, as they had expected and hoped, and continued the attack. Some were arrested, others were shot, and the rest withdrew to regroup. For the next two days, they plotted strategy, engaged in minor skirmishes, and prepared for the final thrust. It came on the fourth day, once again pitting aggressive Weathermen against hostile police.

Why had the Weathermen launched their attack? "The status quo meant to us war, poverty, inequality, ignorance, famine and disease in most of the world," Bo Burlingham, a participant from Ohio, reflected. "To accept it was to condone and help perpetuate it. We felt like miners trapped in a terrible poisonous shaft with no light to guide us out. We resolved to destroy the tunnel even if we risked destroying ourselves in the process." The rationale of the Chicago "national action" may have been clear to the participants, but it convinced few other Americans. There and elsewhere, citizens were infuriated at what they saw.

The New Left was, briefly, a powerful force. Although activists never composed a majority, radicals attracted students and other sympathizers to their cause until the movement fragmented. But while it was healthy, the movement focused opposition to the Vietnam War and challenged inequities in American society.

The Counterculture

In the 1960s, many Americans, particularly young people, lost faith in the sanctity of the American system. "There was," observed Joseph Heller, the irreverent author of *Catch-22* (1961), "a general feeling that the platitudes of Americanism were horseshit." The protests exposed the emptiness of some of the old patterns, and many Americans, some politically active, some not, found new ways to assert their individuality and independence, often drawing on the example of the beats of the 1950s.

Surface appearances were most visible and, to older Americans, most troubling. The "hippies" of the 1960s carried themselves in different ways. Men let their hair grow and sprouted beards; men and women both donned jeans, muslin shirts, and other simple garments. Stressing spontaneity above all else, some rejected traditional marital customs and gravitated to communal living groups. Their example, shocking to some, soon found its way into the culture at large.

Sexual norms underwent a revolution as more people separated sex from its traditional ties to family life. A generation of young women came of age with access to "the pill"—an oral contraceptive that was easy to use and freed sexual experimentation from the threat of pregnancy. Americans of all social classes became more open to exploring, and enjoying, their sexuality. Scholarly findings supported natural inclinations. In 1966, William H. Masters and Virginia E. Johnson published *Human Sexual Response,* based on intensive laboratory observation of couples engaged in sexual activities. Describing the kinds of response that women, as well as men, could experience, they destroyed the myth of the sexually passive woman.

Nora Ephron, author and editor, summed up the sexual changes in the 1960s as she reflected on her own experiences. Initially she had "a hangover from the whole Fifties virgin thing," she recalled. "The first man I went to bed with, I was in love with and wanted to marry. The second one I was in love with, but I didn't have to marry him. With the third one, I thought I *might* fall in love."

The arts reflected both the sexual revolution and the mood of dissent. Federal courts ruled that books like D.H. Lawrence's *Lady Chatterley's Lover,* earlier considered obscene, could not be banned. Many suppressed works, long available in Europe, now began to appear. Nudity became more common on stage and screen. "Op" artists painted sharply defined geometric figures in clear, vibrant colors, starkly different from the flowing, chaotic work of the abstract expressionists. "Pop" artists like Andy Warhol, Roy Lichtenstein, and Jasper Johns made ironic comments on American materialism and taste with the representations of everyday objects like soup cans, comic strips, or pictures of Marilyn Monroe. Their paintings broke with formal artistic conventions. Some used spray guns and fluorescent paints to gain effect. Others even tried to make their pictures look like giant newspaper photographs.

Hallucinogenic drugs also became a part of the counterculture. One prophet of the "drug scene" was Timothy Leary, who aggressively asserted that drugs were necessary to free the mind. Drug use was no longer confined to an urban subculture of musicians, artists, and the streetwise. Soldiers brought experience with drugs back from Vietnam. Young professionals began experimenting with cocaine as a stimulant. Taking a "tab" of LSD became part of the coming-of-age ritual for many middle-class college students. Marijuana became phenomenally popular in the 1960s.

Music became intimately connected with these cultural changes. The rock and roll of the 1950s and the gentle strains of folk music gave way to a new kind of rock that swept the country—and the world. The Beatles were the major influence, as they took first England, then the United States, by storm. Other groups enjoyed enormous commercial success while attacking materialism and other bourgeois values. Mick Jagger of the Rolling Stones was an aggressive, sometimes violent showman on stage whose androgynous style showed his contempt for conventional sexual norms. Janis Joplin, a hard-driving, hard-drinking woman with roots in the blues, reflected the intensity of the new rock world until her early death by drugs.

The music was most important on a mid-August weekend in 1969 when some 400,000 people gathered in a large pasture in upstate New York for the Woodstock rock festival. There, despite intense heat and torrential rain, despite inadequate supplies of water and food, the festival unfolded in a spirit of affection. Some people shed their clothes and paraded in the nude, some had sex in public, and most shared whatever they had, particularly the marijuana that seemed endlessly available, while major rock groups provided ear-splitting, around-the-clock entertainment for the assembled throng. The weekend was not without problems, but supporters hailed the festival as an example of the new and better world to come.

Other Americans, however, viewed the antics of the young with distaste. Their fears seemed vindicated at another festival four months later in Altamont, California. Some 300,000 people gathered at a stock car raceway to attend a rock concert climaxing an American tour by the immensely popular Rolling Stones. Woodstock had been well planned; the Altamont affair was not. In the absence of adequate security, the Stones hired a band of Hell's Angels to maintain control. Those tough motorcyclists, fond of terrorizing the open road, prepared to keep order in their own way.

The spirit at Altamont was different from the start. "It was a gray day, and the California hills were bare, cold and dead," wrote Greil Marcus, a music critic. An undercurrent of violence simmered, Marcus observed, as "all day long people . . . speculated on who would be killed, on when the killing would take place. There were few doubts that the Angels would do the job."

With the Stones on stage, the fears were realized. As star Mick Jagger looked on, the Hell's Angels beat a young black man to death. A musician who tried to intervene was knocked senseless. Other beatings occurred, accidents claimed several more lives, and drug-overdosed revelers found no adequate medical support.

Altamont revealed the underside of the counterculture. That underside could also be seen in the Haight-Ashbury section of San Francisco, where runaway "flower children" mingled with "burned-out" drug users and radical activists. Joan Didion, a perceptive essayist, wrote of American society in 1967: "Adolescents drifted from city to torn city, sloughing off both the past and the future as snakes shed their skins, children who were never taught and would never now learn the games that had held the society together." For all the spontaneity and exuberance, the counterculture's underside could not be ignored.

Gay and Lesbian Rights

Closely tied to the revolution in sexual norms that affected sexual relations, marriage, and family life was a fast-growing and increasingly militant gay liberation movement. There had always been people who accepted the "gay" life style, but American society as a whole was unsympathetic, and many homosexuals kept their preferences to themselves. The climate of the 1970s encouraged gays to "come out of the closet." A nightlong riot in 1969, in response to a police raid on a homosexual bar in Greenwich Village in New York, helped spark a new consciousness and a movement for gay rights. Throughout the 1970s and 1980s, homosexuals made important gains in ending the most blatant forms of discrimination against them. In 1973, the American Psychiatric Association ruled that homosexuality should no longer be classified as a mental illness, and that decision was overwhelmingly supported in a vote by the membership the next year. In 1975, the U.S. Civil Service Commission lifted its ban on employment of homosexuals.

In this new climate of acceptance, many gays who had hidden or suppressed their sexuality revealed their darkest secret. Women also became more open about their sexual preferences and demanded that they not be penalized for choosing other females as partners. A lesbian movement developed, sometimes involving women active in the more radical wing of the women's movement. But many Americans remained unsympathetic to anyone who challenged traditional sexual norms. Churches and some religious groups often lashed out against gays.

The discovery of AIDS (acquired immune deficiency syndrome) in 1981 changed the situation for homosexuals dramatically. The deadly new disease struck intravenous drug users and homosexuals with numerous partners more than any other groups. The growing number of deaths—200,000 by 1992—suggested that the disease would reach epidemic proportions. Advertisements in the national media advised the use of condoms, and the U.S. surgeon general mailed a brochure, "Understanding AIDS," to every household in the United States. As knowledge—and misunderstanding—of the disease increased, many Americans felt that hostility toward homosexuality was justified. Still, homosexuals fought on for a greater governmental effort to find a cure for AIDS. The disease itself began to be better understood when heterosexual sports heroes Earvin "Magic" Johnson and Arthur Ashe were diagnosed as having the virus that causes the disease, and that understanding promised to help the gay cause.

THE ENVIRONMENTAL AND CONSUMER MOVEMENTS

Although many of the social movements that arose in the 1960s were defined by race, gender, and sexual preference, one further movement united many of these reformers across such boundaries. Emerging in the early 1960s, a powerful movement of Americans concerned with the environment began to revive issues raised in the Progressive era and to go far beyond them.

The modern environmental movement gathered momentum after the publication in 1962 of Rachel Carson's *Silent Spring*. She took aim at chemical pesticides, particularly DDT, which had increased crop yields but had disastrous side effects. As Americans learned of the pollutants surrounding them, they became increasingly worried about pesticides, motor vehicle exhaust, and industrial wastes that filled the air. Lyndon Johnson pressed for and won basic legislation to halt the destruction of the country's natural resources.

Public concern mounted further in 1969 when it was discovered that thermal pollution from nuclear power plants was killing fish in both eastern and western rivers. DDT was threatening the very existence of the bald eagle, the nation's emblem. A massive oil spill off the coast of southern California in 1969 turned white beaches black and wiped out much of the marine life in the immediate area. An even worse

oil spill occurred in Alaska in 1989 when the *Exxon Valdez* ran aground.

Concern about the deterioration of the environment increased as people learned more about substances they had once taken for granted. In 1978, the public became alarmed about the lethal effects of toxic chemicals dumped in the Love Canal neighborhood of Niagara Falls, New York. A few years later, attention focused on dioxin, one of the poisons permeating from the Love Canal, which now surfaced in other areas in more concentrated form. Dioxin, a by-product of the manufacture of herbicides, plastics, and wood preservatives, remained active after being released in the environment. Thousands of times more potent than cyanide, it was one of the most deadly substances ever made.

Equally frightening was the potential environmental damage from a nuclear accident. That possibility became more real as a result of a mishap at one of the reactors at Three Mile Island in 1979. There a faulty pressure relief valve led to a loss of coolant. Initially, plant operators refused to believe indicators showing a serious malfunction. Part of the nuclear core became uncovered, part began to disintegrate, and the surrounding steam and water became highly radioactive. An explosion releasing radioactivity into the atmosphere appeared possible, and thousands of residents of the area were evacuated. The worst never occurred and the danger period passed, but the plant remained shut down, filled with radioactive debris, a monument to a form of energy that was once hailed as the wave of the future but now appeared more destructive than any ever known.

The threat to the environment seemed even more horrifying with another nuclear accident seven years later, in 1986. This time the disaster played itself out at a plant in Chernobyl in the Soviet Union. The first reports indicated as many as a thousand people had died following a huge explosion. Though the number of deaths was later scaled down, the airborne contamination affected people thousands of miles away. Europeans plowed up freshly planted crops, warned against drinking milk, and banned imports of livestock and vegetables from the east. Some scientists predicted that one million people would develop cancer, and five years after the accident, estimates of the cancer death toll ranged from 17,000 to 475,000.

As a result of the Three Mile Island and Chernobyl accidents, public opposition to nuclear power has grown worldwide and has made it difficult to build new plants or find geologically safe and politically acceptable places in which to permanently store radioactive waste products produced by nuclear energy plants. In the United States, environmental activists mobilized opinion sufficiently that no new plants were authorized after 1978.

Environmentalists also worried about America's excessive use of water, which had risen from 40 billion gallons a day in 1900 to 393 billion gallons by 1975, though the population had only tripled. American homes, farms, and industries used three times as much water per capita as the world's average, and far more than other industrialized societies. Pointing to the destruction of the nation's rivers and streams and the severe drawing down of the water table in many areas, environmentalists launched an angry wave of protest.

Environmental agitation produced legislative results in the 1960s and 1970s. Lyndon Johnson, whose vision of the Great Society included an "environment that is pleasing to the senses and healthy to live in," won basic legislation to halt the depletion of the country's natural resources (see Chapter 28). During Nixon's presidency, Congress passed the Clean Air Act, the Water Quality Improvement Act, and the Resource Recovery Act and mandated a new Environmental Protection Agency (EPA) to spearhead the effort to control abuses.

Despite growing national sympathy for environmental goals, the movement faced fierce political resistance in the 1980s. Ronald Reagan systematically restrained the EPA in his avowed

effort to promote economic growth. James Watt, his secretary of the interior, opened forest lands, wilderness areas, and coastal waters to economic development and frankly conceded that he saw little reason to save the natural environment for future generations. George Bush initially seemed more sympathetic to environmental causes, but as the economy faltered, he proved less willing to support environmental action that he claimed might slow economic growth. In 1992, he accommodated business by easing clean air restrictions. That same year, he attended a United Nations–sponsored Earth Summit at Rio de Janeiro in Brazil with 100 other heads of state. There he stood alone in his refusal to sign a biological diversity treaty framed to conserve millions of plant and animal species.

Environmentalists were encouraged by the 1992 election of Bill Clinton as president and environmental advocate Albert Gore, Jr., as vice president. The economic recession, however, which had contributed to the defeat of Republican candidate George Bush, also hindered efforts to protect forests, waterways, and wildlife from commercial and industrial exploitation.

Related to the environmental movement was a consumer movement. Americans throughout the twentieth century, particularly in the 1950s, their appetites whetted by advertising, had bought fashionable clothes, house furnishings, and electrical and electronic gadgets. Congress had established a variety of regulatory efforts to protect citizens from unscrupulous sellers. In the 1970s, a strong consumer movement grew, led by Ralph Nader. He had become interested in the issue of automobile safety while studying law at Harvard and had pursued that interest as a consultant to the Department of Labor. His book *Unsafe at Any Speed: The Designed-in Dangers of the American Automobile* (1965) argued that many cars were coffins on wheels. Head-on collisions, even at low speeds, could easily kill, for cosmetic bumpers could not withstand modest shocks. He termed the Corvair "one of the nastiest-handling cars ever built" because of its tendency to roll over in certain situations. His efforts paved the way for the National Traffic and Motor Vehicle Safety Act of 1966.

Nader's efforts attracted scores of volunteers, called "Nader's Raiders." They turned out critiques and reports and, more important, inspired consumer activists at all levels of government—city, state, and national. Consumer protection offices began to monitor a flood of complaints as ordinary citizens became more vocal in defending their rights.

CONCLUSION

EXTENDING THE AMERICAN DREAM

The 1960s, 1970s, and 1980s were turbulent decades. Yet this third major reform era of the twentieth century accomplished a good deal for the groups fighting to expand the meaning of equality. Blacks now enjoyed greater access to the rights and privileges enjoyed by mainstream American society, despite the backlash the movement brought. Women like Ann Clarke, introduced at the start of the chapter, returned to school in ever-increasing numbers and found jobs and sometimes independence after years of being told that their place was at home. Native Americans and Hispanics mobilized too and could see the stirrings of change. Environmentalists created a new awareness of the global dangers the nation and the world faced.

But the course of change was ragged. The reform effort reached its high-water mark during Lyndon Johnson's Great Society and in the years immediately following, then faltered with the rise of conservatism and disillusionment with liberalism (see Chapter 28). Some movements were circumscribed by the changing political climate; others simply ran out of steam. Still, the various efforts left a legacy of ferment on which others could draw.

Recommended Reading

A number of books provide good introductions to the civil rights movement. Harvard Sitkoff, *The Struggle for Black Equality, 1954–1980* (1981), is a short but stimulating overview of the civil rights struggle. Taylor Branch, *Parting the Waters: America in the King Years, 1954–1963* (1988), is a much fuller account of the reform effort. David J. Garrow, *Bearing the Cross: Martin Luther King, Jr., and the Southern Christian Leadership Conference* (1986), tells King's story. William H. Chafe, *Civilities and Civil Rights: Greensboro, North Carolina, and the Black Struggle for Freedom* (1980), is an outstanding study of black southern protest. Anne Moody, *Coming of Age in Mississippi* (1968), is the eloquent autobiography of a young southern black woman who became involved in the civil rights movement.

On women's issues, Sara Evans, *Personal Politics: The Roots of Women's Liberation in the Civil Rights Movement and the New Left* (1979), contains some thoughtful observations about the women's movement in the 1960s and 1970s. Alice Kessler-Harris, *Out to Work: A History of Wage-Earning Women in the United States* (1982), is a good exploration of shifting patterns of employment.

Rodolfo Acuña, *Occupied America: A History of Chicanos,* 3d ed. (1988), is the best account of Chicanos in America, particularly in the modern period. For a thoughtful essay on César Chávez, see Cletus Daniel, "César Chávez and the Unionization of California Farm Workers," in Melvyn Dubofsky and Warren Van Tine, eds., *Labor Leaders in America* (1987).

Alvin M. Josephy, Jr., *Now That the Buffalo's Gone* (1982), is a useful starting point for further examination of recent Indian struggles. Frederick E. Hoxie, ed., *Indians in American History* (1988), contains good material on the modern period.

For the turbulence of the 1960s, see Todd Gitlin, *The Sixties: Years of Hope, Days of Rage* (1987). On the counterculture, William L. O'Neill, *Coming Apart: An Informal History of America in the 1960s* (1971), provides an engaging narrative.

Time Line

1960	Birth control pill becomes available Sit-ins begin Students for a Democratic Society (SDS) founded
1961	Freedom rides Michael Harrington publishes *The Other America*; Joseph Heller, *Catch-22*
1962	James Meredith crisis at the University of Mississippi SDS's Port Huron Statement Publication of Rachel Carson's *Silent Spring*
1963	Birmingham demonstration Civil rights March on Washington Publication of Betty Friedan's *The Feminine Mystique*
1964	Freedom Democratic Party attempts to gain recognition at the Democratic national convention Civil Rights Act Race riots in New York City Free speech movement, Berkeley

1965	Martin Luther King, Jr., leads march from Selma to Montgomery Voting Rights Act United Farm Workers' grape strike Assassination of Malcolm X Watts riot in Los Angeles Ralph Nader, *Unsafe at Any Speed*
1966	Stokely Carmichael becomes head of SNCC and calls for "black power" Black Panthers founded NOW founded Masters and Johnson, *Human Sexual Response*
1967	Urban riots in 22 cities
1968	Kerner Commission report on urban disorders Martin Luther King, Jr., assassinated Student demonstrations at Columbia and elsewhere Chicano student walkouts American Indian Movement (AIM) founded

Time Line (continued)

1969	Woodstock and Altamont rock festivals Weathermen's "Days of Rage" in Chicago Native Americans seize Alcatraz La Raza Unida founded	**1979**	Three Mile Island nuclear power plant accident
1971–1975	School busing controversies in North and South	**1981**	Sandra Day O'Connor appointed to the Supreme Court
1972	*Ms.* magazine founded Congress passes Equal Rights Amendment Broken Treaties caravan to Washington	**1982**	Ratification of ERA fails
		1984	Geraldine Ferraro runs for vice president
		1986	Chernobyl nuclear accident in Soviet Union
1973	*Roe* v. *Wade* AIM occupies Wounded Knee	**1988**	Lauro Cavazos appointed secretary of education
1975	Farmworkers' grape boycott Indian Self-Determination and Education Assistance acts	**1989**	*Webster* v. *Reproductive Health Services*
		1991	Clarence Thomas appointed to the Supreme Court
1978	*Bakke* v. *Regents of the University of California*	**1992**	Bill Clinton elected president *Planned Parenthood* v. *Casey*

....

chapter 30

The Triumph of Conservatism

David Patterson flourished in the early 1980s. An executive in the computer industry, he had risen through the ranks and now directed an entire division of his company. He enjoyed a good salary, a handsome home in the New York suburbs, and two luxury cars. Then, in the middle of the decade, his affluent world collapsed. One Friday afternoon, his boss told him he no longer had a job; his entire division and its fifty employees were all being eliminated. Fortified with but four weeks of severance pay, Patterson was on his own. At first he was optimistic about landing another position, but after nine months of futile efforts, he realized that his family was in serious financial trouble. Although his wife, Julia, had gone back to work, their combined income from her salary and his unemployment check was but a fraction of what it had been. Unable to make mortgage payments, they were forced to sell their house and move into a modest apartment in a nearby town. The emotional costs were even greater. Embarrassed at his plight, Patterson stopped calling friends, and they ceased trying to reach him in turn. He was puzzled and hurt. Computers were hailed as the magical machines of the future, so it was hard to understand the shakedown that affected firms throughout the industry. Why was he having such trouble finding another job? Was there something wrong with him?

Thousands of other executives faced the corporate downsizing that accompanied a continuing economic recession. The cover story in the March 23, 1992, issue of *Business Week* focused on the increasingly pervasive phenomenon of "Downward Mobility" and noted the growing difficulties professionals had finding new jobs as they moved through the 1980s. At the start of the decade, 90 percent of the white-collar employees who lost their positions were quickly hired in similar jobs with the same or better pay. By the late 1980s, the figure was down to 50 percent; by 1992 it had dropped to 25 percent and was still falling. Clearly David Patterson was not alone.

Patterson and thousands of others who lost their jobs were the middle-class victims of a conservative era that was marked by greed and extravagance, especially on the part of those best off. As the nation pulled out of a recession at the start of the 1980s and the economy improved, more affluent Americans prospered most from the initiatives of the Reagan administration. The nation's economic policies widened the gaps between rich and poor; poverty became more widespread; and members of minority groups encountered continued difficulty finding jobs. An even worse recession in the early 1990s brought hardship to the middle and upper-middle classes as well. The national debt skyrocketed, and finally, in reaction to questions about the stability of the economy, the stock market tumbled. At the same time, cataclysmic events shook Communist governments in the USSR and eastern Europe, ending nearly a half century of Cold War.

This chapter describes the enormous changes of the 1980s and early 1990s. It covers the public policies of the new Republican majority, which promised prosperity but brought economic catastrophe to many. It outlines the economic and demographic transformations after 1980 and examines the new role of the United States in a vastly different world order.

THE CONSERVATIVE TRANSFORMATION

In the 1980s, the Republican Party established itself as the dominant force in national politics. The transformation that had begun in the Nixon era was now largely complete. The liberal agenda that had governed national affairs ever since the New Deal of Franklin Roosevelt had lost its broad appeal and gave way to a new Republican coalition determined to scale back the social welfare state and prevent what its proponents perceived as the erosion of the nation's moral values. Firmly in control of the presidency, occasionally in control of the Senate, the Republican Party directed the new national agenda.

The New Politics

Political conservatism became respectable in the 1980s, having gained countless new adherents after the turbulence of the 1960s and the backlash of the Vietnam War. New political techniques that capitalized on national disaffection with liberal solutions to continuing social problems made the conservative movement an almost unstoppable national force.

Conservatives seized on Thomas Jefferson's maxim "That government is best which governs least." They argued that the United States in the 1980s had moved into an era of limits, and that the liberal solution of throwing money at social problems no longer worked. They therefore sought to limit the size of government, to reduce the tax burden, and to cut back the regulations they claimed hampered business competition. In the process, they would restore the focus on individual initiative and private enterprise that many Americans felt had always been the essence of the nation's strength.

The conservative philosophy had tremendous appeal. It offered hope for the revival of the basic social and religious values that many citizens worried had been eaten away by rising divorce rates, legalized abortion, openly expressed homosexuality, and mass media preoccupation with sex and violence. It attracted middle-class Americans who were concerned that they were being forgotten in the rush to assist minorities and the poor. Some members of the new conservative coalition embraced the economic doctrines of the University of Chicago's Milton Friedman, who advocated the free play of market forces and less government regulation of the economy. Other supporters embraced the social and political dictums of North Carolina Senator Jesse Helms, a tireless foe of any forms of expression in art, dance, or literature he deemed pornographic. Many others flocked to the Republican fold because they objected to affirmative action, job quotas, and school busing to promote racially integrated schools. The conservative coalition also drew in religious fundamentalists, ranging from devout Catholics to orthodox Jews to evangelical Protestants, who were worried about sexual permissiveness, the erosion of family life, and the alarming increase in crime. Between 1970 and 1980, the murder rate rose 31 percent, the robbery rate 42 percent, the burglary rate 56 percent, the assault rate 79 percent, and the rape rate 99 percent. The use of drugs spread. Members of the religious right wanted to return religion to a central place in American life and to revive traditional values.

Many of these activists belonged to the so-called Moral Majority. The Reverend Jerry Falwell of Virginia and other television evangelists underscored the concerns of religious fundamentalism and developed large followings in the 1980s. Listeners donated millions of dollars to support the call for the redemption from sin, and Moral Majority money began to fund politicians who held conservative positions on issues like school prayer, abortion, and the Equal Rights Amendment.

Conservatives also understood the importance of television advertising. They became adept at using brief "sound bites," often no more than 15 or 30 seconds, to communicate their positions. They also refined the art of negative advertising in a political campaign. Mudslinging has always been a part of the American political tradition, of course, but now carefully crafted television ads increasingly concentrated not on issues, but on subtly or even openly attacking an opponent's character.

Public relations techniques assumed great importance. Polls, sometimes taken daily, mandated which part of a candidate's image needed polishing most or where one's opponent was most vulnerable. "Spin doctors" moved into action after a candidate made a public statement to put the best possible gloss on what had been said. Small wonder that Americans became increasingly cynical about politics and stayed away from the voting booth in record numbers as the twentieth century drew to a close.

Conservatives likewise led the way in raising enormous sums of money for their campaigns. Richard Viguerie, a young Houston activist in the New Right, organized a huge direct-mail campaign, unlike anything seen before in American politics, to raise money for right-wing causes. His fund raising played a major part in the rise of conservatism as a powerful political force.

But conservatives also understood the need to provide an intellectual grounding for their positions. Numerous conservative scholars worked in think tanks and other research organizations, such as the Hoover Institution at Stanford University or the American Enterprise Institute in Washington, D.C., churning out books, articles, and reports that helped elect Ronald Reagan and other conservative politicians.

Conservative Leadership

Ronald Reagan was more responsible than any other Republican politician for the success of the conservative cause. An actor turned politician, he was elected governor of California in 1966. He failed in his first bid for the Republican nomination in 1976 but consolidated his strength over the next four years. By 1980, he had the firm support of the growing right, which applauded his effort to reduce the size of the federal government but bolster military might. Charging the Carter administration with a "litany of broken promises," he provided a soothing contrast to the incumbent. He showed real wit as he quibbled with Carter over economic definitions. "I'm talking in human terms and he is hiding behind a dictionary," Reagan said. "If he wants a definition, I'll give him one. A recession is when your neighbor loses his job. A depression is when you lose yours. A recovery is when Jimmy Carter loses his."

Reagan scored a landslide victory in 1980, gaining a popular vote of 51 to 41 percent and a 489 to 49 electoral college advantage. He also led the Republican Party to control of the Senate for the first time since 1955.

In 1984, Reagan ran for reelection against Walter Mondale, Jimmy Carter's vice president. For his running mate, Mondale selected Geraldine Ferraro, a congresswoman from New York, the first woman ever to receive a major party's nomination on the presidential ticket. Reagan benefited from the economic upturn and received 59 percent of the popular vote. He swamped Mondale in the electoral college 525 to 13, losing only Minnesota, Mondale's home state, and the District of Columbia. While the Republicans continued to control the Senate, Democrats netted two additional Senate seats and managed to maintain superiority in the House of Representatives.

Reagan had a pleasing manner and a special skill as a media communicator. A gifted storyteller, best at relating one-liners, he seemed like a trusted uncle who spoke in soothing terms. For much of his term, people talked about a "Teflon" presidency—criticisms failed to stick, and disagreements over his policies never diminished his personal popularity.

But Reagan had a number of liabilities that surfaced over time. He was the oldest president the nation had ever had, inaugurated two weeks before his seventieth birthday. Dwight Eisenhower, who left office at just that age, once remarked, "No one should ever sit in this office

Ronald Reagan drew on his experience in the movies to project an appealing, if old-fashioned, image. Though he was the nation's oldest president, he gave the appearance of vitality. Here he is pictured with his wife, Nancy, who was one of his most influential advisers.

over 70 years old, and that I know." But Reagan remained a full eight years beyond that. His attention often drifted, and he occasionally fell asleep during meetings. At times he appeared uninterested in governing. In press conferences, he was frequently unsure about what was being asked. He delegated a great deal of authority, even if that left him unclear about policy decisions. Critics often accused him of being dependent on his wife, Nancy, for advice.

Worst of all, he suffered from charges of "sleaze" in his administration. In a period of several months during his last year in office, one former aide was convicted of lying under oath to conceal episodes of influence peddling. Another was convicted of illegally lobbying former government colleagues. Attorney General Edwin Meese escaped indictment but nonetheless came under severe criticism for improprieties that culminated in his resignation.

In 1988, Republican George Bush sought the presidency after eight years as Reagan's vice president. A businessman who had prospered in the Texas oil industry, then served in Congress, as top envoy to China, and as head of the CIA, Bush gradually overcame his public image of a political weakling by becoming something of a pit bull during a mudslinging campaign against his Democratic opponent, Michael Dukakis. As governor of Massachusetts, Dukakis had turned his state around after years in the economic doldrums. The son of Greek immigrants, he defeated challenges from several Democrats, including the charismatic black candidate Jesse Jackson, in the primaries but proved unable to counter the charges of the Republican campaign.

One particularly devastating Republican advertisement featured black convict Willie Horton, who had benefited from a Massachusetts weekend release program only to commit another brutal crime while away from prison. The advertisement never mentioned race directly, but it encouraged racial polarization and proved a blow from which Dukakis never recovered.

On election day, many Americans, believing that neither candidate had addressed the issues, stayed home to protest the victory of style over substance. Bush claimed a 54 to 46 percent popular vote victory and carried 40 states, giving him a 426–112 electoral vote win. But he did not have the kind of mandate Reagan had enjoyed eight years earlier, and Democrats controlled both houses of Congress.

Bush quickly put his own imprint on the presidency. An unpretentious man, he liked to keep busy, tearing through golf courses and appointments from morning till night. He maintained a wide network of friends and political contacts through handwritten notes, telephone calls, and personal visits. More than a year and a half into his term, he was still on his political honeymoon, with a personal approval rating of 67 percent. Support grew even stronger as he presided over the Persian Gulf War in 1991. Then, as the economy faltered and the results of the war seemed suspect, approval levels began to drop.

Republican Policies at Home

Republicans in the 1980s aimed to reverse the stagnation of the Carter years and to provide new opportunities for business to prosper. To that end Reagan proposed and implemented an economic recovery program that rested on the theory of supply-side economics. This held that the reduction of taxes would encourage business expansion, which in turn would lead to a larger supply of goods to help stimulate the system as a whole. "Reaganomics" promised a revitalized economy.

One early initiative involved pushing through regressive tax reductions. Although all taxpayers enjoyed some savings, the rich benefited far more than middle- and lower-income Americans. As a result of tax cuts and enormous defense expenditures, the budget deficit grew larger and ultimately ran out of control. The gross federal debt—the total national indebtedness—spiraled upward from $914 billion in

1980 to $3.1 trillion in 1990. When Reagan assumed office, the per capita national debt was $4,035; nine years later, in 1990, it was about $12,400.

Faced with the need to raise more money and to rectify the increasingly skewed tax code, in 1986 Congress passed and Reagan signed the most sweeping tax reform measure since the income tax began. It lowered rates, simplified brackets, and closed loopholes to expand the tax base. Though it ended up neither increasing nor decreasing the government's tax take, the measure was an important step toward treating low-income Americans more equitably, but most of the benefits still went to the rich.

At the same time, Reagan embarked on a major program of deregulation. In a campaign more comprehensive than Jimmy Carter's, he weakened agencies of the 1970s like the Environmental Protection Agency, the Consumer Product Safety Commission, and the Occupational Safety and Health Administration. He argued that regulations impeded business growth, and he appointed people like James Watt, his first secretary of the interior, who systematically relaxed enforcement of environmental rules.

Meanwhile Reagan challenged the consensus fostered by the New Deal that the national government should monitor the economy and assist the least fortunate citizens. He had won fame and fortune on his own, and others could do the same. He declared that it was time to eliminate "waste, fraud, and abuse" by cutting programs the country did not need.

Reagan needed to make cuts in social programs, both because of the sizable tax cuts and because of the enormous military expenditures. While calling for economy in government, his administration sought an unprecedented military budget of $1.5 trillion. By 1985, with a budget of $300 billion, the United States was spending half a million dollars a minute on defense and four times as much as at the height of the Vietnam War. The trade-off was clear: reduced spending for social programs.

The huge cuts in some social programs reversed the approach followed under Franklin Roosevelt and endorsed by liberals in the past 50 years. Public service jobs, mandated under the Comprehensive Employment and Training Act, were eliminated, and other aid to the cities, where the poor congregated, was severely reduced. Unemployment compensation was cut back. Medicare patients were required to pay more for treatment. Welfare benefits were lowered, and food stamp allocations were reduced. Many grants for college students gave way to loans. The Legal Services Corporation, which offered legal advice to those too poor to afford lawyers' fees, was gutted. According to the Congressional Budget Office, spending on human resources fell by $101 billion between 1980 and 1982. The process continued even after Reagan left office. Between 1981 and 1992, American spending, after adjustment for inflation, fell 82 percent for subsidized housing, 63 percent for job training and employment services, and 40 percent for community services. Middle-class Americans, aided by the tax cuts, were not hurt by the slashes in social programs. But for millions of America's poorest citizens, the administration's approach caused real suffering.

As a political conservative distrustful of central government, Reagan also yearned to place more power in the hands of state and local governments and to reduce the ways in which the federal government touched people's lives. His "New Federalism" attempted to shift responsibilities from the federal to the state level. By eliminating federal funding and making grants to the states instead, which could spend the money as they saw fit, he hoped to restore a measure of local initiative. But the program never produced the desired results. As critics charged, with some justification, the proposal was merely a backhanded way of moving programs from one place to another, while eliminating federal funding. When a prolonged recession began in 1990, this policy contributed to the near-bankruptcy of a number of states and municipalities, which constitutionally could not run deficits as could the federal government but had been handed responsibility for programs formerly funded in Washington.

Meanwhile, Reagan took a decidedly conservative approach to social issues as well. He willingly accepted the support of the New Right, speaking out for public prayer in the schools and openly demonstrating his opposition to abortion by making sure that the first nongovernmental group to receive an audience at the White House was an antichoice March for Life contingent.

George Bush followed directly in his predecessor's footsteps. Having forsworn his objection to "voodoo economics" as soon as he received the vice-presidential nomination, he faithfully adhered to Reagan's general economic policy while serving in that office and continued it once he became president in January 1989. In the 1988 campaign, he admonished voters to "read my lips" and promised "no new taxes." Though he backed down from that pledge in a bipartisan effort to bring the budget deficit under control, he later renounced his own agreement to modest tax increases when he went back on the campaign trail in 1992.

Like Reagan, Bush systematically prevented spending for social programs. Tireless in his criticism of the Democratic majorities in the Senate and the House of Representatives, he vetoed measure after measure intended to assist those caught in the ravages of a recession that sent unemployment rates up to 8 percent and left one of every four urban children living in poverty.

As president, Bush also firmly opposed abortion, although at the start of the 1980s he had been sympathetic to a woman's right to decide for herself; and his Supreme Court appointments, like Reagan's, guaranteed that the effort to roll back or overturn *Roe* v. *Wade* would continue (see Chapter 29).

The Republican philosophy under Reagan and Bush dramatically reversed America's domestic agenda. Liberalism in the 1960s had reached a high-water mark in a time of steady growth, when hard choices about where to spend money had been less necessary. As limits began to loom, decisions about social programs became more difficult, and millions of Americans came to believe that most of the Great Society programs had failed to conquer poverty and in fact had created lifelong welfare dependency. Conservatism offered a more attractive answer, particularly to those Americans in the middle and upper classes who were already comfortable.

But the conservative transformation also led to a number of serious problems that loomed in the early 1990s. As Bush assumed the presidency, his administration uncovered a scandal at the Department of Housing and Urban Development (HUD) in which highly placed Republicans received large fees from developers in return for helping wealthy clients win HUD contracts. At the same time, the new president had to deal with a crisis in the long-mismanaged savings and loan industry. The Republican deregulation policy had allowed owners of savings and loan institutions to operate without the previous restrictions, and many of them, paying themselves lavish salaries, made unwise high-risk investments that proved profitable for a while but then produced tremendous losses. To protect depositors whose assets had been lost by these questionable lending practices, Congress approved a $166 billion rescue plan (the sum soon rose above $250 billion) that committed taxpayers to bailing out the industry.

Far worse was the role Republican policy played in widening the gaps between rich and poor. Tax breaks for the wealthy, deregulation initiatives, high interest rates for investors, permissiveness toward mergers, and an enormous growth in the salaries of business executives all contributed to the shift. So did more flexible antitrust enforcement and a general sympathy for speculative finance.

The results were clear. "The 1980s," analyst Kevin Phillips observed, "were the triumph of upper America—an ostentatious celebration of wealth, the political ascendancy of the rich and a glorification of capitalism, free markets and finance." The concentration of capital increased, and the sums involved took what Phillips termed a "megaleap" forward. Now there was an extraordinary amassing of wealth at the top levels. According to one study, the share of national wealth of the richest 1 percent of the nation rose from about 18 percent in 1976 to 36 percent in 1989. The net worth of the *Forbes* magazine 400 richest Americans nearly tripled between 1981 and 1989.

Meanwhile, less fortunate Americans, ranging from foreclosed farmers to laid-off industrial workers, were hurting more than they had since the Great Depression of the 1930s. A disproportionate number of women and members of minority groups lost ground in the 1980s, despite the gains of some of the luckiest in all of those groups. While white family income and net worth rose, they fell among African-American and Hispanic families.

The growing disparity in wealth, resurgent racism, and the neglect of the urban poor became horrifyingly visible in the terrible rioting that swept through Los Angeles in the spring of 1992. The year before, Americans had watched a videotaped savage beating of black motorist Rodney King by white police officers, only the most dramatic of a long string of incidents involving police brutality. When a California jury, which contained no blacks, acquitted the policemen, people of all colors throughout the country were astonished and convinced that equal justice under the law had been proved unobtainable by people of color. In Los Angeles thousands reacted with uncontrolled fury. More than a decade of urban neglect lay in the background of the riot and so did tension between African-Americans and Korean shopkeepers and between black and Hispanic urban dwellers, who competed for jobs and living space in the city. As widespread arson and looting swept through many neighborhoods, the police proved unable to control the mayhem. Much of it was led by gang members but involved as well hundreds of ordinary citizens who acted irresponsibly. The riot left 51 dead, 2,000 injured, and $1 billion in damage to the city. It was the worst riot in decades, more deadly even than the Watts riot that had wracked Los Angeles 27 years before. Political candidates from both parties scurried around trying to define new policies to address neglected urban problems.

THE POSTINDUSTRIAL ECONOMY

The Los Angeles riots took place against the backdrop of an economy that frequently appeared more volatile than before. For decades, the Democrats had been trying to use Keynesian tools to stabilize the economy. Now, under Republican supply-side economics, the business cycle began to follow a pattern of moving from recession to boom and back to recession again. As Reagan assumed office, the economy was reeling under the impact of declining productivity, galloping inflation, oil shortages, and high unemployment. Reagan's policies brought improvement in the early 1980s, particularly for middle- and upper-income people, but not for those of lesser means. The recession that gripped the country from 1990 to 1992 only underscored the need for renewed productivity, full employment, and more equitable distribution of wealth.

The Shift to a Service Economy

In the 1980s, the economy underwent significant restructuring. In a trend under way for more than half a century, the United States shifted from an industrial base, where most workers actually produced things, to a service base, where most provided expertise or service to others in the work force. By the mid-1980s, three-fourths of the 113 million employees in the country worked in the service sector—as fast-food workers, clerks, computer programmers, doctors, lawyers, bankers, teachers, and public employees.

In part, that shift derived from the decline of America's industrial sector. The United States, which had been the world's industrial leader since the late nineteenth century, began to lose that position by the 1970s. After 1973, productivity slowed in virtually all American industries; in the early 1980s, during the worst recession since the 1930s, economic growth virtually ceased. Real GNP fell by 0.2 percent in 1980, rose by 1.9 percent in 1981, and fell by 2.5 percent in 1982. In the midst of the Reagan boom it rose 3.0 percent in 1987 and 3.9 percent in 1988, then stagnated from 1990 to 1992 during another recession.

The causes of this decline in productivity were complex. The most important factor was a widespread and systematic failure on the part of the United States to invest sufficiently in its basic productive capacity. During the Reagan years, investment in capital goods—plants and equipment—gave way to speculation, mergers, and spending abroad. Domestic investment declined 5.7 percent in 1990 and 9.5 percent in 1991. Other factors affecting industrial productivity were rising oil prices (see Chapter 28), government policies aimed at curbing inflation by keeping machines idle, and environmental regulations intended to make industries change their methods of operation. Finally, the war in Vietnam diverted federal funds from support for research and development at the same time that Japan, Germany, and the Soviet Union were increasing their R & D expenditures.

While American industry became less productive, other industrial nations moved forward. German and Japanese industries aggressively modernized and reached new heights of efficiency. As a result, the United States began to lose its former share of the world market for industrial goods. Formerly a leader in iron and steel production, the United States found itself importing a fifth of its iron and steel from abroad. By 1980, Japanese car manufacturers

had also captured nearly a quarter of the American automobile market, and they continued to hold that substantial share in 1990. The American auto industry, which had been a mainstay of economic growth for much of the twentieth century, suffered plant shutdowns and massive layoffs. In 1991, Ford lost a staggering $2.3 billion, in its worst year ever. Although the American auto industry subsequently improved its position, foreign competition remained a major challenge.

Workers in Transition

In the 1980s and early 1990s, American labor struggled to hold on to the gains realized by the post–World War II generation of blue-collar workers. The shift to a service economy created problems for many Americans workers. Millions of men and women who had lost positions as a result of plant closings and permanent economic contractions now found themselves in low-paying jobs with few opportunities for advancement. Entry-level posts were seldom located in the central cities, where most of the poor lived, and minority residents often lacked the skills to acquire such jobs. A basic mismatch between jobs and people in the cities became more pronounced.

Meanwhile, the trade union movement faltered as the economy moved from an industrial to a service base. As the United States emerged from World War II, unions claimed 35 percent of all nonagricultural workers as members, but this percentage began to decrease steadily in the mid-1950s and continued to decline in subsequent years. Union membership rose in the public sector, but even this increase did not reverse the general decline in membership. By 1989, only 16.4 percent of nonagricultural workers belonged to unions.

The shift from blue-collar to white-collar work contributed to the contraction. The increase in the numbers of women and young people in the work force (groups that have historically been difficult to organize) was another factor, as was the more forceful opposition to unions by managers applying the provisions of the Taft-Hartley Act of 1947, which restricted the weapons labor leaders could use.

Union vulnerability could be seen early in Ronald Reagan's first term, when the Professional Air Traffic Controllers Organization went out on strike. Charging that the strike violated the law and undermined the "protective services which are government's reason for being," the president fired the strikers, decertified the union, and ordered the training of new air controllers at a cost of $1.3 billion. The message was clear: Government employees could not challenge the public interest. But antiunion sentiments reverberated throughout the nongovernment sector as well.

Everywhere unions encountered hard times. To respond to increasing foreign competition and stagnant domestic productivity rates, unions found themselves forced to make concessions. In 1984, the United Auto Workers (UAW) ended a strike at General Motors after winning a pledge that GM would guarantee up to 70 percent of the production workers' lifetime jobs in return for a smaller wage increase than they sought and also in return for a modification of the cost-of-living allowance that had been a part of UAW contracts since 1948. In the same way, in 1988, General Electric workers in the Midwest accepted a pay cut to save their jobs. That decision was part of a calculated effort to persuade GE to revitalize domestic plants rather than turn more actively to foreign labor. In 1992 the UAW called off a strike against Caterpillar Tractor and went back to the bargaining table after realizing that its contract demands would never be met.

Agricultural workers likewise had to adjust as the larger work force was reconstituted. Continuing a trend that began in the early twentieth century, the number of farmers declined steadily. When Franklin Roosevelt took office in 1933, some 6.7 million farms covered the American landscape. Fifty years later, farm families numbered only 2.4 million. In 1980, farm residents made up 2.7 percent of the total population; by 1989, that figure had fallen to 1.9 percent. As family farms disappeared, farming income became more concentrated in the hands of the largest operators. By 1983, the largest 1 percent of the nation's farmers produced 30 percent of all farm products and had average annual incomes of $572,000.

The extraordinary productivity of American farmers derived in part from the use of chemical fertilizers, irrigation, pesticides, and scientific agricultural management. Equally important were the government's price support programs, initiated during the New Deal to shield struggling farmers from unstable prices and continued thereafter.

Yet that very productivity had environmental costs and led to unexpected setbacks in the 1980s. In the 1970s, as food shortages developed in many countries, the United States became the "breadbasket of the world." Farmers increased their output to meet multibillion-bushel grain orders from India, China, Russia, and other countries and profited handsomely from high grain prices caused by global shortages. Often farmers borrowed heavily to increase production, sometimes at interest rates up to 18 percent. Then, the fourfold increase in oil prices beginning in 1973 drove up the cost of running the modern mechanized farm. When a worldwide economic slump began in 1980, overseas demand for American farm products declined sharply and farm prices fell. Farmers who had borrowed money at high interest rates, when corn sold at $3 to $4 per bushel, now found themselves trying to meet payments on these loans with corn that brought only $2 per bushel. Thousands of farmers, caught in the cycle of overproduction, heavy indebtedness, and falling prices, watched helplessly as banks and federal agencies foreclosed on their mortgages and drove them out of business.

Conditions improved little at the end of the decade. Family farms continued to disappear amid predictions that the trend would continue to the turn of the century. A drought in the Southeast in 1986 led to burned and stunted fields. An even worse drought in 1988 stretched across most of the Midwest. Devastating crops and forcing up prices, it demonstrated how vulnerable farmers remained.

The Roller Coaster Economy

During the 1980s and 1990s, the economy suffered a series of shifts. The Reagan-Bush era began with a recession, moved into an economic boom between 1983 and 1990, and then became mired in another recession as the new decade began. It appeared that the United States had embarked on another cycle of boom and bust, like that of the early years of the twentieth century.

The recession of 1980–1982 began during Jimmy Carter's administration when the Federal Reserve Board tried to deal with mounting deficits by increasing the money supply. To counter the resulting inflation and cool down the economy, Carter cut programs but succeeded only in bringing on a recession. Under Carter, the unemployment rate had hovered between 5.6 and 7.8 percent. During Reagan's first year, the job situation deteriorated further, and by the end of 1982, the unemployment rate had climbed to 10.8 percent, with joblessness among African-Americans over 20 percent. Nearly a third of the nation's industrial capacity lay idle, and 12 million Americans were out of work. Inflation also continued to be a problem, eroding the purchasing power of people already in difficulty.

The recession of 1980–1982 afflicted every region of the country. Business failures, bankruptcies, and plant closings increased. General Electric released almost 10,000 of its 23,000 workers, and International Harvester closed a plant employing 6,500 people. Detroit was one of the hardest-hit areas in the United States. An

industrial city revolving around automobile manufacturing, it suffered both from Japanese competition and from the high interest rates that made car sales plummet. The Detroit unemployment rate rose to more than 19 percent, as the entire city suffered from the decline. The Sun Belt—the vast southern region stretching from coast to coast—initially seemed "recession-proof," but soon it was also stricken. The unemployment rate in California in mid-1982 reached the national average of 9.5 percent, while in Texas it was 7 percent, higher than it had been for ten years. There was more joblessness in Greenlee County, Arizona, than anywhere in the country.

As the rising price of oil led to frantic drilling in many parts of the world, supplies suddenly outstripped demand. The resulting collapse in oil prices disrupted the economy in states like Texas, Oklahoma, and Louisiana. At the same time, worldwide gluts of minerals like copper added to unemployment elsewhere in the Southwest. The threat to the overextended southwestern banking system endangered the entire nation's financial structure. Because many parts of the rural South had never prospered, a gloomy economic picture spread from the Gulf states almost to California. In Jefferson County, Mississippi, 67 percent of the population lived below the poverty line.

Economic conditions improved in late 1983 and early 1984, particularly for Americans in the middle and upper income ranges, but the economic upswing masked a growing undercurrent of poverty. A 1984 survey noted a "staggering" increase in poverty in the South. The Census Bureau reported that the net worth of a typical white household was 12 times greater than the net worth of a typical black household and 8 times greater than the net worth of a typical Latino household. In 1988, the Census Bureau reported a national poverty figure of 13.5 percent. The figure for whites was 10.5 percent, for blacks 33.1 percent. While many families continued to earn a middle-class income, they often did so only by having two full-time income earners. Blue-collar workers often had to accept lower standards of living. Single mothers were hit hardest of all.

The huge and growing budget deficits were another reflection of fundamental economic instability. The doubts those deficits caused culminated in the stock market crash of 1987. After six weeks of falling prices, it suffered a 22.6 percent drop on Monday, October 19, almost double the 12.8 percent plunge on October 28, 1929. The deficits, negative trade balances, and exposures of Wall Street fraud all combined to puncture the bubble. The stock market revived, but the crash foreshadowed further problems.

Those problems surfaced in the early 1990s, as the country experienced another recession. The combination of extravagant military spending, the uncontrolled growth of entitlements—programs like Medicare and Medicaid that provided benefits for millions of Americans on the basis of need—and the tax cut sent budget deficits skyward. As bond traders in the 1980s speculated recklessly, bought and sold companies with an eye solely toward quick gain, and pocketed huge profits, the basic productive structure of the country continued to decline. The huge increase in the size of the national debt eroded business confidence, and this time the effects were felt not simply in the stock market but in the economy as a whole, which drifted into a downturn in 1990.

American firms suffered a serious decline. In an effort to cope with declining profits and decreased consumer demand, companies scaled back dramatically. In late 1991, General Motors announced that it would close 21 plants, lay off 9,000 white-collar employees the next year, and eliminate more than 70,000 jobs in the next several years. Hundreds of other companies did the same, trimming corporate fat but also cutting thousands of jobs. In the New York City metropolitan area, more than 400,000 jobs were lost since 1989. In Manhattan alone, job losses eliminated virtually all of the private sector growth

of the 1980s. In a chilling indication of the city's economic woes, over a million New Yorkers, one out of every seven, were on the welfare rolls in July 1992. Most of the newcomers were unskilled workers who were unable to find jobs during the recession. Meanwhile, for those working, real incomes, after adjustment for inflation, began to fall. The upshot, the New York *Times* reported, was that "most Americans are entering the 1990s worse off than they were in the early 1970s." Around the nation, state governments found it impossible to balance their budgets without resorting to massive spending cuts. Reagan's efforts to move programs from the federal to the state level worked as long as funding lasted, but as national support dropped and state tax revenues declined, states found themselves in a budgetary gridlock. Most had constitutional prohibitions against running deficits, and so they had to slash spending for social services and education, even after yearly budgets had been approved.

After a number of false starts, the economy looked as though it was starting to shake off the recession in mid-1992. But deficits still haunted the nation, and grass-roots opposition to tax increases made it all the more difficult to bring the national debt under control or to balance state and local budgets. Despite some improvement, it was clear that recovery might take a long time.

THE DEMOGRAPHIC TRANSFORMATION

As the American people dealt with the swings of the economy, demographic patterns changed in significant ways. The 1990 census revealed that in the previous decade the population of the United States had increased from 228 million to approximately 250 million. The rise of 9.6 percent in the 1980s, down from 11.5 percent in the 1970s, was one of the lowest rates of growth in American history. At the same time, the complexion of the country changed. As a result of increased immigration and minority birthrates significantly higher than the rate for whites, an all-time high of 25 percent of the population in 1992 was black, Hispanic, Asian, or Native American.

Urban and Suburban Shifts

Urban populations changed significantly. White families continued to leave for the steadily growing suburbs, which by 1990 contained almost half the population. As that transformation unfolded, American cities increasingly filled with members of the nation's minorities. In 15 of the nation's 28 largest cities, minorities made up at least half the population. Between 1980 and 1990, the minority population in New York rose from 48 to 57 percent, in Chicago from 57 to 62 percent, in Houston from 48 to 59 percent, in

San Diego from 31 to 41 percent. Minority representation varied by urban region. In Detroit, Washington, New Orleans, and Chicago, blacks were the largest minority, while in Phoenix, El Paso, San Antonio, and Los Angeles, Hispanics held that position, and in San Francisco, Asians outnumbered other groups.

The New Pilgrims

Another shift occurred as the United States admitted new immigrants from a variety of foreign nations. A fifth of the decade's population growth stemmed from this immigration, which was spurred by the Immigration Act of 1965. Part of Lyndon Johnson's Great Society program, this act authorized the acceptance of immigrants impartially from all parts of the world. Because the national-origins system of the 1920s

Population Shifts, 1980–1990

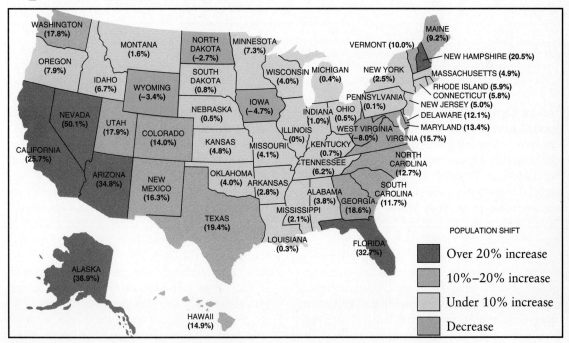

This map shows the population shifts between 1980 and 1990. Note the substantial increases in western regions of the country and the much smaller increases along the Atlantic seaboard.

Immigration: Volume and Sources, 1945-1989

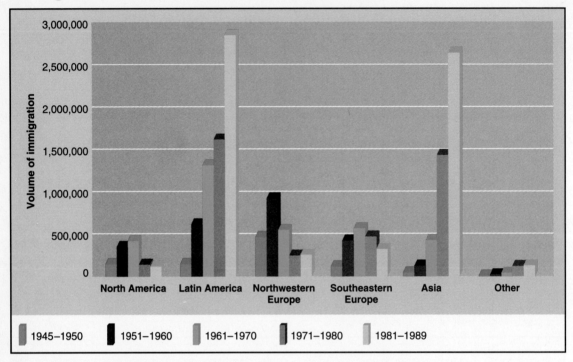

This chart shows the shifting patterns of American immigration in the postwar years. In particular, note the large increase in Asian and Latin American immigration in the past several decades.

had favored western Europeans, most immigrants between 1930 and 1960 had come from Europe or Canada. Between 1977 and 1979, however, only 16 percent came from these areas, while 40 percent came from Asia and another 40 percent from Latin America. In the 1980s, 37 percent came from Asia, and 47 percent came from Mexico, the Caribbean, and Latin America.

As had long been true, the desire for jobs fostered immigration. But foreign crises also fueled the influx. After 1975, the United States accepted more than a half million Vietnamese refugees. In 1980, more than 160,000 arrived. That same year, the nation admitted 125,000 Cubans and Haitians to southern Florida. The

official total of all immigrants in 1978 was higher than it had been in 60 years.

Millions more arrived illegally. As the populations of Latin American nations soared and as economic conditions deteriorated, more and more people looked to the United States for relief. In the mid-1970s, Leonard Chapman, commissioner of the Immigration and Naturalization Service, estimated that there might be 12 million foreigners in the United States illegally. While official estimates were lower, Attorney General William French Smith declared in 1983, "Simply put, we've lost control of our own borders."

Several legislative measures sought to rationalize the immigration process further. In 1986, Congress passed the Immigration Reform and

Control Act, aimed at curbing illegal immigration while offering amnesty to aliens who had lived in the United States since 1982. Turnout for the program was less than expected until the mid-1988 deadline approached. Then 50,000 per week applied, compared with 10,000 earlier in the year, and all-night lines became common at legalization centers.

The Immigration Act of 1990 was even more important. It raised immigration quotas by 40 percent per year, cut back on restrictions based on ideology or sexual orientation that had been used to deny entry in the past, reserved a substantial number of visas for large investors, and provided for swift deportation of aliens who committed crimes.

The United States had once again become a refuge for people from very different parts of the world. The Sun Belt in particular, from Florida to California, felt the impact of the new Asians and Hispanics. In Los Angeles, Samoans, Taiwanese, Koreans, Vietnamese, Filipinos, and Cambodians competed for jobs and apartments with Mexicans, African-Americans, and whites, just as newcomers from different countries had contended with one another in New York City a century before. Throughout the country, in Miami, in Houston, in Brooklyn, the languages heard in the schools and on the streets changed.

These groups left a new imprint on the United States. As blacks and Hispanics became major figures in the urban equation, the number of Asians in the country doubled in the 1980s. In California, they became the largest group of entering students at a number of college campuses.

Growing Up

Other demographic changes also affected Americans' lives. In the mid-1970s, the birthrate began to rise slowly after a decade and a half of decline. The baby boom, which peaked in 1960 with a rate of 24 births per 1,000 people, had created a population explosion in the years after

World War II before leveling off. In 1981, the rate stood at 16, then rose to nearly 17 in 1990, as demographers viewed the new increase in births as part of a long-term trend.

But children less frequently lived in traditional homes. Despite the stereotype of the breadwinner father, the homemaker mother, and two children, the Labor Department estimated that only 7 percent of the nation's families actually matched that pattern in the late 1970s. Divorce shattered the mold, reaching a peak of nearly 1.2 million by 1980, and declining to 1.175 million divorces in 1990. For each 1,000 marriages there were 480 divorces in 1990, compared with 258 per 1,000 in 1960. The social stigma once attached to divorce disappeared, and the nation elected its first divorced president, Reagan. "Nonfamily households" became increasingly common. Between 1980 and 1990, such households increased, and single-parent families, particularly those headed by women, were now common. In 1960, 11 percent of all children lived in such homes; by 1990, the figure had reached 25 percent. For blacks, the proportion of families headed by women was three times as great as for whites. A 1986 study observed that children in such families were more likely to leave school, have children out of wedlock, and end up on welfare.

The rising rate of runaway children became another product of changed family life. According to some estimates, more than a million children between the ages of 10 and 17 were on the run. They left home for various reasons. Some were driven out. Others were victims of physical abuse. Still others fled a violent or stressed family life. In 1974, Congress passed the Runaway and Homeless Youth Act, which established telephone hot lines and temporary shelters. But the shelters served only 45,000 youths a year, leaving countless others without help.

Even more ominous was the rising death rate among the young. The Public Health Service reported in 1982 that the death rate for most

Americans had dropped significantly over a 30-year period, and it continued to drop throughout the decade, but the rate for those between 15 and 24 rose steadily after 1976. Automobile accidents, murders, and suicides caused three out of four deaths for that group.

Growing Old

As concern with the problems of the young increased, awareness of the plight of the old, the fastest-growing age group in modern America, also grew. In the 1980s, the number of Americans over 75 grew by more than 27 percent. Underlying the rapid increase was the steady advance in medical care, which in the twentieth century had increased life expectancy from 47 to 74 years. The "aging revolution" promised to become the most lasting of all twentieth-century social changes. Legislation in 1978 raised the mandatory retirement age from 65 to 70, helping older workers who wanted to keep their jobs, but decreasing employment opportunities for younger job seekers.

Generational resentment over jobs was compounded by the knotty problems faced by the social security system established a half century before. As more and more Americans retired, the system could not generate sufficient revenue to make the payments due without assistance from the general governmental fund. In the early 1980s, it appeared that the entire system might collapse. A government solution involving higher taxes for those still employed and a later age for qualifying for benefits rescued the fund.

At an intensely personal level, American families faced difficult decisions about how to care for older parents who could no longer care for themselves. In the past, the elderly might naturally have moved into their children's homes, but attitudes and family patterns had changed. Children were fewer than in earlier generations, and as women gravitated to jobs outside the home, they were less able to take care of an elderly parent. Retirement villages and nursing homes provided two alternatives, but the decision to place a parent under institutional care was often excruciating.

Margaret Stump, an occupational therapist from Tenafly, New Jersey, agonized over such a decision. For six years she flew to Lima, Ohio, every three months to see her mother, who was over 90 years old. Finally, she decided to bring her to a New Jersey nursing home. "I felt that she'd be better once she got to a home," Margaret recalled. "But I knew she wanted to be in her own house. It was a very difficult decision. I had to wait until I thought she wouldn't know where she was."

The New Students

Another group of Americans were also affected by demographic change. College students were more numerous than ever before. After World War II, partly as a result of GI education benefits, higher education became broadly accessible for the first time in American history. College enrollment, which had never exceeded 1.5 million before 1945, rose to nearly 3 million in the early 1960s and reached 13.7 million in 1990. Women entered college in unprecedented numbers, and students were often older. Students in the 1980s and early 1990s were also significantly more conservative and more willing to work within the system.

Some students, not sure of themselves or their goals, gravitated toward cults, such as the Unification Church of the Reverend Sun Myung Moon, the Way International, and the International Society for Krishna Consciousness. But most students in the 1980s coped with uncertain times by preparing for careers. Large numbers of them chose business or economics courses, while enrollment in the liberal arts dropped sharply. Once in the working world, these young urban professionals, or "yuppies," devoted themselves to upward mobility and material gain. In the

1990s, however, many of these opportunities dried up and left students contemplating further schooling until the economy improved.

THE UNITED STATES IN A CHANGED WORLD

The domestic changes experienced by the American people were in many ways less dramatic than those taking place in the international arena. In the 1980s and 1990s, the United States emerged triumphant in the Cold War that had dominated world politics since the end of World War II. In the most momentous development in modern world history, communism collapsed in Eastern Europe and in the Soviet Union, and the various republics of the Soviet system embraced both capitalism and democracy. Yet the transition to a market economy was tortuous, and several of the Soviet satellite nations fragmented into separate states based on long-standing ethnic divisions. The Soviet Union itself disintegrated into its diverse republics once Marxist-Leninist doctrine and centralized authority no longer provided the cement to keep the once-unified nation together. Similar turbulence gripped the Middle East, accompanied by the rise of religious fanaticism and fundamentalism. South Africa likewise experienced breathtaking change, as black leader Nelson Mandela was freed after more than two decades of imprisonment and led the movement to end apartheid and establish a multiracial state. In the midst of this international tumult, the United States had to shift its assumptions and its traditional approach to the rest of the world and learn to operate with a new multicultural perspective.

The United States and the Cold War

The Cold War was very much alive as Reagan assumed power in 1981. In foreign affairs, the new president asserted American interests far more aggressively than Jimmy Carter. Like most of his contemporaries, Reagan believed in large defense budgets and a militant approach toward the Soviet Union. He wanted to cripple the Russians militarily and economically by forcing them to spend more than they could afford. The massive buildup in both nuclear and conventional weapons helped undermine the Communist state but unfortunately at the cost of tremendously destabilizing budget deficits at home.

Reagan promoted an increased atomic arsenal by arguing that a nuclear war could be fought and won. Discounting scientists' studies that showed that nuclear war would cause cataclysmic destruction, he claimed that the United States could survive. T. K. Jones, deputy undersecretary of defense for strategic and theater nuclear forces, even revived the dormant notion of nuclear civil defense. "Dig a hole, cover it with a couple of doors, and then throw three feet of dirt on top," he advised. "It's the dirt that does it.... If there are enough shovels to go around, everybody's going to make it." That position appeared particularly cavalier as scientists began to speculate about the "nuclear winter" that could end planetary life after a nuclear war.

While promoting defense spending and nuclear superiority during his first term, Reagan persisted in viewing the Soviet Union as an "evil empire." The administration abandoned Senate ratification of SALT II, the arms reduction plan negotiated under Carter, although it observed its restrictions. Instead the administration proposed that Russia destroy certain missiles in return for an American pledge not to deploy new weapons in Europe. The Soviet Union balked at that idea, which was so different from the careful negotiation accompanying previous arms talks. As the arms race escalated, new U.S. missiles were deployed in western Europe, and in both countries, military budgets soared.

Meanwhile, Reagan proposed the Strategic Defense Initiative, popularly known as "Star Wars" after a 1977 movie, to intercept Soviet missiles by means of a shield in outer space. Scientists questioned whether the proposal was technologically feasible. Economists pointed to the extraordinary sums it would cost just to find out. But the administration pressed ahead with the project.

In his second term, Reagan softened his rigid position toward the Soviet Union and agreed to meet with the new Russian leader, Mikhail Gorbachev. Summits in both the Soviet Union and the United States led to an Intermediate-Range Nuclear Forces Treaty that provided for withdrawal and destruction of a whole category of nuclear weapons in both countries. The two nations had not yet resumed détente, but communications were better than they had been in some time.

George Bush maintained Reagan's comfortable relationship with Mikhail Gorbachev. The two leaders met in Malta in late 1989 and in the United States in mid-1990. Together they signed agreements reducing the number of long-range nuclear weapons to a maximum of 1,600 rockets and 6,000 warheads, ending their manufacture of chemical weapons, and easing trade restrictions between the two nations. The Strategic Arms Reduction Treaty (START) they signed in 1991 dramatically decreased the number of long-range weapons stockpiled during years of international hostility. "The Cold War is now behind us," Gorbachev declared at Stanford University. "Let us not wrangle over who won it." But the outcome was clear: In the final years of the twentieth century, the United States would be the dominant force.

Hailed around the world for his part in ending the Cold War, Gorbachev encountered trouble from opposition groups within the Soviet Union. In 1991, he survived a right-wing challenge, but he could not resist those who wanted to go even further to establish democracy and capitalism. The forces he had unleashed within the Soviet Union finally tore the USSR apart. In the turbulence that followed the coup, Boris Yeltsin, head of Russia, the strongest, largest,

and most populous of the Soviet republics, emerged as the dominant leader. Already independence movements in the tiny Baltic republics of Estonia, Latvia, and Lithuania had begun the disintegration of the Soviet Union, and now other republics declared their autonomy and then coalesced loosely in a Commonwealth of Independent States.

Early in 1992, Bush and Yeltsin proclaimed a new era of "friendship and partnership" and formally declared an end to the Cold War. The United States and its allies sought a new role for NATO, the North Atlantic Treaty Organization, and contemplated the extension of aid to former Soviet republics that needed help in reorganizing their economies as free enterprise systems.

While celebrating the collapse of the Soviet Union, the United States found itself facing a vastly different situation in Europe. The liberalization initiated by Gorbachev in his own country quickly spread beyond Soviet borders and soon toppled governments in most countries within the Soviet orbit. Bush spoke of a "New World Order," anticipating international stability, but the fall of communism brought growing disorder as the disintegration of central authority opened the way for intense political wrangling and the rekindling of ancient racial, cultural, and religious antagonisms.

The most dramatic chapter in the collapse of communism began in November 1989, when East Germany's Communist Party boss announced unexpectedly that citizens of his country would be free to leave East Germany. Within hours, thousands of people gathered on both sides of the 28-mile Berlin Wall, the symbol of the Cold War that divided Berlin into east and west sectors. As the border guards stepped aside, East Germans flooded into West Berlin amidst dancing, shouting, and fireworks. All through the night noisy celebrators reveled in what one observer called the "greatest street party in the history of the world." Within days, an outpouring of sledgehammer-wielding Germans pulverized the Berlin Wall, and soon the Communist

The destruction of the Berlin Wall in November 1989 was a symbolic blow to the entire Cold War structure that had grown up in Europe in the postwar years. The dismantling of the Wall touched off joyous celebrations.

government led by Erich Honnecker came tumbling down with it. In October 1990, East and West Germany were formally reunited.

The fall of the Berlin Wall marked a watershed in history. Everywhere it brought in its wake the pell-mell overthrow of Communist regimes. In Poland, the 10-year-old Solidarity movement led by Lech Walesa finally triumphed in its long struggle against Soviet domination and found itself in power, with Walesa as president. In Czechoslovakia, after over four decades of Communist rule, Czech playwright Vaclav Havel became president. But Czechoslovakia soon divided into its two main ethnic components, peacefully forming the Czech Republic and Slovakia. New regimes also swept into power in Bulgaria, Hungary, Romania, and Albania.

Yugoslavia proved to be the extreme case of resurgent ethnic hostility in the face of collapsing central authority. The Balkan region had long been a powder keg, and only dictatorship had held the diverse republics together. When Slovenia and Croatia declared their independence in 1991, the fragile nation descended into chaos.

The decision of the Muslim and Croatian majority in Bosnia to secede from Serbian-dominated Yugoslavia led Bosnian Serbs, backed by the Serbian republic, to embark upon a brutal siege of the city of Sarajevo and an even more ruthless "ethnic cleansing" campaign to eliminate opposition elements of newly independent Bosnia and Herzegovina.

The United States and the Middle East

The Middle East remained equally unstable, as the ancient Arab-Israeli conflict dragged on. In June 1982, the Israelis invaded Lebanon in an attempt to destroy the Palestine Liberation Organization (PLO). Lebanese factions sought Syrian help against the Israelis. In August, U.S. marines joined France and Italy in a peacekeeping mission to restore order and soon found themselves allied with one Lebanese faction against Syria. A year later, terrorist bombs in the American barracks killed 241 servicemen. Humiliated, the United States pulled out its forces, only to station American vessels later in the troubled Persian Gulf, as the Middle East remained as turbulent as before.

In the early 1990s Secretary of State James Baker finally secured agreement from the major parties in the region to speak to one another face to face. Though intense squabbling continued, negotiations struggled forward. A victory in the Israeli parliamentary elections in mid-1992 for Yitzhak Rabin, a less hawkish prime minister, offered further hope for peace.

Another problem in the region drew the United States into a shooting war during the Bush administration. When Saddam Hussein, ruler of Iraq, invaded and annexed the neighboring state of Kuwait in August 1990, the United States took a strong stand. Earlier, between 1985 and 1990, the United States had provided massive military support for Iraq in the war it was waging with Iran. Now, however, the Iran-Iraq war had ended, and Iraq's invasion of Kuwait threatened the flow of Saudi Arabian oil to the West. Equally troubling, Saddam seemed intent on unifying Arab nations, thereby threatening Israel and dominating the region's production of oil, upon which the United States was highly dependent.

Saddam's invasion aroused an immediate reaction. The United Nations Security Council voted 14–0 to condemn the invasion and a few days later endorsed by a 13–0 vote an embargo on trade with Iraq. The American secretary of state and the Soviet foreign minister issued a joint statement condemning the attack. Working through the UN, as Truman had done in Korea, the United States implemented a blockade and began planning for war.

Denouncing Iraq's "naked aggression," Bush mobilized American reserves, including a sizable number of women, organized a multinational army of nearly half a million troops, and secured from the Senate and House a resolution authorizing the use of force. In mid-January 1991, the 28-nation alliance struck at Iraq in Operation Desert Storm with both air and ground forces.

Unlike the costly, drawn-out, and ultimately unpopular war in Vietnam, the Persian Gulf War was swift and engrossing. Television footage showed "smart bombs" being guided to their targets by laser beams. Briefings by General H. Norman Schwarzkopf and other members of his staff carefully released information about the military operations and orchestrated a sympathetic response. Victory came quickly, as the alliance forces completely overwhelmed the Iraqis with sophisticated missiles, airplanes, and tanks. Bush's approval rating soared to 91 percent.

The mood of euphoria in the United States soon soured, however, as Saddam retained power and used his remaining military might to put down revolts of Kurds and Shiites in Iraq. Bush's unwillingness to become bogged down in an Iraqi civil war and his eagerness to bring American troops home left the conflict unfinished. A year after victory, Saddam was as strong as he had been before.

The United States and Latin America

Closer to home, the Reagan and Bush administrations intervened frequently in Latin America. Viewing Central America as a Cold War battlefield, Reagan openly opposed the left-wing guerrillas of El Salvador who fought to overthrow a repressive right-wing regime that was receiving support from the United States. Fearful that another nation might follow the Marxist examples of Cuba and Nicaragua, Reagan increased assistance to the antirevolutionary Salvadoran government, heedless of a similar course followed earlier in Vietnam. Efforts to destroy the radical Farabundo Martí National Liberation Front (FMLN) failed. Reagan rejected an FMLN offer to negotiate and for the next six years poured about $1 million a day into El Salvador. As Americans took over the economy, the CIA sought to prevent either the left wing or the far-right wing, which employed "death squads" to kill thousands of people, from gaining power. That policy failed, and in 1989, the far-right faction, Alianza Republicana Nacionalista

(ARENA), won Salvadoran elections. Peace appeared possible, however, as the government signed an agreement with the rebel FMLN in January 1992.

Nicaragua became an even bloodier battleground and one where Reagan persistently flouted international law and the U.S. Constitution when Congress refused to yield to his efforts to defeat revolutionary reformers. In 1979, revolutionaries calling themselves Sandinistas (after César Sandino, who fought in the 1920s against occupying American troops) overthrew the repressive Somoza family, which had ruled for three decades. Jimmy Carter initially extended aid to the Sandinistas and recognized the new regime, then cut off support to show his disapproval of their curbs on civil liberties and of their alleged efforts to assist rebels in El Salvador. The Reagan administration charged that the Sandinistas were driving out moderate elements, welcoming Cuban and Soviet assistance, and supplying leftist guerrillas in El Salvador. In November 1981, Reagan authorized the CIA to arm and train counterrevolutionaries known as Contras. Although this policy violated United States neutrality laws, the training continued, and the Contras began to attack from bases in Honduras and Costa Rica. As the Sandinistas built up their forces and secured aid from western Europe and the Soviet bloc, Nicaragua became enmeshed in a bitter civil war.

The war went badly for the Contras. Their failures by the end of 1983 led the CIA to assume the initiative in military operations and to mine Nicaraguan harbors in violation of international law. When Congress discovered these secret missions, it cut off military aid to the Contras. In Reagan's second term, Congress insisted on ending military aid, though humanitarian assistance to the Contras continued. American economic sanctions meanwhile disrupted the Nicaraguan economy further and led to a crippling inflation rate, but still the Sandinistas clung to power until peaceful elections in early 1990 drove them out. President Daniel Ortega gave way to Violeta Barrios de Chamorro and her National Opposition Union. Though the economy remained in desperate straits and the Sandinistas still maintained control of the armed forces and continued to be represented in the bureaucracy, the Nicaraguans were ready for democratic change, and the new regime seemed to offer some hope of healing the wounds of the bloody civil war.

The Middle Eastern and Central American crises became entangled in the Iran-Contra affair. In 1987, the nation discovered that the National Security Council had launched an effort to free American hostages in the Middle East by selling arms to Iran and then using the funds to aid the Contras, in direct violation of both the law and congressional will. Commissions and congressional hearings demonstrated the chaos and duplicity in the administration and cast doubt on the president's ability to govern. The subsequent trial of Oliver North, the National Security Council official responsible for the policy, focused on his distortions and falsifications before congressional committees and on his destruction of official documents. Convicted in 1989, North received a light sentence requiring no time in prison from a judge who recognized that North was not acting entirely on his own. His conviction was overturned the following year by the U.S. Appeals Court.

Only on the tiny Caribbean island of Grenada did Reagan win a modest victory. The president ordered 2,000 marines there in October 1983, after a military coup installed a government sympathetic to Fidel Castro's Cuba. U.S. marines invaded the island, rescued a number of American medical students, and the administration claimed triumph.

Bush took the credit for a similar incursion in Panama, ostensibly to protect American lives. The United States invaded Panama, the Bush administration said, to protect the Panama Canal, defend American citizens following a number of attacks, and stop the drug traffic. The incursion resulted in the capture of military leader Manuel Noriega, notorious for his involvement in the drug trade. Noriega was brought to the United

States, charged, and in a lengthy trial convicted of drug trafficking.

The United States and South Africa

Americans, like people around the world, applauded the black struggle against apartheid in South Africa, which grew more militant in the 1980s. Under the rigid policy of apartheid, the white minority, constituting about 15 percent of the population, segregated and suppressed the black majority and denied it voting rights. Under Reagan, the United States followed a policy of "constructive engagement," in which it relied on talk but not economic sanctions to force an end to apartheid. By 1986, the bankruptcy of that approach was evident, and Congress imposed sanctions, including a rule prohibiting new American investments, despite Reagan's objections. The economic pressure damaged the South African economy and persuaded more than half of the 300 American firms in business there to leave.

In 1989, a new president, Frederik W. De Klerk, recognized that South Africa could no longer withstand the pressure from the United States and the rest of the world. The next year he freed the 71-year-old Nelson Mandela, the symbol of militant opposition to apartheid, after 27 years in prison, and announced plans gradually to overturn apartheid. South Africa appeared to be embarking on a new path as the world looked on hopefully.

The Election of 1992

As the world changed, so the United States changed, and the election of 1992 reflected the national and international transformations taking place. After four years in office, George Bush sought a second term and found himself involved in an unusual three-way race against Democratic candidate Bill Clinton, governor of Arkansas, and Texas billionaire Ross Perot, an independent candidate. Overcoming allegations of adultery, marijuana use, and draft evasion, the 46-year-old Clinton argued that it was time for a new generation to take command. Perot pulled out of the race in July but reentered it in the fall.

The three candidates faced a disillusioned nation. A Gallup Poll reported in September that 79 percent of all Americans felt the country was in economic decline, 65 percent believed it was in moral decline, and 19 percent thought it was in military decline. To many, the deficit appeared to be choking both present and future public policy. Despite brilliant technological advances, health care was becoming prohibitively expensive and patently unfair. Crime was becoming a national epidemic.

This campaign, more than any in the past, was fought on television. There were three presidential debates, involving all three candidates, but they told only part of the story. Far more important were the candidates' appearances on talk shows and interview programs. This reliance on the electronic marketplace was visible evidence of the shift occurring in American politics. At times the campaign turned nasty, as when Bush claimed that "my dog Millie knows more about foreign affairs" than Bill Clinton. Despite such rhetoric, the contest was less ugly than Bush's victorious campaign four years before.

In the end, it became a clash of competing visions. In accepting the Republican nomination, Bush underscored his faith in the individual rather than the bureaucracy and insisted, "Government is too big and spends too much." Clinton, in contrast, claimed that the government had a necessary role to play "to make America work again."

On election day, Clinton won 43 percent of the popular vote to 38 percent for Bush and 19 percent for Perot. The electoral vote margin was even larger: 370 for Clinton, 168 for Bush, 0 for Perot. The Democrats retained control of both houses of Congress, with more women and minority members than ever before.

Since the 1960 presidential campaign, televised debates have been a popular way for the candidates to reach large numbers of the American people. In the 1992 campaign, the three major candidates—Republican George Bush, Independent H. Ross Perot, and Democrat Bill Clinton—met in a series of televised debates.

The president-elect moved quickly to demonstrate his intention of shifting America's course after 12 years of Republican rule. His Cabinet nominations included four women, four African-Americans, and two Latinos. He held a televised "economic summit" to explore national options and demonstrated a keen grasp of the details of policy. In his inaugural address in early 1993, Clinton told an eager nation that "a new season of American renewal has begun." Major problems loomed ahead, but a new generation stood ready to try whatever was necessary to resolve them.

The Clinton Presidency

Bill Clinton faced a very different world as he took office in early 1993. The end of the Cold War stimulated complex and rapid changes in countries around the world. Without the familiar framework of Soviet-American competition to guide its foreign policy, U.S. policymakers and the American public were frequently uncertain about what role the country should play in the international arena. What actions were in the national interest? Where did U.S. humanitarian responsibilities lie? These and other questions prompted debate, but no consensus emerged.

Ethnic conflicts posed particularly difficult problems for the United States. In the former Yugoslavia, ethnic and religious violence in Bosnia and Herzegovina worsened. But when Clinton pledged to send American troops to help keep peace, the American public was unwilling to honor his commitment.

Meanwhile, Africa presented other challenges to American policymakers. Somalia, in

East Africa, suffered from a devastating famine and breakdown of political order. American troops, sent by George Bush, assisted a United Nations relief effort there. Six months after Clinton became president, a firefight with a Somali faction led by Mohammed Farrah Aidid resulted in several dozen American casualties. The crisis prompted some Americans, still haunted by the memory of Vietnam, to demand withdrawal. Reluctant to back down, Clinton increased the number of American troops. The soldiers returned home the following spring without having achieved their goals.

Another crisis erupted in Rwanda, in Central Africa, when a fragile balance of power between two ethnic groups—the Tutsis and the Hutus—broke down and led to the slaughter of several hundred thousand innocent people. As the world followed the situation on television, the United States, like many European nations, debated the possibility of intervention on humanitarian grounds but decided to do nothing.

In South Africa, the news was more heartening. Nelson Mandela and Frederik W. de Klerk worked together to ensure peaceful elections in which blacks, who made up the vast majority of the population, voted for the first time. After years of struggle, the African National Congress assumed power and began to dismantle the apartheid system. Mandela himself became president of this nation that was building itself anew.

In the Middle East, Clinton played the part of peacemaker, just as Jimmy Carter had done 15 years before. On September 13, 1993, in a dramatic ceremony on the White House lawn, Palestine Liberation Organization leader Yasir Arafat and Israeli president Yitzhak Rabin took the first public step toward ending years of conflict as they shook hands and signed a peace agreement that led to Palestinian self-rule in the Gaza strip. While extremists tried to destroy the peace process by continued violence, the effort to overcome old animosities continued.

Clinton was similarly successful in Haiti, but just barely. After seeking for several years to restore deposed president Jean Bertrand Aristide to power, Clinton threatened and then authorized an American invasion of the island. At the last minute a delegation including Carter and former Joint Chiefs of Staff chairman Colin Powell secured a commitment from the military dictatorship to relinquish power, and the transition took place. While the United States wanted to nourish democracy and protect its economic interests, Americans remained wary of foreign intervention. American reluctance to become deeply involved abroad posed difficult problems for the president.

Clinton also had his hands full at home. Although the economy finally began to improve, the public gave the president little credit for the upturn. Republicans and some conservative Democrats resisted his initiatives, and he had to fight fiercely for every program he endorsed. He gained Senate ratification of the North American Free Trade Agreement (NAFTA)—aimed at promoting free trade between Canada, Mexico, and the United States—in November 1993, but only after a bitter battle. He secured passage of a crime bill after a similar struggle. But he failed to win approval of his major legislative initiative: health care reform. "This health-care system of ours is badly broken," he said in September 1993, "and it's time to fix it." Particularly troublesome were escalating costs and the lack of universal medical care. Clinton's proposal for a system of health alliances in each state to pay health claims, provide far greater coverage, and trim costs was too complex for many Americans and provoked intense opposition from the health care industry and from politicians with plans of their own. In the end he was unable to persuade Congress either to accept his approach or adopt a workable alternative.

Voters demonstrated their dissatisfaction in the mid-term elections of 1994. They demanded change and supported candidates who promised a smaller government, less regulation, and lower taxes. In a rebuff to Clinton and the Democrats, Republicans gained control of both the Senate and the House of Representatives for the first time in 40 years. Clinton acknowledged that Americans "don't like what they see when they watch us working here." Now the major parties had to see if they could work together for the next two years.

CONCLUSION

THE RECENT PAST IN PERSPECTIVE

In the 1980s and early 1990s, the United States witnessed the triumph of conservatism. The assault on the welfare state, dubbed the "Reagan Revolution," involved creating a less regulated economy, whatever the implications for less fortunate Americans. Policies inaugurated by Reagan and followed by Bush continued the trend begun by Richard Nixon in the 1970s. They reshaped the political agenda and reversed the liberal approach that had held sway since the New Deal of Franklin Roosevelt in the 1930s. There were limits to the transformation, to be sure. Such fundamental programs as Social Security and Medicare remained securely in place.

In foreign affairs, Republican administrations likewise shifted course. Reagan first assumed a steel-ribbed posture toward the Soviet Union, then moved toward détente, and watched as his successor declared victory in the Cold War.

Despite the end of the Cold War, the nation's defense budget remained far higher than many Americans wished, and the nuclear arsenal continued to pose a threat to the human race. Meanwhile, periods of deep recession wrought havoc on the lives of blue-collar and white-collar workers alike. Middle-class Americans like David Patterson, introduced at the start of the chapter, were caught in a spiral of downward mobility. Liberals and conservatives both worried about the mounting national debt and the ability of the American economy to compete with Japan, Korea, Germany, and other countries. Countless Americans were uneasy about the growing gaps between rich and poor. Children wondered for the first time in American history whether they could hope to do better than or as well as their parents had done.

In the 1980s and early 1990s, the United States struggled to adhere to its historic values in a complex and changing world. When the Democrats took command, those basic values still governed, as the American people continued their centuries-old effort to live up to the promise of the American dream.

Recommended Reading

Historians have not yet had a chance to deal in detail with the developments of the immediate past, so fuller descriptions must be found in other sources. Much of the best writing about the years in this chapter appears in the newspapers and magazines of the popular press. But a number of useful treatments about selected topics provide good starting points in various areas.

General and statistical works about this period include Barry Bluestone and Bennett Harrison, *The Deindustrialization of America: Plant Closings, Community Abandonment, and the Dismantling of Basic Industry* (1982); Peter Duignan and Alvin Rabushka, eds., *The United States in the 1980s* (1980); Andrew Hacker, ed., *U/S: A Statistical Portrait of the American People* (1983); Katherine S. Newman, *Falling from Grace: The Experience of Downward Mobility in the American Middle Class* (1988); Kevin P.

Phillips, *The Politics of Rich and Poor: Wealth and the American Electorate in the Reagan Aftermath* (1990); Neil Postman, *Amusing Ourselves to Death: Public Discourse in the Age of Show Business* (1985); U.S. Bureau of the Census, *Statistical Abstract of the United States: 1991;* and U.S. Bureau of the Census, *U.S. Census of Population, 1990.*

On the Reagan presidency, see Lawrence I. Barrett, *Gambling with History: Reagan in the White House* (1983); Paul Boyer, ed., *Reagan as President: Contemporary Views of the Man, His Politics, and His Policies* (1990); Lou Cannon, *President Reagan: A Role of a Lifetime* (1991) and *Reagan* (1982); Ronnie Dugger, *On Reagan: The Man and His Presidency* (1983); Rowland Evans and Robert Novak, *The Reagan Revolution* (1981); Fred I. Greenstein, ed., *The Reagan Presidency: An Early Assessment* (1983); Haynes Johnson, *Sleepwalking Through History: America Through the Reagan Years* (1991); Richard A. Viguerie, *The New Right: We're Ready to Lead* (1981); and Garry Wills, *Reagan's America: Innocents at Home* (1985)

The Bush years are treated in Colin Campbell, S.J., and Bert A. Rockman, eds., *The Bush Presidency: First Appraisals* (1991).

For a closer look at immigration issues, see Roger Daniels, *A History of Immigration and Ethnicity in American Life* (1990); David M. Reimers, *Still the Golden Door: The Third World Comes to America* (1985); Paul James Rutledge, *The Vietnamese Experience in America* (1992); and Virginia Yans-McLaughlin, ed., *Immigration Reconsidered: History, Sociology, and Politics* (1990).

On foreign affairs see Paul Kennedy, *The Rise and Fall of the Great Powers: Economic Change and Military Conflict from 1500 to 2000* (1987); Walter LaFeber, *America, Russia, and the Cold War, 1945–1990* (6th ed., 1991), *Inevitable Revolutions: The United States in Central America* (1983), and *The American Age: United States Foreign Policy at Home and Abroad Since 1750* (1989); Sandra Mackey, *Lebanon* (1989); Robert Scheer, *With Enough Shovels: Reagan, Bush and Nuclear War* (1982); Strobe Talbott, *The Russians and Reagan* (1984); Seth P. Tillman, *The U.S. and the Middle East* (1982); Sanford J. Ungar, ed., *Estrangement: America and the World* (1985); Mary B. Vanderlaan, *Revolution and Foreign Policy in Nicaragua* (1986); and Thomas W. Walker, ed., *Revolution and Counterrevolution in Nicaragua* (1991).

Insight into the period may also be gained from fictional accounts such as the following: Tim O'Brien, *The Nuclear Age* (1985); Anne Tyler *Dinner at the Homesick Restaurant* (1982); and Tom Wolfe, *The Bonfire of the Vanities* (1987).

Time Line

1980	Ronald Reagan elected president
1980–1982	Recession
1981	Reagan breaks air controllers' strike
1981–1983	Tax cuts; deficit spending increases
1982	American invasion of Lebanon
1983	Reagan proposes Strategic Defense Initiative
1984	Reagan reelected
1986	Tax reform measure passed Immigration Reform and Control Act passed
1987	Iran-Contra affair becomes public Stock market crashes Intermediate-Range Nuclear Forces Treaty signed
1988	George Bush elected president
1989	Federal bailout of savings and loan industry Fall of the Berlin Wall
1990	National debt reaches $3.1 trillion Immigration Act of 1990 passed Sandinistas driven from power in Nicaragua Nelson Mandela freed in South Africa
1990–1992	Recession
1991	Persian Gulf War Failed coup in the Soviet Union Disintegration of the Soviet Union Department of Housing and Urban Development scandal uncovered Strategic Arms Reduction Treaty (START) signed
1991–1992	Ethnic turbulence in a fragmented Yugoslavia
1992	Bill Clinton elected president Czechoslovakia splits into separate republics

Appendix

Declaration of Independence in Congress, July 4, 1776

THE UNANIMOUS DECLARATION OF THE THIRTEEN UNITED STATES OF AMERICA

When, in the course of human events, it becomes necessary for one people to dissolve the political bonds which have connected them with another, and to assume, among the powers of the earth, the separate and equal station to which the laws of nature and of nature's God entitle them, a decent respect to the opinions of mankind requires that they should declare the causes which impel them to the separation.

We hold these truths to be self-evident: That all men are created equal, that they are endowed by their Creator with certain unalienable rights; that among these are life, liberty, and the pursuit of happiness; that, to secure these rights, governments are instituted among men, deriving their just powers from the consent of the governed; that whenever any form of government becomes destructive of these ends, it is the right of the people to alter or to abolish it, and to institute new government, laying its foundation on such principles, and organizing its powers in such form, as to them shall seem most likely to effect their safety and happiness. Prudence, indeed, will dictate that governments long established should not be changed for light and transient causes; and accordingly all experience hath shown that mankind are more disposed to suffer, which evils are sufferable, than to right themselves by abolishing the forms to which they are accustomed. But when a long train of abuses and usurpations, pursuing invariably the same object, evinces a design to reduce them under absolute despotism, it is their right, it is their duty, to throw off such government, and to provide new guards for their future security. Such has been the patient sufferance of these colonies; and such is now the necessity which constrains them to alter their former systems of government. The history of the present King of Great Britain is a history of repeated injuries and usurpations, all having in direct object the establishment of an absolute tyranny over these states. To prove this, let facts be submitted to a candid world.

He has refused his assent to laws the most wholesome and necessary for the public good.

He has forbidden his governors to pass laws of immediate and pressing importance, unless suspended in their operation till his assent should be obtained; and, when so suspended, he has utterly neglected to attend to them.

He has refused to pass other laws for the accommodation of large districts of people, unless those people would relinquish the right of representation in the legislature, a right inestimable to them, and formidable to tyrants only.

He has called together legislative bodies at places unusual, uncomfortable, and distant from the depository of their public records, for the sole purpose of fatiguing them into compliance with his measures.

He has dissolved representative houses repeatedly, for opposing, with manly firmness, his invasions on the rights of the people.

He has refused for a long time, after such dissolutions, to cause others to be elected; whereby the legislative powers, incapable of annihilation, have returned to the people at large for their exercise; the state remaining, in the mean time, exposed to all the dangers of invasions from without and convulsions within.

He has endeavored to prevent the population of these states; for that purpose obstructing the laws for naturalization of foreigners; refusing to pass others to encourage their migration hither, and raising the conditions of new appropriations of lands.

He has obstructed the administration of justice, by refusing his assent to laws for establishing judiciary powers.

He has made judges dependent on his will alone, for the tenure of their offices, and the amount and payment of their salaries.

He has erected a multitude of new offices, and sent hither swarms of officers to harass our people and eat out their substance.

He has kept among us, in times of peace, standing armies, without the consent of our legislatures.

He has affected to render the military independent of, and superior to, the civil power.

He has combined with others to subject us to a jurisdiction foreign to our constitution, and unacknowledged by our laws, giving his assent to their acts of pretended legislation:

For quartering large bodies of armed troops among us;

For protecting them, by a mock trial, from punishment for any murders which they should commit on the inhabitants of these states;

For cutting off our trade with all parts of the world;

For imposing taxes on us without our consent;

For depriving us, in many cases, of the benefits of trial by jury;

For transporting us beyond seas, to be tried for pretended offenses;

For abolishing the free system of English laws in a neighboring province, establishing therein an arbitrary government, and enlarging its boundaries, so as to render it at once an example

and fit instrument for introducing the same absolute rule into these colonies;

For taking away our charters, abolishing our most valuable laws, and altering fundamentally the forms of our governments;

For suspending our own legislatures, and declaring themselves invested with power to legislate for us in all cases whatsoever.

He has abdicated government here, by declaring us out of his protection and waging war against us.

He has plundered our seas, ravaged our coasts, burned our towns, and destroyed the lives of our people.

He is at this time transporting large armies of foreign mercenaries to complete the works of death, desolation, and tyranny already begun with circumstances of cruelty and perfidy scarcely paralleled in the most barbarous ages, and totally unworthy the head of a civilized nation.

He has constrained our fellow-citizens, taken captive on the high seas, to bear arms against their country, to become the executioners of their friends and brethren, or to fall themselves by their hands.

He has excited domestic insurrection among us, and has endeavored to bring on the inhabitants of our frontiers the merciless Indian savages, whose known rule of warfare is an undistinguished destruction of all ages, sexes, and conditions.

In every stage of these oppressions we have petitioned for redress in the most humble terms; our repeated petitions have been answered only by repeated injury. A prince, whose character is thus marked by every act which may define a tyrant, is unfit to be the ruler of a free people.

Nor have we been wanting in our attentions to our British brethren. We have warned them, from time to time, of attempts by their legislature to extend an unwarrantable jurisdiction over us. We have reminded them of the circumstances of our emigration and settlement here. We have appealed to their native justice and magnanimity; and we have conjured them, by the ties of our common kindred, to disavow these usurpations, which would inevitably interrupt our connections and correspondence. They, too, have been deaf to the voice of justice and of consanguinity. We must, therefore, acquiesce in the necessity which denounces our separation, and hold them, as we hold the rest of mankind, enemies in war, in peace friends.

We, therefore, the representatives of the United States of America, in General Congress assembled, appealing to the Supreme Judge of the world for the rectitude of our intentions, do, in the name and by the authority of the good people of these colonies, solemnly publish and

declare, that these United Colonies are, and of right ought to be, FREE AND INDEPENDENT STATES; that they are absolved from all allegiance to the British crown, and that all political connection between them and the state of Great Britain is, and ought to be, totally dissolved; and that, as free and independent states, they have full power to levy war, conclude peace, contract alliances, establish commerce, and do all other acts and things which independent states may of right do. And for the support of this declaration, with a firm reliance on the protection of Divine Providence, we mutually pledge to each other our lives, our fortunes, and our sacred honor.

Constitution of the United States of America[*]

PREAMBLE

We the people of the United States, in order to form a more perfect union, establish justice, insure domestic tranquillity, provide for the common defense, promote the general welfare, and secure the blessings of liberty to ourselves and our posterity, do ordain and establish this Constitution for the United States of America.

ARTICLE 1

Section 1   All legislative powers herein granted shall be vested in a Congress of the United States, which shall consist of a Senate and a House of Representatives.

Section 2   The House of Representatives shall be composed of members chosen every second year by the people of the several States, and the electors in each State shall have the qualifications requisite for electors of the most numerous branch of the State Legislature.

[*]The Constitution became effective March 4, 1789.

NOTE: Any portion of the text that has been amended appears in italics.

No person shall be a Representative who shall not have attained to the age of twenty-five years, and been seven years a citizen of the United States, and who shall not, when elected, be an inhabitant of that State in which he shall be chosen.

Representatives and direct taxes shall be apportioned among the several States which may be included within this Union, according to their respective numbers, *which shall be determined by adding to the whole number of free persons, including those bonded in service for a term of years and excluding Indians not taxed, three-fifths of all other persons.* The actual enumeration shall be made within three years after the first meeting of the Congress of the United States, and within every subsequent term of ten years, in such manner as they shall by law direct. The number of Representatives shall not exceed one for every thirty thousand, but each State shall have at least one Representative; *and until such enumeration shall be made, the State of New Hampshire shall be entitled to choose three, Massachusetts eight, Rhode Island and Providence Plantations one, Connecticut five, New York six, New Jersey four, Pennsylvania eight, Delaware one, Maryland six, Virginia ten,*

North Carolina five, South Carolina five, and Georgia three.

When vacancies happen in the representation from any State, the Executive authority thereof shall issue writs of election to fill such vacancies.

The House of Representatives shall choose their Speaker and other officers; and shall have the sole power of impeachment.

Section 3   The Senate of the United States shall be composed of two Senators from each State, *chosen by the legislature thereof,* for six years; and each Senator shall have one vote.

Immediately after they shall be assembled in consequence of the first election, they shall be divided as equally as may be into three classes. The seats of the Senators of the first class shall be vacated at the expiration of the second year, of the second class at the expiration of the fourth year, and of the third class at the expiration of the sixth year, so that one-third may be chosen every second year; *and if vacancies happen by resignation or otherwise, during the recess of the legislature of any State, the Executive thereof may make temporary appointments until the next meeting of the legislature, which shall then fill such vacancies.*

No person shall be a Senator who shall not have attained to the age of thirty years, and been nine years a citizen of the United States, and who shall not, when elected, be an inhabitant of that State for which he shall be chosen.

The Vice-President of the United States shall be President of the Senate, but shall have no vote, unless they be equally divided.

The Senate shall choose their other officers, and also a President *pro tempore,* in the absence of the Vice-President, or when he shall exercise the office of President of the United States.

The Senate shall have the sole power to try all impeachments. When sitting for that purpose, they shall be on oath or affirmation. When the President of the United States is tried, the Chief Justice shall preside; and no person shall be convicted without the concurrence of two-thirds of the members present.

Judgment in cases of impeachment shall not extend further than to removal from the office, and disqualification to hold and enjoy any office of honor, thrust or profit under the United States: but the party convicted shall nevertheless be liable and subject to indictment, trial, judgment and punishment, according to law.

Section 4   The times, places and manner of holding elections for Senators and Representatives shall be prescribed in each State by the legislature thereof; but the Congress may at any time by law make or alter such regulations, except as to the places of choosing Senators.

The Congress shall assemble at least once in every year, and such meeting *shall be on the first Monday in December, unless they shall by law appoint a different day.*

Section 5   Each house shall be the judge of the elections, returns and qualifications of its own members, and a majority of each shall constitute a quorum to do business; but a smaller number may adjourn from day to day, and may be authorized to compel the attendance of absent members, in such manner, and under such penalties, as each house may provide.

Each house may determine the rules of its proceedings, punish its members for disorderly behavior, and with the concurrence of two-thirds, expel a member.

Each house shall keep a journal of its proceedings, and from time to time publish the same, excepting such parts as may in their judgment require secrecy; and the yeas and nays of the members of either house on any question shall, at the desire of one-fifth of those present, be entered on the journal.

Neither house, during the session of Congress, shall, without the consent of the other, adjourn for more than three days, nor to any other place than that in which the two houses shall be sitting.

Section 6   The Senators and Representatives shall receive a compensation for their services, to be ascertained by law and paid out of the treasury of the United States. They shall in all cases except treason, felony and breach of the peace be privileged from arrest during their attendance at the session of their respective houses, and in going to and returning from the same; and for any speech or debate in either house, they shall not be questioned in any other place.

No Senator or Representative shall, during the time for which he was elected, be appointed to any civil office under the authority of the United States, which shall have been created, or the emoluments whereof shall have been increased, during such time; and no person holding any office under the United States shall be a member of either house during his continuance in office.

Section 7 All bills for raising revenue shall originate in the House of Representatives; but the Senate may propose or concur with amendments as on other bills.

Every bill which shall have passed the House of Representatives and the Senate, shall, before it becomes a law, be presented to the President of the United States; if he approve he shall sign it, but if not he shall return it with objections to that house in which it originated, who shall enter the objections at large on their journal, and proceed to reconsider it. If after such reconsideration two-thirds of that house shall agree to pass the bill, it shall be sent, together with the objections, to the other house, by which it shall likewise be reconsidered, and, if approved by two-thirds of that house, it shall become a law. But in all such cases the votes of both houses shall be determined by yeas and nays, and the names of the persons voting for and against the bill shall be entered on the journal of each house respectively. If any bill shall not be returned by the President within ten days (Sundays excepted) after it shall have been presented to him, the same shall be a law, in like manner as if he had signed it, unless the Congress by their adjournment prevent its return, in which case it shall not be a law.

Every order, resolution, or vote to which the concurrence of the Senate and House of Representatives may be necessary (except on a question of adjournment) shall be presented to the President of the United States; and before the same shall take effect, shall be approved by him, or being disapproved by him, shall be repassed by two-thirds of the Senate and House of Representatives, according to the rules and limitations prescribed in the case of a bill.

Section 8 The Congress shall have power:

To lay and collect taxes, duties, imposts, and excises, to pay the debts and provide for the common defense and general welfare of the United States; but all duties, imposts and excises shall be uniform throughout the United States;

To borrow money on the credit of the United States;

To regulate commerce with foreign nations, and among the several States, and with the Indian tribes;

To establish an uniform rule of naturalization, and uniform laws on the subject of bankruptcies throughout the United States;

To coin money, regulate the value thereof, and of foreign coin, and fix the standard of weights and measures;

To provide for the punishment of counterfeiting the securities and current coin of the United States;

To establish post offices and post roads;

To promote the progress of science and useful arts by securing for limited times to authors and inventors the exclusive right to their respective writings and discoveries;

To constitute tribunals inferior to the Supreme Court;

To define and punish piracies and felonies committed on the high seas and offenses against the law of nations;

To declare war, grant letters of marque and reprisal, and make rules concerning captures on land and water;

To raise and support armies, but no appropriation of money to that use shall be for a longer term than two years;

To provide and maintain a navy;

To make rules for the government and regulation of the land and naval forces;

To provide for calling forth the militia to execute the laws of the Union, suppress insurrections, and repel invasions;

To provide for organizing, arming, and disciplining the militia, and for governing such part of them as may be employed in the service of the United States, reserving to the States respectively the appointment of the officers, and the authority of training the militia according to the discipline prescribed by Congress;

To exercise exclusive legislation in all cases whatsoever, over such district (not exceeding ten miles square) as may, by cession of particular States, and the acceptance of Congress, become the seat of government of the United States, and to exercise like authority over all places purchased by the consent of the legislature of the State, in which the same shall be, for erection of forts, magazines, arsenals, dockyards, and other needful buildings;—and

To make all laws which shall be necessary and proper for carrying into execution the foregoing powers, and all other powers vested by this Constitution in the government of the United States, or in any department or officer thereof.

Section 9   *The migration or importation of such persons as any of the States now existing shall think proper to admit shall not be prohibited by the Congress prior to the year 1808; but a tax or duty may be imposed on such importation, not exceeding $10 for each person.*

The privilege of the writ of habeas corpus shall not be suspended, unless when in cases of rebellion or invasion the public safety may require it.

No bill of attainder or ex post facto law shall be passed.

No capitation or other direct tax shall be laid, unless in proportion to the census or enumeration herein before directed to be taken.

No tax or duty shall be laid on articles exported from any State.

No preference shall be given by any regulation of commerce or revenue to the ports of one State over those of another; nor shall vessels bound to, or from, one State be obliged to enter, clear, or pay duties in another.

No money shall be drawn from the treasury, but in consequence of appropriations made by law; and a regular statement and account of the receipts and expenditures of all public money shall be published from time to time.

No title of nobility shall be granted by the United States: and no person holding any office of profit or trust under them, shall, without the consent of the Congress, accept of any present, emolument, office, or title, of any kind whatever, from any king, prince, or foreign state.

Section 10   No State shall enter into any treaty, alliance, or confederation; grant letters of marque and reprisal; coin money; emit bills of credit; make anything but gold and silver coin a tender in payment of debts; pass any bill of attainder, ex post facto law, or law impairing the obligation of contracts, or grant any title of nobility.

No State shall, without the consent of Congress, lay any imposts or duties on imports or exports, except what may be absolutely necessary for executing its inspection laws: and the net produce of all duties and imposts, laid by any State on imports or exports, shall be for the use of the treasury of the United States; and all such laws shall be subject to the revision and control of the Congress.

No State shall, without the consent of Congress, lay any duty of tonnage, keep troops or ships of war in time of peace, enter into any agreement or compact with another State, or with a foreign power, or engage in war, unless actually invaded, or in such imminent danger as will not admit of delay.

ARTICLE II

Section 1   The executive power shall be vested in a President of the United States of America. He shall hold his office during the term of four years, and, together with the Vice-President, chosen for the same term, be elected as follows:

Each State shall appoint, in such manner as the legislature thereof may direct, a number of electors, equal to the whole number of Senators and Representatives to which the State may be entitled in the Congress; but no Senator or Representative, or person holding an office of trust or profit under the United States, shall be appointed an elector.

The electors shall meet in their respective States, and vote by ballot for two persons, of whom one at least shall not be an inhabitant of the same State with themselves. And they shall make a list of all the persons voted for, and of the number of votes for each, which list they shall sign and certify, and transmit sealed to the seat of government of the United States, directed to the President of the Senate. The President of the Senate shall, in the presence of the Senate and House of Representatives, open all the certificates, and the votes shall then be counted. The person having the greatest number of votes shall be the President, if such number be a majority of the whole number of electors appointed; and if there be more than one who have such majority, and have an equal number of votes, then the House of Representatives shall immediately choose by ballot one of them for President; and if no person have a majority, then from the five highest on the list said house shall in like manner choose the President. But in choosing the President the votes shall be taken by States, the representation from each State having one vote; a quorum for this purpose shall consist of a member or members from two-thirds of the States, and a majority of all the States shall be necessary to a choice. In every case, after the choice of the President, the person having the greatest number of votes of the electors shall be the Vice-President. But if there should remain two or more who have equal votes, the Senate shall choose from them by ballot the Vice-President.

The Congress may determine the time of choosing the electors and the day on which they shall give their votes; which day shall be the same throughout the United States.

No person except a natural-born citizen, *or a citizen of the United States at the time of the adoption of this Constitution,* shall be eligible to the office of President; neither shall any person be eligible to that office who shall not have attained to the age of thirty-five years, and been fourteen years a resident within the United States.

In case of the removal of the President from office or of his death, resignation, or inability to discharge the powers and duties of the said office, the same shall devolve on the Vice-President, and the Congress may by law provide for the case of removal, death, resignation, or inability, both of the President and Vice-President, declaring what officer shall then act as President, and such officer shall act accordingly, until the disability be removed, or a President shall be elected.

The President shall, at stated times, receive for his services a compensation, which shall neither be increased nor diminished during the period for which he shall have been elected, and he shall not receive within that period any other emolument from the United States, or any of them.

Before he enter on the execution of his office, he shall take the following oath or affirmation:—"I do solemnly swear (or affirm) that I will faithfully execute the office of the President of the United States, and will to the best of my ability preserve, protect and defend the Constitution of the United States."

Section 2   The President shall be commander in chief of the army and navy of the United States, and of the militia of the several States, when called into the actual service of the United States; he may require the opinion, in writing, of the principal officer in each of the executive departments, upon any subject relating to the duties of their respective offices, and he shall have power to grant reprieves and pardons for offenses against the United States, except in cases of impeachment.

He shall have power, by and with the advice and consent of the Senate, to make treaties, provided two-thirds of the Senators present concur;

and he shall nominate, and by and with the advice and consent of the Senate, shall appoint ambassadors, other public ministers and consuls, judges of the Supreme Court, and all other officers of the United States, whose appointments are not herein otherwise provided for, and which shall be established by law: but Congress may by law vest the appointment of such inferior officers, as they think proper, in the President alone, in the courts of law, or in the heads of departments.

The President shall have power to fill up all vacancies that may happen during the recess of the Senate, by granting commissions which shall expire at the end of their next session.

Section 3   He shall from time to time give to the Congress information of the state of the Union, and recommend to their consideration such measures as he shall judge necessary and expedient; he may, on extraordinary occasions, convene both houses, or either of them, and in case of disagreement between them, with respect to the time of adjournment, he may adjourn them to such time as he shall think proper; he shall receive ambassadors and other public ministers; he shall take care that the laws be faithfully executed, and shall commission all the officers of the United States.

Section 4   The President, Vice-President and all civil officers of the United States shall be removed from office on impeachment for, and on conviction of, treason, bribery, or other high crimes and misdemeanors.

ARTICLE III

Section 1   The judicial power of the United States shall be vested in one Supreme Court, and in such inferior courts as the Congress may from time to time ordain and establish. The judges, both of the Supreme and inferior courts, shall hold their offices during good behavior, and shall, at stated times, receive for their services a compensation which shall not be diminished during their continuance in office.

Section 2   The judicial power shall extend to all cases, in law and equity, arising under this Constitution, the laws of the United States, and treaties made, or which shall be made, under their authority—to all cases affecting ambassadors, other public ministers and consuls;—to all cases of admiralty and maritime jurisdiction;—to controversies to which the United States shall be a party;—to controversies between two or more States;—*between a State and citizens of another State;*—between citizens of different States;—between citizens of the same State claiming lands under grants of different States, and between a State, or the citizens thereof, and foreign states, citizens or subjects.

In all cases affecting ambassadors, other public ministers and consuls, and those in which a State shall be party, the Supreme Court shall have original jurisdiction. In all the other cases before mentioned, the Supreme Court shall have appellate jurisdiction, both as to law and fact, with such exceptions, and under such regulations, as the Congress shall make.

The trial of all crimes, except in cases of impeachment, shall be by jury; and such trial shall be held in the State where said crimes shall have been committed: but when not committed within any State, the trial shall be at such places or places as the Congress may by law have directed.

Section 3   Treason against the United States shall consist only in levying war against them, or in adhering to their enemies, giving them aid and comfort. No person shall be convicted of treason unless on the testimony of two witnesses to the same overt act, or on confession in open court.

The Congress shall have power to declare the punishment of treason, but no attainder of treason shall work corruption of blood, or forfeiture except during the life of the person attainted.

ARTICLE IV

Section 1   Full faith and credit shall be given in each State to the public acts, records, and judicial proceedings of every other State. And the

Congress may by general laws prescribe the manner in which such acts, records, and proceedings shall be proved, and the effect thereof.

Section 2 The citizens of each State shall be entitled to all privileges and immunities of citizens in the several States.

A person charged in any State with treason, felony, or other crime, who shall flee from justice, and be found in another State, shall on demand of the executive authority of the State from which he fled, be delivered up, to be removed to the State having jurisdiction of the crime.

No person held to service or labor in one State, under the laws thereof, escaping into another, shall, in consequence of any law or regulation therein, be discharged from such service or labor, but shall be delivered up on claim of the party to whom such service or labor may be due.

Section 3 New States may be admitted by the Congress into this Union; but no new State shall be formed or erected within the jurisdiction of any other State; nor any State be formed by the junction of two or more States, or parts of States, without the consent of the legislatures of the States concerned as well as of the Congress.

The Congress shall have power to dispose of and make all needful rules and regulations respecting the territory or other property belonging to the United States; and nothing in this Constitution shall be so construed as to prejudice any claims of the United States, or of any particular State.

Section 4 The United States shall guarantee to every State in this Union a republican form of government, and shall protect each of them against invasion; and on application of the legislature, or of the executive (when the legislature cannot be convened), against domestic violence.

ARTICLE V

The Congress, whenever two-thirds of both houses shall deem it necessary, shall propose amendments to this Constitution, or, on the ap-
plication of the legislatures of two-thirds of the several States, shall call a convention for proposing amendments, which, in either case, shall be valid to all intents and purposes, as part of this Constitution, when ratified by the legislatures of three-fourths of the several States, or by conventions in three-fourths thereof, as the one or the other mode of ratification may be proposed by the Congress; provided *that no amendments which may be made prior to the year one thousand eight hundred and eight shall in any manner affect the first and fourth classes in the ninth section of the first article; and* that no State, without its consent, shall be deprived of its equal suffrage in the Senate.

ARTICLE VI

All debts contracted and engagements entered into, before the adoption of this Constitution, shall be as valid against the United States under this Constitution, as under the Confederation.

This Constitution, and the laws of the United States which shall be made in pursuance thereof; and all treaties made, or which shall be made, under the authority of the United States, shall be the supreme law of the land; and the judges in every State shall be bound thereby, anything in the Constitution or laws of any State to the contrary notwithstanding.

The Senators and Representatives before mentioned, and the members of the several State legislatures, and all executive and judicial officers, both of the United States and of the several States, shall be bound by oath or affirmation to support this Constitution; but no religious test shall ever be required as a qualification to any office or public trust under the United States.

ARTICLE VII

The ratification of the conventions of nine States shall be sufficient for the establishment of this Constitution between the States so ratifying the same.

Done in Convention by the unanimous consent of the States present, the seventeenth day of September in the year of our Lord one thousand seven hundred and eighty-seven and of the Independence of the United States of America the twelfth. In witness whereof we have hereunto subscribed our names.

AMENDMENTS TO THE CONSTITUTION*

Amendment I [1791]

Congress shall make no law respecting an establishment of religion, or prohibiting the free exercise thereof; or abridging the freedom of speech, or of the press; or the right of the people peaceably to assemble, and to petition the government for a redress of grievances.

Amendment II [1791]

A well-regulated militia being necessary to the security of a free State, the right of the people to keep and bear arms shall not be infringed.

Amendment III [1791]

No soldier shall, in time of peace, be quartered in any house without the consent of the owner, nor in time of war, but in a manner to be prescribed by law.

Amendment IV [1791]

The right of the people to be secure in their persons, houses, papers, and effects, against unreasonable searches and seizures, shall not be violated, and no warrants shall issue but upon probable cause, supported by oath or affirmation, and particularly describing the place to be searched, and the persons or things to be seized.

*The first ten amendments are known as the Bill of Rights.

Amendment V [1791]

No person shall be held to answer for a capital or otherwise infamous crime, unless on a presentment or indictment of a grand jury, except in cases arising in the land or naval forces, or in the militia, when in actual service in time of war or public danger; nor shall any person be subject for the same offense to be twice put in jeopardy of life or limb; nor shall be compelled in any criminal case to be a witness against himself, nor be deprived of life, liberty or property, without due process of law; nor shall private property be taken for public use without just compensation.

Amendment VI [1791]

In all criminal prosecutions, the accused shall enjoy the right to a speedy and public trial, by an impartial jury of the State and district wherein the crime shall have been committed, which district shall have been previously ascertained by law, and to be informed of the nature and cause of the accusation; to be confronted with the witnesses against him; to have compulsory process for obtaining witnesses in his favor, and to have the assistance of counsel for his defense.

Amendment VII [1791]

In suits at common law, where the value in controversy shall exceed twenty dollars, the right of trial by jury shall be preserved, and no fact tried by a jury shall be otherwise reexamined in any court of the United States, than according to the rules of the common law.

Amendment VIII [1791]

Excessive bail shall not be required, nor excessive fines imposed, nor cruel and unusual punishments inflicted.

Amendment IX [1791]

The enumeration in the Constitution, of certain rights, shall not be construed to deny or disparage others retained by the people.

Amendment X [1791]

The powers not delegated to the United States by the Constitution, nor prohibited by it to the States, are reserved to the States respectively, or to the people.

Amendment XI [1791]

The judicial power of the United States shall not be construed to extend to any suit in law or equity, commenced or prosecuted against one of the United States by citizens of another State, or by citizens or subjects of any foreign state.

Amendment XII [1804]

The electors shall meet in their respective States, and vote by ballot for President and Vice-President, one of whom, at least, shall not be an inhabitant of the same State with themselves; they shall name in their ballots the person voted for as President, and in distinct ballots the person voted for as Vice-President, and they shall make distinct lists of all persons voted for as President, and of all persons voted for as Vice-President, and of the number of votes for each, which lists they shall sign and certify, and transmit sealed to the seat of government of the United States, directed to the President of the Senate;—the President of the Senate shall, in the presence of the Senate and House of Representatives, open all the certificates and the votes shall then be counted;—the person having the greatest number of votes for President shall be the President, if such number be a majority of the whole number of electors appointed; and if no person have such majority, then from the persons having the highest numbers not exceeding three on the list of those voted for as President, the House of Representatives shall choose immediately, by ballot, the President. But in choosing the President, the votes shall be taken by States, the representation from each State having one vote; a quorum for this purpose shall consist of a member or members from two-thirds of the States, and a majority of all the States shall be necessary to a choice. And if the House of Representatives shall not choose a President whenever the right of choice shall devolve upon them, before *the fourth day of March* next following, then the Vice-President shall act as President, as in the case of the death or other constitutional disability of the President.

The person having the greatest number of votes as Vice-President shall be the Vice-President, if such number be a majority of the whole number of electors appointed; and if no person have a majority, then from the two highest numbers on the list the Senate shall choose the Vice-President; a quorum for the purpose shall consist of two-thirds of the whole number of Senators, and a majority of the whole number shall be necessary to a choice. But no person constitutionally ineligible to the office of President shall be eligible to that of Vice-President of the United States.

Amendment XIII [1865]

Section 1 Neither slavery nor involuntary servitude, except as a punishment for crime whereof the party shall have been duly convicted, shall exist within the United States, or any place subject to their jurisdiction.

Section 2 Congress shall have power to enforce this article by appropriate legislation.

Amendment XIV [1868]

Section 1 All persons born or naturalized in the United States, and subject to the jurisdiction thereof, are citizens of the United States and of the State wherein they reside. No State shall make or enforce any law which shall abridge the privileges or immunities of citizens of the United States; nor shall any State deprive any person of life, liberty, or property, without due process of law; nor deny to any person within its jurisdiction the equal protection of the laws.

Section 2 Representatives shall be apportioned among the several States according to their respective numbers, counting the whole number of persons in each State, excluding Indians not taxed. But when the right to vote at any election for the choice of Electors for President and Vice-President of the United States, Representatives in Congress, the executive and judicial officers of a State, or the members of the legislature thereof, is denied to any of the male inhabitants of such State, being twenty-one years of age and citizens of the United States, or in any way abridged, except for participation in rebellion, or other crime, the basis of representation therein shall be reduced in the proportion which the number of such male citizens shall bear to the whole number of male citizens twenty-one years of age in such State.

Section 3   No person shall be a Senator or Representative in Congress, or Elector of President and Vice-President, or hold any office, civil or military, under the United States, or under any State, who, having previously taken an oath, as a member of Congress, or as an officer of the United States, or as a member of any State legislature, or as an executive or judicial officer of any State, to support the Constitution of the United States, shall have engaged in insurrection or rebellion against the same, or given aid or comfort to the enemies thereof. Congress may, by a vote of two-thirds of each house, remove such disability.

Section 4   The validity of the public debt of the United States, authorized by law, including debts incurred for payment of pensions and bounties for services in suppressing insurrection or rebellion, shall not be questioned. But neither the United States nor any State shall assume or pay any debt or obligation incurred in aid of insurrection or rebellion against the United States, or any claim for the loss of emancipation of any slave; but all such debts, obligations, and claims shall be held illegal and void.

Section 5   The Congress shall have power to enforce, by appropriate legislation, the provisions of this article.

Amendment XV [1870]

Section 1   The right of citizens of the United States to vote shall not be denied or abridged by the United States or by any State on account of race, color, or previous condition of servitude.

Section 2   The Congress shall have power to enforce this article by appropriate legislation.

Amendment XVI [1913]

The Congress shall have power to lay and collect taxes on incomes, from whatever source derived, without apportionment among the several States, and without regard to any census or enumeration.

Amendment XVII [1913]

Section 1   The Senate of the United States shall be composed of two Senators from each State, elected by the people thereof, for six years; and each Senator shall have one vote. The electors in each State shall have the qualifications requisite for electors of [voters for] the most numerous branch of the State legislatures.

Section 2   When vacancies happen in the representation of any State in the Senate, the executive authority of such State shall issue writs of election to fill such vacancies: Provided that the legislature of any State may empower the executive thereof to make temporary appointments until the people fill the vacancies by election as the legislature may direct.

Section 3   The amendment shall not be so construed as to affect the election or term of any Senator chosen before it becomes valid as part of the Constitution.

Amendment XVIII [1919]

Section 1   After one year from the ratification of this article the manufacture, sale, or transportation of intoxicating liquors within, the importation thereof into, or the exportation thereof from the United States and all territory subject to the jurisdiction thereof, for beverage purposes, is hereby prohibited.

Section 2   The Congress and the several States shall have concurrent power to enforce this article by appropriate legislation.

Section 3   This article shall be inoperative unless it shall have been ratified as an amendment to the Constitution by the legislatures of the several States, as provided by the Constitution, within seven years from the date of the submission thereof to the States by the Congress.

Amendment XIX [1920]

Section 1   The right of citizens of the United States to vote shall not be denied or abridged by the United States or by any State on account of sex.

Section 2   The Congress shall have power to enforce this article by appropriate legislation.

Amendment XX [1933]

Section 1   The terms of the President and Vice President shall end at noon on the 20th day of January, and the terms of Senators and Representatives at noon on the 3d day of January, of the years in which such terms would have ended if this article had not been ratified; and the terms of their successors shall then begin.

Section 2   The Congress shall assemble at least once in every year, and such meeting shall begin at noon on the 3d day of January, unless they shall by law appoint a different day.

Section 3   If, at the time fixed for the beginning of the term of the President, the President-elect shall have died, the Vice-President-elect shall become President. If a President shall not have been chosen before the time fixed for the beginning of his term, or if the President-elect shall have failed to qualify, then the President-elect shall act as President until a President shall have qualified, and the Congress may by law provide for the case wherein neither a President-elect nor a Vice-President-elect shall have quali-

fied, declaring who shall then act as President, or the manner in which one who is to act shall be selected, and such persons shall act accordingly until a President or Vice-President shall have qualified.

Section 4   The Congress may by law provide for the case of the death of any of the persons from whom the House of Representatives may choose a President whenever the right of choice shall have devolved upon them, and for the case of the death of any of the persons from whom the Senate may choose a Vice-President whenever the right of choice shall have developed upon them.

Section 5   Sections 1 and 2 shall take effect on the 15th day of October following the ratification of this article.

Section 6   This article shall be inoperative unless it shall have been ratified as an amendment to the Constitution by the legislatures of three-fourths of the several States within seven years from the date of its submission.

Amendment XXI [1933]

Section 1   The eighteenth article of amendment to the Constitution of the United States is hereby repealed.

Section 2   The transportation or importation into any State, Territory, or Possession of the United States for delivery or use therein of intoxicating liquors, in violation of the laws thereof, is hereby prohibited.

Section 3   This article shall be inoperative unless it shall have been ratified as an amendment to the Constitution by conventions in the several States, as provided in the Constitution, within seven years from the date of submission thereof to the States by the Congress.

Amendment XXII [1951]

Section 1   No person shall be elected to the office of President more than twice, and no person who has held the office of President, or acted as

President, for more than two years of a term to which some other person was elected President shall be elected to the office of President more than once. But this article shall not apply to any person holding the office of President when this article was proposed by the Congress, and shall not prevent any person who may be holding the office of President, or acting as President, during the term within which this article becomes operative from holding the office of President or acting as President during the remainder of such term.

Section 2   This article shall be inoperative unless it shall have been ratified as an amendment to the Constitution by the legislatures of three-fourths of the several States within seven years from the date of its submission to the States by the Congress.

Amendment XXIII [1961]

Section 1   The District constituting the seat of Government of the United States shall appoint in such manner as the Congress may direct:

A number of electors of President and Vice-President equal to the whole number of Senators and Representatives in Congress to which the District would be entitled if it were a State, but in no event more than the least populous State; they shall be in addition to those appointed by the States, but they shall be considered for the purposes of the election of President and Vice-President, to be electors appointed by a State; and they shall meet in the District and perform such duties as provided by the twelfth article of amendment.

Section 2   The Congress shall have the power to enforce this article by appropriate legislation.

Amendment XXIV [1964]

Section 1   The right of citizens of the United States to vote in any primary or other election for President or Vice-President, for electors for President or Vice-President, or for Senator or Representative in Congress, shall not be denied or abridged by the United States or any State by reason of failure to pay any poll tax or other tax.

Section 2   The Congress shall have the power to enforce this article by appropriate legislation.

Amendment XXV [1967]

Section 1   In case of the removal of the President from office or of his death or resignation, the Vice-President shall become President.

Section 2   Whenever there is a vacancy in the office of the Vice-President, the President shall nominate a Vice-President who shall take office upon confirmation by a majority vote of both houses of Congress.

Section 3   Whenever the President transmits to the President pro tempore of the Senate and the Speaker of the House of Representatives his written declaration that he is unable to discharge the powers and duties of his office, and until he transmits to them a written declaration to the contrary, such powers and duties shall be discharged by the Vice-President as Acting President.

Section 4   Whenever the Vice-President and a majority of either the principal officers of the executive departments or of such other body as Congress may by law provide, transmit to the President pro tempore of the Senate and the Speaker of the House of Representatives their written declaration that the President is unable to discharge the powers and duties of his office, the Vice-President shall immediately assume the powers and duties of the office as Acting President.

Thereafter, when the President transmits to the President pro tempore of the Senate and the Speaker of the House of Representatives his written declaration that no inability exists, he shall resume the powers and duties of his office unless the Vice-President and a majority of either the principal officers of the executive department[s] or of such other body as Congress may by law provide, transmit within four days to the President pro tempore of the Senate and the Speaker of the House of Representatives their written declaration that the President is unable to discharge the powers and duties of his office. Thereupon Congress shall decide the issue, assembling within forty-eight hours for that purpose if not in session. If the Congress, within twenty-one days after receipt of the latter written declaration, or, if Congress is not in session, within twenty-one days after Congress is required to assemble, determines by two-thirds vote of both Houses that the President is unable to discharge the powers and duties of his office, the Vice-President shall continue to discharge the same as Acting President;

otherwise, the President shall resume the powers and duties of his office.

Amendment XXVI [1971]

Section 1 The right of citizens of the United States, who are eighteen years of age or older, to vote shall not be denied or abridged by the United States or by any State on account of age.

Section 2 The Congress shall have power to enforce this article by appropriate legislation.

Year	Candidates	Parties	Percent of Popular Vote*†	Electoral Vote‡	Percent of Voter Participation†
1789	GEORGE WASHINGTON	No party designations		69	
	John Adams			34	
	Other candidates			35	
1792	GEORGE WASHINGTON	No party designations		132	
	John Adams			77	
	George Clinton			50	
	Other candidates			5	
1796	JOHN ADAMS	Federalist		71	
	Thomas Jefferson	Democratic-Republican		68	
	Thomas Pinckney	Federalist		59	
	Aaron Burr	Democratic-Republican		30	
	Other candidates			48	
1800	THOMAS JEFFERSON	Democratic-Republican		73	
	Aaron Burr	Democratic-Republican		73	
	John Adams	Federalist		65	
	Charles C. Pinckney	Federalist		64	
	John Jay	Federalist		1	
1804	THOMAS JEFFERSON	Democratic-Republican		162	
	Charles C. Pinckney	Federalist		14	
1808	JAMES MADISON	Democratic-Republican		122	
	Charles C. Pinckney	Federalist		47	
	George Clinton	Democratic-Republican		6	
1812	JAMES MADISON	Democratic-Republican		128	
	DeWitt Clinton	Federalist		89	
1816	JAMES MONROE	Democratic-Republican		183	
	Rufus King	Federalist		34	

Year	Candidates	Parties	Percent of Popular Vote*†	Electoral Vote‡	Percent of Voter Participation†
1820	JAMES MONROE	Democratic-Republican		231	
	John Quincy Adams	Independent Republican		1	
1824	JOHN QUINCY ADAMS	Democratic-Republican	30.5	84	26.9
	Andrew Jackson	Democratic-Republican	43.1	99	
	Henry Clay	Democratic-Republican	13.2	37	
	William H. Crawford	Democratic-Republican	13.1	41	
1828	ANDREW JACKSON	Democratic	56.0	178	57.6
	John Quincy Adams	National Republican	44.0	83	
1832	ANDREW JACKSON	Democratic	54.5	219	55.4
	Henry Clay	National Republican	37.5	49	
	William Wirt	Anti-Masonic	8.0	7	
	John Floyd	Democratic		11	
1836	MARTIN VAN BUREN	Democratic	50.9	170	57.8
	William H. Harrison	Whig		73	
	Hugh L. White	Whig		26	
	Daniel Webster	Whig	49.1	14	
	W. P. Mangum	Whig		11	
1840	WILLIAM H. HARRISON	Whig	53.1	234	80.2
	Martin Van Buren	Democratic	46.9	60	
1844	JAMES K. POLK	Democratic	49.6	170	78.9
	Henry Clay	Whig	48.1	105	
	James G. Birney	Liberty	2.3	0	
1848	ZACHARY TAYLOR	Whig	47.4	163	72.7
	Lewis Cass	Democratic	42.5	127	
	Martin Van Buren	Free-Soil	10.1	0	
1852	FRANKLIN PIERCE	Democratic	50.9	254	69.6
	Winfield Scott	Whig	44.1	42	
	John P. Hale	Free-Soil	5.0	0	
1856	JAMES BUCHANAN	Democratic	45.3	174	78.9
	John C. Frémont	Republican	33.1	114	
	Millard Fillmore	American	21.6	8	
1860	ABRAHAM LINCOLN	Republican	39.8	180	81.2
	Stephen A. Douglas	Democratic	29.5	12	
	John C. Breckinridge	Democratic	18.1	72	
	John Bell	Constitutional Union	12.6	39	
1864	ABRAHAM LINCOLN	Republican	55.0	212	73.8
	George B. McClellan	Democratic	45.0	21	
1868	ULYSSES S. GRANT	Republican	52.7	214	78.1
	Horatio Seymour	Democratic	47.3	80	
1872	ULYSSES S. GRANT	Republican	55.6	286	71.3
	Horace Greeley	Democratic	44.0	0§	

Year	Candidates	Parties	Percent of Popular Vote*†	Electoral Vote‡	Percent of Voter Participation†
1876	RUTHERFORD B. HAYES	Republican	48.0	185	81.8
	Samuel J. Tilden	Democratic	51.0	184	
1880	JAMES A. GARFIELD	Republican	48.5	214	79.4
	Winfield S. Hancock	Democratic	48.1	155	
	James B. Weaver	Greenback-Labor	3.4	0	
1884	GROVER CLEVELAND	Democratic	48.5	219	77.5
	James G. Blaine	Republican	48.2	182	
1888	BENJAMIN HARRISON	Republican	47.9	233	79.3
	Grover Cleveland	Democratic	48.6	168	
1892	GROVER CLEVELAND	Democratic	46.0	277	74.7
	Benjamin Harrison	Republican	43.0	145	
	James B. Weaver	Populist	8.5	22	
1896	WILLIAM McKINLEY	Republican	51.1	271	79.3
	William J. Bryan	Democratic	46.7	176	
1900	WILLIAM McKINLEY	Republican	51.7	292	73.2
	William J. Bryan	Democratic; Populist	45.5	155	
1904	THEODORE ROOSEVELT	Republican	56.4	336	65.2
	Alton B. Parker	Democratic	37.6	140	
	Eugene V. Debs	Socialist	3.0	0	
1908	WILLIAM H. TAFT	Republican	51.6	321	65.4
	William J. Bryan	Democratic	43.1	162	
	Eugene V. Debs	Socialist	2.8	0	
1912	WOODROW WILSON	Democratic	41.9	435	58.8
	Theodore Roosevelt	Progressive	27.4	88	
	William H. Taft	Republican	23.2	8	
	Eugene V. Debs	Socialist	6.0	0	
1916	WOODROW WILSON	Democratic	49.4	277	61.6
	Charles E. Hughes	Republican	46.2	254	
	Allan L. Benson	Socialist	3.2	0	
1920	WARREN G. HARDING	Republican	60.4	404	49.2
	James M. Cox	Democratic	34.2	127	
	Eugene V. Debs	Socialist	3.4	0	
1924	CALVIN COOLIDGE	Republican	54.0	382	48.9
	John W. Davis	Democratic	28.8	136	
	Robert M. La Follette	Progressive	16.6	13	
1928	HERBERT C. HOOVER	Republican	58.2	444	56.9
	Alfred E. Smith	Democratic	40.9	87	
1932	FRANKLIN D. ROOSEVELT	Democratic	57.4	472	56.9
	Herbert C. Hoover	Republican	39.7	59	

Year	Candidates	Parties	Percent of Popular Vote*†	Electoral Vote‡	Percent of Voter Participation†
1936	FRANKLIN D. ROOSEVELT	Democratic	60.8	523	61.0
	Alfred M. Landon	Republican	36.5	8	
1940	FRANKLIN D. ROOSEVELT	Democratic	54.8	449	62.5
	Wendell L. Willkie	Republican	44.8	82	
1944	FRANKLIN D. ROOSEVELT	Democratic	53.5	432	55.9
	Thomas E. Dewey	Republican	46.0	99	
1948	HARRY S TRUMAN	Democratic	49.5	303	53.0
	Thomas E. Dewey	Republican	45.1	189	
	J. Strom Thurmond	States' Rights	2.4	39	
	Henry A. Wallace	Progressive	2.4	0	
1952	DWIGHT D. EISENHOWER	Republican	55.1	442	63.3
	Adlai E. Stevenson	Democratic	44.4	89	
1956	DWIGHT D. EISENHOWER	Republican	57.4	457	60.6
	Adlai E. Stevenson	Democratic	42.0	73	
1960	JOHN F. KENNEDY	Democratic	49.7	303	64.0
	Richard M. Nixon	Republican	49.6	219	
	Harry F. Byrd	Independent	0.7	15	
1964	LYNDON B. JOHNSON	Democratic	61.1	486	61.7
	Barry M. Goldwater	Republican	38.5	52	
1968	RICHARD M. NIXON	Republican	43.4	301	60.6
	Hubert H. Humphrey	Democratic	42.7	191	
	George C. Wallace	American Independent	13.5	46	
1972	RICHARD M. NIXON	Republican	60.7	520	55.5
	George S. McGovern	Democratic	37.5	17	
1976	JIMMY CARTER	Democratic	50.0	297	54.3
	Gerald R. Ford	Republican	48.0	240	
1980	RONALD REAGAN	Republican	50.8	489	53.0
	Jimmy Carter	Democratic	41.0	49	
	John B. Anderson	Independent	6.6	0	
1984	RONALD REAGAN	Republican	58.7	525	52.9
	Walter F. Mondale	Democratic	40.6	13	
1988	GEORGE BUSH	Republican	54.0	426	50.1
	Michael Dukakis	Democratic	46.0	111	
1992	WILLIAM J. CLINTON	Democratic	43.0	370	61.3
	George Bush	Republican	38.0	168	
	H. Ross Perot	Independent	19.0	0	

*Candidates receiving less than 2.5 percent of the popular vote have been omitted. Hence the percentage of popular vote may not total 100 percent.

†Prior to 1824, most presidential electors were chosen by state legislators rather than by popular vote.

‡Before the Twelfth Amendment was passed in 1804, the electoral college voted for two presidential candidates; the runner-up became the vice president.

§Greeley died before the electoral college met. His votes were divided among four other candidates.

Credits

Page abbreviations are as follows: **L** left, **R** right.

6 Library of Congress **10L** Musée de l'Homme, Paris **10R** Musée de l'Homme, Paris **16** American Museum of Natural History **17** Biblioteca Medices Laurenziana, Florence, Italy **27** Copyright the British Museum **32** Courtesy American Antiquarian Society **37** Julie Roy Jeffrey **41** Gibbes Museum of Art, Carolina Art Association, Charleston **44** National Gallery of Art, Washington, D.C. **54** From the Collection of The Detroit Institute of Art, Founders Society, Gibbs-Williams Fund **64** Peabody Museum, Harvard University **71L** Moravian Historical Society, Nazareth, Penn. **71R** Moravian Historical Society, Nazareth, Penn. **77** National Gallery of Art, Washington, D.C. **86** Copyright Yale University Art Gallery, Gift of Eugene Phelps Edwards **102** Courtesy, Virginia Historical Society, Richmond **106** Massachusetts Historical Society **110L** Library of Congress **110R** The New-York Historical Society, New York City **120** Library of Congress **126** Prints Division/New York Public Library, Astor, Lenox and Tilden Foundations **129** Library of Congress **131** Library of Congress **139** New York State Historical Association, Cooperstown **155** Mead Art Museum, Amherst College, Amherst, Mass. **165** Library of Congress **166** Copyright Yale University Art Gallery **172** The Metropolitan Museum of Art, Bequest of Cornelia Cruger, 1923 (24.19.1) **185** The Maryland Historical Society, Baltimore **192** Historical Society of Pennsylvania **201** National Museum of Natural History, Smithsonian Institution **219** Library of Congress **222** Museum of American Textile History, North Andover, Mass. **224** Public Library of Cincinnati and Hamilton County, Ohio **231** Copyright Yale University Art Gallery, Mabel Brady Garvan Collection **246** South Carolina Library, Columbia, S.C. **250** Library of Congress **255** New York Public Library/Schomburg Center for Research in Black Culture **261** Library of Congress **273** Harry T. Peters Collection/The Museum of the City of New York **279ALL** Sophia Smith Collection, Smith College, Northampton, Mass. **293** Western History Collection, Denver Public Library **295** California Society Library **299** Copyright Yale University Art Gallery, Beinecke Rare Book and Manuscript Collection **309** Library of Congress **313** New York Public Library, Astor, Lenox and Tilden Foundations **316** Courtesy of The Newberry Library, Chicago **319** Bettmann Archive **333** The National Archives, Office of the Chief Signal Officer **336** January 24, 1863/*Frank Leslie's Illustrated Newspaper* **340** Library of Congress **351** February 23, 1867/*Frank Leslie's Illustrated Newspaper* **353** May 26, 1866/*Harper's Weekly* **357** Brown Brothers **359** Valentine Museum, Richmond, Virginia **371** The Metropolitan Museum of Art, Bequest of Adele S. Colgate **374** Solomon D. Butcher Collection/Nebraska State Historical Society **377** Smithsonian Institution **396** The Museum of the City of New York **399** Library of Congress **409** July 16, 1892/*Harper's Weekly* **417** Chicago Historical Society **422** University of Illinois, Chicago/Jane Addams Memorial Collection at Hull House **428** Library of Congress **429** Library of Congress **436** Hawaii State Archives **441** The Granger Collection, New York **444** Culver Pictures **458** Records of the Children's Bureau, The National Archives, Office of the Chief Signal Officer **459** International Museum of Photography/George Eastman House **467** Chicago Historical Society **473** Library of Congress **487** U.S. Signal Corps, The National Archives, Office of the Chief Signal Officer **490** The National Archives, Office of the Chief Signal Officer **493** The National Archives, Office of the Chief Signal Officer **503** Library of Congress **508** From the collection of Whitney Museum of American Art **510** Brown Brothers **514** UPI/Bettmann **525** From the collection of Whitney Museum of American Art **530** Bettmann Archive **533** Library of Congress **551** General Records of the Navy Department/The National Archives, Office of the Chief Signal Officer **554** Library of Congress **555** Library of Congress **562** AP/Wide World **563** The Franklin D. Roosevelt Library **578** Bettmann Archive **589** UPI/Bettmann **598** Margaret Bourke-White/*Life* Magazine/Time Warner Inc. **605** UPI/Bettmann **610** Bob Henriques/Magnum Photos **617** CBS-TV **619** NASA **632** John Filo **633** Sygma **639** Printed by permission of the Estate of Norman Rockwell, Photo Courtesy of The Norman Rockwell Museum at Stockbridge **640** Bruce Roberts/Photo Researchers **649** J. L.Atlan/Sygma **650** Bob Fitch/Black Star **654** Michael Abramson/Gamma-Liaison **668** Michael Evans/The White House **683** AP/Wide World **687** Jeffrey Markowitz/Sygma

711

Index